# ENCYCLOPEDIA

# MENTALISM
# &
# MENTALISTS

## 13 Steps to Mentalism
by Corinda

## Mind Readers
## Masters of Deception
By William V. Rauscher

1878 Press Co.

*ENCYCLOPEDIA*

*MENTALISM*
*&*
*MENTALISTS*

13 Steps to Mentalism is used with permission of
D. Robbins & Co., Inc. Cranbury, N.J. 08512

Mind Readers Masters of Deception used with
Permission of Rauscher / Haversat

Manufactured in the United States of America
Published by 1878 Press Company – A Division of Zanadu L.L.C.
1878press@gmail.com

ISBN: 978-1-4507-6595-4

In Memory

HOWARD THURSTON NOFFKE

*Friendship is one mind in two bodies.*
                    *-Mencius*

# The MIND READERS
## Masters of Deception

WILLIAM V. RAUSCHER

# THE MIND READERS
## Masters of Deception

### The Great Sebastians

Lynn Fontanne and Alfred Lunt as the vaudeville mind reading team of Fssie and Rudi Sebastian. In the opening scene of the play by Howard Lindsay and Russel Crouse they are photographed in performance acknowledging applause from the audience. The play opened at the ANTA Theatre, New York, January 4, 1956 and closed June 2, 1956.

*To my mother,*
*Marie E. Rauscher,*
*who could always read my mind*

# Program

# *Acknowledgements*

Writing is an adventure. To begin with, it is a toy, an amusement. Then it becomes a mistress, then it becomes a master, then it becomes a tyrant. The first phase is that just as you are about to be reconciled to your servitude, you kill the monster, and fling him to the public.

Winston Churchill

Churchill was right. The adventure is trying to discover information about all the people you want to write about. The writing by itself is a lonely venture. The interaction in accumulating data, seeking information, gathering photos and illustrations, and thinking about publication is even more time-consuming. People have asked, "How long did it take you to write this or that?" No estimate can be given of the time, the thought, or the drive that is required to produce a final product.

Although a writer works alone, he is indebted to those who have contributed some tidbit, fact, lead, or conversation. To list all of them would be difficult. However, I must mention the people who have helped, and offer a special thanks to all those who provided photographs included in this work.

For insight, conversation, and assistance, I am appreciative to Stanley Palm, David Booth, Raymond Goulet, Claude Crowe, Arthur Emerson, Lloyd Applegate, George P. Hansen, Marcello Truzzi, Father Cyprian Murray, The Rev. Dr. John E. Bird, Richard Mosey, Ben Robinson, George Daily, Charles Buckner, Meir Yedid, Richard Gustafson, Kenneth Klosterman, Diego Domingo, William McIlhany, Barry Wiley, Phil Willmarth, John Moran, Fred Mitchell, Chris and Nadine Woodward, David E. Haversat, Mario Carrandi, Nick Ruggiero, Del Cartier, Joseph Atmore, McCarl Roberts, Al Cohen, Robert Bluemle, Marya Grossman, Bev Bergeron, Jack Flosso, Cesareo Pelaez, Richard Kaufman, Charles Cotton, Janet Levy, Hannes Höller, David Goodsell, Walter Graham, Bill J. Weldon, Charles Reynolds, Wayne Alan, John Calvert, James Reilly, Doris O'Hagan, John Gaylin, John Booth, George Goebel, Rob Allen, James Hagy, Arthur S. Hirsch, Michael Claxton, Martin Breese, Dennis Ulrich, and Gerald Taylor. A special thanks to Brian McCullagh and David Charvet for sharing material, and to Thomas A. Ewing for his encouragement, support, and time spent with me at the University of Princeton's Firestone Library, and also for supplying numerous items from his collection.

Appreciation is extended to those who have allowed me to quote from their own writings.

I am also grateful to Eugene H. Voshell and his son Blake for their help in scanning numerous photographs, to graphic artist John Bach for his cover design, to artist Kenneth Crocker, and to Blake Voshell for the layout design of this book.

Finally, I extend appreciation to Joan A. Mitchell for her immeasurable assistance in the preparation and editing of my manuscript, and to William L. Broecker for his suggestions.

The author wishes you an interesting visit with a great variety of unusual and intriguing characters, with the hope that you will not repeat what Groucho Marx said when he received S. J. Perelman's first book:

"From the moment I picked your book up until I laid it down I was convulsed with laughter.  Someday I intend reading it."

# *Foreword*

By Cyprian Murray, OFM, Cap.

"Now listen to me closely, I'll endeavor to explain
What separates a Charlatan from a Charlemagne."
*Pippin*
Stephen Schwartz

Since my youth, the world of mentalism has fascinated me. "Nightmare Alley" with Tyrone Power as Stanton Carlisle (The Great Stanton) captured my imagination. It was but a few years previous that Max Terhune performed magic in an old Range Busters film, "Fugitive Valley," and my life was changed forever. Magic, and the magic of the mind, continues to fascinate and thrill me.

Bill Rauscher has researched and assembled an incredible, extensive, and unusual assortment of what I call "mental illusionists." Their individual stories make great reading, but the assemblage provides a pastiche and an insight into the thinking and mystique of the mentalist.

What is it about these people that intrigues and puzzles us? Their apparent ability to know our innermost thoughts, to predict some coming event, to "perceive" what is happening in some remote corner of the globe, to know the contents of a sealed envelope, of a parcel, of a book, a letter, a note, a folded slip of paper? Just what is the deep appeal of the mentalist?

Over the past hundred and fifty years, many performers have taken the stage to baffle and entertain us. From Anna Eva Fay and Washington Irving Bishop to Kreskin, and on and on, the varied parade of men and women runs the gamut - from entertainers to pretenders and charlatans. Whatever your concepts about the powers of the mind, this parade of characters is bound to offer you provocative food for thought, as well as an entertaining read.

Bill raises an important issue: When does a performer pass from entertainer to something else - a charlatan? His reflections may disturb you, but there certainly is an ethical question here. A performing persona is one thing. But when the persona becomes an individual's "reality," what is at issue? Does the individual start to believe in his or her "powers"? If so, that seems delusional. If the individual does not believe in these powers, then that seems to me, at best, to border on charlatanism.

So sit back and enjoy an unusual and fascinating journey through another side of this thing we call reality.

"Mr. Stanton - "
It was the old man who looked like a judge.
"I couldn't let you go without telling you how miraculous your work is."
"Thank you."
"I mean it, my boy. I'm afraid you don't realize what you stumbled onto here.
This goes deeper than you realize."
"I have no explanation for it," Stan said abruptly …
"But I think I know your secret."

Stan felt like shouting. Instead he closed his eyes, the shadow of a smile
passing over his mouth.

*Nightmare Alley*
William Lindsay Gresham

*Father Cyprian Murray, OFM, Cap., is a Past President of the Society of American Magicians, and Chaplain of the Society of American Magicians and of the International Brotherhood of Magicians. He is a well-known collector of and expert on "Magic in the Movies," and a skilled sleight-of-hand artist with playing cards. He is known worldwide as "The Magical Monk."*

# *Overture*

Therefore, if you are to play the role of a mystic, why not claim to be "psychic," but not infallible. This latter is your "out" in case of error. But do not claim any supernatural powers. Claim only God-given abilities and research.

Robert Nelson
"Mindreading vs. Magic,"
Encyclopedia of Mentalism and Allied Arts,
Chapter 3

*It would be almost impossible to write about, or list, all the performers, psychics, mediums, or mentalists who have played a part in the history of magic, spiritualism, and the occult, by acting as readers and message givers.*

*This assemblage is a small selection – a potpourri of unusual personalities, living and departed – who have confused, confounded, and puzzled audiences and individuals for many years. Their talents, skills, performance styles, personalities, and approaches vary greatly. For want of a better term, they are called The Mind Readers, and they are masters of deception. These unusual and intriguing individuals were and are determined to make their audiences believe they possess strange powers. Their ability to use language, psychology, and sheer nerve in accomplishing their purpose is a great lesson in mental dominance.*

*The majority of these individuals want to entertain. At least that is what they say. Those who perform on the stage or in other venues are encouraged by their own belief in their ability to control every possible situation. These men and women prefer to be thought of as members of a kind of "upper echelon" of magic, and not as magicians. They do not always publicly identify with magic, although they may lecture on the subject for magic clubs, and sell their printed routines and methods.*

*Most mentalists role-play on and off the stage. Their approach can be so convincing that the unsuspecting person believes maybe, just maybe, these people really do possess some psychic ability. This puzzling group can easily be encouraged to play a role by receiving adulation, and by encountering lives saddened by misfortune and lost love. Their explanation for their place in life is a lesson in "word conjuring," for they deny they are even a bit paranormal, but instead say they have developed heightened intuition, or sensitive mind patterns – but, NO, absolutely, they are not psychic in the usual sense of that word.*

*May I emphasize here that I believe psychic ability can and does exist. I believe that mystical experience permeates the history of civilization, that the paranormal has a place in this world. I believe that divine intervention can and does occur, and that consciousness can be invaded from without, and directed from within. I believe in a transcendental dimension, and that we possess extrasensory gifts. But I am not writing about the psychic and mystical experiences of ordinary people. I am not focusing upon the paranormal aspects of the* scriptures, nor on the great body of literature regarding the saints and mystics in history. I am writing about performers, stage personalities, and individuals with a body of knowledge concerning trickery, and the ways in which they have presented themselves to the public.

The "mentalists" have made their impact in every age. It was easier to observe fraud in the early era of research into physical mediumship. Although many people were fooled by spirit cabinets, materializations, apports, and even levitations, just as many were not. Slowly but surely physical phenomena faded. Mental phenomena were harder to determine, and the fact remains it is still true today. As a result of the Psychic Revolution, New Age Movement, and New Age Spirituality, mentalism is once again in the spotlight, but in a new format. Gone is the turbaned mystic, replaced by the well-dressed, well-spoken performer who is familiar with the jargon of parapsychology and psychology.

Today the fine line between public mentalism and private readings merges for those who fall victim to their own tempting skills. Now, the real challenge for mentalism as an entertainment is in the area of ethics.

In his revealing book (which is unpopular with mentalists) titled The Handbook of Mental Magic (Stein and Day, New York, 1975), author Marvin Kaye calls mentalism "the aristocrat of the world of conjuring." He also makes the important point that "…basically, people tend to believe in mentalists, but not in magicians." Kaye correctly states, "Unlike magic, very little sleight of hand is necessary to become a good mentalist, and the cost of the equipment is generally far lower than the colorful boxes, silks, and other paraphernalia the conjurer needs to stay in business."

A very capable mentalist once told me, "You magic guys are nothing but box magicians … we have moved beyond all that, and our impact is greater." This same person avoided magic conventions, since he would have nothing to do with "that kind of stuff." He also announced he no longer needed God, because his ego had been enhanced to the point where that need or gap had been filled by his own feelings of power. Unfortunately, this "power" he felt came from his belief that he could dominate other people psychologically. He had also acquired a false sense of academic achievement.

Some mentalists have deluded themselves into thinking that private readings should augment their public shows. Once at a magic convention I graciously asked a mentalist if he thought charging for private readings was ethical, even though he did not believe he had psychic gifts. He became irritated and fumed, "Hell, I don't do anything different than you do when you counsel a person in your church study – and besides, it's none of your damn business!"

I enjoy mental magic shows, which can produce perplexing thoughts for an audience, but they don't necessarily enchant them. These are not shows which children can truly enjoy, whereas classical magic has the power to enchant adults as well as children. Although most magicians include some kind of mental magic in their show, like "divining" the name of a selected card, this mental magic is soon overshadowed by more colorful magic.

The problem within the mentalist fraternity is when the performer crosses the fine line between entertainment and private readings, because they are more rewarding financially.

When this line is crossed, questions can arise pertaining to ethics, integrity, and the role of the trickster mind.

Magicians refer to mentalists as exponents of mental magic, or even psychic entertainers. As a result, these psychic entertainers often refrain from attempting to ingratiate themselves and their efforts into most magicians' organizations. Instead, they prefer their own associations' conventions, and private, confidential publications within the Psychic Entertainers Association.

Since the days of vaudeville and into the new millennium, mind readers have offered their talents both on and off the stage. They are a procession of characters who are colorful, entertaining, devious, and at times, disturbing.

Perhaps you will regard this book as a stage, and consider me your Master of Ceremonies. As you "watch" the various acts, you will meet a most unusual array of clever people who have bamboozled, confounded, and puzzled audiences all over the world. You will find some are true entertainers, as well as others who will cheat and defraud. As a magician friend of mine once said to a psychiatrist about the variety of personalities contained in this book, "I dare you to figure them out."

And so the curtain rises, and I will present the players who will come out to meet you in no specific order. All perform similar acts – each in his or her own way when on stage. You will note similarities in their work, but it is their individual personalities that beckon to the audience. You will encounter message givers, clairvoyant readers, blindfold workers, exponents of physical and mental phenomena, horoscope pitchmen, crystal gazers, spirit cabinet performers, New Age mentalists, and other assorted oddities who represent themselves as possessing extra sensory abilities. As you observe their performances, and learn more about them, you may be left wondering if they believe any part of what they are doing.

Those who are entertainers will relish the various characters described in this book. For the layman, this effort is an introduction to a subculture, and perhaps a safeguard against deception in times of stress, grief, and deepest need.

When the performance is over, you may be left to ponder several questions that are not answered in this book. Do these Masters of Deception merely entertain, or might they possibly provide some additional form of emotional fulfillment that is totally harmless? Do they have room in their lives, or in the lives of others, for true mystical occurrences? Indeed, these Mind Readers are a collection of amazing minds that pose a blurred area within the study of consciousness.

Can you read this book, and still be entertained? Yes, but also enlightened, for you will appreciate the extent of how other minds can control your own, and fill you will false beliefs.

The lights have dimmed, and there is a mood of mystery and anticipation in the audience. So relax – come with me and enjoy the performance as we wend our way through a labyrinth of colorful characters who are committed to making you believe.

# *Act 1*

### *Ladies and Gentlemen –*
### *please join me as we go ...*

## *BEHIND THE SCENES*

DAVID J. LUSTIG, an intriguing man who used the stage name "La Velma," was born on September 4, 1893. Mentalist expert Barry Wiley characterized Lustig as a man who was never without a large cigar and a wide grin.

David J. Lustig
Courtesy of Barry H. Wiley

Throughout his career, Lustig was clever, knowledgeable, shrewd, and capable of offering suggestions on such diversified subjects as crystal gazing, opening lectures for mentalists, and even suggested answers for questions from audiences and sitters. He was familiar with verbal codes, second sight tests, and publicity tests. Most important, he possessed the unusual talent of being able to perfect countless complex ideas, which ultimately fooled people into thinking ESP and thought-reading were real on stage, radio, and television.

Lustig was the author of *La Velma's Vaudeville Budget for Mind Readers, Magicians and Ventriloquists*, published by Robert W. Doidge, Somerville, Massachusetts, 1921; and *Vaudeville Mind Reading and Kindred Phenomena*, also published by Robert W. Doidge, 1929. He also wrote several other books on the subjects of ventriloquism, magic, and hypnotism.

In the August 1997 issue of *The Linking Ring* magazine, Lustig is showcased in an article by Barry Wiley titled "David Lustig – Man of the Theater." He emerges as a man of many talents, but primarily as a backstage support figure for others in the spotlight. His career included the role of mentalist, magician, ventriloquist, scriptwriter, theater manager, and silent movie director. He was a superb wordsmith, with a mind constantly brimming with ideas. He had a sharp mind, and a wonderful sense of humor.

**Vaudeville Mind Reading** and **Kindred Phenomena**

*by*
**DAVID J. LUSTIG**
(LA VELLMA)

Introduction to
First Edition
especially written

for this book
by the late
HENRY HATTON

**REVISED EDITION**

PUBLISHER
R. W. DOIDGE ("Calostro Publications")
P. O. Box 76, Times Square Station
New York, N. Y.

A David J. Lustig 1929 treatise on mind reading
Rauscher Collection

Wiley quotes the humorous lyrics written by Lustig, to be sung to the tune of "Melancholy Baby":

Come to me my alcoholic baby –
Sober up and don't be stewed.
All your drinking's foolish, fancy baby
You know I can drink as much as you.
Every stomach has its silver lining
Yours must be burned right thru.
So, sober up my dear, while I have another beer,
Or else I shall be alcoholic, too!

David J. Lustig
A Self Sketch
Courtesy of Stanley Palm

Lustig's inventive brain made him the perfect unsuspected shadow man for the showman Dunninger, who hired him in 1943 as his "think tank." In that capacity Lustig originated so-called "Brain Buster Tests" that made a great impact on the public. His ability to work secretly with Dunninger as a behind-the-scenes mind engineer was almost as amazing as the performing skills of "The Amazing Dunninger" himself.

In the book *Dunninger*, written and published in 1966 by Charles A. Buckner (a "Sightless Vision" performer), the author quotes Lustig as saying, "It's not what you do – it's what people think you do. Effect is everything." Buckner adds, "Dunninger knew he had to believe he could read thoughts before he could convince others. He never wavered on this, not even with friends." Buckner further quotes Lustig in emphasizing, "Effect is what counts. *Modus Operandi* is secondary. We have proven this on the largest network in America."

Eventually the relationship between Lustig and Dunninger crumbled, but as pointed out by Barry Wiley, Lustig kept Dunninger's secrets to the end. Lustig died in Bridgeport, Connecticut (where P. T. Barnum once lived and died) on September 30, 1977.

Dunninger
Courtesy of Rob Allen

If ever a dominant, commanding, and charismatic character existed, it was **DUNNINGER, The Master Mentalist.** He was a great public performer, and never read privately for individual clients. In fact, to his credit, he was dead set against private readers. He was, indeed, a true psychic entertainer who gave his audiences mystery, puzzlement, and unexplained events.

As a ghostwriter for Dunninger, Walter B. Gibson, the prolific author of magic, was well acquainted with the mentalist, who had incredible verbal skills, but who lacked writing ability. Dunninger impressed people as being a person with authority, one who was highly educated, an individual in control of any situation. It was Walter Gibson who suggested to Dunninger that he should perform his act on the radio, which led to television appearances.

Dunninger once performed at a banquet while Gibson sat at the bar outside the banquet room. Gibson told me, "As I listened I thought, with this kind of thing you don't have to be in the actual room." Blessed with a resonant and commanding voice, and refined with a pinch of a pseudo-British accent, Dunninger was a hit on radio in 1929, and again from 1943 until 1944. A large television audience watched 'America's Master Mentalist' on television in New York from 1948 to 1950, and the whole country talked about him on national television in 1955 and 1956.

Dunninger was a man of great nerve, an outstanding showman – and also a scoundrel. As a youth he was interested in magic, and by 1920 he was a professional magician. In 1928 he discarded all his magician's trappings, and specialized in mentalism. No turbans, no beards or mustaches – nothing out of the ordinary. For his act he wore a business suit and demonstrated a commanding personality. He was the entire show, never tiring of his ability to convince, confound, and cause wonder among his audiences. His publicity was carefully sculptured, and press releases he issued, like the following, appeared in many newspapers across the country:

### DUNNINGER INTRODUCED TELEPATHY TO RADIO AND HAD LISTENERS AGOG

Even the radio editors who are always crying for something new under the sun gasped when they heard that Dunninger was bringing telepathy to the ether waves back on September 12, 1943. Even the most progressive souls smiled politely and shook their heads. It wasn't possible, they said. But the great Master Mind of Mental Mystery, who will give a personal demonstration of his remarkable ability at _____ on _____, accomplished the most marvelous feat ever conceived of in the history of radio. On that Sunday afternoon three years ago, he not only tuned in on thought waves broadcast to him from individuals in the radio studio audience, but he reached out telepathically over a distance of many miles and successfully interpreted the thoughts of persons he had never seen nor talked to. Following his history-making demonstration wires and telephone calls and letters poured into the network mailroom and switchboard from all parts of the nation, and newspapermen hurried to their typewriters, and Radio Life Magazine awarded Dunninger a certificate of merit, and Winchell sent him an orchid!

Since that afternoon three years ago Dunninger has become one of radio's most popular entertainers, most recently having completed a series over the

National Broadcasting Company network for Lever Brothers, and his air experiments are recorded in the archives of radio. On one occasion he scooped the newspaper world by telepathically tuning in on the editor of the New York Daily Mirror, who was three miles from the studio. Dunninger told the radio audience that the editor had just written a headline. He had no way of knowing what was to be the most important news story to be printed in the paper on the next day, yet he announced the headline, and told what page it would appear on in the next day's issue. When the paper reached the newsstands the next morning it was shown that Dunninger had accurately told his listeners the next day's news before it was set up in type.

During another broadcast Dunninger by remote control read the thoughts of a Washington correspondent and told the radio audience from the New York studio that the man in Washington had selected three cards from a pile of 5,200 – and Dunninger named the three cards. The correspondent was 250 miles away. A telephone call to Washington confirmed the accuracy of Dunninger's statement.

Three representatives of Columbia University participated in one unique experiment. Before the broadcast they visited the library and made a mental notation of a phrase in one of the several thousand books in the library. During the broadcast Dunninger, by concentration, was able to determine the book, page and phrase upon which they were concentrating.

During his many radio broadcasts, the mentalist has achieved such seemingly impossible results as conducting a "mental treasure hunt," opening a safe by telepathy, breaking a glass by concentration, describing the contents of a locked and sealed box, and many other unheard of feats.

He has also projected his thoughts to others in the studio and has sent thought waves out over the radio, which a remarkable percentage of his listeners received and sent into the network by mail. He has also received messages from members of his listening audience miles away. All of his studio experiments were conducted under the watchful eyes of a committee of prominent individuals acting as guest judges, and these celebrities have attested to the authenticity of his experiments.

Dunninger claimed he liked skeptics. He said: "They comprise ninety percent of my audience – at the beginning of a demonstration. The ratio is reversed at the end, and the hard-bitten ten percent who remain skeptical can be likened to the Arkansas farmer who, on his first trip to New York upon viewing the Empire State Building, said dourly, 'I see it, but I don't believe it.' "

Dunninger pulled no punches in the press or with his audiences. He declared, "I really read thoughts! I read minds through the possession of extra-sensory faculties." He added that he did "what any child of six could do with 60 years of practice." Like some mentalists today, he insisted that science had substantiated the existence of "other senses." It was not important for him to really believe this, but it was important for the audience to believe, so they in turn would more readily believe him. He emphasized: "Thought reading is a serious science, a latent sense awakening slowly. It is not allied to the supernatural, it professes no cabalistic jargon, it needs no mystic trappings."

Dunninger was so convincing! He set up his audience and let them know that he was "proud to be in the caravan of the progress of science." His ability to control an audience using only his voice and mind – without any formal degree in psychology – made him a kind of super con artist, mind manipulator, and mind reading ringmaster. Evidently he really believed he was somewhat psychic when it came to his personal life (he admitted to friends that he had personal psychic experiences), but his performances were pure showmanship. His words were spellbinding. He would announce: "Ladies and gentlemen, my work here tonight is legitimate. Yes, I really can tune in on your minds, but only if you help me, only if you concentrate. I am not psychic. I make no supernatural claims. I depend upon your concentration." In other words, he first told his audience that he was not psychic, but then he asked for their concentration so he could read their thoughts!

In 1950, Samuel George Soal (1889-1957), the now discredited British parapsychologist and once president of the Society for Psychical Research, described the so-called "Dunninger types." In his 1937 *Preliminary Studies of a Vaudeville Telepathist*, Soal said:

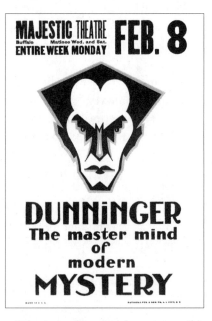

Certain performers, while very careful not to claim that they use genuine telepathy in their stage performances, nevertheless have done their best by indirect means to inveigle the public into the illusion that they really possess paranormal powers. These people would like to be credited with extraordinary telepathic gifts. Instead of admitting that they are entertainers and disclaiming extra-sensory powers, they take refuge in non-committal phrases. (Bulletin of The University of London Council For Psychical Investigation, 1937)

*"Showmanship is that intangible necessity that takes an act out of the ordinary and pushes it up the ladder of success."*

*Dunninger*

Courtesy of Charles Reynolds

Dunninger could really sling words in a firm, strong, and convincing manner. He could refute any accusation, even if it came from a fellow magician, with a statement like, "My work is scientific, and it is not necessary for me to make use of the multifarious methods used by these fakers and tricksters." Or, "Some of you may think that my work is accomplished by trickery, and I say to you that if it is, then it is even more marvelous than if it were scientific."

He often bragged about his "brilliant" childhood and his ability to know all the answers to arithmetic test papers which, according to him, were always marked with "100 percent correct" scores. He explained this phenomenon by saying: "You see, I just couldn't get the wrong answer. I didn't have to work the problems out. The bright children in the classroom just sent me thought waves, and consequently I got everything right."

It was important for Dunninger to state and be accepted more as a "thought reader" than as a mind reader. He did not want to be confused with the old images of vaudeville performers or carnival workers. His confident relaxed personality substantiated believability. He used a wonderful phrase (which I doubt was original): "To those who believe, no explanation is necessary. To those who do not believe, no explanation is possible."

In his heyday, Dunninger often referred to his "rigid test conditions." These were in fact controlled test conditions through which he was in full control, while making his audience feel **they** were in control. Using his magnetic personality, he forced people to believe that his experiments far surpassed any ESP tests conducted at Duke University by Dr. J. B. Rhine – or for that matter, by any other researcher. With Dunninger, positive results always occurred by whatever method he chose to use! Subtly he projected the theory that other so-called magicians were really imitating what he did. Since the participant was uninformed regarding Dunninger's methods, his results always produced a somewhat stunned response from his audience.

Dunninger's performance or demonstration was titled "Mysteries of the Telepathic Mind" or "A Full Evening of Phenomenal Telepathy." As a final declaration of his confidence, he always advertised the names of those he baffled, listing well-known scientists such as Thomas Edison. To fool a famous, prominent person, especially a scientist or an individual who had earned several degrees, is a feat mentalists love and live for. According to Dunninger, he had mystified six presidents, as well as numerous movie stars, mayors, statesmen, and members of the British royal family. He made the most of such publicity, which was in fact a subtle put down that reduced the subject's intellect, while enhancing his own ego.

Dunninger was unique, an icon of many aspiring mentalists. He followed in a long procession of psychic entertainers. In his declining years, he was furious at The Amazing Kreskin, and accused him of "stealing my act!" In his book *Dunninger's Secrets*, as told to Walter Gibson (Lyle Stuart, Inc., Secaucus, New Jersey, 1974), Dunninger doesn't mention Kreskin directly, but instead refers to him as the "Modern Mental Marvel" and "Mighty

Marvel." He demeans the "Mighty Marvel," and treats his work as a mere parody of his own spectacular record.

Dunninger retired in the early 1970's when he developed Parkinson's disease, and seldom left his home in Cliffside Park, New Jersey. He received very few visitors in his retirement, but I visited him one time with Dr. Berthold E. Schwarz, a psychiatrist friend. Dr. Schwarz, who had been one of Dunninger's doctors, addressed him as "professor." Dunninger was aged and obviously not well, but he still retained that indefinable sense of command. During our visit he told Dr. Schwarz that he was "still hearing the knocks in the house." Since I was aware of Dunninger's theatrics, I thought he might merely be performing for the doctor, but he seemed genuinely sincere when he related these incidents. But then it was hard to discern the truth, for Dunninger always sounded so sincere.

Dr. Schwarz believed Dunninger did possess psychic ability, as did Walter Gibson. Gibson knew all about Dunninger, his personality, his tricks, and his clever mind, but in a few instances he thought Dunninger had "hits" or "flashes" of real psychic experiences, based on a few incidents which Dunninger had shared with Walter.

I was fascinated by Dunninger's house during my visit. A dog barked incessantly. His study was a mishmash of books, papers, and Oriental artifacts. His desk looked like it came from the Robert Ripley ("Believe It Or Not") collection. He looked unkempt. The entire house was in disarray. Dunninger regaled the doctor with statements that something must be done to stop Kreskin from stealing his act. Regarding his performances, he said: "I will use any method to accomplish my purpose of entertaining an audience." Then he relayed some stories about Houdini, and gave me a tape of the final séance held on October 31, 1936, on the roof of the Hollywood Knickerbocker Hotel.

I met Dunninger again in Niagara Falls at the Houdini Museum, when he was a guest for the "annual" Houdini Séance. He was weak, thin, and in a wheelchair. Unfortunately there was no car available to transport him from his motel to the museum, so a hearse was used, borrowed from one of the horror museum attractions. It was a sad scene indeed to watch Dunninger being hauled about in such a manner.

Something very strange happened shortly before he died. In my rectory one of Dunninger's signed photos hung on the wall near the kitchen for several years. One evening, while I was sitting in the living room, I heard a crash. The framed photo had fallen from the wall and smashed onto the floor. The next day Walter Gibson called to tell me Dunninger was dead.

One of the best profiles of Dunninger was written by Maurice Zolotow in his book *It Takes All Kinds* (Random House, New York, 1946). Zolotow, who liked to write about odd characters, said Dunninger was one of the oddest he ever met. He did not think the mentalist's success had brought him any inner serenity. Zolotow states in his book, "There is a high price that one pays for carrying out a power operation as complicated and basically hostile to other people as Dunninger's pattern of setting himself up as the world's greatest mental telepathist. The cost is a human cost. It is loneliness, a daily life in which one is shut up alone with one's secrets, not daring to share thoughts or feelings with anyone, lest one's secrets leak out and be exposed. It is a life of constant hazards and threats. But for Dunninger no other way seems possible." (p. 75)

Indeed there is a toll for all those who embark on the path of mentalism, private readings, and/or fake mediumship. A reclusiveness exists in the midst of all the adulation, attention, and publicity, a shying away from open friendships and a necessary protective veneer that must be maintained at all costs. These performers trick the public and their friends. Saddest of all, they trick themselves.

# *Act 2*

**And now, ladies and gentlemen,**
        **for your pleasure, here are ...**

## *FIVE MENTALIST PACE SETTERS*

Ted Annemann
Rauscher Collection

Another great performer in the field of mentalism was **TED ANNEMANN**. Like **La Velma** he created numerous effects, some of which are still used in performances. He is credited by many magicians, including the late, respected Max Holden, and magic collector John Crimmins, as "the one man who probably did more to popularize this branch of entertainment than any other."

In the early stages of his career, Annemann sensed that times had changed, that audiences had become too perceptive to believe in crystal ball reading, wires under rugs, and a parade of odd-looking costumed performers who tried to look mysterious. Instead, he developed a practical approach to mind reading. His methods and ideology reflected the belief that people wanted to hear something personal – that they wanted to be convinced the performer was real, and not much different from themselves.

Annemann's book titled *Practical Mental Effects* (Holden's Magic Shops, New York-Boston-Philadelphia, 1944), now a Dover publication, is one of the finest collections of mental tricks ever produced for the trade. In his book he covers everything from Billet Switching (small pieces of paper with written questions, etc.), Publicity Effects, Book Tests, and Blindfold Reading, to Secret Codes.

Although talented professionally, Annemann's personal life was fraught with problems. Walter Gibson once told me that Annemann was a troubled man, very moody, prone to depression, fearful as engagements approached – yet simply marvelous on stage, leaving the audience stunned by his effects. Those who remember still talk and write about his act of catching a bullet with his teeth. A detailed account of this risky act, which has cost performers their lives, appears in *Twelve Have Died – "Bullet Catching – The Story and Secrets"* by Ben Robinson with Larry White (Ray Goulet's Magic Art Book Co., Watertown, Massachusetts, 1986). Annemann's version, which he performed outdoors, was a real thriller! His performance philosophy and personal approach were very appealing. He once said: "If you act like a normal person with an abnormal faculty, people like you much better. If you act like an abnormal person you become freakish, and people will be afraid to ask you home to dinner."

Theodore John Annemann was born in East Waverly, New York, on February 22, 1907. When his parents divorced, Annemann's mother raised him by herself. She hoped he would pursue an education, and feared that his magic interests were interfering with his future. One day, in a further effort to discourage her son's pursuit of his "hobby," she burned all of his magic books and tricks. Although in later years she regretted it, her son never forgave her. In 1938, when the first 50 issues of his magazine *Jinx,* which he founded and edited from 1934 till 1941, were bound, it is said that he gave a copy to his mother with the following inscription: "Dear Mama – When you look through these pages, I hope you will remember when you burned my magic books in the furnace. That made me try to write one myself. Have you got a match for this? Theo."

Walter Gibson told me that Annemann was an odd man with dark moods. In his chosen field he was a genius, but he was not very successful in daily living. Ted was a sort of enigma. He sported an onyx stone ring with a silver question mark on top that, in some unconscious way, announced this side of his personality. Walter Gibson described him as having thick hair, shaved at the forehead in a widow's peak, and sideburns, cut to a point. Once when Ted was leaving his house, his wife, Jeanette, asked where he was going. Ted scratched something on a piece of paper, folded it, and handed it to her. Unknown to Jeanette, however, he had switched papers. Later when she opened hers, it was blank.

During his lifetime Annemann recorded on paper not only his ideas, but also many ideas and routines of countless other performers. Bound copies of his *Jinx* magazine are still sought by collectors. As a further tribute to his talent, Annemann's followers have produced a 621-page volume titled *The Life and Times of a Legend: Annemann*, which is a compilation and commentary by Max Abrams (L&L Publishing, Tahoma, California, 1992). This work contains every trick created by Annemann – those that were previously published and even some that were not.

Those who knew him described Annemann as a nervous man with a neurotic anxiety and an escalating dependence on alcohol. Today, with proper medication and treatment, he might have been helped with his depression, panic attacks, anxiety, and stage fright. By 1941 Annemann had terrible financial problems, and a serious addiction to alcohol. He had become reclusive, and few had seen him for two years. Despite his problems he decided to attempt a two-night performance titled "Annemann the Enigma" at the Chanin Building Rooftop Theater in New York City. Tickets were printed and sold for this full evening performance, scheduled for January 26 and 27, 1942 – but the show never took place. On January 12, 1942, at the young age of 34, Annemann committed suicide. Leslie May wrote in *The New Jinx*, (No. 52, Vol. V, August 1966): "Ted in pajamas lay on cushions arranged on the floor. The window was open, the phone off the hook. His head was in a rubber cloth bag fitted around the neck with elastic. An electric fan, which had been packed away since last summer, was working. A length of rubber tubing was attached from the gas pipe of the kitchenette range to the weird head covering." Ted was found by his wife, Jeanette, who later arranged for his cremation. His ashes were interred in Glenwood Cemetery in Waverly, New York. The inner demons that had tortured Annemann throughout his life had finally won.

After Annemann's death, editor Bill Madsen of Boston continued publication of *Jinx* magazine, since it was regarded as an important contribution to the trade. Leslie May related an interesting story about Annemann in *The New Jinx* (Vol. IV, July 1965), one of the later issues after Annemann's death. He recalled the time when Bill Neff, a spook show magician, persuaded Annemann to attempt a blindfold drive, since he knew of Annemann's reputation for accomplishing some impressive feats with his eyes covered. May said, "Ted arrived, had a couple of quick drinks, did the drive, got the publicity, and relaxed. Next day driving home on a quiet road, cold sober, he got into an accident, crawled out of the smashed car, looked around dazedly and said, 'If I'd been wearing the damned blindfold this wouldn't have happened!'"

Of all the mind readers whose skills include billet reading, none surpassed the expertise demonstrated by **BERT REESE**.

Born Berthold Reise in Posen, Poland in 1841, he emigrated as a young man to New York in 1861, where he changed the spelling of his name to Reese and lived for 65 years. While in New York, Reese saw and was fascinated by a billet reader called Charles H. Foster, The Salem Seer. Foster was eight years older than Reese, and was also known as a medium. Eventually Reese became his pupil.

As Reese's talent and reputation grew, psychic researchers, including Baron von Schrenck Notzing, hailed him as a remarkable clairvoyant, psychic, and message giver. Reese conveyed to his "sitters" that he had X-ray vision, which enabled him to discern written messages. He never declared himself to be a

Bert Reese
Rauscher Collection

spiritualist, nor did he profess to have supernatural powers. Like many others in his field, Reese suggested that anyone who accused him of trickery should draw their own conclusions, but only after watching him perform.

Over the years, Reese continued to perfect his deceptive skills and "read" for many notable people, including the occultist Aleister Crowley and inventor Thomas A. Edison.

Edison's interest in the mind and its powers was already well known; he had even attended some classes with the renowned theosophist, Madame Helena Petrovna Blavatsky.

Edison met Reese through an unlikely mutual friend – Henry Ford. In fact, after seeing Reese perform, Edison was so impressed with his skills that he provided a written testimonial praising Reese's "psychic powers."

During Reese's career, a rather strained friendship developed between him and Harry Houdini, the master escape artist. Houdini considered Bert Reese to be "the cleverest reader of messages who ever lived," and although Houdini complimented Reese on his skill at deception, he also claimed to be the only one who managed to detect Reese using trickery.

Houdini was critical of Reese after a sitting, and accused Reese of being a billet reader, and not a mind reader. The then aged Reese supposedly begged Houdini not to expose him, and defended his performance and reputation by saying he had never claimed to be a mind reader. As a result, Houdini did not actually attack Reese's reputation until after his death in 1926.

Bernard M. L. Ernst and psychic researcher Hereward Carrington documented the facts of Houdini and Reese's relationship in a book called *Houdini and Conan Doyle: The Story of a Strange Friendship* (Boni, Inc., New York, 1932). Reese fascinated Houdini, who described Reese to author and spiritualist Conan Doyle as merely a magician, with no power to actually read the messages written by his audience on small pieces of paper known as billets.

Ernst and Carrington provide the following apt description of Reese in their book:

> Reese was a remarkable character. He was a short, fat, completely bald, well-paunched, cherubic-faced little Polish Jew, with a kindly heart, keen mind and delightful sense of humor. He reminded one of a little gnome, with his pop-eyes and potbelly. But he was a remarkable personality. He had traveled extensively, and had come into contact with royalty and celebrities in many different countries. His home was filled with presents that these individuals had given him. In his tie was a huge diamond pin, given to him by the late King of Spain; upon his finger an even bigger diamond presented by the Sovereign of another country. In the opinion of many, Reese possessed remarkable powers – though he certainly added to these, whenever possible, by any normal means possible, and his truly extraordinary insight into human nature and human motives. Thomas Edison, the late Dr. William Hanna Thomson, and many others publicly affirmed their belief in his prenatural faculties over their own signatures, in *The New York Times*. (p. 116)

In this same book, Ernst and Carrington also tell the story of Reese's arrest in New York on February 27, 1915 on charges of fortune telling. By then the 74-year-old Reese was (and had been) receiving large sums of money for his "consultations." Judge Rosalsky sat on the bench at Reese's trial. In a privately published monograph titled *The Bert Reese Docimasy* (no date), mentalist Al Mann describes the outcome of the case:

Reese asked the judge to write anything on three pieces of paper, to fold them and to place them in three different pockets, but first mixing them in such a way that no one knew the contents of any particular piece. Then Judge Rosalsky took one of the pellets and pressed it against Reese's forehead. He immediately answered, "You have $15 in the bank mentioned in your question!" Reese then answered the other two questions and Judge Rosalsky acquitted him! (p. 3)

In his monograph, Mann reproduces the tribute to Reese from Edison. He writes:

At the appointed time Reese came over to my laboratory. He asked me to call some of my workmen into the room that he might experiment with them. He had the Norwegian go into another room and write on a slip of paper the maiden name of his mother, where he was born and several other items. The slip of paper was folded and held in the hand of the Norwegian. Reese gave the contents correctly as if he had been reading print from a paper, and remarked in addition that the young man had a ten kroner piece of money in his pocket. I did not know of the coin, and neither did Reese by any ordinary sight. (p. 6)

Edison tells of another incident involving Reese and his friend Dr. James Hanna Thompson, an expert on mental diseases:

Dr. Thompson had denied the possibility of Reese's powers and said he was a faker, etc. This made Reese angry. After some persuasion on the part of Thompson's friend, who had known Reese for a long time, he [Reese] was at last induced to go to Thompson's house. I was not present at this meeting but have been informed what transpired.

Reese met the gentleman in the parlor of Thompson's house and told him to go into the library, write his questions on slips of paper and hide them. During the interval Reese engaged in conversation with the gentleman in the parlor until Thompson came back and announced that he was ready. Then Reese stood in the library door and said: "In the bottom left hand drawer of your desk is a slip of paper with the word *Opsonic*. Under a book on your desk is a slip containing another word *Ambicepter;* another slip shows the word *Antigen*!"

Reese told the location and the words without hesitation. Thompson was astonished, and stated that Reese's performance was inexplicable. (p. 7)

During his lifetime Bert Reese persuaded thousands to believe in his talent, using only his clever mind, his innate sense of psychology, and some small pieces of paper on which messages were written by his believers. His ability to "switch" and read the questions written on the billets, which were then rolled into pellets and hidden on his subject's person, was unsurpassed. Mentalists today continue to praise Reese's skill and extol him as a hero in their craft, while even now attempting to duplicate his feats. He is still fondly remembered as the King of Billets.

When his health failed, Reese returned to Germany in early 1926. He died in Hamburg, Germany on July 8, 1926, at the age of 85.

Corinda
Rauscher Collection

Mind reading is quite different from performing a self-working, mail order magic trick, which may fool some people even without proper practice and with poor presentation. The performers or practitioners of what some call mental magic, rather than mentalism or mind reading, admire the work and contributions of **TONY CORINDA**, the stage name of Thomas William Simpson, who later became a mentalist.

In 1968 Louis Tannen (New York) published Corinda's book titled *Thirteen Steps to Mentalism*. First published as a series of booklets during 1958-1960, *Thirteen Steps* is a remarkable 420-page volume that boggles the mind with its overview of all that is required to enter the profession of mental deception. The British-born Corinda not only describes the secrets of mentalists, but also offers details on how to look, how to act, how to publicize, and how to talk.

Critical in mind reading, Corinda states, is the performer's emphasis on presentation. In ESP, effects, content and delivery define success or failure. Many would-be amateurs and professional mentalists got their start by following Corinda's advice.

Mind reading can be boring. Most full evenings of ESP tricks with envelopes, cards, billets, and long-winded speeches will not hold the attention of a twenty-first century audience. Rare is the performer who can mesmerize a crowd by performing only mentalism. Usually these performers have some dynamic effect that will be remembered by the audience. Some performers can do this successfully. Others try and fail.

Corinda
A 1958 Sketch
Courtesy of Paul Fried

Maurice Fogel
Courtesy of Chris & Nadine Woodward

**MAURICE FOGEL** will be remembered for one startling effect, based on the belief that he used ESP. In 1970 Fogel performed the Bullet Catch and his famous Russian Roulette.

I once witnessed Fogel's dramatic performance of Russian Roulette at the Society of American Magicians Convention in 1978 at the Waldorf-Astoria. This Mind Illusion required six loaded rifles placed on a revolving carousel. Behind him on a stand were six dinner plates. On the stand was an envelope on which a large question mark had been drawn. Six volunteers from the audience were selected and asked to come forward. (Fogel always requested volunteers who were already familiar with guns – especially rifles). One of the volunteers was chosen to select a rifle from the carousel. This person's job was to fire the rifle at a dinner plate, and then replace the rifle on the carousel. Afterward, the carousel was spun so the volunteers were no longer certain of the fired rifle's position. Next, each volunteer was asked to select a card, numbered one through six. They then formed a firing squad and each chose a rifle, but at this point none of them knew which rifle was empty. Finally, all were instructed to aim at the plates, with the exception of one who was told to aim at Fogel's forehead. FIRE!!!

This presentation caused tremendous tension in the audience. The plates would all be smashed. Fogel, who amazingly escaped injury, then tore open the envelope with the question mark to find a card that contained the number of the previously fired rifle. Once again Fogel had predicted the rifle that was empty!

Did he ever make a mistake? Yes. Once he realized that he had the wrong number, and before the instruction to fire he directed the gun to be aimed lower toward his chest. This time when the rifles were fired, blood poured from Fogel's chest, but fortunately he survived. So the question that lingers is – why in the world did he proceed?

This happened again in Rhodesia, and the bullet struck his head. This time the volunteer happened to be a doctor – although why a doctor would participate in such a stunt is another mystery. Fogel was taken to the hospital and a small slug was removed from the brow bone of his skull. Once again, he survived!

I'm acquainted with Fogel's daughter, Nadine, and also her husband, Chris Woodward, who spoke of Fogel at the Sixth Los Angeles Conference on Magic History in November 1999. Even today they are amazed by his talent and abilities.

Fogel's stand-up mind reading work was highly in demand.  Although absent-minded in daily life, he was in total control during a performance.  He was "always on," as they say, and developed unusual effects, like his "Prediction in the Bottle."  His countless engagements and tours took him to the Middle East, Far East – including Hong Kong, Singapore, Beirut, Cyprus, Malta, Israel, and Egypt – and all areas of England.

The son of an immigrant from Poland, Fogel was born on July 7, 1911 in the East End of London.  In his youth he worked for a magician named Rameses, the stage name adopted by Albert Marchinski.  Fogel had a booming voice, and his audience believed whatever he said.  Like many others, he graduated from magic to mind reading and performed in theaters and major hotels.  Eventually he became so proficient that he wanted to attempt even more dangerous effects like "Walking Blindfold Through a Minefield," which the Army discouraged and prevented him from doing.

Maurice Fogel died of a heart attack on October 30, 1981, on his way to a show.  In many ways his talent drove him, but it was also his way of earning a living – and a matter of survival.  He is lovingly remembered by his family, who still marvel at his ingenuity and sheer nerve.

Al Koran
Rauscher Collection

**AL KORAN** (1914 – 1972), whose legal name was Edward C. Doe, was known among magic friends for his creativity.  Some of his best tricks were a mixture of magic and mentalism, but it was his presentation and use of words that sparked admiration for his accomplishments.

As a young man, Koran earned his living as a barber.  Like so many mentalists, he knew he had found his real calling the first time he saw a magician perform.  He quickly became proficient with sleight of hand and manipulation magic; but following an injury to his hand, he shifted his emphasis to mental mysteries.

Facts about Koran's father, Charles Edward, and mother, Lois [Heckman], and details of his childhood in England are sadly lacking.  In Rockford, Illinois, in the Friday, January 15, 1971, edition of the *Register-Republic* (a Gannett newspaper) is an article that announced: "Mr. Koran Captures Audience."  The article continues: "The son of famous British [actually Scottish] spiritualist, Helen Duncan, Al Koran grew up in London, where every Sunday night for twenty years his mother performed before a packed house in Albert Theater."(!!!)  Helen Duncan, who was a famous and notorious spiritualist/medium, actually claimed to be born in Perthshire, Scotland, in 1898 – although records reveal her registered birth date as 1897.

According to researchers, by 1931 Duncan was materializing spirits. She was also involved in all sorts of questionable "research," and was later exposed and tried in court. After nine months in prison, she was released in 1944. In 1956 she was again arrested in Nottingham, became ill, and died five weeks later. (See *Encyclopedia of Occultism & Parapsychology*, Vol. 1, Gordon Melton, editor, Gale Research, Detroit, Michigan, 1996.)

Although Helen Duncan did bear eight children, only six survived – none of whom was Al Koran (sometimes show people claim outrageous backgrounds to enhance their own image). Duncan's remarkable story is related in the book *Hellish Nell: Last of Britain's Witches*, written by Malcolm Gaskill (Fourth Estate, Harper Collins, London, 2001). Incidentally, to my knowledge there is no record of Helen Duncan appearing regularly in theaters (unless it was someone else who chose to use that name).

Strangely enough, in that same January 15, 1971, *Register-Republic*, Koran revealed in a question-and-answer session with a reporter that his first feat of extra sensory perception occurred when he was seven years old. He recalled how an aunt had come to visit from Scotland, and how she told her family she had lost her diamond engagement ring. After hearing her story, Koran told his aunt where to look for the ring when she returned to Scotland. The Scotland connection and so few written facts about Koran's background purposefully create a bit of mystery, which lingers even today.

In *The Magic of Al Koran* (edited and published by Martin Breese, London, 1984), friends recall their impressions of this well-liked gentleman. Koran was considered different from other mentalists, according to writer Charles Goodliffe [Neale], who founded and published a weekly magic magazine called *Abracadabra* for many years. Goodliffe said, "Koran was quiet and reasonably unassuming – not the showman type like Dunninger or Fogel." Goodliffe also offered an interesting insight on mentalists: "Mentalists are great people for trying to kid their fellow mentalists and fellow magicians into believing that they really have supernatural powers. It's a strange thing. I think they convince themselves that they really can do their mind reading when the conditions are right on occasions. And having convinced themselves – perhaps to provide further reinforcement – they try to persuade their fellows that they have these strange powers."

At the height of his career, Koran was billed as "The Fantastic Koran – World's Greatest Mind Reader." According to Koran's publicity, he appeared by Royal Command 25 times at Buckingham and Sandringham Palaces. Winston Churchill thoroughly enjoyed his performances. Princess Grace of Monaco found him fascinating, and several times hired him to entertain at her charitable fund-raising events. He performed in seasonal engagements around the world, in person and as a television guest. He gave countless performances at London supper clubs, and even appeared on the stage of the London Palladium.

Throughout his life, despite the admiration of countless audiences and the worldwide reputation he enjoyed for his outstanding ability, Koran had only a few close friends. In 1969 he moved to the United States, where he died in Chicago on June 12, 1972. His magician friend Billy McComb took Koran's ashes back to England and scattered them from numerous small vials in various meaningful places – one of which was the stage of the London Palladium!

Koran left a wife and daughter, Katherine, along with a legacy of mentalism that is still greatly admired by the mentalist fraternity.

# *Act 3*

## *May I next introduce you to ...*

### *PERSONALITIES –TALENTED BUT CONFUSING*

David Hoy
Courtesy of Raymond J. Goulet

**DAVID HOY** was a charming, bright, and personable man who was born in Evansville, Illinois, on July 21, 1930. He was highly educated, having earned an A.B. and B.D. in Theology, with concentrations in Hebrew and Greek, plus an honorary Doctorate of Humane Letters. He was a great speaker – dynamic, funny, and brilliant. Even Dunninger liked him!

David came to see me at my home in Woodbury, New Jersey, following an appearance on a Philadelphia talk radio show. We discussed at great length his interest in ESP and psychic phenomena. Since he had once been a clergyman, there was a certain natural feeling about him, even though by that time he was media-minded, and an energized performer. Hoy's lecture demonstrations were outstanding, and he loved to make predictions. He had effective public relations people, and his material was totally professional.

Hoy once hosted his own radio shows, called "ESP According to Hoy," and "David Hoy – Inside The Mind." He also conducted seminars on sales and ESP. Many considered him a mountebank, a con, a real fooler, who just happened to latch on to a gimmick with ESP, and who finally left mentalism to become even more well known as a "real psychic."

By 1963, David was known as Dr. Faust. He was striking in appearance – standing 6 feet, 3 inches tall, weighing 250 pounds, and sporting a Van Dyke beard and black-rimmed aviator glasses. With his black homburg-type hat, he looked a bit like "Odd Job" in a James Bond movie.

Hoy wrote a small booklet called *The Bold and Subtle Miracles of Dr. Faust* (Ireland Magic Company, Chicago, 1963). In this booklet he recommends a fun approach to mentalism, where humor and "stunning effects" please an audience. His suggestion is to be BOLD – to come on strong, using the force of one's own personality. Secondly, he counseled, one should take an aggressive approach, using science as a hook (because that was the way the world was moving, and that was his pitch!). Of course, not everyone has the personality of a David Hoy, and it is because of his personality that his approach worked.

David did not approve of the use of envelopes when he made predictions. He felt a performer should predict verbally and claim accuracy. In other words, he "proclaimed" a headline. He told me his discipline was to read every paper, look at every magazine, and then just shoot from the hip. His belief was if he did this often enough he was bound to be accurate some of the time.

David was highly effective when using a blindfold. When he described what someone was holding, or what he or she had written on a board, he did it with gusto. He was an excellent showman, and his performances always concentrated on the paranormal. He would pass out lists of books on parapsychology, offer hints on losing weight through psychokinesis, and even work with the police to try to solve crimes.

David was a dropout from the Baptist ministry, a liberated man who had rejected fundamentalism and preached a kind of psychic gospel. In his prime, he lectured at some 60 to 70 colleges a year. He appeared on numerous television talk shows, including those hosted by Merv Griffin, Mike Douglas, and Dave Garroway. He made records and wrote a hardcover book for Doubleday, *Party Psychic and Other ESP Games*. He authored two other books for Aurora: *The Meaning of Tarot and 49 Notables on ESP*. He believed in the mystical, but there were many fine lines between what he believed and what he actually did.

In a statement for *The New Jinx* (No. 26, Vol. III, June 1964) Hoy wrote:

> Because people are at times "muddle-headed," mentalism as entertainment becomes a possibility. Throughout the history of science, as in most of our human affairs, mysterious or unreal "happenings" have been reported. We can read hundreds of these case histories. And still we do not know a thing about the competence of the individuals reporting the happenings.

> So because people are at times muddle-headed, and because they oft times give inaccurate or highly colored reports of what they have witnessed, mentalism for fun becomes a possibility. And these forays into the world of extra sensory perception, a broad term covering the entire field of psychical research, are fascinating. And because so many want to believe that this nonsense does exist (and I would be the first to say that it does), it is proper that the performer resort to trickery to accomplish his miracles as long as he does not say that he is a genuine telepathist.

Hoy did everything from finding lost dogs to offering advice as a reader (although he never considered himself a private reader). He was, by his own terms, a "practical psychic" from Paducah, Kentucky, and was well known in the magic community and the mentalist fraternity. He was a likable person, and well informed on a wide range of psychic research and parapsychology. In the early days of 1964 he troubled other mentalists when he said in his opening remarks at a lecture, "I'm a mentalist, and I am a fake."

Hoy's weight, drive, and constant activity contributed to his early death on April 2, 1981.

Volta - Burling Hull
Courtesy of Rob Allen

Choosing a stage name becomes a challenge to many performers. The late Burlingame Gilbert Gault Hull, magician, inventor, writer, and mentalist, once told me it was important to have only five letters in a stage name. Hull first called himself **VOLTA – The Man With The Radio Mind**, and later **VOLTA – The Man With The Radar Mind.** (Years ago the words "radio" and "radar" had all the power of an invisible energy reaching out, giving, and gaining information).

Hull was articulate, educated, colorful, egotistical, and charming. He was a magician who incorporated psychic readings into his repertoire as a hired act, giving readings when he performed at tables in some of the best hotels. On stage, as a magician, he also performed his "Miracle Cocktail Bar Act." In this act, all drinks requested by the audience were poured into an empty glass from the same cocktail shaker or water pitcher.

Hull's published works, which were mostly in booklet form, included descriptions of tricks using billiard balls, rope and chain escapes, and methods of seeing while wearing a blindfold. He was a well-known author in magic history, and is credited with over fifty publications on magic and mentalism. His *Encyclopedic Dictionary of Mentalism* and *Encyclopedia of Stage Illusions*, a two-volume mimeographed work, is still widely read. One book that he produced, called *The Billion Dollar Bait*, was an exposé of the tricks and deceptions employed by spirit medium ministers and fake psychics.

Hull was a superb self-promoter, and was a master of his own public relations. When advertised by Hull, a simple trick became a stupendous act. His grandiose use of words helps explain why magicians privately called him

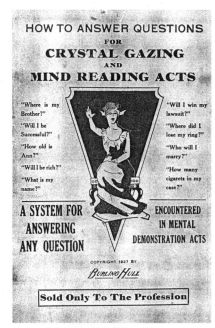

A Burling Hull book cover
Rauscher Collection

-25-

"Hurling Bull." He was very outspoken against private readers, especially mentalists who became private readers.

Hull was fascinated with my role in discovering Lamar Keene, the fraudulent medium. When I finally met Hull in DeLand, Florida, he was in his late eighties, and almost blind – yet still dignified. Just before our interview in the late 1970's, Hull had checked himself out of a nursing home, declaring in the local paper that the home was a "human incinerator."

Hull was always health conscious, and obviously had taken good care of himself when he was younger. At the start of my visit, Hull was slow and soft-spoken. As we talked, an amazing transformation took place. Hull's voice became stronger and more resonant. As our conversation continued, he became animated. By the end of the interview he appeared to me to be back on stage, performing once again!

Because of his numerous magic inventions, Hull was known as "The Edison of Magic." Many of his creations were detailed in his book by the same name, with a biography by Samuel Patrick Smith (Samuel and Lee Smith, Travares, Florida, 1977).

Burling Hull with W. V. Rauscher
Rauscher Collection

Burlingame Gilbert Gault Hull died in 1982.

Anna Eva Fay Portrait
Courtesy of Raymond J. Goulet

**ANNA EVA FAY** was a headline stage performer. She first established herself as a medium by performing physical phenomena – such as having objects move, bells ring, and trumpets sound – but then followed it with mental phenomena, which showed audiences the power of the mind.

Anna had a sense of humor, but always combined it with a certain firmness and total control of any situation. She was of a small build with blond hair, and performed dressed in gowns and diamonds. She answered about three questions a minute, giving direct responses, always in the categories of wealth, health, lost persons, lost articles, and marriage. At the end of her show she would faint, and her husband, David Pingree, would catch her and carry her from the stage to a burst of applause.

Anna Eva Fay in her Edwardian Drawing Room at Heathman Manor, Melrose, Mass. 1927
Courtesy of Raymond J. Goulet

Anna also did a spirit cabinet act. After being tied to a post with cotton bandages sewed together by volunteers, she was placed in a curtained cabinet. Her head could be seen above the cabinet, while tambourines and other items flew about, ostensibly caused by "spirits." For her next act she answered written questions submitted by the audience, collected by her assistants, and delivered to the stage.

Anna Eva Fay Theater Announcement
Courtesy of Bill J. Weldon

John Mulholland, the late internationally known magician/ author/ expert on Spiritism, who amassed a vast collection of magic memorabilia and wrote numerous books on the subject, provides us with the opening stage lecture for one of Anna Eva Fay's appearances in his book entitled *Beware Familiar Spirits*, (Scribner's, New York, 1938). George W. Stock, who once worked as a backstage assistant for Miss Fay and traveled with her for one year, and who was one of Mulholland's friends, is the source of this quote:

Just a few words before introducing Miss Anna Eva Fay. The results may be put before you in this manner: if you think that these experiences are produced through strong will-power, animal magnetism, odic force, electricity, spiritualism, or mind over matter, you have that privilege. These results are simply demonstrated for your kind consideration. (pp. 201-202)

The thread running through all of the supposed phenomena produced by mentalists or psychic entertainers is simply an ability to create confusion in the mind. The words spoken for Fay are a non-explanation of the performer's ability. The spectator is left to ponder whatever he or she may believe or think. This verbal misdirection is still practiced today, and probably always will be.

Houdini once claimed after a 1924 visit with Anna that she told him her secrets –

Houdini with Anna Eva Fay in her garden.
Courtesy of *The Linking Ring* magazine

although there is no real evidence that Anna ever revealed very much to Houdini, other than receiving his visit. After this session Houdini printed a photo of himself with Anna Fay gazing at a sun ball in her garden. He wrote in his book *Magician Among the Spirits* that Anna had revealed to him how she fooled investigator Sir William Crookes in 1875, who believed she was a genuine spirit medium. Anna was very secretive, and researcher Barry H. Wiley, an expert on Fay, states that Houdini's report of his information from Fay "was pure fantasy." (*Yankee Magic Collector*, New England Magic Collectors Association, 1983).

Heathman Manor Today
Rauscher Collection

Anna was a good businesswoman; in fact, it is known that she was the highest taxpayer in her area. Her house, Heathman Manor, in Melrose Highlands, Massachusetts, was large and impressive. She also owned other property and had by most accounts a great deal of money.

Anna was a strong personality, and her act played the best theaters in the United States, England, Germany, France, Spain, Sweden, and the Netherlands. Author and magic historian David Price wrote: "She was unquestionably the most successful act of her kind to ever appear on stage." (*Magic: A Pictorial History of Conjurers in the Theater,* Cornwall Books, Cranbury, New Jersey, 1985).

Anna died on May 12, 1924, and was interred in a mausoleum at Wyoming Cemetery in Melrose, Massachusetts. This is indeed an impressive monument with double glass iron doors. I once visited this site, and as I peered in through the dusty glass I saw a marble bust of this mysterious woman who made a fortune, and always left her audiences wondering.

Anna Eva Fay Mausoleum
Rauscher Collection

Samri S. Baldwin Portrait Poster
Courtesy of Mario Carrandi

**SAMRI S. BALDWIN** is purported to be the father of the question-and-answer act. Originally, Baldwin's career was headed for medicine and theology, but after he saw the Davenport Brothers do their famous "Spirit Cabinet" illusion, he became intrigued by show business and chose a theatrical life. By the 1870's he was doing his question-and-answer routine. (Incidentally, this routine is especially noteworthy, for it is one thing to do a private reading in a living room with time to work through questions and answers, but quite another to do one while performing on stage where time is of the essence!)

Baldwin twisted words and used them as necessitated by his personal needs. He adopted the exotic title "Professor Samri S. Baldwin, the White Mahatma," announcing that the title "Mahatma" had been bestowed on him in India! His ability to improvise titles like "Rosicrucian Somnamancy," used for his clairvoyant work, may have been stimulated by his earlier study of theology.

Baldwin also proclaimed that his wife, Kittie, had psychic powers. One promo listed her as the "Modern Witch of Endor"; another headlined her as a "Wizardess." Kittie's act included astrological readings, memory work using numbers, and book tests where audience members selected a word and page from a book supplied to them, which was then revealed by Kittie.

Like so many of these early personalities, Baldwin was a well-traveled, great showman. Money was never a problem – he made plenty. And like many others in his field, he never claimed supernormal powers.

In the end, Samri S. Baldwin joined a Spiritualist Church, implying that something in him went beyond his efforts toward duping the public. Unfortunately, like many performers, he was penniless when he died at age 72. According to researcher David Price, Baldwin's daughter inherited nothing and was reduced to reading tea leaves to earn a living.

Samri S. Baldwin, The White Mahatma Poster
Courtesy of Mario Carrandi

**SYDNEY AND LESLIE PIDDINGTON** were low-keyed performers who achieved fame as the Australian mind readers for whom people waited all week to hear on the radio. Both appeared to be gentle, charming, believable, and genuine. Sydney had a slight stutter or stammer, and like his wife projected honesty whether on stage or off. Their tag line was "You be the judge."

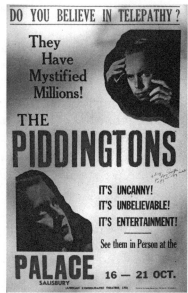

The Piddingtons' radio program in Australia was a prelude to their later programs broadcast over the BBC in London. Their act consisted of tests in which Sydney transmitted thoughts to Leslie. Twenty-two million people listened to their live broadcasts. The press (and even magicians) speculated how they did what they did. Sydney Piddington was masterful in devising these shows, and Leslie was unique by, in a quiet, unassuming manner, doing what she was able to do best – receive her husband's thoughts!

The Piddingtons' Poster
Courtesy of Barry H. Wiley

The Piddingtons toured the British music halls, and even appeared at the London Palladium. They achieved great success, at one point performing two shows a night, six nights a week.

Barry H. Wiley described them in a **Tips and Techniques** bonus insert to *Magick Magazine* (December 4, 1987): "They were the prototype of the modern two-medium act, but an act in which both were central to the effect as a whole, without the sometimes dull repetition that two-person acts can so easily slip into. The effects developed by Sydney Piddington were all marked by simplicity and directness."

Whether Leslie was receiving Sydney's thoughts of a selected line from a certain page in a book that were transmitted to her while she was under water in a diving bell, or whether she was receiving the same thoughts from Sydney while she was in an airplane, the result was the same – a powerful impact on an amazed audience.

After they retired the Piddingtons were asked the secret of their act, and were once offered $50,000 to reveal their method. They smiled and gave one of those classic mentalist answers: "There is nothing to reveal."

The Piddingtons
Courtesy of Barry H. Wiley

The Piddingtons' successful career had strange beginnings. Sydney Piddington developed his act in a Japanese prisoner-of-war camp in Changi Prison, Singapore, with the assistance of fellow prisoner Russell Braddon. Even then, when they tried to entertain fellow prisoners, no one was certain how Sydney's mind reading feat was accomplished.

In my collection is a cassette tape that features an overview of the Piddingtons' career, with excerpts from the "Hindsight" show, aired by the Australian National Radio on February 6, 2000. Sydney had divorced Leslie and had married a 26-year-old girl named Robyn. As his second wife she became his partner in the act in 1974. In response to her grandson's question: "Was it real?," Robyn Piddington responded with a delightful laugh and said, "You be the judge."

Chan Canasta
Courtesy of John Moehring - *Magic Magazine*

Unlike radio and the impact of the Piddingtons, the coming of television produced more reaction to mentalism. Through this medium the viewers could not only experience the amazement of mentalism, but they could also observe the performer and his approach. In England during the 1960's, **CHAN CANASTA**, who was termed a "psychological illusionist," fooled vast audiences with his Book Test. Like the performers who preceded him, Canasta claimed, "I do not read minds. By watching people, I can anticipate their reactions." Here we go again!

Canasta was a natural performer. In his act, a member of the audience was asked to think of a page number and a line from one of 50 volumes of books on the stage. (Incidentally, these books were all different – not merely the same book with 50 different covers.) And obviously, every time Chan Canasta chose the correct book and read the selected line from the volume, he left his audiences dumbfounded by his ability to thought read.

Canasta was so highly regarded that his methodology and techniques were compiled into a book titled *Chan Canasta: A Remarkable Man*, written by David Britland (Martin Breese, 2000). This book explores many of Canasta's psychological secrets – including his astounding Book Test.

The world of ESP has produced some mysterious figures. Among this collection, **JACQUES ROMANO** must be included in the category of mind reader.

Romano did not earn a living reading minds, but he did indeed perform what he believed was ESP. His life so fascinated psychiatrist Berthold E. Schwarz, M.D., that Schwarz wrote a book about him.

*The Jacques Romano Story* (University Books, Inc., New York, 1968) was the result of Dr. Schwarz's intimate knowledge of his subject for a period of six years.

Schwarz admired Romano's multifaceted personality and claimed he was "confidant, advisor, and healer to politicians, royalty, rulers, clergymen, housewives, professional people, and men and women from all walks of life."

Jacques Romano
Courtesy of Berthold E. Schwarz, M.D.

Romano's list of friends and acquaintances seemed to confirm this, for it included such luminaries as Madame H. P. Blavatsky, Gurdjieff, Evangeline Adams, Gandhi, Edison, Einstein, William James, Mary Baker Eddy, and Charles Lindbergh.

Romano was a proponent of good health, diet, long life – and everlasting life. He considered many psychics psychopaths, and spiritualists fanatics who heard only what they wanted to hear. He also believed psychic ability "only picked up vibrations from the past that continually bombard, and that the finite within us cannot communicate with the infinite – yet identity is never lost." His creed included a view of the spiritual life as existing within everyone, but not being understood. Yet he also believed his abilities included the power to become aware of past happenings in other people's lives.

Romano was a popular after-dinner speaker – his audiences were convinced he could read their minds. He was a man consumed with the subjects of body and mind, and his ideas and opinions were eagerly sought.

He also performed various Yogi feats, like slowing his pulse and stopping the circulation in his hand – although whether anyone ever checked his armpit for a rubber ball pressed against his side is not known. As a "healer," he quieted babies, cured headaches, and professed a belief that the body was surrounded by a "mysterious envelope or radiation." Accordingly, people attributed his ability to what they called "Romano's ray."

Oddly enough he knew Zancig the Mind Reader, was aware of the code, and had knowledge of magic. He often performed card magic, and claimed to have experienced numerous psychic occurrences. At times he offered unsolicited psychic impressions that astounded his listeners.

Romano was a respected gentleman whose numerous lectures confounded his skeptics. He also seemed to have a talent for self-hypnosis, and once, under a fluoroscope, caused his heart to stop for New York County Medical Association President, Dr. Milton Bridger.

Romano worked as a chemical manufacturer for his own company called Jamol in Manhattan. Although he may not have considered himself a performing mentalist, he impressed his audiences whenever he decided to exercise his abilities.

Romano claimed his birthday was April 16, 1864, but his viewers continually mistook him for a much younger man. In a series of photographs – assuming they were not repeat photos – he appears to be extremely well preserved well into his 80's and 90's.

In Fulton Oursler's autobiography, *Behold This Dreamer*, (Little, Brown & Co., Boston, 1964), Oursler wrote that he found Romano a puzzling and weird man. Romano had given numerous seances at Oursler parties, but had never once accepted payment. In his book, Oursler says he knew the secret of many of Romano's tricks, and admitted he had served as Romano's confederate at one of his parties. But Oursler also describes watching Romano instantly heal a deaf man, and claims he has no explanation for many other phenomena he witnessed during Romano's performances.

Author Schwarz summarized Romano as follows: "Mystic or magician, holy man or iconoclast? Psychic, after-dinner speaker, entertainer, pioneer, aviator, chemist, salesman, and soldier of fortune – all describe the spry, sharp-witted, little 98-year-old New Yorker, whose vigor and appearance bore witness to his discovery of the fabled fountain of youth."

Romano died in 1962. Like the Piddingtons and so many others, he made no special claims for his puzzling feats and left his audiences to form their own opinions. Meanwhile, like a wise teacher, he subtly influenced his students.

Jacques Romano
and his Wife, Molly - 1915
Courtesy of Berthold E. Schwarz, M.D.

# *Act 4*

***Be wary! Check your wallets!***
***Here come some...***

### *PROMINENT TRICKSTERS*

Washington Irving
Bishop Portrait
Courtesy of Princeton
University Library

**WASHINGTON IRVING BISHOP** was a marvelous exponent of muscle reading. He followed the footsteps of **JOHN RANDALL BROWN**, a man who made this type of act famous. Muscle reading most often involves finding a hidden object, following a selected path, finding a chosen person, or performing a defined action. The person who has hidden the object grasps the wrist of the performer – or the performer may grasp the subject's wrist. The performer is literally led to the object by "being in touch" with the subject, who believes there is no way the hiding place could be discovered.

John Randall Brown
Portrait
Rauscher Collection

John Randall Brown Performing his Mental Wonders
Courtesy of Princeton University Library

Bishop could locate anything by muscle reading. He also performed other exciting acts, including his original Blindfold Carriage Drive. He once served as an assistant to medium/psychic Anna Eva Fay.

Washington Irving Bishop
Sketch rendition of Thought Reading - 1883 London Illustrated News
Rauscher Collection

Bishop was the godchild of author Washington Irving. He was an active 32$^{nd}$ Degree Mason, and belonged to the Knights Templar. In his youth he was nervous and ill, but during his career he created quite a sensation. Unknown to most people he suffered from cataleptic attacks, and during the seizures he would pass out for hours before regaining consciousness. As a medical necessity, he carried a letter stating that he was subject to these "comas."

Washington Irving Bishop in his casket, and his grieving mother
Courtesy of Princeton University Library

On May 12, 1899, he collapsed at the Lambs' Club in New York and was pronounced dead. But was he? An autopsy was performed on the 33-year-old Bishop, because sadly the medical alert letter that warned of his affliction was overlooked. A photograph shows Bishop in his casket, while his mother looks on. On top of his casket is the Masonic symbol.

Muscle reading requires great practice, and audiences find it hard to believe or explain. They mistakenly think that the tensing of the subject's wrist muscles or the racing of his pulse leads the psychic to the hidden object. Actually, the performer can achieve the same result with the subject holding onto a handkerchief or scarf. With the exception of Kreskin, not many performers attempt muscle reading today. Kreskin sometimes uses this practice to find his paycheck, hidden in the audience.

Bishop once had an assistant named Charles Garner. Born in England in 1857, Garner was known in mentalism history as **STUART CUMBERLAND.**

Cumberland learned muscle reading from Bishop, and then later claimed the act was non-contact. In his prime he toured Europe and America, and soon became competition for Bishop. After Bishop died, Cumberland perfected his own performance and is now also remembered in the annals of mind reading history. He not only performed for members of royalty, but made headlines fooling them. He was excellent at muscle reading, and like Bishop, his act included an exposé of spiritualism. A bitter opponent of mediums, Cumberland's negative approach to spiritualism was an odd contrast to his positive approach about his own psychic work.

Stuart Cumberland in performance
Courtesy Princeton University Library

1880

# IMPOSITION DETECTED!
# SPIRITUALISM EXPOSED!

*In response to repeated requests*

## MR. STUART C. CUMBERLAND

*Will LECTURE at*

# STEINWAY HALL,

LOWER SEYMOUR STREET, PORTMAN SQUARE,

MONDAY & TUESDAY, OCTOBER 4th & 5th,

*At 8 p.m., on*

# SPIRITUALISM

*And*

# CLAIRVOYANCE,

REPRODUCING AND EXPLAINING MANY STARTLING

# "SPIRIT-MANIFESTATIONS."

· Prices—Reserved Seats, 5s.     Front Seats, 3s.     Balcony, 2s.

*SPECIAL NOTICE.—Tickets may be purchased at Austin's Opera and Concert Ticket Office, St. James's Hall, Piccadilly, W., and at Steinway Hall, and in order to prevent disappointment and the consequences of a crush, it is particularly requested that intending purchasers will take an early opportunity of securing seats.*

DOORS OPEN AT 7.30.          CARRIAGES AT 9.45.

Stuart Cumberland 1880 brochure
Rauscher Collection

# PRINCES' HALL, PICCADILLY.

**Friday Evening, June 6th, at 8.30.**

**Saturday Afternoon, June 7th, at 2.30.**

DOORS OPEN HALF-AN-HOUR PREVIOUSLY.

*1884*

# Mr. Stuart Cumberland,

### THE CELEBRATED

## ENGLISH THOUGHT-READER,

Whose recent Paris, Vienna, and Continental Successes are unprecedented
in the annals of the platform, will, as above, give

## EXTRAORDINARY EXEMPLIFICATIONS

OF HIS POWERS OF

## DIVINING THOUGHT

BY PHYSICAL AGENCY.

He will also give Expositions of hitherto accredited

## "OCCULT PHENOMENA."

Prices:

**1st Seats (Numbered and Reserved), 10/6 ; Unreserved, 5/-.   Admission, 2/-.**

Tickets at Box Office at the Princes' Hall, and at principal Libraries.

Stuart Cumberland 1884 brochure
Rauscher Collection

Stuart Cumberland 1884 brochure
Rauscher Collection

Like all the past masters of self-promotion and publicity, Cumberland was very explicit in his advertising materials. They stated:

Mr. Cumberland is no "Mystic," and he disclaims all supernatural aid whatsoever. Without pretence and without humbug he gives his various illustrations, which, in order to provide against all idea of confederates or collusion, are only performed with gentlemen of undoubted integrity, chosen by the audience. His attempts at reading thought will embrace the following:

### READING THE NUMBER OF A NOTE
Mr. Cumberland will, under the same conditions as when successful with Baron Henry de Worms, endeavour to tell the number of a Bank Note, provided by the audience.

### LOCATING THE SEAT OF A PAIN
Given a subject suffering from a pain, Mr. Cumberland will, in full view of the audience, proceed to locate the exact seat of the said affection.

### PIN FINDING
A gentleman will be chosen to hide a pin in any part of the hall during Mr. Cumberland's absence therefrom. Whilst blindfolded, it will be Mr. Cumberland's task to find the pin.

### SELECTING A PERSON
To think of some person in the audience will be the part set for another subject. To discover this person, no matter where seated, will be Mr. Cumberland's endeavour.

### HARMLESS SECRETS DIVULGED
Mr. Cumberland will have pleasure in telling the ages, places of birth, and so forth, of his subjects – with, of course, their permission.

### TRACING OUT A ROUTE
"Think of a route you would, in fancy, like to take through the hall," will be asked of a gentleman. This done, Mr. Cumberland will proceed to go over this route, no matter how tortuous.

Cumberland took full advantage of every public appearance, like his historic séance in the House of Commons when he read Prime Minister William Gladstone's mind on June 19, 1884. He claimed other performance achievements in front of a host of notables, including the Kaiser, the Prince of Wales, Alexander Dumas, and poet John Greenleaf Whittier.

Cumberland died in England in 1922.

Pauline
Courtesy of Princeton University Library

Joseph Robert Poulin is another excellent but long-since forgotten hypnotist.

Poulin was known professionally as **PAULINE,** and at one time enjoyed an impressive theatrical career. In his book *Vaudeville: From the Honky Tonks to the Palace* (Henry Holt & Co., New York, 1953), Joe Laurie, Jr. said: "Pauline was tops; he had a fine personality, spoke like an actor and/or a doctor, and always referred to 'this experiment, which I performed before the world's greatest scientists.'" (p.11)

Pauline was known as "The Hypnotic Humorist," "The Man With the Electrifying Eyes," and "The World's Greatest Psychologist and Hypnotist." Like Polgar, he was a skillful contact mind reader, and gained a reputation for his dramatic blindfold drive. He was also quite skilled at opening a combination safe. His performances included appearances at the famous New York Hippodrome and the London Palladium.

Because these performers were tricksters of the mind, many of them were exceptional individuals who were also born psychologists, who basically taught themselves through their own experiences. Unfortunately, like many others of his genre, Pauline eventually got into trouble with the law. According to Joe Laurie, Jr., Pauline threw a waiter out of a window at the Flanders Hotel in London, following a drinking binge. For this violent act, Pauline received a sentence of six months to three years in prison. His sentence was finally reduced, and after his release Pauline managed to rescue his career.

He died in 1942, and is now virtually unknown.

The Zancigs
Courtesy of Princeton University Library

**THE ZANCIGS.** Julius Jensen was born in Denmark on March 7, 1857. With his wife, Agnes, the couple became one of the greatest acts in the history of mind reading. They quietly stated, "We don't claim that our work is supernormal, nor do we claim that we read your minds. We do claim that what one of the Zancigs thinks, the other thinks; what one of them sees, the other sees." The advertised themselves as "Two Minds With But A Single Thought."

1905 Theater Ad
Courtesy of Bill J. Weldon

Julius portrayed a dignified gentleman with pince-nez glasses. Agnes, who was also a Dane, wore pince-nez glasses, and was an appealing woman with a plain, serious face and an upswept hairdo. She was a hunchback, but actually her deformity may have helped the act, since some of the audience felt more apt to believe in the couple's abilities because of her affliction.

The Zancigs worked together for 30 years. Their approach was to demonstrate mental telepathy, and they were superior in their use of complicated codes to convey information. Their act took them all over the world. They rose to the top of their profession – but, like so many mentalists before them, in later years they eventually bottomed out financially.

When Agnes died in 1916, Julius remarried. His new wife, Ada, was renamed Agnes by Julius in order to preserve the act. (Believe it or not, Ada was a devout spiritualist.) They puzzled audiences and the press wherever they worked.

After attending one of the Zancigs' performances, Sir Arthur Conan Doyle went backstage to express his belief in their psychic ability. Julius admitted to Doyle that their act was done by trickery, and that he sent information to his wife through a system they had developed. Their performance was so convincing that Doyle did not accept the explanation!

The Zancigs belonged to the Society of American Magicians. Magicians liked

Agnes and Julius Zancig in their six cylinder Napier motor car
Rauscher Collection

them because they never pretended to be psychic within that fraternity. Instead, they were considered an "act" – and a great act.

In the latter part of his career, Julius gave private readings in places like Asbury Park, New Jersey, one indication of his fall from his former material affluence. These sittings were highly profitable, however, and his sitters believed he possessed legitimate psychic ability. Robert Lund, the late magic historian, wrote with insight of Zancig's last days in *MUM*, a publication of the Society of American Magicians, (Vol. 43, No. 9, February 1954):

> Time is unkind to those who live after their greatness. The days that remain beat and bully whatever is left when youth is gone. The blows are muted. They are struck by Neglect, Futility and Despair. The pain is not padded, but those who suffer the wounds try to conceal them, more ashamed of their vulnerability than their injuries.

Julius Zancig wanted those who remembered him to believe he had "a wonderful place" where he was "doing fine."

The "wonderful place" was in the basement of a building at the corner of 262 South 52nd Street in Philadelphia. The tenant had a street-level window fronting on 52nd and two larger windows facing the side street. The occupant, proclaimed a streamer running the length of the side windows, combined the skills of "psychoanalyst, astrologist and palmist." Below this banner was an exhibit – you had to stoop down to examine it – of faded posters, photographs and programs depicting Zancig at the height of his career, enlarged reproductions of letters from scientists asserting that his telepathic demonstrations were genuine, newspaper clippings, an assortment of crystal balls and a rack filled with copies of a 48-page paper-covered booklet entitled "Crystal Gazing." Zancig was not the author of this pamphlet, although it carried his name.

It was 1928 and Zancig was nearing 72. He put in a long day at the studio. The shop opened at 10 a.m. and closed at 8 p.m., except when he gave shows, when closing time was 9:30 p.m. Private "readings" or "consultations" were available by appointment.

The dream was always the same: to find another Agnes, younger perhaps, teach her the code and return to vaudeville. A male assistant was out, he reasoned, "because a man is never as clever as a woman in a mind reading act."

He put the suggestion in a letter to a lady in London whom he addressed as Daisy. She sharply reprimanded the old man for his familiarity. "Sorry I can't write like you," he apologized, "but explain to your hubby that I am of foreign birth and to excuse me." He asked her if she and her husband would care to take up the mind reading "or would you take it up with me?" He would return to London and introduce the couple as his students, and "I know England would sit up and take notice." It would cost 100 pounds to produce the act, "but after you have worked a year with me you will get one-half of that back. We could give a 90-minute show of magic and mystery."

Daisy declined. She wanted to know if he employed "supernatural power" to accomplish his inexplicable feats. "Now, friends," he replied, addressing the wife and husband. "First of all I want to make myself clear and understood. I teach nothing supernatural. My work is my own, and an original idea on how to transfer thoughts from one to another. There is nothing supernatural connected with it. I don't want you to think I have any power of any sort. When I perform it is all a very clever system."

In desperation he slashed the price of the code to 20 pounds – then the equivalent of $100. The offer was rejected.

Zancig abandoned "the wonderful place in Philadelphia" in the winter of 1928-1929. He moved to Santa Monica, California, where he died July 29, 1929.

And what of Daisy? She wrote an exposé of his methods for a London magazine.

Berol and Belmonte
Courtesy of Princeton
University Library

Without question, the Zancigs were recognized as being superior in their field. But there were also others, like **BEROL AND BELMONTE**. Mentalist and showman C. A. George Newmann hailed this couple as the Zancigs of their day. He praised their striking appearance and the rapidity of their work. They were billed as "The Premier Second-Sight Artists of the World," and played the best venues during their career.

**ERIK JAN HANUSSEN**, born out of wedlock on June 2, 1889 to Jewish parents and named Herschmann-Chaim Steinschneider, ranks among the strangest and most compelling of entertainers.

Erik Jan Hanussen
Courtesy of Phil Steinschneider

Known as "The Mental Wizard of All Ages," and also as "The Man Who Knows All," Hanussen performed stage shows in which he headlined telepathy, prophecy, and hypnosis. He also gave private readings, and was adept at astrology.

By 1934 he was destined to become "The Prophet of the Third Reich." With his Jewish background unknown at the time, Hanussen's success so impressed the upper echelon of the Nazi Party that he became a so-called psychic superstar for what Hitler promised as "The Thousand Year Reich."

Hanussen's close friends were Count Wolf Heinrich Helldorf, Storm Trooper Chief for Berlin-Brandenburg, and his deputy, Herbert Von Ohst. It was Helldorf who arranged for Hanussen to meet Hitler, who we now know was interested in the occult and destiny and was obsessively concerned with his future place in history.

Hanussen Poster entitled The Green Hand, 1919
Courtesy of Charles Reynolds

Hanussen held séances at his lavish "Palace of the Occult," located at No. 16, Lietzenstrasse, in Berlin. Surrounding himself at his residence with an elegant décor, prominent people of the theater, and high-ranking Nazi officials, Hanussen outdid all others with theatrical lighting, hidden microphones, and other built-in methods by which he obtained information.

Hanussen's medium, Maria Paudler, while blindfolded, gave a dramatic trance reading on February 26, 1933:

> I see a vast and distinguished room … Portraits of prominent men of history hang on the walls. They are men who have led Germany through much agony. Are they not the Chancellors of the Reich? Yes, this is the Conference Room of the Chancellery. Noise penetrates through the windows. The Storm Troopers move down the Wilhelmstrasse. There has been a magnificent victory. The people want Hitler. Victory, Victory, Victory!! Hitler is victorious. Resistance is useless. But the noise comes closer. Is there a struggle? Shooting? No … no … it is not that. I see flames, enormous flames … it is a terrible conflagration that has broken out. Criminals have set the fire.
>
> They want to hurl Germany into last minute chaos, to nullify the victory. They are setting fire to a large public building. One must crush this vermin. They want to resist Hitler's victory. Only the mailed fist of an awakened Germany can hold back chaos and the threat of civil war….

One day later, on February 27, the Reichstag burned! Hanussen was a classic opportunist and had many contacts with important members of the Nazi party – he had even lent them money. But just how he knew the plan for the great fire is still a mystery. One theory is that Marinus van der Lubbe, a Hanussen accomplice, may have set the fire, but as a result of his master's hypnotic ability, did not remember doing so.

Hitler quickly moved into complete power, and violence took over. Hanussen mistakenly thought his future was secure, and even anticipated the building of his own "Academy of the Occult." But although guarded by storm troopers, making great sums of money and living as a wealthy man, the egotistical Hanussen began to make enemies. Like

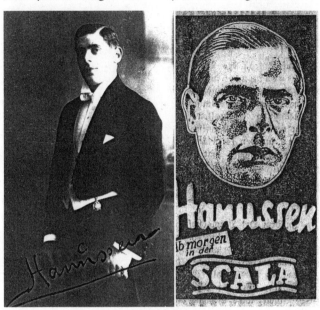

Hanussen and Scala Theatre Poster
Courtesy of Hannes Höller

many mentalists, he had an innate sense of mass psychology, but he could not outwit those he thought were Nazi friends. They considered him dangerous, and felt if he could predict victory, he could also predict defeat. Hanussen eventually became a problem that had to be solved. Ohst, Helldorf, and Hermann Göring all turned against him, not only because he was Jewish, but since he apparently knew too much.

Hanussen was scheduled to appear at the Scala Theater on March 24, 1933, but he never made the performance. Now known by the upper echelon of the Nazi party for his Jewish heritage, Hanussen could no longer be tolerated, and was simply eliminated. Hitler's storm troopers had taken him away, and his body was found south of Berlin on April 7, 1933.

In 1989, Columbia Pictures released a feature film called *Hanussen*, starring Klaus-Mari Brandauer. Its stunning fictional conclusion attempts to secure the reputation of this mentalist. As Hanussen is being murdered by the Nazis, he is challenged to make a prediction while dying. With his body riddled by bullets, Hanussen's last whispered words are, "You will all perish."

In 1998, Wilfried Kugel wrote the biography *Hanussen*, which was published in Germany. Although this publication was written in German, it was reviewed by researcher Martin Ebon in the January 1999 issue of *Magic* magazine. Hanussen's story is so intriguing that an American pictorial biography *Hanussen: Hitler's Jewish Clairvoyant*, was written by Mel Gordon (Feral House, California, 2001). Gordon, who is a University of California (Berkeley) Professor of Theater, presents the dark side of the devious and intriguing Hanussen. His previous book entitled *Voluptuous Panic: The Erotic World of Weimar Berlin*, sets the scene in the 1920's and 1930's in a decadent Berlin amid the rise of Nazism.

Polgar Publicity Brochure
Courtesy of Kenneth Klosterman

Although audiences today recognize Kreskin's feature of "contact mind reading" by which he finds his paycheck, Hungarian **FRANZ POLGAR** accomplished the same feat much earlier. Polgar was impressive because of his foreign accent, academic credentials, interest in the study of consciousness, and appearances from the early 1930's through the mid-1940's.

Polgar styled himself as a lecturer, writer, and master hypnotist. Born in Enying, Hungary, on April 18, 1900, he studied commerce and economics, and claimed his Doctorate of Psychology and Doctor of Economics from the University of Budapest in 1927. He emigrated to the United States in 1933, where he was naturalized in 1944.

Polgar's interest in hypnosis was inflamed by a fascination with Germany's enigmatic psychic/occultist, Erik Jan Hanussen. Although Polgar followed Hanussen's career and closely observed his performances, he distrusted him. In his book *The Story of a Hypnotist: My Adventures in Telepathy, Hypnosis and Memory* (Hermitage House, Inc., New York, 1951), Polgar describes how he shaped his hypnosis act differently from Hanussen's exuberant style, and developed his own performance more as an educational experience. Polgar first saw the strange Hanussen, "The Mental Wizard Of All Ages," performing a two-and-one-half-hour one-man show. After deciphering all of Hanussen's tricks, Polgar later acknowledged Hanussen as the king of tricksters, and described him as one of the greatest showmen of all time. Through his study of Hanussen, Polgar claimed he learned what **not** to do. Later, because of Hanussen's Nazi involvement, Polgar turned against him, calling him the Rasputin of Germany – "a wizard in the service of evil."

Polgar's publicity folder proclaimed him to be "The Amazing Dr. Polgar in Miracles of the

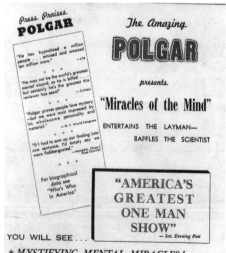

Polgar Publicity Brochure
Courtesy of Kenneth Klosterman

AMERICA'S GREATEST ONE-MAN SHOW

## "MIRACLES OF THE MIND"

*The Most Unusual Entertainment on the American Platform*

### ...ORIGINATED BY POLGAR...

Uncanny Mental Feats . . . Astonishing Mind Reading Experiments
The Photographic Mind . . . The Power of Suggestion, With or
Without Demonstrations . . . Incredible Memory Feats

*. . . Each More Baffling Than the Other! . . .*

**THE PERFECT CHOICE FOR ANY OCCASION**

# POLGAR

**3 WAYS** Whereby
You Can Book Him

(a) **PERCENTAGE—**
for Big Shows
(b) **FLAT FEE—**
chiefly for Clubs
(c) **EN ROUTE FEES—**
for economy

**A CHALLENGE**

Can he read your mind? You may
hide the check for his fee anywhere
in your city. If he cannot find this
hidden check by means of reading
your mind, you owe him nothing.

*Available from Coast to Coast
for Terms, Open Dates, etc.,
write*
**L. F. SHERMAN**
170 Broadway, New York 7.
Phone: CO. 7-3579
*(Inquiries will be forwarded to
nearest regional manager)*

Polgar Publicity Brochure
Courtesy of Kenneth Klosterman

Mind." His show consisted of mental miracles, hypnotic feats, and memory stunts. He received accolades from *The Saturday Evening Post, Life, Collier's,* and the *New York Telegram,* along with statements of praise from various famous personalities.

Polgar's work in the field of hypnotism continued to draw attention. Unlike the contemporary Kreskin, Polgar believed in hypnotism, and used his talent to his advantage to impress doctors, surgeons, and show people. He gained further recognition through his numerous lecture tours, and theater, college and television appearances. As a young man, I remember watching him perform on television. His demeanor and ability to handle a group left a powerful impression on me.

Theater and magic historian Charles Reynolds recalls that Polgar's show always had three parts. The first part of Polgar's show was a complicated effect called "The Magic Squares." Polgar describes it as follows:

I ask someone in the audience to call out a number between fifty and one hundred, which I propose to arrive at in a quite complicated series of additions from a blackboard on which sixteen squares are marked off. Let's say the number ninety-three is posed.

In each square I have a member of the audience write the name of some object, such as shoe, window, table, ice cream – actually anything. The assistant from the audience picks the squares in no particular order but at random. I stand in front of the blackboard so that I cannot see it. Then the words of all sixteen squares are called back to me, also at random, and I in turn answer by calling numbers, such as nine, sixteen, twenty-one, four.

The board filled thus, I name all the objects with the correct numbers and finally turn to it and add up all square numbers, horizontally and vertically by columns and then diagonally. Each totals ninety-three, if ninety-three was the selected number. Of course, I don't have to tell the audience that I have never seen the assistant, who is always a local resident. I tell them quite frankly that this feat is the product of a good memory and plain arithmetic.

Polgar claimed to have a photographic memory, and impressed his audiences with his "memorization" of a magazine that always had more than 96 pages. In this act, the audience would call out any page number, and Polgar would recite the content and details of any article, advertisement, or headline appearing on that page. His facts were so specific that if, for example, there was a photograph of a plate of meatballs on the selected page, Polgar would note the exact number of meatballs on the plate!

Contact mind reading was another segment of Polgar's performance, during which he would locate his check or fee for the performance.

Polgar was frank and open about his belief in telepathy and his interest in ESP research. His segment on hypnosis was always most impressive.

Throughout his career, there was always one side of Polgar's personality that was totally drawn to the academic. But equally as strong was his theatrical side, which sent mixed messages using his mind reading techniques. Early in his career Polgar met Sigmund Freud, and became fascinated with psychoanalysis and its application to medical pioneering. He correctly believed that the medical use of hypnosis would one day become more and more acceptable in the areas of hypnotherapy, anesthesia, pain control, dentistry, and general psychiatric disorders.

Polgar died in 1979. Today, sadly, he is hardly remembered.

Hanussen crossed paths with many entertainers and exponents of mind power. Another of these entertainers was **FREDERICK MARION**, whose real name was Josef Kraus. Born in Prague, Czechoslovakia on October 15, 1892, Marion would eventually demonstrate telepathy and clairvoyance with great prominence during the 1930's.

Frederick Marion
Courtesy of Mary Evans Picture Library

J. Gordon Melton, an expert on religious movements and psychic personalities, said after Marion met Hanussen in the 1920's, he warned Hanussen that he was becoming too involved in black magic, which would result in "disastrous consequences." Melton related in his *Encyclopedia of Occultism and Parapsychology* (Gale Research, Michigan, 1999) that, according to Marion, it was Hanussen who instructed the inner circle of the young Nazi Party in the power of signs and words, and who first proposed the swastika as the party symbol.

Marion, who was well educated, began performing at age 19. He was billed in music halls as "The Telepathic Phenomenon" and "The Man with Six Senses." Inspired in his youth by performances of the magician Rubini, he began to do astounding feats, such as locating hidden objects and describing the contents of sealed envelopes. He was also proficient in dowsing, and during World War II, the Austrian Army commissioned him to an officer whose job it was to find water for the troops.

In addition, by holding his dowsing stick over an enlarged map, Marion could divine maps without having to travel to various locations to find water. He also entertained the troops, and following his army work, returned to the European music halls. Eventually he gave lectures, private readings, and public demonstrations.

Marion claimed he had no spiritualistic experiences, such as seeing lights, talking with the dead, seeing apparitions, or hearing raps. What he was able to do, he claimed, was a result of his own mind powers, with no assistance from the spirit or any other world. He felt he was a telepathist, pure and simple – but yet he was also a public entertainer.

Researcher S. G. Soal investigated Marion, who cooperated on various tests in a series of twenty-five séances. Marion agreed to these same tests with researcher Harry Price, who noted the following:

> His public performances are well worth seeing. He has almost uncanny powers of finding hidden objects: but those powers, brilliant as they are, are not – so far as we have discovered – of a psychic nature. Marion has a charming personality; he assisted the experiments in every way, and I was sorry when the tests were over.

Both Soal and Price were convinced Marion was more than a vaudeville performer. Price writes of Marion in his *Confessions of a Ghost Hunter* (Causeway Books, New York, 1974) that the experiments included finding numerous small objects hidden in a large room within a minute or so. Marion also found a ring hidden in one of six rectangular tin boxes placed in various parts of the room. There were also various card experiments in the dark.

The researchers decided that Marion's ability was a result of *indicia*, or the gathering in some way of information from the audience who already knew the answers. The experiments with Soal and Price were published in 1937 as a bulletin of the University of

London Council for Psychical Investigation called *Preliminary Studies of a Vaudeville Telepathist.*

Marion, meanwhile, tells his life story in the book titled *In My Mind's Eye* (London: Rider, 1949).

Rajah Raboid Portrait
Courtesy of Princetion University Library

**RAJAH RABOID** became well known in several venues. Most notable were radio mentalism and crystal gazing. Born in New Orleans, Louisiana, as Maurice P. Kitchen on January 22, 1896, he was an aggressive publicity hound – and a strange personality.

Starting his career in carnivals as a magician, Raboid called himself "Ray Boyd," and gained experience from the performers he met as he traveled across the country. From all reports, he was a capable illusion performer as well as a good magician. However, his real talent lay in his ability to perform mental acts.

While he worked in the carnivals, Raboid observed many of these mental acts, and believed he could perform better than those he had seen. Obviously he was right, and shortly after his switch to mentalism he anointed himself "Rajah Raboid."

Raboid was tall and impressive in appearance, dressed in a turban, white tie and tails, mustache, and goatee. When I look at his photographs, I am reminded of Lamar Keene, the devious fake medium and subject of the book *The Psychic Mafia* (by M. Lamar Keene, as told to Allen Spraggett; Foreword and research by William V. Rauscher, St. Martin's Press, 1976. Reprinted by Prometheus Books, New York, 1997).

Raboid broadcast on Mexican radio to avoid legal problems that might result from his question-and-answer show. He offered an early version of today's advertised psychic hotline, and listeners willingly sent money to him along with their questions. Regulations were not strict in the 1920's, and he supposedly made $66,000 in one week with his program! He was later censured, but nothing could deter his successful climb to the top.

In New York City, Raboid performed to sold-out houses in theaters and made thousands of dollars each week. Selling books, offering readings, and building his own reputation was Raboid's goal every working day. Magic scholar John Booth reports that Raboid's one-time public relations manager George Marquis told Booth, "Raboid was the first to cash in with the occult on the air." Eventually Raboid became extremely wealthy, and like Lamar Keene, owned a mansion in Miami Beach, Florida.

Ads from Raja Raboid's Dream Book sold during performances for $1.00
Courtesy of Mario Carrandi

Raboid had a strong streak of the carney in him. He was a talented knife thrower and is also credited as being the first man to fly a plane while blindfolded – although the renowned John Calvert gained fame for this same feat.

Whenever Raboid tried something new, his results were impressive. Such was his performance with Johnny Eck. John Gaylin, a friend of the Eck brothers, lectured on their life and experience with Raboid at the 31st Magic Collectors' Weekend held in Baltimore, Maryland on April 28, 2000. As Gaylin told the strange tale …

**The Eck (born Eckhardt) Brothers** were born on August 27, 1910, in Baltimore, Maryland. Robert Eck was born healthy, with no abnormalities; however, his twin brother, Johnny, was born with only half a body, which ended at his rib cage. According to Gaylin, it became Robert's responsibility to take care of Johnny all of his life.

Despite his handicap, Johnny grew to be good natured and affable. In 1928 he met a magician who was so awed by the "half-man" that he offered him a life in show business. Johnny enjoyed magic, but the job he was offered was to be an exhibition in a carnival during his teenage years. He appeared in the 1931 MGM horror classic film *Freaks*, and in 1933 he was exhibited at the Chicago World's Fair. He was later booked by Robert Ripley to appear in his "Odditoriums."

Johnny Eck
Courtesy of John Gaylin

When Raboid met Johnny Eck he convinced him that together they could perform the "Sawing in Half" routine better than it had ever been done before. And so they did, beginning February 25, 1937, at Keith's Theater in Portland, Maine, in a show called

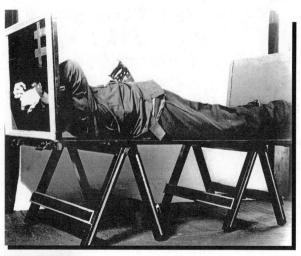

Johnny Eck
On stage with Rajah Raboid
Courtesy of John Gaylin

"Mysteries of 1937." Raboid's prediction was correct – his use of Johnny Eck in his act turned out to be one of the most startling and shocking illusions in the history of magic.

Raboid worked out a hypnotic routine using four volunteers from the audience. Two were stooges who remained on stage following the hypnosis segment. One of the stooges was Robert, Johnny's twin brother. While the audience watched, Robert was seemingly hypnotized, and was then put into a "sawing box." Moments later, unknown to the audience, Robert had changed places with Johnny, who then became the "head" in the box, along with a midget who was dressed in a pair of trousers that covered his body, who served as the "legs."

In an article titled "Magic's Most Unusual Illusion" (*Magic*, June 1977), historian David Charvet explains the clever method Raboid used, as told by magician Jean Foley who traveled with the show:

> When the box was rolled on stage, Johnny and the midget were concealed in the back of the box. As Robert was lowered into the box, he dropped right through the bottom into the table base. The assistants then folded the double back down inside, releasing Johnny and the midget.

> When the box was dismantled at the urging of the stooge, the pieces were set aside, and later stacked on the table base (which contained Robert), after the plank on which Johnny and the midget were lying was placed across the two saw horses. Very casually, the stacked pieces were rolled off stage into the left wing, where Robert was released from the base.

> Then a plant in the audience yelled, "If you're going to saw a man in half, why do you need the box?" So Raboid removed the box, and Johnny and the midget were all set – stretched out on the plank in full view and ready to wow the audience.

(Incidentally, Gaylin once told me transporting Johnny to the theater unnoticed was a problem. As a solution, Robert had a special suitcase constructed and carried his brother, who weighed only about 38 pounds, in it to and from the theater! Later on Robert used a baby carriage to transport Johnny.)

David Charvet continues his vivid description of this strange performance:

> Raboid again began to saw, this time in full view. After the saw had passed through the body, the subject awakened. Then incredibly, the upper half of the man raised himself on his hands – entirely separated from the lower half of his body! This was no mere illusion. Raboid appeared to have done the impossible. The man on the plank kept muttering, "I want my legs! Where are my legs?" … apparently unaware of the rest of his body on the

board. Raboid's assistants brought out a small set of steps that they placed at the edge of the board. Walking on his hands, the man descended the steps to the stage, still demanding to Raboid, "I want my legs!" At that point, the other volunteer ran screaming from his seat at the side of the stage and back up the center aisle. The half-man followed after him, but Raboid stopped him short. At that moment, the disembodied legs on the plank stirred. Then they swung over the edge of the board and stepped on to the stage. It was an unbelievable sight: half a man's body on each side of the stage.

Then the half-man noticed his legs and began running on his hands, chasing after them. The audience was in hysterics at the improbability of the whole scene. As the chase continued, the legs running with the upper half in hot pursuit, the laughter grew louder.

Just as the man was about to catch his legs near the stage wings, Raboid's two assistants grabbed the man under the arms and placed his torso atop his legs; at the same time giving him a quick spin. As he stopped, the man kept telling Raboid, "I want my … I want my …? not aware that he had been restored. Finally, Raboid asked him, "What do you want?" Suddenly realizing his condition, the man said, "I want my coat!" As he left the stage, Raboid remarked, "I'll be seeing you!" In the center aisle, the man turned and quipped, "Not if I see you first!" He then ran up the aisle and out of the theater as the still-laughing audience broke into an ovation

It was in the conclusion of the act, with Johnny scrambling off the plank chasing his "legs" and causing pandemonium, that the stagehands mounted Johnny on the trouser top over the midget who served as the legs. When they spun "the sawed man" around near the wings, Robert, his twin, quickly took his place and stepped out onto the stage. In front of the astonished audience, the whole man had been restored!

Gaylin believes that toward the end of his career the master magician Howard Thurston considered doing a similar act with Johnny Eck. But Thurston had been ill and died before any plans for the performance could be finalized.

Rajah Raboid is primarily remembered for his clever and profitable crystal gazing and mind reading acts. But the performance in which he used Johnny Eck, Eck's twin brother Robert, and a midget turned out to be a fantastic shocker.

As for Johnny and Robert Eck, the brothers retired in 1994 to live in Baltimore. John Gaylin visited them often and helped them in numerous ways. Although they were financially comfortable, both men were compulsively frugal, and after a cruel mugging, became reclusive. Johnny died in 1995, followed by Robert a few years later.

# Act 5

***Our show continues,***
***with a discussion of …***

### *MENTALISM - ON THE STAGE AND ON THE PAGE*

Chandra
Courtesy of Thomas A. Ewing

Fair Sa-Hara
Courtesy of Thomas A. Ewing

In private life, **CHANDRA** and his wife were James S. and Catherine Harte. Before his mind reading and crystal gazing act became a financial success, James also performed as Harto the Magician.

James Harte was born in Webster, Massachusetts in 1868. He met his future wife, Catherine Wren, who was a mind reader and crystal gazer in the Walter Main Show, where she was billed as **THE FAIR SA-HARA**. They married in 1901, and were together until James's death in 1933 at 63.

In 1910 the Hartes were sideshow performers with the Hagenbeck-Wallace Circus. In 1911 they became members of the Buffalo Bill Farewell Tour, a combination of the original Wild West Show and Congress of Rough Riders and the Great Far East Show. The tour was run by Harte's friend, Gordon Lillie, whose stage name was Pawnee Bill.

Although he was primarily a magician, escape artist, and ventriloquist, James would eventually be known for his dramatic mind reading act in the role of Chandra. When Chandra and Catherine were dressed in their stage attire, they became Arabian, or Moorish, or whatever else the audiences imagined them to be. Surrounded by lavish stage settings, their act emanated an air of mystery, set a spooky mood, and used various methods to astound and cause a constant uproar.

In *Two Hartes That Beat As One*, collector and magic historian Thomas A. Ewing (published by Ewing, Yardley, Pennsylvania, 1993) details the Hartes' career, from his early days in the circus and with the 1898 season of the Pawnee Bill Wild West Show. Ewing shares insights from Audley Dunham, Chandra's friend, assistant, and co-worker. The Hartes' costumes were outstanding, Dunham recalls, and can be admired from photographs taken during their performances. The innocent-looking turbans they wore were rigged with wires that produced electric impulses conveying code.

Chandra and the Fair Sa-Hara
Courtesy of Thomas A. Ewing

Late in his career, Chandra put his mind reading act up for sale. The advertisement read: "Worth $100 – Price $5.00." A paid advertisement in the Ewing collection tempts the buyer: "Any questions whispered to the performer, or any article handed to him, is instantly conveyed to a blindfolded assistant on stage without a word being spoken, using no suspicious signs, no apparatus, easily accomplished. This is the best system in the world."

According to Ewing, Chandra's sad ending was due to syphilis, a disease that required numerous injections to control the pain. After Chandra's death in 1933 in an Indianapolis sanitarium, Dunham emptied his storehouse, which had been unopened for eleven years. Dunham was so frightened of germs that he destroyed all of the costumes, rare letters from famous magicians, publicity material, posters, and countless cartons of equipment. The few remaining items were auctioned off in 1944, and the money was given to Chandra's widow, Catherine.

Ewing considers Chandra a most intriguing personage in the field of mentalism, and is convinced that if all his papers and records had been preserved, we would have a much deeper insight into the grand era of mind reading and crystal gazing. Quoting from a letter in his collection, Ewing says Chandra would have likely disagreed with this supposition, for he writes: "I have some interesting experiences to relate, but what's the use – it would only bore you."

One man stands out in the field of radio mind reading, for he earned a fortune doing it. This individual was Wilbert W. Holley, who called himself **MEL-ROY**, Master Mind of Mystery and Apostle of Mental Science.

During the 1920's, in the state of Texas alone, Mel-Roy was reported to have 84 people on his staff whose job was to open envelopes that contained letters and money, sent to him by people who wrote seeking answers to questions about their personal lives and future. Mel-Roy is alleged to have received 17,000 letters in one day from his listeners, and was taking in upward of $5,000 daily from those who believed in him.

Mel-Roy's love of magic later prompted him to leave his radio mind reading act and create a large magic

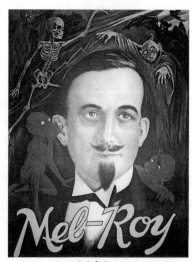

Mel-Roy
Portrait Poster
Courtesy of George Daily

show called "Mel-Roy's Magical Sensations." In 1933, using the money he made from radio mind reading performances, he spent many thousands of dollars to build his show – including a tent that seated 3,000 people.

From the Nelson Enterprises Catalog
Rauscher Collection

**ROBERT NELSON** advertised himself as the greatest name in mentalism for more than 45 years. Nelson rightly considered himself to be the largest exclusive manufacturer of mental equipment in the world. I believe he was – as a young man I remember sending for the Nelson Enterprises Catalog. He also wrote dozens of books and manuscripts, offered routines, and motivated people to read minds – and make money. Many of the Nelson titles are still in print.

Nelson also sold "miracles" like the "Talking Tea Kettle," and "Reaching Rods" for the séance room. From Nelson you could learn how to "Read Sealed Messages," "Make Mind Reading Pay," "Become Psycho, the Telepathic Brain," and "Make Predictions." He also offered ghost show items, guidelines for cold readings, horoscope material, and recordings to teach hypnotism. He designed many acts, and had his own radio mental question-and-answer show for which he called himself **DR. KORDA RA MAYNE**, The Voice of Destiny. He also had a theater ghost show.

Robert Nelson as Dr. Korda Ra Mayne on radio answering some of the thousands of letters containing questions and money
Courtesy of Diego Domingo

Alla Rageh
Rauscher Collection

In his early days, arrayed with a turban, Lawrence, bother of Robert Nelson was known as **ALLA RAGEH**. For years Robert wrote a monthly column in *The Linking Ring*, the official publication of the International Brotherhood of Magicians. Although it is now long after his death in 1972, students of mentalism still refer to his 200 columns and his vast body of work.

Even though Nelson wrote and sold material for pretenders, he personally believed in the world of extra sensory abilities. In his book *Hellstromism* (first published in 1935, describing contact mind reading, or muscle reading, as performed by Alex Vogt, a German who was known as **Hellstrom**), Nelson said about himself:

I am firmly convinced that there is such a thing as "genuine mind reading" and that Hellstrom practiced it many times, and I know I have genuinely accomplished it many times. I am further of the belief that this work, starting with muscle reading and developing it, will some day reveal the possibility of mind reading in a greater scope, or what we may describe as mental telepathy, over great distances and between many people. (p. 17)

Nelson's headquarters were in Columbus, Ohio for over 50 years. Today mentalist and private reader Diego Domingo still thinks so highly of Nelson that he has a kind of shrine to him in his home, and is writing a book describing Nelson's life and accomplishments.

**THE FALKENSTEINS** are modern mentalists. Well educated, sophisticated, suave, and articulate, they are in the vanguard of constant bookings, and they are a pleasure to watch. Glenn and Frances are a two-person act, and perform the best, most astounding spirit cabinet act in existence today.

Frances grew up with parents who were hard-working tent show performers. Her father was Willard the Wizard, and with Joy, her mother, performed a segment known as the "Spirit Cabinet." In this act, the medium steps into a cabinet with an open curtain stretched across the front, sits on a stool, and leans against an upright board. The performer's

Glenn Falkenstein and Frances Willard
Rauscher Collection

hands and neck are tied by volunteer helpers. The ties are nailed to the upright board. The curtain is drawn – and the spirits take over! From behind the curtain tambourines and plates fly up in the air, and bells ring. The next instant the curtain is flung open – and there is the medium, still seated on the stool in her supposed hypnotic trance, with her hands and neck still tied, with all the knots still intact! The grand finale occurs when the curtain is once again drawn shut, and a spectator's coat is tossed over the top of the cabinet. The curtain is immediately opened to reveal the medium *wearing* the spectator's coat – with her hands and neck still tied! Frances learned this act from her parents, and now performs it internationally with her husband Glenn, who is also an accomplished performer of blindfold effects.

The Falkensteins have also perfected the ability to pass information between themselves using the fewest number of words possible – and always with great success. They are entertainers par excellence.

A similar version of the Willard Spirit Cabinet was performed by the late **VIRGIL AND JULIE** for nearly 40 years. They called their act "The London Spirit Séance." As with the Willards' performance, audience members marveled at the speedy opening of the cabinet, immediately after they witnessed plates flying over the top. They were mystified when a volunteer entered the cabinet, closed the curtain, and phenomena happened. When the cabinet curtain was opened,

Glenn Falkenstein and Frances Willard performing their astounding Spirit Cabinet
Rauscher Collection

Julie of Virgil and Julie
The Psychic Enigma
Courtesy of Raymond J. Goulet

Julie
Rauscher Collection

Virgil and Julie performing the Spirit Cabinet
Rauscher Collection

the volunteer was found with a bucket over his head and his pant legs rolled up. The medium was still bound and entranced.

Max Maven
Courtesy of
*The Linking Ring Magazine*

**MAX MAVEN** is known as "The Thief of Thoughts." By the start of the 21st century, he had already established an amazing reputation in the history of mentalism.

Maven is an honor graduate of Brandeis University. At the age of 24 he decided to become a full-time mentalist. His speaking and writing skills are notable, and he has published close to 2,000 tricks, essays, articles, and columns. In addition, he has devised all manner of mind-bending effects.

Maven has appeared on television specials, documentaries, convention shows, comedy clubs, theaters, and in his prepared videotapes all over the world. Like fellow bizarrist **EUGENE BURGER** (who is equally adept at portraying the image of "ancient" magic), Maven dresses in black. He has adopted a demonic look, while Eugene Burger sports a full Santa Claus beard, and round wire-rim glasses. Along with their shaman-type approach to performing, Maven and Burger have appearances that make them easy to remember.

Eugene Burger
Courtesy of
*The Linking Ring Magazine*

Maven has an excellent attitude toward his work. He and Burger are among the most well-known, intellectual members of the magic community.

**THE EVASONS** have it all! Youth, personality, good looks, and a captivating way with audiences. They are most certainly leaders in the new generation of mentalists, as they work a fast and confident 15 to 90 minutes.

Jeff and Tessa Evason are accomplished in nearly all aspects of psychic entertainment – and according to their publicity, they can do anything! They advertise their show as "audience interactive," and cover in it Mind Over Body, Telekinesis, Telepathy, Super Memory,

The Evasons
Rauscher Collection

Levitation, ESP, Spirit Séance, Psychometry, Prediction, Second Sight Illusions, Clairvoyance, Psychokinesis, and additional Illusion. What more could an audience ask?

The Evasons' publicity claims that they are not a magic act, nor do they call themselves psychics. They don't perform hypnosis, they don't claim to have supernatural powers, and they don't ask anybody to believe in the paranormal. But they do think the powers of the mind reach far beyond what most people accept. Both are strong believers in intuition and in the power of belief.

Jess and Tessa began performing together in 1983 in Canada. In his booklet *The Magic of ESP: Unexplained Natural Phenomena Revealed*, Jeff writes that what at first seemed coincidental was really the "beyond," or sharing the same thoughts and ideas, which they now refer to as "Psychic Synergy" at play. He also reveals a change of heart between him and Tessa: "As magicians we were trained to be skeptical. We knew how to trick people by using illusion and sleight of hand. After you've done it long enough, you begin to think that all miracles are fake, and that everything can be explained scientifically."

The Evasons describe their show as a kind of Psychic Vaudeville. They demonstrate many forms of phenomena, and say their show has been called "The X-Files – Live on Stage." Incidentally, they claim many events take place during their show that even they cannot explain!

Their approach has earned them appearances on NBC-TV, and on *Powers of the Paranormal* on FOX TV. The International Psychic Entertainers Association was so impressed by this couple's performance that it awarded them the Dunninger Memorial Award for Distinguished Professionalism in the Performance of Mentalism as a token of their esteem.

Colleges, hotels, cruise ships, and locations around the world proclaim their greatness. Their blindfolded second sight work is especially impressive, and involves conveying unspoken messages about everything from names, dates, and details about people whom they have never met.

I have seen the Evasons work their minds, and can say without hesitation they are a world class act.

If ever there was a contemporary, smooth, and natural mentalist, it is **RICHARD WEBSTER**, a native of Auckland, New Zealand.

Richard Webster
Rauscher Collection

Webster is presented as a well-known international performer, and a master of cold reading.

People meeting him for the first time are immediately disarmed by his gracious, charming, and quiet manner. His talents include nearly everything in the psychic line, and his performance is believable in every respect. He not only earns a living from all types of readings, but also from his published books and tapes. From Webster, an aspiring mentalist can learn about Gemstone Reading, Palm Reading, Hypnotism, and Past-Life Regression. His book *Cashing In On Past Lives*, and his Webster Pendulum Video are but small parts of his professional world.

Richard Webster first became interested in magic when he was eight years old and watched a magician perform. Years later he met a man who read palms, and as a teenager he became interested in hypnotism. Today Richard Webster thanks Kreskin for how he now earns his living.

In an interview published in *Séance: The Quarterly Magazine Devoted to Spirit Magic* (Fall 1989, No. 5), Webster revealed some of his thoughts about his work. When asked, "How did you feel when you discovered that you could be psychic through trickery?" he replied, "I can't really recall. I probably thought it was great, because I could finally actually do it. When I first started doing the horoscope parties, I did have a guilt complex for a while. I was absolutely petrified that someone would discover the clipboards or something like that. That doesn't worry me in the least now. I feel that, hopefully, I'm doing more good than harm. I try to stress that if I'm doing a show, it is entertainment. But when someone comes to me for a private reading, it's a different matter. Then I regard myself more as a counselor, than as a fortune-teller." Counselor?? Hm-m-m.

Webster believes that mentalism is more believable as entertainment – and of course more lucrative. He says, "I do believe in extrasensory perception. Obviously it can't be done regularly enough to make a living. But when I'm on stage performing, if I'm doing an effect of clairvoyance, I believe that I'm actually clairvoyant whilst I'm doing it."

Richard Webster performed séances after attending the Invocationals, promoted by Bizarre Magic. He even rented an old, spooky-looking house with a friend to create a full experience for those who attended. Guests paid their money to Webster's friend, who stood in an old pulpit near the entrance. During these performances all the pseudo-phenomena happened, allowing for a contrived spirit encounter with the unknown. Because of his "Mr. Nice Guy" persona, Webster's audiences believed what they saw and heard was genuine. Any interference from religious groups was ignored, and Webster probably considered them fanatics.

Today he admits that, if approached on questions regarding religion, he quotes the following poem:

Ten Thousand paths may lead to God.
What right is mine to say,
That he who fails to walk with me.
Has missed the only way.

*Séance* Magazine
Summer 1990, No. 8

Subjects covered in Webster's sixty publications include techniques and procedures for reading auras, readings based on numerology, hypnosis, and the use of Tarot cards. Webster claims that Uri Geller described his books as "some of the best how-to books I have ever read."

Today Webster has numerous clients who come to him for private readings, and he is greatly admired in the field of psychic entertainment. He is in the vanguard of that group of puzzling people who play it "for real." An extremely convincing performer, and a great teacher of the trade, Webster is also a prime example of the "psychic business," and unfortunately the layman is unaware of Webster's real psychological secrets.

Perhaps this advertisement for his book titled *Astral Travel*, promoted by Flora Company, says it all:

"*Astral Travel* – Richard Webster's book about how to separate the gullible from their money by helping them zoom around the cosmos. Was $35, a few left for $20, out of print, there ain't no more."

# Act 6

***Watch these performers!***
***See how...***

### THEY AMAZE THE WORLD!

M. Lamar Keene
Rauscher Collection

**LAMAR KEENE** was a unique, puzzling, likable, and sad figure in the history of mind readers. He never belonged to a magic organization, and to my knowledge, never read a magic book. He never took lessons from magicians on blindfolds, or learned formally how to read billets. Most of his knowledge was gained from other fake mediums in the field of Spiritualism, where he himself was a star. The rest was a result of his own creative, devious mind.

Lamar is not listed in the annals of the mentalist fraternity, but these people could have learned a lot from his methods. His pulpit and platform work was dramatic, believable, and based on a religious approach. But he had a dark side – there was a gap in his conscience, and a moral chasm so great that cheating victims and then going to dinner with them became his modus operandi. Money was his god, and obtaining it was his life's work.

Lamar was an expert with the blindfold. He was a classy gentleman, always well prepared with meticulous records, and was "always on" in a quiet, dignified manner. He had a magnetic personality and was an excellent speaker, but there remained a sinister quality about him.

Lamar became quite wealthy as a result of several businesses. He ran an elegant spiritualist church; worked the spiritualist camps; performed thousands of private and group sittings; produced materializations, apports, and pictures on silk; and brought forth music from the spirit world. He was known as "The Prince of Spiritualism."

But in spite of all his so-called success, Lamar was a deeply troubled individual. I knew Lamar personally, and he related his entire story at an especially tumultuous time in his life, when he was about to commit suicide. Fortunately, through my guidance and counseling, he did not take his own life.

At a critical juncture in his troubled, unhappy existence, he met Florence Hutchison, a quiet, elderly lady who came to him for a reading, and also because she had lost an important legal document. Lamar was exceptionally agitated and impatient on the day of her sitting, so he blurted out the first thing that popped into his mind. He told her: "You have a metal file cabinet at home, a portable one, and it has a false top in it. There is a key to the false top in the bottom under some papers. The document is in that false top." Actually, he just wanted to rid himself of this lady, and when she left he thought she would not return again. Instead, when Hutchison returned to her home she found the document exactly where Lamar had predicted – in the false top of her file cabinet!

As a result, Florence Hutchison became a believer in Lamar's talents, and more important, in Lamar himself. Perhaps it was because she saw in him a similarity to her deceased son. Her humility, honesty, and trust had a profound effect on Lamar, serving as the catalyst for his slow rehabilitation. Florence Hutchison and Lamar Keene grew so close that she became a surrogate mother to him. He, in turn, cared for her until her death. (Incidentally, I conducted the funeral of this humble lady.) As a result of their relationship, he never returned to the séance room.

Lamar Keene's life story was documented in a book *The Psychic Mafia*, for which I served as the catalyst. After countless hours of taped interviews, visits to spiritualist camps, and conversations with those who were members of his "church," I wrote the introduction, assembled the bibliography, and saw the manuscript go to print through St. Martin's Press in 1976. The end result was a book by Lamar Keene, as told to Allen Spraggett, who did the final writing. Now considered a classic in psychic research, the book describes in lurid detail how far individuals can descend into the murky

The author in 1973 meeting with M. Lamar Keene at the Haunted Mansion in Walt Disney World, Florida. In numerous interview sessions Keene revealed the secrets of his career as a fake psychic and medium who contemplated suicide.
Rauscher Collection

world of manipulating lives through the use of private readings and numerous other methods for producing fake psychic phenomena.

Lamar Keene was not the first psychic to regret his life's work. Charles Pidgeon (pseud.) revealed similar feelings in his book *Revelations of a Spirit Medium*, first published in 1891; a facsimile edition was published in 1922. In this book, Pidgeon relays the effect he had on his sitters, who realized too late that they had been cheated and defrauded, and had lost their money to a charlatan.

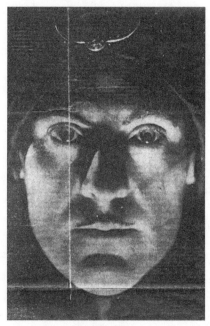

Hermes Trist
Rauscher Collection

A similar self-exposé appeared in *The Sunday Oregonian of Portland* on January 27, 1935, detailing the mentalism work of Hermes Trist, a performer known as **HERMES**.

Hermes had a crystal ball, wore a turban, and considered himself a "mitt reader," or fortune teller who read lines in the hand, or mitt. Incidentally, in Hermes' opinion, all mystics or mental workers were mitt readers.

Young Hermes became interested in fortune telling as a boy. Later, he worked as a reader for 15 years. His carnival training in how to bilk money from the public was by a man called "Pharaoh." As part of this training, Hermes worked as a "dummy." His job was to obtain information from customers while they waited to see Pharaoh, who had a speaker built into his turban through which young Hermes Trist passed along the facts. Pharaoh would then address a person by name even before he or she sat down in front of his crystal ball! Next he would astound this person with the answer to a written question that his guest still held in his or her hand! (A special table allowed Hermes to obtain knowledge of the question the guest wrote before the session.) If a sitter appeared gullible, Pharaoh encouraged the person to come back for an important message in a day or two, thus ensuring a second visit. Hermes eventually perfected the same scam – and others.

During his years of experience, Hermes found that the crystal ball worked better than cards or tea leaves. In his theater performances, Hermes' assistant collected messages from the audiences that were then supposedly burned on stage. Hermes would go to his crystal ball and offer replies to the written questions that had been reduced to ashes. How, you ask? The burning tray that held the messages had fire on only four sides. The actual messages dropped through the middle of the tray into a hollow stand, and then fell through the floor to Hermes' assistant, who sat under the stage. A button activated a final burst of flame and smoke. Hermes then moved to his Crystal Ball Table and placed his feet on a metal contact plate. He wore hidden wires up both legs and into his turban. Contact with the plate activated the speaker in his turban, where he received the messages from his assistant under the stage. The rest was pure showmanship.

Although the real money came from requests for private readings, Hermes did it all. Slates, trumpets floating in the dark, ghostly voices, ridding houses of ghosts – all this was part of his racket. After performing professionally for over a decade, these and other more sordid tricks prompted Hermes to give up his mentalism act. Like Lamar Keene it eroded him, and he felt the need to unburden himself. By 1935 he was sorry he ever had anything to do with mentalism. He hated Pharaoh, and he hated himself even more.

Strangely, despite the fact that Hermes lived a life of fraud, he believed in astrology. He said, "I do believe in what, for want of a more scientific term, is called psychic astrology. I believe in it thoroughly and sincerely."

Kuda Bux Portrait
Courtesy of Mike Caveney

**KUDA BUX**, "The Man With the X-Ray Eyes," performed an act he called "Sightless Vision."

In the 1930's and 1940's, Kuda Bux was at his peak as a world-renowned entertainer. He loved magic, and also performed illusions. I remember as a young man seeing him on television, and reading about him in magazines and newspaper articles. He evoked constant mystery, and no matter how many performers tried to duplicate a blindfold act, they never reached the level of perfection accomplished by Kuda Bux.

Born Khuda Bakhsh in Aknmur, Kashmir, Pakistan, on February 17, 1905 (or 1906, depending on the source), he was one of seven boys, the product of an educated family. When he was 13 years old he saw a magician called Professor Moor, whom he convinced to hire him as his assistant. From Professor Moor, Bux learned to perform "The Linking Rings," but he longed to become adept at what he considered "real magic."

He next studied the power of yoga, admitting that he did so to further his quest for personal fame and fortune, and not for any religious reason. Through yoga, Bux learned about the conscious and the unconscious. For many hours every day he practiced visualization. He said this was the beginning of his "seeing" with his mind.

For the next two-and-a-half years he practiced this art, and he gained a heightened power of concentration. Eventually he attempted fire walking. This feat brought him further recognition, and soon he was the subject of observation by a group of physicians in England. He recalled what his yoga teacher once told him: "Certain holy people have been known to develop so great a concentration that they can see without the use of their physical eyes."

Kuda Bux
Courtesy of Mike Caveney

Kuda Bux became more and more interested in his inner senses and their innate power. He later included a blindfold act in his conjuring; and in 1933, at age 28, he claimed he could read a book with his eyes blindfolded. Many doctors began serious examinations of him, and his fame escalated.

Charles Buckner
Rauscher Collection

(Incidentally, my friend **CHARLES BUCKNER** of Birmingham, Alabama, claims he uses the exact same method as Kuda Bux in his performance, and for years did the "Sightless Vision" act. Buckner also extols the excellence of German mentalist Satori, and says he does a "staggering" sightless performance in the same tradition as Kuda Bux.)

For his demonstrations, Kuda Bux used two large wads of bread dough. Volunteers pushed the dough into his eye sockets, and then covered his eyes with oversized pads of cotton. Next his head was wrapped in 12 yards of bandages. Finally, three large table napkins were tied around his head, over the dough and bandages. Bux then proceeded to drive a car, trace a volunteer's handwriting on a blackboard, ride a bicycle in traffic, identify objects, and even read a newspaper. Not only was his act impressive – it appeared impossible!

One of his most astounding feats was done on September 11, 1937 in Liverpool, England, when, fully blindfolded, he walked the narrow ledge on a roof, 200 feet in the air. Everyone was convinced of his paranormal powers; he was so admired that he became a favorite subject of Robert Ripley's "Believe It Or Not" newspaper feature.

It was the audience's choice to believe whether or not Kuda Bux possessed ESP, clairvoyance, or second sight; he simply and humbly allowed people to draw their own conclusions. But usually his audience was totally convinced – Kuda Bux was really and truly "The Man With the X-Ray Eyes." His viewers were certain he could not see through his blindfold; they knew he saw words and objects with his mind! So impressive was he that author John Godwin wrote eleven pages on this enigmatic man in his book *The Baffling World* (Hart Publishing Company, Inc., New York, 1968).

Placing coins over one's eyes, pasting surgical tape over the coins, and then securing both with a regular blindfold is a method used by many mentalists. It is also common among fake spiritualists who do billet readings from the platform. These performers are easier to expose – but no layman ever doubted Kuda Bux's talent!

There is an interesting incident related in an article from which I gained some of the above information ("The Amazing Eyes of Kuda Bux" by Roald Dahl, *Argosy* magazine, July 1952 issue). In this article are descriptions of events that fool and puzzle scientists – and even other magicians:

"A question? Yes? Can I see through a sheet of metal?

"No, I cannot see through anything, not even my bandages. My eyes themselves are not in use at all when they are covered. Instead it appears to me – although I confess I am not quite sure of this – that it is with the pores of my naked skin that I see on such occasions. I can see anything at all so long as a part of my naked skin is in view of the object. Put a sheet of metal in front of me and I cannot read a book which is on the other side of it unless you allow me to put my hand around the sheet of the metal, in view of the book. Then I can read it. You like to test?"

"I should like to test it," I said, "but I haven't got a sheet of metal. We'll use the door instead."

I stood up, went to the bookshelf and took the first book I saw. It was Boswell's *Johnson, Volume II*. I opened the door and told Kuda Bux to stand behind it. I opened the book at random, propped it on a chair on the other side of the door from him and stationed myself in a position where I could see both him and the book.

"Can you read that book?" I said.

"No, I cannot, of course."

"All right, you may put your hand around the other side of the door, but only your hand."

He slid his hand around the edge of the door until it was within sight of the book, about two feet away. The hand seemed to hover, to quiver slightly, feeling the air, like the antenna of an insect, and it turned so that the back of it was toward the book.

"Read the left-hand page," I said. "From the top."

There was silence for perhaps 10 seconds, then smoothly, without pause, he began, "Pray teach Veronica to love me. Bid her not mind Mamma. Mrs. Trale has taken a cold, and been very much disordered...."

In his later years Kuda Bux was happily ensconced at the Magic Castle in Hollywood, California, which he visited each night to play cards and spend time with his fellow magicians. He wore glasses, but friends thought he might have done better with the blindfold on. He was beloved and remembered as an astounding gentleman.

Walter Gibson told me a great story about Kuda Bux. Bux was performing with his many layers of blindfolds, and, in an effort to trick him, someone turned out all the lights in the room. He responded, "I am aware that the lights have gone out. You must understand that I see not only with my mind, but with your eyes as well. If you cannot see, I cannot see – even though I am blindfolded." The lights were quickly turned on, and Bux finished with a standing ovation.

William Larsen, the late editor of *Genii, The Conjurers' Magazine*, said in the May 1976 issue: "I suppose I must be a skeptic because I feel there must be an answer as to how he does it, but I have watched him time and time again performing at the Magic Castle, and I swear what he does is impossible. You have to see it to believe it. When all the bandages and dough are removed at the end of the act, you have to believe that Kuda Bux has a power that we do not." (However, a magician friend who saw Bux perform as an older man at the Magic Castle said that, with age, Kuda Bux's method was obvious.)

Kuda Bux died of a heart attack on February 5, 1981. In Bux's obituary (*Genii, The Conjurors' Magazine*, March 1981), Jack Hurlbut is quoted:

While visiting Kuda in his apartment, I mentioned the following conversation to him. Some people who had last seen him work in the Magic Castle asked me whether or not he would ever teach anyone how to perform his "Blindfold" feat. I told them I did not think that he would ever teach the secret to anyone and that he would take it with him. In our conversation I asked Kuda if I was right. His reply was: "I will have to take it with me, because there is NOTHING to teach!"

The obit further states:

When you consider that during his last performances at the Castle Kuda was over 90% blind and he was still performing the "Blindfold," it makes the above statement kind of interesting!

Peter Pit made a one hour video tape interview with Kuda in June of 1977 and we hope, someday, to transcribe all of our interviews with famous people into book form. Meanwhile, there was one very interesting statement Kuda made during this tape which I think shows Kuda's real feelings. He said: "I believe in Card Reading but I don't believe in card readers. I believe in Mentalism but I don't believe in mentalists. I believe in Spiritualism, but I don't believe in spiritualists."

Kuda Bux left one son from a marriage that failed; however, he left the legacy of a career that succeeded. Few people in this world have had the privilege of a newspaper headline calling them "The Eighth Wonder of the World" – or "The Wonder of the Century."

John Calvert
Rauscher Collection

**JOHN CALVERT** is a master magician whose name is legendary in the annals of magic.

In May 2001, at 90 years of age, John was given the Magician of the Year award from the Parent Assembly of the Society of American Magicians in New York City. During his stage appearance at this event, Calvert performed the Floating Organ illusion. His wife, Tammy, sat at the keyboard as the console moved from the stage out over the audience. He also did the classic Levitation, Dancing Handkerchief, and other selections from his long-running and touring "Magicarama Show."

Although Calvert is not a mind reader in the tradition of those who only perform mental magic, he has perfected one illusion that casts him as a stage persona of extraordinary powers. The act is called Audio Sharp Shooting, and during his performance for this feat Calvert is blindfolded.

First, Calvert's eyes are covered with coins. Volunteers from the audience then assist in applying numerous layers of wide adhesive tape over the coins, rendering sight on his part seemingly impossible. With the blindfold in place, Calvert is handed a .22 rifle and shoots candles, balloons and sometimes walnuts from the head of an audience volunteer who is seated on the stage in a chair. John's subject volunteers as a target thinking, "This is just a trick – this man would not shoot real bullets at me." But the gun, target, and bullets are real and ungimmicked. Calvert's only guide to the target's location is a clicking sound, made by his wife, Tammy, who holds a cricket clicker over the target's head. To the audience, the implication is that Calvert is able to sense his target's exact position, sight unseen, by a form of mind reading.

John Calvert
Audio Sharpshooting
Rauscher Collection

Calvert performs a similar trick by placing a hatchet on a target pad, with the sharp side of the hatchet facing him. BANG! When he fires, the bullet hits the hatchet and splits in half, with the two pieces of bullet extinguishing two candles positioned on either side of the hatchet.

John Calvert flying blindfolded over Nashville,
Tennessee, April 14,1945
Rauscher Collection

Calvert seldom misses the candles, balloons, or walnuts. Magician friends insist he uses a trick target, but this is not so. As Calvert's biographer and friend, I have had numerous instances to observe this feat and discuss it with him. I, myself, have practiced with him several times, and I can assure all who question or doubt that the bullets are certainly real, fired by Calvert and absorbed into the target pad.

John's performance is unique because it implies a form of mind reading that exists between Calvert and the volunteer. It gives the illusion of a mind reading effect, and is sculptured around a sharpshooting act, with no doubt on the part of the audience that Calvert cannot possibly see. Calvert's act is dramatic, and even more breathtaking when, blindfolded, he flies a plane or drives a speedboat.

The second photo shows John Calvert, blindfolded, piloting a plane over Nashville, Tennessee, on Sunday, April 14, 1985. To the amazement of his observers, John not only flew the plane, but also completed a safe landing. The first photo shows him ready to perform his audio sharpshooting act. To those who watch, John appears to be guided by some inner sense, whereby he sees not with his eyes, but with his mind.

John Calvert is a master of the blindfold and, at the age of 91, still performs with strength, vigor – and class.

Uri Geller
Rauscher Collection

**URI GELLER** can be considered either a clever magician/mentalist, or one of the most complex, successful, and enigmatic figures on the contemporary scene. Today most magicians refer to him as a fellow performer, and classify him as one of their own. Geller would not agree.

I first met Uri Geller in New York City in the early 1970's at the home of Judith Skutch. Robert, her then husband, was interested in healing, but Judy's interests in matters pertaining to the psychic and paranormal were much broader. Beginning in 1968, she explored all phases of these phenomena. She went to mediums, interviewed researchers, sponsored groups for discussion in her elegant apartment dwelling, and raised money for parapsychological research, including experiments conducted in the Dream Lab at Maimonides Hospital, New York. She ran training seminars, sponsored a conference and became what some called "the den mother to parapsychology." Even more descriptively, she was referred to as a "cosmic catalyst" and "The Perle Mesta of Psi."

One afternoon I, along with several others, was invited to meet Geller at the Skutch residence. Uri was casually but impeccably dressed, charming, and disarming. His manner portrayed a kind of innocence, very natural, intense, well spoken. He had marvelous verbal skills, and the questions asked by the guests – as well as Uri's answers – went on forever.

Eventually to demonstrate his ability Geller bent some spoons. Then, to my dismay, he bent my house key. I detected no flaw in his performance, and whatever method I might have suspected was not apparent; nor did I observe any unusual moves as I watched him bend table flatware for the other guests.

It was inevitable that the magic fraternity would find a way to duplicate Uri's feats, and then market all sorts of gimmicks in an effort to accomplish the same results. One item developed was a small, flat metal piece that contained a hole, and was attached to an elastic cord. After the performer placed a key in the hole, with leverage from the unit, the key could be bent using the thumb. The metal piece attached to the elastic cord would then fly up the performer's sleeve and out of sight. But Uri was not wearing long sleeves when I observed him perform that afternoon.

A deluge of articles appeared offering ways to bend forks, knives, and spoons, followed by booklets on the same subject. Soon books appeared about Geller, and his television appearances escalated. He began to demonstrate psychic vision and remote distance vision, predicting what people wrote and hid from him, until his reputation created a puzzle and magicians began to attack instead of embrace his talents. Geller answered all accusations, and, in some cases, even sued his accusers.

Uri Geller is now the subject of numerous books – some favorable, others devastating. Most interesting is the book *Uri Geller – Magician or Mystic?* written by Jonathan Margolis, (Welcome Rain, New York, 1999). In this 291-page biographical work, Margolis brings himself to the point of belief in the Geller phenomenon.

In a private meeting with Geller, Margolis' son David brought an oversized spoon, thicker and heavier than the average. Geller placed the spoon on the young man's hand. Then, after a short period of time, the spoon – by itself, in full view of the father and son – slowly bent to a 90-degree angle, standing up from David's hand "like an upside-down V." On page 58 of his book, Margolis comments:

> To see a spoon bend in Uri's hand, as everyone has on TV, is one thing. It could be a special spoon; he could be in collusion with the TV people, anything. But to watch your own spoon actually in the process of bending and without Uri touching it at the time was truly disturbing. I picked it up to try to feel if it was at all warm, or had some caustic chemical on it. There was clearly no chemical. I touched the bend point to my upper lip, a specially heat-sensitive spot. It was cold.

A psychic's job is to keep convincing others, an endeavor that is surely draining. Geller had apparently convinced Margolis, and, as a result, Margolis went ahead with the creation of his book.

Barrie Richardson, author of *Theater of the Mind* (Hermetic Press, 1999), had a similarly convincing experience. Richardson, a professor of management and dean of The Frost School of Business at Centenary College in Louisiana, has a background in magic and mentalism that spans over 50 years. He prides himself on his knowledge of the methods of mentalism. His popular book is filled with mind-boggling effects.

In late September 2001, Richardson attended a party in London where Uri Geller was also present. In Richardson's words, this is what happened:

> I had a most amazing experience at a private party in London a few weeks ago. Uri Geller asked if I had ever seen him bend a spoon, and I said only on television. He picked up a large spoon from the table and asked me to join him at the bar. He placed the spoon down and began to stroke it. A small bend appeared. He held it up for me to see and then placed it down again. I looked at it closely and the bend was more pronounced. I was astonished since this happened without any misdirection. He asked if I would like the spoon as a souvenir and I said "Sure." He took out a felt tipped pen and signed it. As I walked back to the room I was really taken by surprise. The spoon was now bent at a 75-degree angle. When I tried to bend the spoon, it was too strong for me to move in my bare hands. The bend was not at the weak spot near the spoon, but a few inches up from that spot. Uri is 54 and looks 35. He is clearly a man apart.
>
> — Courtesy of Marcello Truzzi, Ph.D.

Whether this experience made Richardson a believer is not known. The escape clause for mentalists who are fooled, deceived, or even tempted to believe in another reality is simply, "It was a trick, but I don't know the method."

Magicians still debate their belief in Geller, often without any direct contact or observation of him. Many magicians (along with his friends) are puzzled by him. David Blaine, street magician and star of his own TV specials, was so enamored with Geller that he flew to England to meet him. He came away from his visit convinced that Geller is real.

Intellectual British magician David Berglas, a past president of England's Magic Circle, is mentioned by Margolis in his book. He thinks what Geller does is based more on intuition than on psychic ability. Allowing for the unexplained, Berglas says the following about his own career as a mystifier:

Some things in my professional career happened that I don't know how they happened. Something would work because of extreme luck, or you'd made a lucky guess, but again and again and again. It's perfectly possible for a psychic to be a magician and a magician to be a bit psychic. I'm not a skeptic. I have an open mind and like to investigate things. Having been part of CSICOP, I now regard skeptics as scoffers, who are ignorant about magic.

My definitive statement about Uri is this. If the man is a genuine psychic, has paranormal abilities, can bend metal by his mind, can duplicate a drawing that you're only thinking of, can make seeds sprout, can stop and start a watch, can do all the other things that he claims, then he's the only person who can do it and must be respected. In my lifetime, nobody else has ever achieved such international fame and incredible respect. If, on the other hand, he's a charlatan, a cheat, a con man, a magician, a trickster, a crook, and he's achieved that level of notoriety, you must respect him. Whichever way you look at him, he's a phenomenon. Even magicians haven't pinpointed what he does. The public is demanding, and he's done it consistently everywhere in the world. You can't get away with doing something badly and get such acclaim. (p. 236)

(Incidentally, Judith Skutch did a great deal to promote Uri, but then went on to other things. She would later gain fame as the discoverer of the person who "brought through" the now famous *A Course In Miracles*. This unusual work, originally published by Skutch, was the result of an inner voice "channeled" to Helen Cohn Schueman, who was an atheist! Published in 1975, the 1,200-page three-volume book set has been selling well for years. But I digress …)

Uri has never admitted he uses methods of misdirection, sleight of hand, or diversion techniques. Other magicians believe he does so, and are satisfied that he has been fully exposed. The beginning of this exposure must be attributed to The Amazing Randi, who, through public appearances and in his books, has stated facts and attempted to justify his opinions.

The cover of the December 1991 issue of *Magic* magazine features a full-face pastel sketch of Geller, with an image of Randi drawn into the bowl of a bent spoon! Randi, also a skilled magician, proclaims that Geller is also a skilled and clever magician – with methods he can duplicate.

Because of Randi, Geller has been adopted by the magic fraternity. The publishers of *Magic* magazine compiled a survey list of 100 magicians who have shaped the art of magic in the twentieth century. Strange as it may seem, Geller was named on this list, but Randi's name does not appear.

Despite many efforts promoting Geller's exposure he has not been affected by it, and continues performing with calm and charm, and a fervent belief in God. Uri is now a world figure. From bending spoons to dowsing for oil, he has become a multimillionaire and owns a large estate in Sonning, Berkshire, England. He counts among his friends scientists and famous figures around the globe.

Geller claims he is real, and although he continues to have doubters they have changed neither his image nor impact. He remains unflustered by his critics – including his archenemy, The Amazing Randi, who, like Professor Moriarty in the stories of Sherlock Holmes, stalks Uri Geller's career.

# Intermission

Ladies and Gentlemen, we are witnessing a procession of talented performers from the distant past, as well as those who presently work in today's public and private venues.

Those performers from the past who graced the stage lived in an era when live theater was everywhere. They were, and still are, ENTERTAINERS. Were they ethical? Some were. Some still are. Many are not. But all of them worked hard to entertain their audiences in whatever venue they happened to find themselves. Those in the past had the advantage of many theater circuits, and once they obtained a booking they could work long engagements. For them, before movies and television, vaudeville was the way to earn a living, to provide amusement, culture, and unusual novelty acts live, on stage.

Many show business people did not realize the impact motion pictures would have on their lives. The invention of talking pictures not only replaced vaudeville, but also caused thousands of performers to end their careers in what once had been active, sold-out theaters. Without Social Security or hospitalization, many of these performers struggled for financial survival. They all hoped the good old days would return, but they had really lost their means of livelihood. In many cases they had no other skills. Yet they carved a place for themselves in show business history, and contributed to a unique and popular form of entertainment.

Along with the countless acts that had once trod the boards were numerous mind reading acts. But as times changed, these performers had a slight advantage. They could do private readings.

Those who now represent the new age of mind reading are similar to those of the past. They no longer have the stage as a home, but instead use any available venue to exercise their pseudo-psychic demonstrations. Like many of their predecessors, they appear in trade shows, at psychic fairs, in spot television appearances, and at private parties. They give lectures for magicians, sell their methods on videos – and, like their predecessors, some do private readings. Perhaps as audiences become even more sophisticated, these performers will also find it difficult to earn a living.

I remember a play called "The Great Sebastians," presented in 1956 by Howard Lindsay and Russell Crouse, which starred Alfred Lunt and Lynn Fontanne. This production about a vaudeville mind reading couple premiered on January 4 at the ANTA Theater on Broadway. To Sebastian, his act was the only thing in the world of importance. To his partner, Elsie, money was the issue. But to each of them, their act was their life. I think this is true of mind readers today. They love what they do. They are empowered by their own skills, and live in a world where they need to sell themselves constantly, compared to yesterday where a booking might last for months or years.

Listen to Sebastian as he speaks his lines in Act One, Scene 1, in a different world, but with circumstances similar to today:

This time I shall blindfold Madame and come down among you, and
try to send to her across the intervening space the thoughts you put into my

mind. Remember, the little lady makes no claim to occult or supernatural powers. However, if you believe that what you see is caused by odic force, psychometry, metaphysical manifestation, or the simple triumph of mind over matter, you are at liberty to do so. And may I add, we have performed before all the leading scientists of every country in which we have appeared – and Madame has amazed them all.

And now please return to your seats, and listen to the conclusion of a stirring pit orchestra selection. Imagine the fancy signs with large gilt frames that stand on each side of the stage to announce more performers. Prepare to be amazed, and to wonder if you can believe your own eyes! Watch the house lights dim and the curtain rise for the final acts. Join me once more to meet and ponder the names from a ghostly past, and from the present as we rejoin THE MIND READERS – these Masters of Deception.

# *Act 7*

*Are you confused?  Confounded?*
        *Here come some...*

## MORE MIND MANIPULATORS

Tim Conover
Courtesy of Eugene H. Voshell

Some mentalists now work in the corporate field; their acts are more appealing to business groups and trade shows than the walk-about, close-up card trick, spongeball magicians.

**TIM CONOVER** is a corporate performer. He has appeared as an entertainer before employees of Xerox, AT&T, IBM, Westinghouse, and many other large firms.  In 1995 he received the Dunninger Award from the Psychic Entertainers Association.  He is the ultimate in style.

Conover uses a crystal ball in his act, but to his credit, he publicly admits he is a magician and, as such, does not do private readings.

Conover's publicity proclaims:

Birth dates are dramatically unveiled.  Words randomly selected out of well-known books are instantly revealed.   Drawings are duplicated.  Borrowed finger rings are linked together, completely examined, and then visually unlinked in slow motion.  Three members of the audience construct the elements of a dream vacation and find a complete description sealed in an envelope, inside a wallet, that remains in the spectator's hands through the presentation.

Conover further confounds his corporate audiences with blindfold readings:

Tim identifies personal objects you choose at random.  He divines the serial numbers on bills of any denomination.  Personal messages sealed in envelopes are described in intimate detail without ever being collected.  Birthplaces, social security numbers, close friends, birthmarks, important events, situations, and thoughts known only to you are revealed in a delightfully captivating experience.

While company executives and their employees gather about his booth, Conover gazes into his crystal ball, divining the personal thoughts of an individual in the audience. An appropriate corporate message is always central in his act, but he employs old-time mind reading and applies it to the 21st century.

Lee Earle
Rauscher Collection

Tim Conover's Web site is a model for this new approach to mind reading. The viewer is greeted by an open attaché case with a crystal ball inside – illustrating how mind reading has become a business for business people!

Unlike Tim Conover, **LEE EARLE** does not bill himself as, or admit in public, that he is a magician. On April 25, 2001, Earle was interviewed by Bryan Dean on Dean's "Magic & Illusion Chat Room." When asked by Dean if mentalism was a branch of magic, Earle answered:

NO, it is not. It is an allied field with some similarities. With magic, the audience knows the performer is doing tricks, fooling them. With mental magic, it's still a magician doing tricks, with a mind reading theme. Only with Mentalism (and I use the capital M for emphasis), it is perceived differently. The audience must believe what they see is real. The real test is what we ask them to believe.

Lee Earle is a mentalist who offers no disclaimer regarding his psychic abilities. He says,

I don't believe in disclaimers – the stage is my disclaimer. Remember, I want my audiences to believe what I do is real. Real memory, real perception, real subconscious. If I disclaim, then the audience disregards.

A performer for more than 40 years, Earle originally did standard magic shows. Today, his attitude toward magic has changed. He has said in an interview:

The public equates magicians with side shows or fire eaters or sword swallowers or clowns, or whatever else they associate with unsavory entertainment – at least until one gets to the Siegfried & Roy or Copperfield level.

When he entered the field of mentalism, Earle found his fees instantly tripled; now they are even higher. He considers a mentalist more unique and more valuable. Through mentalism, Earle found he was able to "pay the bills, have more money, deal with a nicer clientele, and stay in better hotels." He does not mix magic with mentalism because he wants the audience to believe what they see. He says, "I think magic degrades mentalism."

He does not use the words "Psychic" or "Mentalist" in his work. Instead, he considers himself a "Speaker." This allows him a wider scope, and he says, "At the fees I charge, I don't need to work a lot." Further, he states bluntly, "If I start doing magic (tricks), they may begin to equate me with a magician, who is lower paid. I like the money."

Lee Earle publishes his own material, and is well known for his books, tapes, mental effects, and many issues of *Syzgy, Journal of Contemporary Mentalism.* He is also adept at all forms of psychic work. His private work includes handwriting analysis and cold reading. He is also experienced in conducting séances, and has developed a program called "Manifestations," through which people can book experiences with spirit phenomena.

Along with **LARRY BECKER**, a prolific inventor of mental effects, Lee Earle has toured the country conducting teaching sessions called "Mentalism Super Symposiums" and "Mentalism Master Classes." Together, these two men provide a full day of intense instruction, limited to 50 people, at $95 each. Among their teachings are "New Strategies, Techniques, and Presentations." From these seminars come more and more mentalists, who, when not performing in public, might certainly consider private work!

Larry Becker
Courtesy of Raymond J. Goulet

Both Becker and Earle are well known in the magic community, and have been booked by various magic groups to share their knowledge and experience. Becker is an author of books, and has been featured in teaching videos. A professional mentalist since 1984, his signature effects are Russian Roulette and the Headline Prediction.

Incidentally, at one point in his adult life, Larry Becker felt the call to be an Episcopal priest, but changed his mind because of his age.

Through their careers in mentalism, Becker and Earle continue to do exactly as they advertise: "bypass the usual sensory channels, and transcend mundane reality."

Mark Lewis
Courtesy of Mark Lewis

Former magicians **RUDY VAN LANGEN** and **MARK LEWIS** are two examples of magicians-turned-psychics for a single reason – a better source of income. They are now professional readers who call themselves entertainers, but who are still magicians who have chosen to forsake standard magic for the more lucrative psychic field. Like Lee Earle, they have abandoned magic in its truest sense, but still use its methods.

In his early career, Van Langen created a successful magic trick called "The Classic Vanishing Coke Bottle." Although this trick sold well, its profits did not generate as great an income as possible through doing private readings.

Then Van Langen met Mark Lewis, who was doing psychic readings at the International Psychic, Mystic, and Seers Fair in Toronto. When he was introduced to Lewis, Van Langen says, "I could not help but wonder why he was here! In a booth! Doing something other than magic!"

Van Langen and Lewis are quoted in an extensive promotional Web site. According to Van Langen, "I have been performing as a professional magician for over 28 years, and now I look back and laugh."

After joining Lewis, the "Famous Irish Psychic" (who incidentally is an Englishman now living in Toronto), the duo eventually produced a $300 instructional video called "The Strolling Psychic Entertainer Home Study Series." This study series is highly publicized on their Web site, and reviewed in *Magic* magazine (February, 2002). It is advertised as the most detailed and complete program on psychic readings available in the market place. It is only available by mail or from select magic dealers in Canada, the USA, and Europe. Prospective customers, magicians, clowns, actors, and entertainers are told how to earn up to $200 per hour as strolling psychic entertainers. They are further encouraged to think about a daily income of $2,400 and a weekend income of over $7,000 which is dangled before them through appearances at Psychic Fairs.

Lewis writes to his fellow entertainers, who are mostly magicians:

> "I have been performing magic for over 30 years successfully, and made a damn good living at it, but I found a way to enhance my performing income substantially by making a few small changes to my act. I started doing Entertainment Palm Readings just for fun as an addition to my act after my shows, part time, for free. But before I could finish my reading, I looked up and there were over 30 people standing in line in front of me waiting their turn. I realized then that I had acquired a talent that no other magician had – and could cash in on it big time. I'd like to tell you how I did it."

He continues to say he is "happy to announce that the pie of cash is big enough for anyone who wants a piece to take one."

According to Lewis, the prospective reader can learn all that is necessary to get his piece of the cash pie from his and Van Langen's series of seven videotapes, six audiotapes, and six books. According to their promotional material, if this course is studied properly, a magician can do "iron-clad, risk-free, fool-proof readings."

Both Lewis and Van Langen now market their course to the entire magic community. The potential purchaser is encouraged to think of working parties, trade shows, and psychic fairs, doing everything from Fortune Telling, Palm Reading, Tarot Cards, and Numerology. Hopefully, through the Lewis/Van Langen course, the student will be transformed into "the best Psychic entertainer you can possibly be." They promise the possibility for a student to earn back the cost of the course – plus a profit – after the first performance. By the way, nothing is said in the promotional material about bringing back the dead to a grieving widow – but why not?

Like Mark Lewis, the now ex-magician can be transformed into a new, professional – RICH! – psychic entertainer. As magicians evangelizing magicians, they encourage potential customers to graduate from stage performances of pulling rabbits out of hats and doves out of silk scarves, and instead appear at events like the International Psychic Expo in Ottawa, where 250 psychic and clairvoyants offer readings for $5 to $100. More important, many of these new clients return again and again.

These promoters do not admit to any trickery. Instead, they offer an enormous potential income – and further teach that self-promotion is important to gain access to this money. After all, money is the name of their game, and to hell with sincere, uninformed people who seek out these charlatans for readings.

And woe to the performer who is looking for ethical direction in magic and mentalism. It is not even an issue with these "psychic entertainers."

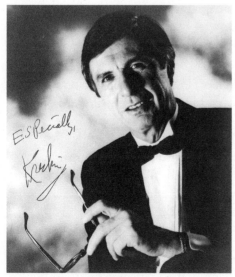

Kreskin
Rauscher Collection

**KRESKIN** is a modern day (born January 12, 1935) mentalist/self-promotion phenomenon who has built his reputation slowly and carefully for many years. A headline in the August 19, 1983, issue of *The Catholic Star Herald* (the official publication of the Camden, New Jersey Diocese of the Roman Catholic Church) proclaimed: "The Amazing Kreskin Calls His Talent a Gift From God."

Kreskin, using his knowledge of psychology – for which he has a degree from Seton Hall University – was quoted as saying that much of his ability lies in "being able to think the way the other person is thinking." Aligning himself with Archbishop Fulton J. Sheen, he adds, "The

Archbishop admitted to me (in letters) that these were the techniques he was using. He became very familiar with my work."

To the faithful who receive *The Herald*, Kreskin, a Catholic, insists his gift is God-given. His talent, though, lies in his development of that gift.

Continued nationwide interest in ESP has been furthered for the general public by Kreskin's performances, as well as by others who are not as well known. Young and old have their belief enhanced by these performances, because they cannot distinguish between truth and fraud. Once during a hospital visit, a patient who knew of my interest in mystical theology lifted his head from his bed and asked, "Have you seen Kreskin? … He's fantastic." His belief was falsely enhanced in a non-physical reality by a mentalist!

In his book *The Amazing World of Kreskin*, wherein psychic research, ESP, performing, and psychology are all tossed together, Kreskin provides no real admission of prior planning by mentalists. He maintains that combinations to safes, for example, are indeed mentally transmitted at a specific time on nationwide television.

The ultimate deception perpetrated by Kreskin rests in the title of his book *How To Be A Fake Kreskin* (St. Martin's Paperbacks, New York, 1996), which provoked a scathing critical review from Jamy Ian Swiss in *Skeptic*, Vol. 4, No. 4, 1996. Swiss, a magician and prominent magic book reviewer, not only called the volume "useless and ridiculous," but also rates Kreskin's work as "quaintly old-fashioned hype."

One of the most preposterous attempts by Kreskin to obtain publicity and involve himself in the national political scene was his March 10, 1998 letter to Janet Reno, then Attorney General of the United States. This was not old-fashioned hype, but bold-faced hype, and typical of fake mind readers now known as mentalists. Kreskin's letter was printed in the July 1998 issue of *Harper's* magazine:

> Dear Attorney General Reno:
>
> I have followed Kenneth Starr's inquiry very closely, and I believe that it has gotten far out of control. Therefore, I would like to formally offer my services as a mentalist. My fifty years of experience as a mentalist have allowed me to develop my abilities to perceive not only the feelings of those around me but their thoughts as well. More important, I have an innate ability to determine whether a person is telling the truth. I propose to save the government millions of dollars by meeting with those involved with the Whitewater investigation and telling you who is telling the truth and who is lying, including Prosecutor Starr himself.
>
> Of course, I understand that the thoughts of the President are a matter of national security, and I assure you that any thoughts detected that go beyond the matter at hand will be kept secret.

As an entertainer I am the highest paid mentalist in the world, but as an American my services could be retained for $1. If you simply contact my office, I will report to Washington for service and we can end this debacle before we spend another $30 million.

ESPecially yours,
The Amazing Kreskin

The public is always treated to great word puzzles when it comes to Kreskin – or, for that matter, any professional mentalist who attempts to legitimize ESP. Kreskin writes:

> Perhaps some of what I do fits into the category of "psychic" so called, under certain conditions. But I think that my particular forms of mental communications, as adapted for the stage, are probably hyper-sensitive or hyper-normal rather than extra-sensitive. In the manner of a concert pianist who has spent much of his life at the keyboard, the communication, a very earthly one so far as I'm concerned, has been developed through years of painstaking practice. (*The Amazing World of Kreskin* – New York: Random House, 1973, p.5).

The vagaries of this statement are too numerous to mention, but perhaps one example will suffice. Kreskin has said that his gifts are "probably hyper-sensitive or hyper-normal, rather than extra-sensitive." Now the prefix *hyper* derives from the Greek, meaning, "over, above, beyond, super." In other words, Kreskin is contradicting himself by implying a virtue that he is outwardly denying. Presumably "hyper-normal" or even "hyper-natural" are acceptable, and serve to confuse the issue.

Kreskin is quite agile in using the mentalist's traditional vagueness. William Poundstone, in *Big Secrets*, a book whose exposure of time-honored stage illusions disturbs magicians (including me!) as well as the mentalists, gives a hypothetical example:

**Kreskin:** Does the date September 11 mean anything special to anyone?
(**Author's note: NOT September 11, 2001!**)

**Subject:** Yes.

**Kreskin:** Is it a birthday, an anniversary?

**Subject:** It's my daughter's anniversary.

**Kreskin:** I see something about your daughter and an automobile.

**Subject:** She just bought a car.

Poundstone then offers this analysis of his example:

> Now think about it. There are hundreds of people in the audience. Everyone has a birthday. Most people have other special days. No matter what date Kreskin names, it is almost certain to draw a response.
>
> When someone claims September 11, Kreskin goes for a second match. This time he has to play it safe because he already has his subject. The subject admitted a daughter, so Kreskin sees something about a daughter and an automobile. Again, almost everyone can think of "something about an automobile." Kreskin is vague, and lets the subject fill in the details. He knows that much of the audience will soon forget who said what first. Many will go home honestly believing that Kreskin divined the date of a subject's daughter's anniversary and the fact that she had purchased a car.
>
> William Poundstone<br>*Big Secrets*<br>William Morrow Co., 1983<br>(pp.172-173

Kreskin does not depend upon shrewd guesses and feedback from his audiences, but he uses a medley of techniques – especially for the reading of Social Security numbers. Poundstone suggests that Kreskin recovers messages that he has his subjects write down and then throw on the floor. The public actually deludes itself by not realizing that if a person were a mind reader he would not need to write material on pieces of paper to begin with. He cites *The Psychology of the Psychic*, a work by New Zealand psychologists David Marks and Richard Kammann (Prometheus Books: Amherst, New York, 1980), who claim they saw Kreskin palm a message and put it in his pocket. Marks and Kammann also suspect that Kreskin's clipboard may be a "magician's tray" – a standard device allowing for a quick read or a switching of messages.

Kreskin's trick of reading Social Security numbers depends for its effectiveness on his use of the television camera. Under the guise of saving valuable air time, Kreskin passes out slips of papers to the audience before the show or during commercial breaks, or he has the completed tape edited to eliminate the dullness of watching people write down their Social Security numbers. Once the numbers are written down, there are many ways for Kreskin to retrieve them – such as through the "stolen message" technique described above.

Kreskin also employs more traditional techniques, similar to ones used by Houdini in his early days – and others before him. While Houdini used to memorize tombstones to prepare for his mind reading act, Kreskin, on walks before a show, memorizes license plate numbers and the makes of cars in the studio parking lot – or else has someone do it for him. Poundstone suggests that "…he may look for bumper stickers and personal articles inside of cars.  Say Kreskin spots a car with a Missouri license plate, a racquetball sticker, a child's toy, and a Szechwan cookbook in the back seat.  It isn't hard to imagine how he could weave this information into a fantastic demonstration of 'mind reading.' " (Poundstone, p. 175)

While some mentalists like Kreskin are intentionally vague about conducting their work, others are unabashedly commercial. One example is **MYRIAM RUTHCHILD**.  In her book *Cashing In On the Psychic* (Lee Jacobs Productions, Pomeroy, Ohio, 1978), the author begins piously enough, assuring readers that she believes in a higher reality, and her book will teach them how to "create the illusion" of that reality. (p. 4)  However, by the time she reaches page 17, her advice becomes more candid:  "Never give medical advice unless you enjoy lawsuits or visits to jail."  She further informs the young mentalist/psychic, "There is only one caution in this business.  Check your local and state laws concerning occult procedures."

Ruthchild does not suggest ways to psychically produce physical phenomena.  She is concerned with mentalist tricks that can be given a patina of the occult.  In teaching a beginner the art of prediction, the author advises sticking to simple "yes" and "no" answers. She goes on to say, "In this way you have a 50/50 chance of being right – and who knows, you may even find yourself making predictions that work." (p. 18)

By the time the author has reached the end of this brief work, she has given up all pretense of being "a true believer in a higher reality" and unveils her true theme – how to get money under dubious circumstances.  She writes: "The field of the psychic is the business of tomorrow, and the person who is the first in a new field is the one who makes the money." (p. 51) Ruthchild leaves little doubt about how to acquire this money, or why psychism is a growing business, as she exhorts the reader:  "Believers look for something paranormal in which to believe.  They will grasp even the most blatant phonies for proof that there is something more.  These people are growing in number.  They are waiting for you."  (p. 24)

As with most mentalist/psychics, Ruthchild is reluctant to associate herself with magicians:  "If people question you about once being a magician, all you can say is that the association with the illusion led you to seek a truer reality."  She further suggests that a budding mentalist should associate only with his or her peer group.

Ruthchild now has a number of Web sites and is known as Myriam Ruthchild de Serna-Maytorena.  She advertises herself as a writer and counselor, and maintains a weekly newsletter called *Manifest Reality*.  A professional psychic, she is also an ordained Universalist minister.  Her appeal on the Web is in the area of e-mail astrological readings, and for a fee of $50 she will send the reader a personal cassette reading, with a two-week delivery date offered.  For $150 a month she offers one-on-one counseling sessions by phone, along with daily e-mail contact.

Myriam Ruthchild de Serna-Maytorena is living proof of her own prophecy:  "The field of the psychic is the business of tomorrow, and the person who is the first in a new field is the one who makes the money."

Like Dunninger before them, Kreskin and Ruthchild never appear at magic conventions or in magic shops, since such associations might detract from the authenticity of their image as a true psychic. For a mentalist to be aligned with a magician is to curtail the impact of what he or she is doing – that their act is really a "gift." Their need to be with like-minded people is fulfilled by joining the secret and selective fraternity called The Psychic Entertainers Association.

The PEA is carefully promoted. The organization announces it is not a magicians' club, nor is it intended for information collectors, but certainly the core group is magicians who have an interest in "mentalism, bizarre magick, hypnotism, cold reading, and allied arts."

Although the PEA professes to support a serious interest in ethical performance, its main concern is in keeping magic trick methodology secret. The members place great emphasis on the word "entertainment." They take no real position on the role of private readers which they consider entertainment – yet they say they promote and support genuine psychic research.

Every effort is made to investigate all prospective members. Following application, the membership screening process takes three months. Frankly, it is more difficult to be accepted as a member of this group than to join the exclusive Everglades Club in Palm Beach! Even Kreskin does not belong to this group, but many do and subscribe to the purposes and goals listed below:

**The Purposes of the Association**

1. To consider and deal by all lawful means with common problems involved in the practice of ethical psychic entertainment

2. To facilitate communication, exchange of ideas and cooperation between those in the field of psychic entertainment

3. The creation of ethical standards and practice for those in the profession

4. To encourage and assist in the prevention of unwarranted exposure of the professional methods of the psychic entertainer

5. To provide a force to exchange ideas with those of a kindred spirit

**The Goals of the Association**

1. To promote the practice of ethical mentalism and psychic entertainment by discouraging the use of the art as a means of creating fraudulently induced reliance, either personal or financial, upon non-existent psychic ability

2. To promote and support genuine psychic research

3. To discourage exposure of the ethical mentalist by those who seek to create their own fame by exposing the methods of psychic entertainers

4. To protect the original creations and routines of members from theft or plagiarism by encouraging extensive use of copyright and patent procedures (**Note:** Even though such procedures will not stop the determined pirate, the promise of expensive litigation to complete his theft will certainly have a discouraging effect.)

As members meet, perform, and share ideas about mentalism, their ethical boundaries regarding fooling others develops thinner and thinner lines. This happens because their egos are enhanced by their ability to convince by deception. This phenomenon is also true of magic, but no real harm is done since the magician is not accepted as a miracle worker.

It is questionable whether or not a professional mentalist would be willing to accept the advice of the late Bruce Elliott, author of numerous works on magic. He stated to be a magician and not a charlatan, one would somewhere in a show have to explain that he or she was using magical methods to read minds.

It is when mentalists graduate from color-perception, book tests, envelopes, and ESP card telepathy tricks to what is known as "cold readings," or providing off-the-cuff impressions about a person or object, that they are edging closer to becoming the fake spiritualists that they profess to rally against.

Walter B. Gibson, the late noted authority on magic, said that the German mentalist **HELLSTROM** (Alex Vogt, 1893-1933) could make "hits" this way. For example, if someone picked a color and you were wearing a blindfold, you would try to think of the color first before you peeked. Often you might be right. Dunninger tried these kinds of things on people before using them on stage. The danger is that the

Hellstrom
Courtesy of Raymond J. Goulet

Hellstrom
Courtesy of Raymond J. Goulet

mentalist may begin to believe in himself more and more, and then it becomes difficult for him to separate the use of his talents when dealing with the public.

Kreskin is an excellent example of today's approach to mentalism whereby the performer uses all the parapsychological terms, weaving them in and out of the act and deluding the audience. This verbal misdirection is the very essence of what creative mind reader and author Robert Nelson wrote about years ago in a monograph called *Mentalist's Opening Lecture* (Mickey Hades International, Alberta, Canada, 1979, p. 1):

This evening I shall present for your approval and consideration a series of experiments in parapsychology – that branch of science dealing with thought transference, subliminal control and extra-sensory perception. Please bear in mind that I am making no claims to supernatural powers, and that I am not a fortuneteller. Science has proven the ability of one individual to direct and influence the thoughts of another. It will be my purpose to direct your thoughts into the proper perspective by influencing, not your conscious, but your subconscious mind by my own mental impulses.

Kreskin is always prepared to fool his audience – in this world, and if possible, in the next. His Web site, *www.amazingkreskin.com*, features a photograph of himself dressed in a black cape, standing at his gravesite and looking like a benign Count Dracula, with the headstone already in place. Engraved in stone are the words, "EVEN NOW I KNOW WHAT YOU'RE THINKING." On the base of the stone is the name KRESKIN.

In addition, he offers the following statement to intrigue his viewers:

I have always used my mental abilities to predict specific events in other people's lives. While looking into the minds of others I have often seen things that I would rather not have seen and, unfortunately, I have often successfully predicted many people's deaths. At first, this bizarre twist to my chosen profession took me by surprise, but as I got used to it I learned how to ignore the bad and concentrate on the good.

Now for my latest stunt, I have set all fear of my own mortality aside and have decided to share my death with the world before it even happens. Hidden on this web site is a thirteen part riddle that, when solved, will reveal the day of my own death. All thirteen clues can be found on my site, and with a little thinking, you will be able to piece them together to solve the riddle.

Currently, Kreskin is not only the most famous mentalist in America, but he is also well known throughout the world.  He delights in appearing on most any television show, and has even been included on the vulgar Howard Stern show (which in itself is surprising for a man of Kreskin's intellect, character, and stature).  In his book *The Amazing Kreskin's Future With the Stars* (Meyerbooks, Glenwood, Illinois, 2001), Kreskin presents predictions of celebrities, as well as his own predictions and stories about his many well-known friends.  In the same book Kreskin describes Howard Stern as a conservative, and calls him "the best social critic/satirist since Mark Twain and Oscar Wilde."  Stern, meanwhile, predicts in the book: "Kreskin will be locked up in a mental institution and carted away in the new millennium." Stern also predicted that Kreskin "will shake hands so hard with a biker that he will beat the crap out of him."

To this I add my own prediction:  Kreskin's career will be eclipsed, if it has not been already, by mentalists such as Marc Salem and Derren Brown, who will be accepted as the leading mind readers – or "psychological mind controllers" as they consider themselves in their peculiar vocation.  Audiences will respond more to their mature personalities and seemingly impossible feats.  Salem and Brown will continually draw sold-out houses, while Kreskin will fade and be remembered as an oddity, an imitation of the renowned Dunninger.

As with David Hoy, who was mentioned earlier in this book, Kreskin shoots from the hip, and from time to time is lucky enough to win a round.  As an example, on page 266 in his book, he says:

> When this book is published, the governments of the Western World will have still failed to notify their people that we are in another war.  The enemy is using the most invisible and insidious of tactics – that of terrorism. The gravest danger the world has faced in the last 100 years will be showing its ugly face before long.  With the ominous possibilities of biological warfare, safety zones will inevitably be set up in schools and government buildings.

Now lest anyone thinks this prediction was a trick, and perhaps added just prior to publication, the publisher pasted the following notice in the front of Kreskin's book:

> Note to the Reader:  The first edition of this work was printed in September 2000 for a select group of contributors.  With the exception of the introduction, this second edition, printed in March 2001, has been left untouched – including Page 266.

Gersh Kuntzman, a columnist for *The New York Post*, reviewed Kreskin's book on November 5, 2001, for a *Newsweek* Web Exclusive, and called him "Hollywood's go-to mentalist" and "America's flesh-and-blood Magic 8-Ball."  (For those unaware, the Magic 8-Ball is a novelty item – a black ball filled with liquid, to which questions are directed. After a question is asked, the questioner inverts the ball and an answer appears in a small window. The catch is all the answers fit any question!)

Kuntzman's recommendation on Kreskin's 268-page book (which was written with Bret Saxon) is, "If you read this book, any faith you have in Kreskin's psychic abilities – or any delight you take in his kitschy television appearances – will fade faster than the golden finish on one of those Sacagawea dollar coins."

One Kreskin mega-event prediction that fizzled miserably was the supposed appearance on June 6, 2002 of what he promoted would be the largest UFO sighting in history. After much long-term hype, this publicity stunt sky show was scheduled to appear above the Nevada desert between 9:00 p.m. and midnight, and anxiously awaited by a crowd, along with a small group who had been pre-conditioned and given a post-hypnotic suggestion. No real UFO's appeared except in the minds of a few hypnotized audience members. Actually NOTHING happened except total frustration for those who gathered in a party atmosphere at the desert area beyond the Silverton Hotel, south of Las Vegas, where Kreskin had performed. One observer, Angela Thompson Smith, said, "Some of the crowd were angry at Kreskin and started cat-calling and saying "Da plane, da plane!" and that many "walked away in disgust." It was reported that people came from as far away as Utah and Kentucky.

(Incidentally, Kreskin had offered a gift of $50,000 to charity if his prediction failed. How generous!)

The problem with tricksters is that one can never be sure of their mixture of truths and falsehoods. As the Roman poet Ovid once wrote, "Skilled in every trick, a worthy heir of his paternal craft, he would make black look white, and white look black."

# Act 8

## And now, may I present...

## A POTPOURRI OF PUZZLERS

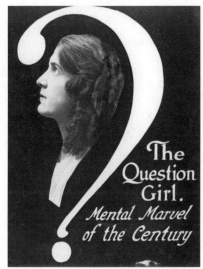

Leona La Mar
Rauscher Collection

Throughout the history of mentalism there have been many outstanding acts. One was **LEONA LA MAR**, "The Girl With The Thousand Eyes."

Leona was a real headliner, according to Bill J. Weldon in his article "Vaudeville Magicians" (*Linking Ring*, March 2000), in which he discusses mentalists who played Cleveland, Ohio, during the heyday of vaudeville. Miss LaMar had numerous repeat engagements in that city during 1922 and 1923. Weldon quotes from a 1923 *Sphinx* magazine article: "An exceptionally fine vaudeville bill. Through her clever twenty-minute offering, she kept the audience deeply interested in her rapid-fire demonstration of seership."

Theater Ad
Leona La Mar
Courtesy of Bill J. Weldon

Miss La Mar claimed she was really the Countess Leona Von Vos Dumar, and that her father was the late Count Alexander Von Vos Dumar of St. Petersburg, Russia. People believed it! Despite the doubtful pedigree credentials and photographs that surrounded her with a question mark, Leona still packed in audiences.

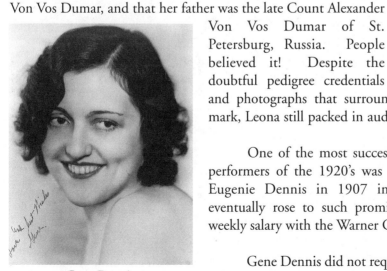

Gene Dennis
Courtesy of Walter B. Graham

One of the most successful women psychic stage performers of the 1920's was **GENE DENNIS**. Born Eugenie Dennis in 1907 in Atchison, Kansas, she eventually rose to such prominence that by 1932 her weekly salary with the Warner Circuit was $2,000 a week.

Gene Dennis did not require written questions, but simply gave answers to oral questions at a rapid-fire pace.

Gene Dennis
Courtesy of Walter B. Graham

She became known as "The Wonder Girl" and "The Mystic Marvel," and grew so popular that Eleanor Roosevelt invited her to the White House on June 3, 1933. During her visit there she stood in the East Room, where a dance in progress had been interrupted to present her. The crowd was delighted to meet her, and eager to ask her questions, hoping for answers to their concerns. One question asked concerned the Lindbergh case: "Where has Gaston Means hidden the money he extorted from Mrs. Edward B. McLean in connection with the Lindbergh case?"

Dennis replied, "In a tin can, but if you want to find it and a whole lot more, you had better think about the woman in the case."

According to a report in *The New Jamaica Theater News* (no date), Dennis was later introduced to President Roosevelt. He, too, asked her a question, and then later they talked alone.

In a January 13, 1933, Palm Springs, California INS report, Dennis was reported to have spent several hours with Albert Einstein. The physicist said of the psychic: "She told me things no one possibly could know, and she demonstrated to me she had a power to do things I can't explain at this time. It was miraculous indeed."

Miss Dennis became a good friend of businessman and magician **DAVID P. ABBOTT** and his wife, Fanny. Abbott created wonderful magic effects, such as "The Talking Tea Kettle." For this effect, a spectator held the tea kettle and asked it questions. When the spectator put the spout to his ear, the answer to his question was whispered from inside the kettle.

Abbott also performed a convincing act called "Balsamo, The Living Skull," in which a skull provided answers to questions by clacking its jaws. He is also credited with solving the riddle of how the Bangs sisters, famous spiritualists in the late nineteenth and early twentieth centuries, produced their much heralded "Spirit Paintings" on canvas. Abbott's version became a magician's stage illusion,

David Abbott and Gene Dennis in 1922
Courtesy of Walter B. Graham

and private performances of this and other illusions in his elegant home were attended by many professional magicians.

Abbott was interested in investigating and exposing psychics, but never considered Gene Dennis to be a medium or a spiritualist. Abbott's dedicated interest in Dennis was sparked in 1922, when Dennis appeared in a theater in Omaha. A skeptic and a very critical man, Abbott kept careful notes on Dennis.

When Abbott died, he left behind an investigative report on Gene Dennis, written in 1922. Magician Walter B. Graham published this report with a commentary titled "The Wonder Girl." There seems to be no doubt that both David Abbott and his wife remained impressed with Miss Dennis; Abbott makes no attempt to expose her, nor does he speak disparagingly of her.

Abbott's work and interests are detailed in *David P. Abbott's Book of Mysteries* (Modern Litho, Inc., Omaha, Nebraska, 1977), a fascinating volume also made possible by Graham. Historian Milbourne Christopher devotes eight pages to Dennis in his book *ESP, Seers and Psychics* (Thomas Y. Crowell, Co., New York, 1970). In this book, Christopher recalls that when Dennis appeared at the Omaha Rialto for three days, Abbott introduced her at every performance.

Dennis also made predictions. Christopher says Dennis described her psychic ability as similar to receiving "a series of pictures to her mind. The images were vivid, like scenes in a movie. Other people thought back, but she thought forward."

Dennis was popular in the United States, and also in Britain. The only visible assistants in her act were ushers in the theater who would go to individuals wishing to ask a question, and then simply repeat the question to Gene, who remained on stage.

Dennis also answered questions mailed to her by her followers. Most times the envelopes contained money. At one point Abbott assisted Dennis in her need for secretarial help, which gave him a chance to watch her dictate answers till she reached the point of her own nervous exhaustion. If a phone number was included in the correspondence, Dennis would call the person directly. She claimed that hearing the individual's voice helped her to answer the questions more easily.

What is not totally clear is whether Abbott concluded Dennis was simply a "cold reader," or if he left a margin for what he considered might be some real psychic ability. He writes in the conclusion of his report:

> I have used the greatest care in checking the facts that I here report.
> By nature I am a skeptic. I suppose I was born such. It is very difficult for
> me to believe in the genuineness of such things as this, but I am driven to

state that these things have actually happened. One who would not acknowledge the facts would not be an investigator. I have endeavored to report the facts with sacred accuracy. At times, she seems to possess a kind of uncanny intuition for saying the right thing. This is the feeling that comes over one now and then, when what she says proves to be correct. As to what part coincidence can play in things like this, or as to how much can be due to systematic guesswork, the reader can judge as well as I. He can even try for himself, and use all his faculties, and see how often he is right. There is no trickery used. I can vouch for that, and for the fact that the persons whose names are given as receiving these tests were given. It would seem to be impossible for anyone to guess correctly anywhere nearly so often as she is correct. I shall no doubt form a definite opinion in time, but now, I have simply presented the evidence. As to what it means, my readers must be the jury. (p.21)

In May 1930, Gene Dennis appeared at Loew's Orpheum in Boston for a series of 40-minute performances. The following excerpts appeared in a May 31, 1930 review in *Billboard*: "Her ostentatious appearance, natural delivery, neat dress, light full up" was noted. The excerpt continues, "She is not bad to look at and depicts herself not only with grace, but with a self-reliant manner that bespeaks a personality that is very sure of itself." Her style of work is also mentioned: "She works simply by having the interrogates raise their hands and ask their questions out loud. No trick here about guessing questions as in other mental turns. She answers the queries, predicts the outcome of the problems presented, and even fills in details not supplied by the questioners."

Gene Dennis left the stage in the mid-1930's to marry J. C. von Herbert, a Seattle theater magnate. She died of cancer at age 41 on March 8, 1948. In her *Omaha World-Herald* obituary, the article recalled one of the startling statements she had made during a reading. "She stopped in the midst of a reading, clapped her hands to her eyes, and said: 'Oh, something terrible is happening! A man is being killed!'" The report continued, "It was learned later that a holdup man had killed a policeman about that time a few blocks away."

Gloria De Voss
Courtesy of George Daily

Large magic shows of the past often featured a woman mind reading segment. In his spectacular show called "Sim Sala Bim," Kalanag (Helmut Schreiber), the German illusionist, presented his wife as:

**GLORIA** [De VOS] and Her Amazing Memory! She has memorized 100,000 telephone numbers from the telephone books of the world's leading cities.

Kalanag Poster with Gloria
Courtesy of George Daily

Gloria performed a mind-boggling feat in which she allowed members of her audience to select a name and telephone number from a display of phone books. Then, did she give the correct name and phone number selected? Of course she did!

In the 1920's, Mysterious Smith (Albert P. Smith) featured his wife **OLGA** as "The Sensation of America." She appeared as part of his "Temple of Mystery" stage show of magic and illusions. Her act complimented Smith's presentation of effects like the Spirit Cabinet and other ghostly illusions.

Madam Olga
Courtesy Princeton University Library

Smith also called his wife "The Psychic Marvel." During her act, while she was seated on an Oriental throne, the audience asked her about lost articles, missing relatives, love affairs, stolen property, marriage, and divorce. Her publicity read:

Madam Olga
On stage with her husband Mysterious Smith
Rauscher Collection

Madam Olga's methods are unique and quite her own. She has many imitators, but newspapers from the territory where the company has been playing frankly state that she has few, if any, equals. The many lost articles recovered, the many business problems solved and the long list of predictions that have materialized have given the friends of Madam Olga supreme faith in her powers. Simply, forcefully and unerringly she answers question after question with amazing accuracy and rapidity.

**EVELYN MAXWELL** performed a similar type of mental act as a segment in the enormous world-touring magic and illusion show of Carter The Great during the 1920's. In this show, Maxwell was billed as "The Psychic Marvel" and "The Psychic Wonder." Publicity proclaimed: "Ask Evelyn Maxwell. She knows all … She sees all … She tells all … Ask her."

The program listed Evelyn as "One who unfolds a chapter from the supernatural in an exhibition of Thought Transference of Mental Telepathy, the result of years of study."

Evelyn was presented as a one-woman "Psychic Phenomenon." Further, the program promised: "Questions written at home and brought to the theater in sealed envelopes are read and answered while still in your possession."

Publicity photographs for a mentalist always help promote a mysterious, intense feeling. This is as true today as when **ZENOLA**, the woman mentalist and crystal gazer, posed in an Illinois studio, staring with total concentration into her crystal ball. Zenola is dressed for the occasion in a flowing gown with an ethereal quality, and appears to be in a dissociated state of mind or trance.

Evelyn Maxwell
Courtesy of Mike Caveney

Zenola
Rauscher Collection

At one time in her career, Zenola was advertised as "The Girl With the Diamond Teeth." Presumably this description was appropriate, because when she smiled on stage in the glare of a spotlight, sparkles of diamond reflections radiated out to the audience.

Less intense was a publicity photograph taken in London of the **MYSTIC MORA**. From 1916 to 1921, Mora traveled the world with her husband, a magician called "Dr." Rowe. In the London photo, she is seated in a rather demure pose and is looking at the viewer instead of at her crystal ball.

Mora specialized in clairvoyance. She also worked fast, and was noted for her accuracy while performing a blindfold question-and-answer act. She did half the show, while Rowe, whose act included manipulation routines using balls, cards, and coins, completed the other half.

Mystic Mora
Courtesy Victoria State Library, Melbourne, Australia; Alma Conjuring Collection

Another highly successful team that performed from the early 1900's into 1940 was The Floyds.

Walter Floyd had been a magician before his marriage to Mary Robinson. After they wed, Floyd's act changed, and Robinson became **MOHALA**. This couple was popular on the Chautauqua circuit, worked constantly, and traveled extensively.

Mohala
Courtesy of Raymond J. Goulet

With his wife at his side, Floyd performed a second sight act. Like Julie of Virgil and Julie, Mohala did blindfold calculations, using numbers written on a blackboard.

All went well until August 21, 1940, when Floyd had a heart attack while performing in front of a bachelor dinner party audience in Massachusetts. He died with Mohala once again by his side.

**EVELYN BENNETT HARRIS** was another sophisticated female mentalist. She played all the first-class clubs during the nightclub era. She also tap-danced.

Harris was a beautiful woman who projected an exotic aura while answering the audience's questions in a serious and dignified manner.

Evelyn Bennett Harris
Courtesy of
Princeton University Library

Madame Mayah
Courtesy of
Princeton University Library

A direct contrast to Evelyn Bennett Harris was the crystal-gazing act performed by **MADAME MAYAH** in the early 1900's. Mayah also chose an Oriental costume, and her act was similar to those of Mahendra, Allah Rageh, and others. Her publicity photo depicts a well-fed woman, seen with her arm resting on a table – apparently thinking only of the viewer!

Performer **MADAM JEWELL** wore an elegantly embroidered velvet dress. We don't know her real name or just how successful she really was, but we do know she was one more theater attraction in a long list of now-forgotten mind readers.

Madam Jewell's publicity advertisements appealed to those who wanted answers to their questions. A large question mark in her ad symbolically covered the many concerns of most people. According to her publicity, Madam Jewell emphasized business issues like "good securities," "bad investments," and "law suits." She also addressed the emotional issues of love, divorce, marriage, and lost articles. She would even help someone learn when he or she would die!

Madam Jewell was promoted as presenting a "scientific demonstration of mental phenomena, supported by fifteen years of experience." All you had to do was bring your name and questions to the theater where she performed!

Madam Jewell
Courtesy of Raymond J. Goulet

Princess Romola
Courtesy of Raymond J. Goulet

Unlike Madame Jewell, **PRINCESS ROMOLA** dressed more like a gypsy, and wore a rich, silk-patterned gown with a matching turban.

Romolo appeared in the famous Circuit Chautauqua variety entertainment shows which performed under canvas during the 1920's. Along with the Lyceum shows, this group brought music, comedy, magic, and lectures by famous speakers to rural areas and towns across the United States.

Today we have no idea what **LOLO**, the Sioux Indian mind reader, looked like, but she probably wore Indian clothes. We do know that in 1910 she was working at the Keith Fifth Avenue Theater in New York. In addition to her second sight act, she demonstrated her skill as a sharpshooter with bow, arrows, and a rifle.

**PRINCESS WAHLETKA** was another Indian mentalist. She was talented enough to play the Ziegfield Roof, along with a host of theaters. She dressed in tribal clothing, with pigtails and an Indian beaded headband.

Princess Wahletka's April 25, 1927, 18-minute matinee performance at the Moss Theater on Broadway in New York City was reviewed in *Billboard Magazine*. J. B. S., the reviewer, wrote:

Princess Wahletka
Courtesy of Raymond J. Goulet

> There is not a dull moment in Princess Wahletka's current vehicle. The "American Indian Seeress" with the aid of a male assistant, worked with speed and precision. The man opened the act "in one," with a brief discourse on the mental gifts of the mind. While the orchestra played the music of the red men, the curtain is raised and the girl is squatted in front of a wigwam.

When the man enters the orchestra floor, the house lights are snapped on and the girl comes to the footlights. The man does not use the conventional slips of paper, but merely calls the questions, and the Princess, in a squeaky and piercing voice, answers the "transposed" queries in rapid fire order. At this performance, a majority of the questions and answers concerned the advisability of entering a new business, matrimonial prospects, and the seeking of information about missing people. Comedy answers are brought into play regularly. Near the close the girl requests that the entire audience concentrate on some item. After a moment or two she calls the first name of certain individuals and informs them what they have been thinking of.

Her pleasant style of delivery, smooth manner of working and uncanny ability kept the interest of the audience throughout. Altogether a very entertaining exhibition.

Magicians are indebted to the late magic historian David Price for insights into the mentalism teams of **CHARLES AND MARTHA STEEN,** and **MILDRED AND HARRY ROUCLERE.**

The **Steens** were telepathists, and although they did a second sight act, they were bold enough to expose fraudulent mediums. Their tours brought them recognition as enemies of

Charley and Rose Steen
Courtesy of Mike Caveney

Spiritualism, while they were performing at the same time as psychics. From 1899 into the 1900's, one of Martha's special effects was to call the totals of numbers that were written on a blackboard while she was blindfolded. She would also call out a number that an audience member wrote down and then touched. Even after the Steens' marriage ended, both Charles and Martha continued on with their acts – but with different partners. Pictured here is the publicity poster of Charles and his second wife, Rose.

Magician and mentalist **Harry Rouclere** learned from the Steens' while working with them in the Charles Andress Circus; he later toured with the couple in 1887. Rouclere became an accomplished magician, and invented a number of illusions. He married Mildred May Searing in 1889, and the couple formed a mentalist partnership known as Mildred and Rouclere. According to Price, at one point in their careers they called themselves Ellington and Cook, and posed as spiritualist mediums. They brought their "mediumship talents" by invitation to the historic spiritualist camp called "Lily Dale, New York." During their act, Mildred and Rouclere would involve the audience. Audience members

Mildred and Rouclere
Courtesy of Thomas A. Ewing

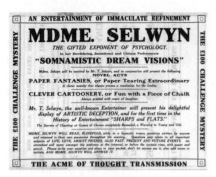

Madam Selwyn
Rauscher Collection

Madam Selwyn
Rauscher Collection

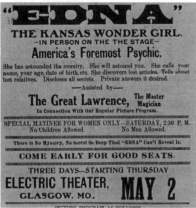

Edna - The Kansas Wonder Girl
Rauscher Collection

Ramon Coran
Rauscher Collection

Helmar
Courtesy of Mario Carrandi

Mazeppa and Zilla
Rauscher Collection

Sedrick Hout
Courtesy of Raymond J. Goulet

would tell Harry what they wanted Mildred to act out, and she would honor the request after Harry sent the message to her telepathically. Rouclere named this act "Mildredism," and also "Psychonotism."

As an example of the couple's cleverness, Price recalls when, in 1897, Rouclere convinced a convict who was sentenced to hang to mention his show from the scaffold. Somehow Rouclere had met privately with the convict, and told him that his séance was able to bring back the dead. With a noose around his neck, the convict's last words were that maybe he might appear at the Rouclere séance. Needless to say, the theater in Winston-Salem, North Carolina was filled the night of Rouclere's performance.

Mildred Rouclere lived to be 69, and Harry reached the age of 76. In their last years they ran a hotel in Ridgewood, New Jersey.

During the era of vaudeville there were more mentalists who were Princes, Mystics, Madams, Professors, Rajahs, and Greats than can be imagined – and they all made their living pretending to read minds. Among these performers were **Edna – The Kansas Wonder Girl, Mazeppa & Zilla, Helmar, Madam Selwyn,** and **Sedrick Hout – The Fourth Dimension Telepathist,** and **Ramon Coran.** Coran, born in Seville, May 14, 1899, promoted himself as the son of Senor Ferdinando Coran, eminent Spanish Psychologist who was well known throughout Spain and Southwestern Europe. His father was supposed to have trained him in the occult sciences. His publicity states that his father suffered a nervous breakdown while playing the old Grand Opera House in Marion, Ohio. Ramon, in his teens, took over and presented telepathic and mental expreiments. His biographical history states that he was astounding! In 1930, Ramon Coran's show booklet of astrological readings stated, "Still a comparatively young man, Ramon Coran is hailed by thousands of people as one of our greatest exponents of psychology and human nature."

There was Prince Ali, Prince Sha Babert, Prince Rajbar, Princess Zulieka, Prince Zomar, Mystic Spencer, Madam Celeste, Madam Anitra Thelma, Professor E'Artis, The Great Kara, The Great McEwen, Thurman, Lady Alice, Lady Bonnaffon, Lady Beth, Lady Ethel, Marjah, Syndu, Omar, Khaldeah, Zolar, Zomah, Khyam, Zandra, Zangar, Zelleno, Rubini, Jove De Le Rajah, Ali-Vad, Rex, Handy-Bandy, and The Van de Koors with Felix, who was costumed as an oversized mind reading duck! There was even a Socrates.

In 1918, like other mentalists of his era, Henri Wilbur, a.k.a. **MYSTIC CLAYTON** projected an image long remembered by his audiences. His publicity photos

Mystic Clayton Portrait
Courtesy of Princeton University Library

Mystic Clayton bedecked
with his medals
Courtesy of Princeton
University Library

show him dressed in brocades, wearing a silk cape, turned-up shoes, and a star-crowned turban emblazoned with "rare gems." His chest was always adorned with medals; whether or not he had legitimately earned these medals remains a question. Regardless of their source, his award medals looked impressive, and contributed to his success.

One fact known about Mystic Clayton is that he was a joiner who belonged to every conceivable fraternal order. These memberships afforded him entrée and friends wherever he went. Clayton was a fine showman and a good crystal gazer, but when it came to ethics he was deficient, like many others in his profession.

Mystic Clayton
A double image
Rauscher Collection

In 1919 it is reported that he was a partner with The Great Leon, a well-known magician who created a production called "The Famous Oriental Miracle Show." A marvelous full-face portrait of Mystic Clayton shows him wearing a large diamond ring and turban. His audiences never realized that his turban was wired inside for audio prompting.

Allah Naxmi
Courtesy of Princeton
University Library

Dressed in a costume similar to Mystic Clayton, but wearing velvet and adorned with chains and occult medals, was E. T. Nellar, who called himself **ALLAH NAXMI.**

Neller was financially successful during the 1920's. He performed with his wife, using a silent code. He retired to his house in California in the 1930's.

Some mentalists chose to proclaim themselves as "Reverend." Some of them even started churches and lived a life of false religion. Such a man was "The Reverend" **LOUIS C. PITZER.** Unlike the previously mentioned fake medium M. Lamar Keene, Pitzer was well acquainted with the spook equipment that could be purchased from magic supply houses.

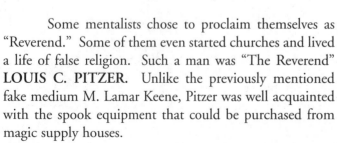

"The Reverend" Louis Pitzer
Courtesy of Princeton
University Library

C. A. George Newmann mentions Pitzer in his scrapbooks, and relates that he was once "pastor" of the Church of Light in Los Angeles, where Newmann attended Pitzer's Physical and Mental Phenomena Circles.  Newmann describes Pitzer as being highly theatrical.  In his act, he included crystal gazing, trumpet speaking, slate writing, a spirit telephone, and materializations.  During these demonstrations Pitzer told risqué jokes and used profane language in a burlesque manner.  Newmann said the vulgarity did not bother Pitzer's "parishioners," because they truly believed in him and in his ability.

His publicity photo in which he wears a turban, frock coat, and a piercing forward stare depicts a man of firm opinions, who could probably be stern and controlling when necessary.

Another performer, whose name was Hugo Lorenzo, but who called himself **SVENGALI**, used a silent code also associated with parts of the body.  When he casually touched some part of himself, his assistant, called "Trilby," knew which song had been selected.  She merely watched him down through her blindfold.

Mercedes and Helene Stantone
Courtesy of Princeton University Library

**MERCEDES** (born Joe Cohen) was another great performer.  In his act, he would psychically convey any song whispered in his ear to his blindfolded wife and assistant, **MLLE. HELENE STANTONE** (Nellie L. Clement).  Stantone, still blindfolded, would then play the song at a piano on stage.

A full-page spread in the July 16, 1914, *Milwaukee Free Press* proclaimed Mercedes as a "New Svengali," and his wife as another "Trilby." Mercedes was considered to be telepathic, enabling him to send music from his brain to his wife's brain. *(Author's note: Svengali, the musician, would hypnotize Trilby and make her sing – all the while employing a silent code.)*

Theirs was a simple act, but it required associating hundreds of songs with a numerical code, one dependent on body language and key words spoken by Mercedes.  The couple was proficient enough with their act to work at the New York Palace Theater in 1914.  They were held over three weeks, and in 1915 did another full week.  While they performed there, it was asserted that Mlle. Stantone could play over 5,000 different pieces of music.

Their billing had a cadence in itself: "Mercedes and the Marvelous Musical Mystic Mademoiselle Stantone." Mercedes' own billings read: "See him take music from your mind and mentally project it through space." The couple's favorite saying was: "Every mind is a human radio."

The act began when someone in the audience gave Mercedes the name of a piece of music. Then Mercedes would quietly think over the first few bars in silence. Or a member of the audience would give a piece of sheet music to Mercedes to look at. Then Mercedes would "send" the music to Mlle. Stantone, who would play it.

This act played all the best theaters, and was one of several great musical telepathy performances. The real mystery was why no one could detect trickery, but that's the advantage of using what is called a silent code.

David Edgar Rice, Ph.D., and his wife attended one of Mercedes' performances at Keith's Palace, specifically to look for deception. He and his wife realized that a code or confederates might be being used, but they could not determine Mercedes and Stantone's method. They even arranged for a private demonstration, and kept Mercedes at a distance of 40 feet. This time instead of whispering the song to Mercedes they wrote their request on a piece of paper. But once again, Mercedes fooled them.

Many other tests were devised in an effort to discover the act's secrets, but Mercedes always outsmarted his audience. Once Mercedes visited the mayor of Syracuse, who requested "The Star Spangled Banner." Meanwhile, Miss Stantone was sitting at a piano in the office of the mayor of Utica, some 50 miles away. Immediately she began to play her rendition of the National Anthem!

Mercedes and Mlle. Stantone puzzled other prominent people, such as Dr. James H. Hyslop, a longtime president of the American Society for Psychical Research. Hyslop was quoted as saying:

> I gave Mercedes the names of a number of classical pieces of music I wished played, and Miss Stantone, whose back was turned to us and who was blindfolded, played them. She was equally successful when I went out of the room with Mercedes. She made some mistakes, but that is no evidence of fraud. I could detect no trickery. I must say, however, that I should need to watch them very closely for probably two months before I could form an opinion whether there was any element of the supernormal in this case.

When acts like Mercedes and Mlle. Stantone attract the attention of important people, they have accomplished their goal. Lyman J. Gage, a former Secretary of the U.S. Treasury, provided Mercedes with impressive headlines. His priceless quote was:

It would be unreasonable to argue that their results are obtained by trickery which no one can explain, rather than by a psychical process, which has been shown on good evidence to be a reality.

According to magic historian and author David Price, Mlle. Stantone was nearly crushed to death in a stage elevator accident at the Paramount Theater in Staten Island, New York. As a result, she and Mercedes retired in 1932. They ended their days as successful travel agents.

Mercedes, "Wizard of the Wonder World," died on July 7, 1966. Mlle. Stantone died on February 5, 1971.

Helene Stantone
Rauscher Collection

*TOURING THE WORLD*

**MR. TREE**
*presents*
**MISS TREE AND MYSTERY**
The Famous Royal Command Personalities

*Have Appeared before*

| | |
|---|---|
| HIS LATE MAJESTY KING GEORGE V | PRINCESS ROYAL |
| QUEEN MARY | PRINCESS BEATRICE |
| KING OF NORWAY | PRINCESS ALICE OF ATHLONE |
| KING OF SWEDEN | PRINCE & PRINCESS OTTO von BISMARK |
| KING OF DENMARK | PRINCESS JULIANA |
| DUKE OF WINDSOR | PRINCE & PRINCESS DE CROY |
| DUKE OF KENT | PRINCE ADOLPH OF SWEDEN |
| Ex KING OF GREECE | |
| Ex QUEEN OF SPAIN | |

*Two minds with but one single thought*

"THE LONDON TIMES" says:
'Words fail to adequately describe one's impressions of their unusually original and delightful entertainment."

"It is really amazing," the King told Mr. Tree

Leo Tree
Courtesy of Gerald Taylor

Another musical telepathy act was performed by **LEO TREE** (born William John Atkins in England on April 4, 1894), with his wife, Myra, who called herself **MISS TREE.**

As with Mercedes and Mlle. Stantone, this couple impressed an incredible number of prominent people throughout their career. Everyone except their magician friends (who knew the truth) accepted them as true psychics.

To their credit, the Trees' act had an impressive list of royal appearances. Like Mercedes' wife, Myra sat at a piano and played music the audience members "thought about." Their career reached its peak during the 1920's, with appearances in the best theaters, for the best people.

Scholar David Price relates an incident regarding the Trees and the Duke and Duchess of Portland, who once asked the couple to perform a test. King George V also was present. With the Duke, the Trees went into the library of Welbech Abbey and chose a book from the shelves. King George opened the book and selected a passage. Then Miss Tree, blindfolded, wrote the passage the King had selected on a blackboard. Imagine the publicity value of such a stunt!

In spite of all their success, Leo and Miss Tree could not resist doing private readings, using everything from graphology to astrology. They eventually retired to Australia, where Leo died in 1957, followed by Myra in 1974.

When it comes to clever, devious showmen, no one can beat our next man, who could easily be called the Aleister Crowley of mentalism.

ALEXANDER, "The Man Who Knows," was born on June 30, 1880, in Alexandria, South Dakota.

Alexander providing his followers
with a mystic gesture
Courtesy of Princeton University Library

Alexander entered the world as Claude Alexander Conlin. Billed as "A Master of Modern Mental Mystics," he was a star performer for over 35 years, and was considered one of the best in his field. He is perceived by many to be "The King of Mind Readers." With great success he mixed magic and mentalism – both professionally and financially. He is estimated to have earned more than a million dollars during his career.

Alexander's poster lithographs proclaimed that Alexander "Sees Your Life from the Cradle to the Grave." These posters – which are now collectors' items – always featured his face, with his penetrating eyes that stared at the viewers, while he gazed in or through a crystal ball. His "face forward" poster is a dramatic representation of a man who fooled countless thousands of people in the theater, as well as during private readings.

Alexander's question-and-answer work was impressive. He was a master of the bluff, and his rather gaunt look, Oriental settings, turban, and robes gave an aura of Oriental mystery. He referred to himself as "The Crystal Seer" and "The One Who Knows, Sees and Tells All." He had so many imitators that in 1917 he registered the name "Alexander" and his titles with the National Vaudeville Association; however, these efforts did not deter the copycats.

From all reports, Alexander was a rather introverted man who had a highly checkered career. He avoided fellow magicians and never attended magic events. He had a strange, charismatic effect on women and was married on record six times – including to one woman who married him twice. Actually, it is rumored that he was really married twelve times! From these marriages came two sons and one daughter.

Alexander
Courtesy of Raymond J. Goulet

Primarily he was a master of psychology without a degree, and a manipulator of people with an innate ability to control individuals and audiences. He was also a 32nd degree Mason and a Shriner, and no doubt he used these organizations to his own great advantage.

Alexander and two assistants gazing in the crystal ball
Rauscher Collection

Alexander was a conjuror of words, and attempted to persuade his audiences and the press of his integrity to allay any suspicions they may have had about what might have been considered questionable methods used in his performances. In an effort to prove his honesty, he included the following in the printed program for his September 19-28, 1918, and June 1-16, 1919, performances at the Metropolitan Theater in Seattle:

> Mr. Alexander desires especially to call to the attention of the audience the fact that in these demonstrations he uses no confederates, no codes, no waxed pads to write upon, no exchange of your questions, thereby permitting the same to be transferred in some dressing room to an assistant to be transmitted to him via a telephone line to nails driven into the stage or wire woven in the carpet under the runways in the stage, connecting with copper wires running to a small telephone receiver concealed in a handkerchief, or other blindfold, or a turban with a plug attachment allowing for the headgear to be removed and shown appropriately. There are no tin globes, no blackboards in footlights and in wings, where the exchanged queries may be written for the performer to read as he answers. These are some of the methods resorted to by alleged performers, irresponsible, aspiring charlatans, pure and simple, who have copied Alexander's billing matter verbatim and have endeavored to imitate him in the smaller houses. There is but one Alexander, the original "The Man Who Knows," whose standing in the theatrical world is consistent with the position in the world of science; and he will be found playing only the best theaters of a city or it is not ALEXANDER!

Conversely, in Darryle Beckmann's book titled *The Life and Times of Alexander – The Man Who Knows* (Rolling Bay Press, Rolling Bay, Washington, 1994), Beckmann reveals that "every method Alexander claimed not to use during his performance, he actually used!" (p.54)

Author Walter B. Gibson, who had an encyclopedic knowledge of magicians, once told me it was not unusual for Alexander to arrange for a car to be stolen, or to plan to have

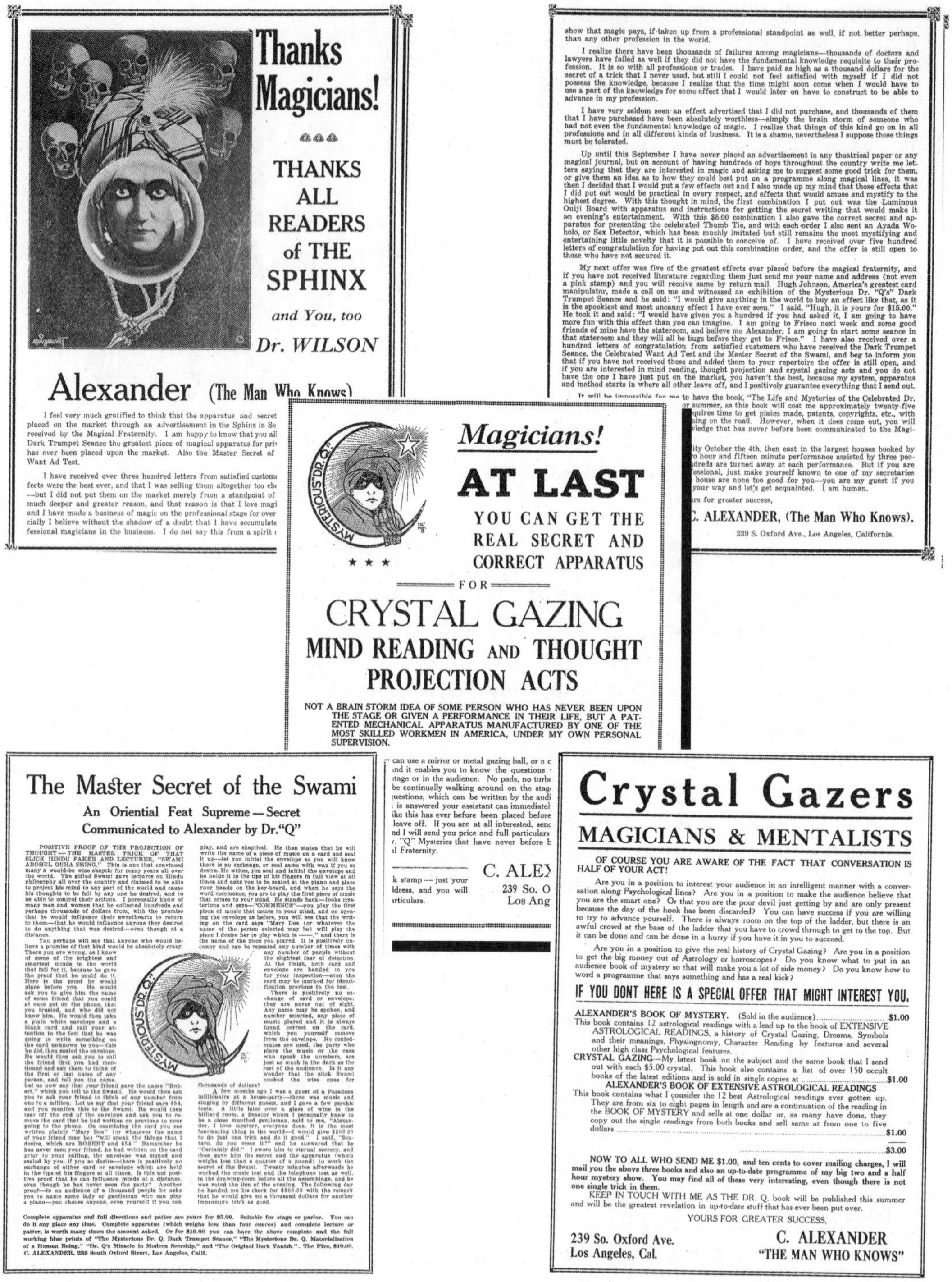

Thanks Magicians!

THANKS ALL READERS of THE SPHINX

*and You, too*

*Dr. WILSON*

Alexander (The Man Who Knows)

I feel very much gratified to think that the apparatus and secret
placed on the market through an advertisement in the Sphinx in Se
received by the Magical Fraternity. I am happy to know that you al
Dark Trumpet Seance the greatest piece of magical apparatus for pri
has ever been placed upon the market. Also the Master Secret of
Want Ad Test.

I have received over three hundred letters from satisfied custom
fects were the best ever, and that I was selling them altogether too ch
—but I did not put them on the market merely from a standpoint of
much deeper and greater reason, and that reason is that I love magi
and I have made a business of magic on the professional stage for over
cially I believe without the shadow of a doubt that I have accumulate
fessional magicians in the business. I do not say this from a spirit

show that magic pays, if taken up from a professional standpoint as well, if not better perhaps, than any other profession in the world.

I realize there have been thousands of failures among magicians—thousands of doctors and lawyers have failed as well if they did not have the fundamental knowledge requisite to their profession. It is so with all professions or trades. I have paid as high as a thousand dollars for the secret of a trick that I never used, but still I could not feel satisfied with myself if I did not possess the knowledge, because I realize that the time might soon come when I would have to use a part of the knowledge for some effect that I would later on have to construct to be able to advance in my profession.

I have very seldom seen an effect advertised that I did not purchase, and thousands of them that I have purchased have been absolutely worthless—simply the brain storm of someone who had not even the fundamental knowledge of magic. I realize that things of this kind go on in all professions and in all different kinds of business. It is a shame, nevertheless I suppose these things must be tolerated.

Up until this September I have never placed an advertisement in any theatrical paper or any magical journal, but on account of having hundreds of boys throughout the country write me letters saying that they are interested in magic and asking me to suggest some good trick for them, or give them an idea as to how they could best put on a programme along magical lines, it was then I decided that I would put a few effects out and I also made up my mind that those effects that I did put out would be practical in every respect, and effects that would amuse and mystify to the highest degree. With this thought in mind, the first combination I put out was the Luminous Ouiji Board with apparatus and instructions for getting the secret writing that would make it an evening's entertainment. With this $5.00 combination I also gave the correct secret and apparatus for presenting the celebrated Thumb Tie, and with each order I also sent an Ayada Woholo, or Sex Detector, which has been muchly imitated but still remains the most mystifying and entertaining little novelty that it is possible to conceive of. I have received over five hundred letters of congratulation for having put out this combination order, and the offer is still open to those who have not secured it.

My next offer was five of the greatest effects ever placed before the magical fraternity, and if you have not received literature regarding them just send me your name and address (not even a pink stamp) and you will receive same by return mail. Hugh Johnson, America's greatest card manipulator, made a call on me and witnessed an exhibition of the Mysterious Dr. "Q's" Dark Trumpet Seance and he said: "I would give anything in the world to buy an effect like that, as it is the spookiest and most uncanny effect I have ever seen." I said, "Hugh, it is yours for $15.00." He took it and said: "I would have given you a hundred if you had asked it, I am going to have more fun with this effect than you can imagine. I am going to Frisco next week and some good friends of mine have the stateroom, and believe me Alexander, I am going to start some seance in that stateroom and they will all be bugs before they get to Frisco." I have also received over a hundred letters of congratulation from satisfied customers who have received the Dark Trumpet Seance, the Celebrated Want Ad Test and the Master Secret of the Swami, and beg to inform you that if you have not received these and added them to your repertoire the offer is still open, and if you are interested in mind reading, thought projection and crystal gazing acts and you do not have the one I have just put on the market, you haven't the best, because my system, apparatus and method starts in where all other leave off, and I positively guarantee everything that I send out.

to have the book, "The Life and Mysteries of the Celebrated Dr.
or summer, as this book will cost me approximately twenty-five
quires time to get plates made, patents, copyrights, etc., with
oing on the road. However, when it does come out, you will
wledge that has never before been communicated to the Magi-

ity October the 4th, then east in the largest houses booked by
o hour and fifteen minute performance assisted by three peo-
dreds are turned away at each performance. But if you are
essional, just make yourself known to one of my secretaries
house are none too good for you—you are my guest if you
your way and let's get acquainted. I am human.

rs for greater success,

C. ALEXANDER, (The Man Who Knows).

239 S. Oxford Ave., Los Angeles, California.

*Magicians!*

AT LAST

YOU CAN GET THE REAL SECRET AND CORRECT APPARATUS

FOR

CRYSTAL GAZING

MIND READING AND THOUGHT PROJECTION ACTS

NOT A BRAIN STORM IDEA OF SOME PERSON WHO HAS NEVER BEEN UPON THE STAGE OR GIVEN A PERFORMANCE IN THEIR LIFE, BUT A PATENTED MECHANICAL APPARATUS MANUFACTURED BY ONE OF THE MOST SKILLED WORKMEN IN AMERICA, UNDER MY OWN PERSONAL SUPERVISION.

can use a mirror or metal gazing ball, or a c
ind it enables you to know the questions
itage or in the audience. No pads, no turb
be continually walking around on the stag
questions, which can be written by the audi
is answered your assistant can immediatel
ike this has ever before been placed before
leave off. If you are at all interested, senc
nd I will send you price and full particulars
r. "Q" Mysteries that have never before b
il Fraternity.

k stamp — just your
ldress, and you will
articulars.

C. ALEX
239 So. O
Los Ang

The Master Secret of the Swami

An Oriental Feat Supreme — Secret Communicated to Alexander by Dr. "Q"

POSITIVE PROOF OF THE PROJECTION OF THOUGHT — THE MASTER TRICK OF THAT SLICK HINDU FAKER AND LECTURER, "SWAMI ABDHUL GUHA SHING." This is one that convinced many a would-be wise skeptic for many years all over the world. The gifted Swami gave lectures on Hindu philosophy all over the country and claimed to be able to project his mind to any part of the world and cause his thoughts to be felt by any one he desired, and to be able to control their actions. I personally know of many men and women that he collected hundreds and perhaps thousands of dollars from, with the promise that he would influence their sweethearts to return to them—that he would influence anyone they desired to do anything that was desired—even though at a distance.

You perhaps will say that anyone who would believe a promise of that kind would be absolutely crazy. There you are wrong, as I know of some of the brightest and smartest minds in the world that fell for it, because he gave the proof that he could do it. Here is the proof he would place before you. He would ask you to give him the name of some friend that you could at once get on the phone, that you trusted, and who did not know him. He would then take a plain white envelope and a blank card and call your attention to the fact that he was going to write something on the card unknown to you—this he did, then sealed the envelope. He would then ask you to call the friend that you had mentioned and ask them to think of the first or last name of any person, and tell you the name. Let us now say that your friend gave the name "Robert," which you tell to the Swami. He would then ask you to ask your friend to think of any number from one to a million. Let us say that your friend says 654, and you mention this to the Swami. He would then tear off the end of the envelope and ask you to remove the card that he had written on previous to your going to the phone. On examining the card you see written plainly "Mary Doe" (or whatever the name of your friend may be) "will speak the things that I desire, which are ROBERT and 654." Remember he has never seen your friend, he had written on the card prior to your calling, the envelope was signed and sealed by you, if you so desire—there is positively no exchange of either card or envelope which are held in the tips of his fingers at all times. Is this not positive proof that he can influence minds at a distance, even though he has never seen the party? Another proof—in an audience of a thousand people he asks you to name some lady or gentleman who can play a piano—you choose anyone, even yourself if you can play, and are skeptical. He then states that he will write the name of a piece of music on a card and seal it up—let you initial the envelope so you will know there is no exchange, or seal same with wax if you so desire. He writes, you seal and initial the envelope and he holds it in the tips of his fingers in full view at all times and asks you to be seated at the piano and place your hands on the key-board, and when he says the word commence, you are to play the first piece of music that comes to your mind. He stands back—looks mysterious and says—"COMMENCE"—you play the first piece of music that comes to your mind, and on opening the envelope as before, you will see that the writing on the card says "Mary Doe (or whatever the name of the person selected may be) will play the piece I desire her to play which is ——," and there is the name of the piece you played. It is positively uncanny and can be repeated any number of times with any number of people without the slightest fear of detection. At the finish, both card and envelope are handed to you for your inspection—even the card may be marked for identification previous to the test.

There is positively no exchange of card or envelope; they are never out of sight. Any name may be spoken, and number selected, any piece of music played and it is always found correct on the card, which you yourself remove from the envelope. No confederates are used, the party who plays the music or the ones who speak the numbers, are just as much in the dark as the rest of the audience. Is it any wonder that the slick Swami hooked the wise ones for thousands of dollars?

A few months ago I was a guest of a Pasadena millionaire at a house-party—there was music and singing by different guests, and I gave a few psychic tests. A little later over a glass of wine in the billiard room, a Senator whom I personally know to be a close mouthed gentleman, said to me, "Alexander, I love mystery, everyone does, it is the most fascinating thing in the world—I would give $500.00 to do just one trick and do it good." I said, "Senator, do you mean it?" and he answered that he "Certainly did." I swore him to eternal secrecy, and then gave him the secret and the apparatus (which weighs less than a quarter of a pound) to work the secret of the Swami. Twenty minutes afterwards he worked the music test and the telephone test as well, in the drawing-room before all the assemblage, and he was voted the lion of the evening. The following day he handed me his check for $500.00 with the remark that he would give me a thousand dollars for another impromptu trick as good.

**Complete apparatus and full directions and patter are yours for $5.00. Suitable for stage or parlor. You can do it any place any time. Complete apparatus (which weighs less than four ounces) and complete lecture or patter, is worth many times the amount asked. Or for $10.00 you can have the above complete and the full working blue prints of "The Mysterious Dr. Q. Dark Trumpet Seance," "The Mysterious Dr. Q. Materialization of a Human Being," "Dr. Q's Miracle in Modern Seership," and "The Original Duck Vanish." The Five, $10.00. C. ALEXANDER, 239 South Oxford Street, Los Angeles, Calif.**

Crystal Gazers

MAGICIANS & MENTALISTS

OF COURSE YOU ARE AWARE OF THE FACT THAT CONVERSATION IS HALF OF YOUR ACT!

Are you in a position to interest your audience in an intelligent manner with a conversation along Psychological lines? Are you in a position to make the audience believe that you are the smart one? Or that you are the poor devil just getting by and are only present because the day of the hook has been discarded? You can have success if you are willing to try to advance yourself. There is always room on the top of the ladder, but there is an awful crowd at the base of the ladder that you have to crowd through to get to the top. But it can be done and can be done in a hurry if you have it in you to succeed.

Are you in a position to give the real history of Crystal Gazing? Are you in a position to get the big money out of Astrology or horroscopes? Do you know what to put in an audience book of mystery so that will make you a lot of side money? Do you know how to word a programme that says something and has a real kick?

IF YOU DONT HERE IS A SPECIAL OFFER THAT MIGHT INTEREST YOU.

ALEXANDER'S BOOK OF MYSTERY. (Sold in the audience) .......... $1.00
This book contains 12 astrological readings with a lead up to the book of EXTENSIVE ASTROLOGICAL READINGS, a history of Crystal Gazing, Dreams, Symbols and their meanings, Physiognomy, Character Reading by features and several other high class Psychological features.

CRYSTAL GAZING—My latest book on the subject and the same book that I send out with each $5.00 crystal. This book also contains a list of over 150 occult books of the latest editions and is sold in single copies at .......... $1.00

ALEXANDER'S BOOK OF EXTENSIVE ASTROLOGICAL READINGS
This book contains what I consider the 12 best Astrological readings ever gotten up. They are from six to eight pages in length and are a continuation of the reading in the BOOK OF MYSTERY and sells at one dollar or, as many have done, they copy out the single readings from both books and sell same at from one to five dollars .......... $1.00

.......... $3.00

**NOW TO ALL WHO SEND ME $1.00, and ten cents to cover mailing charges, I will mail you the above three books and also an up-to-date programme of my big two and a half hour mystery show. You may find all of these very interesting, even though there is not one single trick in them.**

KEEP IN TOUCH WITH ME AS THE DR. Q. book will be published this summer and will be the greatest revelation in up-to-date stuff that has ever been put over.

YOURS FOR GREATER SUCCESS,

239 So. Oxford Ave.
Los Angeles, Cal.

C. ALEXANDER
"THE MAN WHO KNOWS"

Alexander Advertisements from the *Sphinx,* March 1921 and April 1921 issues
He feared no competition, and was not averse to advertising to magicians who wanted to become mentalists.
Rauscher Collection

a window in a jewelry store broken, with these occurrences timed to coincide with his visit to the city in which he was scheduled to perform. Then, while on stage, he would interrupt himself and say: "I must stop! I hear in my mind the sound of breaking glass! I am getting an impression that at this very moment there is a possible robbery taking place at (he named the street). But now let us proceed…" He would also predict where to locate a stolen car (the theft of which he himself had arranged) – and even give the location where the abandoned car could be found! This was nothing new. Other old-time mentalists used the same or similar tactics.

A clever master of the con, with a special appeal to women, Alexander evoked strong feelings – and got away with it! His "Ladies' Matinee" was just one of many ways he succeeded in drawing crowds. Another of his ploys was to suggest that his clients – particularly women in private sittings – invest in stock in a certain silver mine. What he failed to inform them was that he owned the mine!

Alexander
Rauscher Collection

Alexander's real life was stranger than fiction, and bubbled over with intrigue and wrongdoing. We are left to wonder exactly what his personal belief concerning psychic ability really was, but those who have researched Alexander conclude that he was the ultimate cheat, crook, scoundrel, and a sinister, ruthless, and immoral man.

Alexander wrote the book *The Life and Mysteries of the Celebrated Dr. Q by C. Alexander, "The Man Who Knows,"* which he dedicated "To Magicians for the Betterment of Magic and the Truth of Psychic Phenomena." In the book's preface he says he wishes it distinctly understood that he neither affirms nor denies the existence of psychic and spiritual phenomena. He does not attempt to refute researchers, but states his purpose is to deal only with what he knows to be counterfeit, hoping their conclusions may help in the research of genuine psychic phenomena. This from a man who, in his own home, held materialization séances for the bereaved in a rigged upstairs bedroom!

Researcher Beckmann says in his second publication of notes, *The Alexander Story: Some Images and Revelations* (private publication, 1996), that Alexander was probably the top moneymaker in vaudeville. He sold tons of pamphlets, crystal balls, and books on astrology,

Alexander Show
Program
Rauscher Collection

numerology, and sexology. According to Beckmann, Alexander even sold luminous Ouija boards! He advertised a five-volume book set titled *Inner Secrets of Psychology*, and there are those who claim he also dealt in Prohibition liquor, opium, and even white slavery. Throughout his nefarious life the money continued to flow into his coffers, and by his standards that was the name of the game. He was truly a trickster par excellence.

The late magician John Pomeroy was so fascinated by Alexander that he began a book intended to be a definitive work of his life and career. Pomeroy's research discovered an even more secretive life of "The Crystal Seer." Author and magician David Charvet edited and annotated the Pomeroy manuscript, which is titled *The Life and Legends of The Celebrated C. Alexander, The Man Who Knows* (Scheduled Fox Publication 2003).

Despite all of his material successes, when Alexander died on August 6, 1954, at age 76 in Seattle, Washington, only six people attended his funeral. Rather a sad ending for "The King of Mindreaders."

Alla Axiom
Theater Announcement
Courtesy of Bill J. Weldon

**ALLA AXIOM** was a turbaned vaudeville headliner who is now forgotten. Styled in 1918 as a Hindu seer, and dressed like Alexander, Axiom drew crowds in the theater four times a day. Along with other acts like O'Neal and Walmsley, the money also flowed in to these performers through private readings.

Magician and mentalist **G. A. MURDOCK** was yet another Alexander imitator. Featured on the cover of the June 15, 1919, issue of the *Sphinx*, Murdock is seated in a throne chair, staring into his crystal ball. Beside him, his exotic assistant stands over a bowl that will hold the collected questions from the audience.

The *Sphinx* reports that Murdock was a graduate of Morningside College in Sioux City, Iowa. He was trained in dramatics, and made his first public appearance in the legitimate theater in 1910. By 1917 he had a large show, but he soon discarded it in an effort to build a new image. Two years later he was performing Hindu magic with Oriental settings, Egyptian dances and songs, and demonstrations of telepathy.

Murdock's plan was to eventually build a house in Kansas City, which would be constructed with rooms for public and private séance work. Many of yesteryear's mentalist acts tempted members of the audience to seek private readings – today's mentalists often follow this same pattern. Current reading system advertisements that appear in magic publications not only hint at the advantage of giving private readings – they often encourage this direction.

An ad in Brad Burt's San Diego, California, Magic Shop Fall 2001 newsletter is an example. A package of a 120-page spiral-bound book and four audiocassettes by Kenton Knepper and Rex Steven Sikes that sells for $250 is described as "possibly one of the best investments you will make as a magician or a mentalist." The ad continues, "Although the material would seem to be more in line with what a mentalist would use, the fact is that the addition of 'psychic,' 'personality analysis,' etc. readings to the programs offered by a magician can be a HUGE money maker. Consider that on average the mentalist can ask for and get MUCH higher fees than most magicians!"

G. A. Murdock
Courtesy of Raymond J. Goulet

The reviewer offers a final thought: "I had a magician friend years ago who made a great deal of money by opening with a 30-minute magic act. He finished with a terrific mental routine, and then offered to do 'readings' for folks afterward. This was, of course, part of the agreement with the client. He could sometimes pick up as much as $500–$1,000 extra on the evening in tips!"

The Murdocks of the past are the Murdocks of today. Today, G. A. Murdock dresses down for the occasion, and his programs no longer include women who perform Egyptian dance numbers. He does his act, but is not surprised when, afterward, a sincere person approaches him and whispers, "I wonder – would you consider doing a private reading for me?"

Newmann Blindfold Drive Poster
Courtesy of Kenneth Klosterman

**C. A. GEORGE NEWMANN** stands out as an important figure in the world of mentalist performers. Magic scholar and author James B. Alfredson found Newmann so interesting that he wrote a biography titled *Newmann: The Pioneer Mentalist* (David Meyer Magic Books, Glenwood, Illinois, 1989).

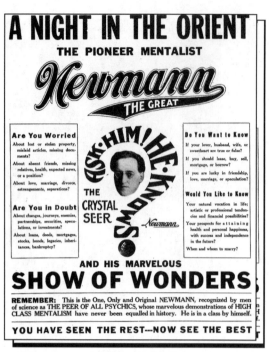

Newmann - A Night in the Orient Poster
Rauscher Collection

An Exhibition You'll Never Forget

(Part Three)

**Newmann's Studies in Scientific Suggestion**
(Psychology Put in Harness)

Mind is the master power that moulds and makes,
And man is mind, and evermore he takes
The tool of thought, and shaping what he wills,
Brings forth a thousand joys; a thousand ills.
He thinks in secret and it comes to pass,
Environment is but his looking glass.

Bonafide local volunteers while influenced by Mr. Newmann's dominant suggestions will offer some of the most amazing and mirth-provoking feats ever seen on any stage. Especial attention is directed to the unusual fact that, (unlike his contemporaries) Mr. Newmann employs no professional subjects, his demonstrations being presented with well known residents of this community.

**Sensitives Do Whatever Newmann Suggests,**
Frequently Producing
**DRAMATIC SKETCHES, OPERATIC SELECTIONS
AND IMPERSONATIONS**
From the Great Orators, Poets and Musicians Of the Past and Present Day

A $50.00 CASH AWARD will be paid to any person who can prove that there has been any private understanding, pre-arrangement or preliminary rehearsal between Mr. Newmann and those who assist him in his Unique and Original Mind Reading Experiments and Hypnotic Demonstrations.

**One of these Great Features is Presented Nightly**
Newmann's Astounding Cataleptic Sensation "THE HUMAN BRIDGE" From 700 to 1,000 pounds is sustained by the suspended body of A Hypnotic Cataleptic. Newmann challenges his numerous Imitators to duplicate this unbelievable feat under like conditions.

THE HUMAN-WOOD PILE & THE AMAZING ROCK BREAKING TEST Marvelous Cataleptical Achievements That Have Captivated the Intelligentsia of Every Community in Which He Has Appeared.

NEWMANN'S UNCANNY CONTROL OF BODY TEMPERATURE, PULSE AND HEART BEAT Local physicians supervise the proceedings thus guaranteeing their genuine reality.

NEWMANN'S ORIGINAL SCIENTIFIC SENSATION— THE GREAT BLOOD TEST An awe-inspiring demonstration in which he controls the flow of blood in various parts of the subject's body by hypnotic suggestion unassisted by the artificial devices employed by his many imitators and professional magicians.

*Two Hours Of Clean, Psychological Amusement, Scientific Entertainment and Mysterious Fun*
*Entertainment and Mysterious Fun*

Newmann 6th Annual Tour
Courtesy of Kenneth Klosterman

Newmann 6th Annual Tour
Courtesy of Kenneth Klosterman

Newmann 6th Annual Tour
Courtesy of Kenneth Klosterman

According to Alfredson, Newmann distinguished himself as an intelligent man who loved literature and was serious by nature, but who had a sense of humor. He enjoyed the fraternalism of magic, but never billed himself as a magician.

Christian Andrew George Naeseth, known as **NEWMANN**, was born on November 28, 1880, in Kenyon, Minnesota. At age seventeen, he entered the field of mentalism, and approached his stage persona in a professorial manner. He was also an excellent hypnotist, and many of his posters read "Master of Mental Marvels." He billed himself as "The World's Greatest Mind Reader" and as "America's Foremost Hypnotist." He was "That Brilliant Psychic Star, Newmann The Great," and performed at all the local opera houses.

Newmann booked his own shows, and since he did not use tons of apparatus, he was able to travel easily. He made his greatest impact on audiences with his mental magic. He also performed a few spook effects, including the "Rapping Hand" and "Spirit Paintings."

Local audiences were impressed with his dignified formal appearance, pince-nez glasses, and his scientific approach to his work. He was called "Doc" by many of his audience members in rural America. The effect of his mentalism and hypnosis demonstrations staggered local townspeople of that era.

Although Newmann did perform a few magical effects, they were insignificant compared with his real talent as a psychic and hypnotist. In his early days, at one outdoor public event he drove a team of horses and a carriage while blindfolded. His publicity poster lithograph depicts the excitement of his guest riders in the carriage, with Newmann, blindfolded, standing up and holding the reins while the horses race along.

He had a great interest in magicians, and became an early collector of magic memorabilia. Today his scrapbooks present a treasure trove of material. A number of photos in this book are from three of the Newmann scrapbooks in the Firestone Library at Princeton University. Newmann not only identified every item in these scrapbooks, but he also wrote a commentary for many of the photos. He also produced manuscripts on hypnotism and mentalism, and was a frequent contributor to magazines and books.

Newmann died in Minneapolis on December 30, 1952.

**SATORI**, "The Man Who Knows Everything," is Wolfgang Voigt. Born in 1947 in Germany, he is a first class mentalist with a renowned talent for contact mind reading, which is the same concept as muscle reading.

Satori has perfected his ability to determine what a person is thinking by touch alone, and his performance is greatly admired

Satori
Courtesy of Richard Hatch

by top mentalists throughout the United States. His repertoire also includes a two-hour hypnosis show.

Satori's personal interests in psychology and the social sciences, yoga, and Zen Buddhism add to his intriguing personality. He was awarded a bachelor's degree in Psychology and the Social Sciences, and writes with incredible insight about his craft.

His performance requires actual physical contact with an audience member who has hidden an object or selected objects somewhere in the theater. Satori has the subject hold his wrist, and is led to the object through the unsuspecting subject's body impulses. He creates such drama throughout his performance that he leaves his audiences in sheer amazement at his "telepathic experiments."

In his book *Satori: Making Contact* (H & R Magic Books, Humble, Texas, 1998), Satori presents an analysis of this fascinating field. The way in which people stand, sit, move, twitch, smile – all these subtle indications contribute to a lesson in "reading" a subject. Satori has finely tuned his ability to sense a volunteer's (the transmitter) involuntary impulses to near perfection. His act may include looking for a known (or even unknown!) object, finding a particular individual in the audience, or carrying out some activity with a person or object. His act is not simply one of questions and answers, or envelopes and psychic card tricks, and he is one of very few professionals who perform a mental act of this caliber.

The members of the magic community agree that Satori is indeed masterful in his technique, and he stands alone in the perfection of his art.

Ted Lesley
Courtesy of Phil Willmarth

**TED LESLEY** is the most internationally known mentalist in Germany.

Lesley got his start as a creative artist in his hometown of Düren, after watching his public school teacher perform magic. Now an award-winning mentalist, author, and performer, Lesley has been voted Gold Star membership in the Inner Magic Circle of London. He also received the Dunninger Award from the Psychic Entertainers Association. In 2001 he was honored to receive the Creative Fellowship Award from the Academy of Magical Arts at the Ebell Theater in Los Angeles. His book *Paramiracles* is noted for its original material and effects.

Lesley's "Wonder Workshop" markets his many effects, including a borrowed wineglass which visibly bends. Think-A-Drink is another of his creations, in which the name of a drink is written on a card and then inserted into an envelope, and Presto! Lesley pours the named drink from the envelope. He also makes a spoon wiggle until its handle looks like a corkscrew.

Lesley's vast repertoire also includes other para-mental effects. One observer remarked after Lesley demonstrated his mind reading ability, "Ted Lesley looks right into your future … and beyond. He can't be a faker!" Ted Lesley fully qualifies as an entertainer, and that's what he is.

Born in Australia, **ARTHUR BUCKLEY** was another psychic performer. He was also an expert with coin and card tricks.

When the money he made from performing magic tricks was not enough to satisfy him, Buckley developed a successful career through an effective two-person mind reading act, assisted by his wife, **HELENA LUCAS.**

In 1918 Buckley was playing vaudeville in the United States; by 1924 he was back in Australia with a card and séance act. Two years later he owned a thriving psychic mail-order business in Sydney, and made thousands of dollars conducting astrological readings and casting horoscopes.

Arthur Buckley
Courtesy of Raymond J. Goulet

Historian Brian McCullagh writes about Buckley in James Hagy's *Perennial Mystics #14*, privately published by Hagy in 1999. McCullagh quotes Australian magician Ken Jaffrey, who was personally acquainted with Buckley. In the mid-1920's, Buckley completed a series of test séances for the renowned Annie Besant, who succeeded the intriguing and strange Madam Blavatsky as head of the Theosophical Society. In a letter to McCullagh, Jaffrey states: "He [Buckley] did not approach Mrs. Besant, but got a friend to slyly drop a hint. When Arthur was approached by Mrs. Besant, he first played hard to get, and finally agreed to be tested, but promised nothing."

Supposedly Buckley gave three séances "under test conditions" for Mrs. Besant. According to the McCullagh article, Buckley was stripped naked and searched. Then in a sealed room, wearing only pajamas, he produced apports – material objects from the spirit world – consisting of large bronze Chinese coins, which fell from the air. At another séance he produced an object that contained salt water, seaweed, and fish. In the third session he brought forth an object of Indian art so hot that it burned the rug! McCullagh says, "Annie Besant gave Buckley a letter stating that, in her opinion, he was a first-class spirit medium."

Arthur Buckley, 1926
Courtesy of Brian McCullagh

Buckley also performed séances in private homes. McCullagh quotes an interesting description of Buckley at his best that appeared in the August 24, 1926 issue of the Sydney, Australia *Daily Guardian*:

> Several ladies of considerable social prominence are deeply interested in psychical research and anything connected therewith, and these speedily seized upon Mr. Buckley's presence in New York and invited him to their homes where his Simla Séances were carried out, and where he answered hundreds of questions from celebrities whose names loom largest in the social register.

Tall, slim, with deep-set black eyes, Mr. Buckley makes a handsome figure in his Oriental robes, and it is small wonder that this handsome Valentino of mystics won immediately a place as an entertainer of society people that few have occupied.

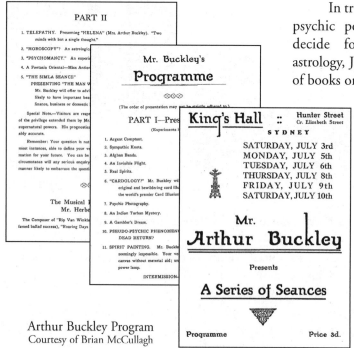

Arthur Buckley Program
Courtesy of Brian McCullagh

In true form, Buckley never claimed psychic powers; rather, he let people decide for themselves. Regarding astrology, Jaffrey said, "He sold thousands of books on astrology. When I asked him what was in astrology, he replied, 'Money!' I said, 'Is that all?' He replied, 'That is all.'"

Like so many performers of his day, Buckley did the usual crystal gazing. During his act, he always encouraged people to send in money for a reading by mail. And the mail arrived by the bag load! According to McCullagh's article, Jaffrey says Buckley could lip-read, allowing him to observe conversations from a distance and gain information. His sister, Madge Best, also obtained information for him by stealing questions that were written by the audience.

Arthur Buckley's psychic moneymaking career was rather short-lived. In 1928 he was prosecuted, convicted, and sentenced in Sydney to three months in jail for money schemes based on his fortune-telling scams. He was eventually acquitted after a confusing trial and sentence, with no jail time served.

In 1929 Buckley abandoned his magic/mentalism profession and returned to the United States. Despite his unethical behavior, he was an intelligent man, and became an engineering consultant. He also wrote books on magic and mentalism until his death in 1953. Even today when most magicians think of Arthur Buckley, they remember his book on card magic, not his background as a mind reader.

In a lecture on mind readers that he delivered in the 1980's at a Magic Collectors Weekend, the late magic historian Robert Parrish said with a smile that Buckley gave up mind reading because he was beginning to believe he really was psychic! Parish went on to affirm that the most successful mentalism performances were question-and-answer acts, since audiences more easily respond to an "oracle" type presentation. Another advantage is that this type of presentation opens the door for requests for private readings.

Buckley was seduced by his own talent, and almost paid the price by going to jail. Today, with Internet Web sites, magazine advertisements, and television psychic hotlines, he would most likely still be in business.

**MARDONI AND LOUISE** was another two-person mentalism act that became well known.

Mardoni and Louise
Courtesy of Rob Allen

Clayton Meryl Hines (Mardoni) was an educated man who graduated from Northern Illinois University in DeKalb. He was a teacher until 1928, when he began performing on the Chautauqua circuits. He did magic, and also jumped from an airplane wearing handcuffs, from which he had to free himself in order to pull the ripcord of his parachute.

In 1928 he married Louise Garman. Their fame as a star attraction mind reading team began when they first saw Arthur Buckley and Harry and Frances Usher.

Scholar John Booth details more of their career in his article "Memoirs Of a Magician's Ghost" (*Linking Ring*, July 1984, Chapter 185). The success of so many of these acts necessitated the performers' swift work and constant practice of their verbal and silent codes when they were idle. This kept their minds sharp, and increased the rapidity with which they were able to work. It also made them attractive to bookers, who engaged them to work in nightclubs and theaters, on cruises, and as an additional act with other performers who were already playing the "Big Time."

Tommy and Betty Tucker
Courtesy of John Moran

So it was also with **TOMMY AND BETTY TUCKER**, a once-famous duo who possessed energy, quick wit, and great verbal ability. Tommy Tucker also offered the Blindfold Car Drive, and was a pioneer in the 1950's in the development of electronic devices used by mentalists.

The Tuckers called their business "ESP Inc.," and their products "Magitronix." They advertised their methodology as "The Easy Way to Learn Contact Mind Reading." Why, they said, spend time memorizing complicated codes when you can use state-of-the-art miniature senders, receivers, tappers, or micro lights? They simply brought up-to-date the bygone days of electric wires in turbans!

It was inevitable that electronics would help revolutionize mind reading, and the Tuckers were in the forefront of a new era.

# *Act 9*

**And still they come!  Some bearing**
**horoscopes for sale – others who influence**
**thoughts.  Here's a group of ...**

## *CHARMING PERFORMERS WITH CLEVER MINDS*

**THE JARETTS** were a successful husband and wife team.  I saw them perform the eyeless vision act in Keansburg, New Jersey when I was a young man.  The couple billed themselves as providing "Thought Transmission Through the Window of the Mind."  Their promotional statements cleverly announced: "He sees things others cannot see.  She not only recognizes objects, but also describes them in detail.  She may suddenly call a stranger by name, tell him his birthday, the nature of his business, and other intimate things, equally astounding."  After their demonstration the Jaretts sold horoscopes.  Sales were always brisk – and like many others, I contributed my 25 cents for the envelope marked "Libra."

The Jaretts
Promotional Brochure
Courtesy of Thomas A. Ewing

**SIR EDWARD** was the pseudonym used by Raymon LaRue, who performed with his wife, **CONSTANCE**.  Dressed in an immaculate formal suit and sporting black hair and a thin mustache, Sir Edward projected sophistication as audiences marveled at his message readings.  During the couple's act, Constance collected written questions from the audience and then placed them in a fishbowl.  From the bowl, Sir Edward, eyes blindfolded, would divine the questions and answer them.  He would also predict happenings two weeks in advance, lock the predictions in a chest, and place the chest in a department store window.  Later he would give the results of his predictions, which might include the current day's headline or ball game score.

In his book *Conjurors and Cornfields:  Magic on the Indianapolis Stage* (published by Thomas A. Ewing, 1999), Ewing talks about LaRue.  Born in West Virginia

Sir Edward and Constance
Courtesy of Thomas A. Ewing

on April 6, 1893, LaRue's career began with mind reading and pitching horoscopes. In 1936 he married Constance, and they settled in Indianapolis.

By the 1940's LaRue was highly successful as a horoscope pitchman. Robert Nelson featured LaRue (as Sir Edward) in his *Catalog No. 20* (Nelson Enterprises, Columbus, Ohio), and described him as a man who gave 36,000 individual readings in 1941. Many of these were done at horoscope booths in "Five, Dime and Dollar Stores."

Nelson marketed many items for use by mentalists, mediums, and astrologers, and also offered "The Sir Edwards' Store Demonstration Sales Plan" for $100.00. Written by LaRue, this plan supposedly taught all you had to know to become another Sir Edward – or as he billed himself "Sir Edwards." Nelson supplied the necessary printed horoscopes, posters, question slips, booklets, and advertising materials. His advertisement read:

> Sir Edwards' demonstration of reading sealed billets is marvelous – holds and mystifies his audiences. It is very, very clever, and above fear of detection. Involves no special apparatus, no codes, no memorization, or suspicious moves. It is thrilling to witness – a convincing argument to any skeptic."

This demonstration, done by Sir Edward while blindfolded, was part of a warm-up to the selling of his individually printed horoscopes, and was preceded by a short lecture. According to the promotional material, "With only one assistant, you, too, can become a lecture/salesman of astrological readings in the stores."

Sir Edward
Department Store Setting
Rauscher Collection

Sir Edward also performed escapes, and his act had all the flair of a daredevil. According to Ewing, Sir Edward was the first man to accomplish a straitjacket escape while hanging from a helicopter. His escape performances continued until he reached middle age; after being dropped on his head (fortunately, landing unharmed) at the Syracuse, New York State Fair, he decided to attempt something less dangerous.

Constance continued to perform with her husband; in one of their acts she allowed herself to be frozen in a cake of ice. Actually, like the contemporary David Blaine, she was put in several large cakes of ice that had been hollowed out. Also like Blaine, Constance was later removed from the ice and rushed to a hospital to warm up!

After Sir Edward abandoned escapes and dangerous stunts, he turned to full-time mentalism, where he gained tremendous publicity. However, he encountered a series of problems with the magic societies when they wanted him to disclaim any psychic powers, and he refused.

Ewing offers an interesting account of LaRue's prediction of his own death: "After his wife, Constance, passed away, it was LaRue's custom to travel to his children's house for Sunday dinner. On Sunday, May 18, 1969, he casually announced that he wouldn't be there the next Sunday because he would be dead. His daughter Nancy told him to stop talking nonsense, but he was adamant. Five days later, on May 23, he passed away."

A performer similar to Sir Edward was a man known as **AKBAR** Warshaw.

According to notes by C. A. George Newmann, Akbar did not appear in theaters, but instead limited himself to performing in large department stores, where he also pitched horoscopes. He sometimes performed at carnivals, but even in these venues he focused his efforts on selling as many horoscopes as possible.

Akbar
Courtesy of Princeton University Library

Akbar worked during the 1940's, when supplies were always available from Robert Nelson Enterprises. At this time, a horoscope pitchman could purchase hundreds of envelopes containing standard horoscope readings. Twelve different envelopes contained information on the twelve signs of the zodiac, arranged by date of birth. Regardless of which envelope one received, every sale that followed Akbar's talk and demonstration was accompanied by Akbar's wishes for a happy future.

Eddie Fields and
George Martz
Courtesy of Stephen Minch

A better-known horoscope pitchman in the mid-1940's was **EDDIE FIELDS** (1915-2001). Born Isadore Feldman in New York, he eventually sold horoscopes in department stores with his partner, Freddie Teschner, and a later partner named **GEORGE MARTZ**. As a team, **Fields and Martz** developed a code act, and for decades worked chain stores like F. W. Woolworth, Grant's, May, and Newberry's.

Fields was an expert on pitchmen, and on psychic oddities and con techniques of this world. A fascinating character, he was the subject of two books: *The Greater Artful Dodges of Eddie Fields* by Jon Racherbaumer (Kaufman & Company, 1997), and *A Life Among Secrets: The Uncommon Life and Adventures of Eddie Fields* by Stephen Minch (Hermitic Press, 1992).

Magician Al Cohen, who was proprietor of Al's Magic Shop in Washington, D.C., was a good friend of Fields. Cohen told me that even into his 80's, Fields was delightful – full of ideas, and a wonderful, colorful guy. He said: "He stood out with his black hair and bulging eyes, and dressed like he just walked out of Sears Roebuck & Co. While Martz was doing the Horoscope Pitch, Eddie would be there in the audience, gaining information and passing it along to Martz. They were a great team, energetic and upbeat. Eddie was truly a funny little guy, and sharp as a tack."

Jon Racherbaumer, magician, writer, and friend of Fields, described Fields in *Genii Magazine* (December 2001) as a "benign, empathetic, dyed-in-the-wool con artist." Then Racherbaumer added " 'Con' here connotes cajolery and swindling deception, not criminal activity."

Racherbaumer also said Fields had "a carny soul" and that two words were key to his credo: risk and opportunism. In the same article, Simon Aronson, who had known Fields for 34 years, wrote, "Eddie was a real character, and he 'played' you [actually, he played everyone] whenever he talked with you."

Dr. Arthur Hirsch, a retired dentist and another of Fields' friends, found him so fascinating that he allowed him to live at his house. In return, Fields taught the doctor his mind reading code. Hirsch told me Fields did a fantastic act in such a natural way that he fooled nearly everyone with his two-person performance.

In Fields' obituary, written by Robert D. L. Smith in *The Linking Ring* magazine (December, 2001), Smith describes Fields as "a mentalist, close-up magician, pool shark, pitchman, and life-long hustler, who was applauded by mentalist Orville Meyer and considered the greatest mentalist he [Meyer] had ever seen."

In every way, Eddie Fields was a colorful character who impressed all who knew him.

Another intriguing mentalist team was **DOC IRVING AND PRINCESS YVONNE.** Doc was a Russian Jew, born 1900 in Kiev. As a young man, I once saw the couple perform on Hamid's Million Dollar Steel Pier in Atlantic City, New Jersey. They worked on a platform decorated with a Zodiac backdrop. To make extra income in combination with their act, they sold Dream Books.

According to Walter B. Gibson, who knew Irving well, Irving was strong-willed and domineering. Gibson told me that Doc was greatly influenced by Houdini, and even had a similar aggressive personality.

Doc Irving and Princess Yvonne
March 29, 1929
Rauscher Collection

Doc Irving and Princess Yvonne
In performance on the Steel Pier,
Atlantic City, New Jersey
Courtesy of Diego Domingo

Princess Yvonne and
Baby Yvonne
Courtesy of Diego Domingo

I met Doc's wife, Princess Yvonne long after her husband's death. At the time of our meeting, I was not aware that she had become an alcoholic. She was a sad figure indeed, and had deteriorated drastically from the once prominent "Oriental Enigma." I learned of Yvonne's addiction when I met her forceful, screaming, out-of-control daughter who was beside herself over her mother's condition. The daughter, once known as "**BABY YVONNE**, The World's Youngest Mental Marvel," had learned her parents' code by watching them perform every day. Eventually her father brought her into the act.

In his younger days, Doc Irving had been influenced by his association with another mind reading team known as **THE USHERS** (Harry and Frances).

In their prime, Harry and Frances Usher were very successful. In 1927 their act was called "Fifty Years From Now." They worked fast, and were sought after in the United States and in English Music Halls.

The Ushers began their career selling horoscopes, and then progressed to private readings. They performed their fast-paced act as a top attraction for nine successful years.

At the end of their career, they were once again selling horoscopes.

Jack Flosso is the son of the late famous magician Al Flosso, who was known as the Coney Island Fakir, and who ran a unique old-time magic shop in New York. Jack, who can relate countless stories of magicians and vaudeville acts, remembers (Richard) **DOC SYLVERS**, another mentalist.

During one of our conversations, Flosso described Richard Sylvers as a tremendous performer who pitched horoscopes and gave great readings before his pitch. Jack met Sylvers in his father, Al's, magic shop. He eventually traveled and worked with Sylvers during the early 1950's after Sylvers' wife died and he needed an assistant. Jack's

The Ushers Promotional Brochure
Courtesy of George Daily

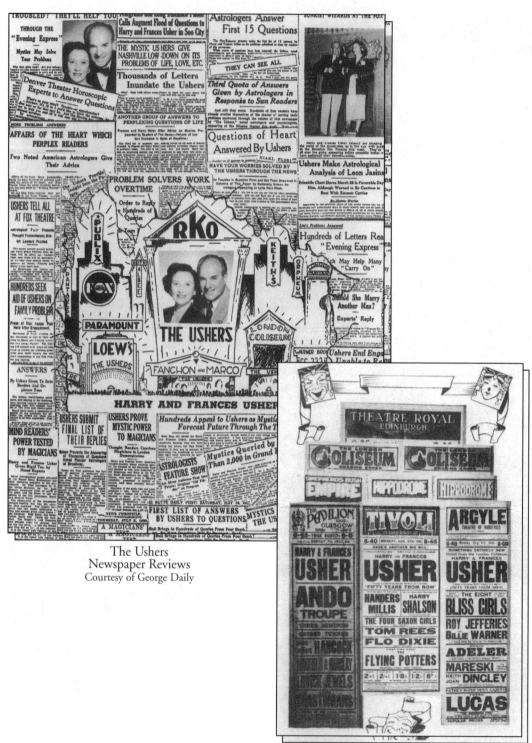

The Ushers
Newspaper Reviews
Courtesy of George Daily

The Ushers Theater Heralds
Courtesy of George Daily

responsibility was to gather information for Sylvers prior to their performances across the MidWest and in countless mill towns.

Jack also told me of his adventures with Sylvers:

"It was a touring experience I will never forget. Sylvers was a short man with a hunchback. His appearance actually helped the act in some places. It might not help in fancy or wealthy venues, but it worked in the places we played."

He continued:

Harry and Frances Usher in 1928
Courtesy of George Daily

"Funny thing about mind reading — economic conditions do not affect the money making prospects. One time in a vaudeville theater I watched Leona La Mar give readings in front of a thousand people. She was terrific!

"A lot of people did mind reading acts. Myrus was especially good because he carried it off in a non-showmanship way. He was low-keyed, and came across looking and acting like a professor. Even my father, in his very early days, did an act with my mother, who was known as **MADAME XENIA**. This was an act and not my father's real thing, as you know.

Madame Xenia
Courtesy of Stanley Palm

"My father knew all the people of his day who did magic, mind reading, and puppets, plus the side show crowd. I remember being with him on the Steel Pier in Atlantic City. We were watching Doc Irving and Princess Yvonne. As Doc was giving his readings and sending code messages to his wife, he was talking out of the side of his mouth to my father. It was a rather hilarious situation. For so many of these people, even during the depression, you could make a buck reading minds. Good times or bad times, the mind reader could make money."

Then Jack reflected:

"Bad times even made it better. I notice that psychics may be doing more business since the September 11th attack here in New York."

Jack Flosso was right, according to an article in the December 16, 2001 issue of *The New York Times*. In this article, "Looking for Solace in a Spirit World," writer Bob Morris describes how friends and relatives of the World Trade Center attack victims were consulting mediums in an effort to reach their missing loved ones. This raised questions of exploitation.

In a related incident, following an appearance on the Larry King television show, British-born best-selling author and psychic Rosemary Altea, who claims to speak with the dead, was hosted by the prestigious William Morris Agency in New York City. Widows of fire fighters, family members of missing or dead World Trade Center attack victims, and six other mourners who were Morris employees attended Altea's performance.

A similar situation was described in the article "Seeking Solace From the Psychics" in the December 24, 2001 issue of the *Philadelphia Inquirer*. In this piece, Amie Parnes states that people are looking for spiritual aspirins from psychics to ease the pain of their own uncertainties, and that fees of up to $100 per hour were not unusual for this "assurance."

Psychics are being questioned regarding potential danger aboard airplanes, whether it is safe to work in tall buildings, or even if mailboxes should be opened. This same article said in the November 2001 issue of the *Sunday Times* of London it was reported that U. S. intelligence agencies had recruited psychics to help predict future terrorist attacks, and to help track down Osama bin Laden. Psychics reported obtaining hundreds of new clients, including relatives of the World Trade Center and Pentagon attacks – and stated these clients could now charge their visits on credit cards. This may now be common practice, but in the past most magicians who are mentalists and who do private readings preferred cash.

It is difficult to judge the results because of the extraordinary circumstances surrounding the World Trade Center and Pentagon attacks, but this search for comfort confirms that in times of doubt or grief, people seek what they think is – or may be – true spiritual help. Usually this assistance is not spiritual at all, but merely an impression, a mixture of the personalities involved, with questionable reassurances and results.

Jack Flosso made one final point in our conversation:

> "My nature is such that I could never do private readings for a living. A person has to live with himself or herself, and some of these people who do this have problems with it that they conceal. It's a lot different when it's just an act."

The list of these performers goes on and on …

Harry Ingalls
Courtesy of
Raymond J. Goulet

Lucille and Eddie Roberts
A prediction from a locked chest
is about to be revealed
Courtesy of Raymond J. Goulet

Lucille and Eddie Roberts
Promotional Brochure
Courtesy of Thomas A. Ewing

King and Zorita
Courtesy of Rob Allen

Lucille and Eddie Roberts
Rainbow Room, Rockefeller
Center program announcement
Courtesy of Bill J. Weldon

Lucille and Eddie Roberts
Courtesy of Rob Allen

**HARRY INGALLS**, "The Wizard of Mental Telepathy," stated in his publicity that he could solve *all* of everybody's problems. How comforting it must have been to his follows when they read Harry's advertisements proclaiming "Why worry? – Ask Ingalls!"

Ingalls ascertained he could locate missing people. He even claimed he could find a husband for the women in his audience! Most reassuring was his printed statement: "I will do anything for anyone at any time, so long as it is legal."

**KING AND ZORITA**, declared themselves "The King and Queen of Mentalists." Zorita, wearing a blindfold, called out first, middle, and last names of audience members in a two-person act with Englishman Harry King. They played night clubs, fairs, and amusement parks during the 1900's.

**LUCILLE AND EDDIE ROBERTS** were well known, and played many of the supper rooms in first-class hotels. They gained the approval of celebrities such as Walter Winchell and Danton Walker. The Roberts' billing asked, "What's On Your Mind?"

Sid and Elayne Marlo
Promotional Brochure
Courtesy of Thomas A. Ewing

Russ Burgess
Promotional Brochure
Courtesy of Thomas A. Ewing

Rudy Saxon
Promotional Brochure
Courtesy of Thomas A. Ewing

**SID AND ELAYNE MARLO** coined a new word when they called their act "Mentalia." The Marlos guaranteed their audiences that they would provide a program long to be remembered. Whether or not they did so is uncertain; however, their work was apparently good enough to amaze stars like Jack Paar, Joey Bishop, Tom Poston, and Hugh Downs.

**RUSS BURGESS** presented himself as a skeptical psychic, and described his mentalism work as "Mental Fascinations." Along with his insights into ESP, he performed a sealed prediction act.

**RUDY SAXON** did a similar act, presenting "Mysterious and Fascinating Wonders of the Sixth Sense." His publicity invited the reader to join him "on a unique adventure into the realm of Psychic Phenomena."

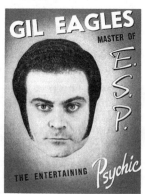

Gil Eagles
Promotional Brochure
Courtesy of Thomas A. Ewing

**GIL EAGLES'** program was called "This Is ESP!" Eagles' publicity promised to take his audience "to the innermost recesses of the human mind." He proclaimed he could "pierce the walls of the future" with his effect, "Visions of Tomorrow."

**MYRUS**, born Harry Carp, had a question-and-answer stage act that used a fishbowl containing questions written by the audience. Myrus answered the questions and offered additional, unprepared "psychic insights," otherwise known as cold readings. His technique of generating these impromptu remarks was greatly admired by other mentalists.

Myrus
Courtesy of Bill J. Weldon

Eventually he appeared on Station WXEL-TV in Cleveland, Ohio, and tickets to his show were scarce. Sponsored by Norge Refrigerators, his show aired once a week at night, and three times a week in the morning.

Myrus fooled magicians and other mentalists, which is a tremendous achievement for any performer. Robert Nelson, who wrote a column in *The Linking Ring*, thought highly of Myrus' mind reading skills. In a 1956 issue, Nelson says, "This boy really rocks 'em with his demonstrations, and knows how to get reams of publicity." He claimed Myrus created a sensation in the Cleveland area. He was also popular in Miami, Florida, where his show on WITV-TV was sponsored by an auto agency.

In 1959, Nelson noted that Myrus was back in Cleveland, and again on television. He recalled Myrus' first appearances in Cleveland in 1958, when he was so successful and created such widespread interest that his admirers renamed the city of Cleveland "Myrus-Town."

In a 1960 issue of *The Linking Ring,* Nelson writes:

> I recently caught one of Myrus' TV shows in the studio. His program consisted basically of answering questions, and several tests. The man does a masterful job of handling and answering questions. Number writers [gambling operators] were interpreting some of Myrus' remarks into numbers, and several "hits" occurred, whereupon the number operators passed cards stating they would pay only even money on any number deduced from the Myrus program. Otherwise, the payoff is 500 to one!

Magician friend Bill J. Weldon knew Myrus, and once appeared with him. He remembers that Myrus, like many contemporary mentalists, was strictly a telepathist and wanted nothing to do with magicians.

Weldon says that Myrus was an expert at obtaining information previously written by audiences on cards. A faded article titled "See – Hear With Stan Anderson" (no date or city) recounts how the proprietor of Monaco's Restaurant once questioned Myrus by writing on a card: "Where is Maggie Wulff?" Myrus gave no indication that he even knew who Maggie Wulff was. He took the card, tore it in pieces, and put it in his pocket. Then he thoughtfully toyed with the question as if he were stumped, using his delay tactic to make his act appear more difficult. Finally he said, "She's sitting three tables to our left."

Myrus
Cotillion Room Appearance
Courtesy of Bill J. Weldon

Myrus' act and one-to-one table work was successful not because of what he did, but how he did it. A man once asked Myrus to tell him his daughter's name. Thoughtfully, Myrus finally replied, "Winnie." The man said, "That's not the way I wrote it." Myrus paused, thought, and at last he said, "Well, if you want to be quite proper about it, your daughter has a double name – Winnie Sue."

According to those who knew him, Myrus was devious, secretive, and always able to convince others that his ability was genuine. He is also reported to have run a mail order psychic business, which eventually landed him in trouble with the law. But that was the way Myrus made his living.

Doc Mahendra
Courtesy of Princeton University Library

With his wife Ann, **DOC MAHENDRA** was another colorful character. Magician Claude Crowe remembers M. S. Mahendra as an early influence in his life of magic. Crowe told me, "Bill, he was a personable guy, but in his own way domineering, fascinated with magicians, fraternal, and very much in command. I found him a bit threatening as a young man, but then again he was in touch with what was going on in magic. Yes, he did private readings, and he did use a crystal ball."

Mahendra, who was Frank B. Sterling, loved magic, and helped organize the Texas Association of Magicians. He was superb at mentalism and also hypnosis. In his 1930's act he wore a turban, as did so many others, and was assisted by his wife, Ann, who was dressed as an Oriental dancer. In their act, Ann would gather the written questions deposited in the theater lobby by the audience members before the start of each performance. She would dump all the questions in a fishbowl on the stage, and then perform an Oriental dance to set a mystical mood just before her husband, the mysterious Doc Mahendra, appeared on stage.

During his lifetime Mahendra interviewed many magicians, and was a frequent contributor to magic magazines. He also wrote routines for card magic and crystal gazing, and a manuscript that taught magicians how to swallow needles and thread, then extract them from the mouth threaded. He performed this trick himself in 1912.

Ann Mahendra
Courtesy of
Princeton University Library

Mahendra and his wife retired to live in San Antonio, Texas, where they operated a health food store. Whether they believed in the value of health foods, or whether they thought the store was just another way to convince people to buy from them based on their power to sell another "audience" is difficult to say.

Mahendra died in 1970.

**STANLEY JAKS,** who was known as "The Incredible Dr. Jaks," is remembered for a special talent.   Born Herbert Siegbert near Danzig in Germany in 1903, he emigrated to the United States in 1946 and became a citizen in 1951.

Dr. Jaks
Courtesy of Rob Allen

Jaks was a one-man mental show whose signature item was a large, red leather book in which he carried the unique small magic props used in his magic performed at tables.  Jaks was serious in his presentations, and excelled in lecture demonstrations given to small groups of people.

Robert Bluemle, the attorney/mentalist known as Dr. Juris, is so impressed by Jaks' life and work that he is writing his biography, which will be published in a red leather book similar to the one Jaks carried to his performance.

The article titled "The Incredible Dr. Jaks," written by Martin Gardner in the October 1954 issue of the *Linking Ring*, describes Jaks as outstanding, and admired especially for his ability to analyse handwriting.  Gardner notes that Jaks could speedily duplicate signatures of spectators upside down and backwards on a blackboard, while blindfolded.

Although he could forge a signature, there is no indication that the signatures in the front of his red leather book were not real.  Supposedly, the autographs were written (at Jaks' request) by prominent members in Jaks' audience after they had witnessed his performance. This list was impressive and included such names as the Aga Khan, the Queen of Spain, Harry Truman, Walter Chrysler, Al Jolson, and Lana Turner.  Since he did table performing using the small and elegant props from his book in clubs like the Copacabana and in expensive hotels, Jaks had no trouble meeting prominent people.

Gardner remembers him as a man who came across like "a distinguished European professor of psychology."  He quotes Jaks' rather prophetic statement in 1954 regarding mentalism's resurgence and future advanced methods:  "I am convinced that modern mentalism is a field that has been only barely scratched.  Annemann opened up many new paths.  But there are paths which even Annemann did not foresee, and the possibilities for the future mentalist are truly unlimited."

Jaks died in 1960.

Ray Raymond
Courtesy of Raymond J. Goulet

Most magicians are not really professional mentalists; however, a large segment of them include some aspect of mentalism in their act, even if only to reveal a selected card. These performers don't consider themselves psychic entertainers. Rather, they are first magicians, who also happen to do ESP tricks as simply another part of their act. Raymond J. Goulet, my friend of many years, must be included in this group.

Ray and his wife, Ann, performed magic as **The Raymonds** on 22 trans-Atlantic sailings of the S.S. United States, and also made appearances on other cruises and in countless top venues. Ray performed illusions, sleight of hand, and comedy; he also entertained with a mental act. Like others, he realized that including a "twilight zone experience" in his act was another way to entertain his audiences.

Ray worked alone in his mentalist act. Publicized as **RAY RAYMOND**, he posed the question, "Extra Sensory Perception – Is It Real?" After watching Ray's performance, his viewers were left to decide for themselves.

Private readings were an abhorrent to Ray. His approach was pure entertainment, sculptured around magician's tricks that always amused and baffled his audiences. Now retired, he possesses a vast knowledge of magic.

Ray Raymond
Courtesy of Raymond J. Goulet

Bob Cassidy
Courtesy of Meir Yedid

Some performers decide that mentalism will be their full time vocation. In the early 1970's, Robert E. Cassidy, a former lawyer-turned-mentalist, made that decision. As **BOB CASSIDY**, he did a version of Russian Roulette, using four pistols. While blindfolded, and supposedly using ESP, Cassidy would attempt to select the single unloaded pistol, then place the gun to his head and pull the trigger. Fortunately he always chose correctly, and is still alive today.

(Ray Goulet, who earlier had been impressed by Cassidy's act, also did a version of this dramatic effect, much against his wife Ann's better judgment. Neither Ray nor Ann minded if someone secretly mixed up their deck of ESP cards when they were not looking, but Ann was always backstage with a close, watchful eye on Ray's pistols when he performed this dangerous feat.)

During the 1970's, Bob Cassidy was especially popular in his home state of New Jersey. In 1978 he became a founding member of the Psychic Entertainers Association. Today he still performs his strong routines, now to a much wider audience. He has worked on Holland America Cruises, in nightclubs, bars, and at banquets, and seems always to take on tough audiences. His methods and techniques are admired by a generation of mentalists who frequent his lectures, buy his videotapes, and read his writings.

Cassidy's 2002 CD contains his complete works and, together with his television and radio appearances, helps define his philosophy regarding mentalism. He gave up private readings over a decade ago, and prefers to be thought of as a legitimate entertainer. His opinion of private readings should serve as a lesson for other mentalists. He says, "They appeal as much to the insecurity of the sitter as to the reader himself."

Friends consider Cassidy an original, with a natural comic touch. His explanation for his ESP demonstrations is similar to that offered by many other entertainers: "It is the result of the applied principles of mentalism, psychology and lateral thinking." He admits to being a firm believer in psychic phenomena – but then again, disclaims the use of any psychic ability in his shows.

Marc Salem
Rauscher Collection

The real success of a mentalist resides in presentation, manner, and material. In the 21st century, **MARC SALEM** has achieved remarkable acclaim on Broadway with a contemporary full-evening demonstration of mentalism called "Mind Games" – a clever title that does not imply any psychic credentials.

Salem is exceptional, and his experiments are presented in a casual, no-nonsense manner. He says, "I don't read minds; I influence thoughts." On the Montel Williams television talk show, Salem performed as an expert in kinetics and body language. He is smooth, and his psychic work never seems to fail.

Mentalists have a way with words. Marc Salem is no different, except that he is a master in his field. In August 2001, his one-man show was a hit when he appeared in Edinburgh, Scotland. He was interviewed for *The Scotsman*, and as usual he was asked, "Are you psychic?" Salem replied, "I'm not a mystic, and I don't do psychic. I work with minds. I pick up things. I don't call it the occult because I'm working on lots of different levels, and occult carries so much weird luggage."

He works on different levels? *What* levels? As a mentalist, it is important to be able to conjure with words. Magicians are thought to conjure with boxes, tubes, dice, and doves, but a mentalist is truly a conjurer with words. And Salem is a master trickster – his statement is a prime example of his talent.

In the same interview, Salem admits: "Eighty percent of the information we convey is not what we say, but how we say it. How I do it is a combination of factors. I work within four areas: I am a psychologist; I'm a sensitive – I do pick up and guide people's thoughts; I'm considered one of the world's foremost authorities in nonverbal communication; and I'm an entertainer."

Salem disarms those who think he is nothing more than a magician with a remarkable defense. He will offer you $100,000 if you can prove he uses a person as a plant in his show. He tells the journalists: "I don't use plants, I don't have any assistants, I don't use electronics. I'm not a magician, either. I don't do conjuring, and I don't bend metal. I walk into a theater and it's just me, a stand, a few books, and the audience."

Most mentalists offer examples of happenings they can't explain. This tends to confuse their listeners, and implies that they have "gifts" they had to learn to harness. As a boy, remarkable Marc Salem knew his parents were taking him on a surprise trip. He even told his parents he knew of their plans, and he told them where they planned to go.

Salem holds a doctorate in Developmental Psychology from New York University. This degree, combined with his twenty years of teaching psychology, is a distinct advantage to his career. He, like Tim Conover and others who have found a life in mentalism, ride the wave of the once psychic revolution – a part of the New Age, Now Generation – and find themselves in the vanguard of Millennium Mentalism in this Biotech Century.

With his suit, vest, and well-trimmed beard, Salem dresses like a lawyer. He lives his mind games when he says, "I do possess heightened sensitivity." He works all venues, and is comfortable in places like the Regency Hotel in New York City. At times he even has an all-woman jazz trio back him up!

Salem has received stunning reviews that serve to enhance his already escalating reputation. His impact in London at the sold-out Hampstead Theatre was a prelude to repeat appearances on Broadway.

The following review by Brian Logan appeared in *The Guardian* on October 10, 2001:

"There is nothing supernatural in what I've done here tonight," says Marc Salem, behavioural psychologist and mind reader. But how else to explain what is happening on stage at the Hampstead Theatre? Salem, a stubby New York academic, who has been "studying the human mind for over 30 years," credits non-verbal communication – the information we give off physically. He begins his show with demonstrations, but soon leaves all reasonable explanations in his wake.  I felt in the presence of weird forces. This is an astonishing show.

Its opening is modest only by comparison with what follows.  The black-clad Salem is spirited suddenly on stage in the show's sole concession to drama, which he punctures by announcing:  "It's only me."  By way of a warm-up, he's soon guessing the three-digit number that an audience member's husband will suggest from the other end of a mobile phone. Next, when five volunteers draw five sketches on stage, Salem ascertains who doodled what by interpreting their physical tics as they lie to him.  The routine is a master class in the ways liars betray themselves.

So far, so amazing – but at the least, at this point, Salem's acts aren't entirely beyond our rational imagination.  After Mind Games' second half, however, this viewer was content to conclude that there's no sleight-of-hand: Salem is actually reading our minds.  Blindfolded, and with 50p coins taped to his eyes, he describes a range of items donated by the crowd, and simultaneously divines the holiday experiences of several concentrating punters.  Not only does he identify the penknife and the pears, but also he knows that the packet of mints contains 15% extra.  Not only can he tell us that Matthew in Row F had a frosty time in Prague, but all of a sudden, that "Jenny, you're thinking of Mark."  He guesses the latter's phone number, to the sound of jaws hitting the floor.

Salem is scrupulously unflashy, and the pace does slacken from time to time.  He clearly knows his skills can stand up for themselves, accompanied by the occasional droll remark and a twinkling-eyed catchphrase:  "Coincidence?  I think not."  He makes you think hard about how people communicate, about what he's doing to marshal our responses. I have seldom experienced such wonder, or such a sense of community, in a theatre.  Mind Games is mind-boggling entertainment – but of course, Salem knew I was going to say that.

For those who like a full evening of mentalism, Marc Salem may be the best tonic for mind reading in the 21st century.  He may also be the best performer today on the boards. In an interview with Lawrence Van Gelder of *The New York Times* on December 11, 2001, Salem is credited as a man "who boggles the mind and tickles the funny bone.  His blend of mental mystery and swift humor makes for delightful family entertainment."

In an appearance at the Duke Theater on West 42nd Street in New York, Salem left a doctor astonished with his ability to stop, slow, and race his own pulse.  He also slammed his hand down on paper bags – one of which "might conceal a sharp knife."  Then, while blindfolded, he identified numerous objects, along with people who had drawn pictures, but who denied so doing.

Salem is the only mentalist to play such prestigious venues as the Regency Room in New York since the early days of nightclubs. How many other U.S. mentalists fill theaters in New York and London, do television specials, and work constantly? "Mind Games, Too" is the name of Marc Salem's latest show in New York, and it has been described by a New York Times theater reviewer as a prime destination for fun seekers.

All the major cities around the globe await Marc Salem. What more could any mentalist ask?

Derren Brown
Rauscher Collection

**DERREN BROWN**, another mentalist whose star is rising, presents a show called "Mind Control." Brown accomplishes amazing feats in his show, but of course disavows possessing any psychic power. Then suddenly his act changes, and the audience members can't help but think that perhaps he does possess such power after all.

Like Marc Salem, Brown considers himself to be a psychological entertainer. He tells his interviewers that he uses "psychological techniques," and that he believes he has discovered a new form of entertainment with this approach. But unlike Salem, at times Brown incorporates magic and hypnosis in his act – a twist that complements his show.

Respected reviewers comment about his show's effect on his audiences. It is thrilling for a mentalist to be able to quote an audience member who says, "I don't think it's quite human, you know," or "I was believing it when it was happening." And Brown makes effective use of these audience comments.

Reviewers believe Derren Brown's talent is powerful. During his 2001 "Mind Control II" special performed in the United Kingdom, he was afforded rave notices. A British *Magic Week* reviewer wrote the following on the Internet:

Using an artist's sketchpad, Derren's predictions were filmed live as he was making them. Viewers saw him commit words to paper for them to be confirmed just moments later by a volunteer, using the pad merely as a means to get his thought down.

In the December 13, 2001 issue of *Stage Newspaper, Ltd.*, reviewer Ben Dowell applauded Brown. He describes Brown's abilities as purely scientific practices, and declares that nothing in Brown's act can be considered supernatural. He says Brown actually represents his own specialty as "messing with your head." Then Dowell proceeds to describe parts of Brown's performance that actually do appear supernatural:

> For example, he asked me to think of the name of somebody I went to school with. I chose a primary school friend of mine called Tola Bashir, partly because it was an unusual name. Despite my best efforts to give nothing away, Brown guessed that name within a minute.

Brown is well educated. Born in the United Kingdom, he attended Bristol University where he studied German and law. However, instead of pursuing a legal career, he became a hypnotist and magician. During a recent interview he said he grew up in his own little imaginative world. In this same interview, he admitted he was formerly religious, but now considers himself "spiritual in that I respond to life, art, and beauty."

Brown has performed for over twelve years. He has three television specials to his credit, with another series planned. He is also working on a national tour during which he will "invade everyone's thoughts."

Like many other performers in the field of mentalism, Derren Brown now shuns the terms "psychic" and "mind reader." In the December 28, 2001 issue of *London Life*, Tim Cooper quotes Brown: "I think mind reading is a lazy explanation. I explore things through perfectly tangible psychological methods." Brown considers his current work a result of his years of focus on psychological techniques, and says he has developed a skill in the field of "psychological magic."

Like Kreskin, Brown says he does not believe in hypnosis in its purest sense. Columnist Tim Cooper quotes Brown describing what he does:

> There's a lot of suggestion. I get people into playing a certain mental game with me that allows me to create a particular effect on them. They give certain things away and become responsive to things I say. There's a lot of intuition involved, but I don't want people to believe that what I do is psychic, because it isn't.

The American publisher of H&R Books was so impressed with Brown's book, *Pure Effect: Direct Mind Reading and Magical Artistry* (originally published as a spiral-bound volume in the U.K.) that they issued the book in hardback. The publisher felt other mentalists could benefit from Brown's tips in the book regarding "presentational strategies, psychological ploys, neuro-linguistic programming techniques, and effects structure," and, therefore, considered the book worthy of a second printing.

Other interesting aspects of Derren Brown's approach appear in his publicity as "psychological illusion," "perceptual manipulation," and "persuasive technique." He is also credited with pioneering a new form of magical entertainment that is unlikely to be imitated for a long time; some say Brown's talents can *never* be duplicated. This places him in a new category of mentalist, since a recurring problem in mentalism is that so many performers do the same old thing, or merely place a different spin on similar effects. For this reason, many mentalists believe they are not viewed as examples of standard magic, but are instead the future of magic.

Finally, some performing magicians – although not necessarily full-time professional mentalists – receive great publicity out of making successful headline predictions. This prediction is usually on paper, and sealed in a box or chest – or even a cake of ice! Their explanations for their ability and success are similar to those of Mark Salem's.

David Copperfield
Courtesy of Thomas A. Ewing

Magician **DAVID COPPERFIELD** created a stir in Berlin on October 13, 2001, when he "predicted" the winning numbers in the National Lottery in Germany. On February 17th of that year, Copperfield wrote down his psychic impression of the winning numbers. His prediction was sealed by a notary, and locked in a box. Newspapers reported that the box was opened during a live television broadcast. There in the box on a slip of paper were the correct numbers – 2, 9, 10, 15, 25, 38, and 4.

With a straight face, and typical of the magician playing the role of a psychic, his words were classic: "It was more an experiment and mental exercise. We only use about ten percent of our brain capacity." Concerning predictions on lotteries, Copperfield said: "I find them boring. I'm not a gambler. I used to try it out by giving friends the numbers, but then it would never work. If the numbers aren't kept secret, it doesn't work."

Copperfield was further quoted during a press interview as saying, "This is not a trick." Actually he said, "This is not a trick like making the Statue of Liberty disappear." Criticism ran rampant, and even the Amazing Randi on his Web site leaped on the magician to announce, "David Copperfield just may have gone over to the dark side." After Copperfield later chastised Randi, and emphasized his actual quote to the press, Randi issued a profound apology.   Regardless, the subtle implication remained that Copperfield, even though later denying his psychic abilities, played mind games when he answered questions about his stunning prediction.

Mentalists all over the world must be encouraged by the success of David Copperfield, who has, with one prediction, gained worldwide publicity.  He also received hundreds of e-mails, letters, and requests from people in despair.  Copperfield said: "There were so many people in tough situations with debts and similar problems."  But nothing was said to dissuade anyone from believing in what they thought was truly psychic, paranormal, and astounding.

Most important, no one thought to ask David Copperfield why he did not openly predict the attacks on the United States before they happened on September 11, 2001.  With his help, along with all the mentalists and psychics of the world, we might have avoided that horrible nightmare – unless, of course, these folks are not genuine.

And so we are left with Copperfield's simple, great words: "It was more an experiment and mental exercise."

Many magicians have performed mentalism not to mention the famous Milbourne Christopher who created a sensation in 1956 when he predicted the winning number 20050 of the pre-Castro Cuba lottery.   Another mentalist that is part of mind reading history is Richard Osterlind.  Noted for his magic effects and mentalist routines he is a prominent name in the field of mentalism.  Mentalism has its own fraternity of stars since the subject is appealing and new performers are always emerging.

# *Act 10*

*Do you still think you can believe your eyes?*
*Then you must meet the following...*

## *BIZARRE AND BENIGN IMAGE MAKERS*

Tony Andruzzi
A favorite portrait by Susan Anderson
Courtesy of Richard Kaufman

Some in the field of mentalism have opted to work in strange areas. Such is the case with **TONY ANDRUZZI**, who was born Timothy McGuire. While a magician he first became Tom Palmer, and in his later years, Tony Andruzzi, and finally Masklyn ye Mage. Like many other mentalists he was a chameleon who changed his persona to fit his latest interests, ideas, and creations.

I met Andruzzi some years ago in a Chicago restaurant, and we talked about private readings. He did not seem interested in discussing the ethics of this type of work, but expounded at length over performing ideas and insights on magic.

Andruzzi began his career by performing regular magic, dressed as a clown magician. Later he graduated to illusions, along with various other tricks. He also did a comedy act where everything went wrong. Throughout the 1960's he was a successful performer at the Playboy Clubs.

Eventually he came to believe that magicians, as they were generally envisioned, had ceased being magicians. In Eugene Burger's book *Spirit Theater* (Kaufman and Greenberg, New York, 1986), the author quotes Andruzzi as saying: "The magician today is, in the words of W. C. Fields when he first saw Charlie Chaplin, 'a son of a bitch who is a toe dancer!' "(p. 85) No longer could Andruzzi tolerate pulling silks out of a tube or rabbits from a hat. Instead he now imagined himself to be a real magician. He considered himself as a kind of dark-side priest, and was able to make people believe that he was, in fact, just that – a "priest" who could do what he did when he did it because he fused with his projected image. Instead of doing tricks, Andruzzi did bizarre things, like sticking needles in his arm. He pretended his performances were real, fooling physicians and others from the medical profession, even though they involved trickery. He adopted mentalism into his act, but included spooky overtones and evil images. He transformed his image from a diviner to an invoker of dark powers.

In the midst of this, he announced that cold readings by mentalists were wrong if the reader took money from people. According to Burger, Andruzzi told people: "I'm a fake, but I'll make a believer out of you." Andruzzi changed magic into an act that was now uncomfortable for his audience. He opted into an eerie, esoteric world with all the trappings of a living tale from the crypt, and referred to himself as an "alchemical magician." Slowly his image changed until he was a caricature of his real self.

Finally, Andruzzi entered the strange world of Bizarre Magic. Bizarre Magic is an avenue that is especially attractive to the trickster mind reader types, and Andruzzi is an admired past guru. Bizarre Magic projects an image of power. It places the performer in a position where he seemingly controls all the dark forces of nature. It does not imply a benign power, but leaves the observer wondering if the person in control is good or evil. In the end, all this is just a trick, but these tricks have a sinister aura. Further, they do not induce a feeling of enchantment, but rather the sense of watching a B-movie horror film, which may even generate feelings of sympathy for the performer.

In this field Andruzzi became known for his weird ways and undisciplined personal life, which was fueled by alcohol. He wrote books, conducted odd mentalist conventions called "Invocationals," and developed devious behavioral patterns that turned Tony into a true trickster figure. Writer/performer Eugene Burger described Andruzzi as "a striking embodiment, a personification of the archetype of the Trickster, who was therefore, among other things, both a sinner and a saint." ("Speak of the Devil: A Conversation about Tony Andruzzi with Eugene Burger and David Parr" – *Genii* Magazine, October 7, 2000).

Andruzzi followed in the footsteps of the late Charles W. Cameron, who was "The Godfather of Bizarre Magic." Both Cameron and Andruzzi treated each day as if it were Halloween, and delighted in presenting themselves as if they were personally in touch with some dark realm.

Tony Andruzzi
In action as Masklyn ye Mage
Courtesy of Richard Kaufman - *Genii* Magazine

Andruzzi contributed frequently to a quarterly publication called *Invocation,* which was devoted to weird and bizarre magic. In 1981 he became editor, and eventually he purchased the publication. From his wacky world of the unusual came some eight conventions called "Invocations," where competition was intense for different, strange, and intriguing material. His eventual character of Masklyn ye Mage was pagan in nature. When he was dressed in his costume, he looked like magic's version of Satanist Anton LeVey (to whom Andruzzi once supplied candles that supposedly dripped blood). His books documenting the field of the bizarre had titles such as *Daemon's Diary, Grimoire of the Mages, The Necromicon,* and *The Legendary Scroll of Masklyn ye Mage.*

There are many stories that relate to Tony and his followers of the bizarre. Some magicians thought he was a genius, although this was at times offset by their uneasiness with his act. For a while, aided and abetted by alcohol, times were good. But his true self slowly disintegrated, despite the preservation of his intellect.

Eugene Burger was so impressed with Tony Andruzzi that he dedicated his book, *Strange Ceremonies: Bizarre Magick for the Modern Conjurer,* to his friend with the following inscription: "To my friend Tony Andruzzi, who urged me to rethink the roots of magic and offered much encouragement along the way."

Andruzzi once told Burger, "The people who produce doves and streamers are on an ego trip. The man of mystery is on a super ego trip!" Andruzzi remained on a super ego trip until his soul trip on December 22, 1991, when he died at age 66.

After Andruzzi's death, a fellow bizarrist who was just as far out continued his strange conventions. This man is known as **DOC HILFORD.** It has been said that Hilford is not just weird in the field of mentalism and the bizarre, but that he's "re-e-ally we-e-ird." He has produced a series of videotapes that package his approach – and also makes money for him! The advertisement for his videos claims that his mind reading demonstrations are "so real that you'll be believing them yourself." As a stage performer, Doc has opened for groups like Weird Al Jankovic, Gallagher, and even a heavy metal group called "Black Sabbath."

Alexander Cannon
September 1961 photo by
John Henry Grossman, M.D.
Courtesy of Marya Grossman

There is no end to the unusual characters in the world of magic, particularly in the field of mind reading. One individual who stands out like a beacon of muddled light casting his shadow in all directions is **ALEXANDER CANNON.**

Cannon was born in Leeds, England, on August 4, 1896. As an adult, he acquired a string of questionable degrees, which he touted throughout his lifetime. These degrees rivaled those of any and all academics. He was affable, gracious, and courteous, and generally enjoyed being around people. He wore a wing collar, vest, bow tie, black coat, striped trousers, and spats, along with various awards from "Foreign Orders."

Researcher and sociologist Marcello Truzzi, Ph.D., calls Cannon "one of the most interesting modern rogues in

Alexander Cannon - 1951
In his home surrounded by artifacts
Rauscher Collection

conjuring." According to Truzzi, even though Cannon was called a magician and hosted many conjurors on the Isle of Man in his home theater called The Enchanted Hall, much of his work qualifies as mentalism (*Vibrations*, September 1998). If Dr. Truzzi develops a complete portrait of Cannon, his work will be a valuable contribution to the description and understanding of a man who called himself, along with dozens of other titles, "Kushog Yogi of Northern Tibet" and "Master – the Fifth – of the Great White Lodge of the Himalayas."

In his article in the September 1998 issue of *Vibrations*, Truzzi reminds us of some of the outrageous things Cannon proclaimed. He cites Cannon's book, *Sleeping Through Space* (Woodthorpe: The Walcot Publishing Co., 1938), in which Cannon gives directions for bringing the dead back to life. According to Cannon: "This is accomplished by administering a severe kick with the knee between the shoulder blades, while shouting Oye, Oye, Oye in the left ear of the deceased." Truzzi quotes Cannon as saying, "It is rarely necessary to repeat the operation before life is again resumed, but this can be repeated up to seven times in long-standing cases."

Truzzi also cites Cannon's technique for inducing hypnosis when the normal induction method fails. As described by Cannon in a 1949 article titled "Some Hypnotic Secrets" (*British Journal of Medical Hypnotism*): "If the patient wakes up at all before I have got my hypnotic sleep suggestion home to him, I place both of my thumbs on his carotid arteries' vagus nerves and carotic body firmly … until he is 'off' again."

If (and when) Cannon's demonstrations did not succeed, he always had a ready explanation. Author Alan Burnett-Rae cites an excellent example of Cannon's glibness in his booklet *Aleister Crowley – A Memoir of 666* (Victim Press, London, 1991).

Crowley, the notorious occultist, and Cannon crossed paths several times. On this occasion, Crowley was present when Cannon was lecturing on hypnotism, yoga, and trance at the Mayfair Hotel in London on a Sunday afternoon in May 1934. As part of his lecture, Cannon attempted to hypnotize a woman and make her levitate across the stage. Witnesses claimed that the subject was indeed in a trance, but that she failed to float. When pressed for an explanation, Cannon told the audience the heavy clothing she wore obviously held her down. He further explained if she had been nude there would have been no problem, but since the hotel would not allow her to be stripped in the ballroom, the experiment was abandoned.

Cannon had a propensity to heap scholastic honors upon himself. He received an M.D. in 1928 through the University of Leeds, and also seems to have legitimately earned an M.B. and Ch.B. (1924). In addition, Cannon was awarded a diploma in Psychological Medicine (DPM) from the Royal College of Physicians and Surgeons (London).

Outside the medical world – and apparently at his own direction – he had people calling him everything from Your Excellency to Dr. Sir Alexander Cannon. A prolific author, he wrote eight books with exotic titles such as *The Shadow of Destiny, Powers That Be, The Power of Karma, The Invisible Influence, The Science of Hypnotism*, and *The Power Within*. For university students he wrote *The Principles and Practice of Psychiatry* and *The Principles and Practice of Neurology* textbooks.

In the United Kingdom, Cannon was falsely considered the father of hypnotism. He is also incorrectly credited with inventing ultraviolet light in 1909, and the polygraph in 1912. His medical specialty was the treatment of mental and nervous diseases in his own clinic, which was presided over by two women – Rhonda De Rhonda and a nurse named Freda Butler. When not busy managing the clinic, De Rhonda also acted as Cannon's medium/psychic during demonstrations in his theater.

During Cannon's blindfold readings, cotton wool and towels were wrapped around his head, somewhat like the procedure of the famous Kuda Bux. Cannon also invented an array of electrical machines that hummed, buzzed, produced static sparks, and gave off what an article in *Lilliput* magazine called "a strong hygienic smell of Ozone" (March 1948). These

Harlan Tarbell
Rauscher Collection

machines resulted from his experiments with electricity, along with some very unorthodox healing methods. In the field of magic, he applied his knowledge of transmitting voices by a wireless phone to a skull that answered questions.

During his career(s) he accumulated considerable wealth and real estate, and created the image of belief in occult powers. Strangely (and sadly) he was indeed intellectual, but fell victim to his own ego. Yet when challenged about the authenticity of his degrees, he always had the answers.

The late magician and writer **HARLAN TARBELL**, who was himself eccentric, was enamored of Cannon's background and apparent abilities, since Cannon's interests paralleled many of his own.

Tarbell was a disciple of philosopher Elbert Hubbard, "The Master Mind of Inspiration" (1856-1915), who, in 1915, founded a handcraft movement centered around the Roycroft Press and the Roycroft Shops in East Aurora, New York. The Roycrofters attempted to emulate the Arts and Crafts movement of the counter-industrialist William Morris, a devotee of the Pre-Raphaelites who had established a firm of decorators in 1861 devoted to the return of the working methods and decorative schemes of the Middle Ages. Tarbell was taken with Hubbard's individualism, writings, and insights on life. (Incidentally, Hubbard died on the Lusitania which sank during World War I.)

Tarbell was a health-conscious vegetarian, with a deep interest in the occult. He was a graduate of the Chicago Academy of Fine Arts, and was called "Dr. Tarbell" by his friends because of a claimed degree in 1917 in the study of naprapathy – a method of therapeutic and rehabilitative exercise and nutritional counseling – which he practiced until his death in 1960.

Tarbell is known for his numerous writings on magic, his performance of feats like "Eyeless Vision," and his classic eight-volume *Tarbell Course in Magic*. Writer Robert Parrish recalls that Tarbell believed magic "pointed to something beyond itself." Parrish wrote in *Magicol* (May 1988, No. 87), the journal of the Magic Collectors Association of America, how Tarbell described to him an experience with Cannon at Laureston Mansion House, his home:

> They laid Doc [Tarbell] on an examination table and Sir Alexander [Cannon] sent his spirit control ten miles above him so she could look straight down through the Doc. Tarbell said, "Oh Bob, it's so far ahead of X-Ray. You know there are certain tricks you've seen me do where at a particular point I have a little trouble with them. Well, she traced the cause right back to my Spanish incarnation."

Harlan Tarbell with Alexander Cannon in his Enchanted Hall, Douglas, Isle of Man
Courtesy of Marya Grossman and daughter Pixie

In 1953 Tarbell spent a week with Cannon. Tarbell loved Cannon's Enchanted Hall with its forty-foot stage, thousands of varicolored lights, music, and voices from the air, as well as Cannon's shows of mental magic. Tarbell claimed in an article that appeared in *M-U-M* (October 1959), the magazine of the Society of American Magicians, that Cannon pioneered past-life regression. He also claimed Cannon's hypnotic work inspired Morey Bernstein, who became famous for the Bridey Murphy case of a past life. He further credited Cannon with inspiring the Zancigs to go on stage as mentalists, and said that Cannon helped them with their code.

The late John Henry Grossman, M.D., famous magic historian and collector, visited Cannon for a week in the early 1960's. Grossman wrote about this visit in *Magicol* (Issue No. 87, May 1988), saying he felt as though he had stepped into "a creepy atmosphere." In a meeting with me Dr. Grossman elaborated, describing the interior of Cannon's house as being littered with gifts from all over the world and loaded with Oriental art objects – Buddhas, carvings, vases – décor that projected an aura of mystery. Grossman and his wife, Marya, also described the interior of Cannon's house as palatial. He wrote that Cannon "believed in occult magic such as teleportation, psychokinesis, telepathy, and all else."

When they arrived, they found their bedroom was huge. In it was an oversized fireplace, a large mantle, and a carved-ivory framed mirror. Before their visit, the Grossmans had been warned that Cannon's house was bugged, but they found no evidence of any hidden listening devices while they were there.

Marya told me, "It was a very formal place. We dressed for dinner each night, and attended lectures in the 300-seat Enchanted Hall." She recalled that their host never ate with them during their weeklong visit, but she attributed this to his being a diabetic. Marya took a photo of Cannon and has kept copies of letters that he exchanged with her husband.

The Grossmans saw the very human side of Cannon, and acknowledge that he was indeed a remarkable figure in the annals of magic. They found Cannon to be a "brilliant conversationalist," and said every evening was devoted to magic. In addition, they revealed that Cannon walked on two artificial legs. Marya said Cannon had lost his legs in an electrical accident during experiments. She also recalled in a conversation with me in March 2001 that during their visit Cannon dropped an object – but when she bent down to pick it up, he quickly said, "I can do that!" She observed, "He was a proud man," adding, "We liked Alexander Cannon very much."

I have found nothing in print describing the circumstances of Cannon's death, other than in the files of the weekly magazine *Abracadabra* (published in England by Goodliffe), which reveals the date as Monday, March 18, 1963 (Issue 8-95, March 23, 1963). A glowing tribute from Goodliffe appeared in Issue 8-96, March 30, 1963, in which Cannon was extolled as a generous, gracious friend, and a grand magical character.

Goodliffe also made a recording for his friend, magic dealer Martin Breese, in England (Magicassettes: Martin Breese, 164 Kensington Park Road, London W11 2ER, U.K.). In it, Goodliffe tells of his friendship with Cannon, offers insights into Cannon's personality, and provides further information later affirmed to me by Marya Grossman. In addition to these reminiscences, there is a recording of Alexander Cannon's own voice, which is similar to the forceful, convincing voices of the old Shakespearean actors. In this recording, Cannon describes a demonstration of illuminating a light bulb using only his mind; he says the bulb is lit because it is filled with the energy of his brain!

Marya Grossman related an unusual incident to me regarding her husband and the death of Cannon. One week before Cannon died, John Henry Grossman dreamed that Cannon was dead. The dream seemed very real and disturbed John Henry, because "he did not believe in any of that stuff." Within a week of John's dream, a telegram arrived from Cannon's ward, De Rhonda (who was, according to Marya, Cannon's adopted daughter), informing the Grossmans that Alexander Cannon had died in his sleep of a heart attack at the Mansion. Marya said, "John was really shook up over that dream – I mean *really* shook up, because it did not fit into his way of thinking."

Did His Excellency Dr. Sir Alexander Cannon, M.D., Ch.B., M.B., K.G.C.B., Ph.D., LL.D., D.Sc., D.Litt, M.A., D.P.M., F.B.P.S., F.R.G.S., F.A.C.P., F.R.S.T.M.&H., S.A.M.S., etc., leave behind one more paranormal mystery for Dr. Grossman and the rest of us to ponder?

Ormond McGill
Courtesy of American Guild of Hypnotists

**ORMOND McGILL** is best described as an entrepreneur of the mind. Blindfold drives, hypnosis, mind reading, magic, and ghost shows are part of this near-legendary individual's career. So extensive is his experience that, in 2002, as an aged gentleman, he still takes part in hypnosis seminars. McGill does believe in the paranormal, and has made a supreme effort to investigate all types of mystical occurrences – both good and evil – on a firsthand basis.

McGill's interest in hypnosis began in 1927 during his days in high school when he saw the Danish hypnotist DeWaldoza. He entered this theatrical venue himself in 1934, after being further inspired by a performer named Elwin Peck, who performed as El-Wyn. Peck offered McGill the opportunity to tour with his show. By 1942 McGill had his own show, a hypnotic spook show called "The London Hypnotic Séance," which he later renamed "The Séance of Wonders." For these performances, McGill traveled under the name of Dr. Zomb. A talented hypnotist, he performed for forty-five minutes and ended with a blackout that produced luminous ghosts. In the 1950's he delved into horror shows, and became even more popular.

Along with his stage work and travels, McGill eventually produced twenty-one books. His knowledge of mentalism motivated him to write a six-volume series on mind reading, *Psychic Magic*. In this, he shares everything from ESP tricks to occult and spiritualistic effects. His other books include *Professional Stage Hypnotism*, a book for aspiring performers, and *Hypnotism and Meditation*.

**THOUGHT CONTROL ENABLES ORMOND McGILL TO PREDICT NEWSPAPER HEADLINES!**

Ormond McGill
Promotional Brochure
Courtesy of Raymond J. Goulet

On his early trips to the Orient, McGill traveled with the late film producer Ron Ormond, and detailed his travels and adventures in books. The two collaborated in writing *Into the Strange Unknown*. On his own, McGill produced a total of forty-two manuscripts and books, including *The Mysticism and Magic of India*, *Hypnotism and Mysticism of India*, *The Secret World of Witchcraft*, and *The Encyclopedia of Genuine Stage Hypnotism*.

Throughout their trips, Ormond and McGill photographed and filmed many experiences, and fortunately a record of their adventures still exists. (Incidentally, years later during a visit to the Ormond residence which I made with McGill's old friend John Calvert, Ron Ormond's wife, June, was still running their business of renting films with a religious message to churches. In her backyard was an old shed filled with tons of motion picture equipment, untouched since her husband's death years before.)

As McGill's experience became more extensive, so did his interest in all phases of mind power. His dedication to the study of Eastern systems of meditation, mysticism, and the subject of healing added to an unusual career.

McGill is also a storehouse of information on the paranormal, and is referred to as "The Dean of American Hypnotists." He also trains hypnotherapists. His seminars and workshops, sometimes called "Quantum Hypnotherapy – A Weekend for Professionals with Ormond McGill," are popular and well attended.

Ormond McGill is one of those rare magicians who opened more doors than are found in a trick cabinet. He is unique, and one of the grand old men of magic and the supernatural.

# *Act 11*

***Do you feel a chill?***
***Perhaps it's because you are about to meet ...***

## *COLD READERS – PSYCHIC ENTERTAINERS*

More and more mentalists are going beyond entertaining to take up cold reading as we move deeper into the first years of the New Millennium. Through the escalating sale of teaching videotapes, DVDs, audio cassettes, and books, the potential "reader" can find ways and means not only to build a reputation, but also to earn a living. This area of performance mentalism disdains all props. It is now necessary, if you call yourself a mind reader, to be just that. A magic trick that merely implies ESP is not enough.

Cold reading instruction focuses on character analysis and how to handle problem situations, offer thoughts for the future, and generally convince the sitter that he or she is being helped by the most astute psychic insight. Cold readings in which the reader pretends to divine what is wrong in the mind of the sitter can be combined with Palm Readings, Psychometry, Astrology, Tarot Cards, Tea Leaves, Aura Readings, and the Pendulum. Better yet, the mentalist might just "get impressions" and/or act as an advisor.

Cold readings are highly tempting to any mentalist who knows all the methods, and who knows how easily people can be manipulated and controlled psychologically.

The Psychic Entertainers Association is aware of this temptation, and in 1991 attempted to deal with the problem. Ken Chandler, then president of the Association, wrote a letter about rumors regarding attempts to oust psychic readers in the organization. Chandler's letter appeared on page 10 in the June issue of *Vibrations*, when he announced he had no problem with "the many members who work under the guise of being 'real' psychics." His position was that cold readings are still a form of entertainment, and that the ethical question was limited to "the kind of advice we, as psychic entertainers, give." He further stated that it was up to the individual to decide his or her position regarding what is or is not ethical!

The PEA has always been more concerned with exposure than with any moral sense of responsibility. Unfortunately the Association still lacks a policy on the subject of private readers. Because of this omission, the most unscrupulous person, if approved, can join under the guise of being an entertainer, so long as he or she does not expose methods. As for any protection for sitters, these individuals are left to their own delusions.

Mentalist Ross Johnson of Ross Johnson Enterprises states his position on this subject in a letter printed in the same June 1991 issue of *Vibrations,* when he writes, "In short, claim to be a psychic if you like, just don't defraud those who believe you." Can they expect everyone to do just that?

These days very expensive mentalism books serve as teachers – and videotapes offer real-life experiences. Electronic devices to aid the mentalist now sell for upward of $2,000. Soon individuals who were psychic entertainers may also become private readers. Unfortunately, these people may delude themselves into thinking they are helping people in the same way that counselors or religious figures offer guidance. However, unlike psychiatrists, psychologists, priests, ministers, rabbis, and trained therapists who may be hired by medical or guidance centers, these mentalists do not have to document case studies or report to a board. They are accountable to no one. Few have taken courses in psychology or have any degree in religious counseling. They answer only to themselves, and yet they are free to offer advice that can alter lives. If questions arise about a loved one who has died, they can be easily tempted to offer thoughts or a message in an effort to provide answers or give comfort. As a result, the mentalist/reader's personal and ethical beliefs, if any, erode, since ethics are unknowingly replaced by the desire to perform and the ability to influence the sitter's situation. The ultimate motivator is money, paid by the sitter to the individual, who now masquerades as a "genuine" psychic reader.

In 1951, Robert Nelson, the futuristic purveyor of mentalism literature, wrote in his book *The Art of Cold Reading:*

> There was a time when people in trouble would turn to their minister or close friends. The materialism of our age has lessened the source of this aid and comfort. More and more people are seeking the psychiatrist's couch, the private reader's crystal ball for guidance. A magical short cut to their problems!

> Psychiatry has made great advances since the last war. It is specifically nothing more than applied psychology. In psychiatry, the operator ASKS the subject voluminous questions about the problem, but with the COLD READER, he must GUESS at these problems and offer counsel.

> Apparently, the cold reader's task is more difficult, but such may not always be the case. The cold reader is trained in DETECTING these symptoms and telling the SUBJECT of the situations that have upset his apple cart.

> Psychiatry is an expensive outlet for the emotions, and is still somewhat terrifying to many people. The "reader" is often referred to as the poor man's psychiatrist. The psychiatrist is usually far better trained for his profession than the rank and file of readers, but too, his purpose is more deliberate and extensive. Both, knowingly and unknowingly, proceed along similar lines.

> Each, aside from any moral argument, fulfills a demand. (p.4)

The mentalist who considers himself simply a psychic entertainer can easily embark upon a journey to cold reading, and may begin a career as a person with more self-confidence in himself as a 21st century mentalist than can be imagined.  This person can buy instruction tapes which offer training on "How to Give Readings with Gemstones," "Techniques for Psychics," "The Psychic Pitch," "Palm Readings" – all of which are geared to making money.  He or she can be taught how to develop this "talent" as a business, to do private gatherings, and even to advance to cold readings performed in department stores, malls, and homes.  This individual will learn how to give specific answers, even create promotional material — and THEN this mentalist eventually will feel the world has been conquered!

Again, the challenge for a prestigious organization like the Psychic Entertainers Association is an ethical one.  Perhaps **TERRY NOSEK**, the PEA's former president (1983-1984) did the organization a delightful favor when he called himself "Dr. Sigmund Fraud."

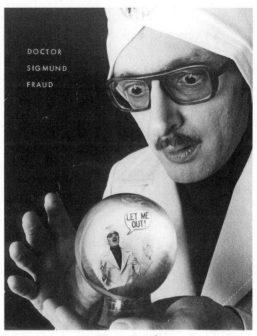

DOCTOR
SIGMUND
FRAUD

LET ME OUT!

Terry Nosek
Courtesy of *The Linking Ring* Magazine

Where do the PEA leaders of today draw the line for their members?  Do they believe that psychic ability exists in any form whatsoever, or is the entire history of civilization – both secular and religious – just one big cold reading?  The term Cold Reading now appears to be an acceptable answer for any and all general explanations of readers, whether they are mentalists, storefront psychics, butchers, bakers, or gurus.

There are those who might even label Jesus himself a cold reader since he offered guidance.  A mentalist might also say that that any counselor, whether he is a priest or psychologist, is a cold reader, and that mystical insight is nothing.

In the Newsweek article "God & the Brain:  How We're Wired for Spirituality" (May 7, 2001 issue), skeptical scientists claim mystical insight and spiritual experiences are self-contained.  These scientists speculate this insight and these experiences are a result of individualized wiring in the human brain.  Not so, according to the wisdom of the ages and religions of the world.  If there is a transcendental dimension – if there are other realms – and if human life is in fact more than horizontal – there *must* be moral and ethical concerns.

For practitioners in all professions, and especially those who live day-to-day under the banner of psychic entertainer, what is ethical or unethical?  Mentalists who specify that they work only as entertainers apparently understand the problem.

Showmen **GERRY & BANACHEK**, who perform six different "Mystical Minds" shows, know all the methods of fooling audiences. Together and solo, as a thought-reading team, they make an important statement that serves as a subtle indictment of any performers who do private readings:

> Many self-proclaimed psychics like to rip off the public by taking money for giving bogus psychic readings and giving personal advice. Some of these phony psychics stoop so low they actually use Magic Tricks or Mentalist Mind Tricks to convince their potential sitter that they are authentically psychic.
>
> They dupe the potential sitter with a trick that looks so real you are convinced that they MUST be psychic, and you fork over your hard earned cash for a reading that is given by a person who is as psychic as a piece of driftwood.
>
> Some phony psychics also use such tactics to take money from gullible people to talk to their dead relatives, locate lost children, and remove spells that are causing bad luck.
>
> Question: If these people are real and authentic, why on earth would they be doing house reading parties or personal one-on-one sittings for a couple of hundred bucks a pop, when they can claim the million dollar prize (Prize offered by the James Randi Foundation) by simply proving that their talents are authentic and not store bought?

In their publicity, Gerry & Banachek devote time to make sure their case for earned skill is not mistaken for true psychic ability. Accordingly, they describe a mentalist as "just an entertainer, who should claim no supernatural abilities." Although many performers make similar statements, Gerry & Banachek emphasize a specific warning to their audiences regarding those who claim to be real psychics. Like others, they hope someday to find a real psychic, but to date admit they have been unsuccessful. They also alert the public to the danger of paying a psychic to solve a crime, and state that phony psychics will not hesitate to fool sitters by using mentalism tricks.

Banachek
Rauscher Collection

Gerry & Banachek proudly announce they have been given permission by the James Randi Foundation to test those who claim to possess paranormal ability.   Banachek, along with Randi, achieved recognition some years ago by helping to expose Peter Popoff, the television evangelist healer. Popoff, it was revealed, actually wore a radio-receiver earpiece through which Mrs. Popoff conveyed information to him about sick people who were members of his vast "congregation." (Incidentally, this disgusting and blasphemous betrayal of spiritual trust by Popoff made headlines, but it did not deter Popoff, who eventually popped right back on the air with his healing services and followers.)

Gerry & Banachek do not expose their own methods, but admit they demonstrate psychic feats only for entertainment.  Their list of credentials includes the study of verbal communication, non-verbal communication, psychological tricks, theatrical hypnosis, theater, magic, visual illusion, mental manipulation, physical manipulation – and straight-faced lying!

# *Act 12*

*Our performance is almost over.*
*But before we leave, let's explore ...*

## *MENTALISTS AND ETHICAL CONDUCT*

Internet Web sites abound, and offer every subject imaginable – including mentalism. It is easy to distinguish which performers offer private readings, and those who are merely entertainers. There are also Web sites for those who claim to be psychics and who offer readings via e-mail. For a fee they will also talk on the telephone. Some mentalists even have their own Web site psychic hotline.

The material offered on the mentalist Web sites is familiar enough. Each site offers the same basic information, but with various twists. Mentalists list their credits, client comments, standing ovation performances, and public appearances, and tout their astounding ability to amaze people with their hidden knowledge of them.

There are only so many things a mentalist can do – and, therefore, that a Web site can include. Mentalists' essential appeal revolves around their claims to read thoughts, minds, serial numbers, names, and projections about money, marriage, love, and travel. However, some Web sites cover even more topics, are more interesting than others, and offer links and parapsychological associations.

Jon Saint-Germain
Rauscher Collection

For example, found in the ever-growing psychic entertainment mentalism Web site world is **JON SAINT-GERMAIN**. For his alter ego, John Riggs apparently chose the name "Saint-Germain" from the 18th century French occultist, healer, and miracle worker. Saint-Germain, with his Lamar Keene-style beard, advertises that he is a professional psychic, but also a screenwriter and producer for Emrys House, a production company specializing in feature films, documentaries and television content. He is also listed as being a member of the "Office of Paranormal Investigation," one of numerous groups with titles that imply the use of scientific methods to prove or disprove unexplained phenomena.

As with most contemporary psychic performers, Saint-Germain says he has investigated the unexplained for years. His self-promotion claims that he is a popular guest on television and radio programs, and a lecturer on metaphysical topics. These topics include palmistry, past-life regression, hypnosis, and self-empowerment. When performing, he demonstrates "the inner workings of the Silent Language" as he answers unspoken questions of audience members, describing concerns in their lives, and revealing details like birthdays and important names!

(Incidentally, Saint-Germain received recognition from the Psychic Entertainers Association in 1977. His contributions to mentalism earned him the Blackwood Award. His academic credentials include degrees from the University of Tennessee and Pellissippi State Technical Community College, where he majored in Studio Art and Mechanical Engineering. He proudly proclaims, "Now I read minds and palms for a living.")

The Saint-Germain Web site offers everything from his palmistry page to a list of *Link* articles, such as "Scientific Approach to Parapsychology," "Scientific Research on Mind Reading," "Some Seek Business Advice from Psychics" – and a *Los Angeles Times* article (December 21, 2000) entitled "Surf Where the Spirit Moves You." This article details the endless number of sites offering guidance and readings for "Surfers Of The Third Eye."

This mentalist's definition of a psychic entertainer is "One who deals with the hidden abilities of the human mind, exploring the subjects of Mind Reading, Hypnosis, ESP, Handwriting Analysis, Palmistry, Numerology, Astrology, and any other area that involves the way we see ourselves and the world around us." He likes to publicize, "It is the brain that sees, not the eyes alone," and he tries to prove this in performance by wearing a self-described solid steel blindfold. According to Saint-Germain, his Mindbender Show is especially designed for the upscale, sophisticated audience. All of the above is part of a package called "The New Millennium of Entertainment."

The upscale and sophisticated can also have their palms read. At parties, fundraisers, and cocktail events, Jon Saint-Germain performs Tarot, Handwriting Analysis, Runestones, and Numerology readings. He is also available for private readings. His book, *Runic Palmistry*, published by Llewellyn, combines classic palmistry with Norse mythology! Promotional material states: "The resulting mixture combines folklore and psychology to help people better understand themselves and others through mythological archetypes."

Jon Saint-Germain is just one example of those who blur all areas of the psychic, but who make no real public commitment to other-dimensional beliefs. Whether or not he actually believes in what he purports to be beyond trickery is not stated in his Web site.

It is indeed surprising that despite all efforts of the well-known Amazing Randi, archenemy of anyone who takes a person on a psychic ride, Randi has left untouched the contemporary psychic entertainers who also do private readings. One must therefore pose the question – why are Jon Saint-Germain, and all those others who cross the fine line neglected or avoided by Randi, who is so intent on dismantling all images of so-called psychic ability?

Most mentalists want to promote any academic credentials they might – or might not – have. In the 21st century, speakers on psychic subjects who sport Ph.D's and claim experience with aura-intensity training, and use letterheads of self-created organizations, should be suspect.

There are individuals in the psychic entertainment field who are well educated, who aim to belong to all kinds of scientific associations and to have friends in the research field who will keep them informed, and establish them for wider acceptance. With their knowledge of trickery, do these individuals help, inform, and instruct the real laboratory parapsychologists in how to avoid being tricked themselves? They may declare something as trickery, but do they teach those who are really exploring the science of consciousness what the methods of mentalism are, and contribute their "secrets" to move research forward? The answer to the question might fairly be stated as rarely – especially on the Internet.

One mentalist who perhaps takes an active interest and involves himself in the real work of parapsychology is **LOYD AUERBACH.**

Loyd Auerbach
Rauscher Collection

Auerbach holds a bachelor's degree in Cultural Anthropology from Northwestern University, and a master's in Parapsychology from John F. Kennedy University, where he also serves as Adjunct Professor of Parapsychology. He is a member of the Core Faculty of Rosebridge Graduate School for Integrative Psychology in Concord, California. He was also Public Information and Media Consultant to the American Society for Psychical Research in New York from 1982 to 1983. In addition, he was president of the California Society for Psychical Study, and Consulting Editor for the 40-year-old *Fate Magazine*, with a bimonthly column called "Psychic Frontiers." His interest in mentalism spans 16 years.

In 1989 Auerbach founded the Office of Paranormal Investigations. Still active in the Parapsychology Association, he continues pursuing his interests by attending conferences. He is an accomplished magician and mentalist, and has an edge on those who seek, but who are not informed about, trickster methods. His credit as a consultant for The Magic of David Copperfield X show establishes his standing as a magician.

Rather than writing about "How To Read Auras," Auerbach produced *Mind Over Matter; ESP, Hauntings, and Poltergeists: A Parapsychologist's Handbook; Psychic Dreaming;* and *Reincarnation, Channeling, and Possession.*

Loyd Auerbach is president of the Psychic Entertainers Association. He is also a performer. On stage he assumes the role of **PROFESSOR PARANORMAL**. In his mentalist mode, he is adept at what he calls "Séance Fiction Theater." This other side of his personality is revealed in publicity photographs, which depict him as a man surrounded by fog, with arms crossed and dark glasses covering his eyes.

One side of Auerbach's persona is in search of truth and falsehood in the realm of the paranormal, and remains ever vigilant in separating the real from the fake. His theatrical side projects strong verbal abilities and performing skills, making him popular enough to be the leader of an organization that contains a large number of mentalist performers – all of whom hold varying attitudes and opinions. He keeps company with many who perpetuate those blurred areas, where on stage and in private they play with a subliminal mystical need, but also distort and muddy the waters.

If Auerbach, as president of the PEA, can sort out the unethical and ethical aspects of mentalism, he will have left behind a remarkable achievement. Magic and mentalism are important to Parapsychology and Psychical Research. But will these two strange bedfellows contribute anything substantial?

# *Finale*

**WHAT IS DECEPTION?** Deception is the purposeful act of persuading, or attempting to persuade, a person or group to believe an alleged fact or set of facts, which are not true. Even more precisely, it is the act of knowingly providing and supporting an untrue argument. The argument need not be elaborate or formal, and may be as simple as a one-sentence lie. The deceiver's intent for the receiver to believe that lie constitutes an attempt at deception – steering the audience away from the truth. Depending upon many circumstances, that lie may require a support system of other lies if it is to withstand scrutiny for very long.

Jason Randal, Ph.D
*The Psychology of Deception*
Top Secret Productions, Inc.
Venice, California, 1982

*As a way of life, can the end result of total loyalty to mentalism bring a variety of rewards? Yes, but they are fleeting. Samuel Johnson, the British lexicographer, wrote, "Almost every man wastes part of his life in attempts to display qualities which he does not possess, and to gain applause which he cannot keep." The private readers within the fraternity of psychic entertainers who may believe in nothing beyond this earthly realm, but who project belief in everything, are indeed enigmatic. They join the chorus of those who can say in the words of Sir Walter Scott, "Oh what a tangled web we weave / When first we practice to deceive."*

*For those who encounter these strange and deceptive members of society, their predictions, their readings, and their endless books that attempt to teach the ways and means of charlatanism, I offer this final thought. After decades of interest in Religion, Psychical Research, Parapsychology, and Magic, a lifetime of exploring the religious life, seminary training, and forty years of ministry in the Episcopal church, counseling every conceivable human problem, and encountering the dark side of human nature in all facets of deception in research efforts and even religion itself, life has taught me to allow for humanness in all others – and particularly in myself.*

*Traditionally, from the earliest time until the present day, recognized Christian churches have frowned upon those who purport to read minds for profit, or who act as mediums. But except for strict fundamentalist groups, Christianity looks kindly upon magic as a form of entertainment. This even includes mind reading, as long as there is an explanation that the acts are being performed as benign trickery. However, Christianity certainly looks down on those who pretend to read minds, give readings for money, and who have no conscience about either. In the eyes of the Christian church, this is considered blasphemy toward the Holy Spirit, especially if one among the departed is used as bait.*

*Fortunately, the law is on the side of those defrauded by psychic and religious scams, and mentalists are very much aware that they must perform as entertainers. Even then the* mentalist/conjuror who hides beneath the mask of a psychic runs the risk of facing the wrath of a disgruntled believer, a former client who has lost his faith in the mentalist/psychic, or a person who may have invested and lost savings as a result of a reading. Any attempt to direct a person's life by psychic means is tricky business, but the commercial aspects of this exercise are tempting, so it will probably continue.

In the end, armed with sensible teachings and spiritual disciplines, one must approach life in a mature, Godly manner and allow a margin for true mystery, not just imitation mystery. Despite all we can learn and all we can accomplish, when all is said and done we are left with only our faith – faith that cannot be found in psychics, mentalists, mediums, and horoscopes, which can misdirect lives by non-spiritual spurious, even if well-meaning, efforts. The faith to which I refer surrounds a higher mystery – a cosmic mystery – revealed in evolved consciousness by so many great souls of the past and present.

# Cast of Characters

# 13 Steps to MENTALISM

SWAMI GIMMICK

PENCIL, LIP, SOUND, MUSCLE, READING

MNEMONICS & MENTAL SYSTEMS

PREDICTIONS

BLINDFOLDS & X-RAYS

BILLETS

BOOK TESTS & SUPPLEMENT

TWO PERSON TELEPATHY

MEDIUMISTIC STUNTS

CARD TRICKS

QUESTION & ANSWER EFFECTS

PUBLICITY STUNTS

PATTER & PRESENTATION

*by Corinda*

# "SWAMI GIMMICK"

## BY

## CORINDA

### STEP ONE

IN CORINDA'S SERIES :—

## "THIRTEEN STEPS TO MENTALISM"

**D. ROBBINS & CO., INC.**
Cranbury, N.J. 08512

# STEP ONE in CORINDA'S SERIES
## " THIRTEEN STEPS TO MENTALISM "

## THE " SWAMI GIMMICK "

## CONTENTS

### PART ONE    TYPES

### PART TWO    TECHNIQUE

### PART THREE    TRICKS

## DIFFERENT TYPES OF WRITERS

When contemplating the use of a Swami Gimmick, the first essential is to discover the type of writer that suits you best. You should examine each variety and test it for your own requirements ; assess the value of any particular model according to the ease with which you can use it—that is the governing factor. Then concern yourself with the other important considerations ; does it fit comfortably ? does it write legibly ? can you get it on and off inconspicuously ? is it firmly held when on the nail or in position? can the lead be replaced? will the lead break in use? and so on. The only really satisfactory way to find out is to try each model, and for what it costs to buy one of each type at the start—is nothing compared with the value of what you get for your pains. The following list gives examples of all the major types of writers ; any that have been omitted are regarded as " special " models that have been the particular fancy of a single performer and not accepted as a standard item :—

A.   Described as " The Swami Gimmick ".

This variety has been appended the title " The " as it is one of the very early models which was used extensively by " Swami's " and Mediums. In general, Mediums made use of writers far more than magicians ; it was quite a common thing for a writer to be the only apparatus used to earn a substantial income as a medium. Slade, the famous fraudulent medium worked a great deal with " spirit writing " produced by trick methods with chalk, and by billet switching and use of a writer. Some examples of his technique were, in our opinion, classics of mentalism. The Swami Gimmick is the smallest type of lead holder you can get. It can be used on the thumbnail or first finger—but usually the first. It is a very small square shaped metal holder which has the lead held in a metal tube mounted on the holder or clamp. It has a leading and important advantage over all other types—its size. Being the smallest it is the type which is least visible, but, unfortunately, it also has a strong disadvantage ; due to its' compactness, it is easily pulled off the thumbnail and may fall off accidentally.   Moreover, the absence of " wings " (see later types) make it unsteady when writing. Provided that you have a fairly long nail upon which it may be fixed firmly, this type will be found practical. The leads can be replaced when used.

B.   Described as " C " Type.

Otherwise, and more commonly called " the undernail writer ". This title is not strictly correct as it is, if you consider, misleading. The lead fits on the holder which jams on the thumb. Part of the *holder* goes under the finger nail but the lead stays on top. Hence the term given should only be applied to the variety of writers that project the lead actually *under the nail*—such as do exist. We would prefer to call it " C " type because it is shaped like the letter " C " —or, as you might say in modern times, this is the " Delta Wing Swami Gimmick ". It appears very much like a delta wing aircraft— though not as large . . . . !

The " C " Type is probably the most used variety. It features reliability when working, fits comfortably and rigidly by virtue of

4

its two wings which project outwards from the main holder, and, running under the thumbnail lock the gimmick firmly on. The addition of wings has to a large extent improved the old type of gimmick. They spread the strain over a wider " gripping area " of thumbnail and in consequence, cut out practically all unwanted movement of the gimmick when in use. Most " C " types are designed to take new leads for refilling but not all. The best are made of a fairly pliable metal which allows you to bend the gimmick to fit your thumbnail with exactness. They should be flesh coloured or made of dull metal—not because they are liable to be seen by the audience, but because they will make you feel happier. The " C " Type is made in several sizes allowing for both short and wide nails. It also comes in two types of lead (disregarding colour) as we have the ordinary medium-soft lead and then a rather extra-special class with thick heavy black lead which has, as an additional improvement, a machined tip-carefully rounded to give thick letters or numbers in use. The difficulty with this type is making new leads.

C.  Described as The Band Writer.

In reply to the question, " Do you use a Swami Gimmick " I have frequently received the answer, " I can't my nails are too short ". It is somewhat surprising how many magicians and mentalists are unaware that several writers exist that do not fit on the nail at all. The Band Writer is an example. This is a pliable metal clip or band that fits on the ball of the thumb or any finger. The band is designed to hold a small tube into which fits the lead. This type suffers from lead breakage in use if you do not take care. It would not be dangerous if you were proficient. The size is much larger than models already mentioned, but being flesh-coloured as *it must be* it is no more visible than a common thumbtip. It does feature one asset over the rest of the family ; because of the clip arrangement, it may be fixed to all sorts of odd positions on the thumb and fingers. Occasionally this may be of use as we shall see. This type is best for fixing on a toe to write on a card in your shoe—as may be done for several good effects, and, funny as it may seem, is quite easy and very practical. Band Writers rarely have facility for replacement of the lead and whilst on this subject, be warned—never use a band-writer that has the lead simply stuck to the clip. Examine it and be sure it is mounted in a tube which goes *through* the clip holding same firmly in position.

D.  Described as the Overnail Writer.

This model is not widely known but has been in existence for about twenty years. It really is a " C " Type plus a clamp which gives just a bit more ' lock ' to the nail. It fits only the thumbnail—and is very firm in use as it features three wings as supports. Two go under the nail and one comes out over the top of the nail. It has a slight draw-back in that it cannot be quickly got into position or removed without considerable force. The leads can usually be replaced when exhausted.

E.  Described as an " Adhesive writer ".

This variety invented by my good friend Eric Mason and sold under the name of " BOON " is a later innovation in the family of

5

Swami Gimmicks. It is a small circular disc which has the lead mounted in the centre. The disc is prepared with an everlasting adhesative which sticks to the thumb or finger. The principle of sticking lead to the finger has been used before, but at no time has a suitable holder been available until the researches of Mr. Mason. The Boon is practical both in size and working. It stays put when stuck on by virtue of continued pressure caused by writing or pressing the lead against paper. It does in fact become more firmly fixed as you progress. It is very easy to remove and there is no restriction as to the place of fixture. Generally speaking it is used on the tip of the ball of the thumb and preparation for getting it on simply involves a quick lick of that part of your anatomy. It is not messy as those unacquainted might suppose. For general use there is no need for this type to be flesh coloured and although the leads can be replaced, its cheapness makes it an unnecessary task.

F.    Described as The Thumbtip Nailwriter.

As a magician you will be familiar with a thumbtip and probably with its use as a nailwriter. It is in fact an ordinary thumbtip with a lead mounted in the end for writing. It is obvious that a good fitting tip gives complete control over the lead and the only drawbacks of this method are, you do not have the same essential mobility as with others and you lose the " feel " gained when writing almost directly with the thumb—as with most other types. It is however a simple matter to get it on and off quickly. In truth, the Thumbtip Nailwriter is regarded more as a novelty than as a widely used Swami-type gimmick. Although mention of this style is made in Annemann's Practical Mental Effects.

### Points to consider with All Types

(1)    Make a very careful examination of the construction of any Swami you intend to use. Be quite sure that when a tube is used to hold the lead—it is very firmly affixed to the clip part.

(2)    Be quite certain that the lead is not so long that it could easily break under pressure and see that it is well fixed in the tube. If need be, stick it into the tube with a good strong glue.

(3)    See that your lead cannot be pushed right through the tube. If you press as though writing and it simply pushes the lead back into the tube, it is useless. You must stick the lead in and seal the end of the tube with strong glue.

## HOW TO USE YOUR SWAMI GIMMICK

As soon as you have inspected the family of Swami Gimmicks and found the type that you think will suit you, the work begins. Long before you go rushing off to show your friends a new field of miracles, you should get well acquainted with tools of the trade. Start off by forgetting all about effects and concerning yourself with the really important things :—

### (a) Getting the Gimmick into position for use

If you can't get it on—you can't use it ! First deal with your " hiding place ", the spot where the gimmick is kept ready for use. If you intend to

6

use it for an opening effect, the best thing is to put it on the nail or in position just before you are due to perform. This way means you know it's on just right. If this cannot be done, you must steal it, magically speaking, just before you want to use it. (Although in many cases you can wear it throughout your act). It does not matter where you hide the gimmick as long as you can get at it without attracting attention and as long as it cannot get lost. It may be as well to mention here that a spare gimmick on your person gives you considerable confidence and accidents can always happen. I have always carried two and have not yet had cause to resort to the emergency one—but one day I shall be very grateful. (That's a prediction !)

The magical fraternity being blessed with magical dealers having nothing but the desire to further your success, has at its disposal what are known as " Holdouts ". A Swami holdout is anything that inconspicuously hides the gimmick and yet delivers it to you when required. Usually a pencil is used. The gimmick fits into a slit designed to hold it conveniently for getting on. Two holdouts designed especially for Boon are presented by Mr. Mason. The first is a small pad which you hold when writing your predictions and the second a magnetic holdout built into a pencil. Both are good if you use Boon but neither can be used to accommodate other varieties. Other holdouts have been fashioned with finger rings, pens (where a special writer that writes in ink is used) a rubber and so forth. These appliances are by no means essential but most have one useful feature. They enable you to see yourself fitting the gimmick on whereas putting it on in the pocket means you work by feel alone. Outside of holdouts you can't go far wrong with having it in a pocket. A waistcoat pocket is quite good because it looks very natural when you stick BOTH thumbs in the pockets. (One in each of course). I use my trouser pocket and have nothing else therein. Fancy places have been suggested which no doubt appeal to the mind as clever, but are, more often than not, impractical. The lapel sounds clever because who would think you had a Swami Gimmick hidden behind your lapel? And who the Devil knows you have one anyway? Don't try and fool yourself—in the long run simplicity pays where complication fails. If you cannot use your pockets and it is not always convenient, put it on a chair or table and pick it up when you want it. A final suggestion that I have considered but not tried over any period—but think it suitable ; have the gimmick on the wrist watch strap then you may acquire it whilst looking at the time or winding the watch a bit. It is perfectly natural which is what it should be. All this is recorded although it may well be taken for granted that you get the gimmick on secretly. However, I have seen many performers look as though they were having a manicure during the process of getting it off and on. You are excused a glimpse whilst getting it on—just to check all is in order—but getting it off is different. You are fully aware of the location of your thumb and must therefore know the position of the gimmick WITHOUT LOOKING and so you take it off, if you must take it off, without looking. Annemann had a suggestion for this and I have another. He used to run his hands through his hair and leave it there and occasionally I have left it in my mouth and removed it with the teeth under cover of the natural position of thumb nail just inside mouth, fist clenched as do so many people when adopting a " let me think " air, you cough it into your hand later—they are indigestible and should not be swallowed. Right ! You have got it on and you are able to take it off, now let us deal with your behaviour WHILST it is on :—

## (b) How to Handle the Gimmick when it is on

The most impressive demonstration of handling a Swami when it's on can be given if you FORGET ALL ABOUT IT until it is actually used. Weigh the odds in your favour.

(1)  No one but you is aware that you have something stuck on your thumb.

(2)  It is very small or flesh coloured and is barely visible.

(3)  The audience do not know what you are going to do—until you have done it—with very few exceptions.

(4)  You are performing and distracting attention from the hands.

Once you have acquired the art of ignoring the gimmick when you have it on, you may attend to the finer points of handling.

We will suppose for the moment that you must write a number on a card. In order to achieve this simple feat, you must have everything just so. The card should be of the right thickness—that is very important—then it must be of a certain size, which also matters considerably ; on top of this, the card must be held in the correct position during the writing process and last but not least, at no time must the audience suspect you have written right under their noses. All points may be regarded as details, but I would prefer to consider each one a major operation if one chooses to progress to perfection.

## (c) What to write on—the Right Type of Card

With a Swami Gimmick and a lot of trouble and risk, you can write on practically anything. With very little trouble you can do it right and take no risks. The very best thing to use is an ordinary white visiting card of fairly thick texture—about double the thickness of common cartridge paper. The size should be $3\frac{1}{2} \times 2\frac{1}{2}$ inches—not smaller. The thickness of the card recommended is such that when writing you have a substantial or rigid surface ; as would be quite different with paper. Even resting paper on a stiff rest is not as good since it involves holding too many things in one hand at once. The size recommended is such that it nicely covers the thumb or finger during the writing process and at the same time, is very easy to hold in the hand in the correct position. You must take it that exceptions will occur.  Should you be using one of the special gimmicks known as a " STYLUS WRITER ", which is used to *impress* writing via a carbon sheet sealed in an envelope, naturally you must write on the envelope and the card by virtue of its thickness would be most unsuitable. However, with or without exceptions, it is a wise policy to adopt one technique and stick to it. I recommend a thick white card of the size given and advise you to use the same thing all the time. From any good stationers you can buy at 2/- per hundred—ready cut unprinted visiting cards and there is nothing strategically wrong in the use of visiting cards printed on one side with your name and address—a constant reminder to the audience and a good advertisement for you. Have a few of these cards blank both sides though, as sometimes you require two sides free.

## (d) How to Hold the Card Before, During and After Writing

We will start with a conclusion ! The best way to hold the card is *naturally*. Idiotically simple as that may sound it is quite a difficult thing to do unless you train yourself. A fault generally develops because you cannot forget that in a moment you must have the card in a certain position and then write on it. This you must do to be natural—you must forget and regard the card with the same indifference that you hold for the Swami —until the vital second when it is in use. The easiest approach to this is to practice mirrorwise without the gimmick on—just practice holding, waving, passing from hand to hand and see what looks natural and what looks unnatural. I prefer to operate this way and give you the effect to show the construction of the plot step by step.

An opening effect of mentalism ; I stand central facing the audience and point directly with the right hand (which has a swami on the thumb) at a person who is seated over to my right. The card I hold is held between the thumb and finger tips of the left hand—held in view without waving it like a Union Jack on Coronation Day. I point to a person and say dramatically, " You sir ! Would you please stand for just a brief moment—thank you. (He stands.) Sir, will you please point to any member of the audience anywhere you like." As the last few words are said, the card is transferred without looking to the right hand to allow the left to wave at the left side of the audience. " Thank you sir ! Madam, the gentleman has pointed to you—he could have chosen anyone here tonight—but for some unknown reason he has asked you to take part—and all I ask you to do is to call out loud—very loud and clear please—the very first number that comes into your head—NOW !" As the last few lines are spoken, the card in the

right hand is manouvered into the " writing position " which is this. The lady calls out her number and immediately you call back " Will you repeat that a little louder please ". And the time it takes you to say those words is the time it takes you to write her number on your card—then instantly spin it out into the audience at the lady and—" Catch ! Take this card please—read out loud everything that is written on it—thank you ! " It reads, " I Corinda predict that the first number you will think of will be 732 and that you will not change your mind. (You had better use your own name !)." It remains 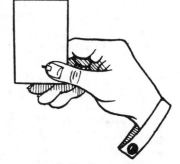 only to mention that during the writing, the card completely screens the thumb—FROM ALL ANGLES—which is achieved by holding it almost against the chest when writing. You should note that the " writing position " is such that most of the card is in view of the audience and it is not obscured in the hand like a palmed playing card. It is held in the writing position for the least possible time—immediately the work is done, the arm shoots out to full length—the card comes to the absolute fingertips—it is not even given a glance.

If the person to whom the card must be given is near to you—within reach, it is a good thing to hand it to them. You do this with your right hand and to hide the Swami Gimmick hold the card between the thumb and second finger and cover the gimmick with the tip of the first. Alternatively, you may clip the card between the first and second fingers whilst they are outstretched, and hide the thumb nail under the other fingers which are bent—exactly as is required for the two-fingered Clubs salute. (Boy Scouts.) Unless it is quite unavoidable, do not change the card from one hand just to give it away.

## (e) The Technique of Writing

According to what you must write, the technique will vary. Fundamentally it amounts to the same principle each time ; gaining time to write inconspicuously or without the audience knowing. In nine cases out of ten you will be able to resort to verbal misdirection by asking a question or giving an instruction :—" Will you repeat that out loud please ". Or, an old dodge is to repeat the number given, incorrectly—they might call " sixty four " whereupon you call back " did you say sixty-five "—and whilst doing so write sixty four. This is best used only when the number given has a phonetic resemblance to another number—as for example—fifty-four and sixty-four.

For longer numbers or words I have developed my own technique which I offer you and promise is very practical and makes a difficult job easy.

" Think of a number—a number of several digits—two, three, four, five you have a free choice. (Do not invite more than five !) I want you to imagine the number written in the air—in great big numbers (or letters for a word). Have you done that ? What did you imagine ? Did you actually see the number like this ". As you reach this point, whatever number was given, with the card in the writing position subscribe their number slowly and deliberately in the air—doing each number separately and, as you do so, writing each number on the card ! Believe me, it's so blessed easy you can't go wrong ! The numbers you draw in the air should be (in imagination) about two feet high. The move is absolutely natural and not only does it help you to form the written number, but it allows you every chance to look at what you are writing. This is one technique that helps to overcome clumsy misformed numerals and letters. Which brings us to our next step—the style of writing.

## (f) The Style of Writing and What to Write

Without considerable practice and experience, you will find it hard to create written numerals that look nicely written. The numbers are badly formed and are not the same size or maybe out of line. These are imperfections which use of a Swami Gimmick over a long period—will overcome. However, you must not worry about this side of it too much—in truth it matters very little as long as your writing is legible. You can do several things to improve the faults. First, as you will realise, the complete prediction is not written with the Swami Gimmick. The " lead up " is filled in on the card and a gap left where the vital facts (such as the thought of number) are inserted. Aiming at a uniform appearance throughout, you write the general prediction or lead up in shaky writing—some performers even write it beforehand with a swami ! The bad writing then conceals the bad figures. Another dodge is to write the lead up with your left hand or, if you normally write with the left—with the right. (And should you be awkward and be ambidexterous—with the teeth). Don't think that can't be done either ! Slade mentioned earlier, fooled Professor Hyslop by writing a message of some twenty lines on a slate whilst both his hands were held. He held the chalk in his teeth—and with a gag he would have done it with his feet with the slate on the floor—he was an exponent of all fakery with writing. The other aids to improved writing are ; first write as slowly as you can when learning to use the Swami, second ascertain the best size figures for yourself—and stick to that size—adjust the swami to the right or the left of the nail until the lead in it points in the direction which you find works best. Again stick to that position once you find it. Last but not least—take it easy—and by that I mean, control ambition and in the early stages of your work, stick to writing numbers—the shorter the better—or to making a simple cross against a list of names and so on. In time you may write sentences with a Swami—but, as I say, first avoid all forms of digital dexterity and stick to that which is practical and of use.

## SECTION TWO : SPECIAL TECHNIQUES

To summarise the position so far, we have dealt with types of Swami Gimmicks, where to conceal them, how to use them and when to use them. We shall now deal with different methods that have been designed to improve the effects created by way of the writer unseen.

### (a) The Use of Different Colours

Occasionally one may add to the perplexity of an effect by writing in a colour such as red. It takes little time to change your normal black lead for a red one. However, as with the black leads, you should select a good quality SOFT red and, as mentioned on page six, make certain that it is fixed properly. I will give you one good effect with coloured Swami Gimmicks you will find it quite difficult to do—but once you have mastered the trick you have a very good effect at your disposal for life. It will cost you ten Swami Gimmicks to do. For that price, you, like everybody else have many pieces of unusable junk which you will never use—and I mean conjuring props.

" Madam ! Call out the first colour that comes into your head ! Red ? Thank you—and now you sir ! Let me have the first figure that you think of—134 ? Sorry ! 154—I thought you said thirty-four. Right sir, take this card please and tell us if you can see anything unusual on it ! You can ? What ? On it is written the number you thought of—ah ! that was luck— but there's more than that—Madam can you remember what colour you chose ? Red—that's right, and what colour is your number written in sir ? Red ? So you chose red and you chose 154—both are right which can't be luck ! " That is the effect.

There are two methods ; the perfect one gives each spectator a free choice and the imperfect limits the selection of colours. For the perfect, you will find that if you approach a serious person (try and choose an elderly lady) and ask that person to name a colour it will be one of the following (these colours are given in order of the frequency with which they occur) ; RED, BLUE, GREEN, YELLOW, VIOLET or MAUVE, ORANGE, BROWN, PINK, GREY and MAROON. You buy a box of coloured pencils and make up one swami with each colour and then buy a small pocket note-book for sixpence from Woolworths, and down one edge (the right hand edge) stick a strip of tape on the top page to make it thick. On this thick edge you " index " your swami gimmicks—simply stick them on the edge as though it were the thumb. The card is lying on the top page. As the COLOUR is called you are holding the book and have plenty of time to look for the correct swami and take it out with the card. As the number is called you have the card only in the right hand with the swami on and write it in. You will very rarely get the minor colours—or last five called and should you be given " black " or " white " immediately reply, " No—a proper colour if you please black and white are not true colours," which is correct. The other method is to limit the colour choice—have four cards ; one red, one blue, one green and one yellow. On each card have the swami of the same colour! Give them a free choice of cards—holding them up for display and discard the 3 which are not wanted. Suppose red was selected, steal the gimmick from the red card, put the card dramatically on show and pick up the white card which can be stuck in the top jacket pocket where it is on view all the time, until it is actually used. The effect seems long—but in effect it is quite snappy—and aside from the speed it qualifies as good mental magic by virtue of the very simple plot—every member of the audience can understand what has happened.

### (b) The Window Envelope

Annemann used this method quite frequently and I am very fond of it because first it is simple and second it is what I call " cheeky ". The idea is to have a card in an envelope which has an opening on the address side. The writing is done directly on to the card through the window and the impression which you convey is that the message or prediction was sealed all the time ! Mention of this technique in various books on mentalism invariably refer to the envelope as " a window envelope " which naturally conveys the idea of the full size standard model. This is not best. I work with home-made envelopes—or rather, home-made windows. I purchase quite cheaply small white envelopes (brown are just as good if not better) which are supplied to accommodate wedding cards. With a razor blade or Stanley Trimmer I cut out a small window on the address side only. (Insert a playing card into the envelope to avoid cutting right through.) I cut the window just where I want it—no larger than is required to write five numbers and just where those numbers fill into the rest of the prediction already worded on the card. My window is about $1'' \times \frac{1}{2}''$ and is central two-thirds of the way down. The envelope is sealed and is slit open when needed with a nail file. A spectator pulls out the card after you pull it out a bit to start with. Obviously it is held flap side upwards.

### (c) The Carbon Impression Technique

Until quite recently I have not considered this method to be worth the trouble because I have always thought the window envelope technique achieves much the same result by easier means. However, having now at our disposal new types of carbon paper, we can, if we choose, iron out the original weakness and make the technique of practical use.

The old method was quite simple. A white card sealed in an envelope and inside the envelope, stuck on the inner surface was a sheet of carbon paper. By using a Swami Gimmick (or sharp fingernail) one wrote on the outside of the envelope making a carbon impression on the card inside. The Swami was the Stylus type or one which had a ball tip in place of the usual lead. Nothing clearly visible was to be seen on the outside of the envelope. Although you achieved writing on the inside of an envelope, you were still faced with the problem that the carbon was inside with the card. Ways to overcome this have been thought up ; the carbon was wrapped in a sheet which was removed by the performer who handed the card found inside the sheet to a spectator and so on. The best effect or better still, the best results technically speaking, were obtained from this method when Air Mail THIN envelopes were used in conjunction with BLACK carbon that gave a near resemblance to black ball-pen ink or heavy pencil.

Today we have on the market a variety of Carbon Paper called " N.C.R." or in full, " No Carbon Required " paper. Sometimes this is called " white carbon ". It is a chemically treated paper supplied in two white sheets which we shall call " A " and " B ". Both papers look like normal typing paper, but when " A " is placed on " B " and anything written on the top sheet—a blue impression is formed on " B " underneath. The colour of the impression can be matched with blue artists pencils. The paper is quite sensitive, does not require heavy pressure, and its only fault is that with age it decolourises at the edges and turns a faint blue. This takes a long time. The process is entirely chemical, the writing forms visibly immediately the impression is made and no developers are required or anything like it.

To utilise " N.C.R." you must make an envelope out of " A " and inside the envelope have a slip of " B " which is to bear the prediction. Be sure you get the order of " A " and " B " right, or you will have writing back to front appear on the inside of the envelope and not the right way round on the inner paper. " N.C.R." is obtainable from most magical dealers and is supplied in pads. .The advantage and improvement of this technique is that the sealed envelope can be given to any spectator who opens it and takes out the inner sheet and you have no worries about carbon paper stuck inside. If you must use a sealed envelope method, this is probably best—but if you have any option I recommend the easier and foolproof way—the window envelope.

### (d) The Ink Writer

To my knowledge, no satisfactory Swami Gimmick that writes in ink has, as yet, been developed. I have seen two types available and cannot honestly recommend either. The first is a version of the Overnail Writer which holds a very short ball pen and reserve ink tube. To my mind the appliance is cumbersome and is not satisfactory. The second a Thumb Tip writer which also had a ball pen tip inserted. I am told a version of this writing in real ink has been made but I have yet to see it. The tip method of the two, was best because you could put a new refill in and it was steady and less visible—but for all that it did not warrant the trouble. In my opinion it makes very little difference whether the prediction is written in pencil, ink or, for that matter—blood. The Swami Gimmick as it is, offers you everything you require without the necessity of so called ' improvements ' which flatter the ingenuity but not the effect.

### (e) Preparation of the Prediction

It is a good policy to have a full message on the card bearing the prediction. You could content yourself with just the number or word—but a " lead up " is a subtle form of misdirection. People are obliged to think that you couldn't possibly write " all that " in a few seconds . . . and true too ! The best place to insert the fact (that is the number) in the prediction —is in the middle. You could have it at the end or at the beginning, but the middle is best. Then you have words before and after the fact. The lead up should be brief—six to ten words is quite adequate and the words should be placed so that the spot where you insert the fact is placed in the exact position convenient for writing with the swami. The spot should also line up with the window if you have an envelope in use. For a straightforward "think of a number" effect, the prediction can be, for example, "YOU WILL THINK OF THE NUMBER . . . . . AND WILL NOT CHANGE YOUR MIND—CORINDA." Below will be found a diagram which shows a typical layout of the wording.

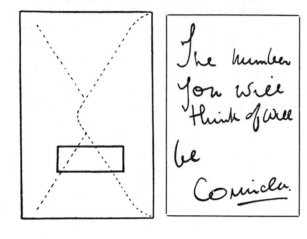

**Diagram :** Showing the spacing of words in the prediction and written so that the "fact" space is conveniently situated and in place for the window envelope.

The card size is $3\frac{5}{8}" \times 2\frac{3}{8}"$.

The fact is written in letters or numerals equal in size to the rest of the writing.

The writing is badly done to offset the like writing with the Swami Gimmick.

The next essential in the preparation of the prediction is to use a pencil which has the same lead as your Swami and which writes with the same thickness of letters. You should keep one pencil especially for this purpose. I always round the tip of the Swami lead and the pencil by rubbing on fine glass paper or, in an emergency, using a nail file. The pencil and the swami lead should be soft. Medium H.B. is not enough and although soft pencils have thick leads—it is worth the trouble to file down a small piece of soft lead for the swami. I recommend a 2 or 3 B. Lead. This writes thick and black, moves easily across the surface of the card and being soft—makes no scratching noise. A round tip to the lead is better than a point or sharp cut off finish. Conrad Haden in America can supply De Luxe Swami Gimmicks which have special soft/black leads with machined leads. The type mentioned can be obtained in this country from dealers who stock the American varieties. You will appreciate the importance of having a pencil to write the prediction that is of the same class as your swami lead.

## (f) The Fingernail

You are not overdoing the issue if you pay attention to the thumbnail or fingernail that is to be used to hold the gimmick. It is easy to forget that the fingernail grows and that it varies in size in doing so. The best length for the nail for most Swami Gimmicks is one-eighth of an inch long. Moreover, you should keep the important nail at that length—do not cut it shorter and do not let it grow longer. A slightly square tip to the nail helps to hold.

## (g) Alternative Methods of Holding the Card

We have explored one method of holding the card—and the chosen one has been that which we found best after considerable experiment. You may discover the technique unsuitable and prefer another :—

1. You can write on the card with your arms crossed.
2. You can write on the card when it is held behind your back.
3. You can write with it in the hand hanging at the side.
4. You can write whilst holding it in two hands.
5. You can write with the card in your pocket.

The method we have given, that is, one handed writing whilst the card is held in view at chest height—is THE BEST. It is also the hardest to do. If you want more information about the techniques No's. 1 to 5, you may refer to a very good publication called " 20 Stunners with a Nailwriter ", by Chapman. I am critical of the alternative methods because :—

1. Crossed arms is a natural but still ungainly pose for a performer on stage.
2. Card behind the back. It is not good to have it from view unless sealed in an envelope. Theoretically you could be using an index, exchanging and so forth. The card in view is to my mind, an essential of presentation.
3. Hand at the side is not angle proof.
4. Two hands used to hold one small card—WHY?
5. Pocket writing has nothing wrong with it. But a pencil stub is as good as a swami and even then it's not on view.

For the reasons given I would advise you to work on the single handed method and do it properly. If you are not prepared to work hard and practise you may as well forget all about Swami Gimmicks because they involve hard work.

### (h) The Visible Pencil

Quite frequently you will want to pretend that you are writing a prediction whilst the audience wait. You take out a pencil and appear to write on the card. Sometimes you may actually write, sometimes you only pretend to write. The important thing is to make clear to the audience that the pencil is not in your hands WHEN the chosen number is revealed. To do this, you make a lot of fuss and bother over the visible pencil.

First, make it a conspicuous pencil—a long white painted one. Then have some trouble finding it—searching through the pockets for a moment. This is good psychology; it convinces the audience you have written the full prediction in full view—and then it remains only to put the pencil away —with great deliberation. Never use a short pencil which could suggest you have it in the hand out of sight. A good move once the pencil has been used is to throw it on a table nearby—do it with a " don't want that any more " attitude.

Some performers make a point of borrowing a pencil—in theory proving that they have arrived without any means of writing. I am of the opinion that this is being too clever. You are liable to be handed a purple copy pencil, a red one, a pen or anything other than a matching pencil to your gimmick. You must then get yourself out of that fix—when it is all unnecessary trouble. Stick to your own pencil.

Another tip with regard to pretending to write. To do this in a convincing manner is not as easy as it would appear. One concrete solution to the trouble is to stick a wee bit of selotape over the pencil lead—which prevents it from marking and cannot be seen. You may then write properly, and if that's not natural—what is? Finally, if you are supposed to be writing numbers only in pencil on a card—do not give them the chance to " Pencil Read "—other people than magicians, know of this principle.

## SECTION THREE : MODESTY AND MENTALISM MIXED

You have come this far through the subject of Swami Gimmicks or trickery at writing and must therefore be interested. It is now my intention to give you a very brief idea of what can be done in the field of trick writing (TO GIVE YOU ENCOURAGEMENT) and to tell what others have achieved (TO KEEP YOU MODEST). Whenever you feel you are the world's greatest trick-writer—come back to this paragraph and see how you compare with :

SLADE.—Inventor of spirit slate writing. Who could write on slate with chalk with his feet (both) or his mouth. Who could write a letter back to front to be read in a mirror—and write it as fast as you could dictate it.

MADAM DISS DEBAR.—Exponent at spirit writing and spirit painting.

Who outwitted the famous magician Carl Hertz in Court when she was being " exposed ". DEBAR was able to draw a picture in colour with her feet in secrecy and could use both hands writing something different at the SAME TIME.

CARL FRANKS : Who is still alive can write with a swami on either hand, write neatly and write full sentences. He is the only person I know of that can use the method of writing in the shoe by having a gimmick on his toe.

KEELER.—Described as the Greatest Living King of Slate Writers. Wrote legibly on a slate or with pencil on paper held behind his back— with his hands tied. Wrote messages backwards for mirror reading—and did them in the dark—and last but not least, CHUNG LING SOO who used a Swami extensively and mentions it in his book " Slate Writing and Kindred Phenomena " Published in 1898.

## CONCLUSION

Mr. Eric Mason inventor of Boon, describes his Swami Gimmick as " The greatest little gimmick in the world ". Mr. Mason is right—and his statement applies to all good varieties of the Swami Family. Nothing so small can be of so great a use to the Mentalist. Its potential uses are incredible. The restriction of its application is on the part of the performer alone ; if he is willing to work hard and practise constantly the result will be something really worth having. To be successful—you must stick at it ; few tricks are worth having that can be done as soon as you pick them up ; technique is vital but is not everything—presentation is the other half. I will conclude with my personal feeling which is, to me, a Swami Gimmick is worth fifty pounds. What it's worth to you—is what you make it. I wish you every success.

TONY CORINDA.

16

# TRICKS WITH A SWAMI GIMMICK

### No. 1. The Spectator as the Telepathist

This is a principle that may be applied to several effects. It is one of the finest tricks you can use as the plot reverses the normal procedure of mental magic—and makes it appear that the spectator reads your mind—instead of you, as normal, reading theirs. It is best performed after one or two effects of Mentalism have been shown. It is offered to the audience as " conclusive evidence " that thought reading must be possible—and proved when they read your thoughts.

After suitable opening spiel, you take the card and pretend to write on it four numbers. The spectator is asked to try and " receive " these numbers as you " send " them one at a time. You hand them another card and a pencil. If you are an exponent of Pencil reading, you have a miracle on your hands—simply by reading each number as they write and filling it in with the Swami. If not, you can work one of two different ways. After you say, " I'm sending the first number now " you pause, then enquire " Have you got it—what have you written " and when the answer is received, gaze at your card and knowingly state " Hmm. not bad—let's try the next ". You can fill that number in while you gaze or, send the four numbers and finally ask as you walk towards the spectator " and what did you get ? " so that by the time you get there, ready to hand over your card, the same numbers are written on your one. The pencil reading method is by far the hardest—but by far the best as you do not ask any questions at any time ! (CORINDA'S " STEP TWO " DEALS WITH PENCIL READING.)

### No. 2. First Variation of the No. 1 Principle

With the same principle of having the spectator read your mind, to get away from numbers—if you want to (there is nothing really wrong with using them) you may work on a name, sending it letter by letter. To add to the value of the effect it is a good thing to have the two cards handed to another spectator to check.

### No. 3. Second Variation of the No. 1 Principle

A date is to be transmitted ; as a precaution that you cannot exchange coins once the experiment is started, you record on a small slip of paper the date you have in mind. This is then sealed between two pennies and held at the fingertips. You adopt the same sending procedure as for No. 1. To perform this effect you will require a special penny that I believe was invented by B. Hull. It is like one coin from a stack of pence, having a round hole cut from the centre. You place the written slip on an ordinary penny and cover it with the fake. You can then write on the slip through the hole.

## No. 4.  Straight to the Point

The next few tricks are more or less " quickies ".  They come straight to the point and therefore make good opening effects.  Before I deal with the tricks, I would like to point out that there are numerous variations of this principle and there is no necessity whatsoever to copy effects used by other people.  A leading Mentalist in this country makes a point of using a variation of this principle and I am constantly disgusted that so many must copy the one effect he uses when there are so many equally as good variations.  Try and be different.

As soon as you have finished your " Good evening, Ladies and Gentlemen" point straight at one person—shout " you sir—close your eyes—call out the first number to enter your head "—write that on a card you are holding in view and toss is to him to read and call out loud.  That effect should take about 15 seconds.

As variations of this technique, you can call for colours, names, words and so on.  Another slightly longer variation is the Change in the Pocket.  You ask a person to count how much they have in loose change and that amount is predicted.  The same " straight to the point " technique can be used when several spectators are involved ; one man is asked to stand and add up mentally any numbers called by the audience (digits) after about six to ten are called he declares the total which you have on your card as a prediction.

## No. 5.  A Stage Trick

You have three cards, on each one you pretend to write something and then put them aside in full view of the audience—but not showing your supposed writing.  The backs of the card which the audience see, can be numbered 1, 2 and 3.  You have nothing visible in your hands—point to any person and call for any colour—point to another—and call for a city—point to the last and ask for a date.  In the time it takes you to pick up the card and say " You sir, were number One and you called out the colour Red "—you have the answer " Swamied " on !

**No. 6.**  The impact of the Swami Gimmick used in Mentalism is so strong that at times it appears you must be using a stooge.  You can help to eliminate this hypothesis by making it obvious your assistants are selected by chance.  A method is to have numerous ping pong (table tennis) balls.  Each is numbered differently from one to ten.  Throw them into the audience and ask a person who has not caught a ball to call out a number—whoever has that number is used.  This is quite a useful dodge when you are getting paid for the time you are on ! Throw the balls out—when you have the spectator chosen, ask him to gaze at the ball and imagine it to be a globe—suggest a globe of the world.  Tell him he can see places ; countries, cities, towns and villages—tell him to travel in his mind and keep moving until you call stop.  At the moment when your showmanship thinks best, call " stop " and then quickly " Name the place where you stopped ".  That place you record gracefully on a card sealed within a window envelope.  The ping pong ball has thus served its purpose in two good ways and warranted its use.

18

### No. 7.  A Card Trick

In the normal course of things, I would not offer you a card trick for Mentalism, I feel however, that you will agree this earns its place as a Mental Effect.  A deck of cards is borrowed.  Ask someone to assist you and ask their NAME—you make a show of writing their initials on one card—fan them and appear to put it on the face of a card—don't write anything really.  Have the card replaced anywhere without showing its value.  Have the pack truly shuffled by two people or one, if in a hurry.  Ribbon spread them on a table if you have a table and if you can ribbon spread (!) or, if not, fan face downwards before the spectator who gave his initials.  Ask him to touch any card and remove the one he touches yourself holding it back towards him and stating " Somehow I knew you were going to touch this one  that's why I put your initials on it before we started ! "  As you speak you jot on the card his initials.  The full value of this effect is gained when you do not have the cards in your hands when he is told to touch any one.  Otherwise your audience may suspect you forced the card at that point.

### No. 8.  Living and Dead.

To be quite honest, I am not overwhelmed with Living and Dead tests.  To me, they seem clever but morbid for general use with entertaining outside of the seance room.  However, I am obliged to include this item because it is a classic example of simplicity and to my mind is one of the top class L. & D. Tests.  The idea is a product of that great man Al Baker.

On your visiting card, down the left hand side write the numbers 1, 2, 3, 4 and 5.  Hand the card to someone you do not know and tell him to fill in the name of a dead person against any number.  Turn your back whilst this is done or, if you cannot or should not—get him to turn round.  Next tell him to write a name of a living person against each of the other four numbers.  Take back the card, take out your pencil and seen be making a tick against one name.  Actually you mark nothing.  Put the pencil away very deliberately and then, and only then, tell him you have marked the dead person's name with a tick and for the first time will he tell everybody what that name was—as soon as you hear, tick it off on the right and hand the card quickly to another person and say " and what name have I marked as dead ? "

### No. 9.  A Close up Quickie

This is an effect that I have used quite a lot and can assure you that it goes over very well.  It is quick, simple to understand and looks impossible.  Ask an unlooker to take any coin from his pocket and to hold it from sight in his clenched fist.   Then for a moment to hold his fist containing the coin against your forehead.  Think a bit and look intelligent.  Tell him to take it away and then bring out your pencil and jot (apparently) a date on your card.  Holding the card in view and putting the pencil away—tell him to show the coin to another person and to say what date it is.  You write that on the card and will find you have time to lay it on the table face downwards and step away for them to pick it up and read.  NOTE : For this—do not have a full prediction—the effect is not a prediction—it is more of the X-Ray Eye class and the date alone is used.

### No. 10.  Two Person Telepathy

The principle used in this effect is based on an idea given in that excellent booklet " 20 Stunners with a Nailwriter ".  I think it is most ingenious and that it is just right for Mentalism. In a friend's home you ask him to take any book he likes and whilst your " medium " wife, girl-friend or grandmother is out of the room to choose any page—then any word on that page and to underline it. You lend him your only pencil to do that ! When he is satisfied you, in telling him to mark it clearly and showing him how, note the word. You then step well away—take out a packet of cigarettes and a *book* of matches. Light one and put the word inside the book matches on the cover. Drop same on the table and leave the room by another door or go into a corner and be quiet. In comes your medium who ponders a bit, asks the spectator to draw a cross on a bit of paper—has a good look at it, decides it reveals all that is needed so tears it up and burns it. When your medium burns the paper using the matches from the table she will have a hell of a job not seeing what you have written !

## No. 11.   A Mediumistic Effect

To my knowledge, the only time this effect has been published elsewhere is in Joseph Rinn's " Searchlight on Psychical Research " which is a book dealing with the work of Rinn and Harry Houdini in the field of exposing Fraudulent Mediumship. It is an ideal trick for serious demonstrations of mediumship under what may be suggested are ' test conditions '. The effect is this. A name of a dead person is asked for and the sitter is told that a message from the other side may be obtained from the deceased. The medium is brought in and does not know the name. To impose test conditions which prevent signals and codes, she is put under a heavy blanket whilst seated on a chair. As a suitable time she calls out to the effect that she has a message coming through—" they " are asking her to write the message. (Although she is in the dark as far as the audience know, it does not appear to matter to them that she writes in the dark). As the medium calls for a pencil, the performer hands one to another person to give her. She has a thick card to write on with her and has a small pocket torch. The pencil given by the performer has a cap ; one of those removable chrome tips that some ordinary pencils have. In that tip is a slip of paper rolled up and put there by the performer and on it is written via the Swami what name was given. The medium writes a suitable sure-fire prediction and signs it with THE name. This is a trick which was used by a professional medium for many years and the method was a closely guarded secret. Presented before the right type of audience and in a mediumistic manner it will be accepted as conclusive proof of psychic ability—it was for many years.

## No. 12.   Time and Space, An Informal Effect

You know as well as I do that presentation makes the trick. Your technique from a performing point of view is important but ability to apply your skill is also important. Few things enhance the presentation so much as a good plot. This is nothing except the use of a swami to write the name of a place —but it is dressed up into a presentable trick.

Start an argument about thought reading, that's a good way to get an excuse to prove by demonstration your point of view ! Sooner or later some bright spark will speak of time and space—whereupon you leap in with a suggestion of your own :—" Time and Space are important—if telepathy exist—it must be, as the projection of thoughts involves distance and therefore space and, moreover, if there is no sympathy of time—the recipient will miss the thoughts—it's hard to describe, but easy to demonstrate if you will allow me !" They will—you can bet on that ! Turn to someone and say, " Will you help me in an experiment—it is only an experiment and nothing may result—but do try, it will be interesting ". You take out a card and a pencil—thy Swami is on. " I am going to write a city on this card (pretend to write) and I shall now ask you to close your eyes and do just as I say. You are travelling through space—not in an aircraft, imagine you have the ability to fly through space projecting yourself through the air. You are moving fast, looking down you can see towns, trees, people— you fly out of this country and go abroad—in your mind you can go anywhere but now you are so high only the big places become visible—you will fly along and see the cities of the world—you are in space." If the spectator suddenly floats up in the air at this point, you stop your trick and turn to the others and say—you see what I mean ? If not, carry on—" Now you are in space—so I will deal with time. In a moment I will say stop—and when I say stop tell me the nearest city you saw—keep flying until I say stop. Right Stop !" He tells you the city and you write it on the card and then say, "Which proves my point because I was concentrating on that very city and telling you to stop at the time when you reached it—read what I wrote at the start ". Which is what I call making a mountain out of a molehill— but the audience love it.

## No. 13.   The Card in Glass

This is a trick which utilises a technique which is new and which is the result of work done by Mr. Eric Mason. It is not at all easy to do, but is well worth the trouble taken in practice.

The effect. The Mentalist writes the name of a playing card (or a number, word, colour, etc.) on a small white card. This card he drops into an empty glass which stands on a table. The audience then decide upon any playing card and then the card in glass is tipped straight from the tumbler into the spectator's hands. He reads the name of the chosen playing card on the prediction card !

The method is to have a glass with a fairly large oval hole cut near the base on one side. The Mentalist can write on the card whilst it is in the glass by pushing his thumb through the hole. The card should be a tight fit in the glass and will then hold steady for writing with the Swami. The fact that the card is visible all the time in the glass precludes all suspicion of trickery. The half pint tumbler size of glass is used.

## No. 14.   The Week Ahead Prediction

Again the principle of this effect may be applied to other tricks. You send a letter to a friend which has inside a sealed envelope with instructions in the letter to say that the sealed envelope should not be opened until you arrive a week later. Inside the envelope you have given them is another smaller one ; it is a window envelope as described on earlier pages. In the window envelope is a card in the proper position for filling in the facts, and on the card is written your prediction.

*Dear Mr. Williams. I am writing this now and in a week's time you will be reading it ! When I meet you, I will ask you to name any person you have met during the week and . . . . will be the name you say ! You can keep this card. CORINDA.*

The prediction is on one side of the card, your name and address on the other for future bookings ! Needless to say, you arrive and as soon as you meet the person Mr. Williams, say " Hallo—before you say anything—name someone you have been talking to this week—better be someone I don't know ". Later ask for the sealed envelope and open it yourself and take out the next envelope the *right way up ;* whilst reminding him of the name he chose you fill it in, then slit open the small envelope and partly pull out the card—allowing him to pull it right out and read it. This is a very good publicity stunt.

### No. 15.  Another Publicity Stunt

" *I predict that when I perform at the Gala Club on Tuesday next, . . . will be seated in the third seat of the front row,*" today's date 1/7/58. Mr. X."

When you are sure that you will play before a seated audience and that you are going to have rows of seats this prediction is quite astonishing. It is sent as with trick No. 14 to the organiser and acquired at the beginning of your act.   The lady or gentleman in the third seat left or right—it matters not) of the front is asked, " Madam, yes you ! Have we ever met before ? Will you agree that I have never seen you before and that I couldn't have known you were coming here tonight ? Thank you Madam, would you be good enough to tell me your name ?" The envelope is opened as above and the card handed to the lady and then read out loud for all to hear. It is not a good trick for the theatre where seats in the front row can sometimes be reserved under a name.

### No. 16.  The Seven Chairs

A rather novel effect for stage is published in Darlings " I'LL READ YOUR MIND ". It has nothing to do with swami gimmicks but the effect can be achieved by use of this apparatus. On the stage you have seven empty chairs in a row. On each one hangs a ticket numbering them one to seven. In your hands you have and show seven cards—playing card size—and each has a number on it from 1 to 7. You mix the cards and select one and hold it number-towards-you at the finger-tips.   Any spectator is invited up and is told to sit on any chair. When they sit down you turn round your card and on it is the number of that chair !

This is a very simple effect. You have eight cards and show seven. The spare card is blank. You select this one and put the other seven aside in a pile. As the spectator sits down you write his chair number largely on the card. This is not too risky to repeat with another person—and will need nine cards to do.

### No. 17.  Any Date of the Year

A quick pocket trick. Have two pocket calendars which have all months of the year on one sheet. Give one to a spectator and tell him to choose any month of the year—and then any day in that month and to " ring " it in pencil. You appear to do the same on yours—ask him to call out his date and then hand your calendar to someone to show the same date ringed.

### 18.  The White Swami

In my booklet " MINI SLATE MAGIC" which dealt with tricks with Pocket Slates, I described a special Swami Gimmick which I called " the white swami ". It was nothing more than an ordinary gimmick but had artists white pencil lead in the tip. It is an appliance for writing on black surfaces—such as pocket slates and if you do have the slates this is quite a good trick to perform.

You have two pocket slates—no flaps are required. They are shown clean, examined if you like, then banded together with elastic. A spectator thinks of a dead name whilst holding the slates to his forehead and trying to impress that name on the slate. You ask, after a suitable period, " I think I heard writing—what name did you think of ? Take back the slates, open them and show both sides—they are still clean ! " Sorry, I must have been mistaken, try again " you say—but before you reband the slates you jot the initials of the dead person on one slate. Next time you ' hear ' writing, they open the slates and find the initials !

### No. 19.  The Sex Detector

You should never miss an opportunity and you will have to wait for this opportunity to occur ! When someone you know is due to have a baby, prior to the birth send them a letter with the sealed envelope inside (see effects No's. 14 and 15). Have a prediction inside on friendly terms such as :—*Congratulations on the Birth of your baby* . . . (insert boy or girl). *If you take my advice you will call the baby* . . . . . . (insert the name). —*CORINDA.* Make sure that in your letter you give instructions that the envelope must not be opened until you have *seen* the baby !

### No. 20.  Headline Predictions

To perform this class of effect you must be proficient with a Swami Gimmick. The idea is to send a sealed envelope to someone of importance and the prediction in it tells the Headlines in the Prominent Local Paper of that day. The letter is sent or handed over well before that day. There is no short cut, to do this you have to be able to write a sentence—although headlines are invariably brief—and the sealed envelope technique for tricks No. 14 and 15 will do. However, as an extra precaution you would be wise to lock the envelope in a 10/- steel cash box calling it a " safe deposit "— which can be obtained at most stationers.

### No. 21.  Topical Effects

Topical effects are always good ; the Football Pools offer you considerable scope for work with a Swami because you have only to write the single signs " 1, 2 or X " to signify results. A simple effect is to have two coupons and pretend to fill in a result for the Three Draws—marking nothing in fact. The other coupon is then handed to a spectator who calls out which teams he thinks will draw. (Specify the Pool they are to select from). You fill in an " X " representing a draw against the teams they call and then show your result to be the same as their choice ! If you care to take this a step further, you may fill in eight " 0's " to predict or forecast the winning result of the Treble Chance Pool which usually pays out in thousands of pounds. The general public know the odds against winning the pools.

### No. 22.  A First Class Newspaper Test

A spectator is given a choice of any three newspapers. You write a prediction on a card and put it face down on the table. They select ANY page from their newspaper. They then tear it in half and choose ANY half ; then tear in half again and choose ANY piece. From that piece, from EITHER side they choose and underline a word—ANY word. You have predicted THAT WORD. At no time have you touched the newspapers and they are all ordinary. Your prediction is worded ready to fill in their chosen word with the swami as you hand the card to be checked. This is an exceptionally clean and strong mental effect—I strongly recommend it.

## No. 23.  Dartboard Prediction

A good stunt that you can pull in a pub or social club is to predict the total score made by someone who throws three darts at the board. To add to the fun of the effect, the last dart should be thrown with the spectator having his eyes closed—which also proves he is not a stooge.

## No. 24.  Matches or Cigarettes

Another stunt for close up work or table work is to predict the number of matches or cigarettes in a box taken by a spectator from his pocket and put on the table. With these close up quick effects, you need not resort to window envelopes or any complicated technique. Simply forecast the total on the card and have the result declared and fill it in as you hand the card to be checked by another spectator. It is also a good thing to keep the prediction as brief as possible—make it of five to six words—straightforward, like : YOU WILL SELECT THE .... OF .... for a card trick, or THE TOTAL WILL BE .... IN THE BOX for matches.

# " Pencil, Lip, Sound, Touch and Muscle Reading "

## BY

## CORINDA

## STEP TWO

IN CORINDA'S SERIES :—

## "THIRTEEN STEPS TO MENTALISM"

STEP TWO in CORINDA'S SERIES

" THIRTEEN STEPS TO MENTALISM "

# CONTENTS

## PART ONE   PENCIL READING

## PART TWO   LIP READING

## PART THREE   SOUND READING

## PART FOUR   TOUCH READING

## PART FIVE   MUSCLE READING

# PART ONE: PENCIL READING

Pencil Reading is the Art of standing some distance away from a person who is writing with a pencil, and being able to discern from the visible movement of the pencil, what is being written.

A simplified explanation of the Art is that, by keeping a careful eye on the movement of a pencil used in writing, adding to that the movement of the hand and elbow, you can very often tell what is being written.

The Art of Pencil Reading is not new, its existence has been realised for many years—but its application is by no means extensive. In fact, it would be reasonable to say that the average well-read Mentalist *knows about* pencil reading, but has never tried it. The reason why the average mentalist has never tried it is because first and foremost, it sounds like hard work and that is enough to scare him, and secondly, in so much as that it is known to be uncertain, the element of risk deters any who may otherwise be interested. To some extent both of these things are true; it is hard work, but not terribly hard and it is liable to fail—but you can by certain measures increase the odds for success substantially in your favour. In order to satisfy yourself that this is perfectly true, now is the time to prove the point. Before you read on and find out how to make the work easier—and how to eliminate the danger of failure, get someone to sit down some ten feet away from you and to write a few numbers on a piece of paper. See how many numbers you can get by watching the movement of the pencil as they write! When you have done that—you may be more inclined to agree that it is not easy and that, shall we say politely, "you slipped up just a little"?

It occurs to me that in case there should be any misunderstanding at this early stage, I should state that when the Art of Pencil Reading is being applied, you do not see the actual writing. If you were able to see what was written—either during or after—you would have no need to resort to pencil reading.

Before we concern ourselves with "how to do it"—shall we see if it is worth while anyway? Let us have a look at the virtues of the art and see if time spent on a little study will be rewarded with something of practical gain to our knowledge.

I invite you to consider for a moment that to an enormous extent, Mentalism relies on something being written. Half the apparatus available to the mentalist is concerned with something written. Think of Clip Boards, Billets, Fake envelopes, Slates and so on. Invariably, these appliances are contrived to convey to the mentalist the word or sentence written by the spectator. We must therefore agree that the importance of the written word in Mentalism—is very great. Now think; wouldn't it be wonderful if you could tell what was written—without any appliance? If we have someone simply think of a word, write it down fold the paper and drop it in their pocket—then without touching the paper or handling any apparatus—you tell them what they have chosen? I am a perfectionist—or I like to think I aim at the very best, and to achieve this sort of thing to my mind—is approaching perfection in Mentalism. Let us be honest, if you could go one step—and one step only further—get it to the point where they do not have to *write*—but just *think*—then you would not be a Mentalist—you would be a genuine thoughtreader.

If Pencil Reading will do this for you—do you think it is worth your time and trouble? I do—that's why I am going to tell you how!

# TECHNIQUE OF PENCIL READING

## (1) When to do it

On the face of it, the title "when to do it" seems a bit silly. You would easily suppose that you do it when you want, but no you don't! You do it when you are in a position to do it—which is not always when you would very much like to do it. Pencil Reading is governed by conditions—and without the favourable condition you cannot afford to try it. As you will see, it involves a chance of failure and if you should be unwise enough to attempt it under unfavourable conditions, you naturally increase the chance of failure and must blame it on what amounts to nothing less than your bad judgement. I propose to analyse the favourable and unfavourable conditions in order to keep your chances of failure to a minimum.

### Favourable Conditions:

When you are performing at close quarters with the audience. At home, in the drawing room, etc.

When you have an excuse to hand the spectator a pencil to use—because we have a special type of pencil that makes it all much more certain.

When you have an excuse to hand the spectator the right type of card to write on—because we have a special card which helps.

When the spectator is seated and you are standing.

When the spectator and audience have no indication whatsoever of the effect they are to expect—and when the writing of the word seems to be the least important part of the proceedings.

When you can get at least four to five feet away from the spectator whilst he writes—making it clear that you do not see what he is writing, or so it would seem.

When you are sufficiently practised to be in a position to try it.

### Unfavourable Conditions:

When the spectator is so near to you—that there may be a good reason to suspect you saw what he wrote.

When he is so far away—you cannot see the pencil used in writing.

When there is a mirror behind the spectator (goodness knows why, but many people wrongly suppose that every mentalist is quite capable of reading in the mirror).

When the spectator uses the wrong type of pencil or pen and writes on something which screens the pencil from view (*i.e.* rests on a large book).

When the spectator is standing.

When the audience, or the spectator *suspects* or anticipates that the writing is of the greatest importance to the effect.

When you are not practised enough to inflict your immature skill on the public.

Having propounded various "when's" and "when not's" I feel I should add that you are not obliged to wait for favourable conditions to occur—although they do very often—thank goodness! You can make them. If you have a large audience and you would not be able to see someone write if they stood up in the back row—you can bring them on to the stage, seat them down (favourable position) out of "politeness"—hand them your pencil—out of "courtesy" and give them the card for "convenience". All very satisfactory steps to getting the favourable condition and everybody will conclude you are a very nice chap for making your assistant comfortable and seeing that you have your equipment at the ready! Which prompts me to slip in here that a golden rule of mentalism is to *be natural*—and you have just accomplished a hell of a lot in a natural manner. After all, instead of seating the spectator, you could stand on a chair yourself to achieve the height difference, and instead of bringing him on to the stage, you could use a telescope to watch his pencil—*this* gentlemen would be unnatural!

To summarise the position of "when to do it". If the favourable conditions are existent, do it. If they are not and you can change them—change them. If you cannot change unfavourable conditions—don't do it.

## (2) The Pencil used for writing

Let's start with the best and work down to the worst. The very best pencil for experiments and performance is undoubtedly what is called a CARBON DRAWING PENCIL (the grade HB made by Wolff's I find entirely satisfactory). You will have to use this pencil to realise why it is so good, and yet the way in which it helps you immensely—is not obvious. The carbon drawing pencil has no lead—in place it has a thick black carbon centre. It writes a good thick black on white paper but this is the important part, being carbon it drags considerably on the surface of the paper and *it is virtually impossible to write quickly with this pencil*. I claim full rights for this discovery which to my mind alters Pencil Reading from a risky dodge to a reliable principle. When you hand a pencil to someone and tell them to write a number, you have no idea (most of the time) how quickly they will write their number. No matter how good at the Art you maybe, the quicker they write—the harder it is to read. Slowing down the writing by such subtle means gives you an enormous advantage over the average worker. It is one of these quiet simple little secrets that make all the difference between success and failure—and as the reader you have a right to know—but join me and keep it quiet.

The carbon drawing pencil maybe obtained quite cheaply from any good shop which supplies artists materials. It looks like an ordinary pencil in every respect and having used it for the purpose of pencil reading, I have never yet had a comment from the one person who may realise it is not ordinary lead. The rest of the audience should never know. In two minutes you will be able to think up ten good excuses should you ever get a query— I do not make excuses!

The size of the pencil is the next thing to consider. After quite a bit of trial and error, I find that a pencil five inches long is most suitable. It is a bit tricky deciding what is best; if you have it very short, almost a stub, you get much more hand movement—which helps a lot—BUT the pencil itself may become screened from view. If you have it full size, normally six-and-a-half inches long—you are almost sure to see the pencil—but not so sure to see hand movement which is restricted. The answer is to meet it halfway; five inches may be regarded as the optimum length.

Having read this, you will appreciate that if you allow the spectator to take out his pen or pencil—you involve the chance of failure because he may well come out of his pocket with a pencil some two inches long. On the other hand, having practiced pencil reading (and pen) with a five-inch pencil you have at least trained yourself to read the most probable length of pencil that may be procured at random. Have a look in Woolworths and see how many ball pens which are commonly used—are about five inches long, then you will appreciate what I mean.

If you are an expert, within reason any writing appliance used by the public can be "read" by you. However, faced with a degree of uncertainty during an important reading, the expert will resort to the safety checks I recommend in section (5) of Pencil Reading Technique, and eliminate the degree of uncertainty by a confirmation of fact process.

### (3) The Card used when writing is done

I am taking trouble to give you these painstaking details because you can take my word for it that a lot of headaches can be avoided by doing the right thing. When you have the chance you should hand the spectator a card to write on. This card should be thick enough to remove the necessity of resting on anything else whilst writing. You could not hand a sheet of paper to a spectator and expect them to write on it without resting on something. The size of the card is very important since it may well screen the pencil from view if it is too large. The maximum size should be postcard size and from that you may work down to a normal visiting card. You will find the spectator invariably rests the visiting card in the palm of their hand—but the pencil remains clearly in view.

The alternative is to use paper BUT restrict the size or better, the danger of screening, by providing a rest for the spectator. Suppose you do not have a card with you and you want to pencil read. Tear a piece of paper into a piece about $4 \times 3''$ in size—THEN pick up something small for a rest and hand it to the spectator. Your wallet is about the right size—BUT your wallet or anything similar suggest a carbon impression apparatus—so preferably select something like a small book from their bookshelf; their wallet, their cigarette packet etc. In any event, do not approach the resting apparatus when you have no need to do so.

### (4) The Distance between you and the spectator

Here again it is a matter of proficiency and discretion. It should be obvious that the further away you are from the spectator who writes, the better it looks and the harder it is to do. Once you get the hang of it, you will amaze yourself that from some twenty feet away you can pencil read. I work more or less according to conditions, but when I have the choice I prefer a distance of ten to twelve feet away from the writer. You will also find that it is much easier to pencil read when the spectator is facing you—although you can do it from a side-on view.

### (5) Safety Checks to eliminate errors

When you get down to work at pencil reading, one of the first things you will do will be to study the pattern made by the hand and pencil when writing numbers. You will then find that there are cases where two numbers have very like patterns, such as, for example, six and nought. In order to combat this difficulty, I have devised a system of checking what was written—by means that do not inform the spectator what is happening. It is very simple—but practical:—

Suppose we are pencil reading. We hand the card and pencil to the spectator and request that he thinks of any number of three digits and writes them down. We watch in a casual manner and we *think* we see the number 356 written down. But shall we say that the last figure was doubtful—there is a suspicion that it could have been an "O"? We know the first two are correct—they happen to be almost unmistakable—but we are stuck on the last. So you proceed. "Now I would like you to do a bit of simple mental arithmetic please, simply add seven to the number you have chosen and then write down that total". Again you watch as the total is written and by that total you will know all the facts. If the spectator writes "363" you know it must have been 356, if they write "357" it must have been 350. Bear in mind also that since they can only write one of two figures for the total and *you know them both before they start*—it makes pencil reading a very simple matter to say the least.

You may think that by telling the spectator to add a number you are imparing the effect. If so, you have the option of turning to another spectator and asking them to call out the first number they think of—which is then added to the original figure. It would be obvious to any audience that the original figure could in no way be discovered by simply adding one digit at random. On top of this, you do not ask for the result of the addition—you tell it!

## (6) Pencil Reading of Numbers

If you have never done pencil reading, take my advice and start by working with numbers only. Get as many different people as you can to help you practice, it is no good working with one person only, you become accustomed to their style and very few people write the same way. Study the patterns made by writing the following numbers:—1, 2, 3, 4, 5, 6, 7, 8, 9, 0, and of these, pay particular attention to the numbers 2, 6, 7 and "0", these numbers have the most variations. Number nine is found to have two variations, one when it is drawn by one continuous curved line and two, a composite of curves and straight line. Both are easy to detect. Both four and five have the asset that they are invariably drawn in two stages, the pencil leaving the paper to complete the number—with most other numbers this does not happen—and very, very few people draw four or five in one line. In general, watch for curves and straight lines, bear in mind the time—as for example it takes less time to write "1" than it does "8", and last but not least do not make the mistake of assuming that everybody writes as you do yourself.

## (7) Pencil Reading Words

This is not easy, in fact it is very hard for a normal person but it can be done. To attempt to read any word written in any manner would be fool-hardy. You have far too many odds against you from the start; the word may be written or printed, may be one of millions and unlike our numbers you have 26 patterns to cope with and a much more extensive range of variations. If you are going to pencil read words, you must first alter the odds in your favour.

The first thing is to have the word printed in block letters—not written. The next thing is to confine the range of words so that to some extent you know what to expect. For example, ask your assistant to think of a girl's name and print it on the card. You have thereby limited the choice from millions to maybe a hundred. And let us suppose that you asked for a girl's name and that your first sighting showed you the letter "M"—before the next letter is written you can anticipate names like Mary, Maude, Muriel, Mavis, May and so forth—which has restricted the hundred down to perhaps a dozen. Now the odds are in your favour!

Another important approach to pencil reading words—is to make a habit of counting the number of letters as you go. Knowledge of the number of letters in the word can very often help to reveal what the word is; Suppose you were reading and were doubtful about the girl's name—was it "May" or was it "Mary"? If you had counted the letters you would know.

## (8) Pencil Reading by Position

This will be a lot easier to demonstrate than to tell you—so draw the numbers one to ten on a postcard in two rows of five and get a pencil. The

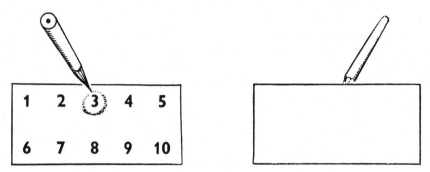

numbers, by the way, should be evenly spaced running more or less along the top and bottom edge of the card. Now hand the card to someone and tell them to look at the numbers and then to encircle any one they like. You will be able to tell which number they choose by the POSITION of the pencil on the card during writing. That is the principle, now we may progress it a step farther. Make a long list of say twenty cities of the world, and memorise it—or have a duplicate list. After a bit of practice, you will be able to tell any city that it underlined simply by watching carefully the position of the pencil when used.

## SUMMARY

Annemann states in one of his works (One Man Mental & Psychic Routine) which is one of the very few places which refer to Pencil Reading in print—"This is one of the most valuable accomplishments in the Mental Field. It takes practice, but is worth every minute spent". Annemann, as usual, is right. I have tried to make it a lot easier for you by giving all the important features of The Art, I honestly hope you will take the trouble to study and perform pencil reading because I know you will be very pleased with the trouble you have taken. As a last line on technique—I think it important to summarise the most likely means of success—that is practice.

## TRICKS ACCOMPLISHED BY THE ART OF PENCIL READING

### (1) "Get-outs Gallore"

If you want to do a trick where *it must work*—or when you happen to be nervous that one method may fail, you may like to try this effect—or principle that I have used. The trick can be a very simple plot; a person thinks of a word and writes it down. From thereon you must be sure to find out what that word is.

Stage one—you hand them any of the popular carbon impression apparatus to rest on while writing.

Stage two—you tell them to write their word and try to pencil read what is written. If you fail, you tell them to fold the paper in half and in half again.

and then proceed to perform the centre tear. (Step Six; on Billets tells you all about this) which brings you to:—

Stage three, you blunder this and fail to read the billet so you pick up the carbon impression apparatus—and read what they wrote! And when you pick that up and find the carbon paper was missing so it didn't work you calmly take out your Swami (Step One) and . . .

Stage four—pretend to write their word on a card, ask what it was then fill it in!!! If the Swami lead breaks, you go back to magic and learn up ways and means to vanish people—particularly mentalists!

## (2) Strange Coincidence

You and the spectator each have a card and a pencil. You suggest that for a change, he must try and read your mind. You pretend to write down a number and ask him to write down what he thinks you thought of—but watch to see what he writes. You fill in the number he has just written, which you see by pencil reading, then say you have written another—actually, as we say, you were writing his first. He writes his next number and you record that as your third and so on. You are in fact one behind him all the way. I credit this effect to Annemann who to my knowledge was the first to publish it in the book mentioned on page 33.

## (3) The Total Result

This particular effect I have devised is good for those wishing to use pencil reading without the necessity of staring at the writer all the time. You hand a card to one spectator and tell him to write any number at the top, then to pass it on to the next who adds a number underneath. It is passed like this from four to five spectators and finally handed to one who adds the total. Whilst the card is en tour from spectator to spectator—you have no need to look and when it reaches the final person then you turn and watch for the total to be written. By this time, the audience will have noted that you are not interested in what is being written and will be off guard at the last spectator.

## (4) A Debt Repaid

This makes a good item for drawing room work. It is quite easy to do and the plot is strong and amusing.

Hand a spectator the card and pencil, tell him to imagine that you owe him a sum of money—it can be as much as he likes—but since you are not a very rich man, suggest it be under £1,000 pounds. Tell him to write down the amount you owe him so that later you can sign it as an I.O.U. Note what he writes. Now tell him he is absent minded, and that he has forgotten to allow for some money you paid him back—tell him how much and have that deducted from his bill. Now you tell him to drop the bill in his pocket and come over to you. When he arrives you hold out your hand the fingers holding something which cannot be seen—and ask him how much you owe? He will say two shillings and a halfpenny—whereupon you open your hand and there it is in hard cash—which you give to him for his trouble! The method, in case you can't see it, is very easy. See what he writes in the first place and then mentally subtract from that amount enough to leave 2/0½d. as the amount outstanding. Call out the sum he must subtract and there you are.

## (5) The Swami and the Pencil

Using pencil reading in conjunction with a Swami Gimmick you can achieve some incredible effects.

You hold a card up and write something on it—but do not show for a moment. You hand the pencil with another card to a spectator and tell him this is silent thought transmission. You will ask him to think of various places in the world, preferably places he has visited, to watch you and when he sees you hold your hand up—to write down immediately the name of the place he has in mind. You stand still for a moment then hold up your hand, he writes you pencil read then fill in on your card with the Swami Gimmick. You have a miracle on your hands.

## PART TWO:  LIP READING

Lip Reading is the Art of watching a person's lips move when they are talking and by doing so, telling what they say. You do not hear what is said, you only see.

You know as well as I do that there are hundreds of incapacitated people in the world today, who are able to lip read with a very high degree of skill. I refer to deaf people who have been forced to learn lip reading; and some of these people have reached an amazing standard—up to the point where it is not infrequent for a good lip reader to be able to read from anybody they meet and at a considerable distance away from the speaker.

In the general run of things, it would not occur to a person gifted with the normal senses to attempt lip reading. However, from the point of view of the Mentalist it can be another means to an end.

You need not be concerned with learning to lip read up to the high standard we have just mentioned—but it is very handy to be able to decipher numbers and simple names. I think you will be surprised how much information you can acquire simply by watching two people talk. You have every chance to practice—since there is no shortage of people who talk! Study the way the lips move when the numbers one to nine are spoken and in no time you will be in a position to perform effects achieved by lip reading.

Just one final tip, practice with a friend who acts as the speaker and learn to lip read from full face and profile positions. Most of the time you will be using the profile or side view position. Do not allow your friend to try and help you by slowing up his speech or exaggerating his lip movements. You must learn to read the movements as they would be done naturally.

In part One, speaking about pencil reading, we stated that you can make your job a lot easier by limiting the choice—bringing the odds of success into your favour. The same applies to Lip Reading; by confining the subject you can anticipate to a large extent what may be said—the Lip Reading then becomes confirmation of your ideas and you are not obliged to guess wildly. The first effect will elucidate.

## TRICKS ACCOMPLISHED BY THE ART OF LIP READING
### (1) Any Card Called for

Somewhere in the vast mass of magic in print, this effect has been published. I read about it quite a long time ago and it was in fact the very thing that inspired me to try lip reading in the first place. I wish I could give full acknowledgement to the original source—but unfortunately I have lost trace of it so I will state that to whosoever invented the idea—I hand my sincere thanks.

The effect is this. You have in your hands a pack of cards. A spectator thinks of any card—he does not have to see the pack, whispers his choice to another spectator so as to confirm his selection then tells you he has made a final decision and has a card in mind. You do a "mental act" on him! After looking for all the world as though you were counting the brain cells in his cranium, you take from the pack one card and hold it high. You put the rest of the pack down. You now say "For the first time will you say what card you chose?" (It is not the first time—it is the second, but obviously you do not say so). Whereupon you show the only card you hold and that is it! Since you can do this anywhere at any time, with a borrowed pack and no preparation at all—we might fairly consider it to be a first class mental effect—what do you think?

The method as you will have guessed is observation. You wait until the spectator turns to whisper his choice to the next spectator and at that point you lip read. Really this is quite simple. To start with you have limited the choice to fifty two, fifty three with the joker and in all you have only to cope with eighteen possibilities; ten numbers, then Jack, Queen or King and four suits—which amount to seventeen, the joker being the last. Remember that people *always* say the value first—then "of" and end with the suit. When you find someone that says "Diamonds the four" you have met a magician! Fifty per cent of the people will say "The" in front of the value—don't mistake this for three.

An analysis of this effect would not be complete without mention of the means that may be introduced to cut out any number you find difficult to lip read. Suppose you keep slipping on six—just for example, well all you have to do is to take out all the sixes from the deck—which is then handed to the spectator who is asked to look at any card he sees . . . . as long as the pack does not appear unusual, it doesn't matter how many duplicates or missing cards you have. There is no justification for having the deck examined.

## (2) **Reconstructed Evidence**

Effect. Two spectators take part. One thinks of a geometric shape and the other thinks of a colour. The shape is then drawn in that colour on a slate. After it has been drawn it is shown to the audience but not to you. The slate is then well cleaned and people are invited to see that no trace of the original drawing remains. You are blindfolded and the slate is given to you. (You may prefer to do away with the blindfold and have it held behind your back). The test now is for you to try and reconstruct the picture that was on the slate—and as you run the fingers over the surface, you get impressions of shape and colour, eventually you name correctly the original design.

The method calls for several delicate steps. Provide two spectators with a slate and a piece of WHITE chalk. Start off by telling one of them to think of a *simple* geometric design, suggesting in other words the square, triangle, circle, rectangle and so forth—if you say "any" geometrical design you invite something like a "tetrahexagon" whereupon the other fellow has to work out just how many sides that monster should have! Make the suggestion of a simple design in an offhand—almost indifferent manner as though it is of no importance. When the first spectator has thought of one (don't give him much time) tell him to whisper it to the second man who should draw that shape on the slate. This having been done, you now tell the chap with the slate to hand it to number one and then ask him to think of a colour. When he has done this, he whispers that colour to number one, the fellow with the slate who takes up the chalk and writes the name of the colour in the design. You may turn your back whilst this is done and explain to the audience who are waiting that white chalk is used because you could easily see what colour was "thought of" if you had coloured chalks on the table. By now you know all the facts you have to know—having managed to lip read the design spoken to number two and the colour spoken to number one. You can therefore pay very little attention to the next stage of cleaning the slate and having it examined. It is more convincing if you have the design obliterated first by scribbling with chalk then rubbed out—but you must remember to say that you "feel a lot of scribbling—but there is a distinct design underneath . . ."

### (3) The Whispering Buddha

For this you will require, simply as a matter of presentation, a brass Buddha. You will find the "Made in Birmingham" variety can be purchased in England quite cheaply, or from abroad as "originals" quite expensively! If you cannot get a brass Buddha—you can use any small statue in place.

You must give this effect a great deal of build up. Before, during and after the trick, you do what professional mentalists call "spiel"—that is churn out a load of verbal nonsense that sounds good. Tell the story about the mystery of the Buddha—how people confess their sins and make their wishes to the Buddha—(which is true up to a point)—tell how it always seems as though Buddha sees all, hears all—and says nothing. (By the way—it was a brass Buddha not a brass monkey!!). Now with uncouth wickedness you infer that the Buddha may well talk—but only those who know how, can hear what it says. Suggest an experiment:—

"In a moment I will let you make a wish, no matter how silly this might appear to you—please do as I say. Take the Buddha and hold it in your left hand. It must be the left hand because that is the hand of fate and fortune—the hand which governs your destiny and the hand which is your success in life . . . now I want you to tell the Buddha a few facts—but these facts are private, they concern your life and you personally so you need only whisper into one ear of the Buddha. First introduce yourself, tell your name and what city of the world you were born in. Then give the Buddha an outline of your personal and occult likings—whisper your favourite colour—tell what you think is your lucky number. Buddha will want to know your occupation, so whisper the name of the work you do and how long you have been doing it. I think Buddha knows enough about you to be able to give a reasonable answer to any wish you have to make—if you have a personal trouble, worry or need—whisper it to the Buddha and we will see if you can get an answer".

Up to now, the inference has been that the Brass Buddha is going to do the talking at the end—well it is! Only it is going to tell you the answers! You ask to listen to what the Buddha has to say and from the substantial

37

amount you have learnt about your victim, you dish him up with a very bright future and weave in the facts he has presented as though they were told to you by Buddha. You have been lip reading his talk to the Buddha, and know at least something about the spectator. You should know his name, the city where he was born—and therefore his nationality, his favourite colour—his lucky number, his job and how long he has been at it—from which you may judge his position. and you may know his wish or trouble. The latter, being the most he had to say may have been missed—but this makes no difference since a sure-fire prediction covers that angle. Make the answer to his wish or trouble—strictly favourable. Tell him "things are around the corner—he will soon know what you mean"—and be careful that you do not commit yourself to stating any facts.

I have used the word "him" referring to this effect, but it may equally as well be performed on a "her"—in fact most ladies would love it.

## PART THREE: SOUND READING

Sound reading is the Art of listening to the noises made by something being done, and by telling from those noises what it is. This may apply to an action or to something being written. You do not see what the action is.

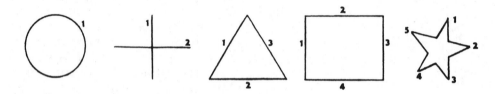

### (1) Written Information discovered by Sound Reading

A few years ago I was holding a seance to demonstrate fraudulent medium-ship at the Magic Circle Headquarters in London. I was half way through the programme and had reached a point where "E.S.P." tests were being conducted. I was under what may honestly be called "test conditions"—blindfolded, seated in a chair some distance from a blackboard upon which members of the gathering were to draw various E.S.P. designs. The test conditions as such didn't worry me very much because I had made preparation to use a special electronic apparatus to convey the information to me. The first design was drawn and I "received" it, before the next was selected my electronic apparatus was inadvertently disconnected from the mains and I was stuck. It was the fault of my negligence and not the apparatus which was foolproof if allowed to work properly. Anyway, I thought the next best thing to saying I was due to go wrong—was to guess—so I waited. The next committeeman went to the board and on it he drew a square. Without thinking how I knew—I also duplicated his design—and immediately realised I could hear, and from what I could hear—I could tell which of the five possible designs they would choose.

I relate this story because I would like you to know that I am not suggesting "grand theory" when I write about Sound Reading; it is very easy, very practical and it has been tried and tested with favourable results.

Since the days when I first encountered sound reading by accident, I have made a careful study of the Art and the following facts will help you to do it the easiest way with the best results:—

(a) Have the writing done with chalk on a blackboard.

(b) As with Pencil Reading and Lip Reading, confine the subject.

(c) Have the designs drawn very big.

(d) Stick to using designs which make different noises when being written.

(e) Keep within a sensible hearing distance of the blackboard (or slate).

(d) Confine your attempts to reading certain designs and numbers only.

## The Designs to Use

When you Sound Read, you listen for three things. First you listen for *curves* which make a different sound from *straight lines*. Second you listen for straight lines which make a different sound from curves and last you listen for "breaks" or pauses in the writing (*i.e.* in order to draw the number 4, most people start by drawing an "L" then remove the chalk and come back again to cross it downwards to complete the figure; you get the break in between the two stages). On a piece of paper draw the following designs:— A circle, a cross, a triangle, a square and a star. Observe that the following analysis is correct. The circle is composed of one line, more often than not drawn in one continuous movement. The cross is composed of two lines which makes it necessary to make a break when drawing. (It can be drawn without the break but only by going over the same line twice which is not done). The triangle is composed of three straight lines—which may be drawn in continuation or with two breaks. You will however get audible pauses at each corner. The square has four straight lines—drawn continuously or with three breaks; sometimes the square is drawn with two breaks effected by drawing two letter "L's". The star is recognised by the *time* it takes to be drawn, which is more than the others and by the considerable amount of drawing involved.

Now if you care to get out a slate and a piece of chalk and have a friend draw any of these designs whilst you turn your back and listen, you will find that without any practice—you will score a good 75% correct. With practice you can get 99% correct.

## The Numbers to Use

If you have to rely on the differentiation between the sound of curves and straight lines coupled with breaks, you cannot use all the numbers available because some sound too much alike. Those which are not likely to sound similar are:—1, 3, 4, 5, 6, 7, 8. Two is omitted because it sounds like seven when written, and nine because it sounds like six or seven depending on how you write it. Fortunately, you can tell after some practice the following letters of the alphabet: C.H.S.D. which means that numbers, although incomplete are of use—since playing cards can be used to confine the choice and of the fifty-two available only eight number or spot cards have to be removed and a simple instruction covers the court cards which can be left in the deck: "Choose any card you like—but to avoid complexity, I advise you to ignore the court cards".

## (2) Sound Reading Applied to Action—Not Writing

In addition to using sound reading to discover a written number or shape drawn on a board, there are other principles which are of use to the Mentalist.

When we have a trick which is accomplished by sound reading something that is done by the spectator, we call it action. For example, one of the tricks on the market today is based on the sound caused by paper being unfolded:

Archie Byford has invented a Living and Dead test which goes as follows:— Five pieces of paper are handed to the spectator, on four he writes the names of living people and on the fifth the name of a dead person. The spectator then screws up each piece into a small ball and mixes them before handing to another. That second person unfolds the paper balls one at a time and holds each slip to their forehead. At one point you stop them—and declare that they are holding the dead name slip in their hand at that moment. This 2nd spectator does not know which is the dead name so could not help you—and the other confirms it to be correct. At no time have you handled the paper slips after the effect was commenced. The method which I am able to tell you by courtesy of Archie Byford the inventor, and L. Davenport & Co.—who supply the special papers required, is very simple and is a good example of action sound reading. Four slips of paper are the same and one is different. The difference is that the two types of paper used make a clearly definable sound when unfolded and the two types make *different* sounds. In fact four unfold quietly and one, being of different texture, makes considerable noise. It is the noise of this one, which has the dead name on it, that enables you to perform the trick.

Then we have another aspect of action sound reading. Three boxes are on a table, the performer turns his back whilst a spectator drops a coin into any box and then locks it. You know which box contains the coin. This time the method is sound reading of "clicks" either one, two or three, which are made by each box being especially constructed or "designed" for that purpose. As the box is locked it makes a clicking noise, the first box will click once as the key turns, the next twice and so on. A poor man's version of this effect may be constructed by having three boxes which are respectively lined in their bases with tin, wood and baize. You are able to tell from the noise of the coin falling on to the base into which box it has been locked. In fact it may be as well to mention that with sufficient practice, it is possible to tell the value of any English coin by the noise it makes when it is placed on a hard surface—such as a polished table.

Another application of sound reading is one that is quite well known and some writers have claimed that it has been used extensively. I refer to spinning a coin into the air—and telling by sound whether it will fall heads or tails. The coin, in this country a penny, is faked with a small nick at the edge on one side only. If the nick is made on the tail side, after the coin had slowed down and just before it stops spinning, it will give off a different tone when it is going to land tail side up. The variation in sound is caused by the coin beginning to spin or travel on the imperfect edge. It is better to spin the coin on a hard flat surface rather than throw it into the air which does not assure the correct spinning position required. You will have to accustom yourself to the "head" noise and the "tail" noise and be able to tell the difference—which is not so difficult. Even if you slip up once or twice —you will change the odds of a fifty-fifty gamble to 90 to 1 in your favour— not bad gambling odds!

Last but not least we have a considerable range of code systems for two person telepathy which are based on the transmission of sound. To mention two of the applicable ones, signals given by way of a chair that creaks, and the well known "finger-click" transmission, caused by pressing the first finger nail against the thumbnail. However, we shall not deal too deeply with these things as they are not regarded as true examples of sound reading.

To summarise Sound Reading as a principle of Mentalism we can say that like seeing for Pencil Reading and Lip Reading, it is a question of using your natural ability to advantage. The essential thing is to practice, experiment and always try to improve your ability.

## TRICKS ACCOMPLISHED BY THE ART OF SOUND READING

### (1) Tapping Card Location

Three people devised this effect, Alex Elmsley, Jon Tremaine and myself. We were discussing sound reading and as a result of the conversation we devised the following effect.

A deck of cards is borrowed and given a mix. During the mixing you note the bottom card. You then proceed to do the Hindu shuffle, but hold a break with four cards on the bottom of the deck. The spectator calls stop during the shuffle and you show the bottom card which we shall say is the queen of hearts. As soon as you have shown this card and the spectator has been asked to remember it—you complete the shuffle and end by throwing the four "controlled" cards on top of the deck. By this action you have forced the queen of hearts and positioned it four cards down from the top. The deck may now be given a false shuffle or false cut before it is handed to the spectator. When he is given the pack he is told to deal cards face down from the top in a row on the table. After seven cards have been dealt, you stop him casually by saying, "I think that will be sufficient". Next you hand him a pencil and instruct him very clearly to wait until you turn your back, then to start from either end of the row he likes and to tap on the cards with the pencil—two or three times on each card. You turn your back and wait. From the handling of the cards, you know that the queen of hearts is in the middle of the row of seven—from either end. However, you must stop him *when* he is actually tapping that card—and since he is allowed to tap as often as he likes it is not a question of counting but rather a matter of listening for the distinct "sound breaks" that occur as he stops tapping on one card and starts on the next. That is why it is important that he taps down the row without missing any cards. You listen carefully and wait until you have heard three breaks and the tapping which follows this must be done on the face down queen. When he reaches this card, you call—"tap that one again please" (as though it mattered) and then say—"drop the pencil on that card please to mark it for a moment". You turn round, gather up the other six cards first—to make it less obvious that his card was central from either end, ask him to name the card "he thought of" (which you forced) and turn over the queen to show that it is his card.

The effect takes much longer to describe than to perform and it will withstand some pretty shrewd thinking before the means is discovered.

### (2) Paranormal Precognition

This is a stage effect which presented well, will cause quite an amount of controversy as to the means by which it was done.

You require a fairly large blackboard, five cards with the designs mentioned on page 38 drawn on them, some white chalk and a table to rest the board on when performing.

Two spectators are asked to take part. One is asked to hold the blackboard upright whilst it stands on say a card table—with the edge facing the audience. He should be told to hold it firmly so that writing may be done on both sides at once. Next you take the five sign cards and show them to the audience as all different. You then hand them to the second spectator and give him a piece of chalk. He is then told to stand on one side of the board, whilst you go and stand on the other; the audience can see both of you.

You start by telling the spectator to take any of the five cards and to draw the chosen design in the middle of the board. Next he chooses another card and adds that design on top of the one he has just drawn, then another which he puts underneath—and drawn so that it just joins the middle drawing, then one more to *his right* (your left) and finally to his left. All designs have therefore been drawn in an order chosen by the spectator. When it comes to the last one which you know before he draws, draw it to the right and then stand back and give the final instruction. The complex structure of the finished drawing helps considerably to misdirect from the fact that only five designs were offered. In many cases your audience will presume by forgetfulness that you duplicated a compound geometrical drawing. Page 38 gives you all the information you need to know about sound reading designs drawn on a blackboard.

### (3) A Pocket Trick

This is a very old effect which is still good enough to fool those unacquainted with the secret.

You have two small coloured pencils—say red and blue. One of them is hollow inside and has a small piece of solder or a little mercury in it. The hole is sealed at the end so that the fake pencil looks the same as the real one. Both pencils are given to a spectator who is asked to drop any one into a matchbox (they just fit) and close it, then to hide the other one from view. You can always tell what colour is in the box simply by picking it up and turning the box the other way up. If it is the fake pencil, you will hear a little noise as the weight falls to the other end of the pencil—and you will get the feel of the impact—which although very little is easily detectable. With the genuine pencil nothing happens of course. It is considered necessary to use some misdirection when handling the matchbox so, if, when you turn round he has it in his hands, take it and place it on the table—reading as you do so; or if it is on the table, place it in his hands—reading again during the necessary movement.

### (4) Clean Cut Card Trick

A deck of cards is fanned and a spectator told to look at any card he likes and remember it. He is then handed a slate and told to write the name of his card on it. You pick up the pack and remove one card, he then shows his slate and you show the card. They are the same. See page 38.

### PART FOUR: TOUCH READING

Touch Reading is the Art of gaining information by feel or sense of touch. The Art is used quite a lot by mentalists and magicians in one way or another —but it is not always recognised as being touch reading. A good example of this is, of course, the common pocket index for playing cards.

Since the basis of touch reading is the same in all cases, and the technique only varies, we will content ourselves with a selection of tricks which utilise the principle so that a fair indication of its value may be given.

# TRICKS ACCOMPLISHED BY THE ART OF TOUCH READING

## (1) Sujan Location

This principle may be applied to several tricks. It is already used for two or three items on the market. Obtain five pieces of coloured card which are all of the same thickness. Each of the five pieces should be of a different colour. Make up a solution of starch in water and mix to a fairly thick paste. Then with a clean brush, paint across each card in a straight line about half-an-inch wide from any two opposing diagonals. That is, for example, from the top left corner in line through the middle to the bottom right corner. Allow each card thus treated to dry whereupon the starch will become invisible. The effect of this treatment is that two corners of the card will become stiff—while the remaining two are normal or soft. The cards may now be trimmed to a convenient size—say playing card size. If you like the effect which can be done with these cards, you would be advised to purchase a good supply from your favourite dealer—those marketed by dealers are of a high standard compared with the usual home made jobs. If you take the top right-hand corner of any card and bend it back very slightly, you will feel a certain tension—either stiff or soft. Arrange all the cards with the stiff corners at top right and bottom left. Place the cards in a row on the table and invite any person to turn one over while you turn your back. Now it makes no difference which way they turn, that is from top to bottom or left to right, because either way will bring the soft corner of that card into the position just occupied by the stiff corner. The cards are now gathered up by the spectator (to prove that the effect is not achieved by noting special positions) and handed to you after they have been carefully mixed. Your job is to locate the card that was reversed. Take them all and deal them in a row once more, and as you do so hold each card by the top right corner and bend it back a bit as you place it down. You will find it very easy to tell which one is their card because of the tension on the odd card against the other four. Now take the spectator by the hand, and move his fingertips along the row several times passing his card—but eventually stopping at it and declaring that it is the one he selected.

After this, the first suspicion to enter the mind of any onlooker is that the cards are marked—which would be a solution. You therefore do it again—but this time seal each card in a paypacket. Even though the cards are in the envelope—the stiff and soft corner principle is easy to detect. Finally, if you like the principle, you should get in touch with the Supreme Magic Co. in Devon, England who have a very clever effect called "The Ultimate Living and Dead Test" which is based on this principle.

## (2) With a Pinch of Salt!

There are dozens of tricks based on this principle, we will give you a new one to demonstrate the technique. The effect is a version of 'Just Chance'—but it has features which, as a mentalist, you may find attractive. It is not likely to be copied by any who do not understand the handling properly—because one slip and you lose your money. No slips—and you are as safe as you will ever be.

### Impromptu "Just Chance" by Corinda.

When you arrive somewhere and someone asks you to perform a trick—and you have nothing with you—of the fifty or so good tricks you could do—this is one. Borrow three envelopes. Request the help of two sporting people to take part in a gamble in which they cannot lose. From your wallet remove a £5 note (or £1, according to your wealth). Seat one spectator to your left and one to the right. Start by explaining to all that you intend to have the five pound note sealed in one of the three envelopes, in the other two will be a piece of newspaper the same size as the note—once the envelopes are sealed and mixed, no one will know which contains the money. To be sure that you have no choice in the matter—hand the £5 note and the three envelopes with two scraps of newspaper to one of the spectators—and tell them to seal the note in one and put paper in the others. All envelopes should be the same, all are sealed by the spectator, and while this is done, you turn your back! Now we will explain the method so that the last stages can be followed with a complete understanding of the effect.

Before you introduce the trick, a few seconds preparation has to take place. You take a small bead, or, break the tip off a pencil and use that; this you fix to one corner of the £5 note with selotape. It is held firmly there and cannot be seen since your thumb covers it when showing both sides of the note at the onset. Having produced the note and shown it to be genuine, fold it in half—as if demonstrating what should be done with the pieces of newspaper. Then fold in half again and be sure that the bead is folded  inside. Hand the note and the papers to be placed in envelopes. You will note that regardless of the fact you cannot see where the note goes, you have a very secure check because when you handle the envelopes as you will—the bead may be felt with ease. Thus touch reading locates the whereabouts of your money.

The next step in the routine is to state quite honestly that all the envelopes have been sealed and mixed by the spectator. The second spectator is now given all three and told to choose one, this he keeps and hands you back two. Before giving the first spectator the choice of one of these, feel on both envelopes for the bead, the chances are two to one that you have it in your hands and if so, you use the simplest possible force you know to make the first spectator take the dud envelope. If you do not have it—then you know who does and must get it. You approach this problem by first and foremost conducting the normal "Just Chance" procedure of advising a change of mind. If this comes off—and you should try and be very convincing, stay put with the one he gives you having checked by touch reading that you are right and have the fiver. However, rather than end the presentation abruptly—offer the chance for both spectators to change before you settle—that exchange cannot effect you. However, we have one thing more to contend with—what happens if he cannot be persuaded to swap for your dud? Then you have two more options, maybe you can get him to exchange with the other spectator then you work on him, or, you perform the bare hand envelope switch advised by Corinda in Step Four. To run through that manoeuvre briefly.

Approach the spectator in the following manner, "Now sir, I will give you the chance once more—and this must be your final decision—will you have this envelope in place of yours?" He replies "No thanks". You smile as though very pleased with his reply and answer, "Right, that's it! And to show you how wrong you were I intend to let you see how I knew this one (yours) had the money in it—look". You hold your envelope in the right hand and raise it to the light showing the shadow of the contents. "You see the way the contents are folded? Well that's how you know the note! Now take a look at yours—". Here you reach forward and take his from his hand—don't ask—take. You hold his up to the light whilst holding your own in the left hand for a moment. "You see your envelope has a small shadow (immediately bring the hand down putting the envelope on top of your one and then lifting that very same one back again) whilst my one has a large one". To all intents and purposes what happened was this, you showed him yours first, then showed him his, then showed him yours again and gave him back his. That all sounds very complicated but it takes thirty seconds to do—if that, and any fool could do it. For all that it is amazingly convincing. By now you have his envelope with the money whether he likes it or not. Again you end with offering both spectators the chance to swap with each other.

To climax the proceedings, the envelopes are to be opened. First the spectator on your left—then the one on your right. Whilst this is done you place your envelope on the floor in front of you. When both newspapers have been shown, invite both spectators to come forward and open your envelope and see that you did indeed leave the five pound note in circulation. You did!

### (3) Marked Playing Cards

According to John Scarne, who may be regarded as good authority, the marking of playing cards so that they can be indentified by touch, is an old gamblers' ruse. The markings are made with a pin or tack; it is only necessary to make a very small prick to mark the card. To read the marking, you must run the finger over the surface of the card and the "bump" will be felt with ease. This process is called "Pegging" and apart from pin-pricks made directly through the card, other methods have been devised. Another, for example, is to make minute notches along the edge of the card. By running the fingernail down the edge it will be found that the notch is easily felt. Several people have worked out systems of marking a complete pack of cards both by Pegging and Notching so that every card could be indentified by touch reading alone. Further reference to this matter will be found in "Scarne on Cards" by John Scarne.

### (4) Psychic Sorting

Take an ordinary pack of playing cards and discard the two jokers. Divide the blacks from the reds. With a razor blade make a minute "V" shaped notch two-thirds of the way down on the right-hand long edge, and two-thirds of the way up the left-hand edge, on everyone of the *Red* cards. This having been done, sort the reds into two piles, hearts and diamonds. Take the hearts only and make on every card another very small notch, this time opposite the other notches which now take the shape of a square. Finally, divide the thirteen hearts into odd cards and even cards. Regard the Jack as eleven (odd) the queen as twelve (even) and king as thirteen (odd). Take all the even hearts and make another notch in the middle of the top and bottom short edge. The diagram below shows you the markings as they would appear on three cards. The notches illustrated have been considerably enlarged to show their position:—

## Showing Notch Positions on Face Down Cards

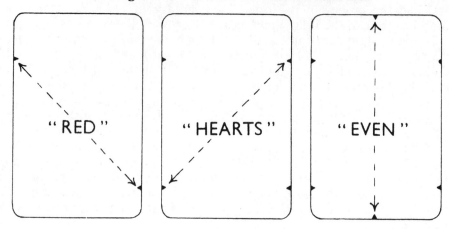

The system of marking given above was originally conceived by me and was intended for the market as a trick pack called The Ghost Deck. Whilst in the experimental stage, I consulted a person whom I regard as a card expert and it was his opinion that the deck would not be very useful for card magic. In time I learnt to agree—but since then I have found it a very convenient standby for mentalism. It is to be understood that the notches are so small that they are practically imperceptible. You do not have to see them, you feel them. The exact handling is as follows: to read any card it must be held either naturally or out of sight (we will come to that later). For natural handling, take the card, face downwards in the right hand with thumb on top and face resting on the bended fingers below. With the first finger you run the *nail* down the edge of the card—not the ball of the finger, but the nail as though pointing directly at the edge and as you pass the notch you will feel a very distinct bump. This "reading" movement may be made in the fraction of time that it takes to deal a card on to the table.

Now to simplify the reading process, you make no attempt to read all the notches at once, this would involve a dangerous amount of finger movement and is by no means essential. The following effect indicates quite clearly a typical example of handling and application for mental magic.

The complete deck is used for one or two effects and then handed to a spectator to mix thoroughly. It is as well to do a couple of tricks first which tends to neutralise the suspicion that a special deck was produced for the effect. As long as the edges of the cards are dirty, the spectator has no chance of seeing the markings. You have no reason to ask for the cards to be examined.

When they have been mixed you take the pack and hold it behind your back. Then you immediately bring forward cards one at a time and place them face up on the table in two piles. Before you actually turn the card to place it on one of the piles—you declare its colour. "This is a red one—and

46

this is a black one" etc. Half way through, you stop, have the remainder reshuffled and hold them above your head where all but you can see. You continue to sort them into blacks and reds. This should be done with all the speed you can muster without becoming inaccurate. As soon as you have 26 reds in one pile and 26 blacks in another, pick up the red ones and proceed to shuffle them—inviting the spectator to shuffle the blacks. You will not use the blacks, but you do want the spectator to have them in his hands because in a moment, while sorting hearts from diamonds, he will examine those black cards (they do every time!) and he is going to find them all ordinary—because they are all ordinary.

"Let me go a step farther, which will you choose next—black or red?" Whatever he answers—you keep the red. "Black" he may say, so you reply "right, take the black and try and do as I do with the reds—guess the suits". Or he may reply "red"—whereupon you say "very well, let me see if I can find the different suits". The classic phrase "That leaves" does not enter the conversation!

When is what necessary for you to decide one factor—black from red, you had only to concern yourself with the position of one notch. The one that indicated colour—so your finger should have been guided to within half an inch of that point before it actually touched the card. You do not have to go through the unnatural motion of running the finger down the full length of the card. Our next concern is to differentiate between two red suits, this we do by approaching the suit indicator or notch (see diagram 2). The cards are again mixed—first by you, then after a few have been dealt into two piles, a little more mixing is allowed by the spectator. As a diversion at this point, you may take the deck below table level, bringing the cards up one at a time and naming them before they reach sight.

Finally we have two piles, each contains thirteen cards of one suit. By the same means as was used to force the reds from the blacks, you now force the hearts so that you may divide the odd from the even. You do not encourage the spectator to handle the diamond pile as they are faked. Normally they will have had enough of examination after running through the blacks earlier on—so simply place them on the bottom of the black cards. Run through the odd and even sorting and when complete infer that you could now go the last step and name each card individually. By now they will have had enough—but you are in a very favourable position to perform a master move of magic. Pick up the red cards and add them to the bottom of the deck. Take the full pack and give it a good false shuffle. Immediately proceed to perform "Out of this World" which, in the circumstances, could not be a better effect. By the time the spectator has sorted the cards themselves you have finished a pretty good routine that's going to take a lot more sorting out before the method is uncovered! (Note: Paul Curry's "Out of this World" may be obtained from your favourite dealer; should you be one of few people who do not know it—my advice is hasten to get it now).

### (5) Colour Conscious

Using the Ghost Deck described above, divide the cards into black and red to start. Have any red card chosen and placed by the spectator amid the blacks. Holding the cards under the table, you quickly locate it and then count how many cards are on top of it. Square up the pile and bring it to the table top putting it down in the middle of the table and saying "That's funny, I'm sure I could do it—lend me a bit of paper, I must see where I went wrong". Take any bit of paper and quickly jot down a few meaningless calculations—ending up with the announcement "I cannot understand it—my calculations show it must be the fifteenth card from the top" (for fifteen, insert however many cards were above the red). "Would you check it once more please"—hand the pile to the spectator who counts down to the fifteenth card and finds it is the red one. Within five seconds you are going to have everyone who can add two and two trying to work out how you can calculate the position of the red!

I should mention that the cards when dealt by the spectator should be placed face down on the table, the last one of the count then turned over and shown. If they are dealt face up, it looks very suspicious that you get a run of fourteen blacks before you reach the first red—which happens to be theirs!

## (6) Another Version of The Princess Card Trick

From the ghost deck remove the following four cards: Ace of Spades, Five of Diamonds, Seven of Hearts and Eight of Hearts. Make these four cards into a fan and have any one mentally selected. Next have the four cards mixed by the spectator and handed to you in a pile face downwards. Before you start the effect you should have one extra card in your lap—the rest of the deck is on the table. Take the mixed cards and hold them below table level. Say that you think you can tell two things, the mentally selected card and which of the four it is. Keep all four below but bring up the extra card without showing it—and say that is the one you think was the chosen card—place it face down in the middle of the table and cover with your handkerchief. Ask now for the chosen card to be named—and while recapping on what has happened you feel for their card amid the four held below the table. Immediately you find it—drop it in the lap and bring up the left-hand palm upwards and empty. An instant later the right hand brings up the three other cards and drops them on the outstretched left palm in a face down position. This hand now extends to pass the three cards to the spectator to check. Whilst the left hand goes forward with the cards, the right returns to the lap picks up the selected card and palms it—then comes up again, goes to the hankie in the middle of the table and the left hand, now empty because the spectator has taken the cards lifts the corner allowing the right to move under a bit and appear to take out the card. The palmed card is withdrawn and thrown face down to the spectator who goes to turn it over, allowing you a fraction of time to pick up the hankie and the tabled card and place same into your pocket. There are no sleights in this routine; the moves given are all natural and the handling is such that both hands have been shown empty at a vital point. The last point is to explain that the four cards we name are each distinctive in the Ghost Deck. To find the Ace of Spades, check immediately for the "red" notch only. For the Five of Diamonds—feel in the "red" and "Hearts" position, if is "red" only—it must be diamond. For the Seven of Hearts check the "Hearts" and "even" position only—if it is "Hearts" only it must be the Seven. For the Eight of Hearts—the only even card, check "Even" only. It is as well to do the checking before you pretend to remove the chosen card (the fifth) so that their order is known and as soon as the chosen card is named you can drop it to the lap immediately.

48

### (7) **Another Application of the Touch Reading Envelope**

It is an easy matter to slip a few grains of sugar (white granulated sucrose) into an envelope, and it is just as easy to feel the sugar grains through the envelope. The ability to identify one envelope by touch puts you in a position to perform many effects. To give you some examples, the envelope can be used for identifying the right key in the "Seven Keys to Baldpate" mental effect. It can be used to identify a "plant" question when performing a series of "Question and Answer" effects—the plant envelope allows you to get a "One-ahead" system in operation. It can be of use for several versions of the "Living and Dead" test, where it contains the only dead name amid several living ones, and it will serve to locate a playing card sealed from view and mixed with other envelopes containing cards.

According to the effect I vary the technique of using grains of sugar. If the envelopes are very thick—the heavy manilla kind, it is as well to use a small bead in place of sugar; if the envelopes are ordinary the sugar is quite adequate. To make the touch reading part much easier, I frequently stick the grains inside in one corner with selotape. However, some effects require that you tip out the sugar to have the envelope examined, so then it must be loose inside. If you consider, it would be quite a simple matter to work out an index system with envelopes and sugar. A simple version would be to have grains in four separate corners of four envelopes. You are then able to identify four envelopes by the position of the sugar, and, as we have said, the grains may be fixed in position with selotape.

As an example of the value of this idea, suppose you were doing an effect which ended in such a way that the spectator would name one of four cards. To cover all, possible contingencies, you had four envelopes each containing one of those cards. Suppose it was necessary that you had all four in one pocket, so now we come to the vital point. The card is named and you produce one envelope—that envelope is supposed to contain their card. Can I ask you quite honestly, how many times have you seen a performer go astray here—and because his index system was unreliable or without safety checks, he got the wrong envelope? You need never have the embarrassment of that situation because you can check that you are right by feel. Do not make the error of supposing that a grain of sugar is too small to bother with; the grain touch reading principle is one of the valuable standbys of mental magic. Moreover, the last example will serve to illustrate my contention that when you are sure a trick will work, you can relax and devote more attention to presentation and less worry to technical points. A Mentalist must irradiate an air of confidence which cannot be achieved when you are not confident. You cannot be too fussy when it comes to getting your tricks in working order—take my advice and always know what you would do if a trick went wrong—before it goes wrong; and better still—work on it to make it so perfect that it can hardly fail. It was my pleasure to witness a failure performed by a well known mentalist and I say it was a pleasure because I think that about three people out of many hundreds knew the trick went wrong. When it failed he continued his presentation twisting the result so skillfully that the audience presumed that his climax was the climax intended —such nerve, presence of mind, skill and knowledge make that man one of the greatest in my opinion. The only time you can appreciate his ability, is when you have failed with a trick whilst performing—and know what it is like. Let it be an example not a story.

# PART FIVE: MUSCLE READING

There have been a lot of books written about Contact Mind Reading or Muscle Reading, some of them propound absurd theories as to the way in which it works and others seem to make sense. I do not propose to offer reasons or causes to explain why it works, I would rather content myself with thinking it is a form of suggestion and, more important, the so-called impulses which guide you are purely physical. As far as I am concerned, it is a variety of touch reading and I'm not going to do anything more than give you the technique of one method. The method I use and the method which I find works. If you wish to explore the whole field of Contact Mind Reading, you would be advised to consult a specialised work on the subject. Edward Dexter's "Contact Mind Reading" is a good starting place.

The easiest way to understand Muscle Reading is to try it, so start right away with a couple of experiments. Get a friend to help, an outsider is just as good, if not better. Tell him to hide a penny anywhere he likes in the room —but instruct him that it should be within reasonable reach and not hidden on his person. When he has done that, he should come and stand by the door and call out to you that he is ready. You wait outside and don't peep!!

When he calls out "ready" you come in. Some people now say you should look at his feet to see which way they are pointing to act as a starting guide. In my experience, the subject does his best to face anywhere but where the coin is hidden so I should forget it. When you arrive, take the subject by the left arm, put his hand with fingers outstretched on your hand. Support the weight of his arm with your other hand and tell him to relax, bend his arm at the elbow and let you carry the weight. Now position your right hand over his wrist and hold it fairly loose. Before you move an inch with him, start the mental propaganda! Tell him you *must* have his co-operation, that the success of the experiment depends entirely on his will power to make you go to the coin. Tell him that he must not attempt to lead you— just relax the arm and forget about it—but keep saying to himself—"Its under the clock—we must go this way" etc., etc. Proceed to walk him slowly to the middle of the room and when you get there say, "Now forget for the moment the exact location—just concentrate on the *direction* from here—say to yourself, we must go towards the fireplace" etc. When you have done this, look carefully at his hand and very, very gently push it in one direction, if you feel him resist—try another direction, but if you feel no resistance, go that way. The whole art depends on your ability to tell when he is stopping you or letting you go on. It is not a conscious movement on his part—it is probably the result of autosuggestion—but what matters is that you do get this resistance or encouragement from the subject. When you become an expert, you will be able to tell the

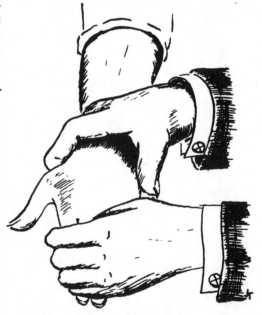

path without the gentle push to test the direction—the encouragement will be enough to guide you, but to start with apply this technique.

Having got some idea of the first direction, you now work on the place. Move him towards the mantlepiece and when you get there say, "Now we must deal with an exact area, imagine we are drawing a line from your hand to the penny, will me to move along that line". Almost immediately you will find his hand moves slightly in the desired direction—but frequently it does not indicate the height at which the object is hidden. Suppose you arrive at a bookcase, you now say "We must deal with the height—say to yourself, we must go up or we must go down to find the penny—keep saying it". Sometimes it helps if you tell him to close his eyes when he is very near to the object. This confirms that you are on the right trail without asking "Am I hot?" When you finally feel convinced it is within a certain area—say a shelf, use your left hand to touch objects—but do not lift them until the right hand, holding his wrist, gives you a distinct tug. When you touch anything very near to the coin and he can see you do it, the movement on his part is very strong—then you lift the obstacle and there should be the penny underneath. His eyes should be open for the very last stages—he need only close them whilst he concentrates on telling you where to go.

It is almost certain that you will fail to get positive results if your subject treats the matter as a joke. He must do as you say—and should be serious. When you have worked with several people, you will find that there are good and bad subjects. Some seem so sensitive that you find the object at an incredible speed; others are not so good. The worst type is the person who deliberately misleads you—but you will soon learn to spot any fakers. The best subject is a person who believes that you can do it—like hypnosis, if they believe—half the battle is won. As for the sympathetic subject who thinks you are a crank and helps you with an occasional pull in the right direction—well, they get you out of trouble—but don't do your ego or your personal progress any good, because you cannot learn to do it when you are being guided.

There is a particular feature of Contact Mind Reading that should appeal to the Mentalist. It amounts to this: when you have discovered the hiding place of the object, and you are quite sure it is there, you have no need to say so immediately. In fact, when the chance occurs, you would be wise to wait your time, continue the presentation so that the climax appears to be nothing short of an impossibility. The following example will serve to illustrate the procedure.

We shall suppose that a penny was concealed in a room, and that you have gone through the preliminary steps and arrived at the "very near" stage. We shall say that your attention becomes directed to one shelf, in moving the hand over the articles you may have noticed that one of them was not standing flat on the shelf. You may even be able to see the edge of the coin. Taking into consideration the places it could be hidden and the places which were improbable or impossible, you could arrive at a pretty firm decision. Instead of making the final move—and saying that you have found the penny, you go on. Without showing any signs of your discovery, slowly move away and lead the subject to another spot as though you had missed it. Then, lead the subject to the centre of the room and announce that you are having great difficulty so you will try by another method. Let go of the arm and tell the subject to stand with their eyes closed, and to concentrate on the exact spot where the coin is hidden. After due deliberation, and having apparently read their thoughts, you declare the exact spot and allow another person to go and collect the penny and show it to all.

If you would like to make a habit of this form of presentation, and it is indeed a very good method, you may resort to an old dodge which helps very often to see where the article is hidden. You use a threepenny bit instead of a penny, the first being substantially thicker causes a wider gap under the article when it is stood directly over the coin. Of course, this does not effect cases where the coin is dropped into something.

### Advanced Forms of Contact Mind Reading

Since this work cannot hope to deal with a comprehensive study of Muscle Reading, we shall give mention to some advanced forms of the Art and deal briefly with them.

### The Copper Wire Contact

Some exponents of muscle reading are said to be capable of judging the impulses from the subject when the only contact between you and him is a length of copper wire. You each hold an end. I have not seen this done successfully, but I have it on good authority that it has been done and can be done. One specialist would make a point of going anywhere in town from the theatre—leading the subject to the place where a borrowed ring was hidden. Sometimes he walked, sometimes he sat with the subject in a cab (horse drawn) and would order the cabby to turn in the desired direction. It is claimed, and I believe it to be true, that his information was gained from the subject via contact mind reading with a copper wire. The distance involved was quite frequently more than a mile.

### Action with the Chosen Object Following Location

Another advanced technique is to have an object chosen for the test and then to have the committee decide upon some specific action that must be done with that object. I can offer first hand information on this subject, having had the pleasure of watching a well known Mentalist perform the test. On quite a number of occasions, I have had him in my studio conducting various experiments and tests which I proposed. On one occasion, in the company of a group of well known magicians we decided to try him out. He was sent from the room and did not know what test was proposed and had no assistants. One person acted as the subject. He went fairly quickly to a shelf by one wall; from that shelf he removed three dice which he carried to a card table across the other side of the room. Here, after much deliberation he set them in a row with the numbers 4, 5 and 6 uppermost. This was the exact test that was proposed by a visitor who I can add did not help the Mentalist. The same person has allowed me to underline in my mind a word in a book; he has gone to a bookcase, removed the correct book from about ten or twelve in the case, found the right page and then the exact word on that page and then, for the first time actually underlined it in pencil!

The result of this advanced form of contact mind reading is often so good that even those "in the know" cannot believe that trickery was not used. However, if you remember that a subject is capable of leading you to an object—and does so without any conscious encouragement, then it is not so difficult to understand that he can lead you on to do something with the object. As long as *he knows* what has to be done, he will indicate whether you are doing right or wrong. Finally, if you wish to test a mentalist for contact mind reading to see if he is genuine or not. Have the object hidden on the subject—it then becomes almost impossible to find by genuine reading.

Another good test is to act as the subject yourself. Deliberately hide the penny somewhere in the room—but when he comes in—think of another place and in your mind, stick to that place. If he locates the real penny— he has seen it hidden or has an assistant in the audience. If he arrives at the place you are thinking of—and only you know that place, he is a genuine contact mind reader on that occasion.

### When to Use Contact Mind Reading

I have no doubt that what I am about to say will cause a lot of disagreement. However, my opinion is formed after some pretty careful thinking, performing and watching others perform; you are not obliged to stand by my opinion. I do not think Muscle Reading is suitable today for stage work. I think it should be used for small gatherings, at home or in the office, for publicity stunts with three or four reporters or at a party. But when it comes down to using it as it WAS used—when conditions permitted that sort of entertainment, I think it is out. The last time I saw a Mentalist running along the aisle of a theatre, climbing over people in and out of rows of seats to find a pin stuck in somebody's lapel—I made a firm resolution that I would never do it or advise it. The same applies to any place where you have a large number of people seated in such a position that you cannot get at the hiding place without causing an alarming disturbance.

Contact mind reading is a wonderful thing, worth every second you give it in practice but learn not only *how* to do it—but also *when* to do it.

### The Blindfold

Some performers like to work whilst they are blindfolded. It is questionable as to whether or not it improves the presentation—there are points for and points against. Nevertheless, if you choose to use one, be sure you can at least see down the nose—or better to have a fake blindfold and be able to see through it. I do quite a bit of contact mind reading and I do not use a blindfold and I do not think it makes much difference.

### Hellstromism

In case you don't know, Contact Mind Reading or Muscle Reading is sometimes called "Hellstromism" after Hellstrom—the professional Mentalist. In a book by the name of "Hellstromism" it is claimed that a contact mind reader was able to define the thoughts of a spectator while standing five feet away from him and without any contact whatsoever! Sounds like the touch reading envelope—it should be taken with a pinch of salt!! If anybody cares to make some money doing that on me—let me think of something, stand five feet away from me and tell me what I'm thinking—I'll add fifty pounds to the one thousand pounds they can collect from the Occult Committee of the Magic Circle.

## The Blackboard Test

This has been a very popular form of demonstrating muscle reading, today it is rarely seen performed.

The spectator writes a number on the blackboard for all to see, then rubs it out and you come in. You are blindfolded properly and have to duplicate their number by working on encouragement or resisting impulses from the subject. It is more advanced than straightforward work, but not very hard to do. The easy way out recommended by S. Edward Dexter in his book on the subject, is to have the digits one to nine written in a row on the board, then all you have to do is to run the chalk along the row and you will get a strong impulse on the first number chosen. You do it again for the next and so on until the four or five figure number is discovered.

## Conclusion

I refer once more to S. Edward Dexter's book on Contact Mind Reading where he makes a very strong point of the fact that you should not, under any circumstances reveal that you are using contact mind reading. Let the audience form their own conclusion—but keep the technique and Art a strict secret. I having nothing to add to that—other than to wholeheartedly agree.

# "MNEMONICS AND MENTAL SYSTEMS"

## BY

## CORINDA

### STEP THREE

IN CORINDA'S SERIES :—

## "THIRTEEN STEPS TO MENTALISM"

STEP THREE in CORINDA'S SERIES

" THIRTEEN STEPS TO MENTALISM "

" MNEMONICS AND MENTAL SYSTEMS "

# CONTENTS

# INTRODUCTION

To the Mentalist, Memory Systems are indispensable; they are part of his equipment and the means whereby he can be called upon to perform at any time—and give an impressive demonstration. They are the best type of equipment you can have as there is nothing to carry and no apparatus to prepare. The skill lies in the training of the mind, in conditioning the mind to operate to maximum advantage, and once trained, that skill remains with you for life, ever ready to be applied.

Before we concern ourselves with individual systems, we should understand at least to some extent, the whole art of Mnemonics. To get a general picture we may consider the mind and look upon it for the moment as a machine. The history of mankind has shown that there are great thinkers and there are imbeciles, it has not shown whether the difference between the two is brought about by two types each in possession of vastly different minds—or two types, having the same mind—but one applies his to thinking whilst the other does not. If the mind happened to be a machine, a vastly intricate machine, perhaps something like an Electronic Brain, it would be rational to suppose that the output of the machine would be governed by *how it was operated* and, of course, its ultimate potential. We need not involve ourselves with the ultimate potential of the human mind as it is far beyond our requirements and we are in no position to estimate such a factor. We do however concern ourselves with how to use the mind—and the reason is that we shall use our machine more than does the average person.

This does not mean that we can add to the mind anything more than is there already. Practically everybody has the ability to apply memory systems and it amounts to a very simple thing; getting to know new methods of using your natural ability. Fortunately, not everybody knows about mnemonics and since they exist in the mind only it is difficult to tell when they are being used, which of course makes it a good thing for the mentalist. Your protection against discovery is to make every effort to keep the science a secret. It is tempting at times to tell your audience that you have not used trickery as they suppose—but used a memory system which you have developed in the mind. Let me put it this way. You will have seen the well known effect called the "Giant Memory" where some twenty or thirty objects called out by the audience have been memorised by the performer. This is a wonderful thing, it is very impressive, it appears incredible—but if every member of your audience knew that given a week's practice they could do the same— how good would be the effect? Don't try and fool yourself that the ability to do the "Giant Memory" is an outstanding achievement. It is not. Any person of average intelligence could do it with twenty words after a few hours study. The only thing that you have got that they have not—is the knowledge of how to do it—and if you keep that a secret the effect remains as it is—a masterpiece.

The word "mnemonics" is derived from a Greek word meaning "to recollect". If you have read "The Republic of Plato" you will know that the science of mnemonics was well known to the Greeks, and if you care to search further you will find that mnemonic principles have been used for as long as man has been civilised. There have been many claims by magicians and mentalists to the invention of mnemonics; some of the claimants have been world-famous performers—and none of them have a right to their claims. A large number of the systems developed by the magical fraternity have drawn their material in one way or another from the work done by Gregor von Feinaigle of Baden, who specialised in the science and lectured throughout Europe around 1807.

Some more sincere magicians have certainly developed and improved the old systems—and deserve credit for their improvements. As, for example, Al Baker who published in "Magical Ways and Means" a mnemonic system which happens to be a modern application of the Feinaigle System published in 1812. An effect in Al Baker's book called "The Polish Psychic" is a creditable example of the application of mnemonics for two-person telepathy. This effect shows how you may use the system for other purposes than straightforward memory feats—it is in fact used as a code system.

Another example is the Nikola Card System. Here we have a basic mnemonic principle being applied in an original fashion, and there are many more examples that could be given. It is the work of these sincere magicians that makes it possible for me to give you in "Step Three" a selection of mnemonic principles and mental systems that will serve you well as a performing mentalist.

You must understand that the Science of Mnemonics has been developed to such an advanced state, that this work cannot be expected to cover the subject in its entirety. "Step Three" aims at giving you a wide selection of various principles, covering many different fields and dealing with the systems which are of most use to the Mentalist and which are usually most popular with the audience. There will be nothing new or sensational in the selection given; each one is a time-tested, audience-appealing effect. Most of them are very simple to learn—and appear complex on paper only. The mentalist would be well advised to learn as many different systems as possible and he will then find that they can be used in conjunction with each other. This does not mean that you should learn two ways of doing the same thing, it means you learn several systems—one for each field of mentalism or mathemagic. I would go so far as to say that it is dangerous to learn two ways to do the same thing—you are very liable to confuse your mind. Once you have developed your system—stick to it for good, which means you should consider very carefully what system you intend to use—before you learn it. The use of two systems used in conjunction is exemplified again by the Nikola Card System which is founded on the memorisation of words and of numbers. Moreover, the ability to cope with several fields (*i.e.* words, objects, numbers, dates, names, etc.) allows you to present your personality to the full. If you are working in a drawing room to a private gathering and you perform, shall we say, a demonstration of memory, wherein you are given long numbers and succeed in remembering them, you will be credited with "an amazing knack for remembering numbers". If, however, you then proceed to deal with twenty objects and perhaps conclude with a few rapid calculations—there can be no question of "a knack"—you are a genius—the owner of a phenomenal mind! You convey the impression that you could go on all night and after what they have seen, their imagination will have you doing things which even mnemonics could not achieve. With Mentalism, like Magic, it is an important feature of presentation to convey the impression that it is not so much what you *have done*—as what you *could do*—if you had the time!

# THE AMAZING MEMORY TEST

This is probably the most popular application of a memory system in use today. It has every qualification you could hope for as a mentalist; no props to carry, do it anywhere, on stage, cabaret, the drawing room office or walking down the high road. It can be performed before any size of audience—one or two—or thousands; it is positively sure to work, is easy to learn and last, and most important of all, it has a terrific effect on the audience. What more could you want?

There are about six standard methods by which you may perform the Amazing Memory Test. The idea of the test is to have the audience call out some twenty or thirty objects and for you to remember those objects and their order. I do not propose to give you more than one method as first it is confusing and second it is unnecessary; the technique I have chosen is the one most used and the one which I find has served me well for years. Before I give the actual working, I should point out that the system can be progressed to cover unlimited number of objects. If you wanted, you could go into hundreds—BUT twenty to thirty objects is enough. It takes considerable time to deal with this number and it is sufficient to make your point with the audience.

**The First Stage:** To learn the system, the first stage is to memorise a "KEY" for all the numbers from one to thirty. The "KEY" is an object which you, in your mind, can always associate with a certain number. To make this easy we choose objects which have something to do with the number—more often than not, an object which rhymes with the number. The following table is an example, it can be used but there is no reason why you should not compile your own table—for, what sounds logical to one person does not always make sense with the next. The table given is the one that I use:—

"Number one is a GUN"
"Number two is a SHOE"
"Number three is a FLEA"
"Number four is a SAW"
"Number five is a HIVE"
"Number six is a TRICK"
"Number seven—GOES TO HEAVEN"
"Number eight is a GATE"
"Number nine—is OUT OF LINE"
"Number ten is a PEN"
"Number eleven—COMES FROM DEVON"
"Number twelve is a SHELF"
"Number thirteen is SKIRTING"
"Number fourteen is COURTING"
"Number fifteen is LIFTING"
"Number sixteen—is SWEET SIXTEEN"
"Number seventeen—CANNOT BE SEEN"
"Number eighteen is BAITING"
"Number nineteen—is PINING"
"Number twenty is SENTRY"
"Number twenty-one is IN THE SUN"
"Number twenty-two is PAINTED BLUE"

"Number twenty-three is OUT AT SEA"
"Number twenty-four is ON THE SHORE"
"Number twenty-five is BURIED ALIVE"
"Number twenty-six is ON TWO STICKS"
"Number twenty-seven GOES BACK TO DEVON"
"Number twenty-eight ARRIVES LATE"
"Number twenty-nine is ON THE LINE"
"Number thirty is DIRTY".

**The Second Stage:** This is the next stage. Having memorised the code you then create a "picture" to go with the number so that it is impressed even more into the mind. It is what I call "The Action Key"—and means doing something—always the same thing—with the key. For example let us take No. 6 The Key is "Number six is a trick". We could stop at that— but we can improve the system considerably by adding an action, so:— Number six is a trick—and whenever we have this number, we *always* think of a magician pulling something out of a top hat. The "trick" suggests a top hat and should always be remembered.

Other/Action Keys to reinforce the number code are as follows:—No. 1: Always shooting at something. No. 2: Always putting something into a shoe. No. 3: Always an object with a flea hopping about on it. No. 4: Always something being sawed into two pieces. No. 5: Always a hive, with bees swarming over an object. No. 6: Always a top hat with something being produced. No. 7: Always two angels carrying an object to Heaven. No. 8: Always an object standing on a farmyard gate. No. 9: Always three objects, and you find yourself trying to look down a row and get them in line—but one is always out of line. No. 10: Always writing something on an object with a pen. No. 11: Always unpacking a box which contains something. No. 12: Always something standing on a shelf on its own. No. 13: Always something hanging on a nail knocked into the wooden skirting that runs around a room at floor level. No. 14: Two people trying to kiss—always something comes between their lips! No. 15: Always an object which you try to balance on the outstretched finger. No. 16: Always pouring treacle or honey (sweet) over an object. No. 17: Always looking down a micro-scope to try and see something very small. No. 18: Always pulling a fishing line out of the water to see an object hanging on the hook. No. 19: Always at the Lost Property Office reporting the loss of an object. No. 20: Always a Sentry standing on Guard with an object in place of his rifle. No. 21: Always covering something with Sun-tan lotion. No. 22: Always painting with a large brush an object in bright blue. No. 23: Always something floating on some high waves out at sea. No. 24: Always an object lying on the beach at the seaside. No. 25: Always something being ceremoniously buried in a coffin. No. 26: Always something balanced on two matchsticks. No. 27: Something you must always parcel up to send back to Devon. No. 28: "Arrive late" an object always standing on top of a big clock on the mantelpiece. No. 29: Always an object placed in front of an oncoming train on a railway line. No. 30: Always something which you must give a good wash with detergent.

## The Application of The Amazing Memory System

For stage work, have everything written on a big blackboard so that all the audience can see—for small audiences, simply have the objects written on a sheet of paper.

Take a piece of paper and write a column of figures from one to thirty down the left-hand edge. Now invite anybody to call out any object they like for "Number One". The audience should remember their objects. As soon as you hear what object is chosen, you quickly work out your "Key" for "Number One"—(That is—"Number one is a gun") and immediately associate your key with their object in your mind. Don't worry about being sensible—the more stupid the picture you create—the better it will be. Suppose we were given as the first object a MOUSE. We could think of a little white mouse standing in a begging position whilst we tried to shoot at it with a gun.

Having created a vivid picture, associating your key with their object, you immediately FORGET IT, and go on to the next, number two and do the same. Every time you get an object, taking them in correct order, of course, you make up this mental picture and then forget it—until finally you have completed the thirty. Each object given by the audience is recorded as it is given on the sheet—a task which may be given to any member of the audience to do. Be sure you remember the "Action keys" and always do the right action with the object selected by the audience. This will make it a lot easier for you when you come to the next stage.

## Calling the Objects Back

When you have "accepted" the thirty objects, hand the sheet to someone who acts as "Scorer". He is to tick off every time you are right. The audience are now invited to call out ANY number from one to thirty. You immediately call back the name of the object given for whatever number they say. It is very easy. As soon as you hear the number—think of your "Key" and the very moment you remember your key—you will find you also remember their object! When you do this for the first time—you will be amazed that it really works. That is all there is to it—and a very good effect can thus be performed.

To conclude the performance, you may if you wish run through the complete list of objects backwards, starting from thirty. You may also have an object called here and there—and you give the correct number. One aspect of presentation that improves the effect is to enlarge in detail on one or two objects as they are given. For example, suppose at Number 8 we were asked to accept "CAT" as the object. We could say, "Any particular type of cat?" And even though you are told it is a Cheshire Cat wearing a yellow spotted cravat and dancing the Hornpipe"—you will still get it! Moreover, it adds comedy to the presentation. Such is the Amazing Memory.

## QUICK CALCULATIONS: MENTAL ARITHMETIC

There are several methods whereby the Mentalist can render an impressive demonstration of his ability by a show of rapid calculations. The business of mentally squaring or cubing a number, or extracting the square or cube root can cause quite a stir amidst intelligent people.

### (1) Squaring

Since it is very easy to square small numbers in the head we shall not bother to deal with anything under twenty-five. Most people, having to square say 15—could do so with little trouble. However, dealing with numbers from twenty-five and up to a hundred (which is more than enough):—

*For numbers from 25 to 50.* First take the difference between the number and 25 for the hundreds and square the difference between the number and 50 for the tens and units. As for example, to square 39:—

> The difference between 25 and 39 is 14. The number 14 gives the first two numbers of the answer.

> The difference between 50 and 39 is 11. Which when squared gives 121:—
> To 121, we add fourteen hundred from the first step, and the answer 1521 equals 39 squared.

*For numbers from 50 to 100.* First take twice the difference between the number given and fifty for the hundreds and then square the difference between the given number and 100 for the tens and units.

## (2) Extraction of Square Roots

The performer must first memorise the following table which shows the square of the digits one to nine:—

| Digit | 1 | 2 | 3 | 4 | 5 | 6 | 7 | 8 | 9 |
|---|---|---|---|---|---|---|---|---|---|
| Square | 1 | 4 | 9 | 16 | 25 | 36 | 49 | 64 | 81 |

Suppose we are asked to extract the square root of the number 3136. First we consider only the two starting figures; the number nearest to 31 in the above table is 25—it must be *more* than 25 but not greater than 36. The table shows that 25 is represented by 5. Hence 5 will be the first figure of the square root of 3136. The last digit of this number is 6. There are two squares terminating with 6 in the above table and the number opposite them is one that will end the answer. However, we must be able to tell which of the sixes to use since one represents six and the other four. Take the answer to the first step—which was 5, multiply this by itself giving 25, deduct this from the first two figures in the original number (31) and six remains. This figure six is larger than the one we have multiplied (5) so select from the above table the larger of the two numbers terminating with six. The figure opposite then gives the second number in the root; the root of 3136 is 56.

## (3) Cubing

To find the cube of any two figure number, you must first know or work out the cube of the units one to nine. It will pay you to learn these because they can be used for other calculating effects shown later:—

| Digit | 1 | 2 | 3 | 4 | 5 | 6 | 7 | 8 | 9 |
|---|---|---|---|---|---|---|---|---|---|
| Cube | 1 | 8 | 27 | 64 | 125 | 216 | 343 | 512 | 729 |

Suppose now you are requested to find the cube of the number 62.

Cube the first figure—6 and put it down in thousands, to the left of the cube of two. That is of six, 216, and of two, 8, which equals 216,008. To this add the product of:—

$$62 \times 6 \times 2 \times 3. \text{ } i.e. \text{ } 62 \times 36. \text{ equals } 2232.$$

Place this under the first number, moving the units figure one step to the left and add the two lines together.

```
62.   216008
      2232  (62×6×2×3 equals 2232)
      _____

      238,328 equals 62 CUBED.
      _____
```

## (4) Extraction of Cube Roots

Of the various calculating systems given so far, this is probably the most effective and oddly enough, the easiest. The table shown for Cubing Numbers is used and it can be made to reveal the cube root of any number from one to a hundred. For higher numbers, the extraction of cube roots of numbers resulting in more than a hundred, it is only necessary to add noughts to the cubes accordingly.

Ask a member of your audience to work out the cube of any number (say "Two figure number") under one hundred. Suppose their answer came to 804,357. To find the number cubed is very simple:—

Refer to the table for Cubing. The first three figures are 804—greater than 729, the highest possible number. 729 represents the unit 9, so this will be the *first* figure in the answer. Next take the last number in the total given by the audience—7. Find the cube which *ends* with seven in the table, it is 27—represented by three—so 3 will be the last figure of the answer. Therefore the cube root of 804,357 is 93.

## THE MAGIC SQUARE

I am obliged to say in the first place that the Magic Square has nothing to do with the Magician who doesn't like Rock and Roll! It is in fact a very, very old form of brain-teaser that is worth knowing. Of the various sizes of Magic Squares that can be used, we shall concern ourselves with the five by five square. The problem is to draw out a square containing twenty-five divisions and to insert in each division a number. When totalled across and down, the sum of five divisions in a row must all be the same. To make it more complicated the answer or total of the rows of five can be determined by a member of the audience.

Draw out a square and divide it so that you have twenty-five equal squares, five across and five down. Have a member of the audience choose a number (it must be above sixty and under five hundred) and write it down outside the square.

You must now fill in a series of numbers to add up finally to their choice. This has to be done quickly for effect, and can be done quickly if you know how.

Suppose the audience select the number 65.

You must find the starting figure—the lowest number that goes in first. This is easy, deduct sixty from their figure and divide by five. Hence:—

65 chosen number for total, we deduct 60 leaving 5, and divide by 5 to get 1. We must therefore start with the number 1.

Begin with the first figure inserting it in the middle square of the top line, and then proceed to fill in 2, 3, 4, 5, 6 etc., etc., travelling diagonally upwards to the right. Imagine that it is possible to arrange the square in cylindrical form in both directions. Where the square upwards and diagonally to the right is occupied, and the square below is free, take that for the next number. This takes very little practice as you will see and you will soon reach a high speed. Example squares are given in the illustration which if studied closely, will show how to fill in properly. However, we must allow for certain numbers given by the audience that will not fill in as straight forward as the above example. When the number given has had sixty deducted and cannot equally be divided by five, the remainder must be added en route to certain "key squares". These are marked in the diagram with a star and their position should be thoroughly memorised in case you have to use them.

If you use the Key Squares, say you were given 248—you first subtract 60 which gives you 188, divide this by 5 giving you 37 which means you are left with a remainder of 3. You start at 37 and go on to 38, 39 and 40, continuing until you reach a Key Square where you add the remainder each time. Continue as normal otherwise.

(A)

| 17 | 24 | 1 | 8 | 15 |
|----|----|----|----|----|
| 23 | 5 | 7 | 14 | 16 |
| 4 | 6 | 13 | 20 | 22 |
| 10 | 12 | 19 | 21 | 3 |
| 11 | 18 | 25 | 2 | 9 |

(A : Totals 65 All Directions)

(B)

| | | | | |
|----|----|----|----|----|
| | | * | | |
| | | | | * |
| | * | | | |
| | | | * | |

(B : Position of Key Squares)

(C)

| 52 | 61 | 38 | 45 | 52 |
|----|----|----|----|----|
| 60 | 42 | *42 | 51 | 53 |
| 41 | 43 | 50 | 57 | *57 |
| 47 | *47 | 56 | 58 | 40 |
| 48 | 55 | 62 | *37 | 46 |

(C : Totals 248 Uses " Keys ")

(D)

| 101 | 108 | 85 | 92 | 99 |
|----|----|----|----|----|
| 107 | 89 | 91 | 98 | 100 |
| 88 | 90 | 97 | 104 | 106 |
| 94 | 96 | 103 | 105 | 87 |
| 95 | 102 | 109 | 86 | 93 |

(D : Totals 485 All ways)

NOTE: Examples of the five by five Magic Square given here are as shown by Fred Barlow in his excellent book called "Mental Prodigies". This publication is strongly recommended to those seeking accurate detail of History and Technique of the Science of Mnemonics. I am indebted to Mr. Barlow for adding considerably to my knowledge of the subject.

# THE KNIGHT'S TOUR

The American Magician Harry Kellar made this startling trick popular many years ago—and today, it remains as good as ever. The effect is that the Mentalist must call out numbers which represent the squares of a chessboard. Every time a number is called, a knight is moved to that square and the tour from square to square is such that the knight must cover once only every square of the board (64) without touching the same square twice. Additionally, the knight must always be moved in the correct fashion for the knight's move in the game of chess. As most of you will know, this is regarded as the most complicated move of all the chessmen—being one forward and two to the side in any direction. All other men and pawns move in a straight line in one direction or another. The feat therefore becomes more than just a demonstration of your ability to memorise sixty-four numbers in a given sequence (which is quite something) but adds to this the knowledge of a "path" or "route" which weaves intricately around the board.

To the Mentalist this may not mean much, but to Chess-players it means a great deal and to any intelligent lay-audience (non-chess-players) the feat appears incredible. The audience need not have knowledge of the game of chess to appreciate your accomplishment. If they do—the effect is doubled. I have been a keen chess-player for many years and know that this effect performed before a chess club or group is nothing short of dumbfounding. It has been done by pure skill on the part of one or two outstanding chessmasters, but you will be able to do it without so much as having to learn a thing!

To present the effect you need only a piece of paper which is ruled off into a square divided into sixty-four sections ($8 \times 8$) representing the chessboard. Starting from the top left-hand corner, number the small squares from one to sixty-four. (For large audiences you may use a blackboard). Next inform the audience what you intend to do; emphasise the incredible number of variations and diverse paths for the knight's tour, and how you must remember sixty-four squares and so on. Next designate a member of the audience to mark off the squares as you call them out. You do not actually need a knight, it is enough to make a small tick to show that "the knight" passed that way. To add to the presentation, we now permit the audience to decide which square shall be used as the starting point for the tour. They can pick any square on the board—simply call out the chosen number which is encircled to show it as the first square. From then on it is easy, you turn your back (so that you cannot cheat and cannot be seen!) and stand well away from the chessboard. To perform the knight's tour, all that remains is to call out a string of numbers reading them from the chart given in the illustration. It is as well to copy this chart out on to a small card which can be concealed in the hand when in use. (Eric Mason has the numbers written on the edge of his spectacles!) As soon as you receive the starting number, look it up quickly and then read off down the rows and as you reach the end of one row, start again at the top of the next. When you reach number 18—you start at the top of the first row again—number 1. So, for example, we were told to start at number 54. We look it up and then call out 48, 63, 46, 56, 62, etc., etc. You should remember the starting number so that you know when all sixty-four have been called.

Add to the presentation towards the end by quickly counting the remaining numbers and saying: "I see we have nine squares to go—it's getting really difficult now!"

| | | | | | | | |
|---|---|---|---|---|---|---|---|
| 1 | 60 | 37 | 53 | 23 | 32 | 62 | 49 |
| 11 | 45 | 20 | 43 | 8 | 47 | 52 | 34 |
| 21 | 39 | 26 | 33 | 14 | 64 | 58 | 17 |
| 4 | 29 | 36 | 27 | 24 | 54 | 41 | 2 |
| 10 | 12 | 30 | 44 | 7 | 48 | 51 | 19 |
| 25 | 6 | 13 | 61 | 22 | 63 | 57 | 9 |
| 35 | 16 | 28 | 55 | 5 | 46 | 42 | 3 |
| 50 | 31 | 38 | 40 | 15 | 56 | 59 | 18 |

## CHESS TRICKERY

Aside from the "Knight's Tour" there are other swindles concerning the game of Chess that are of use to the Mentalist. The next two items are extracts from my publication "Chess Trickery" which has been on sale for some years now. Neither of the items require any skilled knowledge of the game of chess.

### The Foolproof System at Chess

The origin of this principle is somewhat remote and subject to argument. I know that the effect was used by a little girl playing against Dr. A. Alekhine (ex-World Champion) and another player of good strength—and the little girl forced a draw. However, having published the effect and used it as part material for my "Chess Trickery" it then appears that the effect is credited to a magician. I discussed the subject with Dai Vernon on one occasion and he told me that Martin Gardiner had worked on it some time ago. Although magicians may have improved the presentation, I do not think they can claim the right of invention in this case.

**The Effect.** The mentalist is able to play as many games of chess simultaneously as he likes, and although having no knowledge whatsoever of the game, is able to guarantee a draw on the complete match.

This must have a profound impact on chess-players because:—

First, since they must know the game in order to play you, they will appreciate the difficulty of playing several games at once.

Second, it makes little difference what strength of play or opposition you meet—in other words, you could play against a panel of twenty people—all international champions—and still draw. Under these circumstances, a draw is a notable accomplishment and in the game of chess, the title holder is considered the winner in the event of a draw—since his opponent must do better than to equalise the tournament.

### The Method

To simplify the explanation we shall describe the technique of playing just two games at once. Later we shall deal with more than two.

It is very easy; to play two people at once, you would have two chessboards, two tables and two sets of chessmen. On one board (which we shall call "A") you are supposed to play with the WHITE PIECES. On the other board ("B") you play with the BLACK. Both opponents sit opposite you.

Now the rules of Chess demand that the player holding the WHITE pieces ("A") must always make the first move. So when you are ready to commence the match, you wait until your opponent on board "B" (playing the white against you) makes his move. As soon as he has made it—you make exactly the same move on board "A". After a while the opponent on this board makes a reply, and this reply you duplicate on board "B". In effect, instead of playing the opponents yourself—you have turned the tables on them—and set them *playing against each other*! Now, if you consider for a moment, you will realise that the outcome of this match can only be three possibilities:—

(1) "A" wins. (So "B" must lose, you win on one board and lose on another therefor it is a DRAW).

(2) "B" wins. (So "A" must lose and the same as above occurs).

(3) "A" and "B" draw. (You draw on both boards which equals a DRAW as tournament result).

There can be no other possibilities. Even if one player resigns the outcome would equal a draw—hence you cannot lose.

It is practically out of the question that the players will discover this ruse as first and foremost, there is no suspicion of trickery. Second, the players are, or should be seated quite a way apart. Third, the position on one board is in reverse to the position in the other—and it takes a chessmaster to glance at a board from white's point of view—then again from black's and say immediately—they are the same on both boards. Fourth, you must remember that chess is a gruelling game—and takes the undivided attention of the players. Fifth—you may say that it will be obvious in the opening stages of the games as only one or two pieces will be moved out of position. It will not because chess-players more often than not resort to standard openings and gambits and similarity in the opening play between several games is commonplace. (I have looked up the Hastings Chess Matches of 1947 and find that out of some two hundred games the opening P-K4 or P-Q4 took place 87% of the time).

## To Play Unlimited Games at Once

If you have more than two opponents (multiples of two are required) you seat them in a long row and mentally number the boards from one onwards. Now instead of playing two opponents sitting next door to each other against themselves, you play them against another person some boards down the row—which makes it quite out of the question that they can see what's going on. The system I used to use was this:—

1 2 3 4 5 6 7 8 9 10 11 12

The boards (twelve) are divided into three groups of four. The colour set up from one to twelve should be (Your men) First two BLACK next two WHITE, next two BLACK, next two WHITE and so on. As you will see, at the start you go to the first board and await your opponent's opening move, when he makes this, you do not reply (make your move) yet—you pass to the next board. Again you have black so you wait for the first move to be made. Now you reach board three where you have the white and must move first—so you simply duplicate the first move as was made by board ONE. On the next board, four, you make the move from board two—

and so it goes on. Outside of remembering a couple of moves for a few seconds and being observant enough to make the correct moves—there is no skill required at all. If you forget the move—you can always look back a couple of boards and check.

A few final tips on this subject; do not allow the matches to be recorded by chess notation as they sometimes are during tournaments. If you do so, your ruse will be discovered as six games will be alike. If you are moving quickly and you arrive at a board (say No. 5) and your opponent has not yet decided his move, simply miss him out and also miss out his partner (No. 7) on that time down the row. You only make one move each time you move along the row—and each time you reach board number twelve, you then go back to number one and start over again.

## The Mate in One Problem

Many years ago Tartakower a famous chess-player walked into "The Gambit" a well-known chess club and restaurant in London, and bet with all present that he could show them a Mate in ONE problem—that they couldn't solve. He won. Chess problems for a mate in two, three or four are commonplace—but mate in one is unheard of. It is taken for granted that the position would be so simple that it would be obvious. However, this position, although painfully simple—will defy the brains of the greatest chessmaster—as the answer is a trick! It is well worth knowing as it makes a very good publicity stunt to perform when you meet a chess-player.

The exact position is this:—

The ruling is "White to move and mate in One" (*diagram*) (Moving up the board).

**(BLACK)**

Black in Black
White Shaded

R = Rook   P = Pawn
K = King

**(WHITE)**

70

The answer is this. The rules of chess at the time when Tartakower made his bet stated quite clearly that "a pawn advanced to the "8th" rank could be exchanged for any other piece excepting a King". There was no mention of what *colour* that piece should be! Consequently, white plays his pawn on one square (P-N8 equals Black N) and calls a BLACK KNIGHT which is mate in one. For those wishing to keep a record of this position, I will give the problem in Forsythe Notation:—

r7/kPR5/8/1K6/8/8/8/8. (White to move and mate in One; P-N8bn‡)

## A DAY FOR ANY DATE

**The effect.** The performer invites members of his audience to call out any date they like; upon hearing the date, the performer gives the exact day of the week that that date falls on and delivers his reply within seconds. Everything is achieved by a quick calculating mental system.

Before we deal with the technique, a few words of introduction are required. First of all the system given can be used only for periods within the range of the Gregorian Calendar (*i.e.* from 1753) as prior to this, the Julian Calendar was in force. The only real difficulty in the system is the learning of the values to represent each month. Mnemonics are recommended to overcome this problem.

It is first necessary to learn a simple code whereby each month of the year is represented by a number:—

| *Month* | *Value* |
|---|---|
| June .. .. .. .. .. .. | 0 |
| September and December .. .. .. | 1 |
| April and July .. .. .. .. .. | 2 |
| January and October .. .. .. .. | 3 |
| May .. .. .. .. .. .. | 4 |
| August .. .. .. .. .. .. | 5 |
| February, March and November .. .. | 6 |

Exception to this code is made in Leap Years when January and February values are reduced by one. Now suppose the Mentalist is asked to name the day for the date, October 5th, 1888. If the method is fully understood, the reply can be given in seconds . . . "Friday". Moreover, although the method looks complex it is indeed very simple.

We shall take October 5th, 1888, as an example. Start by taking the last two digits of the year (in this case 88) and add a quarter (22) making the total 110. Next add the value for the month (October is 3) bringing the total to 113 and to this add the day of the month—("5th") giving us 118, this number we divide by seven and we then get a remainder of 6.

We now have a code number for each day:—

| *Day* | *Value* |
|---|---|
| Sunday .. .. .. .. .. .. | 1 |
| Monday .. .. .. .. .. .. | 2 |
| Tuesday .. .. .. .. .. .. | 3 |
| Wednesday .. .. .. .. .. | 4 |
| Thursday .. .. .. .. .. | 5 |
| Friday .. .. .. .. .. .. | 6 |
| Saturday .. .. .. .. .. .. | 0 |

When our calculation was made we were left with a total of six and this represents the day—in this case FRIDAY as will be seen in the above table.

When the last two digits of the year given by the spectator, cannot be divided exactly by four, take the nearest lowest number divisible by four as, for example, the year 1827, we take 24 as the lowest number and add a quarter of this (6) to 27 giving the answer 33 to which the value of the month is then added.

The sample given has been for the nineteenth century 1801-1900. When the date occurs in the twentieth century you must *deduct* two from the final remainder and when the date occurs in the eighteenth century you must *add* two to the final remainder.

## SUMMARY OF THE DAY FOR ANY DATE SYSTEM

(1) Take the last two digits of the year and add a quarter again.
(2) Next add to this total the code value for the MONTH.
(3) To this add the day of the month.
(4) Divide the total by seven.
(5) The remainder tells you the DAY according to the day code number.

**Further Examples:**

Date given: *April 4th*, 1931. Equals 31 plus 7 (one quarter) plus 2 (for April) plus 4, equals 44. Divided by 7 gives a remainder of 2. Less 2 for the twentieth century date given, leaves us with 0 which indicates a SATURDAY.

Date given: *January 8th*, 1900. Equals 8 plus 3 total 11. This minus 2 gives 9 which divided by 7 leaves a remainder of 2 which indicates a MONDAY.

Date given: *August 5th*, 1752. Last two digits of the year are 52. Divided by 4 gives us 13, which added to 52 equals 65. To this we add the code value for the month (August is 5) and we add another 2 for an eighteenth century date so:—
65 plus 5 plus 2 equals:—72.
To this we add the day of the month which is "the fifth" so:—72 plus 5 equals 77. We then divide by 7 which goes exactly so we have "0" for the remainder and "0" from the day code represents a SATURDAY.

## PERFORMANCE OF THE "A DAY FOR ANY DATE" EFFECT

The best method of presentation is to build the effect up slowly. Start off by giving an introductory talk in which you explain how quickly the average person forgets time. Ask how many people can remember exactly what they were doing on January 23rd, 1957—or how many people can even remember what day of the week it was? You would like to prove that it is possible to keep a mental record of what you do and when you do it—and will demonstrate for example, by calling out any day for any date of the PRESENT YEAR. All members of the audience are asked to take out their diaries and to turn to any page and call out a date—you will attempt to name the exact day for that date.

You run through about half a dozen dates in this fashion which is a good way of proving to a large number of people at the same time that you are right. Now you invite those people with diaries to turn to the small page at the front or back that gives you a calendar for last year and next year.

You run through a few of these and you will find that people in the audience who call out dates, are those people that know what day it was because invariably it was a day of some importance to them.

Having dealt with the diaries you now invite anybody to call out:—

> Their birth date.
> Their date of marriage.
> The date of their twenty-first birthday.
> Any other date as long as they are quite sure what day that date fell on.

So you progress through the ages! To add amusement to the presentation you can inject asides and witticisms which give an element of comedy. For example the patter might go:—

"Now what date did you want? January 8th, 1900—right! Now if I remember rightly that was a wet and windy day—it was a Monday and it was the same day as the famous Leeds Convention" . . .

"You sir! April 4th, 1931—let me see! Ah yes! I always call that day 'the Black Saturday' because of the African uprising which started then—yes it was a Saturday" . . .

The asides or apparent "facts" are utter nonsense—but you go so quick and make such non-commital remarks that no one is in a position to dispute your suggestions. This adds considerably to the effect. Another point is to keep an eye open for special dates like December 25th (Christmas Day), November 5th (Guy Fawkes) and so on . . . you will gain a lot of material from these.

Watch out for the "wise guy" who sits in every audience. When you get "I want February 30th, 1942" you have met him. Get to know how many days are in each month (including Leap years) and watch out for catch-questions. The best thing is to have a ready-made answer for these—something which makes a fool of the spectator and gets a laugh at his expense—he has asked for it. I said—get a laugh—don't be rude, please.

Example: "What day was June 31st, 1905?"

You could reply: "That's an easy one! It was the same day as the famous haunting by the Ghost of Cowley—right?"

And in no time back will come the answer "Oh no it wasn't—because June the 31st never existed".

To which you may reply: "exactly what I meant—neither did the Ghost!"

Or: "What day was September 31st, 1952?" reply: "Were you born on April 1st?"

## SIMPLE CARD SYSTEMS

### (1) The Stacked Deck

The "Stacked Deck" is a pack of cards that has been arranged in a special order according to a system which enables you to know the position of every card in the deck. This may be applied to a few cards or to the complete pack of 52—according to requirements. The principle in itself, is well-known to magicians and it is incorporated here for the benefit of the newcomer—who will find it quite invaluable.

To arrange a pack of cards in some specific order—presents a bit of a problem. If the system or order is simple, something straightforward like arranging the cards in numerical order, then it becomes obvious to the spectator. On the other hand, if you use a "mixed" system which is not obvious—then you have to find a way of remembering it and it must also be one that functions quickly in use. (*i.e.* You can work out where any card is within reasonable time.)

To overcome this little problem we resort to our old friend the "memory system" and in order to remember the "key" to the system, we utilise the following rhyme:—

"EIGHT KINGS THREATEN TO SAVE—NINE FAIR LADIES FOR ONE SICK KNAVE"

| 8 | K | 3-10 | 2 | 7 | 9 | 5 | Q | 4 | A | 6 | J |
|---|---|------|---|---|---|---|---|---|---|---|---|

You will notice that the words in the rhyme have a phonetic resemblance to the numbers printed underneath. The Queen is represented by "Ladies" which should be pretty easy to remember! Now that we have allowed for the thirteen card values, we must deal next with the suits. To do this, we bear in mind the word "CHaSeD" and you will note that the four consonants represent Clubs, Hearts, Spades and Diamonds and since we must keep them in a fixed order, we take them as they appear in the word CHASED.

Using the value rhyme and the suit order as given, we now "stack" the complete deck. Start with the 8 of Clubs, and place it face upwards on the table, on top of this, always face upwards, place next the King of Hearts and then the 3 of Spades. You will see that each time we move along the words of the rhyme, we move to the next suit. We go on like this until every card is in its proper position. When the pack is completely assembled in order you will note that every fourth card is the same suit and every 13th card is the same value. Just one thing more, every time you reach the end of the rhyme (the Jack) you start again at the beginning (Eight).

Now that the deck is stacked it must be kept in this order very carefully. To do this you handle the pack with reasonable care, see that cards removed are replaced in the right position (see below) and always cut the pack and complete the cut properly to mix. In actual fact cutting the pack will not disturb the stack at all as long as it is a normal method. You may false shuffle but you must be pretty sure of yourself in order to do this.

Let us deal with a simple trick in order to illustrate how to handle the stacked deck and how to work it properly.

The pack is pre-arranged. After it has been given one or two completed cuts it is fanned face downwards and a spectator is invited to remove a card say, from the centre. As soon as they remove their card, break the fan just above the position of their card and casually put the top half of the fan on the bottom half—in effect, dividing the pack in two for an instant and putting the top half on the bottom. Having done this, the bottom card of the pack will naturally be the card that preceded the one that was removed by the spectator. Suppose we see the Two of Hearts on the bottom—we can quickly run through the rhyme and find that the two is always followed by a SEVEN (". . . threaten to save") and since the bottom card is a Heart— the next suit in the order CHASED would be a SPADE so we now know that the spectator holds the Seven of Spades. With a bit of practice you will be able to work all this out in a matter of seconds—it becomes almost automatic.

Once you know the card you are in a position to do one of many good tricks—and it is best to built it up into an effect before you declare what the name of the card maybe. It is not enough simply to have a card chosen and then to name it; throughout this series you will find dozens of tricks that can be performed once you know what card a spectator has chosen.

Before we deal with one or two more tricks, it might be as well to point out that when you look at the bottom card—some sort of mis-direction should be used. If you just turn the pack over and glare at it—you are asking for trouble. One method is to casually place the deck aside—placing it face upwards on the table and hardly giving it a glance. Another is to "accidentally" drop the bottom card on the floor—and look at it when you pick it up. Another technique is to use anything that reflects—such as a mirror, highly polished table knife, or spoon, cigarette case or lighter—when the pack need not be reversed at any time.

Last but not least—a method using powerful misdirection. The spectator holds his card, you tell him to look at it and remember it, then you say "now so that I cannot possibly see your card—hold it flat against your chest like this . . ." and holding the pack in the left hand you bring it up to your chest to demonstrate the position and note the bottom card as you do so.

Having revealed the name of the chosen card you take it back. Now it stands to reason that this card cannot be pushed at random into the pack if the order is to be maintained. It must go on the bottom or the top—bringing it back into sequence. If you have had several cards removed—pick them up from the table in the right order and drop them one at a time on top setting the stack as you go.

## Some More Tricks Using the EIGHT KINGS STACK

(a) Cut a Queen—any Queen—to the bottom of the deck and then deal out a "Pontoon" hand for two people; the spectator and yourself. You deal out from the top two cards each in the order, him, you—then him, you. He will get a six and a four and you will get "Pontoon", an Ace and a Jack—the top winning hand! If he wants to "twist" on his hand of six and four he gets an Eight—and if he twists again he gets a King and must lose.

(b) Hand the pack to the spectator and tell him to do exactly as you say. Take the cards behind his back and cut them—completing the cut. Then to take the top card and to reverse it anywhere in the pack, to square up the cards and then place them face up on the table. You will see the face card of the pack and can therefore name the card he reversed somewhere in the middle—since the spectator does not know himself it will seem a real miracle.

(c) Have the spectator take any three cards in a row. These he places in his pockets—each goes in a separate pocket. Cut the pack as he takes his group of cards and note the bottom card when placing the pack aside. Turn your back on the spectator and tell him to remove any card from one of his pockets. You now know that this card must be one of three—to find out which one—you work by a method known as "pumping". Suppose he took the following three cards:—

Eight of Clubs, King of Hearts, and Three of Spades.

You start off by saying "you are holding a black card" . . . and make it sound as though you were telling him and not asking him. If he says "No"—you can reply immediately—sorry—I always have trouble with court cards—it is a red King the King of Hearts. Take out another please. This time you most certainly have a black one—I think it is a spade?" If he says "yes"—straight away you say "and it is the three—which leaves the last card still in your pocket—and that is the eight of clubs". Or, if he said "No"—you reply—"you are you know! You are holding it in your pocket—the three of spades—I thought I would tell you that first before naming the one in your hand—the eight of clubs!"

## (2) Si Stebbins Stack

This is another system of arranging a full pack of cards in order. You may prefer it to the Eight Kings System, although by nature they are very similar.

The cards are arranged in the following order:—

3C 6H 9S QD 2C 5H 8S JD AC 4H 7S 10D KC 3H
6S 9D QC 2H 5S 8D JC AH 4S 7D 10C KH 3S 6D
9C QH 2S 5D 8C JH AS 4D 7C 10H KS 3D 6C 9H
QS 2D 5C 8H JS AD 4C 7H 10S KD. (The top card in the pack is the Three of Clubs, face down).

The suits rotate in the order Clubs, Hearts, Spades and Diamonds (see "Eight Kings") and to work out the value—all you have to do is to ADD THREE to the last card. You value a Jack as Eleven, a Queen as Twelve, and a King as Thirteen.

To operate the Si Stebbins stack, proceed the same way as for Eight Kings and when you see the bottom card—simply add three to the value and rotate the suit forward one.

## (3) The Fourteen/Fifteen Set Up

First discard the Ace of Hearts and the Ace of Spades. Now set up the remaining 50 cards in this order:—

7C, 8C, 6D, 9S, 5C, 10H, 4D, JS, 3C, QS, 2D, KS, AC, KH, 2H,
QC, 3D, JH, 4S, 10C, 5D, 9C, 6S, 8S, 7S, 8D, 6H, 9H, 5H, 10D,
4C, JD, 3S, QH, 2S, KD, AD, KC, 2C, QD, 3H, JC, 4H, 10S,
5S, 9D, 6C, 8H, 7H, 7D. (Bottom).

There is no "Chased" suit order in this set up as it is not possible. Now if the pack is cut anywhere, the two cards at the cut will always total either fourteen or fifteen. The deck may be given as many complete cuts as you like before using. This can be of considerable use when it is necessary to force a number as for example for a book test. If you know the fourteenth and fifteenth word on a page—by having two cards removed (together) from somewhere in the deck—you force those numbers.

## (4) The Odd and Even Set Up

As a magician you will have spent many hours handling a pack of cards. I wonder if you know how many odd cards there are in a pack? Twenty six? No! There are twenty eight—and there are twenty-four even cards—you work it out!

This is a very simple set up—and it is almost impossible to see at a casual glance. Put all the odd cards (King is 13 and Jack is 11) on top of the pack and put all the even cards (Queen is 12) below. Any cards removed from the top half and replaced in the bottom half will be clearly visible. This may also be done by having all the blacks at the top and all the reds at the bottom—but it is of course more obvious.

# THE MNEMONIC NUMBER CODE

One field of Mnemonics, sometimes called the Science of Artificial Memory, deals with a system for remembering numbers. This system can be invaluable to the Mentalist. One of the early pioneers of this system was Gregor von Feinaigle of Baden who published a treatise dealing with it in 1812. Since then it has been dealt with in several magical works. The system, like The Amazing Memory with objects, is based on the "association of ideas" principle, and consonants of the alphabet are used as the "keys" to represent numbers:—

The first step is to learn the following code—wherein each number is allotted a letter:—

| 1 | 2 | 3 | 4 | 5 | 6 | 7 | 8 | 9 | 0 |
|---|---|---|---|---|---|---|---|---|---|
| d | n | m | w | f | s | v | g | p | z |

In order that they may be committed to memory with ease, we have additional "keys" (as with the Amazing Memory Test) to assist us:—

No. 1. The letter "d" has ONE stroke.
No. 2. The letter "n" has TWO strokes.
No. 3. The letter "m" has THREE strokes.
No. 4. The letter "w" is made up of FOUR lines.
No. 5. The letter "f" begins "five".
No. 6. The letter "s" begins "six".
No. 7. The letter "v" appears only in the spelling of "seven".
No. 8. The letter "g" appears only in the spelling of "eight".
No. 9. The letter "p" gives a mirror image of that number.
No. 10. The letter "z" starts "zero".

Having mastered the above code—you are ready to work. To use, simply take whatever number you wish to remember and mentally work out what consonants represent that number. Suppose you wanted to deal with the number 6731—the consonants are S-V-M-D. Now we are allowed to insert as many vowels as we like—in any position we like in order to make those consonants into a word or several words. We must however keep the consonants in their proper order. We could make S-V-M-D into "Save Mud"— two small words. It is not necessary to make sense or find sensible—long words—in fact, the more absurd your efforts—the better it will be. You find the "key word" as quickly as possible and commit it to memory. Should you be dealing with a lot of these key words then you can utilise the Amazing Memory system to remember them. Nevertheless, for one or two simple words it is hardly necessary. Remember the secret to this system is to find short simple words as quickly as you can.

Now we shall deal with the next step—which is a method for speeding up the working and giving you a wider range of letters to choose from; first, however, I want to translate a sentence into numbers—and will ask you to refer back to it again in a moment or two:—

"Oh what a tangled web we weave—when first we practice to deceive".

The consonants of this sentence equal the number 4281444742564917 by the above method.

If you consider for a moment, you will realise that the speed with which you can translate the numbers into words is dependent upon two things. First, complete familiarity with the letters representing the numbers and second, the range of letters available. Obviously, the more letters you can use—the easier it will be to compile the words; suppose therefore that we enlarge our code:—

No. 1 is "d" or "l" again with the key or one stroke.
No. 2 is "n" or "b" phonetic Shakespeare "to be or not TWO B" (!!!)
No. 3 is "m" or "k" composed of three strokes.
No. 4 is "w" or "r" the last letter of "four".
No. 5 is "f" or "q" five precedes the Queen in the Eight Kings Stack.
No. 6 is "s" or "x" the last letter of "six".
No. 7 is "v" or "y" which has the written appearance of "seven".
No. 8 is "g" or "t" the last letter of "eight".
No. 9 is "p" or "c" where "c" stands for Cat with NINE lives.
No. 0 is "z" or "h" as the letter "h" appears in "nought".

You do not have to adopt the letter I suggest — if you can sort out the alphabet in such a way that you find a code more suited to yourself—then use it of course. The difference that the extra set of letters makes to the code can be seen by translating the sentence I gave at the beginning of this code; originally we had sixteen numbers—now we get thirty:—040882814244-740254684949898197.

Moreover, taking the original example number (which was 6731) instead of having four consonants to work with (S-V-M-D) we now have eight:—

$$S \& X - V \& Y - M \& K - D \& L.$$

Our first effort working with four consonants was "SaVe MuD". This time it could easily be:—"Say Kid—Sieve Mad—Axe Yokel—Suave Mole or Save Mud". So as you will see, we are able to form the number into a wider range of words and the little extra time it takes to learn the second set of key letters—makes all the difference in the long run.

## THE APPLICATION OF THE MNEMONIC NUMBER CODE

(1) When performing "lightning calculations" instead of trying to over-burden the mind with numerous sub-totals, convert them to a word which can be quickly brought to mind when required.

(2) For "telephone" tricks—have a number written by a spectator; convert this into a word which will pass as a name. Send the spectator to tele-phone your medium and tell them what name to ask for. When the medium hears what name you have called her—she immediately knows the number chosen. The friend or medium can have a written copy of the system ready to work it out. A clever application of this principle, that is, using the Feinaigle System *in reverse* making numbers indicate letters, will be found in a fine book, "Magical Ways and Means" by Al Baker—the effect is called "The Celebrity Feat".

(3) The performer works with an assistant. The latter is seated and blind-folded. On a blackboard are written about two dozen numbers—with at least one of each from 1 to 9 (and "0" included). The performer takes a stick, says nothing but points to a number, the assistant calls it out. He then begins to point in rapid succession to various numbers—and each time the assistant calls out the correct one. On one occasion he points to part of the blackboard that is blank. The assistant calls out "there is nothing there!" In the course of about two minutes—the assistant has called out perhaps fifty to one hundred numbers accurately. This is very impressive. To conclude, the performer points

to one number and says "what is this added to this?" and points to another. Then he goes on "and multiply this by this—subtract this from this, add up these three", etc., etc.

Both performer and assistant have memorised the complete order of numbers to be used for the Act. When the performer points to a number —it is the number pre-arranged in the mental system and the assistant calls it out. It is literally impossible to make a mistake and since the assistant does not have to see the board—he should sit with his back to it and make no effort to turn during the performance.

As a very good climax to this effect you can have a spectator come up to the blackboard and write down two rows of figures and then add them up. As soon as the total is seen by you—you declare to the audience: "And now Ladies and Gentlemen, we will conclude with the "................." test—a very difficult feat where my partner will try and tell you the total of this sum written by the spectator. Whatever name you call the *test*—tells your assistant the total on the blackboard.

(4) Corinda's "Fourteenth Book Test". This was an effect that I used to use and it went over very well. It is necessary for both performers to know the Mnemonic Number System—and when you get a team working on a double mental act, it certainly pays in many ways to learn this system.

One of the team, called "the medium" leaves the room. The audience decide on a word in any book, note the page number and the line and then the position of the word in that line. Your medium now comes in and picks up the book and locates the chosen word. It is done by a code method. When the medium comes in, you turn to the spectator that chose the word and say "now we will not mention the word—but suppose it was "dog"—imagine you are writing that word on a blackboard". The word "DOG" keys your assistant—page 18. Your medium turns to page 18 and then appears to have some difficulty. You turn to the spectator again and say, "your conscious mind is confusing the picture—I want you to rub out the imaginary word and write something else like Bat or just a letter like K" . . . Now you have coded the line number (Bat equals 28) and the position of the chosen word in the line (K equals 3). Because the conversation is so natural—devoid of such usual classics as "Please now this what is it" (!) there is never a suspicion that a code system has been used.


**Take My Word**

Another effect I have used with this system. Have about ten words thought of by the audience whilst your medium is outside. Then have one of them chosen. (They should be written in a long list). Suppose the fifth word down the list is selected, just before you leave the room by another door—or go and stand quietly in the corner, say "I'll just add a couple more to make it difficult"—and add any two words to the bottom of the list—but the very last word starts with the same letter that indicates the chosen word from the top of the list. For five you may use "f" or "q" so you add something like "fig" or "quality" to the bottom of the list.

It may then be taken a step in advance of this by having very many words written on a list and still doing it. Several words can be chosen and as long

79

as you and your assistant both know the key word you have a good effect on your hands. Remember that not a word is said or a sign given and that you can be out of the room. If you cannot leave the room—there is nothing to stop you sending the list out to the medium.

## THE PHOTOGRAPHIC MEMORY

This effect is the application of the Mnemonic Number System in all its glory. You will have to be well practiced to do it—but the trick is really fabulous.

You have a blackboard and work alone. You invite people in the audience to take out a ten shilling or one pound note and hold it up. You point to any one and ask them to call out the number on their note—you write it on the blackboard and ask them to check that what you have written is right. Whilst you write it—you gain a few seconds to translate their note number into a word or two. You then ask for their initials—and quickly form a word with them in your mind. Now the number key and the initials key are associated with No. 1 in the Amazing Memory System—and then everything is forgotten. This takes a long time to describe—but the well practised mentalist will be able to do it in about three to five seconds.

Suppose the bank note number was 347531—immediately we know the key letters are MK—WR—VY—FQ—MK—DL. And something like "Mary Female" soon springs to mind. Then our spectator tells us his initials are B.N.—we then make up any word very quickly—there is nothing to think about, B.N.—we will say BUN. Now we instinctively know "Number one is a gun" in the Amazing Memory Code (see page 61) so we associate Mary Female and Bun with Gun. An absurd picture is created—A woman named Mary, unmistakably female (!) is trying her skill at shooting a bun through the middle. We create the picture and then we forget it.

You turn back to the spectator in the audience and say, "I will call you number one—will you remember that please?" Then do just the same with another person—calling him number two—and another—number three until you have covered about ten or twelve. By that time you have a pretty formidable list on show on the blackboard. Now you give a brief explanation about the so-called "photographic memory", pretend to study the board carefully for the first time, turn it round and call out "Number One—will you hold your note up please—let me see—your initials are B.N. and the number on your note is 347531—correct?" Would anybody now like to call out the number I gave them and we will see if we can recognise you".

Be sure the audience call out the LAST SIX numbers on the note—and if you "accept" twelve altogether the blackboard will show seventy-two numbers all in special order and about twenty-four to thirty letters (some initials may be three letters)—and to add to this—you have given each spectator a number and also remember that!

If you have never handled mnemonics, this sort of effect will quite possibly scare you! Believe me, you have no idea until you try—just how easy and effective it is. When you start to learn and apply mnemonics, the first person to be amazed is always yourself. As I said at the very beginning of the book, the best equipment that the Mentalist can have—is knowledge carried in the mind—there is more magic in your mind than there is in all the dealers' catalogues put into one volume!

# PREDICTIONS

## BY

## CORINDA

### STEP FOUR
IN CORINDA'S SERIES :—

## "THIRTEEN STEPS TO MENTALISM"

# STEP FOUR in CORINDA'S SERIES

# " THIRTEEN STEPS TO MENTALISM "

## CONTENTS

### PART ONE  INTRODUCTION

### PART TWO  TECHNIQUE

### PART THREE  PREDICTIONS FOR THE STAGE

### PART FOUR  PREDICTIONS FOR THE DRAWING ROOM

## PART ONE: INTRODUCTION

TO PREDICT is to tell beforehand—to prophesy. In order to avoid any confusion we should understand right from the beginning what is, and what is not a Prediction. What the Oxford English Dictionary means by "Prediction" and what Mentalists mean by "Prediction"—are two things far apart. A mentalist may put the Ace of Spades in an envelope and give it to someone. He may then force that person to select the Ace of Spades—and when the envelope is opened and the matching card is found, it *appears* that a Prediction has been made, moreover, it is *claimed* that a Prediction has been made—BUT nothing of the kind has been done. It was a force presented as a prediction.

We are not concerned with dictionary definitions—we are concerned with what is meant by a Prediction in the magical sense of the word. To cover this, we might say that any effect wherein the performer makes it appear he knew what was going to happen—before it happened—is an effect called a prediction.

PREDICTIONS are one of the strongest forms of Mental Magic—because they work in the future—and not in the present or past. To understand this, let us take an example of the same trick presented three ways:—

(*a*) THE PAST.     The spectator is told to think of any place he has visited during the last two years—and the performer names it correctly.

(*b*) *THE PRESENT.*     The spectator is told to think of the town he lives in—or the city—and by some means or other this is named.

(*c*) *THE FUTURE.*     The spectator is told to think of any place he would like to visit one day—and by some means or other that is named.

There can be no doubt that the best presentation is the last (*c*). It is plausible that you know *where he has been* and *where he lives at the moment*—but beyond any doubt, you cannot say *where he will go in the future*!

It is somewhat easy to overlook that some forms of Mentalism are more powerful than others. With so many tricks to choose from, and such a wide variety of methods—the mentalist is liable to be confused himself—and cannot see the forest for the trees. The only way to evaluate an effect is to judge it by the impact it has on an audience. What might seem very clever to you—may well be an utter bore to the spectators.

The abstract nature of Predictions make them a subtlety of presentation; we can judge their value on the audience by comparison of technique using a pack of cards. You can shuffle a pack and following time-honoured technique say, "Take a card—look at it—and put it back". Because the technique is time-honoured and the audience have seen the approach so often—all that remains to be known in their mind—is by what method you will reveal the card *this* time. The trick has degenerated to a puzzle before it is half done. On the other hand, if you tell the spectator you know what card he will choose before he takes it, run through the cards face upwards and tell him to touch one and then show that his card is the only red-backed card in a blue-backed pack—then you are using a more powerful technique. Hence Predictions are of great value to the Mentalist.

The Art of Predicting is by no means a newcomer to Mentalism. The human race seems to have a lust to know what is going to happen before it happens. Millions of pounds and dollars have been made out of telling the future. Throughout the ages we have been "gifted" with prophets, seers, soothsayers, astrologists, crystal-ball readers, sand-readers, Tarot readers and clairvoyant mediums. We have records of Predictions in religion (The Bible) and in classic literature (Shakespeare's 'Macbeth'). However, the Mentalist likes to operate a different way from the horoscope-worker. He likes to see his prediction proved correct in a short space of time—which brings us to the subject of trickery!

## PART TWO: TECHNIQUE

### (1) The Billet Pencil by Corinda

The apparatus consists of a hollow metal tube six inches long with a slit partly down one side. Inside the tube is a small plunger operated from the outside by a button making contact through the slit. At one end of the hollow tube, the tip of an ordinary pencil is fixed—the other end is left open. The complete job is finished to look exactly like an ordinary pencil—you cannot tell the difference unless you handle it. (Marketing rights are reserved on this apparatus).

To load the Billet Pencil, a piece of thin paper about the size of a ten shilling note is rolled tightly into a tube and then inserted after the plunger has been pulled back. Another method of dealing with the paper is to fold it in zig-zag fashion, like a continuous letter "W" (WWWW) so that when it comes out it expands. If tightly rolled, a £1 note can be loaded into the pencil. To operate the pencil when loaded, it is only necessary to push on the button with the thumb—and the billet shoots out completely.

There are very many uses for the apparatus—especially in the field of Predictions. We are dealing with tricks later on, but to give you an idea of the principle it is this. The Mentalist leaves a sealed envelope with a Newspaper Editor and tells him to keep it safe and unopened until he calls about a week later. When he arrives a week later he asks for the envelope, verifies that it has not been opened and then slits along the top and hands it to the Editor asking HIM to remove the contents and read it. Inside is found a piece of paper which predicts word for word the Headlines of the newspaper for that DAY. The Editor himself did not know what the headline would be until twenty-four hours previous! It appears that the prediction was written a week ago—a very good effect. The method of course is to have nothing in the envelope—and to shoot the billet in when you use the pencil to slit along the edge. If the billet is folded in the zig-zag manner, when it is in the envelope, if you run your fingers along the outside—pressing slightly—you will find the billet practically comes out flat. If you use the rolled method you must adopt some form of misdirection to excuse the appearance of the billet and to overcome the danger that the Editor may well feel the sealed envelope and find or feel nothing in it:—

(a) The billet may be rolled and then placed in a very small rimless test tube—which is then corked or sealed. The test tube and billet complete are loaded into the pencil and when desired the "message sealed in a little bottle" is shot into the envelope. It is natural for the paper to be rolled if it is in a small bottle, and the fact that it is in a bottle—gives extra conviction to the fact that all was sealed beforehand.

86

(*b*) In the presence of the Editor you write something (calling it a prediction) on a slip of paper and then ROLL IT UP and seal it in the envelope. He watches you roll it—so later when he sees the billet in rolled form, it is nothing more than he expected. When it comes to opening the envelope, obviously you have two billets. You use the pencil to open the envelope and shoot the second one in then. However, as you do so you grip the first through the envelope—and having slit it open, you appear to tip out the rolled billet on to the table or the Editor's hand. Whilst he unrolls that one to read it—you quietly remove the first and then put the envelope on the table for examination.

(*c*) The first billet—a piece of paper the same size as the second is written with the message: " 'I certify that the prediction enclosed in this envelope was written by me on May 16th, 1958'—signed Corinda". Now, this is very important, this piece of paper is rolled into two little rods—one piece of paper shaped like the letter "S" with one roll at the top and one at the bottom (see diagrams). When this is in the envelope—it feels like two pieces of rolled paper —actually it is one. Later, when the real prediction goes in you tip out, or they take out—two. They are told to read the "S" message first—and then to see if you have made a correct prediction from the other slip!

(*d*) This is one of the best methods—as it removes all danger of anyone tampering with the envelope in your absence. You start by simply showing the envelope sealed and telling the Editor that inside in a prediction concerning something that will happen in a week's time. You have him put his signature on the flap and then you lock it in a steel cash box and keep the key yourself. The lock may be sealed with wax to aid the precautions and the effect. This steel cash box is simply one of those strongly made cash boxes that cost about ten shillings and are obtainable from many office equipment companies and stationers. He cannot feel the envelope if it is locked in a cash box—and the sealing of the message under such elaborate conditions makes the trick so much more impressive. However, from your point of view—it is just as easy to perform. If you use this method—call the cash box "a safe deposit box" which sounds much more impressive—and should the trick receive any publicity in the press—the wording "safe deposit" could easily be mis-construed as "locked in the vaults of a bank"!! I mention this— because that is exactly what happened to me on one occasion.

To summarise the Billet Pencil—it is a beautiful thing. It is the very essence of natural behaviour—using natural apparatus. That is Mentalism.

## (2) The Billet Knife—Dr. Jaks

This is a dealer-item on the market so I am not in a position to give you constructional details. However, I can say that for occasions when you are able to use a Paper Knife as an excuse to open an envelope this is a very good appliance. It works on the same principle as my Billet Pencil, that is, shooting the prediction into the envelope—but it has the drawback that you cannot carry a paper-knife as an everyday object in the pocket. The billet is unloaded from the tip of the knife—and it has been made in wood and metal.

### (3) The Billet Knife—Sackville

This is a variation of the Dr. Jaks Billet Knife which shoots the billet from the side instead of the tip of the knife. It will accommodate a much larger billet and there is much less finger movement during operation than there is with both the Billet Pencil and Jaks Knife. The mechanism was designed by Neville Sackville and it works by a series of cross levers which operate from a button. When the operating button is pushed about one quarter of an inch—it forces out the billet which may be anything up to the size of a One pound note. Again it has the drawback that a Paper knife is not commonplace as a pocket item. Like the Billet Pencil, this item is in my catalogue as a Magical Dealer and so I have had every opportunity of examining the knife in detail. It is absolutely amazing how by moving one little lever a fraction of an inch—the knife shoots out a billet about three inches long—the principle is very ingenious and yet very simple. It is so powerful—that the billet can be shot out for a distance of two or three feet when the ejection mechanism is operated.

### (4) The Impromptu Billet Knife

This is not something that you will use as a standard technique—but it is well worth knowing for an emergency. Any fairly wide table knife can be used as a Billet knife. On one side of the blade you must have something sticky to hold the folded billet. Chewing gum works like a charm—and in my experience is equally as good as any magician's wax I have encountered. The billet is stuck on the knife and the knife is used to open the envelope— after which, the billet is retained by finger pressure and the knife removed. If you must show both sides of the knife, you can use the "Paddle move"— but there is no reason to show both sides of the knife.

### (5) The Pocket Index

This piece of apparatus consists of several bits of cardboard stuck together to form a miniature filing cabinet for the pocket. It is used to hold playing cards in a known order, and little tabs sticking up make it possible for you to count by feel to the position of any card in the index. The Pocket Index is a very useful piece of apparatus—it can be the *modus operandi* for many mental miracles. However, if you have ever bought one from a dealer— the chances are you got an instruction sheet which said something like— "put the cards in the index and when you want to remove one, count along the tabs and pull it out". That is an easy thing to write—and a very hard thing to do. Bearing in mind that more often than not—speed of location and accuracy are vital to the success of your trick, it stands to reason that your index must be well constructed and that you must be well practised. I can help you quite a bit on this subject as I have used a pocket index for a long time—and know the snags. On top of that I will give you the constructional details of a special pocket index for playing cards—that you will be able to make. This will reward you for the price you paid for this copy of Step Four, as the index I am about to describe is normally sold by me for 14/-.

CORINDA'S BILLET PENCIL

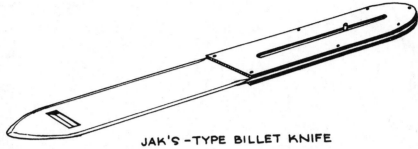

JAK'S -TYPE BILLET KNIFE

SACKVILLE BILLET KNIFE

BILLET

IMPROMPTU BILLET KNIFE

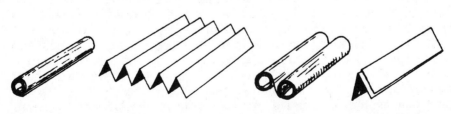

ROLLED
BILLET

ZIG-ZAG FOLDED
BILLET

"S"-ROLLED
BILLET

FLAT FOLDED
BILLET

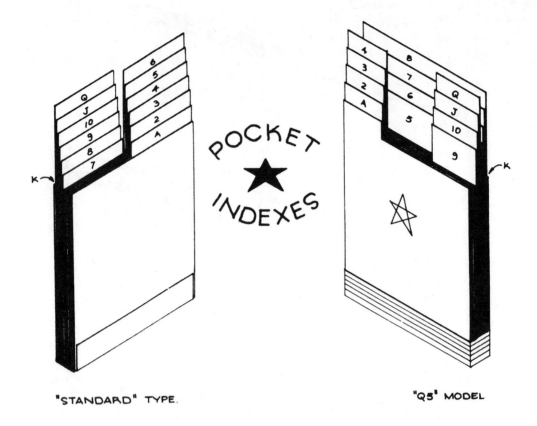

"STANDARD" TYPE.                                    "Q5" MODEL

On the left you see a diagram of the Standard Pocket Index. Most indexes are of this construction. On the right you see the type I recommend. It was invented by a little fellow that knows a lot of magic—Patrick Page, and it has been sold by our Studio under the title "The Q.5 Pocket Index".

If you look at the standard model, you will see that you have two main sections. Each section (one to the left and one to the right) has seven compartments. Some models have only six on one side. Into each of these sections you put the cards in some known order (usually A, 2, 3, 4, 5, 6, 7). One card goes into each compartment. The tabs on the index stick up one above the other—so that by feeling along the row and counting the tabs—you can find any card. Remember you are working by FEEL alone—so if you miss a tab—or count two as one—you will withdraw the wrong card. To limit this problem the Q.5 Index has special constructional features which reduce the finger-counting to a minimum. So little in fact, that you can reach ANY card within a maximum of two counts. Instead of having two main sections—the Q.5 Index has three—and a separate partition at the back. Each section of three has four individual compartments which allow for twelve cards. The last card—a King—goes into the separate compartment at the back. To see the difference, look at both diagrams and work out how you would go about reaching the 4 (say of Spades). In the Standard model—it would be situated in the middle of the left-hand section. You would have to count 1-2-3-4 (four counts) or coming down the index backwards, 6-5-4 (three counts). To reach the same card in the Q.5 Index takes ONE count.

I am not quoting the number four as a favourable example to the Q.5 Pocket Index because you can work out any number you like—and you will find it can be reached in a count of one or two—no more. The next example is a Seven. We know that each section has four compartments, and that they go in the order:—Left Section: A, 2, 3, 4; Middle Section: 5, 6, 7, 8; Right Section: 9, 10, J, Q—and the King at the back which can literally be forgotten as it can be removed immediately. Number seven we know, will be in the middle section and since we can always count from one of two ends—we always take the shortest distance and simply go 8-7 (two counts).

To make the Q.5 Pocket Index use thick strong paper or board. The thickness should be a little more than that of a playing card. The index will have to take a lot of wear and tear in the pocket and unless it is strongly made—it will soon fall to pieces. To index a full pack of cards you require TWO pocket indexes—so make two whilst you are in production. Each index requires fourteen pieces of card cut to a size $2\frac{3}{4} \times 5\frac{1}{2}$ inches. Having cut fourteen pieces of card—making sure they are all square, take five pieces and spread them out so that each piece overlaps the next by about a quarter of an inch—longways. Take a pair of scissors and cut right across the last section to overlap. Now you have five pieces of card each one a quarter of an inch shorter than the next; put the very shortest one to the back—this is the King section and then bind those five cards together with sellotape by running a strip about half an inch wide around the bottom. As all the cards are square at one end—you get a series of "steps" at the other—that is the first part of your index—actually it is the middle counting section. The next section to make is the right-hand counting block. Take four of the cards left and stack them in the overlapping position again. This time cut out a large corner which is two-thirds the width of the cards and $1\frac{1}{2}$ inches deep. Bind those four together with tape just as you did for the first block. For the last section, the one that goes to the left, take the remaining five cards and stack them with the quarter-inch overlap. Cut out a large corner on the opposite side this time two-thirds the width of the card and—note carefully—$1\frac{1}{4}$ inches deep (a quarter of an inch less than the previous block). Bind these cards like the others. Now assemble the three blocks in order, the first one you made goes at the back—the second in the middle and the last on the face. Square up all three and then staple them at their base together and bind over the staples with more tape. You should hammer the staples out flat before putting on the tape and then you will not get any bumps sticking up.

The constructional details sound a bit complicated because it is hard to describe clearly—but follow the instructions and look carefully at the diagram and it will take you about twenty minutes to make a pair. Having assembled the complete index, I always bind each tab with sellotape to give it added strength.

To load the index ready for use you pair off the cards into two groups. In one index you put the Hearts and Clubs, and in the other the Diamonds and Spades. In the first compartment in Index One, you put the Ace of Hearts and the Ace of Clubs. Two cards go together in the same compartment. However, you must be sure that you can tell which is which—so we always put the red card to the BACK—in other words, the Club on top of the Heart. In the next compartment (see the Diagram) we put the Two of

Hearts and the Two of Clubs—and so on. At the back we put the King of Hearts and the King of Clubs. We do the same with index number two—this time putting the Diamonds (RED) to the back and the spades to the front. The only thing that remains is to put one index in each pocket—and to know which way they face when in the pocket—that is important. We put them with the Kings nearest to the body which makes it easier to reach the tabs for counting. Unless you have to—do not have two indexes in one pocket as they cause too much bulk and do not index 52 cards if the effect could just as well be done using 26. The blacks and reds are spread between two pockets so as to avoid having to pull cards all of the same colour from one pocket—which could look suspicious when many cards are produced. When not in use keep a strong elastic band around each index to retain it in compact condition. Face the cards in the index so that when they are removed from the pocket they come out showing the BACK of the card—you can see it first to be sure you are right and at least have the chance to change it if you are wrong. Finally, it sometimes pays to seal every card in a small paypacket so that it is produced in an envelope. If you do this, I suggest you do as I do, and mark each envelope with a small dot to tell you which card is inside.

If you have never used a Pocket Index, you might wonder if it's worth all this trouble. I can assure you it is. There are dozens of very good effects—including some first class Predictions that you will be able to perform using them. It is like having 52 "get outs"—the need to force a card becomes unnecessary—you cover every possible contingency in your pockets. We will deal with some tricks later on, but let me give you just one as an example.

The Mentalist shows a small sealed envelope and puts it in his wallet which he lays on the table. He tells the spectator that in the envelope is sealed a card—one card that he thinks will be the same as the one that the spectator will now choose. To obviate any trickery—he suggests that the spectator merely thinks of a card—and tell his choice to everybody so that there can be no disputes. When he names his card you reach into your pocket and take out the card named which is already sealed in an envelope the same as is in your wallet. You palm this envelope (it is not much larger than a playing card) and keep up the patter. Casually reach forward and pick up your wallet and appear to take out the envelope you hold in the palm. This is not by any means difficult as the wallet screens your hand. Throw the envelope on to the table and have the spectator open it and show the card inside. Whilst this is done—you may, if you wish, remove the other envelope from the wallet in case they want to inspect it to see what else is inside. If you do the card in wallet effect—using the slit wallet principle, this is a wonderful version. Have the card thought of by the spectator, take it from the index and load it into your wallet as you take it from the pocket. Hand the wallet to the spectator who removes the only envelope inside—which contains a card he thought of—a stunning prediction. Do not do this if you have the type of wallet that shows up the slit very clearly. This should be sufficient to portray the value of the pocket index for the time being.

## (6) The Billet Index

This is also a Pocket Index—but to avoid confusion with the index used to hold Playing Cards, I will refer to it as the Billet Index as it is used to hold Billets (small pieces of paper) in a fixed order.

There are several types of Billet Indexes. It all depends on how many pieces of paper you want to arrange in order. The first use of an index to hold pieces of paper bearing the names of cards is attributed by Annemann to Al Baker. The early models were blocks of wood with holes drilled in rows and billets stuck in the holes. These do not appear to have been very satisfactory—although I have never used them myself so I cannot give an honest opinion. The method I suggest for working with billets to cover playing cards—is a smaller version of the Q.5 Pocket Index. However, in some cases you will require an index to deal with only a few billets and the easiest way to do this is to put one billet in each pocket and remember which pocket contains which billet (See "The Body Index System"). Before developing the Billet Index I use, which is a small version of the Q.5, I used to work with the type invented by Annemann which is described in full on Page 79 of Annemann's "Practical Mental Effects". I found that model entirely practical and changed to the Q.5 only because there was less counting involved.

To load the Q.5 Billet Index you use the same order as you would with cards. However, each billet (size $3 \times 2$ in.) is first folded once each way and since they are smaller than cards, we stack one upright and one sideways in each compartment—so that the two suits do not become mixed. It is important to push each billet well down into the index so that it is held tightly in position. You must remember that if the billets are written in pencil—to use pencil when performing—and if in ink, to use ink.

The Q.5 Billet Index can be used for a wide range of things. The billets can cover numbers, cards, colours, names and so on. Fifty-two possibilities cover a pretty wide range if you consider some of the things you can use.

### (7) The Cigarette Packet Pellet Index: Tremaine-Corinda

Under the title "Mind over Matter" in Part IV of this book, you will find a Prediction effect that is in a class on its own. The trick seems so utterly impossible, that it cannot fail to bewilder those who see it. In order to perform this masterpiece, you will have to prepare a special pellet index. However, you will be able to put this to good use for other effects so your time will not be wasted.

The drawing shows the constructional details of the Pellet Index. The theme is very ingenious. It is presumed that in order to "index" fifty-two pellets, which are very small pieces of paper, the first problem is to find some means to keep them in order and second, how to find any one quickly. Both of these difficulties are nicely removed in the Cigarette Packet Pellet Index; the papers are held firmly in position and since you are able to remove any pellet WHILST LOOKING (instead of working by feel) you can hardly fail to locate the correct one in a matter of seconds. When the packet is properly set up—one cigarette is placed inside and it is under cover of removing this and lighting it—that you steal the pellet. A natural move in itself and the apparatus (a cigarette packet) is hardly subject to suspicion.

You require two Players Cigarette packets—the twenty size. Remove both drawers and from one cut off the bottom flap and the very top flap. On the other drawer you line out four columns in ink (a drawing pen is best) and then divide each column into thirteen sections. For each of these sections you make a small slit with a razor blade and into these slits you place a small unfolded slip of paper—size about $\frac{3}{4} \times \frac{1}{2}$ in. leaving just the top of each slip sticking out of the slit. On each slip is written the name of one card. The wording should be 2 of Hearts . . . but write "2 of" along the top edge—and the suit diagonally below. This means that each slip will show the name of the card it represents as it sticks out of the slit. Added to this you write the name of each slip alongside the slit actually on the packet and arrange it so that you have all the hearts in one column running from Ace to King—then the Diamonds and so forth. Write the suit at the head of the column—as you cannot tell this from the index. The drawing gives you a very good idea of what the Index should look like. It remains only to say that when you have the slips in place, you stick the second drawer (with the missing flaps) over the back of the Index drawer. The sticking is done at the top only and this now forms a flap which keeps all the pellets in place—and yet it may be lifted when you want to reload the index.

To avoid confusion it is stated once more that when referring to an index for playing cards, we call it "A Pocket Index"—for Billets (paper slips size about $3 \times 2$ in.) we call it "a Billet Index" and for very small papers—"a Pellet Index".

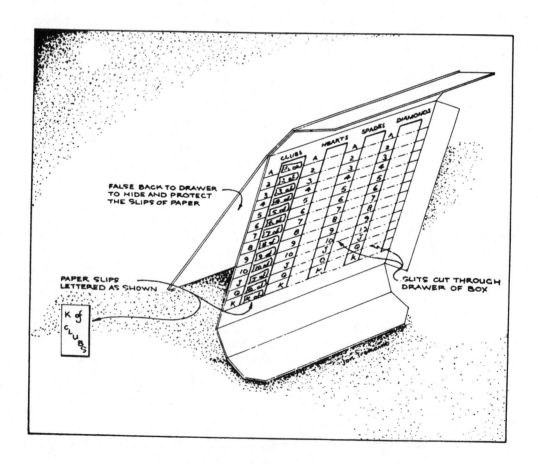

### (8) The Body Index (Corinda)

Later on in this series we shall be discussing a "Mentalists Pack"—which is a pack of cards containing duplicates so that the maximum number of different spot cards is only ten. With such a pack, or with any trick where the possibilities can be confined to ten—we are able to index the cards by distribution on our persons and since this requires no apparatus whatsoever—we will find it a good standby for emergencies:—

Consider the EFFECT—a pack is handed to a spectator to mix they are then fanned and the spectator told to remember any card *he can see*. The deck is placed aside and then the Mentalist asks that the card be named. No sooner is the chosen card declared—than the spectator is asked to reach into the Mentalist's jacket pocket and pull out the contents. He removes one card—the only card in the pocket and the same one as he thought of a moment ago. There are very many variations of revealing the chosen card from the index—this is but one.

To index the cards, as we call it, "on your body"—start with the lowest value and place that down the *left-hand side* of your left ankle (just tuck it into the sock) it should face the leg. Put the next one (in value order all the time) down the *right-hand side* of the left ankle, put the third down the left side of the right ankle—the fourth down the right side of the right ankle. To show any one of these cards—without revealing the others is a simple matter. Suppose it was to be the Ace—situated down the left side of the left ankle. You would turn the body to face the left side to the audience, make sure the left leg was pointing directly at them, then slowly pull up the trouser leg and raise just enough for all to see a card stuck in your sock! Since they cannot see through your leg they will not get a chance to see Number Two on the other side.

From the legs or the ankles, we move up the body to the pockets; keeping to our system of going from left to right we start with the trouser pockets. In the left goes number Five—and in the right, number Six. Then up a bit more to the outside jacket pockets—left number Seven—right number Eight. We now come right up to the top jacket pocket—the handkerchief pocket for number Nine—and number Ten goes into the wallet on the inside pocket (jacket) or it may just stay in that pocket. It takes you two seconds to think where any card maybe found and if you present the effect correctly—no one will suspect that you ever had anything BUT ONE CARD. Some performers may prefer to have each card sealed in a paypacket or to use index cards that have a different coloured back to the deck in use.

The application of the Body Index System during a routine will be seen in Part III under a stage trick called "Quadruplication" by Corinda.

### (9) The Swami Gimmick

A survey of the Technique of Predictions would be incomplete without mention of the Swami Gimmick. However, Step One of this series gives you precise details of this small apparatus and further writing would be superfluous. There are many good Predictions included in the Step One book—and you would be advised to run through them.

### (10) The Switch and The Force

Many Predictions rely on the technique of switching an envelope or forcing a card or other things. There are very many methods by which this may be done—but there is no necessity whatsoever to know them all. The most

95

you should try and master is ONE good way to switch (or exchange) say a Billet, ONE good way to switch an Envelope, ONE good way to switch a Pack of cards and so on. Never mind about variations—there is no necessity to search constantly for new and better ways—if you work hard enough on any solitary method—you will get it down to a fine art. The same applies to Forcing. Learn ONE good card force and use it—for it is better to find different ways to present an effect by forcing a card, than it is to find different forces to present the same old effect.

We will give a few examples—but it is as well to mention that you have at your disposal a more detailed examination of Billet Switching in Step Six and Card Forcing in Step Ten.

(a) To switch an Envelope, a Billet, a Pellet or Playing Card—there are two outstanding requirements. Misdirection and Timing. We will analyse the Scarne Pellet Switch as an example.

## Scarne Pellet Switch

The Scarne Pellet Switch is an ideal way of exchanging two pellets. It is easy to do, hard to detect, almost impossible to do wrong and is not widely known. Basically it is this. You have one small rolled pellet (a cigarette paper) on the table. You have one in the hand, moreover, you must now swap one for the other without anyone knowing. The one in the hand we shall call Pellet "X"—the one on the table Pellet "Z". Hold "X" pinched between the second finger and ball of the thumb—the first finger extends a bit. Go to "Z" and pick it up with the first finger and ball of thumb and at the same time drop "X". In effect you swap over fingers on the ball of your thumb and at the same time pick up and drop a Pellet. So we know the MOVES—but there is more to it than that. Our next consideration is how to cover the move — Why should we pick up the Pellet in the first place? Scarne utilises this switch in his 'Think-a-Card' routine (a good mental effect) when the Pellets are used in conjunction with cards. The pack is spread face downwards and a card withdrawn. The Mentalist has just written a prediction and dropped the Pellet on to the table. The card is taken and placed over the Pellet—so that it cannot be touched! Now we have our MISDIRECTION, for when we want to get the Pellet later to see if it predicts the card correctly, we can reach forward, lift the card slightly, bring forth the Pellet and drop it bang in the middle of the card. It would appear that you have just taken the Pellet and put it from underneath the card to the top. The switch is performed then. It remains now for us to consider the TIMING. If we dropped the Pellet on to the table, immediately covered it with a card and then without so much as a pause lifted it out and put it on top of the card—we will have to work out why the card was placed over the Pellet in the first place. It is not right—we must allow time to pass to make the move logical and then, accompanied by suitable patter and action—all in the right tempo—we make the move. (You will be able to use the Cigarette Packet Pellet Index to perform this trick).

Our analysis shows the rudiments of the switch. If we understand the general principle—we can switch anything within reason. You don't have to go reading through dozens of magic books to find a method—it is much, better that you construct your own switch. If you start by saying to yourself— "Now I want to exchange this piece of paper for that—how can I do it"— solve that and then say "Now how can I hide the moves under cover of mis-direction and timing". You will find that when you get the switch—it is the one which suits you and your style as no other switch can—because no other switch was made for you. Bear in mind that Misdirection comes in many shapes and forms—in Patter, Sound, Action, Facial Expressions—especially the eyes—and if you use misdirection you will be able to perform anything equal to the most complicated sleight in existence. We will consider two more examples.

## The Switch of a Pack of Cards

We shall deal with this from a purely theoretical point of view. The spectator has seen the deck and we want him to hold it—but at the same time we desire to switch the deck so that he really holds another pack. We have the second pack in our left jacket pocket. We take the pack he has seen and say "Now I want you to put the cards in your jacket pocket and hold your hand over the flap like this . . . ." following the action to the words you SHOW him what you want, put the pack in the left pocket, let go, take out the hand and hold down the flap apparently securing the cards in the pocket—reach back—take out pack No. 2 and give it to him—where-. upon he immediately puts it in his pocket.

If the action was performed in a natural manner—it would not seem unnatural that you should show the spectator what to do—that is why the right patter with the right movements is of the greatest importance. There is a degree of boldness in this type of work—and boldness should not be scorned; as long as the switch is not blatant—you can be as cheeky as you like.

## The Bare Hand Envelope Switch

This serves as another theoretical example—although you will find that the method is used during a "Just Chance" routine published in Step Two. It is a case of having two envelopes on show and wanting to switch one for the other. The technique is the height of boldness—you literally exchange them under their noses! BUT IT WORKS. You have no stack of envelopes—no mechanical apparatus or gimmicks—the only requirement is the Mentalist's Best Friend—personal ability.

The spectator holds envelope "X" you hold "Z" and want to swap. You go up to him and ask him to be sure that he still has the folded paper sealed inside—and instinctively he begins to feel the envelope. Immediately you reach forward and take—I repeat—take it from him saying "look if I hold it up to the light you can see the shadow of the paper inside—right?" You hold his envelope "X" in your right hand and "Z" in the left. Without much waiting you continue, "and the same with this one—you see the shadow again?" Timing the move (if it can be called a move since you do nothing) you bring down his envelope and for a second bring the two together, one on top of the other—then show him "X" AGAIN—but at the same time you say "and you see the shadow again"—as though you were showing number two. You cannot detect when the envelopes are together—whether they are switched or not—and to prove it—you will see the spectator's eyes go straight back to your left hand which he honestly thinks holds his envelope —this one you give him.

These few examples should be sufficient to illustrate the general principles of switching. It would be pointless to overburden you with dozens of varied techniques and since it all depends on what you want to switch, the best approach is to understand the simple rules and apply them to the best of your ability.

(*b*) **Forcing.** Here again we can only deal with the matter by analysis and cope with general principles. I will, however, step out of line from other writers and probably make a few enemies by advocating that you discard some accepted methods of forcing. I refer to such methods as those which involve weird and wonderful apparatus and quaint sayings. I refer to such classics as the Drawer Box and the Changing Bag. Doubtlessly these items were good in their day—but their day is past and outside of doing a Mental Act in a Cathedral I wouldn't go within a mile of a changing Bag. If apparatus has to be used to perform a Force or a Switch—it is essential that it is in keeping with Mentalism and that it does not in any way resemble a conjuring appliance. One of the cleanest mechanical switches available to the Mentalist is the Dunninger-Annemann Routine using a changing tray as is described on page 133 of Annemann's "Practical Mental Effects", the tray may also be used for Forcing.

Aside from unsuitable apparatus (and there are a lot more examples that could be given) we are bound to reject the peculiar approach which always ends with the tag line "That leaves". This is an utter waste of time and a lot of nonsense. Suppose you have to force one of three books. You lay them all in a row on the table and say "kindly select any two" and if they leave the force book—go straight ahead without saying "that leaves this one"— what else could it do? If not, you say, "thank you, give me one of them"— if you get the force book you make it appear that this one was selected for the test, if they keep it, you say "right, that's the one you have chosen so that's the one we shall use".

As for cards, the easiest way to force a card is to use a Forcing Pack and after that there are many methods and as long as you know ONE good way— that's all you need to know.

Other forces achieved by the use of Dice, coins etc. may be used, but generally speaking they do not improve the effect. I detest Book Tests that start off by the throwing of a pair of dice and then go into a long involved counting-location of one word. I would sooner use a Swami Gimmick and do away completely with the force in the first place. All these things you must judge for yourself—and as a general guide to forcing—make it quick, clean and simple and above all, make it *convincing*.

## (11) The Prediction Chest

This is usually a costly affair. A special box bestowed with the title "Prediction Chest" and if you can afford the luxury it is a good thing to have. There are two or three types available, Nelson Enterprises (Magical Dealers, U.S.A.) market one variety, and there are others you can buy or make. The principles vary. Sometimes the billet is shot from the key into the chest when the lock is undone—sometimes the billet is written on whilst it is in the chest and sometimes the billet is switched although the chest is locked. If you want a really reliable model you would do best to buy one rather than risk a home made model.

## (12) Trickery with Envelopes

## (a) The Carbon Prediction Envelope

This can be a very good technique and with the right sort of trick and presentation you have one of the best methods of working.

The idea is to have a specially prepared envelope. Inside the envelope is stuck a sheet of BLACK carbon paper, it goes on the address side with the glossy side outwards so that when you put a card in the envelope and then impress from outside, the writing is duplicated by carbon impression on the card inside. However, it is as well to dress the plot a little more and to have a letter or fully worded prediction in place of a plain card in the envelope. If you "line up" the wording inside so that you know the exact spot above the spaces in the prediction, you can write on the envelope and fill in as you go. Further details about this type of thing appear in Step One—which also covers work with N.C.R. white carbon envelopes and paper, and Stylus writers.

Under the heading of Stage Tricks Part III we give an example effect using this technique.

### (b) The Nest of Envelopes

There are three ways that you can use the Nest of Envelopes. First, you can have them all sealed at the start and by having the middle one prepared as for the Carbon Prediction Envelope you can press hard with a ball pen to get the writing-copy on a Prediction in the middle of the Nest. Or, you can have them all nested but open ready to drop the small card into the middle one and then seal quickly. For this you use a Swami to write on the card and then produce the envelopes under cover of misdirection loading the card inside. Third, you may transfer a carbon impression of some writing into the centre envelope.

To seal them all quickly you may use Rubber Cement along the edges so that the envelopes seal on impact or by slight pressure, alternatively you may use the "Seal-easy" type paypacket which is obtainable from stationers in various sizes and which require no preparation. You just press the flap down to seal—no licking is required.

Three nesting envelopes are usually considered sufficient although Robert-Houdin describes an effect which uses six.

Under the heading Part IV. Drawing Room Tricks, we give an effect to illustrate this technique.

### (13) Stooges

This is no place for an argument about whether or not you should use stooges. All I'm going to say is this. I use them—quite a lot, and I'll list a few of the dodges that come in useful—and if you want to copy them good luck—and if not—suit yourself.

You can classify Stooges into two groups—those who volunteer and those who have no choice. I rather like the second group as they act normally up to the last minute! This is a simple effect that was taught to me by "Teddy" Love in a lecture some time ago—I believe he credited it to Al Koran. The effect literally paralyses an audience—it's incredible. You ask for any two people to help and any two come on to the stage. You have three packs of cards and give each person a free choice of one pack. They stand behind you and both are told to open their cases and to remove any card from the pack and put it in their top jacket pocket back outwards. You do the same with a card from your pack. You then take each deck and fan to show that every pack is made up of different cards. Then you turn to the left spectator and say—"and what did you choose" he shows the Four of Clubs—you you turn to the one on the right "and what did you choose", he also chose

99

the Four of Clubs and you then show the one card in your pocket,—The Four of Clubs! Alternatively, you show your card first and the spectators show theirs afterwards. The method is very simple. The face card in every pack is a joker which has a gummed label reading "LOOK! Help me to fool the others—take the Four of Clubs and keep this a secret between us— thanks"; the label is stuck over the face of the joker. There are one or two finer points. You glance back to see that both spectators are reading the joker-fake when they take their cards out and, to make it easy for them to find the black Four of Clubs quickly—you put it near the face of the pack and surround it with all red cards so that it stands out clearly. Finally, you avoid showing the fake-joker when fanning the cards to the audience.

A similar technique has been used by various people including Annemann when a pocket watch is handed out to the audience—one spectator gets it and is asked to set it at any time. You have predicted that time. On the face of the watch is a small label reading "Please set the watch to 8.45 and keep this a secret". The label is such that it can be removed easily—and any of the self-adhesive variety will do.

## Summary of Technique

It may well be said that no Mental Act is really complete without at least one Prediction. The importance of this type of trick has been stressed in the opening. We have seen that there are many ways and means to produce this type of effect and we have covered a selection of apparatus generally used for this work. Needless to say, there are other methods and pieces of equipment—but the selection I have covered have been chosen as represent- ative of *basic technique* and there is nothing like sound, time-tested procedure.

Finally, a word or two about presentation. Predictions are not the easiest of effects to work—that is, to work properly. There are three common failings which can quickly reduce the trick to a low level of entertainment. First, the plot—unless it is easy to understand the audience cannot fully appreciate the achievement at the end. It is very easy to slip into a complex, involved preparation that so confuses the audience that they *forget* what has occurred. You probably know what I mean—it is the sort of effect that goes like this:—

> "Take a card, sign your name on it, put it in this envelope which I will now mix with the other six I have here. Now I will number each envelope from one to seven and I will ask you to mix them all so that I do not know which one contains your card. Now I would like to draw your attention to that slate which is standing on the table—please remember it is on show all the time. Now we will have another person take a card from this pack which has a different coloured back from the one you used. Will you please take a card and sign your name and then also place it in this envelope. Again I shall mix your envelope with six others and number them so before you mix them. Now both of you have a stack of seven envelopes—and . . . ."

I won't burden you with any more of that nonsense—but that's how it goes—and you should never be guilty of such an offence to Mentalism. Keep the plot clear and if possible—quick. Avoid unnecessary distractions— misdirection is the only excuse for diverting attention.

The second common failing is lack of good timing. Far too many magicians and mentalists do not pay sufficient attention to the tempo of the trick. They will deal to the nearest split second with the running time of their act—but forget that each trick has a running time of its own. More than that—it is not just a matter of how long it takes to do the trick. It is also very important to know *at what rate* to perform the effect. With every Prediction effect there is always one crucial moment when you are in the best position to end the trick. You do not necessarily end the trick just as soon as you have completed the mechanics—you always end when interest is at its maximum—or, with an element of surprise—just before the audience anticipate the conclusion. It is generally a good policy to increase the tempo towards the end so that the added pace becomes part of the build up to the climax. Remember that varied tempo makes presentation interesting and that never changing rate is like never changing speech—monotonous. No book can really convey a proper understanding of perfect timing—it is a thing which experience alone can teach.

The third common failing is what I always call "The re-cap complex". Unfortunately, most predictions have to go through several stages of preparation. Aware of this, the performer frequently reminds the audience of all the various things that were done so that they may understand at the end—just what was achieved. Sometimes there is no answer to this—recapitulation—it has to be so; but on other occasions it is not necessary. From what I have seen I suppose that there are Mentalists who think that recapitulation is part of presentation. In my opinion it is not. It is both boring and frustrating to see a person go through several stages—and then turn round and keep reminding you what he did. Unless it adds to the impact of the effect—or simplifies the understanding of the trick—try and talk about something other than that which everybody knows you have done; it is as well to remember that the audience have nothing better to do than to sit and watch you perform—so you should *expect* them to know what is happening. If they do not—your trick is due for reconstruction.

The next two parts of this Step deal with a selection of Prediction effects. They have been divided into two classes—those suitable for stage and those suitable for drawing room or more intimate gatherings. Most of the tricks have been chosen to illustrate some particular approach or technique for the performance of Predictions. As far as possible I have given credit where it is due, and I am grateful to the many people who have contributed effects and suggestions in this Step.

## PART THREE: PREDICTIONS FOR THE STAGE

### (1) "A Million to One" by Corinda

If ever a book on mentalism was named appropriately, the Cook & Buckley effort called "Gems of Mental Magic"—was rightly named. The book is indeed full of gems—and it was from an effect called "It's a small world" published in the book—that gave me the original idea of this trick.

The original effect, as an effect—was excellent. However, the method required the use of an assistant and a large globe of the world—which could be costly. It was a Prediction. The performer wrote out his prediction in full view, sealed it in an envelope and then had a spectator stick a pin anywhere into the globe. When the name of the nearest town or city was announced—it was shown that the Prediction also gave that name! There's nothing wrong with that for a stage trick!! However, I so much liked the plot that I decided to work a little harder to try and simplify the mechanics—and as a result I call this variation "A Million to One"—and give my thanks to "Gems of Mental Magic" for the inspiration.

**The Effect.** The performer asks for the assistance of a member of the audience who comes on to the stage. He then writes something on a card, which in turn is sealed in an envelope and signed by the spectator. The envelope is then handed to the spectator on the stage—who is told to put it in his pocket and on no account let you (the performer) touch it again.

You now draw attention to a large board upon which is pinned a map. This can be a map of the world—but we prefer to have it a map of England which does away with large areas of sea—see?!

You explain that you have made a Prediction of something that will occur very soon but you do not indicate exactly what it will be. You go on to say that in a moment your assistant, the spectator, will be invited to stick a pin anywhere he likes into the map—but just in case some members of the audience may be a little suspicious—you will blindfold the spectator who will then stick the pin in and arrive at a town or city by pure chance.

You blindfold the spectator—with a genuine blindfold so that he cannot see. You then lead him across the stage and stand him in front of the map. You put a pin in his hand and tell him now to wave his hand round in three big circles and then to jab forward and stick the pin into the board. This he does. As soon as the pin is pushed into the board you bring out a small pocket torch and light up the surrounding area—at the same time telling the spectator to take off the blindfold and call our loud the nearest town or city to the pin-pointed position. This he does. We will suppose he calls out "Birmingham" . . . .

He is told to remove the envelope from his pocket—check his signature—open it himself and read out what you wrote on the card. It reads, " 'It's a Million to One if you do it—but I think you will arrive at Birmingham'—signed Corinda". That is the effect, now for the modus operandi—and be warned—this is mentalism—there's nothing to it, the working is absurdly simple and yet bold. If you are a bit weak hearted—this is not a trick for you I can tell you that!

**The Method.** You will require as a minimum of apparatus, a map of England size about $3 \times 2$ ft., which may be purchased for a few shillings from any good stationers, a board large enough to hold the map and best covered with a sheet of cork to hold the pin in position, a blindfold—and the card and envelope for the prediction. Lastly, you require the means by which the trick is achieved—this gentlemen—is another pin!

Before you laugh at me—all I ask is that you try what I am about to say. Get a map and stick it on the wall. In the middle stick a pin—just an ordinary 1 in. long pin. Stand five feet away and you will not see the pin—so what chance have the audience got—when they are not even looking for it? That's just how it works. You prepare by sticking a pin into the map—making sure it goes right into some town or city. This place you record in the prediction. When you have the spectator come up keep him at the other end of the stage, away from the board. When he is due to go near the board—YOU BLINDFOLD HIM! He is the only person likely to see the second pin—and somehow I think the blindfold will make that a bit difficult! So you give him another pin—and you stand him right in front of the map with his back to the audience, now they cannot see through him so until he stands aside they can't see where the pin goes—and he can't see because he's blindfolded. The swindle ends when as he sticks in his pin you quickly bring out the torch with the left hand and shine it on to *your* pin—for a second the right hand rests on the map as you lean forward to look closely at the position . . . the right hand now pulls his pin OUT of the board and all that remains is to allow the spectator who, by now has disentangled himself from the well-knotted blindfold—to read out the name of the pin-pointed town. As a last word I might add that should the Two Million to One event occur—and the spectator sticks his pin on top of yours you then leave them both there and show how great minds think alike . . .

## (2) "Quadruplication" by Corinda

This is a trick for a skilled performer. The methods, there are several, involve a certain amount of skill and work. The effect is well worth the trouble in my opinion—but you judge for yourself.

**The Effect.** A spectator is asked to go to the table and choose any card from a pack which lies there—ribbon spread face upwards. Just before he goes however, you hand him a small envelope and tell him to stick it in his top jacket pocket. He takes a card. You ask him to replace the others in the case and then to sign his initials on the card he chose. This done, he sticks it back into the pack which he drops into his pocket—the preparation is ended—the presentation begins . . . .

"Now sir! Let me see, you did have a free choice of any card? Well before I try any clever stuff I must see if you are a suitable subject. Do you read minds? NO! gracious me—how do you know—look, I'll write something on this slate—now, be honest do you know what it is? No? RIGHT! (You turn the slate round and on it is written a large "No"). You see— you are a mindreader! But then, so am I . . . is the card you chose the Nine of Spades? It is?—funny thing that, because it also happens to be the only card I took from another pack before I came this evening" (Performer reaches into pocket, removes one card—the Nine of Spades, then turns out the lining to show that otherwise the pocket is empty) "and what is more odd than that is the fact that I gave you a small envelope remember? May I have it—inside here is a card—I would like you to read it out loud . . . (it reads) "I've a sneaking suspicion you will select the 9 of S". Now that's incredible—but these things do happen don't they? You agree—good—but even then, if it so happened that all those cards were Nine of Spades—it would have been very easy—but let's make sure—you have them in your pocket—can I have them. Look—they are all different—and here we have your nine—and I believe those are your initials on the face? Excellent— well just in case you doubt me you might be interested to know that you happen to have chosen the only card with a black back in this pack— look . . . (performer shows all the backs—only the nine is black) which more or less proves that I knew which card you would choose—don't you agree? You do—I don't blame you!!"

**The Method.** You will require a pack of black backed cards made up of any ten cards repeated five times. You require a duplicate set of these ten set out in the Body Index System which I describe on Page 95 of this book. You require an ordinary pack of 52 cards with red backs—but the case should be the same as is used for the ten-card set up pack. You require a prediction written on a card set in a window envelope ready for use with a Swami Gimmick, described on Pages 12 and 13 of Step One. A slate and some chalk, a pencil, a table and a chair.

The set up pack is ready spread on the table the case lies beside it. You ask the spectator to choose a card and, as an afterthought remember the envelope so hastily place it in his top jacket pocket, window facing inwards so that it cannot be seen and leave it there. You time it so that you remember the envelope just after he has pulled out his card—so that you may see what he takes as you approach to give him the envelope. You must now play for time, so first get him to place the remaining cards in the case which you take. You ask him to put his initials on his card—and whilst searching in various pockets for a pencil—simply exchange the blue-backed pack for the ordinary red-backed one—which, by the way, is best done slowly and without any fuss. Simply have the pack ready for switching in the left jacket pocket. Reach into various pockets with the right hand and at the same time put the left hand in the left pocket for a moment and exchange the decks. Turn the body to screen this pocket as much as possible and keep talking all the time. Hand the spectator the pencil and tell him to initial his card. Tell him also to sit down—there is no need for him to stand and he has probably paid to sit! Hand him the ordinary pack and have him push his card inside—but keep near him to see that it goes in the right way up—although the trick is not ruined if it goes in upside down. Tell him to drop the cards in his pocket and begin the spiel leading up to the "No" slate gag. When you write "No"—to make sure they cannot guess go over the same lines several times—as though you were doing a drawing and be absolutely sure you word the question to the spectator very carefully . . . you must get the reply "No"— not "I'm not sure—or I haven't got a clue" . . . control your spectator to answer as you want him to answer. This part of the routine gets a laugh which is not easy to get with mental effects—and I am indebted to Fogel who first introduced the gag to me—it always works well.

The second stage cashes in on the Body Index System—which in this routine works very well—because should it happen to be one of the cards down the sock—you get a second laugh—and even if not, you still have created quite a stir . . . you reach to the right position and remove the card and show it.

The third stage uses a limited amount of skill. You refer back to the envelope but do so *only* when you are near enough to reach forward and take it from the spectators pocket. Whilst you explain what it contains (instead of recapping on the fact that he had it before he chose a card!) you use a thumb-writer to write his card by the brief initials like those we gave for the Nine of Spades . . . 9 of S. the rest of the prediction has been given already. Having covered the technique of this method in the greatest of detail in Step One, I feel justified in giving you the bare working on this at the moment—I am sure you will agree that space is saved. Just one important point—you don't want him to say 9 of S—so you lean forward and when he gets to the initials you say "Nine of Spades"—so that it is quickly interpreted in a favourable manner.

The last stage is comparatively easy. You remove the cards from the case and fan them to the spectator holding up the fan to show him the faces. Naturally you will see the backs and will therefore see the odd coloured card very quickly. You pull this up and out and ask him to confirm his initials. Then show the backs. There is very little chance of the spectator noting the duplicate of his card amid 52 others when shown them for an instant. That is the effect—or really what I should call the routine—I hope you will like it.

It is a good effect to illustrate a point mentioned earlier; the plot should be simple and quick—the revelation of the Prediction comes in four stages, but each one is designed to beat the last—so that a mounting interest is formed and a good strong climax awaits you at the end. There is a healthy balance between the four sub-tricks; the comedy gets you off to a good start and the Index card revelation introduces the first signs of what may be called skill. Following this, we step away from cards again for a brief instant (we did so first with the slate) and deal with the written prediction in the envelope. Here you will note the friendly theme is maintained with the wording of the Prediction which although accurate is also light-hearted. There is no necessity for a pompous declaration that reads like the Riot Act. The final revelation can leave no doubt that your trick was a Prediction and to draw the full benefit from the only black-back card in the red-back pack—you must, of course, show the deck to the audience—simply by fanning to disclose the faces and the backs. The last few words of the patter—should be on the lines suggested—to end the routine on the friendly basis that has been maintained throughout. You will use your patter to suit your style, but I would not advise you to make this one of those "show the whites of the eyes and look like a Frankenstein monster" effect—you do not have to present every mental effect with Svengali-type dramatisation and light-heartedness makes a pleasant change.

### (3) "De Profundis" by Corinda

From an idea applied by Dunninger, from a title used by Oscar Wilde and by the help of Maurice Fogel—comes this—De Profundis, or "Out of the Depths" . . . .

**The Effect.** A spectator assists in the experiment. They are told to hold one end of a length of rope—perhaps some five feet long. On to the rope is threaded a ring which has a clip attached to hold a crystal clear box. Inside the box is seen an envelope. The performer holds the other end of the rope and slides the crystal box to the middle where it remains suspended in full view of the audience.

The performer now counts out loud from one to ten—and tells the spectator to call stop whenever he feels that he gets a "mental vibration on any number". This is repeated three times—so that a number something like 854—is finally selected. Following this, the performer runs quickly through a list of colours and then names of cities throughout the world—and each time the spectator calls stop. The performer writes the selections on a large slate or small board standing close at hand so that everybody can remember with ease what was chosen. We will suppose that we end with the selection "854—Green—Paris".

The box has been left suspended all the time—the performer now holds his end of the rope up high—causing the box to run down the rope into the spectator's hands. The spectator is told to remove it and open it, take out the envelope and read aloud the contents. Inside is a Prediction which reads, "You will receive mental inspirations to choose the number 854—the colour Green and the city—Paris".

**The Method.** Again I shall have to ask you to try this out before you laugh at the modus operandi and see for yourself that it really works. You will require a large slate or small blackboard and something to act as a rest. Some chalk (white), five feet of ordinary conjurers' rope, a platelifter (one of those joke things that is made out of a long thin rubber tube with a rubber bulb at each end) a clear plastic or perspex box about $6 \times 4 \times 3$ in.—large enough to hold an envelope. A prediction sealed in an envelope.

If I tell you what happens first, you will understand more about the simple making of the apparatus. It is a force. Inside the rope is the platelifter and you each hold an end. When you call over the numbers from one to ten, if you want to force say number five, as you reach that number you squeeze hard at your end and the spectator immediately reacts—more often than not with a jump! Oddly enough, they do not always associate the "vibration" with the rope—and even if they do, they don't know why and the audience have no idea that anything like it is happening.

106

To make the platelifter rope, buy the best quality platelifter you can get, and an extra length of fine rubber tubing. Take one bulb off and push the tubing through the rope and then replace the bulb. You will now find that the bulb can be drawn back into the rope (fray it out a bit to loosen) and although this restricts the full expansion of the bulb—it still acts enough to give a decent "pulse" when the other end is pressed. You will appreciate that the rope can be coiled in a natural manner and the rubber tubing bends with the rope—making everything look as it should be. The very tips of the rope may be bound with white cotton and a little paste to stick them neatly.

The crystal box is an easy matter. From Woolworths for two or three shillings you can buy a neat food container which is a box made in clear plastic. Fix a clip to the top so that it may be hung from the ring you thread on the rope. Tie the box with the Prediction inside—with a neat bow of red ribbon. The lightweight box will not obstruct the air-passage of the rubber tubing—a heavy box may do so.

The final details are these. When the spectator comes up to assist stand him so that all the audience can see the suspended box. Have the slate on a stand nearby so that you can write on it without letting go of your end of the rope. Lastly, be quite sure that you "control" the spectator. You frame the instructions to him in a very careful manner—you make it quite clear that he must not guess—he is to wait until he "receives" some distinctive impulse, if he gets nothing to say nothing and if he really feels a "reaction"— to call stop immediately, and do be sure that you give the spectator the "receiving" end of the platelifter rope—otherwise he might be telling you what to do!

If you feel inclined, you may switch the rope whilst attention is on the opening of the box and envelope—and end by throwing the rope into the audience, I don't think it is really necessary.

## (4) "The £75,000 Test" by Corinda

We shall use this effect to illustrate the application of the carbon envelope technique which was described on page 98 of this book.

**The Effect.** The Mentalist is frequently confronted with the question "if you are so clever—why don't you predict the winner of the Derby horse race —and make yourself a fortune?" A good question deserves a good answer and this effect serves to prove why or why not.

"Ladies and Gentlemen, for many years I have applied the simple laws of para-psychology to demonstrate that it is, to some extent, possible to predict the future. It is natural therefore that I am constantly asked, Why don't I win the pools and make a fortune? Now I appeal to your good sense of judgment—do you think I wouldn't do that if I could? Of course I would—and by predicting say the Treble Chance pool correctly, you know as well as I do that I would acquire something like £75,000—and I'm not ashamed to say that it would come in handy!

No, I'm afraid the matter is more complicated than it seems. To make a proper Prediction it is essential that I work with a sensitive person, a suitable subject. You cannot get results with anybody, you must have the right person who is mentally attuned to similar wavelengths—like identical twins. I'm going to try a simple experiment but I must have the right subject so I will try out a test first of all. I have written a number on this slate, when I point to you will you call out the first number to enter your head please? (The performer points to two or three people until any one calls out "7"—whereupon he turns the slate round and shows it bears a large figure 7) Thank you sir, you seem to be in harmony with me—now we will try something really astounding. Keep your seat please, I have here an ordinary football coupon and I would like you to call out eight different numbers between one and fifty which just about covers all the teams I have here for the Treble Chance Pool—I will fill in an "O" to indicate your selection—ready?" (He calls out eight numbers which you write in on the coupon).

Good—now please take this coupon and hold it for a moment. I would like to draw your attention now to the envelope which most of you may have noticed clipped on my slate. That envelope contains another coupon and last night I filled in what I thought would be a winning line for the Treble Chance Pool—I would like you madam to take this coupon and to check our results. You sir—call out your first number—13? Good, and what is my first number—13? That's luck! Now what is your next number sir? 26? And what is mine Madam? 26! That was coincidence! The next? 27? And mine? 27! That is extraordinary! The next—31—and mine? 31—that's incredible! The next 33? And Mine—33! That's fabulous! Next? 39 and mine please? 39! That's phenomenal—next? 44—and mine 44! That's impossible! And the last? 49 and mine 49! That's a miracle . . . . .!!

Each time the gentleman calls out a number—the lady calls out the same, this is repeated eight times and the exclamations from you increase in surprise. You go:—(1) Luck! (2) Coincidence! (3) Extraordinary! (4) Incredible! (5) Fabulous! (6) Phenomenal! (7) Impossible! (8) A Miracle!

**The Method.**     You must first prepare a carbon-envelope (see page 98) and next insert a football coupon carefully folded so that the Treble Chance Pool is uppermost to the carbon paper—which, incidentally, should be jet black. Before the envelope is sealed it is essential to line up another coupon on the outside—so that both Treble Chance Pools lie directly in line. The easiest way to do this is to make three pin holes on the inner coupon and then by holding the envelope up to the light you will be able to see through the pin holes and line up on the light. When it is set exactly right, put a paper clip at the top to hold them dead in line.

You also require a hard pencil, a slate with a bulldog clip holding a dummy envelope clipped to one side and the number seven chalked on the other side. A card table or chair and another coupon. The last one does not have to match the other two—it is not examined.

You begin with the opening address and whilst you are talking you casually take the unprepared coupon from your pocket and show it in your hands—then put it away when it comes to picking up the slate for the number test. When the test is completed you remove the prepared coupon from the pocket. Now if you have made it correctly, the envelope, being smaller than the coupon, cannot be seen as it is hidden behind the coupon. You look for a rest—pick up the slate again and lay the coupon out flat on the chalked side . . . this means that the audience see the dummy envelope on the other side all the time, and that you can show the coupon resting on the slate—the carbon envelope now being hidden below. As you fill in the numbers—from time to time you wave the slate to show the coupon in the writing position—everything looks perfectly normal. When it comes to the last number, fill that in and then prepare for a simple switch of envelopes. The fake coupon is lifted with the right hand for a moment and the left arm drops to the side with the slate. Talking continuously, the performer turns the slate round and brings it back resting the coupon this time over the dummy envelope. He turns the slate to show the coupon side to the audience and whilst telling them about the envelope clipped on the slate—reaches under the coupon and pulls out the carbon envelope. Immediately the slate is turned back and placed on the chair or table—with the dummy still clipped in position—but the other hand removes the coupon and hands it to the gentleman.

You now go over to a lady seated near the front, show the envelope both sides under pretext of having trouble to unseal it—open it and remove the coupon. Hand this to the lady, screw up the envelope and drop it into your pocket and all is set for the eight-point finale.

### (5) "Astronomical" by Corinda

**The Effect.**  An envelope is handed to one of four spectators who have come along to help you. The spectator is told that it contains a prediction and that he should keep it in his possession from now on—and let no one touch it. You stand in the middle with two spectators seated on either side of you. You hand a card to the first, and tell him to jot down a row of five figures. You then take it back and hand it to the next who does the same and likewise with the third. When the third person has finished, you tell him to add another row of five—"just for luck". The last person (the fourth) is asked to add the total of the rows and to write it below. He is then told to take out the envelope and open it—inside he finds another envelope, this one he opens only to discover another inside that. When the third and last envelope is opened a £1 note is removed and written on it is a message saying:—"The number of this note will be the same as the total of your figures—please check". It is.

**The Method.**  This is a very easy Prediction to perform and mostly it is a matter of presentation, the only work being a simple switch. The effect illustrates how a switch can be smooth and trouble-free and how we can utilise a Nest of Envelopes to build up the effect.

You will no doubt know of the classic force where several people write down rows of figures and the last person adds up the total—you of course switch the sheet for a set of prearranged figures before he adds, so that *your* total is declared. On many occasions when I have seen this method in use, the performer has gone down into the audience to collect the four rows of figures. I think it is much better to work on the stage all the time—if you can, and with this force—you can. Seat the four spectators two on either side of you—and don't have them too close to each other or one may see what the other writes.

I am going to suggest that you use a simple non-mechanical way to exchange the papers. However, there are some very good mechanical ways of doing this and if you want you can use them instead.

Purchase a sixpenny packet of ordinary postcards (size about $3\frac{1}{2} \times 5\frac{1}{2}$ in.). Take five of these and trim off about an eighth of an inch from the ends. (Not the sides). Add to these one unfaked card so that now you have one long card and five shorts. Stack them with the long card second from the top. Now each card is plain on one side and has "Post Card" printed on the other side. The top two, face "Post Card" side downwards, the bottom four face "Post Card" side upwards.

Take a One Pound Note and copy out the serial number—the six numbers that follow the serial letters are used. You must now work out four sets of figures that add to this number. This is quickly done—simply divide the serial number by four and write the answer out four times; now to conceal the similarity between the four figures, subtract a few hundreds and units for one group and add them to another. This will increase one set and decrease the other without altering the final total. Should there be any remainder after the initial division by four—you may add it to any of the four figures. When you have settled for four figures that will add to the same number as the serial number of the note—take the second (long) card from the stack and write them there. You place them in a column of four and each row is written in a *different handwriting* excepting the third and fourth—which are the same handwriting. When you have done this, replace the card in the stack with the numbers face upwards, covered from view by the top short card. Put the cards thus prepared into your jacket pocket and have a pencil in one pocket ready for use.

Now go back to the £1 note. Write a prediction on the note which reads "The number of this note will be the same as the total of your figures". Fold the note and put it in a small envelope and seal. Put that envelope inside a slightly larger one and seal again—and finally put the second inside a third and seal again. You are all set to perform.

You will remember you have two spectators seated on either side of you. Start by handing the sealed "envelope" to the last spectator on your right (No. 4). Then remove the cards and pencil from your pocket and explain that you want each person to think of any five numbers at random and to write them in a row on the card. You hand the TOP (short) card—blank side upwards to spectator No. 1 seated on your left. He writes five figures—immediately you take the card and pencil and hand to No. 2 the other person on your left and tell him to write his row of five BELOW as though to make it a sum. Next you hand the card to No. 3 and he writes a row of five—but when he has done, as though you had an afterthought—tell him to "add another row of five, just for luck". This done you take back the card and start to explain that the last person must now add the total—but halfway through your explanation you turn back to No. 3 and say "By the way, did you sign the card?" Look straight at him as you say this and he will look straight at you. In that fraction of time you turn over his card and offer it to be signed—but what really happens is this.

The top card on the stack in your hands is their card bearing the proper numbers. The next card is your force card. Whilst talking you square up the cards and when it comes to turning the card to be signed on the "Post Card" side—you double lift. This is made very easy because the second down is a long card, so by gripping it by the short ends you can double lift and turn without looking. As soon as the card is turned, you pass it to No. 3 who writes his name on the back. You then tell him to pass it himself to No. 4 to be added. The card that No. 3 signs is really the back of your force card—but he cannot tell as it is upside down! What has taken ten minutes to describe—takes ten seconds to do. The switch is remarkably convincing and the last person No. 4 hasn't got a chance. He is handed the card by another spectator—not you, he has no idea what numbers were written by the others and the card he holds bears the signature of No. 3. Lastly, he opens the envelopes himself and he checks the £1 note. That is all there is to it.

### (6) "The Mentalist's Four Ace Trick"—Corinda-Tremaine

**The Effect.** One, the stage is a card table, standing on which are four drinking tumblers and two packs of cards. A spectator takes part. The Mentalist explains that he will attempt an experiment to demonstrate "sympathetic relationship between two minds". He stands at one side of the table, the spectator stands opposite. He picks up one of the packs, removes them from the case and shows that his pack has red backs—and that they are all different. He looks intently at the spectator and then moves four cards placing one in each of the tumblers with the backs facing the audience. He next removes the other cards from their case and spreads them face down on the table. The spectator is now invited to push out ANY four cards, and this done—he is told to show that the backs of his pack are all black and that the cards are all different. He is then told take his four cards which lie face down on the table and drop one into each tumbler.

111

Reaching into the first glass, the mentalist removes the two cards and shows that they are both the Ace of Diamonds. He takes them out, holds one in each hand to show the red back and the blue back first—and then dramatically turns them round. As soon as they have been shown, he hands them immediately to the spectator for examination. From the next glass he takes the Ace of Clubs and the Ace of Clubs . . . from the third, the Ace of Hearts matched by an Ace of Hearts and finally the Ace of Spades, with the duplicate from the fourth glass. That is the effect.

**The Method.**    Take two packs of cards, one with red backs and one with blue backs. From the blue-backed pack remove the Four Aces and stack them Diamonds, Clubs, Hearts and Spades. The Diamond on top. Put these four cards down the right side of your right foot—by tucking them into the shoe—the trouser turn-up may be allowed to cover them until you are ready.

Have the audience on your left, the table in front of you and the spectator standing opposite. Have four ordinary glasses standing in a row along the back of the table (audience viewpoint). Have both packs in their cases on the table and you are ready to perform.

Pick up the Red cards, remove from case and fan faces to audience and spectator—show also the red backs. With apparent indecision, select four cards. First the Ace of Diamonds—which you place in the glass nearest the spectator (No. 1) do not show it, simply put it in the glass back outwards. The next card (Ace of Clubs) goes into No. 2, the glass next to No. 1. The third (Ace of Hearts) into No. 3 and the last (Ace of Spades) into the glass nearest you. Return your cards to the case and put the case down so that it just overlaps the edge of the table on the side nearest to the audience.

Pick up the red-backed pack, do not show them—but spread them in a row, face down, in front of the spectator. Tell him to push out any four cards. When this is done pick them up with the left hand, one at a time, counting aloud "one, two, three, four". Each time the left picks up a card—it is dropped face down on to the right palm. As soon as you have them all together in the right hand you turn to the spectator and say, "Now just to satisfy yourself and the audience that you had a perfectly free choice—would you kindly examine the rest of the pack and show the fronts and backs to the audience". He picks up the pack to examine them—whilst he does so, you lean forward on the table and "accidentally" knock the red-backed case to the floor. The left thumb catches it as you lean forward—a natural motion. You immediately stoop to pick up the deck and as you bend down the left hand picks up the case—but the right hand, containing his four cards goes to the right foot. Here you quickly drop his four cards sideways into your turn-up and pull out the four aces from the shoe! You stand upright again, casually drop the four aces face down IN A PILE in front of the spectator (who is busy showing the cards to the audience) and wait. When he is ready—point to the four Aces and say "now please put one card in each glass". As you do this you point very slowly and clearly to No. 1 (first), No. 2 (second), No. 3 (third), and No. 4 (last). His cards are in a pile—so naturally he takes the top one first—which because they are stacked is the Ace of Diamonds—this one he must put in glass No. 1 and he will do so if you have handled the instructions carefully. Watch him to see that he does as is required—and should he try to put the wrong card in the wrong glass—push the right glass forward. I have done this trick many times and so far I have never had the spectator do anything wrong. You could of course pass the glasses to him one at a time—but the effect is not the same—consider it: You removed four cards and you alone knew what they were. He chooses any four cards—they happen to be the same. Then he appears to have put the same cards in the same glasses—and there are no duplicate aces* left in his pack—and he examines the cards at the end and you have a pretty good trick. (*Note.—If performed close-up—somebody may wish to examine his pack).

### (7) Novel Adaption of the "Card in Balloon" by Corinda

**The Effect.** An opening trick; the performer walks on holding an inflated balloon which is on a small stand. He points to one person in the audience and calls "Give me ONE number"—then to another—and another. "6-3-5 —six hundred and thirty five has been chosen—how strange—" He pulls a pin from his lapel and bursts the balloon. Inside is seen a card standing at the top of the frame. The audience see a big query drawn on the card. He walks forward and invites somebody to take the card and turn it over— it reads "6—3—5" . . . . .

**The Method.** This I feel, is an excusable use of weird apparatus and to my mind is indeed a novel application of a conjuring prop. You require one of those self-working Card-in-Balloon appliances and it must be the type that has a tray at the base designed to hold a pack of cards. This is a pretty standard model these days and they are not hard to get. You draw a big question mark on a plain white card—which should be the same size as an ordinary playing card—so that it will fit the loading mechanism. You turn the card upside down and load it into the tray—clipping the edge into the clamp ready to fire. You inflate a balloon and place it in the frame at the top. You have a Swami Gimmick on the right thumb and hold the apparatus in the right hand.

The construction of the apparatus is such that you have a ready-made platform to hold the card in a perfect writing position. Moreover, the hand is completely screened from view making it a very easy matter for you to write their numbers on the card before you burst the balloon.

When it comes to the "Bang"—we avoid the magical presentation—where the balloon appears to burst automatically—and take a pin from the lapel and with one deliberate swipe appear to jab it into the balloon. However— timed along with this action you release the "fire" mechanism of the Card-in-balloon—which really bursts the balloon—and at the same time, transports the card to the top of the frame. To be on the safe side, put your finger over the point of the pin from the lapel so that it cannot burst the balloon before the trigger goes off . . .

One detail. The "writing position" is such that the apparatus must be held back to front from the "Firing position". Having written—walk forward transferring the apparatus from one hand to another and turning it round as you do so. Hold it high when firing and the card cannot be seen in the tray—the apparatus looks like a stand designed to hold a balloon.

Since the trick will take no more than fifteen seconds to perform from start to finish—it makes a good, quick opening number—that goes off with a bang!

## (8) "Psi Function" by Corinda

**The Effect.** A blackboard stands on an easel in the middle of the stage. It faces away from the audience. A spectator comes on to the stage to assist. He is told to go to the blackboard and await your instructions. You take a pack of cards and shuffle them. Lay them face down on a tray and have any member of the audience take any card. He is to look at that card himself, and then to try and convey an impression of it to the man behind the board. The man behind the board is told to draw a picture of a playing card. When this is done, you ask the member of the audience to name out loud his card and to show it—you then turn round the blackboard and it is seen that a large drawing of the same card has been sketched by the other spectator.

**The Method.** We are going to use the easiest possible means—and if you don't like the method then don't do the trick—that's all there is to it. On the board is written a message in chalk:—"Be a Sport—draw a large picture of the Two of Diamonds and then rub this out *when you have finished*— keep this secret please!" Hanging on the blackboard in readiness is a duster. You hand him the chalk in full view of the audience when you say "go and stand behind the blackboard I want you to do a simple drawing in a moment".

Next you must force the two of diamonds. You have a forcing pack—all two of diamonds, you shuffle it without showing the faces. You jumble them face down on a tray and have someone take any card. You tell this person to look at the card but not to show it yet—and to try and transmit a mental picture of the card to the other spectator. The Two of Diamonds is chosen as the card for this trick as a diamond is the easiest suit to draw— and the two can be drawn pretty quickly.

I am one of those quaint people that think the effect is twice as important as the means. Whether you like the means or not—you will agree that in this case the effect is sensational—and yet, not beyond the realms of possibility. If you feel so inclined—you could write the "be a sport" message on a ten shilling note which ends the message with "keep this for being a sport" . . . you then place the spectator under a moral obligation to co-operate. In mentalism, honesty was never a good policy!

## PART FOUR: PREDICTIONS FOR THE DRAWING ROOM

It would be an error to suppose that every Prediction is suitable for presentation on the Stage, and likewise suitable for the drawing room. The "Million to One" effect for example, is strictly a stage trick. Performed in the drawing room where you can expect to be at close quarters with the audience, there is every chance that the trick would fail because they see the first pin.

When we consider tricks that are suitable for the Drawing Room, we find that the use of Billets, Playing Cards and Various Indexes are more suited. The size of the apparatus becomes reasonably proportionate to the size of the gathering—a point which is clearly understood if you consider what it would look like if you tried an effect using Pellets—on the Stage.

The following effects are classified as suitable for the Drawing Room and in general, they may be used for any intimate gathering—of the magical kind!

(9) Effects from Step One (Swami Gimmick) No's. 4, 5, 6, 7, 12, 22 and 24 are all Predictions suitable for the Drawing Room.

## (10) "Mind Over Matter" by Corinda

**The Effect.** A pack of cards is taken and shuffled then dealt face down on the table into a big square—every card being separate. The Mentalist writes

114

a Prediction on a small slip of paper which he rolls into a ball and hands to any spectator. The spectator is invited to place the Pellet under any card he likes. This having been done, the card is turned over and the pellet read aloud by the spectator—it names correctly the chosen card; a Prediction has been made! All the other cards are different and a complete pack is used.

**The Method.** You require a Stacked Deck (see Step Three) or a marked deck. You also require the Tremaine-Corinda Pellet Index as described on page 93 of this book. To start, if the cards are marked—have them shuffled and dealt into a square. If they are stacked, false-shuffle yourself and deal them out in order so that you know by position the name of any card. There's nothing to that so I will not waste time with explanations.

Tell the audience you are going to make a Prediction and write "3 of Hearts" on a slip. Roll up the paper and give it to the Spectator telling him to place it under any card. If he puts it under the Three of Hearts—which could happen—you allow him to remove it for the climax, making the most of your good luck. If not (which is somewhat more likely!) you take the correct Pellet from the Index, roll it and switch it as you reach forward to turn the card face up. (See page 95  (10) "The Switch and the Force".) It's a case of mind over matter—"you don't mind and I don't matter!"

### (11) "My Word!" by Corinda

Before I describe the effect I would like to say that this is a creditable example of simplicity and boldness. You might think it too simple to work—but if you do as I have done, try it out, you will find that the "obvious is not always apparent!" You cannot judge any effect from paper. It must be performed before you can really tell whether or not is is any good. Tricks that look like miracles in print—sometimes flop badly in practice. This is the reverse; it looks silly in print and works like a charm.

**The Effect.** A spectator is given a sheet of paper which bears three words. "Page, Line and Position". He is asked to imagine that he has a book in his hands and that he opens it to a page and sees the number at the top. He is handed a pencil and told to write the page number alongside the heading "Page". He then imagines that he counts down to any line—and fills the number of lines alongside "Line". Finally, he counts along the line to any word and fills in the Position number. All this is done "in imagination". Whilst this is going on, you hand a book to another spectator and tell him to wait a moment. You now take the numbered sheet from the first person and hand it to the spectator with the book. He opens the book at the selected page number, counts down to the chosen line and finds the word at the given position. He calls out that word. You proceed to turn round a large slate which has been on show all the time—and on the back is seen written the chosen word!

**The Method.** Take a piece of paper and in ink write at the top "Page........." below this write "Line........." and below this write "Position.........", now take a good thick book and open it anywhere in the middle. With a PENCIL and in DIFFERENT HANDWRITING fill in that page number on your form. Count down seven lines and put Line 7 on the form and finally count along three words and fill in a three alongside Position.......... Prepare a second form with the three headings written in ink—but leave it blank. Look to be quite sure what word is at the third position on the selected page and write that in bold letters on your slate.

Turn the slate with the blank side towards the audience so that the word is not seen until the climax. Fold the prepared sheet once each way to reduce it to a convenient size for palming. Hand the unprepared slip to a spectator near the BACK and be sure that the book goes to someone near the front. Choose two people that are seated as far apart as possible. Have the person with the slip fill in his numbers, telling him to show no one for a moment and to fold his paper when done. You take it and fold once more and then whilst walking from the back to the front (the greater the distance—the more time you have) simply exchange the two slips—handing YOUR prepared paper to the book man. He does not know what the other person chose and until afterwards, does not know what is going to happen. You tell him to open the book "at the chosen page"—count down to the "Chosen Line" and call out the "Chosen Word". The other spectator does not know that his numbers are in your pocket. That is all there is to it—excepting the switch. You have so much time to perform this essential move, that there is no call for complicated switching of papers—simply EXCHANGE them and put the other one in your pocket. Be sure that you hand a Pencil to the spectator who decides upon the numbers.

If you don't mind hard work, look carefully through many books and sooner or later you will find the same word in the same position in three different books. You may then give the second spectator a choice of any of three books which adds to the effect. The occurrence of three words the same in identical positions is not as unlikely as it sounds—you can find "and, of, the, etc.," in many books—but try and find something better than anything so commonplace as these words.

Should any of my readers feel that the trick may be discovered, perhaps they would care to try the same effect another way:—Have the numbers called out loud and the page found as the number is called—finally when the word is called write it on a card with a Swami Gimmick. (Step One will tell you how to do this!)

## (12) "The Third Choice" by Corinda

Perhaps I should have called this trick "The Trick With a Thousand Inventors"!! Because after I put it on the market about three years ago—along came countless people to tell me that they had invented it. I will therefore make a timid plea that this is my presentation of the trick which I was first to sell—and, by the way, having sold a few hundred by demonstration, I can rightly suppose it fools some of the people some of the time. I like it, I hope you will also.

**The Effect.**   You lay five cards in a row face up. You look intently at the chap who stands in front of you and then write a Prediction, fold it and give it to him. You next seal each card in an envelope and mix them. You then hand all the envelopes to the spectator and tell him to throw away four. The last one you open and show the card—he then reads the Prediction which names that card.

**The Method.**   You require five Aces of Spades and four ordinary cards. Strip the four ordinary cards and four of the Aces by soaking in warm water for twenty minutes and then peeling them in half. Next stick them together again with an Ace facing one side and an ordinary card on the other side. You have made four double-faced cards and they will be the same thickness as an ordinary card. When they are dry—iron them to make them

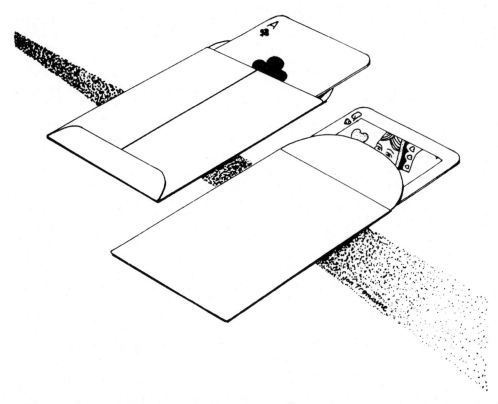

nice and flat and if needed, polish them. To perform, lay the genuine Ace face up in the middle of the five cards. On either side put two of the double-face cards—with the Ace side downwards. Place alongside five envelopes. Write the Prediction which reads, "You will hold the Ace of Spades in your Hand". Fold it and give it to the spectator. Now begin to explain that you will place one card in each envelope, pattering about the fact that they are not marked envelopes or anything like that. Each card is slid into the envelope held flap side upwards all the time. As you reach the middle card— the real Ace, you cough and whilst politely bringing the hand to the mouth, accidentally show the one and only BACK of the real Ace! Don't say any-thing—it registers psychologically. Finally mix all the envelopes and hand them to the spectator telling him to discard any four. Take the fifth from his hand and take out the card whilst holding the envelope flap side down-wards—this means it will show an Ace whatever envelope he gives you. Should he give you the real Ace it will come out showing the back—so you will know immediately, then you can make the best of your luck. This hap-pens very often as the odds are so few. You can have another set of four cards in four envelopes ready to switch whilst he reads the Prediction—so that he can remove the other cards to check everything is above board. I have never found it necessary.

### (13) "The Lottery Routine" by Corinda

This is an exceptionally good routine. It is extremely baffling, interesting to watch and adds to your popularity at the climax; there are few tricks which have so many virtues as this and I strongly recommend it for those interested in entertaining the audience.

**The Effect.** Standing on a table is a glass with an envelope inside. This is on show all the time the routine takes place. You patter about raffles and lotteries suggesting that sometimes it is possible to know what will win before the draw.

You have a book of 200 raffle tickets which you throw into the audience asking that two or three people will examine them to be sure that they are all numbered properly from one to two hundred.

After a reasonable examination has taken place, you ask the person who is left with the book to tear out the tickets and to drop them into a large goldfish bowl which you pass to the front row to be handed back to him. He places the counterfoils in his pocket and then gives the tickets in the bowl a very good mixing. To save time, they are not folded as is usual.

The next step is to invite the spectator to take the bowl to any three people in the audience. Each time they are to reach in and without looking remove a ticket. As a ticket is chosen, the assisting spectator takes it, reads it, calls out the number for all to hear and then returns it to the person who selected it from the bowl. This is repeated three times and can be done in a matter of thirty seconds. The spectator with the bowl sits for a moment whilst you explain to the audience that you could have in no way influenced the choice—and now, just in case you have made a correct prediction, you will need some prizes! At this point you call for your own assistant to bring in a tray upon which stand three prizes. Since these are to be given away, they should be reasonably cheap and suitable for male or female. Chocolates and Cigarettes are two good ones and I always use a cheap Ball Pen as the third.

All is set now for the draw—you make clear that the envelope contains three tickets which you think should be the winning numbers. If any of the three people in the audience have one of those numbers—they will get a prize. The interest is thus built up long before the trick is revealed!

You call for the spectator who is holding the bowl. He comes up and puts the bowl aside (anywhere will do as long as it is out of the way). You ask him to bring the envelope from the glass which he does. You slit it open and tell him to remove the contents. Inside are three tickets—a different colour from those used by the audience, each one corresponds to a ticket held by the three spectators. They are all winners and as you hand the prizes to the spectator to give back to the winners—you also hand him a packet of cigarettes "for his valuable services".

**The Method.** Standing outside the open door to the drawing room is your own assistant who has a tray containing the three prizes. The reason why she is outside is because you want to create a pleasant surprise with the prizes—or so you infer. She also has a book of Raffle Tickets numbered from 1 to 200. They are a different colour from the other book that you have. With this, she has Corinda's Billet Pencil (see page 86 (1)) and as soon as she hears the numbers called by the spectator, she removes their duplicates from her book and loads them into the pencil. She lays the pencil on the tray and when she comes in you call for the envelope and slit it open shooting the three tickets into same. You must give your assistant time to load the pencil, so that is the point when you really explain what is happening—timing is very important. This trick costs you two books of Lottery Tickets and four prizes—an outlay of about 7/- ($1.00) which, for what it costs, is a winner—you try it.

## (14) "The Prophesy" by Corinda

**The Effect.**   A pack of cards is shuffled and handed to a spectator who is told to deal about twenty cards in a row on the table. Two rows of ten will do, and the cards are dealt face downwards. The mentalist speaks about the Art of Fortune Telling and of Seeing into the Future, as practised by Romany Gypsies.   He asserts that a friend of his, a gypsy, wrote a prophesy naming something that would happen tonight. She told the mentalist that he must place a row of cards on the table and have any person of dark complexion come and choose a card. Her prophesy was written and sealed in an envelope—and that envelope is now produced and placed on the table.

Following the instructions given by the gypsy, the performer stands back and invites the spectator to pick up any card and put it in his pocket without looking at it. When this is done, the performer opens the envelope and reads out from a card found inside "This is the prophesy of Gypsy Nialo. The man of dark complexion will choose a card of fate. A red card with the number that governs destiny—a three. The suit will bring that man a money gain during the next three days--it is a Diamond—The card will be the Three of Diamonds". The performer waves the card to show the written prediction and then turns to the spectator asking him to remove the card from his pocket and look at it for the first time.  He must call the name aloud—he calls "The Three of Diamonds".  The pack may then be examined.

**The Method.**   To use a current colloquialism, this is a "Diabolical liberty!" However, for all that it is quite a reasonable effect and the story adds to the presentation.

Take twenty cards and arrange them in any order you like—simply A-2-3-4-5 etc. will do—or "Si Stebbins" order. Stack them on top of a deck. False shuffle a bit—mixing the bottom cards but leaving the stack intact and put the cards on the table. Tell the spectator to deal them face down in a row—see that they go in order from left to right and when twenty are down say "that will do thank you".

Now introduce the envelope which in actual fact contains a prediction written on the lines given—naming any one of the twenty cards. It does not matter which one! Having explained what is to happen, stand well back and turn round facing your back to the table. Tell the spectator to choose a card and put it in his pocket and not to look at it for the moment. Having given him reasonable time to do this, turn round and say "Right done that? Good, now push the other cards back on the pack please". As you point to the "other cards" look for the BLANK position which shows where his card WAS! By this you know which one he chose. That is why you must either use one straight line of twenty or two exact rows of ten. The reason being that if an end card is taken—you will also note the space. The necessary information is obtained at a mere glance—after that you avoid looking at the table.   Now for the prediction—suppose his card was the Nine of Spades and your Prophesy covers the Three of Diamonds—without batting an eyelid, you open the envelope and MIS-READ the name of the card—wording the prediction as you go with suitable spiel to cover his card! To do this with utter conviction—pretend you have a wee bit of trouble deciphering the writing at some point and for goodness sake LOOK at the card when you are supposed to be reading it.

119

After that—turn the card and wave it casually so that all may see it has SOMETHING written on it—but no one will be able to see what!

Finally, tell the spectator to remove his card and call out the name—which he then shows to the audience. As a last word, should the spectator choose the card which corresponds to your prediction—it is obvious that you allow him to open the envelope and read the card aloud.

If you haven't got the nerve to try this trick the way I suggest, you can always end clean by having nineteen predictions in a Pocket Index ready to switch the card after it has been mis-read—so that a card bearing the correct prediction can be handed to the spectator afterwards—I'm glad you thought of that!

## (15) "The Informative Joker" by Corinda

This is a quick card trick which ends on a light hearted note. It is a novel idea for close up card workers—not suitable for performance as an effect for large audiences.

**The Effect and The Method.** You force the three of clubs and have it returned to the pack. I said this effect was for Card Workers—so you do not need me to tell you how to force a card! You now explain that the joker is the one card that sees all, hears all and tells everything! You take out the joker and pretend to listen to him— suddenly your eyes light up— "He tells me you took the Three of Clubs". You look at the spectator and wave the joker at him, " is that Correct?" He will probably smile and say yes—and you then look very serious and say—"You don't believe it I can tell that, but let me tell you that he told me and *showed* me—look, he knew what card you would choose! You drop the joker on the table and it is seen that in one hand he holds a card—it is the Three of Clubs!

Some Jokers are pictured as a clowned man standing with one arm in the air. Draw with ink a small card in this hand and let it resemble the Three of Clubs. When you wave the Joker to show it during the routine, put your thumb over the drawing to conceal the card in his hand.

## (16) "Double-Impact Prediction" by Corinda

**The Effect.** "I want you to imagine that I have a pack of playing cards and that I am showing them to you now. (Make an imaginary fan and show). You look along the cards and you see one that you fancy—what do you see? Good, now would you count along from the start here (indicate an imaginary starting place) and tell me the position of your card? Fourteen? Thank you, and the card was the Eight of Spades—correct? That is a very odd thing— because here I have an envelope and on it, as you will see, is the number fourteen—have a look and see what's inside". He takes out the eight of spades! Please don't rush to tell me it's a good effect, I've been doing it for years—and I know it's good!

120

**The Method.** Use a Pocket Index and a Swami Gimmick. All this I have discussed before!

### (17) "The Matchbox Mystery" by Corinda

**The Effect.** The performer writes a prediction on a small slip of paper which he folds and drops into an empty cup. He then throws a box of matches on to the table and invites anybody to remove as many as they like. This done, the remainder are counted and then the prediction is read. It tells the exact number of matches that will be left in the box—and is correct.

**The Method.** Write a prediction—fold it twice and appear to drop it into a cup. In actual fact you palm it out leaving the cup empty. Have a box of matches with no more than 52 matches in it and drop it on the table. When the total of the matches left is declared—reach into a Billet Index where you have in readiness 52 predictions and palm out the appropriate one. Pick up the cup and drop the billet in as you do so—passing the cup to a spectator to read the billet inside. Effect No. 24 (Step One) is a variation of this trick.

### (18) "The Mystery of the Chest" by Corinda

**The Effect.** On a table stands a nicely decorated chest and beside it stands a drinking glass. To the left of these are two or three items which include seven keys and seven numbered tags. A committee of seven people take part in the proceedings and they are invited to come on to the stage or to one end of the room. Now this is very important so please read carefully. This is one of those rare effects where most of the work is done by the assistants and practically none by the performer. In this case, our performer stands well to one side and calls out his instructions to the committee.

To start the routine, the Mentalist explains to the audience and assistants that the box on the table is a chest—containing something which will surprise everybody (you do not say what it is). You explain further—that on the table are seven keys and that only one of them will open the chest—which at the moment is locked. Next you tell the audience that the committee must be numbered and then must each select a key. You instruct each member of the committee to:—

> "Go to the table, select any number tag you like (they run from 1 to 7) and pin it on your lapel. Next choose any key and test it—should it be the one that unlocks the chest—relock the chest after testing. Whether the key does or does not fit—when it has been tested it must be dropped into the glass".

This is done up to the point when the last person comes to the table. After he has dropped his key into the glass—you ask him to shake them all up and then take them himself along the row of assistants—and have each person remove one. He takes the last one—the one that is left after everybody has had a choice.

Once more the committeemen are called to try their keys and see who has the one that fits the lock. One at a time they come to the table and see if their key fits. Since all the keys look alike—there is no way of telling until they are tested in the lock. No matter who has the key that fits—every key is tried to prove that six do not unlock the chest. The assistant who takes the right key stands aside—the others return to the side of the stage. Now you approach the box for the FIRST TIME and ask that it be unlocked. From inside the chest you remove an envelope and tearing it open, ask the assistant left with you to remove a card from inside—and read it aloud. It reads:—

"It is my Prediction that whoever chooses to call himself number three —will also choose the only key to open this chest—Corinda".

Everybody can see that the assistant standing beside you wears a tag No. 3 and you have not influenced their choice in any way. This is my effect, which although somewhat long (as with most versions of the "Seven Keys") is well worth the preliminaries. I would suggest it is more suitable for the drawing room where the use of seven spectators draws a good number of the audience into the effect—thus giving the trick a personal interest.

**The Method.** In the Chest is an envelope. It is a window envelope as described on page 12 of "Step One" and it is prepared with a pre-worded prediction as told to you on Page 14 of the same book. The trick is painfully simple. When you see who gets the key that opens the lock you look at his number. When you take the envelope out of the chest, with a Swami Gimmick—fill in his number so that the full prediction reads accordingly! To do this, even though you are not proficient with a Swami Gimmick—is childs play—you must be able to write any one of the numbers from one to seven—is that hard? In view of the method you will understand that the chest is unfaked, the lock ordinary, the keys ordinary, there is no force of the number tags and it does not matter who takes part—if anyone criticises this I will send them a pint of my blood!

## (19) "X—Marks the Spot"

**The Effect.** The Mentalist writes a Prediction naming a card. He folds it and gives it to the spectator—telling him to drop it in his pocket. A pack of cards is taken and shuffled. It is explained that one must be chosen—and that the choice must not only be free of any influence—but also, no one must know what is selected. To achieve this—you tell the spectator to hold the cards behind his back and to mark any one on the face with a cross. You give him the cards and a pencil. After that, the cards are examined and the marked one is found—then the prediction is opened by the spectator and read—it names what card has been chosen.

**The Method.** This is an adaption of a trick given in Thurston's Book of Magic and there are many uses for the principle. The secret is very simple— it is the pencil. Although it looks absolutely normal—it will not write. It is just a dowel rod painted up to look like a pencil—or a real pencil with a gimmicked tip. On the sly, you mark one card on the face with a cross. That card you predict. You mix the cards and give them to the spectator with suitable instructions so that he will apparently draw on the face of a card. Give him the fake pencil—and be sure to recover it afterwards. As an added touch, you could switch the fake pencil for a real one—just in case!

## (20) "Nicely Suited"

**The Effect.** The performer shuffles a pack of cards and places them on the table. He declares that he knows what card is most likely to be chosen— before it is chosen! This he proves to be true—a card is chosen and in a striking manner it is revealed.

**The Method.**  I have found this of great use to me with card effects.  It is a definite improvement on the old verbal force which was used to make the spectator take any card you wanted him to take.  Prepare by putting the Three of Clubs on top of the pack, the Three of Hearts you reverse in the middle, the Three of Spades goes to the bottom of the deck and the Three of Diamonds you put into your pocket.  By this arrangement you will observe that whatever suit is chosen—you have what is called a "get-out"—or a suitable card.  The deck is placed on the table in this condition and you must now force (verbally) the number three.  To do this quickly—suggest Court Cards are ignored—deal first with "odds or evens"—force the odds and eliminate to the three.  At this point you stop to explain that there may be some doubt as to the method of selection—so you will give the spectator a chance to call out any suit he likes—and whatever suit is called will be accepted . . . If it's Hearts—Spread the deck face down and show that the only card reversed is the Three of Hearts.  For Clubs—simply turn over the top card; for Spades pick up the deck and show the bottom card—for—have the spectator reach into your pocket and remove one card—his card!  Sometimes the little things make a lot of difference and somebody once said 'Long live the little difference' (misquote).

# BLINDFOLDS & X-RAY EYES

## BY

## CORINDA

**STEP FIVE**

IN CORINDA'S SERIES :—

## "THIRTEEN STEPS TO MENTALISM"

**LOGIC —**

CHILD. "Mummy, what's that man doing up there?"

MOTHER. "He's putting on a Blindfold, my dear".

Child. "What's a Blindfold, Mummy?"

Mother. "Something you wear so that you cannot see".

Child. "Why's he wearing one, Mummy?"

Mother. "So that he can tell us what he's looking at . . ."

— *CORINDA.*

STEP FIVE in CORINDA'S SERIES

" THIRTEEN STEPS TO MENTALISM "

## CONTENTS

### PART ONE    TYPES

### PART TWO    TECHNIQUE

### PART THREE    TRICKS

# PART ONE  TYPES

## Introduction

There can be no doubt that the use of the Blindfold considerably adds to the presentation of many Mental effects. It is one of the few ways of dramatising the performance of Mentalism and, if anything, it is perhaps not fully exploited in these times. Aside from the fact that it adds to the impact of the effect, the Blindfold can of course be the modus operandi of many good tricks and because of this—I feel justified in devoting a full "Step" to the subject.

In this Step we shall deal first with a few types of Blindfolds, then with various aspects of Technique—which will cover the finer points of technical detail and we shall end with tricks and routines. No attempt has been made to give a detailed account of every available Blindfold; there would be conflict with dealer items, repetition and space wasted on impractical ideas. The emphasis has been placed on a selection of standard models with the overall consideration of how they can be used for effect. The most important thing is the tricks you do—not the Blindfold.

Before we commence I feel that personal acknowledgement should be given to Will Dexter for allowing me reference to his book *Sealed Vision* and for the considerable advice he has so freely given.

## (1)  The Unfaked Mask

This is used for effects where a blindfold is used simply because "it looks good"—or where you need only peek "down the nose" to see—or rely on sound or touch. You cannot see straight through the mask, it is very comfortable to wear and can be donned and removed very quickly. I have used this type quite a bit and mine is made of a double thickness of black velvet. It should be about 4 inches wide and eight to ten inches long. It should NOT cover the ears—as it would make hearing difficult and it should NOT have ribbon for the purpose of fixing—it should have elastic sewn firmly in a complete band. I say this because I recently attended a show where a good friend of mine was using a blindfold with tapes which had been tied so tightly— that at the end the knots could not be undone—and he was compelled to finish his act with the blindfold pushed up on to his forehead like a turban! It might happen once in fifty performances but with elastic—it can never happen.

I would say that this type is one of the best for stage work. To read about cotton wool, dough, medical plaster and bag blindfolds

129

for the stage—is one thing. But to cook to death with the heat is another, and it is not what I call a good thing to end your act looking as though you have just stepped out of a Turkish Bath—dripping with perspiration and gasping for air. Why be cruel to yourself when you don't have to?

With this Blindfold on you can see from your chest downwards, a complete table top when standing, and about a yard in front of you on the floor. That's enough for many miracles. When wearing it, if you want to look you glance downwards keeping your head upright—not tilted back or forward, and if you do not have to look, you shut your eyes and keep them shut—thereby effecting a more natural performance of loss of vision. You always close your eyes before you put it on and you always have your eyes closed when it is taken off—that applies to all blindfolds.

### (2) Reverse Crease Blindfold. (Will Dexter)

This works on the same principle as the Unfaked Mask—excepting that the material is three thicknesses of felt which have been deliberately creased down the middle so that one way the blindfold fits snugly to the face, allowing practically no vision downwards and the other way—it doubles the gap by the nose allowing extra space for seeing. The diagram illustrates the principle showing how the fold or crease causes the extra gap. Should you wish to have the Blindfold tested—you put it on a spectator in the snug fitting position—but reverse it when you yourself come to wear it! A cunning and practical idea—easy to construct (about the same size as the Unfaked Mask) and easy to work with.

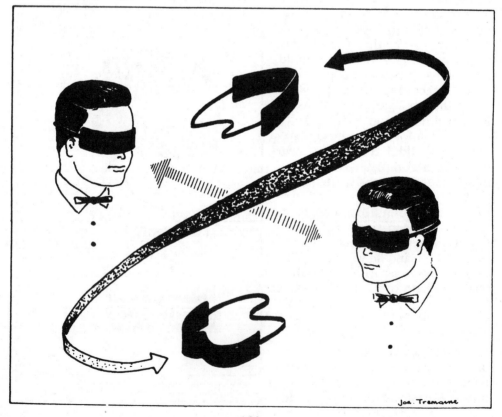

### (3)  The Felt Mask—Faked

This Blindfold is wider than the first two. It is made to cover the front of the face right down to the mouth. A single thickness of black felt is ironed out flat with a very hot iron—so as to singe the material making it compact and brittle. After this, a red hot pin is used to make two very small holes positioned to correspond with each eye. Suitable bands are affixed to the felt to hold it in position.

In use, by peeping through the two pinholes a surprising range of vision is made possible. However, the Felt Mask—Faked should be used discreetly as it will not withstand examination. When donning the mask, care should be taken to avoid having a strong light behind you and in the action of bringing the mask to the face, allowing pinholes of light to appear through the material. This applies also to the types of Blindfold which function on the principle of a sliding panel inside.

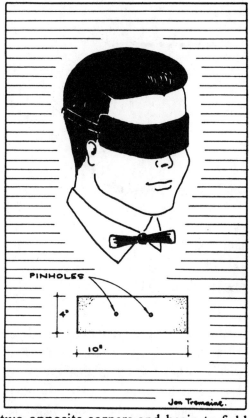

### (4)  The Folded Silk Blindfold

There is much to be said for this type of Blindfold. Probably the simplest form there is, it consists of an eighteen inch square of silk folded in such a manner that vision is possible both by peeking down the nose—and, more important, through the material. A fine silk or nylon is used, sometimes a good grade handkerchief will suffice. The manner of folding is as follows.

Lay the silk out in a square, take two opposite corners and begin to fold inwards in steps about 2 to 3 inches on each fold. The centre of the silk remains one thickness which enables you to see through with ease. Bring the two outside folds right up to the centre and just before donning the Blindfold, push back the folds allowing about half an inch gap. Rather than allow people to see you fold the silk in some special manner, it is better to have it ready folded in the pocket and carefully unrolled when required. Will Dexter advocates that you hold with Blindfold across the outstretched palms of the hands—and bend the head forward when coming to place it on. If you bring the blindfold to the face—the folds are liable to fall out of position.

131

Annemann made use of this Blindfold quite a bit for both stage and close up work. For stage work I recommend that you use thin black silk material —and for close up, thin white silk—looking as though you had improvised

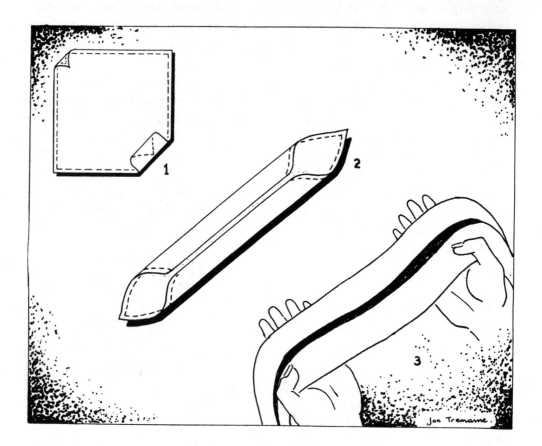

with your pocket handkerchief. If you have not used a Blindfold before and you are not sure what type to try first—I suggest this model is your starting place. It has every qualification for Blindfold Work. With a good light you can see many yards ahead—see downwards and obtain a substantial glimpse to each side—in reality, your vision is hardly obscured at all! The important points to remember are: have the square large enough to enable you to tie the ends behind your head (no tapes are used), make the choice of material with care so that it gives you maximum transparency without looking unduly thin—and most important of all—ACT BLINDFOLDED when wearing it.

## (5) The Bag Blindfold

As the name suggests, this is a bag made large enough to fit completely over the head. It is made from fairly thin black material and is designed so that really there are two bags, one inside the other. If the head is put into the centre bag—because of the double thickness of material all round—nothing can be seen. If the head is placed between bags one and two—so that you get three thicknesses behind the head and only one in front of the face—then you have a reasonable vision if the material is thin enough.

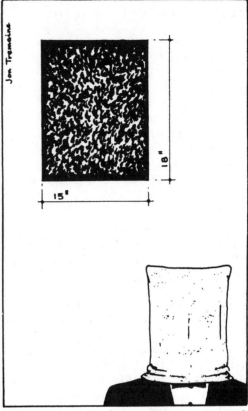

Frankly, I don't like this type at all. The idea behind the double wall principle is supposed to be that the bag blindfold could be tested. In actual fact it may be tested—but anyone with an ounce of common sense would soon see how it worked. The principle of a Bag Blindfold is very good—the idea that the head is fully covered is basically sound. I would therefore suggest that as an alternative you have two bag blindfolds—one very thin through which you can see—and one very thick through which you cannot see. You have the latter examined (if necessary) and then switch for the other one—which honestly does not present much of a problem. By this method, both bag blindfolds are single bags as there is no need for the double principle.

This type of Blindfold is suitable for the Blindfold Drive, Sealed Letter Delivery and such stunts. It has the big drawback that is hard to overcome— inside a bag you can get very hot—very quick and it is rational to suppose that the average magician breathes!

Apart from the drawback—it has an asset over other types. It is a model which may be used by performers who have to wear spectacles to see. The glasses can be in the bag before-hand—put on when the head is in the bag and removed and left in the bag before it is taken off. No one knows that you were wearing spectacles! Many people have said to me that they cannot do Blindfold work because they wear glasses—well here's the answer. It is not just an idea—it has been tried and proven successful.

### (6) The Sheet or Blanket Cover

In many respects, this—though simple—is one of the most convincing methods. The medium or Mentalist's Partner is seated on a chair and is then completely covered with a large blanket. Under such conditions it is quite impossible for the medium to see—and so effects are chosen carefully so that in actual fact there is no need to be able to see. At times, this can be very convenient—especially when the medium wants to do something and not be seen doing it! For example, under the blanket, by the light of a pocket torch she is able to read sealed messages. It would be safe to say that when a blanket is used—the audience are at a disadvantage more so than the medium. The simple things are usually best in the long run.

## (7)  The Bucket

From time to time, those in search of new ways to convince their fans that it is possible to see without looking—have resorted to wearing a bucket (if it can be said that one "wears" a bucket!). To add to the general authenticity of the experiment—the bucket is first filled with water and as no fluid escapes it is implied that there are no holes. Now the bucket is to be worn, but first it is advisable to remove the water—and since most stages do not have drains it is as well to have another bucket nearby. In an emergency, you could drink it—which of course, would prove it was water! Having thus emptied the tested bucket, you invert it over your head and looking somewhat like a hybrid of a Martian crossed with a Robot—you do your party piece.

I am of the honest opinion that, although doubtlessly convincing, the bucket blindfold is dangerously funny. I am sure that it would look so ridiculous that half the audience would snigger throughout the act.

## (8)  Cotton Wool, Dough, Coins, Plaster and Suchlike

In general, I dislike the use of the above named means of blindfolding. Rarely it can be said that there is justification for their use. It depends very much on what you are doing. For a simple blindfold effect—perhaps part of a Mental Routine where you do a spot of X-Ray Eye work or Psychometry—there is no need for imposing what appear to be test conditions fit for experiments in Psychical Research.

For a challenge Blindfold test—yes—use everything you can—have the eyes first sealed with surgical plaster, then covered with bakers dough, padded with cotton wool and have the head mummified with bandages. But use this sort of restraint for publicity stunts—where the effect is specific, based entirely on the fact that you will do something when beyond all doubt— you are blindfolded.

The Mentalist who wants to make sightless vision part of his act cannot afford the time for these elaborate and often messy procedures. For if they are to be done properly, a committee must be called to examine the materials and to take part in the blindfolding and this means time—valuable time during a mental act.

I would be prepared to argue that a good actor wearing an ordinary black velvet mask—would be just as convincing as anyone who used dough and plaster. We cannot say that these elaborate measures are entirely useless —as many famous performers have used them with great success. However, there is no need to get carried away with enthusiasm and forget the underlying feature—you are there to perform effects, not to demonstrate varieties of blindfolds.

For those wishing to study the use of fake coins, surgical plaster, cotton wool and dough, I recommend The Tarbell Course in Magic and Will Dexter's *Sealed Vision*, which deal so comprehensively with the subject that repetition here would be superfluous.

## (9)  Summary

We have considered a few methods of Blindfolding and have said enough to imply that it is not so much what type of blindfold you use—as HOW

134

YOU USE IT. The wise performer would devote more time to handling and presentation of the blindfold than to elaborate techniques which theoretically prove he cannot see. It is far better to convince your audience psychologically—that you cannot see, than it is to try and do so—physically. Little twists of presentation and subtleties during performance will register psychologically and will be remembered by the onlookers.

If you are really keen on using Blindfolds—and you want to learn a lot very quickly, get hold of the one man who can teach you more than any book or magical society—have a heart to heart talk with a man who is really blind—you will be amazed at what he can teach you. Moreover, if the matter is dealt with tactfully, your blind teacher will enjoy offering his services.

## PART TWO   TECHNIQUE

### (1)   Downward Glimpse

We are concerned at this point in Step Five—with the finer points of presentation and technique. Consequently, we must consider the proper use of the Downward Glimpse. Undoubtedly, it can be misused; a fault which is commonly caused by bad timing.

Imagine that part of your Blindfold routine called for the reading of a word written on a card. The card is taken and held to the forehead—or well up in the air. By acting you appear to see the word and begin the patter which leads up to the naming of the word. THEN you drop the hand to the chest position for glimpsing and find out what it really is—at a time when the attention of the audience is on the off-beat. Alternatively, you glimpse the word and wait your time before revealing what it is. Never make the mistake of holding the card at chest level whilst you tell the word. Work "one-behind" or "one-ahead" and get the glimpse when it is not expected.

In practice, I have found it better to create the impression that I know the word—long before I do—and glimpsing when the timing calls for a visible relaxation. This is a very deceptive form of misdirection.

A further example will clarify the point:—

On a table you have six objects placed there by members of the audience. You are blindfolded and approach the table near enough to get a good look at the objects. These you memorise. Next you move well away and request that a spectator bring any object to you. When you receive it you hold it high above your head—in such a position that it would be impossible to see even if you were not blindfolded, and from this position you divine the object. By feel it will be easy to recognise which of the six objects you have been given, and if you have been lucky and have a good memory—you will be able to add one or two details about the object. (*i.e.* it could be a £1 note —and you note the last three figures.)

You must try and pay attention to details such as mentioned above—because it adds so much to the effect. Suppose you are given a key which you hold up—when you name the object as a key, people are a little impressed but some say to themselves "so he felt the shape". These people sit bolt upright when you add "A Yale key—and it has the number 432 on it".

Can you imagine how much less effective this would be if you stood *over* the table inviting the suspicion that you are "peeping"?

## (2)  One Ahead System

After some thought, it will be realised that the One Ahead System used in conjunction with the Downward Glimpse—forms a very powerful combination. Working with a stack of envelopes—say giving answers to sealed messages, it is obvious that by holding one envelope in the air and appearing to read its contents, you have every opportunity to read others held casually in the hand at chest level. Attention on the part of the audience is naturally focused on the envelope in the air and you have ample misdirection for your work. You are not left to find out how to read sealed envelopes, it is explained in this series.

Apart from envelopes, we have cards and an effect by Hans Trixer illustrates the application of the One Ahead System and Downward Glimpse used together (Step Ten). We may therefore, conclude that the One Ahead System and The Downward Glimpse have homologous qualities for Blindfold work.

## (3)  The Magnetic Blindfold

I consider that it is my good fortune to know Punx the German Mentalist. Mr. Punx is responsible for many simple, yet highly practical ideas and this is one of them.

Working with Type I. The Unfaked Mask (*i.e.* you cannot see through it) and preparing first by sewing a small powerful magnet in the blindfold, you can perform many effects. The magnet is set so that it fits into the socket of the eye when the blindfold is worn. This disposes of any visible "bumps" showing through the blindfold. It is actually sewn into the material so that it cannot move from its position.

The application of this blindfold can be illustrated by one effect; once you grasp the principle you will understand that it has numerous possibilities.

You have five paypacket size envelopes and one of them has a pin stuck in the bottom. The trick commences when you hand out five cards, telling four people to write a name of a girl and the fifth person to write the name of a boy. Each person is given an envelope and told to seal their card inside. The person who writes the boy's name is given the envelope that contains the pin. All envelopes are then collected and mixed by a spectator. You are blindfolded and the envelopes are given to you. One at a time you hold them to your forehead (!) and eventually you locate the odd card—bearing the boy's name. If you can visualise the position adopted by the performer when he holds an envelope to his forehead, and at the same time, checking for a slight—yet detectable magnetic pull from the envelope with the pin, you will appreciate the beauty of the mechanics. The position is natural, holding something to the forehead as if obtaining some impulses or psychometric vibration—and it visibly precludes all suspicion of glimpsing or markings as one cannot see; this can be confirmed by having the blindfold tested by holding it over a spectator's eyes. It would not be advisable to let them handle it with the magnet inside.

Other subtleties include the use of five paper clips. Four made of brass with a nickel-plate finish and one of ordinary steel. The brass ones are non-magnetic and yet all look identical. The same can be applied to keys for performing a variation of The Seven Keys to Baldpate.

It is possible to insert shim-steel (about 2 thou' thick) into a playing card. The card is first stripped in two and then the thin steel stuck inside with an anhydrous adhesive such as "Evostick". If you use ordinary glue that

136

contains water you will find the steel rusts inside the card causing yellow rust spots to appear on the surface. By judicious positioning of the shim-steel in various corners of different cards, you will be able to identify any one of several cards by feeling the magnetic pull in certain positions. Hence you can identify say five different cards sealed in envelopes. The effect would be better presented for Mentalism if you were to use Zenner Cards (see Step Two) with signs rather than Playing Cards which are overworked.

The above examples should be sufficient to make it obvious that a Magnetic Blindfold is worth having and using. Like all good things in Magic and Mentalism, it is simple and therefore reliable.

### (4)  The Stacked Deck

Of all the forms of Mentalism wherein one may resort to the use of Playing Cards, perhaps Blindfold Work is the one field where to a large degree—cards are excusable. The conditions of performance appear to be so rigid that it seems to matter very little what media you choose to use.

To the man with "X-Ray Eyes" there can be no doubt that a Stacked Deck is a very valuable standby. We have already dealt with four systems for setting up cards in Step Three and there is no need for further description. Tricks with the deck are given and further effects will appear obvious when worked in conjunction with some of the blindfolds suggested herein.

### (5)  Marked Cards

A good marked pack is another useful standby. The Ghost Deck which is described in detail on page 46 of Step Two can be exceptionally good for blindfold work as it functions on *touch reading* and not visible markings. For that matter, most of the principles of Sound and Touch Reading, will be found of use for Blindfold Work.

Ordinary marked cards (visible reading from the back) will also be helpful and you will find that the handling is much easier working with them blind-folded as the audience cannot see your eyes staring at the backs—as they do in normal use. I have experimented with several types of standard marked cards, both printed and hand-marked, and I find that the marking does not have to be exaggerated for blindfold work. It is just as easy to see with or without the blindfold. If you want to mark your own cards, I suggest a commonplace pattern of geometric design. Use good quality Indian Ink on black backed cards and fill in dots to indicate value. For suits, I usually scratch out from the original print using a fine and very sharp surgical blade, although a new razor blade will do if handled with care. When scratching out, the ink alone is lifted from the card—no grooves are made into the stock because these show up at certain lighting angles.

### (6)  Annemann's One Way Deck

I once introduced this pack to a Magic Club and the best part of those present thought it a very funny joke. Little did they know that it is a very deceptive and cunning idea. The aim is to make a pack "one way" and to put people off the scent (especially magicians!) they are marked ON THE FACES. I know it sounds ridiculous—but you try it and laugh afterwards.

With a sharp blade as described for marking cards, you make a small scratch on the index pip of the suit of every card—at one end only. The diamonds you cut off a wee bit from the bottom of the diamond. The hearts, you exaggerate the line down the centre. The clubs and spades you make a small gap between the stem and main body of the pip. Remember, these markings are made at one end and on the small suit pip which stands just beside the number—the index suit pip.

To operate, a card is taken and you reverse the deck under cover of closing the fan (the neatest way to do it). It is replaced anywhere and they are mixed by an overhand shuffle. The cards are spread face up and you look for the odd one to tell which was chosen. Commonsense tells you that if you are blindfolded, from the audience point of view, it does not make any difference which way the cards face as you (apparently) cannot see them at all. There are not many people who will have the brains to work that one out for themselves!

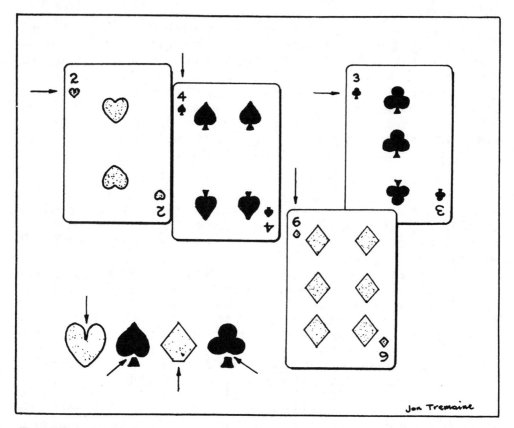

Jon Tremaine

### (7) Mirrors

When performing in a Drawing Room and use is being made of a see through type of blindfold, it should not be overlooked that a mirror can be of considerable use. Mirrors are generally to be found on the walls of a drawing room and they are not liable to be suspected when you perform blindfolded. Aside from mirrors that, by good fortune, are to be found in the place you perform, there are other devices which act as reflectors which you can take along with you.

### (8) Reflectors and Shiners

I have spent quite a bit of time exploring the use of shiners and have examined most basic types such as miniature mirrors built into finger rings, pipes, brooches, etc. Of these, I cannot say that any have proved really successful. In my experience, the use of such deliberately faked equipment, causes one too much concern when performing. You get over worried about someone seeing the gimmick and spend more time hiding it than using it.

Knowing that shiners can be of great use, I decided to try out new methods and after quite a bit of trial and error I find a well-polished cigarette lighter gives me all that is required by way of a reflected picture. Other very good and inconspicuous items include a well-polished spoon and table knife. A heavy chrome table knife resting on the blade edge gives you a terrific amount of scope and in it one can tell with ease—playing cards, bold writing, dates on coins (with a bit of practice) and, obtain a pretty wide view of the room. I consider it far better to utilise such things as knives and spoons—than the specially prepared gadgets. No one ever looks twice at a knife lying on a table and since it can be used to open an envelope, it serves its purpose as far as the audience are concerned—if they are concerned.

I understand that certain wrist watch faces can be adapted to act as reflectors. As yet, I have not seen one that I would care to use. There are special fittings in the form of black discs that go over the face of the watch forming a mirror surface. You might have some luck with this type of apparatus—but, as I say, up to now I prefer working with everyday improvised equipment.

It is generally a good rule to suppose that with any type of reflector, if you can see it—so can the audience. In view of this, I maintain that it is best to use things which although seen are not suspected.

Whilst on the subject of reflectors I may as well tell you about a good swindle that you can use to fool fellow magicians (or lay people). To perform it, you must both be seated at opposite sides of the table and you must not have anyone standing too near you.

You borrow his cards and mix them. You don your blindfold and then have him choose any card from the middle of the pack, which he places face down on your hand. You feel the back of the card with the fingertips of your other hand and finally name it correctly. You do not turn the card over. He knows they are not marked because they are his cards. Your only requirement is a sixpenny birdcage mirror from Woolworths. This you place on your knee when seated and that affords you the reflection of the card index seen through the open fingers of the hand. There is nothing to it, but you can make a lot of it!

## (9) Self-Working Effects

As you know, there are many tricks which are called "self-working" and these effects can be made use of by the blindfold worker. The important point to remember when doing, say a self-working card trick, is that you cannot see to check that the spectator is doing as you tell him to do; and you must therefore be extra explicit with your instructions. Eliminate ambiguity or vagueness in your orders so that he does not make a mistake because of your instructions.

It annoys me to see a trick performed and when it goes wrong the performer turns round and tells the spectator "it was your fault, you made a mistake". There is no such thing as a mistake on the part of a spectator. Every stupidity on their part should be catered for in your presentation, you know what you are doing—they don't.

## (10) Prior Observation

A skilled performer is always wide awake, ever on the lookout for something that can be used to cause that extra little miracle. When you visit a

139

drawing room or club, there are dozens of things lying about that can be casually examined before you perform. Get a good look at one or two items and remember any outstanding features.

You might be visiting a friend to show a few tricks at a party. When you arrive suppose you spot a mantlepiece over the fireplace. Stand there a moment and have a look at any brass monkey "Made in Birmingham", or a photograph of a young man in uniform perhaps bearing a signature. Half an hour later you can do something with this knowledge. Don't waste your time gazing into a glass of gin—the Spirits won't help you!

Let us consider an effect to illustrate the usefulness of "prior observations".

We will take the magical effect conceived by Bob Hummer and improved by Al Koran of locating a ten shilling note under one of three ordinary cups, which has to be found by the performer without looking under the cups— and adapt it to use for a Blindfold trick.

The first thing is to obtain three cups. They should appear to be the same. The next thing is to place them in a row on the table and then to look at any one and detect a marking which will identify that cup from the others. This will be very easy as every cup has imperfections, a small crack, one-way trade mark on the base or some obvious feature. You can safely borrow three cups without much fear of getting a set of three that are perfectly identical. Having located your mark, the next step is to remember the position of that cup. The other two do not matter. We will suppose that from left to right the positions are called "A, B and C". Moreover, our mark for the sake of this description appears on "A" the first cup on the left.

Next we borrow a ten shilling note and screw it into a ball. When explaining what is to be done to the spectator (see "Self-working effects") you actually run through the moves so as to make everything painfully clear. If they get mixed up—so do you!

The note is to be placed under any cup. This having been done, *the other two*, whichever they may be, are to be exchanged. That is, suppose the note goes under "B"—then cup "A" is transferred to position "C" and cup "C" to the place previously occupied by "A". Likewise, if it went under "A" then "B and C" would be exchanged and if under "C" then "A and B" are the two transferred.

Having demonstrated the point and ascertained that you have made yourself understood by the spectator, you replace the marked cup at position "A" and leave them in a tidy row on the table. The note is given to the spectator and you turn your back and blindfold yourself whilst he does the exchanging. When he tells you he is ready, you turn round, take his hand and ask him to guide your hand over the tops of the cups without touching them. With a moment or two of mentalistic fumbling—you stop over one cup and declare that under this one is the note. It is. If it is not, you have either been cheated by the spectator or you are an oaf!

The method, in case you do not know, and many people do know—is simply a process of reasoning from a known factor (the marked cup at a known position at the start). We started with the marked cup at "A". When we turn round we glimpse down the nose until we see the position of the marked cup again. We can tell from that position which one hides the note.

Remember the spectator was told to move *the other two*, so if the marked cup remains at "A" it is obvious that it has not been moved, which means

140

that the other two were moved, which means that "A" hides the note—it was unmoved. Suppose the marked cup now appears at position "B". We can reason that if it appears at "B" then what was at "B" has been moved to the vacant space at "A". Since both "A and B" have therefore been moved —the unmoved cup must be "C". Lastly, the marked cup turns up at position "C". Again we reason that "A" must have been vacant when the first cup was moved, and since it is now at "C" that cup must have gone in its place. Therefore "B" was not moved and must hide the note. Fogel suggests you end by telling the number of the note!

It does not matter at what position you start with the marked cup as long as you know where it was before you turned your back. A few minutes work will teach you the system which is very simple and yet good enough to fool many an intelligent audience. You may even care to progress further, and have the cups moved several times before you turn round. This can still be done as long as you remember the relative positions and after the first move the spectator calls out the number of exchanges and what they are by position "A, B or C". It is sufficient to show that by prior observation, a simple matter of noting a mark on a cup, the means to perform something which greatly entertains and baffles is made possible.

Another aspect of Prior Observation worth mention is that you cannot always identify a person by their faces when you are blindfolded—but very often you can—by their boots or shoes. Watch the spectators shoes when you are blindfolded, you can tell which way he's facing. Watch an assistant's shoes and you have as good a code system as you will ever need for fake Muscle reading, Blindfold walks, and when he stands next to another person, identifying a member of the audience. Last but not least, I have no doubt that you know Patent leather shoes make a reasonable reflector. Or did you!?

### (11) Memory Systems

As part of a blindfold act, if you are lacking material, it should not be forgotten that most of the memory systems can be brought into play as effects. The Knight's Tour or Giant Memory Feat are good examples and these, with others, are fully described in Step Three. I have known people capable of performing the Giant Memory of some twenty objects—who can do it at an incredible speed and yet never could get up and perform because they just couldn't face an audience. Blindfold that person and when they cannot see the audience—they perform. I have no doubt that you like me, could think of quite a few people that would look better doing their complete act blindfolded!

### (12) Patter and Movement During Performance

This is a very important aspect of the Technique of Blindfold Work. Probably too little attention is paid to it and nothing is more likely to lead to a second-rate performance than inattention to presentation.

You must watch your wording pretty carefully. I recollect seeing one Blindfold act where the performer, doing a book test, insisted on the ridiculous phrase "I can't see the word very clearly—it's becoming visible now"—and "I can see the word 'Cardiac'—is that right?" If you are blindfolded you cannot see "period!"

The mediumistic gambit "I see" is well used by mentalist and often with good reason and effect. However, you must avoid it and similar absurdities during blindfold performances.

141

On the other hand, there are many subtleties of phraseology that can go a long way towards improving the authenticity of your lack of vision. When you need a pack of cards from a table and you stand blindfolded to one side of the stage, you say to the assistant or spectator, "there is a table over there and on it a pack of cards, will you please take them and remove them from the case". Through your blindfold you watch him, do just that and wait until he has them and starts to remove them before you add "they are in the middle of the table, have you found them yet?" You know he's got them—but the question at the right time helps to show that you do *not know*. Don't exaggerate this sort of misdirection too much, use it a lot in quick simple plots with words and action and don't make it obvious.

By "obvious" it is meant that when you tell him to bring the Goldfish Bowl and seconds afterwards you get a deafening crash of breaking glass, you will alter your usual tag line from "Now have you found it" to something which clearly shows you heard the blessed thing drop! Sometimes one has to alter or remake the patter according to the misfortunes of performance.

The next consideration is movement. On this subject a lot could be said as there is much to consider. However, in brief, one should always behave with dignity whether blindfolded, unblindfolded or even doing a fan-dance. To move with dignity and grace and still appear blindfolded is not easy. You have to mix the need to walk cautiously with the need to appear graceful. To fall head over heels over a chair would be a positive way to prove you couldn't see, and would also reduce you to a ridiculous level as a performer. (Unless doing comedy). To extend the hand feeling for a chair just as you arrive at it—is just about enough acting. *You cannot do better than stand still* when you have no important reason to move. As said very early on, keep your eyes closed when you want to act blindfolded and know the position of all your props and the chairs and tables. To entertain is one thing, to break one's neck is another.

The combination of well-acted movement and appropriate patter will do more to convince your audience that you cannot see, than would a microscopic examination of the blindfold. There is one particular stance that seems just right. When you are talking to the spectator (wearing the blindfold) you do not turn your face to him. It is as though you have misplaced the point at which he is standing and you appear to address an empty space nearby the spectator. When you refer to a table "over there", point, but make the pointing a casual wave which misses the exact spot where the table stands. When you approach a blackboard or any piece of apparatus, create the impression that you are feeling for it; the hands go ahead. fingers outstretched feeling for the impact telling you that the board is there. These minor points make the act, and the demonstration rise above trickery and ascend to what seems to be supernormal.

Finally on the subject of technique, don't be afraid to make a deliberate mistake. Some Mentalists are inclined to aim at absolute success with every effect, and if anything, this is by no means essential or good. There are times when one mistake is worth a hundred successes! To be right most of the time and nearly right now and then—is perhaps the very best. Nothing seems to give greater assurance that the whole thing is genuine—than a few mistakes.

If you are going to do a blindfold act, work out the routine and effects until everything is just so. Then look through the programme and find one or two places where a mistake can help. Sometimes it can be used to bring laughter, as for example, you have two assistants from the audience, a Lady and a Gentleman. At one point in the routine, you turn to the gentleman and say "Now Madam!". As one line of print in a book it looks cold and weak. Put the same line in patter at the right point in the performance and it can be your greatest success. Let us take another example. You are mixing some cards, one drops to the floor. If you look downwards and pick it up— you are finished. You drop the card, you pause as though you know something has happened, allow one of the assistants to pick it up and hand it to you, and, as this is done, refuse it saying "did I drop one? Never mind we don't want that one it's the Ace of Spades!".

## PART THREE   TRICKS

### Introduction

The following is a complete Blindfold Routine which has been given to readers of this book by Joe Elman. The routine is one that has been performed very many times with great success and Joe is left to describe it in his own words:—

#### "SIGHTLESS VISION" a complete Blindfold Routine by Joe Elman

For many years I, Joe Elman, have been presenting my "Sightless Vision" to audiences under all conditions, and to specially invited members of the medical profession, wherever possible borrowing all the requirements from the audience, yet making no claims other than that this could be done by anyone who has had the benefit of the proper training.

I wish to acknowledge that my first contact with this subject was through the instruction of LENZ (Len Allen) and that I still use the original method shown to me, not having found anything which is so convincing to a lay audience.

The requirements are:—

A chair, for the performer to sit on.

One or more newspapers, menu cards or programmes, to form the first stage of the blindfold.

Two table napkins (large), tea towels or scarves to form the second stage of the blindfold.

A tray, for collection of objects.

A writing pad or menu back, as large as possible to be used for the written word test.

A crayon pencil, or at the worst a ball-pen.

Plenty of showmanship.

143

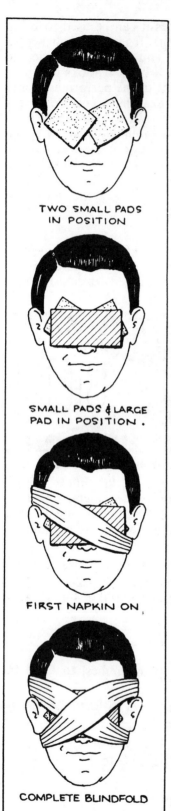

TWO SMALL PADS
IN POSITION

SMALL PADS & LARGE
PAD IN POSITION.

FIRST NAPKIN ON

COMPLETE BLINDFOLD

Jon. Tremaine.

The chair is placed in a position which is well lit from above, as this makes the task much easier. The tray with the requirements in this order, from the bottom upwards, is on the chair:—

Pad and crayon pencil.

Table napkins.

Newspapers.

The performer tells the audience that he wishes to demonstrate the powers of "Sightless Vision", using some rather technical language about physical phenomena, without becoming facetious, and then invites two members of the audience to come up and assist him, laying stress on the fact that members of the medical profession are particularly welcome to assist. The assistants are placed either side of the chair and invited to hold and examine the newspaper and table napkins.

The performer then takes the newspaper and separates it into sheets, folding them to make three pads:—

One twelve by six inches.

Two six by six inches.

These are then handed back to the assistants to be further examined. The table napkins are folded diagonally to make them about six inches wide and handed back to the assistants. Placing the tray on his lap, the performer then sits on the chair and does not rise from it until the very end of the demonstration. The performer closes his eyes. Taking the two small pads the performer places one over each eye, making the edges overlap over the nose, but the bottom corner can come below the nose. The long pad is then placed over the two smaller pads so that at least two layers of pad cover each eye, the bottom edge should come to the tip of the nose.

Whilst this is being done, but before the long pad is placed in position the performer lowers his eyebrows and screws up his eyes and keeps them in this position until the blindfold has been completed and examined by the assistants.

The two table napkins are then tied by the assistants across the face—one napkin over the left eye and round the right ear, the other over the right eye and round the left ear, and the assistants are asked to make sure that the knots are really tight. They are then invited to examine the blindfold and to assure the audience that it would be impossible to see at all using normal vision.

At this moment the performer raises his eyebrows, whilst turning his head from side to side, and ensures that he has a clear "peep" down one side of his nose. This is quite easy with practice, and the tighter the blindfold the easier it is to get the "peep".

It is essential that the performer does not touch the blindfold with his hands at any time during the following demonstrations.

One assistant is asked to take the pad and crayon pencil from the tray whilst the other one takes the tray itself. The one with the tray is asked to collect six articles from the audience, if possible, articles such as driving licences, bank notes, engraved jewellery, club cards and keys which have identification marks or numbers, and to return the tray with the objects to the performer. The second assistant is asked to get a member of the audience to write a word in a foreign language on the pad and to return with the pad to the performer. The assistants are asked to stand slightly behind and each to one side of the performer and to place the tray on the performer's lap.

At this stage the showmanship must come in, to convince the audience that the objects are identified whilst held by the performer in front of his blindfolded eyes and I advise anyone trying to get up an act of this nature to rehearse, rehearse and rehearse before trying it out even in front of the family. If humour comes naturally, it can be used in describing the articles, use speed on the uninteresting but dwell on the articles of interest, such as an endorsement on a driving licence, a key or an unusual object. Always leave an interesting and apparently difficult object to last. Return the objects to the tray handing the tray back to the assistant.

The second assistant is then asked to hand over the pad, which is "peeped" and then he is asked for the crayon pencil. Holding the pad at normal eye level the performer turns his head slightly away from the audience and immediately, slowly and deliberately copies the word. It is as well to make some reference to the handwriting, or if possible the origin of the word, or maybe some appropriate reply.

The pad and pencil are handed to the assistant and the applause, which is never missing if this is done properly, is cut short by the performer raising his arms sideways and in a loud voice requesting the assistants to remove the blindfold.

At this moment the performer must close his eyes very tightly and keep them closed until the blindfold is completely removed, so that his reaction to light will be that of a person who has been in the dark for a long time.

He rises from his chair, asks the assistants to return the borrowed objects and "props" and with some further remarks about "well you too could do this if you knew how" takes the final applause.

To gain the maximum effect of "Sightless Vision" it should not be part of a conjuring show but rather included in a demonstration of mental magic or pseudo-psychic phenomena.

A word of warning — if there is a chance that the audience will be able to experiment and try to reproduce your miracle immediately after your performance, be careful to finish the show with something quite away from "Sightless Vision", or the observant will be showing their friends how you did it.

145

I contend that the chief requirement for a good presentation of "Sightless Vision" is showmanship accompanied by a thorough knowledge of what you are going to do and the methods you wish to employ. In this particular field the know-how is the least important requirement and every effort must be made to convince the audience that you too are convinced that you are demonstrating a power which they all have.

## (1)   Psychical Research versus Mentalism.   Corinda

For many years I have dabbled in what is called "Psychical Research" and during that time I have encountered many people and societies concerned with the subject. About two years ago I met with one group of investigators who called themselves by a name that suggested they would prove the existence of supernatural phenomena. In order to prove their point, it was claimed that their various tests and experiments were conducted on scientific lines, which supposedly eliminated chance, luck and trickery. This to me was a challenge because I am a firm contender that scientific training cannot make an investigator competent to deal with experiments that could involve trickery. A well trained magician will soon baffle a well trained scientist! The only man to do the job is someone skilled in both fields—magic and research.

At this particular time, the organisation who shall remain nameless to avoid any embarrassment, were dealing with a series of card guessing experiments, conducted along the lines of Dr. Rhine's work using E.S.P. or sign cards. At two ends of a table sat the subjects a distance of about seven feet between them. Across the middle of the table was erected a screen of plywood. On one side of the screen the first subject ("the transmitter") was given any one of five cards. Each card had a different design. The transmitter looked at it and attempted to project a mental picture of that design to the subject at the other end of the table (the "recipient") Research officer stood by taking records of correct and incorrect "calls" and doubtlessly on the look out for cheating.

One day I "discovered" a medium, a young lady with highly developed "psi faculty" and her "sister" who likewise had strange mental abilities. The society "tested" the two under their scientific conditions and two months later published their findings to the effect that these ladies were capable of controlled telepathy.

This is the first time the truth has been told, and the method divulged. The swindle, as such it was, having been performed not simply to make a fool of a group of investigators, but more so to show them that "findings" of psychical research mean very little when supplied by unqualified investigators.

One girl was seated at the end of the table behind the screen. Acting as transmitter, she was to convey thoughts to her sister at the other end of the table. The latter girl, the recipient, was blindfolded by the investigators and she was given a pad and pencil with which to draw her impressions. Twenty-five cards were used, the pack consisting of five designs repeated five times. The designs were:—A circle, a cross, a triangle, a square and a star. The cards were mixed in a box, withdrawn one at a time by different investigators who did not look at the design until the medium herself had attempted to "send" it (this was to prevent the recipient from reading *their* thoughts!). The medium took the chosen card, looked at it, put it down on the table and simply nodded. The investigator would tell the other girl the card had been seen and did so every time by saying one word "Now". Every time five cards had been dealt with, two people were asked to leave the room so that in turn, everybody was outside at some point in the experiment. The score as a result of the test was twenty three correct out of twenty five. It could have been twenty five correct—but the little difference convinced everyone it was genuine.

The method, as you will have guessed, is a code system—but I wouldn't mind a little gamble that it would fool you if you did not know. I had to devise a simple code that would survive their test conditions. It was sound—and the sound was made by the playing card being dealt on to the table! Practically the only thing the medium could do—was to look at a card and then put it down. The table top was hard polished wood—so get a card and see what you make of this. The five designs can be remembered as 1, 2, 3, 4 or 5 by their construction (see page 38, Step Two). If it was No. 1, the card was placed on the table without any noise. If No. 2, it was caused to make one click simply by bending slightly as it is put down. No. 3 makes two clicks by putting the index finger in the middle, holding both short ends with fingers and thumb and letting one end go after the other. If it was No. 4, the card is put down without noise, then picked up again in such a way that it makes a sliding noise and one click, then it is looked at and again replaced quietly. No. 5 was the same as No. 4 for the start—but instead of replacing it without noise it was put down as No. 1 with a single click. That is all there is to it!

There were times during the experiment when the silence of the room seemed to be broken by the deafening crash of a little card hitting the table, but no one could hear the noise because THEY were not listening for it. Now to adapt the trick with perhaps even more mystery—you can have two subjects and blindfold both. As long as one can see the cards given to her—perhaps by peeking—it will be easy to do.

I have gone to some lengths to describe this plot as the principle is undoubtedly terrific, and if it was given in a couple of words—you may pass it by. With the full circumstances telling of its use, you will appreciate more how something so simple can be worth its weight in tons of gimmicks. It is a method which embodies an essential of good Mentalism—and that is *natural behaviour*.

### (2)  "Mental Masterpiece" by Maurice Fogel

Anyone who has had the good fortune to witness "The Amazing Fogel" performing a series of Mental miracles. will know that it is not so much what he does, as how he does it. With showmanship, almost unrivalled throughout the world, Fogel will slay an audience with the mere trifle of a trick. This effect is one that he has used with great success and I am endebted for his contribution in this Step. The effect is a Prediction which is performed partly whilst blindfolded. Two persons are invited on to the stage to assist. One is given a sealed envelope containing, as you say, a card upon which is written one word—a word that you predict will be chosen. On one table is a pile of about twenty different newspapers. In your pocket you have a red pencil and nearby stands a blackboard with chalk ready for writing.

When the two assistants arrive and one has been given the sealed envelope to hold tightly, the other is told to go to the table and choose any newspaper.

You do not appear to pay any attention to his choice, and whilst he does that, you put on a blindfold. However, in actual fact you make a very careful note of the paper he chooses. When he is ready, you tell the other spectator to take the red pencil that you will hand to him, to open the chosen newspaper at any page and to underline any word. You stand near enough to be able to peek what word he underlines. This having been done you move casually away and tell him to note the name of the paper and then to mix it with the others in the pile.

Next you point out that whilst blindfolded a paper has been chosen and a word freely selected from many thousands. You ask to be lead to the table and when there, go through the actions of finding the chosen paper. You take two or three, hold them in the air as though trying to get some "feeling" from them, discard one and then another until you are left with the chosen one in the hand. You display the name of this paper to the audience so that they can see that you are right also. Then hand that paper, unopened, to the first spectator. Tell him to hold it for a moment whilst you show the complete audience what is written on the card sealed in the envelope. Take the prediction from the assistant and cross over to the black board; there rip open the envelope, remove the card and look at it and then MISWRITE the name so that you spell out the word chosen in the newspaper. The audience do not know what it is yet! Have something written on the card so that you can casually flash something written. When you have the word written in bold letters, tell the man with the newspaper to open it and find the word underlined in red and to call it out. This he does. You immediately ask the other person to confirm that this was the word he actually chose—it is, so he must agree!

The blindfold is removed as you get to the blackboard. You are supposed to look at the card to check your prediction. Make nothing of the card—and the audience will forget it ever existed.

An alternative method of sighting the underlined word is to glimpse it when you run through the papers to locate the chosen one. If you can do this without appearing to open the paper, the effect is so much the better.

The advantage of asking the spectator to check through the paper and find the word underlined is that you get a time lapse which helps to withdraw attention from the fact that you copied the card writing (apparently) on to the board. You make sure that the man who does the final check is not the man who actually underlined the word. Otherwise he knows where to look and it would be found too quickly. Lastly, when you watch him underline a word with the red pencil, you can also take the opportunity of looking at the top of the page to see the name of the paper—just to confirm that your original glimpse was right.

### (3) "X-Ray" Eyes by Corinda

This is another one of those little things that its nice to know because you can use it impromptu and it has an astounding effect upon onlookers. A pack of cards are borrowed. any seven are removed and any one is chosen for the experiment. The seven are taken by a spectator and mixed, given to you, and then your hands are immediately covered completely with a handkerchief. Your hands are in the middle of the table away from the lap (!) You appear to have "X-ray" Eyes—because from under the handkerchief you will pull out one card and that one is the chosen one. It can be examined microscopically as it IS NOT MARKED in any way. The effect can be repeated indefinitely—with those cards or with another seven from the deck.

The method is a principle that I have used widely with playing cards and have found it extremely useful and deceptive. I call it location by "negative reasoning", and it will serve you well to apply it when performing mentalism with cards. When you know the method you are liable to question its probability to fool, but you will only have to use it once or twice to realise how good it is.

You have seven cards and must locate one. The one you must locate is the centre of attraction so you leave it alone and mark the other six! By negative reasoning you have no idea which is his card—but you can soon find out which it is not!! Somehow the average man does not think to look at the others, logic makes him examine the card you found and it is beyond reason to think that you really found six and the one left was the chosen one.

The method of marking the cards is one that I found myself. I daresay it is not new and most methods of marking cards have surely been discovered. However, it serves its purpose and that is all that matters. In Step Two, writing about a trick pack called the "Ghost Deck" I have given drawings on page 46 which show a fingernail running down the edge of a card. This is the marking method. At the same spot on each of the six cards you press slightly with the nail directly on the edge. The pressure causes the edge to expand very slightly—but not enough to be seen. To read the marking, the card is run through the ball of first finger and thumb and if it is marked a distinct bump is felt, against a smooth edge if it is unmarked. Make the marking exactly where you know where to feel later. It can be done so quickly, and with such natural handling, that six cards can be marked as they are dealt on to the table one by one.

Under cover of the handkerchief— be sure to check both ends for markings as the cards may have been reversed in the shuffle by the spectator. If you wish, when everybody is examining the chosen card afterwards, you can dispose of the marked six on to the deck and then cut it, or switch them for six unmarked ones or, if you like, remove the markings by squeezing the marked edge through the fingertips. I have never yet found it necessary to worry about the other six.

As alternative forms of presentation, you can locate the card whilst holding them all behind your back, under the table or above your head. It can be done blindfolded, with the cards in a bag or hat, spectator's pocket or in total darkness.

### (4)  A Gem of Mental Magic by Corinda

For many years one principle has been exploited by my enthusiasm from every conceivable point of view. It is the principle of the Centre Tear or Torn Centre. I would say that this is one of the greatest things of Mentalism —if not the greatest. I have encountered many good ways of doing and using the Centre Tear and it is used to grand effect in this trick.

Step Six on Billets gives you all the basic technique for doing the Centre Tear. Once the timing and misdirection is mastered the steal is perfect. So easy in fact, that it can be done with your eyes closed or blindfolded—and that is what you have to do for this trick. Should any be in doubt that this can be done with success, I am ever willing to do it if you care to ask.

149

The spectator is given a small square of paper and told to think of any word or person's name. To wait until you are blindfolded and then to PRINT it down. To fold the paper and give it to you. (You should consult Step Six for the exact patter, paper size and preparation of the billet). Whilst blindfolded you take the paper slip and hold it undamaged to your forehead attempting to "read" the name. After what appears to be a mental struggle—you shrug your shoulders and proclaim, "Sorry, somehow I am getting interference from another place—it is *your* handwriting and not another persons'?" When you started you said "print it" not write it so you can argue that it should have been handwritten and not printed. Appear to give up, say "Never mind, take another bit of paper and do it again, but please be sure to use your own handwriting . . ." as you talk you casually tear up the other billet and do the Centre Tear as you go. He thinks it is done with so for a moment his attention is off the billet. Drop the scraps in front of you on the table and whilst he writes the second billet—read the first.

When he is ready, tell him to ROLL his paper into a ball and hold it against your forehead. Now you tell him what he has written when the billet is in his own hands and then you have done something! I always give the torn centre a couple of extra tears after reading and then add it to the other bits on the table—just in case he should be intelligent enough to look there!

### (5)   The Bartender's Nightmare!

It does not take a census poll to discover that quite a lot of magic is done by performers who are supported by the saloon bar. Quick tricks that can be done for light entertainment in "the pub" are worth knowing. This one you could also do at the Townswomen Guild Tea Party or for that matter, whilst playing Croquet with the Vicar on the Parish Lawns.

You blindfold yourself with a handkerchief. You ask the barman to take a pound note from his pocket and roll it into a ball, then to give it to you. You take it and for a moment hold it to your *forehead*—then immediately give it back. Still blindfolded you reach into your pocket and remove your visiting card and a pencil. On this you jot down three numbers. You whip off the blindfold, ask the barman to unroll the note and call out the last three numbers. This done, you hand him the card and let him see that you have written those three numbers on it.

The Method? Swami Gimmick—Step One!

### (6)   The Blindfold Drive and Location of Objects Hidden at a Distance

Effects of this type, although requiring the use of a Blindfold, have been left to Step Twelve "Publicity Stunts" where they can be given a wider explanation.

### (7)   Corinda's "Money Box"

**The Effect.**   A small black money box stands on a table and it contains an amount of real money. One spectator is asked to take part. The performer is blindfolded and stands about ten feet away from the box. The spectator opens the box and removes as much money as he likes. That is, he can take it all, leave any amount or if he likes—take none and leave it all. He closes the box and locks it and then tells the performer that he is ready.

Remaining at a distance of ten feet away from the box and spectator and without asking any questions, the performer correctly names how much money has been taken and then tells the exact date on every coin held in the spectator's hand.

There are alternative variations for presentation and we will deal with them when we have first considered the apparatus.

**The Method.**   A box is so designed that when coins are placed in it, they form an electrical contact across two terminals. This contact lights a small torch bulb which shows a pin-point of light through a hole in the back of the box. Altogether, there are four sets of these terminals and four coins are used to make contact. The design and construction of The Money Box is comparatively simple. Having made and sold a good many, we know most of the potential snags and these have been eliminated in the plans given in the drawings.

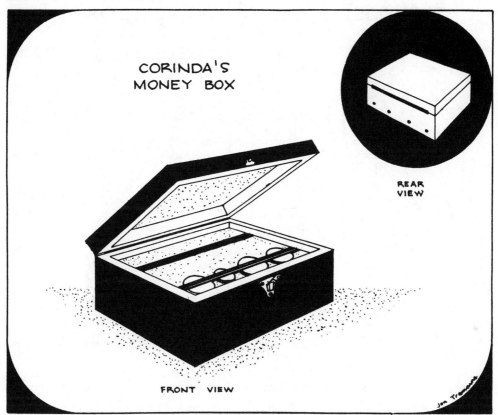

CORINDA'S MONEY BOX

REAR VIEW

FRONT VIEW

## Constructional Details

The box is made of wood. The thickness about one quarter of an inch. With observation, you may be able to find a box ready made that will do— and that can be adapted. It should be about 7 in. long by 5 in. wide and 4 in. deep. The lid is hinged and may be locked by a small catch at the front.

Inside the box, on the base at the back is stuck a strip of wood $\frac{1}{2}$ in. square. This strip has four holes drilled through of sufficient diameter to accommodate a small 2.5 volt torch bulb. In line with the centre of these holes, running right through the back of the box are four pin-holes. They should be made with a 1/32 in. drill or a hot needle. The pin-holes are so small that they are practically invisible—and yet, when the light shines through them, it can be clearly seen.

The fact that the four bulbs are pushed into a hole makes the box literally lightproof—which is an essential feature.

To the strip that holds the bulbs is fixed a set of adapters. The bulbs screw into these adapters. On each adapter is two terminals and we shall deal with the simple wiring system in a moment.

The bulbs, adapters and battery must obviously be concealed, so we make a false bottom to the box which will cover the mechanism inside. A section of three-ply wood is cut to fit just inside the box and good fit cuts out any stray light. It can be supported by small strips of wood running around the inside of the base compartment.

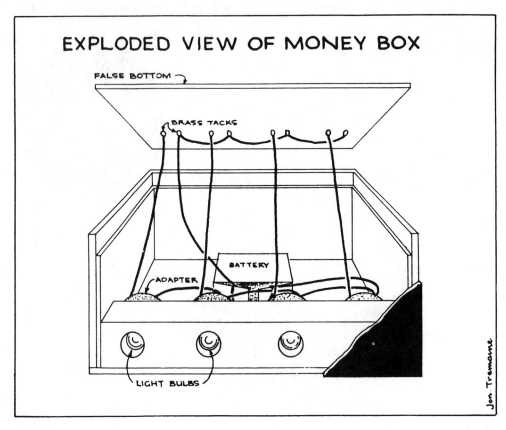

EXPLODED VIEW OF MONEY BOX

FALSE BOTTOM

BRASS TACKS

BATTERY

ADAPTER

LIGHT BULBS

Jon Tremaine

When the false bottom has been made, cover it with a green baize material. Next nail eight small brass tacks in a line across the middle of the false bottom. The heads of these tacks will act as terminals and when a coin is placed across two of them it will complete one circuit. Let the pointed ends of the tacks go right through the wood as these will act as contacts for the circuit inside.

To conceal the heads of the tacks, we fix a strip of elastic across the row, nailing it down between EACH PAIR of terminals. This elastic serves two purposes, it hides the terminals and it pulls the coin down making and maintaining a good contact. If the coins were just left to lie on the terminals, the slightest jar would break the contact and ruin the trick. As it is, they are locked quite firmly in position and they have to be removed before it is possible to put out a light. With this arrangement we have tested a Money Box by shaking violently—and still you maintain a perfect contact. You will appreciate that sending them to my customers through the post—has been a pretty good testing ground!

All that remains now, apart from painting the box black, is to insert a 4½ volt torch battery and wire the circuit. To make this easily understood we will describe it as follows.

First use one piece of wire to join *every other* tack-head terminal together and lead that wire to any one of the battery terminals. Fix it there, as with other joins, by soldering or using a radio twist.

Next join *every other* adapter terminal with one length of wire and lead this to the other battery terminal.

You are now left with four tack-terminals and four adapter terminals. Using four separate pieces of wire, join these together so that you have one of each linked—a tack-terminal with an adapter terminal. That completes the necessary wiring, however, the diagrammatic circuit drawing will make things clear should you be confused.

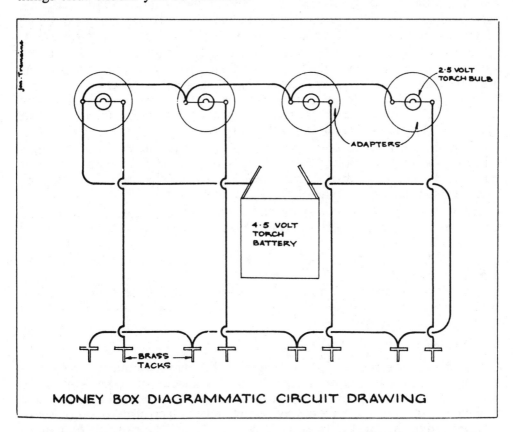

MONEY BOX DIAGRAMMATIC CIRCUIT DRAWING

To test the box when made, insert four coins under the elastic band so that each coin hits two terminals. Look at the back of the box and see if you have four pin-holes of light. Check that they go out one by one in the correct order from left to right as a coin is removed one after another.

When everything is set you are ready to use the Money Box.

The box gives out these small lights when the coins are in, therefore set them ready for use. You use four coins, a Two Shilling Piece, One Shilling, One Penny and One Halfpenny. Put them in order of value so that you can remember with ease. Copy the dates of the coins with Biro-ink on to your thumb, or remember them. Set the box on a table in such a position that the back faces you only. The spectator approaches from the front of the box. Because the pin-lights are so minute, you have little to worry about and unless you are dead in line with the holes—the lights cannot be seen—even from the back. From the top, bottom, front or sides—there is no chance of seeing the lights.

Your instructions to the spectator must be clear, well timed and carefully construed to make the rest of the audience imagine the Box is *full* of money. Stand well away and blindfold yourself with any type which permits your vision straight ahead.

Call out your instructions so:—

"Now Sir. I want you to open the box—and there you will see some money. Correct?" (When he says "yes" you know he has done as he was told) "Now listen carefully please, you can take all of it—or just as much as you like, or leave it all behind—do it now, take what you want and then close the box please". Without more than five seconds delay continue, "Have you done that?" This forces him to hurry—which is what you want.

He holds the money in his hand and you look at the row of lights to see which pinpoints are still alight. By their order you know what coins are left in the box. When you know what he has got—you check the dates because the audience do not know there was only one of each coin to be taken. You tell him the exact total in his hand and then add the correct date for each coin. He confirms you are right.

Alternative methods of presentation are :— First you may have four people take part—each one takes a penny (you use four pennies instead of four different coins) and holds it in their clenched fist. You come along and tell which person has which coin—naming the dates to prove it.

Second alternative is to have one man choose four coins, one at a time, which he puts into different pockets. You tell him into which pocket he has put which coin.

That is the Money Box which when handled with care can be made into a feature trick of any act. It has one outstanding snag—something which is difficult to overcome. The effect is so good—that it is hard to believe that it was achieved without the use of a stooge; that is the price one has to pay for being clever!

## (8) "Evidence" by Corinda

We have said sufficient when dealing with Technique to make it clear that it is not so much the nature of the trick that makes for success—it is the showmanship used to perform it. This plot is quite strong and has a dramatic element which tends to become evidence that the performer cannot see—and yet proves he must have some power (only if it be skill) as he cannot afford to make a mistake:—

**The Effect.**    A One Pound Note is borrowed from the audience and the last three figures remembered. It is sealed by the spectator into an envelope. Likewise four other envelopes have pieces of newspaper of the same size as the note sealed in them. The performer tells the audience what is being done so that they may understand the nature of his ordeal in a moment or two.

The five envelopes are brought on to the stage or floor. The performer is blindfolded and stands to one side of a table. The spectator with the envelopes stands to the other side. The performer now ready to do his stuff asks for the five envelopes, he holds them above his head for the moment, and they should have been mixed by the spectator before he got them. The assistant (spectator) is told to light the candle standing on the table and then to pick up the long needle. (Use a knitting needle)—one at a time the performer is going to hand him an envelope, each time he gets one, he is to stick it on the pin and immediately set it afire. Let the ash drop into a bowl on the table and say when it is fully burnt!

There will be considerable scope for humorous remarks, false apologies and excuses to the spectator who originally lent the note. It is easy to understand that you are blindfolded and may well have the envelope containing the note burnt to ashes.

Fortunately you will have read Step Two and know all about marking envelopes for touch reading with salt, sand and beads. Or you can adapt the "Impromptu Just Chance" effect from that Step applying it for a Blindfold trick.

That is really all you have to know. One envelope, the one in which the £1 note is sealed, is marked in the corner with a bead—which you can easily feel. The rest is showmanship and making the most out of a situation which offers plenty of scope to a talented performer.

### (9) Card Stab by Hans Trixer

Until I saw this method, shown to me by my good friend Hans Trixer, I always thought the best card stab trick was to use a Svengali Deck and be done with it! However, I am obliged to admit that this is *it* as far as the "Stab" trick goes and I think you will agree that the method is very subtle.

**The Effect.** The Mentalist shows a pack of cards which are all there and all different. He wraps the pack in a one pound note and then asks the spectator to name ANY CARD. He takes a knife and stabs through the note. The cards are cut at the point where the knife divides—and there is the chosen card! The effect may be presented as an "X-Ray Eye" trick—the performer seeing into the deck.

**The Method.** The pack is stacked (see Step Three) and you have prepared a £1 note in such a way that to miss their card would be improbable. You find out just where the note will touch the pack at the edges when it is used to wrap the deck. At this point you mark out very fine pencil lines to graduate the deck. In other words, the £1 is a ruler—and when you go to stab, you have calculated where the card will be (because the deck is stacked) so you look at the graduations and stab in the right position (see diagram). To save continuous calculations, Hans has developed a master chart which is simple, a small piece of celluloid cut out with groves. Each grove represents a line of the graduations. The chart is put on any £1 and a pencil is run through the groves—in no time a note is prepared. The same deck should be used each time as different packs will need different graduations.

### (10) Blindfold "Noughts and Crosses"

This makes a neat item for a two-person telepathy stunt. Your assistant who acts as medium is seated on a chair and blindfolded. In front of her, to the right, is a blackboard. A member of the audience comes up to play "Madam" a game of "Noughts and Crosses"—but to make it interesting—Madam is blindfolded and will not be told what moves are made by the spectator!

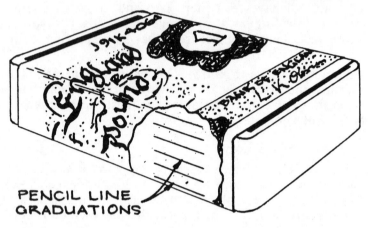

CARDS WRAPPED IN
A POUND NOTE

PENCIL LINE
GRADUATIONS

# THE HANS TRIXER
# CARD STAB

CELLULOID FAKE

Jon Tremaine

The performer stands by the blackboard and fills in the "Crosses" when called by the medium. The spectator fills in his own "Noughts". Each square is numbered and the medium calls out the number of the square she wants to use.

**The Method.** A silent code is used. When the performer stands by the blackboard he stands to the right and has his right hand on the edge, thumb at the front and fingers behind. Madam can see his fingers through a fake blindfold and whatever number he signals—Madam calls out. The performer, in actual fact does all the playing in the game and to be quite honest, Madam hasn't got a clue what's going on! The signals are very simple and easy to learn—any will do, but I have used:—

Count Index finger as No. 1, Second finger as No. 2, Third finger as No. 3 and "Little finger" as No. 4.

Square No. 1.  Show No. 1 and curl other three fingers.
     „     No. 2.  Show 1 and 2, and curl 3 and 4.
     „     No. 3.  Show 1, 2 and 3—curl 4.
     „     No. 4.  Show all 1, 2, 3, 4, *but keep them together*.
     „     No. 5.  Show all 1, 2, 3, 4, but divide between 1 and 234.
     „     No. 6.  Show all, divide between 12 and 34.
     „     No. 7.  Show all, divide between 123 and 4.
     „     No. 8.  Curl all.
     „     No. 9.  Remove hand from the board.

It will only take a few minutes practice to become fast and accurate at the code. One important thing. When the spectator has made his move, the performer should let the medium know by giving one loud knock on the blackboard. He does not say anything which could spoil the effect. I suggest that to conclude this performance, madam comes forward and does the next trick:—

### (11)  The Blackboard Test

The performer, or his medium, blindfolded, has members of the audience write simple sums on the board which he successfully works out and writes in the answers. It is amazing how anything so ridiculously simple can be made to appear so terrific when performed. Of course you use a fake blindfold and simply fill in the answers. Now and then you make a mistake to build things up and you can do some weird stunts like writing the answer backwards or upside down—which make people wonder. (I also wonder what they wonder!). You have to bear in mind all the time—that you are supposed to be without vision and it is natural that the minor feats seem miracles *under the conditions*.

### (12)  The Three Cards by Corinda

Again we resort to simplicity and think about the effect rather than method. This trick, fitted into a Blindfold routine will give you all the applause you want.

**The Effect.** Performer hands a pack of cards to his assistant who takes them to any person in the audience. They examine the pack and then remove three after they have been mixed. These three are dropped into a box which is locked and again examined. The box is taken to the performer who is by now blindfolded and waiting to receive it. He holds it to his forehead, names three cards and then hands the box back—still locked. The spectator removes the three cards he named—and they are correct.

157

**The Method.** The pack is ordinary. Have it examined and then mixed. After that have any three cards freely chosen whilst the deck is face downwards. These three are dropped into a box. It is an ordinary flap changing card box, loaded on the other side of the flap with three cards known to the performer. It is locked with a small padlock AND THEN EXAMINED by the spectator, who really is concerned with holes, trapdoors, etc.—and not what is inside. That's all there is to it—not much to worry about and yet it's good material for a man who knows what he's doing.

**NOTES**

# NOTES

# BILLETS

## BY

Corinda

## STEP SIX

IN CORINDA'S SERIES :—

## "THIRTEEN STEPS TO MENTALISM"

To my
friend ...
with best
wishes
N. Jaks.
1954.

DR. JAKS

# STEP SIX in CORINDA'S SERIES

# "THIRTEEN STEPS TO MENTALISM"

# CONTENTS

## PART ONE: TECHNIQUE

## PART TWO: TRICKS AND ROUTINES

# PART ONE:  TECHNIQUE

## Introduction

A "Billet" in the magical sense of the word, means a small piece of paper which is used generally in the performance of an effect of Mentalism.

This piece of paper may be of any texture and of any size, although it is usually conceded that a Billet is about the size of a Playing card or smaller.

In order to assess the value of working with Billets, we should survey the field of Mentalism as a whole, and consider how many effects depend on the principle that something is written. Either of two occurrences are commonplace; you write something and then have the spectator think—or, the spectator thinks and then writes his thoughts. A moment's reflection on your part will prove beyond all doubt that more Mental effects involve the *written* word (or number, etc.) than any others. Even more than Card tricks—of which there are painfully too many! In view of this, it would be fair to say that we are dealing with the most important *principle* of Mental Magic.

To work with Billets, you have to be able to switch them, tear them to pieces and retain certain parts, force them and locate them from indexes. All this involves hard work, considerable practice, a lot of confidence in your own ability and nerve. Few aspects of Mentalism call for manipulation—but working with Billets does involve quite a bit of digital dexterity and like most other forms of manipulative skill, you need an acute sense of good timing. To discourage the lazy Mentalist further, I might add that without a fair knowledge of misdirection, your chances of success are pretty awful.

At this stage, some may be prompted to ask "why bother if it's that hard?" to which the reply is, "*don't*—unless you happen to be one of those people that love Mentalism as an Art, and think that in its purest form you come down to working with practically no props; relying on personal skill and showmanship to make a miracle out of a little bit of paper". A complicated and gigantic prop may produce the wonder of wonders—by the mere push of a button, but it will never give you as much personal satisfaction as the little swindle where you switched papers right under their noses!

You can take my word for it, every hour you work to study the use of Billets, will reward you with years of pleasure. Give them enough practice and find out what you can do with them, and I'll lay ten to one you will chuck away the suitcases of props and walk around with a small pad of paper and a pencil in your pocket! People often say to me, "what do you think is the best mental effect?" and when they ask, I always reply the same—"to me, I have met nothing yet which will replace my esteem for the Centre Tear". For a good many years this one trick with a Billet has stood me in good stead. I've used it everywhere under almost every possible condition and never once has it failed to do me more good than any other three tricks I know. If you want to get one thing out of this book—and can't be bothered to read the lot—don't waste any more time because you will find nothing better than the Centre Tear—that's worth the price of the full Thirteen Steps.

For those of you who remain, we must get down to work! This Step deals first with Technique and later with tricks. I wish you lots of luck and as much success as Bert Reese, Foster and Morelle had, with "bits of paper" —it was their living.

——::——

## (1) A Few Simple Rules for Working with Billets

(a) Never call a Billet a "Billet" when talking to the spectator.

(b) If you treat the Billet with indifference—so will they.

(c) Look at the spectator when you switch a Billet—not your hands.

(d) Never tell them what you are going to do—unless you have to for the effect.

(e) Don't rush; take your time. Slow and sure is better than fast and failure.

(f) When the spectator has written something, say "what you are *thinking*" NOT "what you have *written*".

(g) Never repeat the same trick immediately—do a different one for an encore.

(h) When you mis-read a Billet—look at it.

(i) Work hard until you find a good trick and when you have that, discard it and find a better one!

## (2) The Centre Tear (Corinda Variation)

There are lots of versions of the Centre Tear (or "Torn Centre") and some of them are good—others deplorable. This is not so much a "variation" as a "routine". It is the exact handling that I use and is the result of continuous performance. Because of this, many of the snags and possible errors have been eliminated. I should mention that, although there may appear to be many details, there are none that could be called superfluous:—

### The Effect

The spectator is invited to think of a word and write it on a slip of paper. The paper is burnt and from the ashes the Mentalist reads the chosen word.

### The Routine and Technique

(A) See that you have a piece of paper that is not too thin. It should be larger than two inches square and smaller than three inches square. In an emergency, borrow a used envelope and rip a square out. Make the paper as square as you can without bothering to achieve geometric exactness.

(B) See that you have a pencil, preferably with a soft lead, or a Ball point pen ready for use. An ink pen is not a good thing since the Billet cannot be folded until the ink is dry.

(C) See that there is an empty ashtray in the room, preferably on the table. If not, look for a suitable container that can be used to hold burning paper and ash.

(D) See that your right hand trousers pocket is empty—but for a box of matches or a lighter and see that your jacket coat is unbuttoned.

This preparation all takes place before you even suggest that you should try an experiment. Miss any one of the above details and you will feel an idiot at some part in the routine.

(E) Propose that you conduct "an experiment". Never call it a trick or an effect. Explain that you will attempt to do something shown to you many years ago. Say that it is simply an experiment with the mind, something that works under the right conditions—and sometimes fails. Make the trick *uncertain* then it is more effective when it works—which it always does!

(F) Ask the audience to relax whilst you prepare for the test. If you approach it correctly, they will expect you to start—when in fact you have finished!

(G) See if you can borrow a pencil and if one is offered, produce the paper (from now on called "the billet") and immediately draw a circle about $1\frac{1}{4}''$ in diameter in the middle. It should be as central as you can make it without appearing to bother too much. As you take the pencil, look at it, put down the Billet and say "I suppose it does write?". Immediately, as if to test it, draw the circle. For some unknown reason, people usually laugh when you say "I suppose it does write". Let them laugh at the pencil—you worry about the circle! If you cannnot borrow a pencil—use your own (*see* B) and again say something, perhaps, "O.K. now if the lead is not broken . . . . ."

(H) Put the Billet in front of the subject and hand him the pencil. Walk away, well away—five to ten yards and call out your instructions. Pay particular note to these instructions because this is where you can meet with trouble:—

"Do exactly as I ask you please, first think of a word—any word you like in the *English* language—it makes no difference what you think of—when you have done that, print it in *block letters in the circle* please".

Although this instruction appears to make blatant demands from the spectator, I have yet to find anyone who remembers what you said after the trick is done. Why you emphasise "English language" is because you will do the Centre Tear ninety-nine times and you can read what you see. One day, the billet is opened and for the one hundredth go you find yourself looking at hieroglyphics which could be Chinese or Uro-Afghanistani; you may not be educated. You also emphasise "in the circle" because if you don't, and they write outside, later on you will have to be psychic because their word is in ashes—really! You say "block letters" because the word on the billet has to be read with a glimpse lasting a fraction of a second. Have you ever tried reading a doctor's prescription in 0.5 seconds? You cannot read bad handwriting quickly.

(I) Having given the instruction—add quietly, "tell me when you have done that".

(J) He tells you he is ready. Without approaching the table yet, say casually—"very well, fold the paper in half please" wait a moment, and then add—"Can you see through it?" He will look and whether he replies "yes" or "no" add, "well to be sure—better fold it once more—in half please . . . ."

(K) Walk back to the table and if necessary collect the ashtray on the way and put it on the table. If it is on the table, move it to the centre —don't say why or anything, just move it. You want to telegraph psychologically that fire is going to be used.

(L) As soon as you arrive at the table—ask for the pencil if it is yours, saying, "that's how I got it . . ." You see there is no rush to get the Billet.    You worry about an ashtray and a pencil—towards the Billet you are INDIFFERENT.

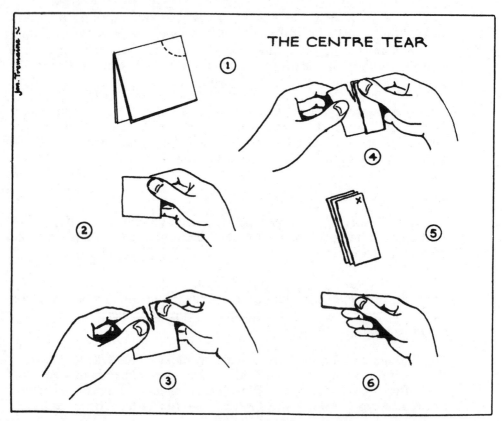

THE CENTRE TEAR

(M) Look at the billet in his hands and sight the centre corner. Diagram No. 1 shows where this will be, the dotted line representing the circle on the inside. You say to the subject "thank you" and at the same time reach forward and take the Billet in the right hand between thumb and first finger, holding it by the centre. (No sharp torn edges are on the centre corner).

Push the Billet between the fingers so that the ball of the thumb and finger give full protection to the centre corner. Diagram No. 2 shows the holding position:—

(N) Proceed to tear the billet into strips. Tear two-thirds off with a downward pull of the left hand. Immediately place the centre corner strip on top of the other pieces and tear the bottom strip again—making it three strips in all with the centre corner held on top of the stack under the ball of the thumb. Diagrams 3 and 4 showing first and second tear and Diagram 5 showing enlarged view of the stack after two tears—the centre corner being marked with a cross.

(O) Turn all the strips sideways keeping the centre corner under the thumb and on top, tear off two-thirds and stack again, as always, centre corner bits on top. Tear for the last time and stack as before. Diagram No. 6 shows the strips held sideways ready to commence the third tear. Altogether you have made four tears, forming nine sets of pieces, you have them all stacked in one pile and the very top piece is the folded centre corner.

Generally speaking, keep the hands open during the tearing process —and do it "at the fingertips". It takes very little time to do, when you know what you are doing, and you don't have to look all the time.

(P) Hold the pieces in one block at the fingertips (thumb and first finger) of the right hand. Keep the other fingers close together and gently curled. Face the back of your right hand straight at the spectator's face (which is the best guide to angles you can get) and with the left hand pull forward the ashtray. "Now I think we can burn them in here . . . ."

(Q) You are about to perform the only hard move in the routine. You must "steal" the centre corner without him knowing it.

Look him straight in the face and say "have you got a match please —oh! never mind, I've got one here . . ." Timing is ESSENTIAL. As you ask him for a match he is distracted by the question and with half a second delay you follow up with the line "never mind . . ." As you say that, pinch the stack a bit pulling the ball of the thumb with the top section (centre corner) back a bit; take all the other pieces into the left hand—holding them at the fingertips, and quickly reach into your pocket with the right hand. Without *any pause whatsoever*, drop the centre tear into the pocket and bring out the matches and give them a shake. (*See* D).

(R) Drop the matches on to the table and drop all the pieces of paper into the ashtray. Brush your hands together as though rubbing off some dust—to show them empty without saying "examine my empty hands . . . ." (*See* C).

(s) Strike a match and set light to the papers. As they begin to burn say to the subject "they might unfold as they get hot—so you burn them and tell me when there are ashes only left". Stroll away and turn your back. Put your right hand into your right trouser pocket and do what is called the "umbrella move". That is, slip the thumb into the folded Billet and push it open. Hold it in the fingers (there is no call for palming) and bring it out. Cough and cough again; on the second cough, bring your hand up to your mouth and on the way down with that hand, look into the palm and read their word. If it should be upside down, drop the hand to the side, twist it round and repeat the cough-move.

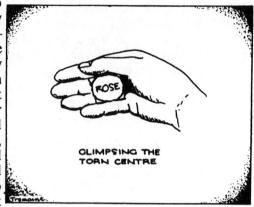

GLIMPSING THE TORN CENTRE

(T) Never get flustered over reading the centre Billet. Take your time—never do it as soon as you get away, relax, wait and be natural.

(U) You have read their word—remember it. Drop the Billet back into your pocket and return to the table saying, "have you done that yet?" Make sure that most if not all of the paper is in ashes—tell them to use another match from the box on the table if necessary. Once the pieces are in ashes—the evidence of your trickery is destroyed.

(V) Ask the spectator to crush the ashes and to give you any one small particle of ash. Take it on your open palm of the left hand. Take another piece of paper and the pencil again. Tell the subject to put his fingertips on the ash—forming a complete circle between you, the ash and the spectator. This, you will say, creates the basic harmony required to establish psychometric vibrations . . . . or some such twaddle!

Tell him you are about to begin the experiment! Everything depends on his power to co-operate. Remind him that up to now test conditions have been imposed . . . "you chose any word out of many thousands, you wrote it down, folded the paper—tore it up and burnt it. All that we have is a small piece of ash to establish contact". You deliberately alter what happened as you remind him—and played skilfully, he will think back later and swear blind that at no time did you touch the paper.

(W) "Now this may sound silly, but please do exactly as I say. Close your eyes and imagine that you are going into an empty room. There is nothing in that room excepting a blackboard. You go to the board and take a piece of white chalk from your pocket. Now write your word on that board—do it in your mind, only *think* of your word and write it in your imagination . . . ." Wait a moment and say, "have you done that?"

(X) Do not omit to say that last line, "have you done that?" it is important. If not, you may write his word before he has done so in his mind and he will certainly tell you "I've not finished yet".

Say "have you done that—the *same word*?" This gives you a warning if he is a clever boy who waits until you write the word on his billet and then tells you "ah! but the word I wrote on the board was a different one . . ."

(Y) Tell him, after the first attempt, that it is not quite right. "Do it again please in larger letters—keep your eyes open this time".

Look him straight in the eyes and holding the pencil in the right hand begin to print the letters of his Billet-word on your paper. Don't look down—it looks very good if you appear to be doing automatic writing. He will see your pencil moving but continue to stare into his eyes and he will still look at you. When you have written his word, drop the pencil and cover the paper with the right hand. Say, "now will you please say what word YOU WERE THINKING OF —out loud please"—and as soon as he speaks, hand him the paper and say "and read that out loud".

(Z) That is the complete routine. One trick—worth its weight in gold. Every detail is here, follow the moves carefully, practice it time and time again and in doing so, do justice to one of the greatest mental effects you can use.

## (2) Centre Tear (Punx-Mier Variation)

Punx has some brilliant ideas and this is just a simple move, but such a move can make all the difference to a practical Mentalist. The word is written as normal and the Billet folded twice. The performer takes it and without the slightest hesitation licks it and sticks it, still folded, on to his forehead. Punx tells me the originator of the move is Mier.

Now the performer begins to give a reading. He sees letters and finally a word. He names the first word that enters his head—but adds that it's "pretty vague".

If the spectator tells you that you are right—you faint! If not, say, "no, I knew something was wrong it was very vague—never mind, try again, write it again but write it backwards this time please because I get a mirror image when it works . . ." Take down the billet, tear it up and throw the bits away—and in doing so, perform the Centre Tear!! He thinks the billet is done with and pays no attention to your action but begins to write it out again. You read the Centre Tear and this time when he has re-written the word and folded his paper, say "will you hold it please to my forehead". Whilst he holds the billet in his own hands—you name the word!! The "off-beat" misdirection of this subtlety is so cunning and natural that it will fool magicians who use the Centre Tear. Such is the simplicity of the Punx move. In using this variation, since no burning is involved, I have found it a good dodge to refold the centre tear after reading and give it a couple of extra tears—then drop it amid the other pieces on the table. If the spectator should be a deep thinker he's going to find it disappointing when he finds ALL the bits on the table in the old pile!

## Centre Tear (One Hand Variation)

From time to time during the performance of a Mental effects with Billets, you will find it necessary to hold a Billet in each hand, and yet one of them has to be used for the centre tear. With both in view at the same time this could present a cumbersome problem. However, this variation solves the problem and it will be found a clean and convincing version.

Several effects with Billets have made use of the Centre Tear Variation where the end on an oblong billet is torn off. Usually the move involved a two-hand operation; the Billet was held by the end in the left hand and it was taken in the right, the torn end being left behind as it was taken. This principle is made use of in Ron Baillie's "Universal Mind". That is the two-handed operation.

Discussing this matter with Al Koran one day, he taught me a handling which to my mind is superior to the original handling and quite useful as it is a one hand tear—without any trouble and very little practice.    A piece of paper is cut to size about two by six inches. The paper should be a brand that tears easily and yet is not too flimsy—as for example, ordinary duplicating paper which is ideal:—

(a)   The folding of the billet by the spectator can be done erroneously. To prevent this, you pre-fold the Billet so that he will follow the creases made by you when he comes to fold. Fold the paper once in half long ways and in half again long ways. Then fold once in half so that the six-inch strip is three inches long. Open out the paper again and you will have creases in the position shown by dotted lines in Diagram No. 8.

(b)   The next important thing is to be able to control where the spectator writes on a fairly large strip of paper. To do this, draw three circles, and with some suitable explanation, write your name in one of the end ones and his name in the other. The centre circle leave blank—that is where he writes his word. Diagram No. 9 shows the Billet ready to be given to the spectator.

(c)   Have the spectator write in the blank circle a word, number, name, etc. . . . and tell him to fold the paper when he has done that. Take the folded Billet from him and hold it by the fingers of the right hand just so:—Ball of thumb pressing the middle of the billet on to the first joint of the index finger. Centre tear section of the billet resting on the second joint of the second finger. Billet is seen sticking out

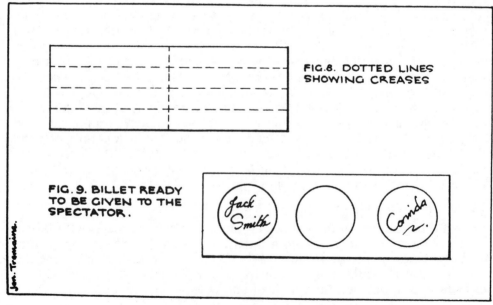

FIG.8. DOTTED LINES SHOWING CREASES

FIG.9. BILLET READY TO BE GIVEN TO THE SPECTATOR.

of the hand. Hold tight with the thumb and first finger and clip the very bottom of the Billet with the edge of the third finger. Now, if you curl your last three fingers the end of the Billet is torn off and carried into the hand all in one move and the visible part of the billet does not move. Diagram No. 10 shows how the spectator sees the billet being held at the start, and No. 11 shows how they see it after the tear. Diagram No. 12 shows the hold before the tear from your point of view, and No. 13 shows after the tear.

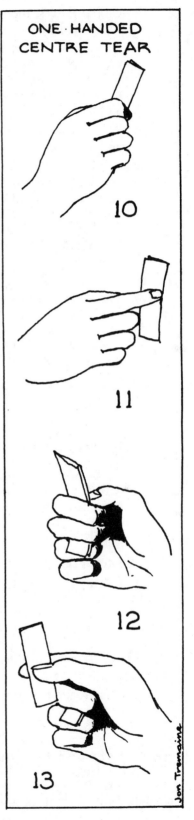

ONE·HANDED CENTRE TEAR

10

11

12

13

(d) The tear is accomplished under cover of misdirection which is gained by moving the hands towards a clip or stand. It is a good thing, for example, to be holding a bulldog clip pinched open in the left hand. The right seems to put the billet into the clip. It does, but performs the tear on the way. See section which deals with Billet display stands and clips.

**(4) Centre Tear** (Corinda's "Backward" Variation)

This is a gag. I've had lots of fun with this idea and although I meant it to be a laugh when I first invented it, from time to time it has been taken seriously and caused a sensation! It's strictly for the Magic Club or gathering of magicians—and means nothing to a lay audience.

Get a friend to act as a stooge—or, for those with high morals—use an impression pad or pencil reading (!). Arrange that he will write "Sausage". Work the routine like this:—

(a) Stand up and say you will show a new trick that you saw published a week ago in "The Fishmongers' Gazette"! Ask for an assistant and state that you would prefer a Mentalist or someone interested in mind reading. Your friend gets there first.

(b) Take a piece of paper and very carefully tear it into a small square. Then take a pencil and with a lot of trouble, draw a circle in the middle.

(c) Give the paper to the assistant with a pencil and say, "I want you to think of any word you like, then to write it in the circle, I repeat, in the circle, in bold capital letters, then fold the paper exactly in half and in half again so that it is just a quarter of its original size".

Great deliberation on the instructions from you are given with painfully obvious details that indicate the Centre Tear. Those only half in the know, will recognise what you are doing and, with knowing nods and whispers to each other, will declare "old stuff"—it's the Centre Tear . . . . .!

(*d*) Stand away with your back turned to the spectator (assistant). When he has done as told you bring in the surprise!

"Now before you came up to assist me I asked for a Mentalist and you came. By that I would suppose you are acquainted with the basic principle of Mental Magic? You are, good. Then you will know roughly perhaps what is meant by the Centre Tear! You do—excellent—then please do it with the paper you are holding". At this stage things go very quiet as the bright boys are quite taken aback by this display of unexpected frankness. Quietness is usually followed by laughter from those who appreciate what you are doing.

(*e*) The assistant does the Centre Tear—usually a diabolical performance —but he does it! You say, "have you done it? Excellent, are you sure you have the bit that matters—you know what I mean! You have, good—then hand it to the President for safekeeping and then kindly give me the *other bits*". These you take and hold above your head perhaps making a false glimpse as you put them there. Slowly and melodramatically you reveal the chosen word. Remember it was "Sausage"—so we go something like this:—

(*f*) "I'm getting an impression of a living object, it's living and yet dead! It seems that you have written something connected with an animal, it could be a dog. Has your word any animal connections?" (Ask the assistant) "Don't help me! You have written a word connected with food—it's Fried Kipper, No—nearly right . . . Sausage!! Will you check that please Mr. President . . . ."
(*Note.*—I am aware that the similarity between a Kipper and a Sausage is only skin deep—AUTHOR).

### (5) Centre Tear (Preparation of the Billet)

(*a*) **Folding.** Some Mentalists find that more satisfactory results are obtained if the square of paper is pre-folded before it is handed to the spectator. The theory being that the spectator, when told to fold the paper, will follow your creases and do so correctly. It invariably works. Most performers who use this preparation feel that it does away with the necessity of telling the spectator to fold in a specific manner. If you feel inclined to use it do so. With my routine for the Centre Tear I do not find it necessary.

(*b*) **Misdirection for the Circle.** Here again, ways and means have been devised to excuse the drawing of a circle and to hide the reason why they should write their word in the middle. Some call it a mystic symbol and write or draw additional signs around the outside of the circle, so that you have no choice but to write in the blank space—the centre. Others call it "A Magic Circle" which is downright ridiculous for a mental effect. A good excuse that I once favoured was to call the circle a globe of the world, and to tell them to think of any place in the world and to write the name on the globe—like marking a map. These days I do not find any of these subterfuges really necessary. A casual mention of "in the circle" during your instructions and they do as they are told and I have yet to meet a spectator who remembers the details of your instructions.

As a change for your own personal entertainment, if you use the Centre Tear a lot you might like to use this idea which I thought up and found impressive.

Draw a square instead of a circle and tell them that it represents a mirror. Ask them to imagine that they have a stick of lipstick and that they are going to write a word on the mirror. When you come to reveal their word after doing the usual routine, write it—but write it *backwards* and explain that you received a "mirror image"—a nice touch for presentation and a reason for the square.

### (6)  Centre Tear (Reading the Billet)

I think it would be safe to say that the reason why the Centre Tear is not used as much as it should be—is because most performers cannot find a comfortable way to glimpse the billet when it comes to reading the word or number. Having done a bit of research on this trick I find that throughout the pages of magic in print there are literally dozens of means suggested.

"Look at the billet whilst lighting a cigar (or cigarette if you are a Magic Dealer!)—look at it in the lap, under cover of a notepad", and so on. Take it from me, if you use the method I give in my routine you wont bother with these alternatives. Wait your time, open it, look at it. Sometimes one is tempted to try and be too clever and I can give you a wonderful example of applied stupidity achieved in an effort to be over keen.

A friend of mine, a good friend but stupid all the same, was with me and performed the Centre Tear on another person. The spectator was the only other person present except myself. He got up to the point where he had to do the steal and did this by taking it from the ashtray on the end of the match (another diabolical variation). Having done that, and made himself really nervous, he subjects himself to further torture whilst he manipulates the centre billet to the second sheet down in his notepad. The top pad he scribbles on, tears off and chucks away and then sees the word. From the manipulation that followed you would suppose that not only was the billet upside down—but also that it was written inside out! So he gets to know the word and then, telling the spectator to close his eyes and think hard he reveals it letter by letter. He followed a routine that has been published—and I say it stinks because if you are going to tell someone to shut their eyes—then *that is not a bad time to read the billet.* With one person it cannot fail. Don't murder Mentalism—just do it!

### (6)  The Billet Switch (Bare Hand Method)

The next few paragraphs on Technique will deal with a variety of methods that can be used to exchange one billet for another. Before we begin, I should explain that several methods are given because what suits one person is not always adaptable to another. However, it would be a mistake on your part to learn all methods. Run through them and try them out until you discover which one suits you best and then stick with that one and practise it to perfection. You cannot use two methods at once and since they both achieve the same effect you waste your time learning more than one.

175

The Basic Billet Switch as suggested by Theodore Annemann in his *Practical Mental Effects* requires that you first learn to finger palm a dummy billet. The Billet size is of some importance and also the method of folding. The size should be $2\frac{1}{2} \times 3\frac{1}{2}$ inches and should be folded once the long way and then twice the other way. This forms a small slip of folded paper which can be finger palmed as shown in Diagram No. 14.

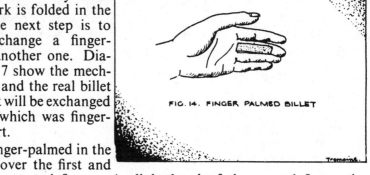

FIG. 14. FINGER PALMED BILLET

You will appreciate that if dummy billets are to be folded in a special manner, then so must the real ones. Consequently, see that every billet for this type of work is folded in the same manner. The next step is to learn how to exchange a finger-palmed billet for another one. Diagrams 15, 16 and 17 show the mechanics of the switch and the real billet is shown in black; it will be exchanged for the white one which was finger-palmed at the start.

The dummy is finger-palmed in the left hand, clipped over the first and second joint of the second finger. A slight bend of the second finger tip keeps it in position. The hand is held at waist level, palm facing the body when the switch is executed.

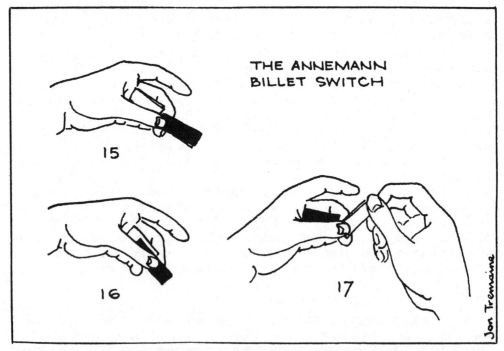

THE ANNEMANN BILLET SWITCH

Hold the dummy finger-palmed. With the same hand, pick up the real one holding it at the fingertips. Using the ball of the thumb, draw the real one back on top of the dummy and further still until you get it as far back as you can, then using the thumb and fingers, manipulate the dummy into view, retaining the real one from sight.

In order to perform this move smoothly and faultlessly, one must be expected to practise it for a considerable while. The essential move of drawing back a billet into the finger palm position, and then pushing it—or another into view again, has to be practised time and time again. Work with one slip to start with, learn to control that using either left or right hand and then introduce the second. You will discover that for experimental purposes, highly gloss paper is best as it has a smooth surface which allows the slips to pass over each other with ease. Later on, when proficient, you will work with any paper.

During the performance of the basic switch, it is a good thing to keep the hands in motion and to avoid looking at them. As for misdirection, it is always a good thing to know that if you look straight at a person and ask them a question—they will look at you—which is enough. Al Baker, using his own Billet switch, always asked "Did you write it in English?" at the vital moment when the change took place.

**(7) The Billet Switch** (Bare Hand Method—Corinda)

I have had a great deal of success with this method and I think it is the easiest one to learn. The Billets used are size $3 \times 3''$ or thereabouts. They are not folded—but rolled instead into a tight ball. This makes the handling in general ten times easier than a slip of folded paper. The ball, being about half an inch in diameter, gives you something to get hold of—and can be retained in the Classic palm as well as the finger palm. Like sponge balls used in magic or other small objects used in Cups and Balls, there are many possible sleights available and some of them we find adaptable to Mentalism. Care should be taken to avoid any move which in itself suggests a sleight.

To exchange two rolled balls of paper (which have the same appearance) the following simple moves are made:—

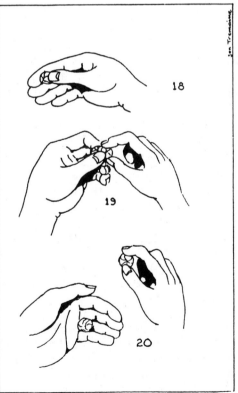

(a) Practise with balls made from slips of rolled up newspaper.

(b) Hold a dummy just out of sight at the fingertips of the right hand. (Diagram 18).

(c) Pick up the real one with the right hand pressing the dummy on top as you do.

(d) Transfer both to the left fingertips pushing the real one on top out of sight and leaving the dummy showing.

(e) Tell the spectator to "roll them really tightly" showing them what to do by squeezing the dummy (Diagram 19) and under cover of this motion let the real one drop into the palm leaving one only at the fingertips of the left hand.

(f) Take the ball from the left hand (dummy) and give it to the spectator. Diagram No. 20 shows the position just before handing the dummy back in place of the real one.

Those of you who are acquainted with Slydini's Torn and Restored Cigarette Routine (Published in *The Stars of Magic*) will recognise the opening moves.

### (8)  The Billet Switch (by lapping)

Mention of Slydini automatically brings to mind lapping! There are several good uses for lapping when working with Billets—not only for switching, but for reading them also. Since a lot of Billet work is done at the table, these things will be found useful and you will get the opportunity to apply them.

We cannot deal technically with the Art of Lapping here—for two reasons; I have neither the space nor the knowledge! However we can cover the Billet switch by Lapping—that I have used!

Make sure that your audience cannot see the lap. The best time for this switch is when you are seated opposite the spectator. Have a dummy billet held at the fingertips of the right hand and have the other billet/s lined up near the edge of the table nearest to you. Make a slight sweeping motion bringing the right hand over the table and towards the billets, appearing to pick up one. In actual fact, you sweep one into your lap, over the edge of the table and bring the hand up without a pause; display the Billet you held at the start.

### (9)  The Billet Switch (Magnetic Clip Method)

Billets size about $3 \times 4''$ are folded twice and sealed with an ordinary paper clip. They are dropped into a cup, shaken and then tipped out. They are all switched or any number of them have been exchanged.

In the bottom of a cup stick (with Araldite or Evostik) a powerful magnet. Buy some paper clips made of steel which you will find are magnetic. Buy or make some more (brass that is nickel plated) that are non-magnetic. Put non-magnetic clips on those you want to act as dummies and have them in the cup to start with. Give the spectator steel clips to put on his billets. Drop these also into the cup. Shake the lot—holding it of course above eye level so that no one can see into the cup, and then boldly tip upside down shooting the contents on to the table. All the billets with a steel clip are held back by the magnet.

This sort of switch is handy for a Living and Dead test where it is expected that you will mix a number of billets.

### (10)  The Billet Switch (Corinda's Billet Pull)

Whether or not Billets appeal to you—and whether or not you try anything told to you in this Step, please do one thing for me—try this out. Even if you do not see fit to use it (which is doubtful) I can assure you that it will give you an awful lot of fun. You will get carried away with the many moves and applications of the simple gimmick—it might entertain an audience—but it is sure to amuse you!

The apparatus consists of our old friend, a piece of elastic acting as a pull. Get a piece of elastic about two feet long. (Adjust to the exact length during use.) On one end tie a small safety pin and on the other end, a paper clip. With that done—the apparatus is ready. Fix the pin to the inside of your right jacket sleeve—just under the armpit. Run the other end down the sleeve and see that the clip hangs about three to four inches from the end of the sleeve. Always have the shirt sleeve rolled up past the elbow when you intend to use the pull. It affords an easy passage up the sleeve which would otherwise be different with the sleeve down.

The Billet pull is designed to help you switch billets. In some respects it has a limited application, because it is not possible to obtain the switched billet back from the clip, without a little manoeuvre which takes a second or so with both hands behind the back. However, there are a large number of effects where one does not have to read the stolen billet immediately, and for that type of trick, this apparatus is ideal.

You will have to work with this gimmick for quite a long time (a few hours) before you acquire sufficient proficiency to use it in public. The handling is much the same for any of the moves.

First, learn how to get hold of the clip simply by putting both arms behind your back and, with the left hand, pull down the clip to the fingertips of the right hand where it is gripped between thumb and first two fingers.

Next, learn how to hold the clip without displaying the elastic. If you keep the back of your right hand facing the spectator—you are reasonably safe. Lastly we come to a few of the various moves.

Number one is what I call the throw. This is possibly the most amusing and yet startling switch of all. Have a dummy billet ready folded to size $1 \times 1\frac{1}{2}''$ held sideways in the right hand. Our drawing shows you how to do this. Pick up the spectator's billet and clip it; that is, put it into your pull-clip. Swing the right hand upwards in a small half circle and show the billet in the clip as seen again in the diagram. Now we come to the release and the exchange and we need to time things very delicately. Move the hand in a small circular motion in an anticlockwise direction. When it reaches the bottom of the circle the billet points to the floor and the back of the hand at the spectator. Bring the hand upwards in a straight line towards the spectator and at the same time let go of the clip. At the same time open the hand and allow the dummy to travel forward towards the spectator.

The swinging motion looks like an ordinary throw—and at no time is there a pause especially when the hand begins to travel upwards. The dummy billet will have a clip like the pull clip of course. Performed correctly, this move is absolutely indetectable—and I defy anyone to say they can see it. Any slight noise of the elastic is covered by a well-timed cough!

Number two variation is the "slap down switch". More or less the same handling as the first method is adopted—only the billet is slapped on to a table instead of being thrown.

Number three—"on to the spectator's hand". Yes, you can even switch it in their hands! Tell them to hold out their hand—don't say why, show the billet and place it on to their hand telling them to hold it tight!

Number four—"the hand to hand pass". You appear to put the billet from your right hand into your left and exchange it as you go. All these moves are so simple that I save space by avoiding details.

Number five, "into the glass switch". This is pretty—but you have to get the timing right again. The billet is shown and dropped into a glass—you release just as the hand covers the top of the glass. This looks best with a tall beer glass which allows the audience to see the billet leaving your hand and falling down to the bottom.

Number six, "putting it on display". This is also very good—if not the best of the lot as you have a logical reason for the clip. You have a Billet Display stand as described in this book and the exchange is made as you put the Billet on to the stand. As a final tip—when you first practice make the billets out of fairly thick card—that makes it easier to handle.

The Billet is regained from the clip after the exchange—by the same method as the clip is obtained in the first place. Both hands behind the back—or, if you can turn your back on the audience with some suitable excuse, do it then with your hands in front of you. I will give you some more uses for this Pull in Step Ten.

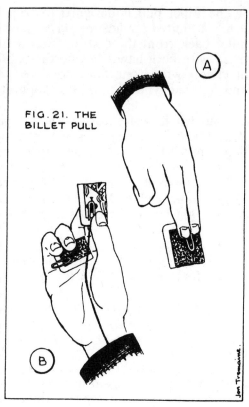

FIG. 21. THE BILLET PULL

### (11) The Billet Switch (The Matchbox Switch—by Will Dexter)

It might not always be logical to burn a billet—but logical or otherwise—it's darn convenient! You find a better way of destroying the evidence of your sins. So for many effects we just have something written, the paper folded and burnt. From the ashes, etc. . . . you read the question. To burn anything requires matches—and this method is a switch which is made possible by a fake matchbox which exchanges the billets (i.e. real one for a dummy) as you remove a match and strike it ready to burn the billet. Natural moves with apparatus above suspicion.

The box is made with both the drawer and case part faked. The drawings show how. You have the dummy ready held under the box in a cut out clip arrangement. It has a section cut away to allow the fingers to pull out the billet later. The same part of the box has one side cut away with a slot large enough to allow your billet to pass inside the case part when the box drawer is open. The inside of the case part is lined with black paper or painted black.

The diagrams show you how to make one of these matchboxes. Drawing No. 22 shows the case part looking at the side—showing the slot for the billet. The other side of the case is left intact.

The next drawing, No. 23, shows the underside of the case part. By attaching an extra piece of casing from another box, we form the holder for the billet and we see the cut out part which allows it to be removed easily.

Drawing No. 24 shows the construction of the drawer itself, seen from a side view. You will note a recess is made to allow the billet room inside the

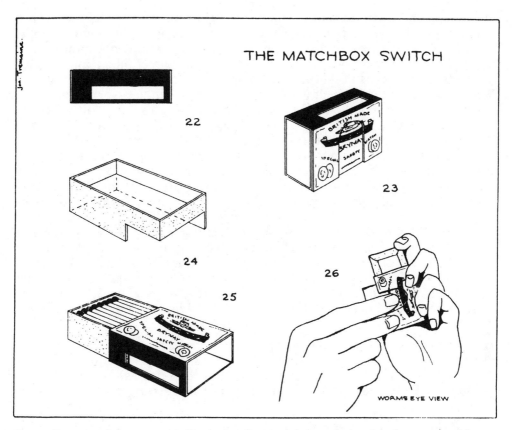

THE MATCHBOX SWITCH

22

23

24

25

26

WORMS EYE VIEW

box. In actual fact, a small piece of wood is stuck in the drawer making a false bottom so that matches go on top and the billet goes below. No. 25 shows the drawer in the box, open ready to remove a match. The real billet slides into the slot at the left side of the box—which can be done only when the drawer is open. As the drawer closes, the right hand slides the dummy from under the box (out of the holder) and that one is burnt. It appears as though you have simply dropped the matchbox with the billet into your left hand, removed a match and then pulled the billet from under the box and set it alight. There is nothing to be seen as you put the box away— the real billet is now inside and can be tipped out into your hand when you want to read it. Drawing number 26 shows the right hand removing the dummy billet.

**(12) The Star Trap Billet Switch** (Eric Mason)

This method will be found of use for effects that require the handling of few billets. It is more or less limited to working with two billets only. A good example of its use would be the trick where the spectator takes a £1 note from his wallet, rolls it into a ball and throws it to you; without un-rolling it, you hold it to your forehead and call out the number of the note— then throw it back to be checked.

Obtain one of those plastic or rubber "star trap" towel holders. Stick this on a small square of cardboard which may then be pinned to the lining of your jacket—in such a position that when the right arm hangs naturally at the side, the fingertips of the right hand arrive level with the Star Trap. Just behind the side jacket pocket is the place.

181

Eric Mason advocates that in the act of performing the switch—a drop is made to give the necessary misdirection for the exchange. Although dropping and picking up of articles is a clumsy affair—one cannot question that in doing so, you create a very powerful form of misdirection. I am inclined to condone the means in this switch—having seen it done and tried it myself. You must decide for yourself if it is something you can use—or if you would rather find another method. However, you are going to work fairly hard to find a move which all in one, is natural and deceptive. In your right hand hold a £1 note that has been rolled into a ball. The number of this note— you know and have memorised. Ask the subject to lend you a note, tell him to roll it tightly into a ball and take it from him with the right hand. At some point early on in your patter, appear to drop his note to the floor. In actual fact, drop your note with the known number and draw his back from sight into the right hand. As you drop the note—look down at it in surprise and immediately bend forward reaching across the body with the LEFT hand to pick it up. As the left hand picks up the note, the right hangs naturally at the side for a moment—and as it does, it sticks the borrowed note into the Star trap. By the time you are standing upright—a matter of perhaps three seconds, you have one note in your left hand, the number of that note you know and the right hand is empty. You are all set to perform.

I suppose it is obvious that at the start you make no mention to the spectator that you intend to deal with the number of his note. He must not look at his note because the one he gets back is not the same as the one he gives. Hasten the proceedings at the start and you will have no trouble.

### (13) Eclipse Billet Switch (John Henley)

The following is the basic effect as the audience sees it, but without dressing of any kind. An assisting spectator examines a piece of paper, about $5\frac{1}{2} \times 2\frac{1}{2}''$, folds it twice and secures it in a small Bulldog clip. He then signs his name on the billet which is dropped, complete with clip, into a tumbler. When next he examines the paper, the spectator finds written on it the name of a chosen card, colour, number or design, as the mentalist pleases.

A few points to note are as follows: (a) the mentalist has no need to touch the paper at any time, except of course, when handing it for examination at the beginning; (b) the piece of paper the spectator signs is the one on which the writing appears; (c) the spectator removes the billet from the glass and unfolds it himself.

The switch gains its title from the gimmicks that are used. To perform the effect the following items are needed:—2 ECLIPSE magnets, 2 pieces of paper about $5\frac{1}{2} \times 2\frac{1}{2}''$, 2 $1\frac{3}{8}''$ Waverley Bulldog clips, a *short* pencil and a glass tumbler.

For the sake of argument we shall assume that ESP cards are being used and that the spectator is going to 'choose' the triangle design. First, empty the back pocket of your trousers and put one magnet in one bottom corner and the second magnet in the other. You may find it convenient to place a box of matches between them to prevent their clinging together. The pencil is also kept in the back pocket.

Now take one of the pieces of paper which, incidentally, should be thick rather than thin, and draw a picture lightly in the centre area. Fold the paper into four and secure the four narrow edges with one of the clips, remove your jacket, let the clip cling to the left hand magnet through the cloth of the back pocket and you are ready to begin. The tumbler is on a nearby table.

Having selected a suitable subject, hand him the other piece of paper and ask him to examine it, fold it twice and secure it with a clip. At this point indicate the end you would like clipped as it must go on the same end as on the duplicate billet. The following actions must be rehearsed until they become natural: (*a*) Take the billet from the spectator by the clip with the left hand, which is then held waist-high, and feel with the right hand in the right trouser pocket as though looking for the pencil. (*b*) Withdraw hand and swap billet from left hand to right, again holding it by the clip. (*c*) This is when the switch is made. As the left hand feels in the left pocket for the pencil the right hand moves behind the back and as it passes the back pocket is leaves the clip attached to the right-hand magnet and immediately removes the duplicate clip and billet from the left-hand magnet. (*d*) As the left hand is withdrawn the right hand comes to the front, swaps billet from hand to hand as before and the right hand goes behind the back, removes the remaining billet and clip which is adhering to the back of your trousers, drops it into the back pocket and removes the pencil. This method of disposing of the billet was suggested by Slydini, and as you can see, leaves the performer "clean".

You give the spectator the pencil and after he has initialled the paper ask him to drop it into the glass. He now selects a symbol and it is up to you to impress upon him that he has the power to transmit his thought-of design to the nearby tumbler. Patter theme, however, depends on individual choice and is not, therefore, dealt with here. Build up a certain amount of tension without overdoing it, and then let him remove the clip and billet from the tumbler. DO NOT HANDLE THE PAPER YOURSELF as, after the effect is over he will remember, when speculating, that *he* put the billet in the tumbler, and also *he* was the one to take it out.

Although the moves surrounding the switch have taken many lines to describe, their actual execution is completed in less than half a minute, and as stated at the beginning, this is only the basic handling without dressing or elaboration. The design, card or colour is of course forced, and the spectator must be given the impression that the clip is used only to eliminate your handling of the billet. A short pencil is used as it is more natural to have difficulty in finding this than a full length one. The writing on the duplicate billet has to be light as, even on thick paper, it tends to show slightly when the paper is folded. Working without a jacket helps to convince your helper that no switch could be made without his seeing it, although, of course, you do not actually say so. In any case you will find it more difficult to make the switch whilst wearing a jacket as the cloth will tend to impede the smoothness of the move, and may also dislodge the billet before the switch is made.

One thing to remember is that the confusion in looking for the pencil must appear natural and not hurried. As far as the spectator is concerned the trick does not start until he has put the billet in the glass, by which time, unbeknown to him, all under-the-counter handling has been completed.

183

*Note by Corinda.*—This particular switch has the disadvantage that it fringes on the magical appearance of writing on a blank piece of paper. For Mentalism it must be questioned whether or not this is a good thing. However, for those seeking effects which are suitable for demonstrations of mediumistic abilities, this switch then comes into a class on its own, and utilised to perform Living and Dead Tests—where the dead name appears written by The Spirits, you have one of the best methods available.

### (14)  Summary of Billet Switching

Somewhere one must draw the line; I can go on and give you a dozen other methods and at the end you will be so confused—you won't know which one to use! Enough has been said, you have a fair selection of methods of skill and mechanical self working ways.

As I have said before, and must stress again, it is not essential to know different techniques—but it *is* essential to understand and apply the same basic principles of Billet switching, no matter what method you choose to use. To summarise those principles in a few words:—

(*a*)  Be able to do your billet switch when your eyes are closed—so that you need not look at your hands.

(*b*)  Go steady—not fast and not slow. A sudden quick move which noticeably changes the tempo of your performance—is the deadliest way to inform your audience that something is being done. They may not know what—but they know something has happened. It is better to go slower than faster.

(*c*)  Pay attention to the section in this book which tells you how to mark your billets so that you can recognise the dummy easily. If you don't, one day without fail, you will land yourself in trouble.

(*d*)  Wait your time for the switch. Many a clumsy switch is caused by lack of good timing. When you take a billet from somebody— THEY EXPECT YOU TO DO SOMETHING WITH IT—otherwise why would you take it? So you do nothing. Take it hold it and show it whilst you talk—let them wait until they no longer know what is going to happen—and then switch. Never fall head over heels trying to do the switch as soon as the billet arrives in your hands.

(*e*)  Never forget that misdirection can do more for you than anything else. Faith can move mountains—and misdirection will move them back again—neither time will you see them go! Learn six stock questions or requests like "do you mind if I use that ashtray over there?" and "Will you see what you have in your right jacket pocket and remove it please . . ." These stock questions and requests are your standby to put the spectator off his guard for the switch. Do not wait until you are performing—learn them first—they don't always come to mind when you have other things to think about.

(*f*) Have faith in yourself. Never worry—you cannot do Mentalism in any shape or form without confidence. Remember they are at a disadvantage all the way—they do not know what you are going to do—whereas, it is hoped that you do! Always remember that an occasional FAILURE makes things look much more legitimate than constant success. You can afford a mistake—it's good publicity.

(*g*) The best way to learn billet switching is to perform with billets until you have made every possible mistake and general blunder. That will teach you more than fifty books—and you will remember what matters!

## (15)  Marking of Billets

This is important—read it and remember it. Whenever you intend to use more than one billet, make a habit of secretly marking the dummy. Suppose you are doing a trick with three billets—a question and answer effect. On the table are the three billets each one folded and ready for you to read. To do this, you will probably use the "one ahead" system. This means you must switch one of the real billets for a dummy which will leave two questions and one blank on the table. You proceed through the routine, secretly reading the stolen billet and applying that question to one of the others—a normal one ahead technique. BUT you have to know which of the three on the table is the blank—if you get mixed up at any point in the proceedings, you are quite liable to pick up the blank and end your performance abruptly because you cannot read the next question.

Don't rely on luck—play safe all the time and mark the dummy so that it can be left without fail, to the last.

To mark a billet for the one ahead system, I usually fold or roll the billet as usual—but taking one corner of the dummy, give it a tight twist forming a tail which although small and inconspicuous, stays put regardless of how much handling it gets, and can always be seen if you know where to look. Moreover, if done properly, it can be detected by feel which occasionally comes in handy.

Other methods include nail nicking and folding in a special manner known to you only. These methods are alright as long as the billets are not going to be handled to the extent that they may become accidentally marked in a similar manner.

Whatever method you decide to use, it should be one that is good enough to avoid suspicion and yet one that allows you to choose the marked billet from any other ten—at a glance.

## (16)  Billet Stands

A Stand, designed to hold and display a billet can serve more purposes than it might appear to! Primarily, it helps with the presentation—but behind the scenes, it affords you the chance to DO SOMETHING with a billet; an opportunity to do something is an opportunity to switch. Either in the act of taking the billet off the stand—or putting it on in the first place, you have movement and cover all with reason and cause.

The stand should have two or three essential qualities. It should appear simple and unlike a conjuring prop in every respect. The best type is easy to make and meets all our requirements for Mentalism.

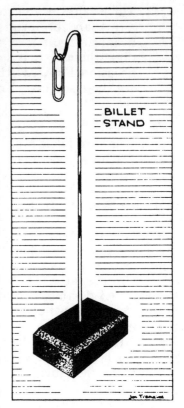

BILLET STAND

Take a ten inch 14 gauge knitting needle and nip off the nob at the end. Bend the pointed end to form a loop as illustrated in the drawing. Get a block of wood to act as the base and drill a hole (slightly smaller than the diameter of the needle) right in the centre. Into the hole jam the needle— your stand is made.

In use, a Billet is folded and then clipped with an ordinary small paper clip which is then hung on the stand. It looks good—it is good!

You will be able to put the stand into your pocket—making it easy to carry. To pack down, simply pull out the needle and it becomes two parts both easy to carry.

*Note.*—Those of you who are familiar with the Ostin switch using a Bulldog clip, will find this stand more than useful!

FIG. 28. LAPEL BILLET CLIP

Another means of displaying a Billet which again offers you considerable scope for trickery—is to have a Small Bulldog Clip attached to a little safety pin. This clip can be pinned on your lapel where the billet can be held on show clearly visible to all and yet not in your hands. Alternatively, the clip may be pinned on to the spectator's lapel and the billet left there—which can be very useful on occasions when you would rather not trust the billet into his hands!

### (17)  The Use of a Crystal Ball

Of the many means that have been devised for the purpose of secretly reading a billet, the use of a Crystal Ball is one of the best. A good ball magnifies the writing which helps, it seems a natural thing to hold in the hands for this type of work and simply by holding a billet open in the hand and reading through the crystal ball you can see everything. From time to time you will find that with careful handling of the crystal ball, you can let the subject look himself and see the answer to his question, etc.

The use of miniature playing cards for the last mentioned principle, offer you a wide range of effects where the spectator "reads" the name of his card in your crystal.

**(18)   References on Technique with Billets in Other Steps**

## PART TWO:   TRICKS

**"The Crystal Locket"** by Dr. Jaks (New York City)

Dr. Stanley Jaks needs no introduction to the world of Mentalism having established himself as a first-rate performer.  This effect is one of his favourite close up tricks and the routine is just as was written by Dr. Jaks for this Step.

An interesting crystal locket is shown and placed on the table.  It is one of those pendant lockets that hangs on a chain and should be an attractive ornament, it is also necessary that it opens so that you can put a slip of paper inside—but most types of pendants are made to hold a small photograph so you will have little trouble getting one.

Next you tear off a sheet of paper from a notepad.  This sheet is prepared for the trick by having faint pencil lines ruled on it.  The size of the pad should be three by five inches.  The top sheet has five lines ruled across the width on one side, and two lines ruled along the length on the other side (Diagram No. 29).

Having removed the top sheet the performer takes a pair of scissors and cuts along the five short lines making six slips of paper.  On the back of each of these slips will be two lines running the other way.  The slips are handed to six people and each person is asked to write the name of a male or female friend on their paper.  However, it is important that you emphasise that the name should be written across the lines covering the full distance between the three divisions, and you say that you will explain the reason why in a moment.

187

The scissors are placed on the table and the performer turns his head whilst the writing is done. Still without looking, he tells each spectator to take the scissors and having written the name, cut along the two lines dividing their slip into three sections, and when this has been done, to turn all the slips writing side downwards and to mix every one together in a pile in the middle of the table. When that has been done, he turns round again.

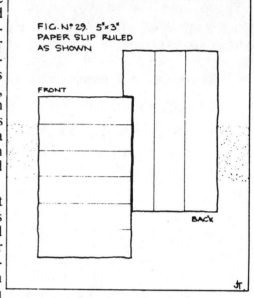

The performer picks up the locket and begins to talk about the powers of a Pendulum. The spiel is patterned along the lines of the old sex detector trick, and the locket is used to demonstrate that a Pendulum swings in circles to indicate a male, and in straight lines to indicate a female. (Diagram No. 30).

Holding the chain so that the locket swings about two inches from the eighteen slips of paper, the performer moves around until suddenly there seems to be some reaction. The locket begins to swing back and forth in straight lines—over one piece of paper.

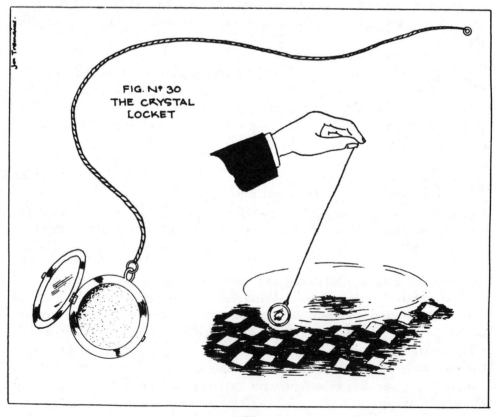

188

Triumphantly the performer siezes this piece and folds it without looking at the writing on the underside. He puts this piece in the locket, closes it, and then explains that it will act as a locator for the pendant.

Again he holds the locket over the slips on the table and moves round until he finds another piece which reacts the same way—and then another. These two are pushed to one side. This done, the piece in the locket is removed and added to the other two. These three are lined up to form one piece again—but left face down on the table for the moment. The locket is held above them and this time begins to react immediately. This, says the performer, shows without doubt that the name was written by a lady. All the ladies are told to hold out their hands, and one by one the pendant is tested over their palms. One of the hands give a reaction and the performer asks this lady if she will admit that the name she wrote was a Female friend. She agrees that it was so.

This lady is now asked to turn over the three slips on the table and she finds that out of all the eighteen pieces, mixed and identical in appearance, the Crystal Locket has located the three bits of paper that spell out the name of the woman friend written in her own handwriting!

## The Method

Based on an idea of Stewart James, I think that it has been hoccussed beyond recognition. Consider, what do you really have to know? You must be able to identify one slip of paper, and you have to know who wrote on it in the first place—that's all.

When you remove the top sheet from the pad, hold it with the five pencil lines towards you. As you cut off the first slip, make sure that you cut slightly above the pencil line so that this piece of paper HAS NO LINE ON IT. Give this piece to a lady and remember that she has that slip. Put it on the table in front of her with the white side down—the two lines showing uppermost. Go back to cutting the other slips from the big sheet and do so in the same manner which will have the result that the next five pieces all have a pencil line along one edge. This is your means of identification—simple and sure.

When you turn your back, instruct the first lady with the blank-back slip to write a name—the name of a female friend. Tell the others to write the name of a male friend. When you hold the locket over the eighteen pieces of paper, scattered across the top of the table, you will have ample opportunity to look for the three pieces that do not have the faint pencil line across them. These must be the three that matter.

The routine requires a lot of presentation—in Mentalism EVERYTHING is presentation and even though you told the lady to write a female name, they will be amazed how you found out—and how the pieces all came together. The effect could of course be presented as a Living and Dead Test, but I personally never liked those effects.

## Three Little Questions (by Corinda)

I have used this routine for many years and I have found it indispensable for the occasion when one is called upon to display one's strange faculties to ladies. It is not my trick—the effect is as old as the hills—going back to the days when Fraudulent Mediumship was big business in America. However, this is my handling and my routine and it is the result of trying out many variations to find the very best.

## The Effect

The Mentalist condescends to give a lady a private reading. To try and receive inspirations which may answer any three personal questions the lady may like to ask. No positive results are guaranteed and the questions should be serious and private. The lady writes three questions and the performer answers them. Having done that, the lady will never forget you!

## The Routine

Get ready before you offer to give the reading. Prepare by taking a sheet of paper size 5 × 4 inches (or thereabouts) and tear it into four equal pieces. One of these will be your dummy billet and must be marked. Roll it into a tight ball and screw a tail on it to mark (*see* page 185). Drop the dummy in your pocket for the moment and with the three slips and a pencil on the table you are ready to begin.

Hand the three slips to the lady with the pencil and tell her to consider any three personal questions she likes. Emphasise that she must be serious and that she has a free choice of any subject—no embarrassment will be caused. The lady is told to *print* one question on each slip of paper and to tell you when she has done that.

You walk away—well away and make no effort to see what is written. However, if you do happen to pencil read all her questions by looking in a mirror—don't pass it by! Whilst waiting, take the dummy from your pocket and hold it in the right hand. When she tells you she has done that, call out—"roll the pieces into a ball please, each one separately". Give her time to roll up the first and the second but arrive at the table as she is rolling the third. Immediately pick up one and say—"No—roll them really tight please—like this". Switch that one as per the instructions given under Section 7 of Technique in this book.

Put the dummy down and tell her then to take all three in her hands and to mix them thoroughly so that neither of you know the order (that's why you mark the dummy!) As she does this, sit down opposite her and holding the first real billet in your lap—read the question. Tell her to follow your instructions very carefully. Look at the three billets now on the table and see which are the two real ones. Push one of these forward with your finger and say "hold that to your forehead please". Now this is important from the point of view of presentation. Whatever the first question may have been—answer if favourable but also indirectly. NEVER let it be known that you know the exact wording of her question. Suppose she wrote:—

"Should I go and see Mary or will she visit me".

Start your reading by saying that you have no idea what questions she has asked or which question *she* has chosen and is holding now. Say that you receive "ideas" and "feelings" that could mean something regarding any of the questions so if you say anything that fits one of her questions—she must say yes, and acknowledge that she understands what you are talking about.

Your first remarks are deliberately vague and gradually you build up the reading to make it obvious that you are answering one question, finally you deliver an answer which is a mixture of the unbeatable reply—a sure-fire prediction, a happy ending, flattery, etc., etc. The answer may be something like this:—

"As soon as you held that paper to your forehead—I got an inspiration which suggested a clock. Does that have anything to do with any of your questions? You can't place it—never mind. Now I also see what appears to be a calendar, would I be right in saying that somehow you are concerned with time? Don't answer yet—I also get a letter—a friend —a message from someone who has been away for a while—you are waiting to hear from someone—is it a friend?" (She will place the question by now) "I can see a rather unexpected event here, you think you are going to meet someone—a lady—but this lady can't be just where you think she is. You must meet this lady—she wants to see you, you have a lot in common—especially your intellectual tastes. I cannot say exactly what the question is—but I feel I should answer it by telling you that you must see a lady—and that there will be a letter concerning this matter. You understand what I mean—I could go a bit further but I feel that this matter is really too personal to discuss openly—you know what I mean don't you? Let me read what you wrote please . . . ."

At this point you reach forward and extend your hand. She drops the billet into your outstretched palm. You open it, appear to have a little difficulty reading it and then slowly read out loud the exact wording of her FIRST question. At the same time you note and remember this question— which is the next you will answer. Look at the billet and make the misreading convincing. Smile as though to say "well I was almost dead right!" Immediately screw up the paper again and drop it into your pocket—with indifference.

Point to number two on the table, the only real billet left, and tell her to hold that one to her forehead. During the reading of this one, which is done on similar lines to the first, you exchange number one for number two in your pocket and drop the first question on to the table. Do this as though you are not thinking.

When you end the second reading, do the same stunt, open it and misread the question thus learning the third question. At the end she will be holding a blank piece of paper to her forehead—but for the climax we add a nice touch.

When the reading has finished—have number three question in your hand. Take the dummy as though you intended to read it aloud like the other two—but change your mind and giving it back to the lady say, "read it out and tell me what you wrote". You switch the dummy for the third question at this point and give her back the proper slip of paper. The other two questions lie on the table in case she should look and you have the dummy back in your pocket.

It's the One Ahead System—one of the oldest and one of the best. The effect will do you more justice than fifty card tricks—you wont find much better anywhere and it's nothing—a rigmarole with a few bits of paper and lots of spiel. That is Mentalism.

**"It's a Record" by Corinda**

**The Effect**

A gramophone record is seen displayed. A catalogue of records is produced, any page selected and that page torn into small pieces. Any piece is selected and the title of any record taken from that piece. The title is announced—and when the record is played—it is the same one as was selected. Nothing more than a prediction like a newspaper test disguised as a coincidence.

## The Method

Obtain a catalogue of gramophone records which can be got from any dealers for nothing. Sort through your records and find one that most people will recognise when they hear it. Locate the title of this record in the catalogue and remove that page. Tear out the section with the title until you get a piece of paper about one sixteenth the size of the original page. Fold this twice and have it in your pocket—this piece shall be the dummy billet.

To perform, have a gramophone ready and one record on show. Take the catalogue and explain what it is and that it contains no fewer than seven thousand different titles. Count them if you wish to be exact! Hand the book to someone and tell them to tear out one page—take it from them as soon as it has been torn out.

Tear it in halves and in halves again—once more tear and again until you have a handful of pieces. Go to another person and ask them to take any piece and fold it twice. Drop the other bits aside and then take the chosen piece and hold it up whilst you explain that the choice was one in thousands . . . switch this piece for the piece in your pocket (by any of the methods given) and hold it yourself. Go to a spectator and open it up—hold your thumbnail right under the title of your record and say to him, "Will you read that title out loud please". He does—leave the paper with him—return to the gramophone—show the only record and play the first few bars . . . .

## Presenting the L & D Test.  Corinda

As Dr. Jaks says—"Living and Dead Tests and not everybodys' favourite effect"—but this presentation does make any of the standard methods amusing and interesting. You have four living names written on slips of paper—and one dead name written on another. By marking the dead name billet you keep track of it. Now we come to the location of the dead name. The five billets are mixed and laid in a row. You get one of those novelty key-chain skulls that are on the market and have it on a chain. Much the same as the sex detector trick—you use that, acting as a Pendulum to locate the dead name. It's a nice touch—appropriate and a bit better than the usual "deep trance" revelation.

## "Great Minds Think Alike" by Punx
### Introduction

In every hundred or so new tricks that come along each year, one finds that ten of them are really any good. Out of that ten, we are fortunate if we find one that is distinct and really exceptional. This is one in a hundred—I would go further and say, one in a thousand. A veritable miracle of mental magic and a secret that up to now—four people in the world know.

Six months ago Punx the German Mentalist walked into my studio and performed this trick. When I had seen it—I had two words to say—"How much?" But it was too good to be bought or sold and after six months' persuasion Punx gave in—and for the first time in print—here is the Punx Test or "Great Minds Think Alike".

192

## The Effect

Two strangers are used. One leaves the room and one stays with you. You ask him to think of anything he likes—a word—a number—a drawing, he has a free choice. He writes down what he thinks of—rolls the paper into a ball and drops it into his pocket. YOU DO NOT TOUCH HIS PAPER. The other person is called into the room, given a sheet of blank paper and told to gaze at it and try to get an inspiration of something. You don't suggest anything. If he sees anything—and he must not guess—he is to write it down and roll the paper into a ball. He does as he is told. Both subjects now exchange their papers, open them and read them—THEY ARE THE SAME. No known method is used—it is a new development by Punx.

Never mind about the method for a moment. Can I ask you quite honestly—do you know of a better effect for Mentalism? What is there so near to the real thing—so clear and unbelievable? There is nothing—this is one of the best—a classic.

## The Method

I have promised Punx that every detail of working will be given so that his trick will not be ruined by bad workmanship. I ask you to follow the details and be sure you stick to the book. No unnecessary moves are made. First you require a special type of paper. The best is called "Art Paper" and it is a matt white finish—like paper coated with white poster paint. The second best is a cheap grade white duplicating paper. The special paper is such that if you run your fingernail over the surface, it leaves a shiny line which becomes visible when the paper is tilted to the light. The paper must be white—coloured art papers are too effective and should not be used. When you get the right paper, test it to be sure it is alright and then cut a few sheets and put them in your wallet. The size should be about $3 \times 5$ inches and the surfaces must be undamaged.

Get your two subjects and explain that you want to perform a test. Two total strangers are best. Tell one of them to go away and return when you call him. He can go into another room or stand a good distance away.

Bring out your wallet and open it. Pull out the papers and take one sheet. With your pencil draw a small circle about $\frac{1}{8}''$ diameter in the middle and put a wee dot in the centre of the circle. Do exactly this—do not put a cross which is sometimes misconstrued as the Roman numeral for ten.

Hand this paper to the subject with you and ask him to look at the dot and to try and get a picture from it. Suggest that he may be able to see a number—say "like 983 or 46—anything". Wait a moment and then say, "What can you see?". If he says "Nothing" say to him—"Well imagine you can—what do you see now?" He tells you what he can see—and we will suppose he replies "Seventy two". "Right" you say, "well take that pencil and write a big seven and a two like that . . ." Now this is it. As you speak to him, telling him how to do it, you draw on another piece of the paper a big "72" using your fingernail (either thumb or forefinger). You are actually writing his number under his nose—but he cannot see it and thinks you are showing him what to do. He will never remember that you did this. Because the paper leaves the shiny line—you have marked it perfectly. Don't hurry, behave just as you would if you were showing him with a pencil in your hands. When you come to mark the second paper, see that it does not rest on any other sheets or a carbon may be suspected.

193

When he has written his number over the small circle and dot, tell him to roll the paper into a tight ball and drop it in his pocket. Note please, a *tight ball* and not folded. Call the next person over and ask him if he knows what has happened. He will say no. Tell him you want to try an experiment —something which may or may not work.

Take the second sheet lying in front of you and repeat the same preparation as before. Draw the small circle and put a dot in the middle. Hand this sheet to him and tell him to go and look at the dot from all points of view, and to try and get an inspiration of a number. Emphasise that he must not guess—if he sees nothing—to say so, and yet, if he sees a number—a distinct number, to write it down and then screw the paper into a tight ball.

When you put the dot on the paper it serves two good purposes. It is good misdirection and it makes them look at the *right side* of the paper.

The writing becomes easier to see in artificial light so send the subject to a spot where he will stand under an electric light. It will work in daylight but artificial light is better.

Be sure to watch him and if he seems in doubt tell him to look at it from all points of view—"sideways—tilt it about—the numbers will slowly appear . . ."

Sooner or later he sees the shine and then realises that a number is to be seen. He writes this down and screws the paper into a ball as told. He returns and you have them exchange papers and open them to read.

It is a strange thing, but the person who sees the number on the second sheet—does not seem to know why. No doubt you are thinking—well he knows how it works, but they don't. Sometimes they get an idea that you must have written the number and the second man is partly wise, but the first man never knows and more often than not they are both lost. I have asked the second subject afterwards, "What did you see" and a common reply is "Nothing at first—and then the numbers slowly came out of the dot".

However, the perfect trick has a perfect finish. When they open their paper and read them, they know that both are the same—but they can never prove *why*, because if you screw the paper into a ball—it destroys the surface and the number on the second sheet then disappears! They can take both slips home with them . . . . it's too late.

## The Flames of Zor

This is an old principle that has been applied in many shapes and forms for both mental and magical mysteries.

Five slips of paper are given out and on each one is written a name. One is dead. The slips are rolled into small balls—and then dropped one at a time into a glass of water. Four of them burst into flame and disintegrate when they are in the water—one remains; that one bears the dead name.

The effect may be modified to any type of trick—where one billet is located from a number of other billets. It is a method of enhancing the presentation and not so much an effect in itself.

The answer is very simple. You have four prepared billets ready rolled into small balls of paper to look like the proper ones. Each of the prepared ones is made from a small slip of Flash Paper and inside is a SMALL pellet of sodium. When the pellet hits the water, after a few seconds the sodium

194

ignites and the flash paper goes up in flames. Alternatively, you may use potassium metal in place of sodium—but whichever you use, take great care as both are dangerous in any quantity when exposed to air. If you wish to perform the effect without using water—you may resort to phosphorus—which will ignite when dry. Never use any more than a piece the size of a very small pea—because these metals are liable to explode in larger quantities.

### A Card and Billet Routine (Corinda-Fogel)

### The Effect

The performer hands out about ten slips of paper. He goes to each person with a slip and fans a pack of cards before them—telling them to look at them and mentally note any one. He stands back and asks all to write on their slips—the name of the card they saw. Whilst this is done, he arranges the cards on a cork board so that the backs face outwards.

The billets are folded and collected. A lady is invited to choose any one and then to impale it on a dart. She does this. Next she is invited to stand in front of the board and to throw the dart at any card. This she does. She removes that card (which now imprisons the billet on the dart) and shows it. Then she opens the selected paper—and reads the name of the card—they are the same. A chance in a million!

### The Method

The first step is to impress upon the audience that all the cards are different —and yet to do so without drawing attention in an obvious manner. The slips are a convenient size for a billet switch. Hand out ten slips and then go to each person and fan the cards showing the faces. Now and then bring the fan up to let everybody see the different faces.

Stand back and tell the people with the slips to write the name of the card they selected. Whilst this is done, go to the board and prepare to place the cards on the simple wooden racks made to hold them. However, just before you start you switch the complete pack for any forcing deck (say Nine of Clubs). You make nothing of this. Simply put the deck in your pocket—move the board a bit using both hands, and then remove the forcing pack. As an alternative switch, have two "Terry" clips on the back of the board. As you move it a bit, put one deck in a clip and take the other from the second clip. Have the board made of cork so that the dart is sure to impale into it.

In your pocket have one folded billet and on that billet have the name of your forcing card, *i.e.* Nine of Clubs. Collect the ten billets when they have been folded—mix them and give them all to the lady. Ask her to choose one and take that one. Draw attention to a dart and at that point—perform a billet switch returning the prepared billet and now the dart to the lady. Tell her to stick it on the dart—and from now on it is obvious.

Should the lady miss a card on any throw—tell her to collect the dart and throw again—she can hardly miss. After the billet switch you do not touch anything—you don't have to!

### "Inexplicable" by Al Koran

### The Effect

One person is given a slip of paper and told to think of a name. The name should be a place—a town or city—village—in any country in the

195

world. To create a vivid picture of that name in their mind, they are told to write it down and then fold the slip.

You take the slip and put it in a clip on display.

Attention is now drawn to a Brandy Glass standing on a table. It is seen to hold several small pieces of folded paper. The performer tips these out and invites another spectator to choose any three. Then to hold a lighted cigarette to them all—and in doing so, he finds that two disappear in a flash and one remains.

All that remains now is for the performer to open the slip on display and read out the name for all to hear—the writer confirms that was his choice. Now the other spectator opens the last billet on the table and reads out a name written by you before you started. It is the name of the chosen place.

**The Method**

Fold up about six small billets of Flash Paper and drop them in a glass which you stand aside on a table ready for use later. Have a display clip that pins on to your lapel—as described in this book. Hand the slip to the spectator who is to decide the name of a place. Choose a person that is seated some way from the glass on the table. The slip you hand him is prefolded in readiness for the One Hand Centre Tear (described in this book).

Have the name written and the billet folded. Take it and under cover of putting it on display in the clip, steal the end. Patter a while and cause sufficient distraction to allow you to open the end tear, glimpse the word and refold the paper. This done, go to the glass and in picking it up and tipping out the slips drop the end tear amongst the other flash paper slips. Have three chosen and see that your end tear is one of them. If there is any indecision, they may all be used. Invite the spectator who is, of course, a different person from the writer of the slip, to hold his cigarette to the slips. The one that does not burn is the end tear—tell him to hold it for a moment.

Come away and take the billet from the clip. It will be in two pieces so you must take care to make it look whole. Open one of the sections and appear to read out what is written on it. In actual fact, call out the name you glimpsed on the end tear. Ask for confirmation that this was written and then tell the other man to open his slip and read out what you wrote earlier that evening! Naturally he reads what the other man wrote—but who suspects that is the case—they have just seen you read the slip!

For obvious reasons, you would be wise to select two people who are seated far apart. Another point is that you may, if you like, have fewer slips in the glass. The only thing is that with six or seven, it is quite impossible that any observant person may have counted the number there at the start. With two or three it is probable.

# "BOOK TESTS"
# and
# SUPPLEMENT

## BY

CORINDA

## STEP SEVEN

IN CORINDA'S SERIES :—
## "THIRTEEN STEPS TO MENTALISM"

STEP SEVEN IN CORINDA'S SERIES

"THIRTEEN STEPS TO MENTALISM"

"BOOK TESTS AND FOGEL INTERVIEW"

## CONTENTS

## SUPPLEMENT

SID AND ELAYNE MARLO

# "ZARKAMORTA II."
## (The Ceremony of Reincarnation)
## By Corinda

**Introduction**

This is a complete routine and as such, it must be performed according to the book. The ingredients of this programme are—one third trickery and two thirds presentation. In essence, this is nothing more than a book test but the dressing makes it such that you could be acclaimed an Ipsissimus of The Left Hand Path—

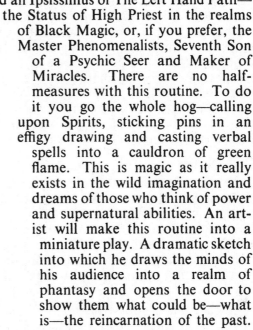

the Status of High Priest in the realms of Black Magic, or, if you prefer, the Master Phenomenalists, Seventh Son of a Psychic Seer and Maker of Miracles. There are no half-measures with this routine. To do it you go the whole hog—calling upon Spirits, sticking pins in an effigy drawing and casting verbal spells into a cauldron of green flame. This is magic as it really exists in the wild imagination and dreams of those who think of power and supernatural abilities. An artist will make this routine into a miniature play. A dramatic sketch into which he draws the minds of his audience into a realm of phantasy and opens the door to show them what could be—what is—the reincarnation of the past.

You can work this routine alone — that is without any trained assistants. You will need some help, but people present take part to overcome this; it takes some preparation but not much, however any work at the beginning is well rewarded at the end. It costs next to nothing to do—except your valuable time which will be spent in hours to perfect the patter and presentation. It is limited to some extent—to performance in the Drawing Room or in such places where you are close to your audience. It could be done from the stage but part of the intimate atmosphere of a drawing room is necessary to create the dramatic picture. The last thing is the trickery involved. Oddly enough, this is the easiest part of all, something which I am confident you will master in ten minutes.

So I will describe the routine as it is performed, and in doing so, I call upon you to use your imagination to visualise the setting and actions. I have used the programme on many special occasions and this is my way of doing a Book Test!

The first thing you do is to wait until you are invited to "do some tricks". On the presumption that you are visiting friends as a Mentalist or Magician, it is rational to suppose that this will happen sooner or later. When the invitation takes place—you take your stand and rather to the surprise of all present—you decline to perform (as usual) and say that this time you would rather tell a story. You allow the audience to force you to do something and get them ready for the story. This you begin to tell—but half-way through, carried away with your own enthusiasm—you cunningly ask . . . "I could show you—but I don't know if I dare". There was never a more certain way to get people curious and wanting to see what they shouldn't!! And so your story continues—but twists slightly so that now it is accompanied by a demonstration—a performance of one of the rare and secret Occult Ceremonies—a weird, fascinating and entertaining display. At the end, your story finishes and as it does the demonstration ends. Here now the audience are confronted with a powerful mystery, what you have done is well beyond the powers of normal happenings and yet even you, so you say, cannot explain the strange reason or force that has achieved this remarkable event.

**Performance**

"Much as I appreciate your request—tonight I am not really happy about showing you the sort of thing I usually do, I would rather forget about doing things myself and tell you a story. I promise you the story will amuse you—it concerns Magic and Magicians of a sort—although I suppose I should warn you that I say "magicians" in a very lose way—I really mean Black Magicians—people that really dabble in Occult Arts—it is the Story of a secret rite a strange and rather unusual tale. Would you like to hear it?

"Please make yourselves comfortable, relax".

The story teller pulls up an armchair and seats himself comfortably. He sits in front of the group and begins the tale.

"In some ways, I suppose I'm taking a big chance in telling you this story. However, I might as well—and in any case, I could do with your opinion, you might even be able to help me.

It's difficult to know where to begin. It was all so strange and I know you wont believe it. I suppose I should tell you about the Rectory first—then you will understand.

To be brief, it happened about two years ago. I was visiting a friend who like myself is interested in Magic and what we call Mentalism. My friend was an expert on what we call Mentalism and happened to be an authority on many other associated arts. He knew a thing or two about Witchcraft and Medieval Practices—he had studied Spiritualism and other cults which concerned themselves with the Living and the Dead. Regardless of his strange interests in life—he was still capable of shrewd judgment, and in fact, he set himself the task of investigator of all weird and wonderful happenings. He was busy all the time exploring haunted houses, chasing poltergeists and watching luminous green trumpets floating around seance rooms. That was my friend, I say "was" because he is no longer with us—and so I feel justified in telling this story—which, but for him, would never have been told. Before I go on—could we have those back lights out please?"

The lights are switched off leaving one only to play its beams around the story teller. People begin to look at the shadows!

"One day I had arranged to pay him a visit. When I arrived I had hardly been with him for ten minutes before he asked me to step into his "den" for a word in private. One day I will tell you about this den—it was a fantastic junk heap of old props, weird inventions and apparatus all mixed up with what looked like a laboratory—but that's another story!

When we arrived at the den he seemed more excited than usual and told me he was "on to something big". As a fellow mentalist he always confided in me and he told me that he had "fixed" it for both of us to get in on a meeting where certain very rare ceremonies were due to be performed. I wasn't too happy about the idea, but eventually he persuaded me to go with him and that is how we came to visit The Rectory. Shall I go on?"

We went to this meeting—thirteen people turned up and most of what we saw turned out to be nothing much—that is with the exception of one thing. I don't think it wise to discuss the meeting too much, I can leave it to your imagination and I might add that I shall never go to anything like it again. It was one particular ceremony that I cannot forget—something which really is too fantastic to believe. It is really a very simple Rite, nothing obviously supernatural or ghostly—in fact it is done simply with a book and what are supposed to be a few Magic Spells; the whole thing is physical, you see it all and I have tried it two or three times myself and it always works. There were of course many strange Rites—but this particular one was called The Ceremony of Reincarnation and although you will find it hard to believe, it is designed to alter *time*—and things which are done in the past are moved back in time so that in fact they were never done at all! I can see you laughing! I don't blame you—I also thought it was a lot of tripe—until I tried it. Really you know, I should do it—not talk about it. I would like to see your reaction when you examine the evidence—I would like to perform the Ceremony—it takes but a few minutes and it is quite amusing—but I am not sure if I should do this—what do you think—shall I?"

The story teller now becomes the performer. He reaches for his brief case and removes a book which he places on a table. With this go two or three sheets of paper, a green pencil, a brass bowl and some matches. All is ready.

"In order to guarantee the success of this experiment, I shall need the help of a few friends here tonight. Stay where you are for the moment, I'll tell you what to do when I am ready; there is nothing to worry about, everything will be under my control throughout the Ceremony—as long as you do as I say. Now the first step is to have a sheet drawn with the Personal Outline. I'm going to run through the pages of this book—will you please hold out your arm. As I run through these pages—I want you to suddenly drop your arm, imagine that it suddenly becomes as a lump of lead, heavy, too much to support; wait until I begin to move slowly through the pages— as the movement of your arm will be the signal for me to stop".

The performer takes a copy of The "Reader's Digest" from the table and standing in front of the assistant from the audience, he begins to run slowly through the pages. Suddenly the man at his side drops his arm and without a second's delay the performer calls out the page number and immediately hands the book to the spectator telling him to tear out that page.

"Seventy-Two! Here—take the book please and remove the chosen page. Tear out page Seventy-Two—but be careful not to remove any others or damage them. Good, we can forget the book for now and this page will act as The Scroll for Marking the Personal Outline. Bring the paper to me please.

You have chosen page number Seventy-Two and I have made a crude drawing of a man which, as you will see is drawn in green—the colour essential to this Ceremony. Next I shall ask another friend to help us. Will you remain please, it takes two assistants to deal with the next step. Will you please hold those two corners of the paper—and you hold the other two. Hold the paper out flat, level with the floor—so that the man in the drawing is lying down. Now we come to the pin—the next step is for one of us to mark the outline with the Curse of Pain. I think I had better do this as should there be a mistake, the Curse may well go astray and become diverted from a simple paper drawing—against one of us. I must mark the drawing with a pin—please hold the paper still as I must not look and I don't want to stick the pin in your hand!"

The performer closes his eyes, his hand moves to make mystic signs in the air and then jabs downwards sticking the pin into drawing.

"There! It is done—let us see where the mark has been made—hold the sheet to the light and find the pinhole. We must remember the exact spot—so tell me if there is a word by the pinhole.

Good, we can remember that, the mark is made on the left arm, just by the elbow where the word JUDGMENT is to be found on that page. Remember that all of you please—page Seventy-Two and the word is Judgment.

Now we may begin the Ceremony of Reincarnation. First, The Destruction. Fold the paper in four and tear it into exactly four pieces. Keep one quarter yourself, give another to our friend here and give the other two pieces to any other two members of this gathering".

Whilst this is done, the performer removes a small packet of powder from his pocket which he drops into the Bowl on the table. This he sets afire and it begins to burn slowly with a Green Flame.

"We are ready to begin the Destruction. For this I must have nothing but the light of the Green Fire. I will have all other lights out please—and when it is so, I want you people with the pieces of the page—to come to the Bowl and tear your paper—dropping the pieces into the Green Fire. Please move over here in readiness—it will be hard to see where you are moving in the dark. Be sure that all the pieces go into the fire—none must remain. Are we ready? Then out with the lights".

The performer stands behind the table, the green fire gives off enough light for the audience to see him moving his hands over the bowl—making mysterious signs as one by one, the spectators come forward to burn their papers. When this is done the lights are again put on and the bowl covered to extinguish the fire.

"Allow me now to remind you all of what we have done. So far you have seen nothing—except that we have provoked a curse which in itself is evil. This must not be left but must be lifted. Everything we have done will now have a reason and I am about to perform the last Rite—and then you will see something quite incredible. These are the ashes of the papers—The

204

Paper has suffered destruction but the Curse remains—it will be lifted and you will see why".

The performer takes some of the ashes and places them on a sheet of white paper. The paper he rolls into a small ball which he stands upon the "Reader's Digest" which still lies on the table. He next invites one of the assistants to hold a match to the white paper ball and as this is done there is fire and it disappears—all that is left is the closed book.

"Ah! as you see, the Black Ashes have been dissolved in the purity of the White Paper and so the curse is destroyed. If that is so—then our Ceremony has been successful and we have moved back in time. I cannot say how far we have gone—maybe in part or maybe further than we anticipated. Will you take the book from the table and do as I say. The book you hold was the one we used for the Ceremony. Our friend there chose Seventy-Two—our drawing with the pinhole through the word Judgment was through the arm of the figure. Now turn to page Seventy-One and tell me—is the next page STILL MISSING?

Page Seventy-Two of The "Reader's Digest" is back in the book properly affixed to the binding. The edges of the page are slightly charred otherwise it is undamaged with the exception of a pinhole—found through the word JUDGMENT on that page.

## The Method

One of the safest ways to make a good performance is to have tricks which work so easily, that mechanics can be forgotten and every attention devoted to presentation. In this routine we do just that. The climax is enough of a trick without trying to introduce more mystification en route—we shall adopt the easiest possible means.

You have two copies of the same edition of "Reader's Digest". Page Seventy-Two (or any other you prefer) is selected and prepared. In one book only, the edges of this page are charred by singeing with a match. A drawing which resembles the outline of a man is made on the page with green pencil and a pinhole is made in some prominent place—right through a distinctive word. You make a similar pinhole on the same page in the other book, otherwise, that book is untouched.

At the beginning of the routine—when the performance starts you have to force that page and word. Remember the force page has to be Seventy-Two. Run through the pages waiting for the spectator to signal stop as given in the presentation. As he drops his arm stop properly wherever you are and open the book at that page. Look straight at that page number and whatever it is say "Seventy-Two" . . . in other words, misread the page number. It may be diabolical but it achieves our aim without any trouble. As soon as you have read aloud the page number—close the book and hand it to the chosen spectator telling him to tear out page Seventy-Two. He will open it at that page for you!

Take the page back and draw the outline of a man in green—making it as near the same as the other drawing as you can. Having done this, get your two spectators to hold the page by the corners, the paper parallel with the floor and take a large pin from your lapel. Make one or two mystic passes, after the fashion of a tic-tac man giving the odds at a race meeting (!) and jab downwards. Before the pin reaches the paper—your fingertip covers the point which makes quite sure that only one pinhole is going to be found—the one you made before you started. Again make nothing of it. Forget about classic methods of forcing and systems which are sure to prove it was a free choice. At no time do you suggest it is a free choice anyway. The audience have no idea what is going on—they only know what you intend to do when it is too late to pay attention to the method of choosing a page and a word. As a Mentalist, you must become accustomed to perpetrating these outright swindles—without so much as a twinge of conscience.

Hence we have arrived at a page and a word is marked for the selection. Our next step is to consider how to switch the books ready for the climax. This complicated feat is achieved by putting out the lights and doing it under cover of darkness! You will recollect that in the routine, the page is torn into four pieces and a green-fire bowl is ignited. The lights go out whilst each spectator comes forward to tear his pieces of paper and drop them into the fire. Whilst this is going on, you have more than enough time to pick up the "Reader's Digest" from the table and stuff it down the back of your trousers belt—taking the other from there and substituting it on the table. After you have done that the trick is as good as done.

The making of green fire is simply a chemical mixture which any chemist will prepare for you. The formulae is as follows:—

    Half a dram of powdered shellac
    Half a dram of powdered charcoal
    One dram powdered Mercurous chloride
    One and a half drams powdered Sulphur
    Three drams Potassium chlorate and
    Six drams powdered Borium nitrate C.P.

This mixture is tipped into a nice ornamental brass bowl and will produce Green Fire. To give added effect, you may utilise Joss Stocks for creating a heavy scented smell and a few pieces of smouldering conjurers rope give out mysterious wisps of smoke.

The very last thing is the disappearance of the ashes in the sheet of white paper at the end of the routine. This is flash paper of course—but no doubt you have guessed! As soon as the paper has burnt away—quickly brush aside any few pieces of ash that remain before the sudden glare fades away—allowing people to see more clearly.

That is the working of The Ceremony of Reincarnation—not a lot of work for such an effect; there is one thing left to tell you. Of course, we don't believe in real Magic, Black, White or Grey; but one day at the end of a performance I opened the book to find the pinhole I had made in the arm—now through the head—and the drawing looked remarkably like me. But that's another story!!

## A CLASSIC SWINDLE—MAGAZINE TEST.

For this you will require six magazines the *size* of "Life" or "Picture Post". They have to be prepared so that the COVERS are all different and yet the insides are all the same. For best effects, obtain six copies of the same edition of "Life" and five different magazines of the same size. Choose those which have bold covers which are obviously different from a good distance.

Remove five covers from the "Life" Magazines, and recover with those takes from the odd five. With this done you are ready to perform, however, it would be as well to mention that this effect is best performed on a stage but a drawing room will do as long as you are careful to remove the other magazines afterwards.

Lay the six magazines in a pile on the table. Have a spectator come up to help you in an experiment of the mind. Tell him that he must follow your instructions very carefully—in fact show him what to do!

"Now sir, on the table here you will see six various magazines. You have a free choice of any one you care to select, don't let me influence you in any way. I want you to take one and stand over there so that I cannot see what you do".

You allow him to take one—but as you are talking at the start, pick the magazines up and display the front covers to the audience, showing that they are all different. When he has made his choice and moved to the spot you indicate, you deliberately pick up a magazine yourself and turn to him and say . . .

"Now the first thing I want you to do is to think of a number—any number you like say under fifty. What would you like?" (He tells you) "Excellent, number twenty-three, then do as I say please, turn to page twenty-three like this . . . (casually run through your copy showing him!) and when you get there look at any prominent word, a heading at the top of the page. If there is a picture on that page, remember that also please—and just for good value, have a look at the very last word on that page. (Each time you say what he is to do, you casually gesticulate with a wave at your open magazine and in doing so, you taken an outright look at the prominent words at the top of his page, any picture and the last word on the page!!). Since your copy is the same as his—you must be right.

After that it becomes a matter of presentation. Drop the magazine on to the table and pick up a slate. Tell him to commit these facts to memory, close the magazine but keep his finger in the chosen page in case he forgets the words.

"The first thing we shall try is to get an impression of a picture . . . I want you to visualise any pictures you saw. Suppose it was a person's face, imagine you are looking at that person—try and help me, make the picture strong.

You quickly sketch something on your slate—a rough outline of the picture and show it to the spectator saying:—

"Say nothing, I get this rather vague shape. It seems like a drawing or a photograph of a building. There is a large square with birds and a statue here".

Point to the slate and the outline drawing as you patter about the scene. Having delivered enough facts to make it certain that they will appreciate you are on the right trail, say to the spectator. "Would you be good enough to tell us all which picture you looked at and what was it?" When he replies "there was a photograph of St. Peter's Square in Rome " . . . you have made your point.

"Now let us deal with the headline—you looked at some prominent words . . . think. Send the words to me—imagine you are drawing the letters on a blackboard".

Write the prominent words on your slate—and others if you are doubtful as you can always say, "this is difficult, I get several words mixed up, is one of these what you have in mind?" . . .

Lastly, the surefire final word on the page. Here you cannot go wrong as it is one word only. Tell him to look once more at the last word then to close the book and lay it on the floor. Tell him to concentrate on this word ONLY—nothing more. Write it on your slate and hand the slate to him saying, "I have written one word on that slate, I want you to turn it round and show it to the audience, but *before* you do so—don't look—will you please call out loud the word you *thought of*? He calls out "revolutionary" turns the slate and all see the word "Revolutionary" written boldly across your slate  Another miracle is done!

# IMPROMPTU BOOK TEST SIMPLIFIED
## By Corinda

It is always as well to know a couple of good effects that can be done on the spur of the moment. In this effect, a Book Test, I have again resorted to the easiest possible means—and, I might add, the cleanest. When you talk about impromptu effects you forget about forcing a word with dice, playing cards and what-have-you—nothing is more likely to make the whole thing appear prepared.

**The Effect and Method**

Being a Mentalist you will anticipate that sooner or later you will be asked to do something! Prepare for this event a few minutes beforehand by finding a good size book. Preferably one from a selection of many that may possible be found on a book shelf. In an emergency, you can utilise practically anything, a directory, office invoice book, diary, etc. . . . but choose a book if you can.

Carry with you at all times a ten shilling note, the serial number of which you have memorised. Here again, if the trick must be done entirely impromptu, you can work from scratch using any ten shilling note, one-pound note or dollar bill. However, you make it easier for yourself if you use the same one each time.

Look at your ten shilling note and note that you have six figures in the serial number. The first two numbers of the six—will represent the PAGE number. The next two the LINE number and the last two—the position of the *word* in that line. Because of this, you would do best to choose a note with the first two figures around the fifty mark (*i.e.* 47) the next two around the twenty (*i.e.* 23) and the last two very low around nine or ten, but not more, as there may not be that many words in the line. A serial number like 472305 would be perfect.

With this foreknowledge, choose a book on the premises and on the quiet look up page number Forty-seven, line number Twenty-three and find the Fifth word in that line. Remember this word and then replace the book. Have the ten-shilling note folded to a convenient size for switching. (*See* Step Six).

When the time arrives to perform—say that you will try something that might be of interest. First ask for the loan of a ten shilling note (or one the same as whatever currency you are using). Next look around for a book and move about a bit before you choose the predetermined one. In moving around the room, obviously getting ready to do something, you have every chance of switching the two notes.

When you get the book hand it to the host and tell them you will try a novel test with their property! Look at the note and say, "we have six figures on this ten shilling note you have given me. Let's take the first two as a page, the next for a line and the last for the word. Look (show them), the first figures are forty-seven—turn to page forty-seven. Take the note also because I don't want to be anywhere near you when you see the word".

Guide them carefully with clear instructions (*i.e.* "disregard the title heading on the page if there is one") until they find the word. From then on it is just a matter of revealing the word by some dramatic presentation or other. Don't just tell them the word—build it up—write it backwards with lipstick on the mirror, in ash on your arm, spell it out with matchsticks—anything that leads up to something more than just saying "And the word is Mouse", to which the host may justifiably retort "So what!"?

Last but not least—looking ahead, you will make a sly effort to recover your ten shilling note and replace it with another. I suggest that the easiest way to do this is to follow with any trick which uses a ten shilling note!

## "A LESSON IN MENTALISM"
### By Corinda.

In a moment I'm going to talk about dice and playing cards, other horrible things which all tie up with the routine for this rather unusual Booktest. But bear with me—there is a deliberate purpose for using the offending materials and if you bypass this effect you will miss something good; aside from which, the knowledge of the dice force involved will come in handy, time and time again.

Is it not true that throughout the career of every performing mentalist, there are constant requests for "show us a trick" and following that "show us how it's done". This time we are concerned with Showing How to do an Effect of Mentalism! That is why I have titled the routine "A Lesson in Mentalism"—it is a standby routine which fits the occasion from every point of view.

First we must consider the ethical side of the problem of teaching a trick to members of the public. You cannot reveal anything of importance and yet you have to do something which pleases them—and perhaps satisfies their demands. I am of the opinion that it is an error to teach anybody anything at anytime—unless they are "one of us". So we get round the problem in true mentalists' fashion—show them a routine presenting it as a demonstration of Mentalism and having arrived at a surprise climax we now go further, explain the methods by running through the trick backwards —but each time you go to illustrate what you did—an even more surprising occurrence is discovered!! Another name with this routine would have been a "Trick with two climaxes!"

**The Routine**

After a few introductory words in which the performer mentions a few basic principles of "Theoretical Mentalism"—speaking about the diversity of ways to perform mindreading, dual-control, long distance telepathy, etc., he prepares to give a demonstration, a single example to show what must be done in order to achieve the results he usually displays!

Four things are laid on the table. A slate, a glass, a book and a pack of cards. The performer explains that this type of experiment is called a Book test, and enlarges the description by explaining that this means a word has to be chosen and the manner must be free of any influence. For scientific purposes the best way to have a word chosen is to isolate the human element and leave it to chance. Which brings us to dice, and cards—for what is more chancey than such things?

He takes about six dice from his pocket and drops them into the drinking tumbler. Whilst talking, he gives them a good shake; finally he hands the glass to one onlooker and tells him to give a real good shake and then to add the top numbers and call out the total.

The number twenty-one is called and the dice put aside. Taking the cards from the case the performer lays them face down in a pile on the table. He explains that the spectator must count to the twenty-first card and then look at it. Whatever it may be—that card will be used to locate a page and word in the book. The cards are counted off and the twenty-first is turned over and found to be the NINE of diamonds—a NINE. (The performer has explained that the suit will be disregarded—whatever the value, if it should be a six, for example, we would take the page number six and sixth word along in the top line).

The spectator takes the book, turns to page Nine and counts to the Ninth word. He reads aloud that word "Unmentionable". This done, you explain that this is how a mental *test* is conducted—and add that if done properly, the results would be like this . . . . the performer picks up the Slate and turns it over. There is chalked the word "Unmentionable".

Normally of course, the test would end there—but this time you intend to show how the preliminary tests are mentally guided so that you are sure to get good results. "Let us go back" says the performer, "Let us see how we arrived at this word which I predicted".

He takes the book. "This is page Nine, the word is the Ninth word in the line. We arrived at that because you selected a card numbered Nine. He puts the book down and points to the cards. The Nine was chosen because it happened to be at the twenty-first position in the pack, had it been any other number it may well have been any other card—do you agree? The number was twenty-one—again by chance as with six dice (he throws them back on to the table) there could have been any total between six and thirty-six—a pretty good range. Therefore the only real problem was to mentally control the dice to make you arrive at the number twenty-one. This I did—and of course you will be doubtful—so I may as well prove it. Your card was the twenty-first—it couldn't have been any other card as now you see (turns pack face up) it happened to be the ONLY real card in the pack—all the others are blank!" Everything may now be examined—there is nothing to be found.

**The Method**

Find a book with a good word at the ninth position on page nine and copy that word on to your slate. Have a blank face pack of cards with the Nine of any suit at the twenty-first position from the top. Now you require twelve dice and an ordinary drinking tumbler. Keep six of the dice in one pocket ready for switching at any convenient point in the routine. You have plenty of time. Divide the other six into three sets of two. Take them in pairs and give each the same treatment:—

With a good strong glue stick the pairs together with the following numbers matching on each of the four long sides of the block, 5 & 2/4 & 3/5 & 2/4 & 3, on the short ends the numbers 1 and 6 will appear. An alternative combination of 4 & 3/6 & 1/ repeated with 5 & 2 at the short ends. The outcome of the preparation is that no matter how much the dice are shaken, the top number will always be Seven on one set. With three sets it will always come to TWENTY-ONE!

At the point in the routine where you introduce the dice, you remove the three "doubles" from your pocket and just drop them into the tumbler, shaking them idly as you patter. When it comes to having the spectator shake them—BE BOLD—don't look twice at the dice—simply say "put your hand over the mouth of the glass and shake them up". When he has done that—and you will see how unbelievably deceptive the noise and movement makes the force, take back the glass and add the top total asking somebody to check that. If, after the shake, one pair should settle upright, give the glass a tap before starting the count. When you have had the total checked, simply tip the dice back into your hand and drop them into your pocket.

Keep the secret of this dice force up your sleeve. If you want to use it more extensively, you can obtain an extensive range of numbers by adding one or two single dice, sticking them to the bottom of the glass. Again you will have to try it to realise that anything so stupid can be so effective. The combination of two or three "Doubles" and one or two permanent singles give you a lot of scope for forcing numbers. I have worked on this principle for quite some time and I know that there is much to be done with it yet.

The end of the routine is, I suppose, obvious. You explain how very easy it would be for them to look up a word, write it on a slate, put one card at a known position in the deck. All that remains is knowing how to Mentally Control six dice—but that's another Lesson!!

## THE CROSSWORD PUZZLE
### By Corinda.

This trick draws the basic idea from an effect devised by that Mastermentalist, Ted Annemann. In Practical Mental Effects, Annemann describes a clever adaption of The Centre Tear to a Newspaper test. Much as the effect is good, and the method reasonable, I have found that getting a spectator to underline a word and then folding the

211

paper so that their word is correctly positioned for the Centre Tear, can offer a bit of trouble. Deciding that the effect and method were worth the trouble, I have experimented with the result that the following method makes it quite infallible.

**The Effect**

A spectator chooses any book—preferably one that is his own property, but a cheap one that you can afford to tear. He chooses any page and tears out that page. He is then instructed to *rule* two lines across the page—right across from corner to corner both ways, forming a large Cross.   Next he looks at the word to be found in the middle of the cross at the point where the two lines meet and then, having committed the word to memory (no writing) folds the sheet in half and half again and gives it to you. Upon receiving it, you tear the paper into shreds, drop the pieces into an ashtray and set it alight.  After that you are able to reveal the chosen word.

There is little to describe.  The drawing of two lines guarantees that the word to be selected is going to be near, if not exactly in, the centre of the page.  Since this is so, when the page is folded twice, you are sure that the chosen word is precisely where it has to be for the Centre Tear which you do as you tear the page into shreds. (Step Six on Billets gives a detailed account of The Centre Tear).

I don't see that the drawing of two lines is any distraction to the effect. No more so than would be underlining a word or drawing a circle around one.  It is enough that they can choose any book and any page—and you may excuse the action by explaining that you want them to "navigate" at random to find the position of a word in millions.  Another thing, you can tell which side of the paper to read when you glimpse the torn centre as it will be marked with two crossing pencil lines.  This is the sort of trick that I would recommend to you for keeping on one side as a standby for emergencies.  As long as you can get a book—you can do it.  A valuable effect to any Mentalist.

# NOVEL REVELATION OF A SELECTED WORD
## By Corinda

Originality in Presentation will always add to an effect. Method is unimportant compared with dramatic presentation.  A superb trick poorly presented will not receive half the ovation that a weak trick will get—if dressed up with showmanship.  This is another method of revealing a chosen word.  It is quite useless knowing fifty ways to force a word—unless you know some good ways to reveal that knowledge.  Your aim should be to learn fifty ways to reveal a word and one way to force it!

A page is torn from a magazine or a book, a number is forced and the word which corresponds with that number is found.  You are not supposed to know the number.  The page is now mounted on a simple stand—something like a large Billet Stand as described in Step Six.  The page is left open wide, hanging from one or two clips.  You tell the spectator to imagine that his word, whatever it may be, is written on a slip of paper and then dropped into a glass of water.  You take a match and set the page alight—it burns falling in ashes with the exception of one small circle of paper. At that point it seems to be fireproof—and when the slip is examined, right in the middle is found the chosen word!

This effect cannot be performed with a large sheet of paper as there is nothing left to support the small fireproofed area. Alternative to the stand, is an ashtray, fold the sheet in half and open out again so that it can be made to stand upright in the tray. If the ash is not disturbed during the burning, the unburnt section hangs in position and stands out clearly to be seen.

To prepare, wet about an inch of the paper which surrounds the force word using a fire-proofing solution like Potassium Alum dissolved in water. Reading through this myself I find it is one of those effects that looks a bit weak when written on paper—but having done it to try it out, I can assure you that it is well worth knowing.

# TELE-DIRECTORY TEST.

## By Corinda

Another "Booktest"—but this time we choose to find more than a word. From any one of the four Volumes in The London Telephone Directories—one subscriber is selected and via the media of mindreading—you discover their Name, address, Telephone exchange and correct number! There are no forces.

The method is an application of a time-tested principle. Basically so simple that people just don't think of that—when in actual fact, it should be one of the first things that come to mind as an explanation. It has been used in many shapes and forms in Vaudeville, so much so—that one professional Lady produced and maintained a highly successful act—using the very same means as we use in this test. Aside from using the principle in Vaudeville —it finds its application even today—in Broadcasting and Film Studios.

Essentially, this is a Stage effect. In a moment you will see why. Your apparatus consists of two large slates, three volumes of Telephone Directories with another three duplicates and these should have different colour covers—so that any one chosen can be identified at a distance with ease. Nothing more is needed—with the exception of chalk and a table and chair.

The chair is placed to one side of the stage—fairly near to the footlights. The table, centre stage—well back near the backcloth. Three directories are ready on the table along with one slate and your chalk. In the wings stands an assistant and she has a slate, chalk and the duplicate books.

Any person is invited on to the stage. Having greeted them, seat them on the chair and take the three directories and give them to him. Tell him to have a look at them and then choose any one. Stand nearby his chair and take away the two books which he does not want. Return to the table and place the books there. Because the books are coloured (as they always are nowadays) your assistant can tell immediately from what two are left in sight—which directory has been chosen by the spectator. The assistant is in the wings at the same side as the seated spectator but cannot be seen because the volunteer assistant has his back to the wings. She selects the duplicate book to the one he chose.

Now to play safe and enhance the presentation—making the choice of subscriber obviously free of trickery, we ask any audience member to call out a page number say between One and Five hundred. (If the numbers have to be limited to the selected book—tell them what range they can choose from). Take your stand near the centre of the stage where by appearing to look at the seated spectator, your eyes can travel past him to where you can see your own assistant. From his point of view it looks natural—and likewise for the audience.

Holding your slate and chalk ready, repeat aloud the page number called by the audience and instruct him to turn to that page. As soon as he finds it—hurry him so as to avoid delay, say, "and now we have three columns as with every telephone directory—will anyone please call out—first, second or third?" If several people call at once, don't stand for any tomfoolery, point to one lady and say "Madam, everybody wants to have their mind read—let's leave it to you—which one shall we use?" Whatever she says—repeat it loud (to your assistant) appearing to instruct the seated spectator. Finally, the exact position of the subscriber—same thing again, have any number say under thirty called and tell the spectator to count very carefully to the chosen line.

When he has it, tell him to think hard of the Subscriber's name—appear to concentrate during which time your eyes roam to a slate held high by your assistant in the wings. On that slate in bold letters—she has chalked the name of the subscriber. As soon as you get it—write the name boldly on your slate and tell him to call out the name. Show your slate as correct. Do the same now with the address—but when it comes to the Exchange and number, we finish slightly differently. Explain that names and places are not so hard to transmit or mindread, they have personal connections which makes it fairly easy—but what is hard is to deal with a few random numbers—like, for example, the Subscriber's Telephone Number.

Whilst you are making this explanation, your assistant has time to chalk the Exchange and 'phone number on the back of her slate—and hold it up again for you to see and memorise. A discreet cough signals her that you have it, so she now disappears from view in the wings.

The spectator is instructed to look very carefully at the Exchange and 'phone number. To memorise them—then to lay the book still open, face down on the floor (this is in case he forgets). He comes to centre stage where you stand. He goes to one side of your slate—and you stand the other. Each of you hold the slate with one hand and write with the other, starting when you call "go".

For your climax, you have the correct Exchange and Number written boldly on both sides of the slate. However, since you are going to be left with a spectator on stage, it would be as well to routine this effect into the programme—where your next trick will need another spectator to help. If you want to close on this effect—you must get rid of the spectator before you show the writing. To do this, have two slates and each of you write on them. This having been done, take the spectator's slate and hold it in your right hand and your own slate in the left. Thank the spectator and ask him to take his seat and then turn his slate first to show what he wrote —followed by yours. Stand near the table when you do this—so that having shown the two slates—you can discard them quickly ready to take your final bow without an armful of props! One must think of everything.

The important points to remember with this routine are:—Talk loud when you call back the selected page number, etc. . . .giving your assistant a good chance to check up accurately. Give her time to do her share of the work—in other words learn some patter and reserve patter for emergencies. See that there is sufficient light in the wings to illuminate her slate for you to read. Use soft chalk which does not talk (*i.e.* white Artist Crayon) just in case the spectator should hear some scratching going on behind him. A mere glance at the slate held by your assistant will be enough—let your glance sweep the theatre—passing the wings en route when you see all you have to see. Don't stand and glare into the wings, it is not necessary.

Finally, you must always be ready for a mistake. It's no good thinking you will deal with that misfortune when it occurs. Suppose you write the name "Williams" and the spectator tells you "No" . . . this is how we deal with it.

First, never show your slate and what you have written before you have told him to call out loud the name only of the subscriber. If it should be wrong, say "I thought that's what you would say—because you are thinking about the wrong person! Can we have a check please—page number 179 was chosen—have you got that correct? Good—and it was the First Column—right? Then we were told the third one down—well are you still sure it is Williams? No? Well what is it? "Wintergarden"—that's better—now we know who we are talking about! (show your slate with Wintergarden). On the re-check your assistant likewise makes sure she is right—although doing it often, she shouldn't be wrong. However, if she has made a mistake she rubs out the name and writes now the Correct address instead. This signals you to get out of that one! "Right you say the name is Williams—good, now on this slate I have written his address (your slate but don't show!) just before I show it will you read his address once more to yourself—and let me check that I have it right?" Concentrate, then suddenly say "ah! Just as well I checked—I have the district wrong—" immediately clean the slate with your hankie or a duster, and quickly write in the correct address of Mr. Williams—THEN show. Don't be afraid to worry about an effect. It gives you grey hairs and makes you look dignified as a mentalist!!

## ULTRA-MODERN MENTALISM

### By Corinda.

A few years ago a fellow mentalist wrote to me and said he would give me a terrific trick. It was an idea from the brain of Bob Harbin—who seemed to do nothing else but invent wonderful ideas! (Nowadays he works!). The letter read—a terrific trick! All you want is a pencil, a piece of paper and a Tape-recorder! The sudden impact of the last unexpected accessory knocked me for six and if I remember rightly I said something like "only one tape-recorder?" However, times have altered a bit and these days there are more people who own recorders and they are not so rare that any effect with them would be wasted.

By the last remark you may infer that this requires a tape-recorder. Personally, I think the effect is worth the trouble—but you decide before you either buy or make a tape recorder. (ahem!)

It's a Booktest Supreme presented as a knockout Prediction. Out of six books one is chosen. The lady who chooses the book tears out a page and hands it to a gentleman. The gentleman arrives at a word which he under-lines. For good value he writes his name across the page and the lady writes her name on the cover of the book. All this has been done—whilst in the centre of the stage is seen a tape-recorder—it stands on a table alone.

Before you switch it on—there is one other thing to be done. You explain that in a moment you will switch on the tape recorder and they will all hear something which should be a surprise. Before that however, you would like another person to choose any one of a dozen cards you offer. On each one is the title of a wellknown piece of music. The Blue Danube IS chosen!

Now we come to the little bit that I think will surprise the audience AND YOU!

You open the lid to the tape-recorder and remove it. You switch it on and stand back. Loud and clear comes forth the music of the Blue Danube— the chosen card bears the name of this piece so you call to the man "is that what you chose?"—He replies yes—and hardly has he had time to say so— when the music fades out and a voice speaks from the recorder . . .

"Fancy asking him if that was right—did I ever make a mistake? Now let me handle this will you please—move aside—no, well away—I want to see the audience!" You stand to one side and shrug. "Good evening Ladies and Gentlemen, you are listening to the only thought-reading tape-recorder this side of Mars. May I deal with the book first. Madam, I'm talking to you—you chose the book out of six didn't you? I'm sorry, I didn't hear you reply! You did—good. Well you nearly cheated you know. You were told to take the first one that you liked and you changed your mind twice! Never mind—you made a wise decision and you selected a book called "How to Pick Pockets" is that correct? (She answers yes). Very good—I hope you learn something from the book—and now the gentleman —you sir received a page—think of the number will you? Look at me— hold the paper up in the air—the page that's it—I can't see with all this tape going round in circles! (Drawing attention to the moving spools). It's a bit of a distance—but I would say you are holding page Twenty-three from How to Pick Pockets—is that right? (*Another* "yes") and out of the very many words on that page—you have underlined one—let me see, that would be TRAVELLING—right—the word you have chosen is Travelling? Well, well, well—that's it, Ladies and Gentlemen—another successful performance and I think we should give a big hand to our two assistants—The Lady— by the way your name is Mrs. Watson—correct? (Yes), and you sir—thank-you Mr. Harrison—that is your name correct?"

That is how it goes—like it? Like most of the things I work out—there's a swindle in it somewhere! This time it's a piece of cake. Any six books— any one can be chosen, any page and any word underlined—it doesn't make any difference and whatever the names of the two spectators—that too is handled with ease.

You have been lead to think—as the audience will think—that the tape-recorder plays back the message. It does nothing of the kind. The only thing it really plays is a half-minute recording of The Blue Danube—then the spools still run, but there is nothing recorded thereafter, so all is quiet. Where does the voice come from? From the tape-recorder! You will find that you can plug in a microphone to your recorder and adjust the output so that the machine works like an amplifying unit. An assistant backstage does all the talking direct into the mike—projecting his voice through the machine. Some of the minor models of tape-recorder will need a Mixer unit to make it possible to speak through and yet still play the music from record—back at the start.

The working at the start has to be quick and straight to the point. Offer six books and whatever is chosen, write the title on a blackboard. Ask the lady to call out any page number and write that on the board whilst she tears it out and gives it to any gentleman. Ask him to name any word on that page and to underline it. Again write it on the board. The writing on the blackboard serves two purposes and they are: first, your backstage assistant can see what's written and check up the facts—dotting them on a piece of paper ready for his part later. Secondly, when it comes to the "revelation"—everybody can hear what the recorder says and everybody can see it is right; otherwise just two people are in on the act.

Having selected a Lady near the front row—you will be able to get near enough to her to say—what is your name please, speaking in a low voice so that as few people as possible hear. Immediately write it in bold letters on a slip of paper and show it to her—saying "write it like that across the book please". The man will be nearby since the lady passed the page to someone, so do the same with him and then you have two copies of their names. Screw these papers up and drop them in your pocket. When you go to switch the recorder on, you suddenly see that the off-stage plug is not connected. Picking up the cable you hand it to "someone in the wings"—at the same time, pass the two paper slips bearing a copy of the names to your assistant. By this method, the audience are given a very surprising climax when the tape-recorder *names* the two spectators!

Last, but not least, have about twelve small cards—printed on every one is the title "The Blue Danube". When you come to the card force, simply tell what they are "about a dozen cards each with a *different* title of some well known music, for example we have . . . ." and you read through about five cards looking at each one as you read but miscalling for various titles. Finally, fan them face downwards and have the third spectator choose The Blue Danube. Don't work out complicated force systems for this part of the routine—it is not needed.

That's the routine—full of surprises and with novel presentation which makes it something they haven't seen before. Bear in mind the strength of the trick. You get *yes* to the book—*yes* to the line, *yes* to the word, and *yes* to the music at the start AND the two names at the end.

In case you haven't noticed it—when I worked out this routine I allowed for anybody in the audience that might have a clue as to how it was done. You see, with music at the start and with the spools moving all the time—you have pretty powerful misdirection—or do you suppose people think you have the London Philharmonic Orchestra backstage playing The Blue Danube! That is another reason why you draw attention to the moving spools—remember the patter?

# THE CLIP BOOK

## By Vivian St. John

### The Effect

A book is handed to a spectator who is told to open it anywhere and look at any word on any page. He is asked to impress that word on his memory by writing it in capitals on a piece of paper you hand to him. He then folds the paper and puts it in his pocket.

The performer now produces a dictionary and explains that since it is a comprehensive volume, somewhere on one of the pages will be found the word that was selected quite freely from the other book. He continues, explaining that there is an art called Muscle Reading, and gives a brief outline of what is to happen. The spectator is first to guide the Mentalist to the section of the Dictionary that deals with the first letter of his word. Then to the right page. When at the right page, the performer decides that the last step should be done by remote transmission and not direct contact; he asks the spectator to merely think of his word and he finds it on that page.

When the spectator guides that Mentalist by "Muscle Reading" he holds the wrist of the Mentalist's left arm, the Mentalist, using his other hand, moves the pages back and forth appearing to get a guiding impulse which eventually leads him to the correct page. Suppose the word was "Renegade" ... he would first arrive at "R" and then turn over the pages until he reaches "Re" and so on ... when the word is seen on the right page, he tells the spectator to let go and think of the name of his word—or visualise it in large letters, the Mentalist's finger moves down the page and finally stops at one word—RENEGADE.

This is one form of presentation out of many that will be found possible with a very simple and yet practical piece of apparatus. The apparatus I am about to describe was first revealed by Vivian St. John, published over fourteen years ago, but still good. The "Cornish Pixie" of May 1945 gives the constructional details of what is called a "Clip Book". It is a simple thing to make and it will be found useful for many routines and effects. Although a Carbon Impression is used, it is well concealed and the apparatus is easy to handle.

### The Clip Book. (*Reprinted by permission of Vivian St. John*)

"The word written by the spectator COULD be obtained by means of one of the many types of Clip Boards or Carbon Methods, but carbon paper even with the best of the clip boards has not been to me, very satisfactory, so make your own carrier in this way:—

Take a book not less than eight by five inches and remove the dust cover. Mark a square out on the front cover leaving about one inch as a border all round, and cut that section right out. You may now do two things. Stick that cardboard cutout on to the first page inside, in line so that when the book is opened or closed it fits back into the gap and also comes out. Or, discard the cardboard cutout and replace it with one of those permanent carbon note pads; the type that have a carbon sheet (actually a jelly) covered by a sheet of celluloid. When you write on the celluloid the lettering appears, to remove the writing, you pull down a small metal bar which separates the carbon from celluloid again—and the writing disappears. One of these, the same thickness as the book cover, and as near as possible the same size as the gap is stuck on the first inside page.

If the first method was used, a sheet of good quality carbon paper is now stuck inside the dust cover (front) if the second method is used, it is not necessary. The dust cover is replaced in either instance, and if the direct carbon method is used, you must insert a sheet of white paper to take the impression.

The book looks perfectly normal, it is handed to the spectator front side up (the proper way) and he is told, "open it somewhere in the middle and look at any word then close the book". You give him time to do this and then place a sheet of paper over the front dust cover and say, "Now write the word in capitals to impress it on your memory". He does this and folds the paper, putting it into his pocket. You casually take back the book, glance through the pages and glimpse the word-impression as you do so. From then onwards it is a matter of presentation to reveal the word by some powerful effect. Make this neatly and you have a clip board much better than those you have paid many a dollar for".

# THE MISSING LINK
## CORINDA

"Book Tests" are generally conceded to be effects wherein a *word or line* is found in a book. There are countless numbers of them already and that is why emphasis in this Step has been placed on Tests which have a slightly different approach from the normal run of things. This is a trick with a book and it might be called a Test. It does not involve words but numbers—the page numbers of a book.

The performer has a glass bowl (or any other container he chooses to use) which is said to contain approximately one thousand small slips of paper. This is true. On the table lies a thick volume—something like a Telephone Directory or an Encyclopaedia.

Nothing is said about the book for the moment. A spectator is invited to roll up his sleeve and dip his hand into the bowl, mix all the slips and then remove a handful. Having done this, he is invited to keep any one of the slips he holds and to throw the others away. Hence one is selected at random. Now the book is introduced; it is explained that the Volume is Seven of the Encyclopaedia Britannica alleged to contain some two thousand pages. He now opens the slip of paper that was selected from those in the bowl and it is seen to hold a printed number, in fact the paper is the corner torn from the page in a book. Suppose the number was 348. The spectator is told to turn to page 348 in the Encyclopaedia and when he gets there, lo and behold! the corner of that page is missing—the piece in his hands matches exactly. No other corner is damaged, just that very one. It would seem that out of all the pieces in the bowl, our spectator has selected the one corner that fits a damaged page in the book on the table!

### The Method

Get about four old books and give yourself ten minutes work during which you tear off each and every corner, screw them into a ball or fold them and drop them into a bowl. Next take the key book to be used for the experiment, and remove a page corner from somewhere near the middle. The thicker the book, the more impressive the test. This corner treat the same as the others, either roll or fold—but drop it in your pocket where you can get at it quickly and easily. Now all that has to be done —which is practically nothing!) is to switch the corner he chooses from the bowl—for the corner in your pocket. Step Six on Billets gives you a good dozen methods of switching so we need not bother about that here. But I will make it easier still for you and tell you how to do it when they least expect it. Have the spectator mix the pieces, choose a handful and then make a final selection of one piece. Up to now, no mention has been made of numbers, you alone know what is happening. You suddenly make an announcement, telling everybody that every piece of paper in the bowl—is the corner of a page torn from a book. Say "about twenty different books have been used—to collect the three or four thousand slips you see in the bowl. Now I want you all to be satisfied that these slips are well mixed, different and that the choice was free. Will you Sir, kindly pick up about three or four slips from the bowl and open them, read out loud the page numbers as you pick them out". Then add as though it was an afterthought, "you had better give me that piece in case you get it mixed" (!) Reach forward and take the selected piece from him and have the other (real corner) ready in your hand to exchange at any time you like during the next half a minute when all attention is focussed on the spectator calling out numbers. Under these conditions, it becomes so easy that you can hardly call it a Billet Switch. You have so much time and so much misdirection that a child could do it.

The last touch is to get the corner back into his hands—without drawing too much attention to the fact that you have been holding it. As soon as he has checked through about four slips from the bowl, stop him and draw his attention (and the audience) to the book on the table. "That will do thank you. Now let me draw your attention to this book on the table, it has been here all the time and has not been touched. Take your paper please and bring the book here". Hand him the real corner and wave him towards the book. After that it is left to your personal (and undoubted) talent to make Much Ado About Nothing!

## SUMMARY OF BOOK TESTS

In this Step, we have been forced to alter our usual approach dealing with Types and Technique before Tricks, as Book Test cannot be classified under such general headings as Types—and technique varies in almost every case. However, rather than publish half a dozen bare effects, we have given in this Step, ten routines which can be applied as Book Tests. That is more than enough, quantity means nothing—quality everything.

Any Mental programme is the better for ONE Book Test—provided it is reasonably short, direct and stunning. Anyone who thinks in terms of two or three book tests for one programme—is asking for trouble. The choice with the Ten Routines given in this Step is pretty wide, and I think it safe to say that if you cannot find at least one Book Test out of this lot— that you can do, then any others that exist wouldn't suit you either. There will be one or two more Book Tests to come in further Steps—but they will be specialities, like the big one due for disclosure in Step Twelve (Publicity Stunts).

Remember that a good Mental programme must be varied. One good Book Test is as valuable as one good Prediction. However, in choosing which book test you intend to use, bear in mind what sort of effect it looks like from the audience point of view. For example, you might do a book test where a word is located and is later revealed written on a Slate. If this is so, you would naturally avoid a Prediction which involved a word written on a slate. Don't excuse repetition by telling yourself "well one is a Book Test and one is a Prediction". As far as the audience are concerned they are the same.

Another thing to watch particularly with Book Tests is that you offer CLEAR instructions at all times. Whenever you do something which is going to involve counting to pages, lines and words—there is scope for the human element of error. Your Test can be ruined because the Spectator, not understanding your instructions, counts to the wrong word (*See* Step Five). Likewise it is as well to remember that when one man looks at a book and finds a word, he alone can see it and the audience are left to suppose he is telling the truth. Whenever it is practical—get the word in writing on a Board so that all can see, or have someone check it. Remember you are performing to an audience and not one man.

Lastly, whether you are using a fake book or an ordinary book, avoid any of the ridiculous phrases that are commonly used in these experiments. Never use such terminology as "I have here a perfectly ordinary copy of the Reader's Digest"—what else is there but a Perfectly Ordinary Copy— unless you have a prepared one?

It is amazing how the psychological suggestion of trickery can be "telegraphed" to an audience—by trying to "Over prove" that everything is innocent. Unless it is imperative, never have anything examined—that's another point. If something is given for examination in order to prove that it is not prepared, the audience are justifiably liable to think—"well he didn't find out how it works". *The most likely time for anybody to think a thing is faked, is when you tell them it is ordinary*!

## AN INTERVIEW WITH FOGEL

The text of a tape-recorded discussion between Fogel and Corinda on the subject of Mentalism.

222

## AN INTERVIEW WITH FOGEL.

Some while ago it was considered that a lot of practical advice would be necessary in order to complete the "Steps". The subject of Presentation is dealt with as a specialised topic in the last Step, but when the chance occurred to get some first hand opinions from Maurice Fogel, an interview was arranged and tape-recorded. In the following script, the interview has not been edited in any way. The questions are as given and the replies as recorded on the spot. Bearing in mind that Fogel has been earning his living and doing well for very many years as a Mentalist, I feel that there is a lot to be learnt from his experience. I do not have to introduce Fogel; if you have not seen him work—you have missed something. Those who have seen him perform don't have to be told he's one of the best. We are thankful for the opportunity to publish this interview for the benefit of our Readers.

— o O o —

(Q) Fogel, you have been practising Mentalism for quite some time—I believe as a Professional; can you tell us how long you have been at it and under what sort of conditions have you worked?

(A) I've been a professional entertainer for over twenty years. Regarding conditions, I've worked under all sorts of conditions, from small barrack-rooms, small billets to the largest of theatres. Also, of course, Music Halls, Cabaret, Club, Dinners—and you know what!

(Q) Now have your activities been confined to England?

(A) No. I've been practically all over the world—excepting Russia and Australia. I've been to Africa, Japan, Malaya, Singapore, Hong Kong—The Continent and I've been over to The States. Naturally I've worked a lot in the British Isles.

(Q) Right! Well I'm going to ask you some questions on Mentalism which I think will help the readers of this book. Please understand that what-ever you say—you say as you like, we don't want to influence you in any way; in other words—let's have it straight!

(A) Don't worry—you'll get it straight!

(Q) The first question I have to put to you is a very important one. Do you think there is any future in Mentalism?

(A) Yes—definitely a future. It's mystery and a good mystic effect well presented is always acceptable.

(Q) Coming down to the actual performer; what outstanding qualities do you think go to make a Mentalist?

(A) Well that's a very big question really. Foremost what one has to keep in mind is to be an Entertainer. People want to be entertained—especially today. But I should imagine one of the greatest things to cultivate is a *commanding personality*. Mentalism naturally calls for that.

(Q) Now to rather a tricky question. Do you think it is a good thing to mix magic and mentalism during the course of a performance. I think we had better say during the course of a Mental Act?

(A) No—I don't think it is a good thing because in presenting Magic, naturally the people, even though you are presenting an apparent miracle— know that you are using trickery. So therefore, if you mixed magic and you come to a Mental Effect the shine has been taken off by yourself because the conclusion with a great many of the people would be "well, it's just another form of trickery".

223

(Q) But I think I would be right in saying that a magician can of course put in a couple of mental effects to add to his performance. Would you agree to that?

(A) Yes—definitely, because that is exactly the way that I started. That was until I realised that Mentalism was far stronger, or had a stronger appeal than my magic—which was probably no good at all—so therefore I went in and specialised in Mentalism.

(Q) Thank you. Now the next question, again I feel you can give a pretty good answer to this. What about Comedy in Mentalism; do you think it necessary to have some light relief?

(A) Yes. This is based again on experience. There was a time when I was the very, very strong Mentalist—but it can reach saturation point and create too high a tension with an audience and where possible to bring in Comedy Relief without lowering the dignity of the performance— it can be a very good thing and a great asset.

(Q) Now, what do you think is the best attitude to adopt towards an audience. By that, I mean, do you think you should try and fool them that you are a genuine mindreader—or infer that they must form their own opinions—or what?

(A) Well—if my experience can help I would suggest that you do not take on too strongly that you are genuine. That was one of my pitfalls in life—although I never made the claim—the claim was made for me and I paid very, very much for it. So if that can be a lesson to any of your Readers and it can be driven home, it would be a good thing for them. So therefore, what it amounts to is—Present Mentalism well, be the Actor, same as David Devant always suggested; after all a magician is an actor. But Mentalism is a very, very tricky subject—no puns meant— so therefore treat it lightly.

(Q) By that do you mean you should tell the audience that what you are doing isn't in any way Genuine Mindreading? Or do you say that the best thing is to say "You must judge for yourself—is it trickery or is it genuine?"

(A) Yes. I agree with you on that only partly. Meaning, a great deal can be done by *inference*. You don't have to say openly "now look I leave it to you to judge what I do" that's been done quite often and to an extent it almost smells apologetic. No, be forthright in your Present-ation—infer as much as you like, but don't come out in the open!

(Q) Excellent! I think I agree with you. Now let's get on to a slightly different field; how about mixing Mediumistic effects during a Mental Act. Do you think this is a good thing?

(A) Again it's dangerous ground. Meaning, you must keep at the back of your mind you're an Entertainer. There are people in this world (includ-ing myself) who are great believers in the Hereafter. Although I'm not a Spiritualist—there are people who are—and many genuine and sincere in their belief; now for you to come along with the aid of gimmicks and to take advantage of that, and to bring in Mediumistic effects—do so— but be careful.

(Q) Now the next question. Do you think that *age* matters if you want to be a Mentalist?

(A) Well for pure Mentalism, naturally, as I said at the beginning, you have to have a commanding personality. Well straight away that does suggest that you have to be of a mature age, although the youngster who wants to come into Mentalism—I don't want him to be thrown off because of this. By all means do it, as a youngster you can still present it and with experience you will learn a lot for a really good Mentalist Presentation I would say you should be of ripe mature age—round about thirty and onwards.

(Q) Actually Fogel, what I had in mind was appearance. That is to say, even if you do get a young chap with a commanding personality (which is possible) do you think the audience will accept his Mentalism if he looks "too young"?

(A) No—certainly they will accept it. As I say, primarily, if he remembers he is an Entertainer and his stuff is presented well—neither age or appearance matter to that extent.

(Q) This more or less goes back to one of our earlier questions but it is a specific question. What about the use of magical locking props on a Mental Act—good or bad?

(A) In a pure mental act—definitely bad. The whole thing has to have the appearance of impromptu; for instance you will recollect, and those who have seen me work will know, that even the boards that I use—the blackboards—I could have quite easily had possibly a frame or a plated border, something bizarre ; no, it was wise to keep them as plain looking as possible. If you were a genuine thoughtreader you wouldn't need anything—keep that in mind.

(Q) Contrary to that I suppose you agree that a bit of Mentalism can be slipped into most magic acts—with or without props?

(A) Are you asking me or telling me?

(Corinda) Asking you!

Fogel. Well—let's have a cup of tea then I'll agree!!

(Q) OK. Now we get on to the next question. Supposing you are doing an act. Which trick do you think is most important. The first or the last?

(A) Both. I think they are equally important. At the opening you must naturally remember that most of them are seeing you for the first time and you have to create an impression, the audience have to accept you. With your finale you must be very strong, very strong because you have to leave them with a good finish.

(Q) In other words, you would say that the first and the last effects of the act are indeed the most important?

(A) Well I would say in every sphere of entertainment that is so. You'll find it with the juggler, the dancer and the singer just the same.

(Q) I see. Now what would you say would be an "ideal" running time for an average act. Shall we say the type of act aimed at dinners or maybe club work?

(A) Fifteen to twenty minutes for a Mental act.

(Q) Not more?

(A) Well you can. I've presented Mentalism for a longer time—but experience, which is something that you cannot learn, helps you to present a longer act. At the beginning I would suggest fifteen to twenty minutes.

(Q) Next question is—would you say it is a good thing for a mentalist to dress up in costume or to appear in any other way than well dressed?

(A) I have seen Mentalism and Magic presented in evening dress—wearing a turban. This seemed quite in order, it didn't seem wrong, but generally speaking it is safe to dress respectably in evening wear. Certainly avoid dressing in Oriental garb and speak in obvious Oxford language. That would be stupid.

CORINDA   And my next question is will you have another cup of tea?

FOGEL   Yes—you've read my mind!

(Q)   Right, now we get on to rather a difficult question, one which I think you will be quite capable of answering—that is; roughly *how many* tricks would best make up a ten to fifteen minute act?

(A)   Well, again that's very, very difficult to answer. It is possible, keeping in mind your introductory effect and your finale, to present just three. That is your opening, something in the centre and something to finish with. On the other hand you can present a few quickies. You cannot give a direct answer on that—that's my feelings.

   The main thing is—get *strong* effects. Get good strong effects and then, vary them, meaning it would be unwise for instance to put in two book tests in one programme. You see it would be just as silly to put in two Predictions. So we must keep in mind that with Mentalism you are limited. After all, what is Mentalism but reading of the mind or Predicting into the future? So keep the effects strong and allow for variety on the programme.

(Q)   From that I suppose we may conclude that it is not the number of tricks that we do—but the strength of the effect that is far more important?

(A)   That's it. Aim at quality and not quantity.

(Q)   Now I want to get down to analysing the two most important tricks in the act. You have said the first and the last are the prime effects so can you give us an idea of what essential qualities are needed for a good *opening* mental effect?

(A)   Essential qualities? Well you must aim to establish yourself and although it might appear contradictory to what I said earlier, get away from the idea that an effect is necessary. I think in mentalism the *approach*. From the moment you walk on with the majority of audiences you are treated with a certain amount of suspicion; it's something they don't know whether to believe in or not. So right from the beginning from, your walk on, you are meeting your audience—*that* is your opening, especially in mentalism more so than with magic.

(Q)   So the first thing is to establish yourself with the audience?

(A)   Yes. I mean—consider your patter. This might seem exaggerated but I don't think it is—with your "Good evening Ladies and Gentlemen", I think you can establish a great deal. The way you walk, the slight nod, the slight bow—it's all *production*. Regarding effect, if you can get over something good, quick, snappy—so much the better, but the main thing to keep in mind is your impact, the opening as you walk on, remember all the time that they are looking at you.

(Q)   So it's the way you walk and what you say that are equally as important as the first trick you do?

(A)   Yes.

(Q)   Thank you. Now let's get to the other end of the act. What about the closing effect, what are the important things to try and achieve for your finale?

(A)   Well to leave a good impression, a good mystery is essential. Right, so we are dealing now on the finale, let's take it that you have your opening and you have established yourself well, your centre material which for want of a better word we will call "padding"—but it should not be padding—not thrown away stuff. (Everything, today especially, has got to be strong.) And we are coming on to your finale. Now what's got to be the finale? The only way I feel I can help you is—imagine a chart in front of you. You start off, for arguments sake, at fifty per cent, that has got to work up like a barometer until you reach a peak—and once you reach that peak, that is it. So therefore, as far as I'm concerned, I'm not worried about what your finale is, I couldn't care less, but *get everything possible* so that first you leave a very good impression—it's got to be sold to the utmost. That's what I mean when I talk about presentation. Every ounce, everything within you has got to come up to a peak—and remember that barometer chart! When it gets to the top—that's when you leave them and you can't go wrong.

(Q) Now a question about tricks. How important is it to try and be original?

(A) Again let's be worldly on this. In every sphere in life originality counts a great deal, it pays off, but let us be fair with ourselves. Rather, let me be personal and be fair with myself.

For myself I try my utmost to present effects, some of them original ideas, but very, very few—because I'm limited. I admit this openly. But even so, there are effects on the market—get them, play with them for some time, and try and get an original approach and it will pay off in the end. Once in a blue moon, it's very rare—but you'll get someone who can be entirely original. Personally I've never come across such a performer. But there are ways of disguising effects—and you get a great deal of personal satisfaction if you get an original approach. It does not always mean the patter—say you, but a trick and you can't find anything better than the patter they suggest, work on it—remember that it's elementary in dramatics that a line in a play can be read in dozens of different ways. One line, pauses, flection in voice—do that with your effects.

Another instance. They suggested I had an original approach with the way I handled props—the way I handled the boards and threw the chalk away. To be absolutely truthful with you I never realised it, I had not planned it, it was *me* working; you can do the same thing—just be NATURAL, and always try and get some original approach and you will find that people like you for that.

Whilst on this I do suggest strongly that if you do see a performer working an effect, and getting away with it, I know there's a great temptation to pinch it. Don't. It's sinful—on this I'm very superstitious, you will never have any luck with it—that is definite. But if that performer has inspired you, by all means be inspired and let that be a help to you. There is no need to take that effect away from him because believe me from experience I can assure you that every move means a lot of hard work. After all there is so much you can find. Some time ago I had to give a lecture on this and my suggestion was again based on personal experience. I advise, go down to the markets, watch the market people working, you will learn a lot from them. Remember they have to earn a living; watch two stalls selling the same product, for arguments sake, crockery or china. One fellow is taking a lot of money and the other fellow isn't. Analyse it—why? They are

227

selling the same product, possibly the same price and possibly the fellow who is not taking so much is selling his stuff cheaper? Why? Yet the other fellow can sell it—and the reason is showmanship; again inflection of voice, there's that en rapport with the public, also experience.

Another thing, don't go and watch entirely Magical performances; those who know me intimately will tell you that I see very, very few magicians because I know that temptation of wanting to take something that is really good and I would rather fight shy of that. But I can learn a lot by going and watch the Ballet or going to a good Opera. You will learn a great deal about showmanship and presentation.

(Q) I think that's very good—but I think you must also agree that it's not much good introducing mental effects into a production of Swan Lake!

(A) I agree with you Corinda—and in the same voice somehow I don't think a chappy dressed up in tights would look well as a Mentalist. But what I'm trying to tell your Readers is to get the inspiration from these Classical productions; go and see a really excellent show away from magic—you'll learn a great deal. Watch all the time—the newspaper men selling papers, shop workers—everybody. Watch and learn.

(Q) Still another on tricks. This time I want to ask you—how can you tell if a trick is good or bad?

(A) Well my answer to that Corinda is this. There are very, very few indeed in the catagory of bad tricks. Meaning there are tricks which appeal to people so naturally you buy them. But like clothing apparel, what suits one man does not necessarily suit another. The same with tricks; what you think is a bad trick another fellow will make a miracle with it. Although I do agree there are some alleged tricks which should never have come on the market. They're no good at all—but there are very few. In the majority a trick is a trick—it may not suit you but it might suit somebody else.

(Q) Don't you think that the acid test would surely be to try it out on an audience and then judge the reaction by the audience?

(A) That's all right to a point. I'll only go with you part of the way on that. So let's start from the beginning; you get your catalogue or you visit a magical dealer's place and there's something that appeals to you, you like it and in your mind you can see yourself presenting it. Well, you have gone more than half way, I do suggest you buy it. Now when you suggested a moment ago that you try it out on the audience to see the reaction and you base it on that reaction as to whether the trick is good or bad, that is not the acid test—again I'm talking from personal experience and I find that there are several tricks and effects which have taken me a long, long time to find out where and how it could be presented properly. Sometimes it was a matter of a word—again presentation, and inflection of voice or sometimes to stop sooner than you originally intended—or work it a bit longer. Therefore you cannot judge it on one, two or three showings. If you like the effect keep at it.

(Q) Now to change the subject. Can you give us an example of a good effect that a Mentalist could do if called upon to do something on the spur of the moment?

(A) Well outside of the dealers' items which we wont mention, the greatest standby for absolutely impromptu stuff has been Muscle Reading. But of course you have all the advantages of Billets and say the Centre Tear if you can use the necessary materials. There's a lot of fun and valuable experience to be gained from finding out for yourself—I don't think I should advertise or spoil the fun for your readers.

(Q) Perhaps you are right. If I may say so, I have always got along with the Centre Tear and when no apparatus has been allowed, I have just used my natural psychic powers—as you know I'm mediumistic!

(A) (At this point Mr. Fogel came out with some quaint old English phrases which might not look so good in print).

(Q) Now another question, this time on a much debated topic. How do you feel about using Playing Cards for Mental Effects, or for that matter, anything that is easily associated with conjuring. For example a magician's wand, silks, boxes and so forth?

(A) Well first of all I'll say straight away the Magic wand is out. Definitely out—that's elementary, we all realise that. Other than that, any gaudy looking props that are definitely the property of a magician—they should be out. Such things won't be a help to you, they will be a deterrent—which should be obvious.

However, regarding Playing Cards, handled properly they can be an asset because remember this—there's a great mystery regarding Playing Cards. Although they are used a great deal by magicians, remember that your Fortune Tellers, Seers, Tarot Readers—some of them use cards as their main stay and they are accepted for that purpose. So therefore you need not be afraid to use Playing Cards—but handle it right. Don't do anything which is obviously manipulation—there is a wide space between juggling and thoughtreading!

(Q) I think the next question is one that few people could answer properly. I'm putting it to you. Most mental acts call for an assistant or two from the audience, can you give us any tips on handling this situation. In other words how do you go about a sure method to get people to come up?

(A) This is again a very important question and is hard to explain, but what has to be done—has to come from within you. Again we must start from the beginning, possibly I missed it earlier on; one of the greatest things is to be sincere. We go back to Houdini again who says a Magician is an actor—acting magic—and remember as a Mentalist you are an Actor presenting Mentalism and you've got to be sincere about it. Furthermore, if your whole presentation is sincerity, you should have no difficulty in getting people to help you. I have found that this has helped me a great deal, and to give you an example, on occasion in Music Halls which as you know are suffering a great deal, I had in large theatres very few people in the audience. Most of the artists backstage felt it and could not gain an atmosphere. You can imagine my feeling before coming on the stage—when I depend on audience participation— I'm wondering in my mind how I'm going to get a committee! But I've never failed and I do put this down to being sincere. It will ooze out of you and you'll attract people to you; after all they are part of the audience. You know as well as I do—that without audience participation you haven't got a Mental Act.

Further on this theme of sincerity, another thing which is worth bearing in mind is that you must have the complex that you are *not going to fail*. You see, it might sound contradictory—but it isn't;

earlier on I said that I felt a complex about getting a committee up—before I went on, but once I get on the stage that feeling goes immediately, *I'm the Mentalist* and this is the only secret—inwardly think, "I'm going to succeed" and you will. Occasionally the response wont be as quick as usual, well don't be lost for words. Always have something to say and always at the back of your mind have the complex that you are going to have your committee and that you will succeed in your mentalism. All this wrapped up together means that you must succeed. That is my experience.

(Q) I'm going to go a bit further with this Fogel. Suppose I'm doing my Mental Act and after a few introductory remarks I ask for two assistants and find that they do not appear to be coming. What do you think I should do—stand there and talk or move about and be seen doing something—trying not to appear worried about the situation?

(A) Yes, obviously you have learnt your lesson already in saying those words, but to deal with that situation from a personal angle. Let's start "Ladies and Gentlemen I would like two people to come up", etc., etc. . . We find the response is not too good so now's the time to get in a bit of light relief. Let me give you an idea now—something which I have done on these occasions. The first thing is to play for time, talk about the way up "the stairs to the stage are on my right—come along up the steps there", look expectantly and smile saying "now don't all rush up together!" continue, "Just take it easy one at a time please", and by that time you'll find that you have broken the ice—but if not you can continue "I'd rather you came of your own accord because if I singled anybody out there would be even more suspicion than there is right now". Phrases in that nature, light friendly remarks will soon solve the problem. Never be insulting—remember, be commanding and yet remain humble —such a thing is possible. Take Sir Winston Churchill, one of the greatest orators of our time—he was commanding and when occasion demanded he was humility itself.

(Q) Do you think it's a good or bad thing to do what is often done. When the Mentalist has asked for assistants and they don't come up, he turns to the audience and says "Well, if somebody doesn't come up I can't get on with my act, I've got to have assistants"?

(A) Well I don't think anything of it. You want to keep your book off the "X Certificate" so I won't say exactly what I've got in mind at the moment. But never confess defeat—that's idiotic; and remember whoever has engaged you—has done so because you are supposed to succeed. You should never be there if you are going to use those sort of words. Never insult your audience in any way, be the master and be humble—the perfect gentleman and be courteous—remember that.

(Q) Another hard question—suppose you do get a couple of people up OK. But what happens if one of them turns out to be an awkward so-and-so. What's the best way to handle that?

(A) Naturally that's happened to me—it happens to everybody and I have my tricks of the trade on that—one of the things is that you must remember again—you must succeed and the audience are with you, they are there to be entertained and if you've got someone with you who is going to spoil it they are on your side. You have to remain the master, on occasion I've held him by the hand and asked him to step back,

I'm smiling to the audience but the heel of my foot has crushed on to his toes, my fingernails have dug deeply into his hand and under my breath to him, on the side, I've used the worst of barrack room language and that has sobered them up—believe me that is definite!!

(CORINDA)  Well Fogel, I've asked you a good score or more questions and think that's enough for the time being.  However, you might have a couple of important things to add—what do you say?

(FOGEL)  To round off this interview—because Mentalism is really a very big subject and is well worth discussing, I enjoyed this interview very much.  But to finish it off, the thing that comes to my mind right now is, let's imagine a situation that has happened to me—one that can be dire. In mental magic a great deal depends on getting information—we agree on that?  Now imagine that everything has gone wror.g, your gimmicks have failed you and you haven't got a clue as to what the fellow has in mind; can you imagine anything more disasterous for a Mentalist?

Well my last point will deal with that—and again my answer is based on experience.  The first thing is be brave; it might sound simple or seem easy to read, but believe me you have to be brave and do this.  Say "I don't know".  Admit it!  This took me a long time to realise and on occasion I've had everything fail and I've tried to get out of it somehow. You know the old saying in Magic, "if a trick fails you show them something to distract their attention"—well naturally I have tried that approach because I know my magic, but I don't think it scores in Mentalism.  The great thing is that you can admit in three small words "I don't know" and although you have failed—if done properly you will get applause.  This is not given because the audience are entirely sympathetic—but more so because you are genuine and sincere.  So take it from me—this is a wonderful tip, small as it might seem—have the courage to admit you are wrong if ever you are in trouble—but then, I hope you never will be.

CORINDA  Well thank you Fogel for your opinions and impressions.  I'm pretty sure that much of what you have said will be useful to my readers and although some of the things you say are subject to argument, I don't think there's much doubt that at any time, anywhere, you can practise what you preach.

JON TREMAINE

# TWO PERSON TELEPATHY

## BY

## CORINDA

### STEP EIGHT
IN CORINDA'S SERIES :—
## "THIRTEEN STEPS TO MENTALISM"

STEP EIGHT in CORINDA'S SERIES

" THIRTEEN STEPS TO MENTALISM "

" TWO PERSON TELEPATHY "

## CONTENTS

### PART ONE: MAJOR SYSTEMS

### PART TWO: MINOR SYSTEMS

### PART THREE: ROUTINES

# "TWO PERSON TELEPATHY"

# INTRODUCTION

Well on the way now, in our Course of Step by Step Mentalism, we arrive at one of the major subjects in the series. To compile a book which allowed for all the methods for performing two-person mental acts, would take more space than five steps. Here, we can but hope to give a selection of good material and with a bit of luck, we shall manage to sift the best from the not so good. At least, we will have sufficient material to enable any two people to start cold and end up with a two person act; that is the basic requirement of this Step.

Technically speaking, we have to sort out the various effects into some resemblance of order. To simplify matters we can boldly differ two classes, the first we say is the type of two person telepathy that is a complete act, and the second, two person telepathy where partners do one or two effects together either on stage or as a party piece. The first is generally an application of a two person code of some type or other, the second can be any trick which takes two people to perform in order that it may be done. Following the usual pattern of the Steps, we shall deal first with method and then with application.

Before we get down to dealing with various methods, let us consider how very important is this field of mentalism. Moreover, let us acknowledge that it is probably the most advanced and most difficult to learn.

If you cast your mind back over the brief history of Mentalism you will find that when you come to think of outstanding performers—a lot of them will be two person teams that got to the top. The use of a code wasn't new when the famous Zancigs were making a mountain out of a molehill—it's old, very old, but anyone who tells you it's out of date is talking through their hat. A lot of people tell me that they think the days of the two person code act are finished—which is utter tripe. Last night in London I saw two people perform the same type of act as was performed by the Zancigs—and it went like a bomb. The reason was, they had done the job properly—and the audience didn't know they were using a code. That's where the fault lies, if any. Today, very few teams seem to take the trouble to work as hard at it—as did the others who made this form of mentalism so successful.

It is by no means an easy task and if you are half-hearted about working out a two person mental routine, then for the sake of Mentalism don't do it at all. Commonsense tells you there is *twice* as much work to be done— as there would be with a solo act. *Two* people have to be successful instead of one and the only consolation is that although it may be twice as hard— when you get there and do it right—it's twice as good! Another thing is that *both* partners must be good, very good. If one is an expert and the other not—it will spoil the act. Both are performers with equal status and importance; neither could do without the other, therefore both should receive the kudos.

Lastly, a word for those who are thinking about starting a two person code act. The essential requirement is a partner and it would be an easy mistake at the beginning to choose the wrong one. Don't be short sighted in your outlook, bear in mind that you must have someone who will be with you for a long time. It is going to take a long time to get the code into working order. Bear in mind also that you will have to be with your partner a lot in the early stages—as the more often you are together, the more you can practice. Without any doubt, the best person if you are a married man—is your wife, as long as she has the ability and the desire. There's more in this than meets the eye! Bring the wife into the act and you avoid many of the common home troubles caused when you devote too much time to mentalism! Added to that, you can practise a lot, and most important of all, having worked for six months on a code—you are not in danger of having the partner walk off leaving you to start again with a new pupil. Practically all the successful two person code acts were man and wife—and most of those working today are as well. There must be something in it; marriage is a high price to pay for a code act—but it's the safest!!

# PART ONE: MAJOR SYSTEMS

## (1) The Code Act: VERBAL.

There is nothing harder in mentalism than a two person code act worked on a verbal exchange. You have quite a lot to learn and memorise in the beginning you have to spend hours and hours at rehearsal and you have to be a performer to put it over. It has to be performed really well, being one of those routines that dies horribly if it's anything but good. We must therefore consider the things that make it good or bad:—

(a) Both partners must know the code inside out and be able to translate it at a high speed.

(b) The code must be up to date and comprehensive. By "up to date", it is meant that the code allows for modern day objects such as plastic materials—as an example. You should be able to send *any word* or *any number*.

(c) The code must be indetectable. If the audience know you are using a code it's no good.

(d) When performing—one thing makes more for success than anything else—that is SPEED. It's got to be fast—almost too fast for the audience to keep up with it all.

(e) Outside of using the code, both performers should have the ability to add to the presentation by injecting humorous asides and a gag now and then. A few laughs are important and keep things going happily along.

In a few paragraphs time, we are going to give you a complete two person code, one that has been tested and found excellent. The system devised by Walford Taylor is reprinted by permission from "Telepathy for Two". It allows you to gain all of the above requirements but like any other verbal code, it is but a framework upon which *you* build the routine.

Before we give the System, we will say a word or two about the way to present this type of act. One good method is better than six potentially good ideas. We therefore choose the method that is usually practised. Two people, usually a man and a woman (though not necessarily) perform the act. The man acts as compere/performer and the woman as Medium or Mindreader. Both enter together and the man gives a short but direct preliminary lecture. Without wasting much time, the Medium is blindfolded and sits or stands. Whilst the performer goes down into the audience and moves quickly amid the people, taking or touching various objects that they take from their pockets.

To be sure that there is a plentiful supply of objects to be named, the performer tells the members of the audience to "take objects from the pocket"

238

—such things as coins, ornaments, wallets—and if they have anything unusual, so much the better. If such an announcement is made before the
performer leaves the stage, practically everyone will have something ready
before he arrives. This has two advantages; it saves time and equally as
important—it offers the performer the chance to look around and *pick
which objects he wants*.

Quite obviously, there is little fun in it if every time you are offered a
coin. You should seek as wide a variety of objects as you can. When you get
a wallet or anything which holds printed matter, make the most of it. For
example, should you receive a Railway Season Ticket—don't stop at coding
"Season Ticket"—work on it so that on one small item you run up a quick-
fire cross question exchange of words with the medium—have her call the
colour, the serial number, when it expires, what it cost to buy and what
stations it covers. All this information is printed on such a ticket.

Remember that no matter what you are given—you are reasonably safe.
Even if you should be handed something quite rare, maybe you don't even
recognise it—you can still ask "what colour is this?" and "what is this
made of?". Now and then when you do get something very unusual it
pays to transmit the full word if it is outside the code—and letter by letter
name the object for the medium. The audience are naturally more impressed
with the ability to determine the unusual rather than the commonplace—
therefore don't be afraid to accept odd objects.

It is a bad policy for any performer to leave the view of his audience.
When you go down into the audience, head for the main gangway and work
to people who are within easy reach. Never get tangled in a row of seats—
you don't have time to move along rows as it takes too long getting in and
out. If there is a gallery avoid going too far to the back of the house or
you become a voice and nothing more. Working to the first three seats on
either side of the gangway—going back ten to twelve rows from the front—
means you can deal with some fifty to sixty people—which is more than
enough as a rule.

Speed, as we have said, is the great thing with this type of work. It's
got to be done at a breakneck rate to be really good. The slower you go—
the more time you give them to think. Whilst the Medium is calling back
one object the performer, not wasting time, is rapidly looking ahead and
getting ready to code the next. The Medium should always commence
talking the very moment the performer stops. Even if she cannot name the
object immediately, she can come in with a standard patter line whilst in
the mind she works out the code. Therefore a good stock or parrot-phrases
like "I get the impression of . . . , this is going to be . . . , as far as I can
tell it is . . ." just simple words that fill in the precious seconds before the
mind clicks to name the object. There is no silence.

You need some sort of a climax to end this sort of performance and since
the performer must be on the stage for the finale—the introduction of one
good closing mental effect is recommended. Make it in keeping with the
type of act, a simple—straight to the point E.S.P. test—with a good punch
finish. There are many such tricks printed in this series. Lastly, take great
care to avoid the temptation of over-running on the code routine. Know
when to stop—it's good up to a point and then it becomes so repetitive
that it will head for boredom. Stop when they still want more—that's a
good rule for any aspect of entertainment.

# "TELEPATHY FOR TWO"

## by

## Walford Taylor

## INTRODUCTION

The basis of this system is old, but it has been carefully revised and elaborated in order that all unnatural phrases should be eliminated, and, for the sake of easy memorisation, the code words are cut down to a minimum. Even so, every effort has been made to make the sequence of code words logical as will be seen; thus the code is essentially practical, leaving nothing for the reader to work out or alter for himself.

It is advisable to read through the system once quickly and then master each section in the correct order.

One more word. At first sight there may appear to be a lot of memory work involved. There is not. Learn the ten code words in Section 1 and the position of each letter of the Alphabet and the hard work is done.

**Section 1**       **THE BASIC NUMBER CODE**

| | | |
|---|---|---|
| I | signals | 1 |
| TRY or GO | signals | 2 |
| CAN | signals | 3 |
| WILL | signals | 4 |
| WOULD | signals | 5 |
| PLEASE | signals | 6 |
| PERHAPS or QUICKLY | signals | 7 |
| NOW | signals | 8 |
| NOW THEN | signals | 9 |
| SEE | signals | 0 or 10 |

NEXT signals that the previous figure is to be repeated.

(*NOTE* that where practicable the number of letters in the code word corresponds with the figure it represents).

**Examples**

*Q.* What is the number of this gentleman's house, PLEASE?

*A.* The gentleman lives at number 6.

(The Medium quickly scans the sentence in her mind's eye until she comes to a code word—in this case the word PLEASE which means 6).

Again: *Q.* WOULD you tell me the number of people in this row?

*A.* There are five people sitting in the row.

Once the Basic Code is mastered, the Performer and Medium will be able to tackle questions as to the age of people, page numbers, dates, ticket and serial numbers, etc.

## (A) Telling a Person's Age

The performer goes to any member of the audience and asks him his age. He then codes the age to the Medium by saying two code words in one sentence in the correct order. Thus:—

*Q.* I'd like you to tell me this gentleman's age, NOW.

*A.* The gentleman's age is 18. (I means 1, NOW means 8).

*Q.* CAN you tell me NEXT this gentleman's age?

*A.* Yes. He is 33.

*Q.* WOULD you know this gentleman's age, I wonder?

*A.* In spite of his youthful appearance, the gentleman is 51.

## (B) Ticket Numbers

Suppose the numbers were 1427, the performer would say: I want you to tell me the first two numbers, if you WILL. The Medium would say: 1, 4. The Performer would continue: GO on, PERHAPS you know the last two numbers as well. GO means 2, PERHAPS is 7, so the Medium knows that the numbers are 2 and 7.

Once the performer is experienced, however, he would code all in one sentence: I'd like you, if you WILL to TRY and tell me QUICKLY all the figures on this ticket.

In all cases I advocate that the coded sentence should be spoken in a quiet and easy manner.

## (C) Dates

### Days of the Week

| | |
|---|---|
| 1. SUNDAY | 4. WEDNESDAY |
| 2. MONDAY | 5 THURSDAY |
| 3. TUESDAY | 6. FRIDAY |

7. SATURDAY

*Q.* CAN you tell me what day of the week this was issued on?

*A.* It was issued on a Tuesday. CAN means 3 and the 3rd day of the week is Tuesday.

### Months of the Year

(Each month is coded by signalling whether it is the 1st, 2nd, 3rd, etc. month in the year).

| | |
|---|---|
| 1. JANUARY | 7. JULY |
| 2. FEBRUARY | 8. AUGUST |
| 3. MARCH | 9. SEPTEMBER |
| 4. APRIL | 10. OCTOBER |
| 5. MAY | 11. NOVEMBER |
| 6. JUNE | 12. DECEMBER |

241

Thus: *Q.* WOULD you tell me in what month this lady was born?
*A.* The lady was born in May.
*Q.* You're quite right. What about her daughter, NOW?
*A.* Her daughter was born in August. (If the Medium wished this could be preceded by a short Horoscope.)

Suppose the Performer is handed a Dance Ticket, from which it is seen that it is to take place on Wednesday, 28th July, the Performer would say: WILL you tell me on what day the dance is to be held. The reply would be: It is to be held in the middle of the week—on a Wednesday. GO on, tell me the date NOW, PERHAPS you know the month as well. Medium: Yes. The date is 28th of July. The first sentence gave the date and the second gave the month.

The reader must next learn how to code COINS.

**Section 2**                        **COINS**

**(A) Coin Code**

Again, each coin is represented by a number, that number being signalled to the Medium. The list which follows need hardly be memorised since it is, for the most part, logical.

1. means 1/- piece.
2. means 2/-.
3. means 3d. piece.
4. means ¼d. (4 farthings in 1d.).
5. means halfcrown (5 6d.'s in 2/6d.)
6. means sixpence.
8. means a penny.
9. means a halfpenny.

No. 7 is not used to signify a penny, since the code word PERHAPS, would be too obvious.

Remember that for a foreign coin, no code word is included in the performer's question. Later on in this book you will find how to signal this foreign country.

A 10/- Note is signalled by the word SEE (10).

A £ Note is signalled by SEE, NEXT (10/- Note repeated).

*Example*    *Q.* SEE if you know what the NEXT coin is.
*A.* It is not a coin. It is a £1 Note.

**(B) Coin Dates**

As the coin will normally be of the 20th Century, the last two numbers only are coded. Thus:—

*Q.* CAN you tell me the date on this coin, PLEASE?
*A.* The date is 1936. CAN means 3, PLEASE is 6.

If the coin is in the 19th Century, it will normally be obviously so, *e.g.* "NOW CAN you give me the date" could only be 1883. If, however, there *is* any doubt, the performer should add some word of caution, *e.g.* WILL you give me the date QUICKLY. Be careful on this one. The reply would be: the coin has on it the head of Queen Victoria. It is dated 1847.

If the coin is foreign, no code word is included in the sentence, *e.g.* What is this coin.

**Examples.** Try to answer each question before reading further.

*Q.* NOW tell me what coin this is.
*A.* It is a penny.
*Q.* CAN you give me the date, WILL you? (Lower the voice when saying "WILL you" in an enquiring tone.

242

A. The date is 1934.
Q. You're right.  SEE if you know this.
A. That is a 10/- Note.
Q. Right Again!  I want you to give the first two serial numbers on the note, PLEASE.
A. The numbers are 1 and 6.
Q. CAN you give me the NEXT two, or WOULD you rather SEE if you could get all four at once.
A. I think I know them all.  They are 3, 3, 5, 0.
. . . . . . and so on.

## Section 3             COLOURS

Each colour is associated with a number.  The following list is not difficult to learn, for the first three colours are RED, WHITE and BLUE, and the rest follow in alphabetical order.

THE COLOUR CODE

| | | |
|---|---|---|
| 1. RED | 4. BLACK | 7. GREY |
| 2. WHITE | 5. BROWN | 8. ORANGE |
| 3. BLUE | 6. GREEN | 9. YELLOW |

The performer walks amongst the audience, choosing his questions. Examples follow:
Q. I'd like to know the colour of this lady's dress.
A. It is a very nice shade of red.
Q. Correct.  What colour is her handkerchief, PLEASE?
A. It is a green handkerchief.
Q. Right. NOW THEN tell me the colour of this gentleman's shirt.  I'd like the colour of his tie as well.
A. Yes.  I get a clear idea this time.  His shirt is yellow and his tie red! (ugh!)

## Section 4             MATERIALS

The MATERIAL CODE as set out below, is a little more difficult to learn, and if the reader has little time, he may, at first wish to omit the list or learn only the first five.

| | |
|---|---|
| 1. GOLD | 6. GLASS |
| 2. SILVER | 7. PAPER |
| 3. CHROMIUM PLATED | 8. PLASTIC |
| 4. METAL | 9. LEATHER |
| 5. CLOTH | 10. WOOD |

*Example*    Q. I'd like to know what this watch is made of.
             A. The watch is made of gold.

## Section 5             THE ALPHABET CODE

Once the Alphabet Code is mastered, almost anything may be coded to the Medium.  It is first necessary to associate each letter with its number in the alphabet.  The task of learning these positions will be simplified by remembering the key word "EJOTY".  These letters are 5th, 10th, 15th, 20th and 25th, respectively.  From this it is a simple matter to work out the position of any letter, and, of course, with ten minutes practice there will be no need even to have to think about it.  Thus, if the letter S is stated, the performer must know immediately that it is the 19th letter of the Alphabet.

To signal a letter, therefore, its number is transmitted to the Medium as explained before. First, here is the alphabet set out in list form. In the right-hand column are the code words for the numbers to be incorporated in the performer's questions, in order to remind the reader.

| | | | | | |
|---|---|---|---|---|---|
| 1. | A | I | 14. | N | I, WILL |
| 2. | B | TRY/GO | 15. | O | I, WOULD |
| 3. | C | CAN | 16. | P | I, PLEASE |
| 4. | D | WILL | 17. | Q | I, PERHAPS/QUICKLY |
| 5. | E | WOULD | 18. | R | I, NOW |
| 6. | F | PLEASE | 19. | S | I, NOW, THEN |
| 7. | G | PERHAPS/QUICKLY | 20. | T | TRY/GO, SEE |
| 8. | H | NOW | 21. | U | TRY/GO, I |
| 9. | I | NOW, THEN | 22. | V | TRY/GO, NEXT |
| 10. | J | SEE | 23. | W | TRY/GO, CAN |
| 11. | K | I, NEXT | 24. | X | TRY/GO, WILL |
| 12. | L | I, TRY/GO | 25. | Y | TRY/GO, WOULD |
| 13. | M | I, CAN | 26. | Z | TRY/GO, PLEASE |

To aid the memory further, the letter L has two strokes and is No. 12; M has three down strokes and is 13; while W, which is M upside-down is 23. Again, U is all in one line and is 21 and V is two strokes and is 22.

**Example**

*Q.*   PLEASE tell us the initial on this gentleman's cigarette case.

*A.*   The initial is F.

**Important.**   To signal two or more letters, SEPARATE SENTENCES MUST BE USED FOR EACH LETTER THAT IS CODED.

Thus: *Q.*   I am thinking of two letters NOW. TRY and tell me what they are, CAN you?

*A.*   The letters are R and W. (18 and 23).

Now that the Reader is able to transmit any letter, the next section will deal with signalling objects.

**Section 6**                              **OBJECTS**

In the first place, each letter of the alphabet is assigned an object which begins with that letter. *E.g.* H stands for Handkerchief. Thus to signal a handkerchief it is only necessary to transmit the letter H—in other words by coding the number 8 to the Medium (H is the 8th letter). The list below has been very carefully compiled and is capable of being mastered in about 10 minutes. When this has been done, 26 common objects may be coded by signalling one letter only.

Here is the list. On the right are specimen code sentences.

|   |   |   |
|---|---|---|
| 1. | ASPIRIN          .. | I want you to tell me what this is. |
| 2. | BADGE ..          .. | TRY and say what this is. |
| 3. | COIN       ..          .. | CAN you say what this is. |
| 4. | DIARY    ..          .. | WILL you tell me what this is. |
| 5. | EAR-RING       .. | WOULD you tell me what this is. |
| 6. | FOUNTAIN PEN | PLEASE tell me what this is. |
| 7. | GLASSES          .. | PERHAPS you can say what this is. |
| 8. | HANDKERCHIEF | NOW tell me what this is. |
| 9. | INSURANCE    .. | Tell me what this is, NOW THEN. |
| 10. | JEWEL   ..          .. | SEE if you know this object. |
| 11. | KEY        ..          .. | I'd like you to tell me the NEXT object. |

| 12. LIGHTER .. | .. | I want you to TRY and get this object. |
| 13. MATCHBOX .: | I want you to tell me this object if you CAN. |
| 14. kNIFE .. | .. | I want you to tell me this, if you WILL. |
| 15. postal Order | .. | I want you to tell me this, if you WOULD. |
| 16. PENCIL .. | I'd like to know this article, PLEASE. |
| 17. cheQue book | .. | I'd like you to give me this object, QUICKLY. |
| 18. RING .. | .. | I want you to tell me this, NOW. |
| 19. STAMP .. | .. | I want you to tell me this object, NOW THEN. |
| 20. TICKET .. | TRY and SEE if you know this one. |
| 21. tUbe .. | .. | TRY and tell me what I have here. |
| 22. VISITING CARD | TRY the NEXT object. |
| 23. WATCH .. | .. | TRY this, if you CAN. |
| 24. X—CROSS or |
| CRUCIFIX .. | TRY this, if you WILL. |
| 25. Y—A BAG ..⎫ | These are given for usefulness as there are no |
| 26. Z—Cigarette Case ⎬ | common objects beginning with Y or Z. |

## Section 7      THE FINAL OBJECT LIST

All objects not included in the list above must obviously be coded by 2 or more letters. The list which follows has again been carefully compiled. It is COMPREHENSIVE and NOT DIFFICULT to learn.

## THE LAST OBJECT LIST

| | | | | | | |
|---|---|---|---|---|---|---|
| ALMANAC or CALENDAR | Al | | MEDAL .. | .. | .. | M1 |
| BANGLE (BRACELET).. | Ba | | MEASURE | .. | .. | MZ |
| BILL .. | .. | .. | Bi | NAILFILE | .. | .. | N1 |
| BOOTLACE | .. | .. | Bl | NATIONAL SAVINGS.. | Na |
| BICYCLE-CLIP .. | .. | By | NECKLACE | .. | .. | Nk |
| BOTTLE .. | .. | .. | Bo | NEEDLE CASE | .. | Nd |
| BOOK .. | .. | .. | Bk | NEGATIVE | .. | .. | Ng |
| BOX .. | .. | .. | Bx | NOTE | .. | .. | Nt |
| BROOCH .. | .. | .. | Br | NEWSPAPER | .. | .. | Np |
| BUSINESS PAPERS | .. | BP | NAIL-VARNISH | .. | Nv |
| BUTTON .. | .. | .. | Bt | PHOTO .. | .. | .. | Ph |
| CASE .. | .. | .. | Cs | PIN .. | .. | .. | Pi |
| CARD .. | .. | .. | Cd | PIPE .. | .. | .. | Pp |
| CHARM .. | .. | .. | Ch | POSTCARD | .. | .. | Pc |
| CERTIFICATE .. | .. | Ct | POWDER PUFF | .. | Pf |
| CIGARETTE | .. | .. | Cg | PROGRAMME .. | .. | Pm |
| CIGAR .. | .. | .. | Ci | PURSE .. | .. | .. | Pr |
| CLIP .. | .. | .. | Cl | PASTILLE | .. | .. | Ps |
| COMB .. | .. | .. | Cb | PUZZLE .. | .. | .. | Pz |
| COMPACT .. | .. | .. | Cp | RAZOR | .. | .. | Ra |
| COUPON .. | .. | .. | Cn | ROUGE .. | .. | .. | Rg |
| ENVELOPE | .. | .. | En | RUBBER .. | .. | .. | Ru |
| FACE CREAM .. | .. | FC | RIBBON .. | .. | .. | Ri |
| FLOWER .. | .. | .. | Fl | RUBBER BAND | .. | Rb |
| FILM .. | .. | .. | Fm | RAZOR BLADE .. | .. | Rz |
| FLINT .. | .. | .. | Ft | SCISSORS | .. | .. | Sc |
| GLOVES .. | .. | .. | Gl | SACCHARIN (SUGAR) | Sg |
| HAIRPIN .. | .. | .. | Hp | SAFETY PIN | .. | .. | SP |
| HAIRSLIDE .. | .. | .. | Hs | STRING .. | .. | .. | St |

| | | | |
|---|---|---|---|
| JAR .. .. ., | Ja | SWEET .. .. .. | Sw |
| KNITTING .. .. | Nt | SHARPENER .. .. | Sh |
| KEY WALLET .. .. | KW | SCARF .. .. .. | Sk |
| LETTER .. .. .. | Le | TELEGRAM .. .. | Tg |
| LIPSTICK .. .. | Lp | THIMBLE .. .. | Th |
| LOCKET .. .. .. | Lk | TIN .. .. .. | Tn |
| LICENCE .. .. .. | Lc | TOBACCO .. .. | Tb |
| MAGNIFYING GLASS .. | MG | TWEEZERS .. .. | Tw |
| MEDICINE .. .. | Md | TORCH .. .. .. | To |
| MEMBERSHIP CARD .. | MM | UMBRELLA .. .. | Um |
| MONEY .. .. .. | Mn | VEGANIN .. .. | Vg |
| MIRROR .. .. | Mi | WALLET .. .. .. | Wa |
| MANICURE TOOL .. | MT | WHISTLE .. .. | Wh |

and

B.D.C. .. BLOOD DONOR'S CARD !

If you are thinking that the list is extremely long, I can only say that the effort made in memorising it is more than repaid in the added confidence which one gains by having a COMPREHENSIVE object list. If you wish, you may "prune" the list yourself.

**Objects** (*Continued*)

Again it is stressed that each letter is coded by a separate sentence. The first sentence asks what the object is and the second asks for a description or for the size, shape, etc. Alternatively, the first sentence is addressed to the helper and the second asks what the object is. Two examples may clarify the position:

*Q.* TRY and say what this is, CAN you? I wonder if you know what it's used for? (Wa).

*A.* It is used for carrying things in the pocket; it is a wallet.

*Q.* (to helper) Concentrate on your object PLEASE. (to Medium) CAN you say what this is?

*A.* That is some Face Cream.

In other words, in the first example the first sentence signals W and the second signals A.

All that is required now is PRACTICE to gain speed and have at the fingertips a really practical and worthwhile system. The sections which follow enable more detail to be given and therefore add interest to the Act. Perhaps it is necessary to point out that wherever possible the Medium should describe the objects. This is already possible in the case of colour, material, numbers, dates and letters.

**Section 8**                    **CARDS**

It will be easy to see from the list below how any card may be signalled. The suit of the card is signalled first in the sentence according to the code for suits which is given below. The rotation of suits is easily remembered by the usual mnemonic—CHaSeD—Clubs, Hearts, Spades and Diamonds. The VALUE of the card is coded second in the sentence.

| | | | |
|---|---|---|---|
| 1. ACE | I | 5. FIVE | WOULD |
| 2. TWO | GO/TRY | 6. SIX | PLEASE |
| 3. THREE | CAN | 7. SEVEN | PERHAPS/QUICKLY |
| 4. FOUR | WILL | 8. EIGHT | NOW |
| | | 9. NINE | NOW THEN |

10.     SEE
JACK    JUST
QUEEN (Name of Medium; see example)
KING    No signal.
    1. CLUBS          I
    2. HEARTS         GO/TRY
    3. SPADES         CAN
    4. DIAMONDS   WILL

Thus the 5 of Hearts would be signalled by: TRY and tell me what this card is, WOULD you.

The King of Clubs would be: I'd like you to tell me what this card is.

The Queen of Spades: CAN you tell me the name of this card, Walford (or whatever the Medium's name is).

## Section 2                    COUNTRIES

It will have been seen how great is the importance of sub-division in coding objects. To signal any country, the continent is first coded and the second sentence gives the actual country. To signal the Continent, the code below is used. The second sentence gives the country by coding its *initial* letter only. Since England, Scotland, Wales and Ireland are countries frequently named, they are the first on the list.

A list of the most common countries to be given in each continent is also given, together with their initials. Learn those which are most well known first.

(A) THE CONTINENTS LIST
  1. ENGLAND          2. SCOTLAND          3. WALES
  4. IRELAND          5. EUROPE            6. ASIA
  7. AFRICA           8. The AMERICAS      9. CANADA
 10. AUSTRALASIA     11. The ARCTIC

(B) SUB-DIVISIONS INTO COUNTRIES

No need to learn these as a list. Most of them come to mind automatically when the initial letter is heard.

| EUROPE | Austria | .. | A | Italy | .. | I |
|---|---|---|---|---|---|---|
| | Belgium | .. | B | Jugoslavia | .. | J |
| | Czechoslavakia | | C | Luxembourg | | L |
| | Denmark | .. | D | Norway | .. | N |
| | Albania | .. | Al | Poland | .. | P |
| | France | .. | F | Portugal | .. | Pt |
| | Finland | .. | Fi | Russia | .. | R |
| | Germany | .. | G | Spain | .. | S |
| | Greece | .. | Gr | Sweden | .. | Sw |
| | Holland | .. | H | Switzerland | | Z |
| | Hungary | .. | U ('Ungary) | | | |
| ASIA | Burma | .. | B | Japan | .. | J |
| | China | | C | Malaya | .. | M |
| | Persia | | P | Singapore | .. | S |
| | India | .. | I | Tibet | .. | T |
| AFRICA | Egypt | .. | E | Rhodesia | .. | R |
| | Kenya | .. | K | Sudan | .. | S |
| | Nigeria | .. | N | Uganda | .. | U and so on . |

THE AMERICAS

| | | | | | |
|---|---|---|---|---|---|
| South | .. | S | North | .. | N |

(Again with further sub-division if required for such places as Brazil, Peru, Chile, etc.)

AUSTRALASIA     Australia .. A

  New Zealand  Z   Tasmania .. T

ARCTIC  Greenland .. G   Iceland  .. I

## Countries (*Continued*)

Now let us see how this system works. Let us suppose that the performer has been handed a cigarette case which was made in Austria. The coding could be as follows:—

*Q.* WOULD you concentrate on where this object was made. I want to know the country.

*A.* It was made in Austria.

Suppose a gentleman is requested to write any country on the blackboard, and he writes PERSIA. Here is a suitable sentence.

*Q.* Tell us the country on the blackboard, PLEASE.
*A.* I believe it is a country in Asia.
*Q.* Quite right. I wonder if you know which one, PLEASE.
*A.* I get the impression that it is PERSIA.

**Section 10**    **CHRISTIAN NAMES**

The same system may be used to code Christian Names, and if the reader will take the trouble of learning the following section he will have a valuable addition to the Act when it comes to describing Car Licences, Diaries, Envelopes, etc.

Again each letter has a common name assigned to it and where there are two names beginning with the same letter, the second one in alphabetical order is signalled by coding two letters.

There are separate lists for Ladies and Gentlemen. See the illustrations which follow them.

GENTLEMEN

| | | | | | | | |
|---|---|---|---|---|---|---|---|
| A | Alan | Fd | Fred | R | Richard (Dick) |
| Ar | Arthur | G | Geoffrey | Rg | Roger |
| B | Bert | Gg | George | Rn | Ronald |
| Bi | Bill | H | Harry (Henry) | S | Sam |
| C | Charles | I | Ian | T | Tom |
| D | David | J | James (Jim) | To | Tony |
| Dg | Douglas | Jo | John | Sd | Sidney |
| E | Edward | M | Michael | V | Vic |
| F | Frank | P | Peter | W | Walter |

LADIES

| | | | | | | | |
|---|---|---|---|---|---|---|---|
| A | Anne | Dn | Doreen | Jy | Joy |
| B | Beryl | E | Eileen | Jf | Jennifer |
| Bt | Betty | H | Heather | M | Mary |
| D | Daphne | Hl | Helen | Ma | May |
| Dr | Doris | J | Jean | Mg | Margaret |
| Dy | Dorothy | Jn | Joan | R | Rosemary |

**Christian Names** (*Continued*)

*Examples:* Q. CAN you tell me this gentleman's name?
A. His name is CHARLES.
Q. SEE if you know this lady's name.
A. The lady's name is JEAN.
Q. WILL you give this gentleman's name? PERHAPS you had better attempt the Christian name only.
A. He is DOUGLAS.

## CONCLUSION

With the information contained in this System, it is possible to give a really mystifying performance of Telepathy. It is up to the reader to make his performance ENTERTAINING. Although the basis of the system is old, let me again say that I hope that I have made the code words far MORE NATURAL than those sometimes heard in the Halls today and have kept it within the reach of amateurs who, like myself, have little time to learn complicated codes and yet appreciate the need for a comprehensive system.

Learn a little at a time. Perhaps the most valuable code for impromptu use is the coin code, together with their dates.

In the Appendix which follows is set out further information, hints and tips. Let your motto be

*'PRACTISE, PRACTISE, THEN ENTERTAIN'*

## APPENDIX

### (A) Further Codes

*Metals.* Refer back to page 243 and you will see how the sub-division principle can be employed in respect of metals in the material code. The example shows how the following code works.

| | | | |
|---|---|---|---|
| A | Aluminium | I | Iron |
| B | Brass | S | Steel |
| C | Copper | T | Tin |

Thus: Q. Will you say what this is made from?
A. Metal.
Q. Go on, what kind of metal?
A. Brass.

*Designs.* Similarly, designs on brooches, badges, etc., can be described by other simple codes.

| | | | |
|---|---|---|---|
| A | Animal | F | Flower |
| B | Bird | L | Letter |

Further sub-divisions may be made for coding the exact type of design.

*Example:* Q. I'd like to know what the design is.
A. It is an animal design.
Q. Yes. I'd like you to say, CAN you, the particular animal? (M)
A. It is a Monkey.

*Tickets.* In the case of a ticket, a further question may be asked as to the kind of ticket. If it were a bus ticket the letter B would be coded: "GO on, what kind of ticket?"

| | | | |
|---|---|---|---|
| BUS | B | RAFFLE | Rf |
| RAILWAY | R | WEIGHT | W |

*Pens.* Again, the Medium can tell the make of a particular pen:

| | | | |
|---|---|---|---|
| BIRO | B | MENTMORE | M |
| CONWAY | C | PARKER | P |
| SWAN | S | SCROLL | Sc |
| | WATERMANS | W | etc. . . . |

*Example:*   *Q.*   Please tell me what this is.
         *A.*   It is a pen.
         *Q.*   Yes. What kind of pen PLEASE?
         *A.*   It is a PARKER.

## (B) Procedure

I suggest that the performance commences with a very short demonstration of telepathy with cards (section 8) followed by signalling the name of any country written by a spectator on the blackboard. Keep the telepathy of objects until the end of the show. Don't forget that the performer should at all times talk in a natural manner and, if possible, introduce amusing asides, all the time coding the objects to the medium. Don't forget that you can code words even though not addressing her yourself. *E.g.* WOULD you mind concentrating on your object". And don't forget that with the owner's permission the contents of a wallet are always interesting. So also are tickets, driving licences (dates of expiry, etc.), cheque books, stamps and designs on brooches. If they are not handed to you then ASK if anyone will hand you his wallet, etc., until you have collected a number of articles. If you *should* get a difficult object then at least get your partner to say what it is made of, the colour, where made, and any initials on it, if nothing else!

Try and end on a strong note, and don't go on too long.

## (2) Sub-Miniature Radio Equipment

There is nothing new about the use of Radio Equipment for mental magic. However, there are many new developments in this particular field and although space does not permit technical details, we can offer a few hints and practical suggestions.

Modern day two-person radio equipment consists of a double unit. One is a very small transmitter and the other a very small receiver. The latest improvements on this type of apparatus include transistorised apparatus which considerably reduce the weight and size. Such appliances are available as for example the Corinda new "Mastergimmick" and Nelson's "Secret Invention". If you know a lot about the subject you can make your own—but for reliability it is advisable to get a dealer model which is guaranteed to work all the time. This is not sales talk—but sound advice to anybody who contemplates the use of this apparatus. You have to bear in mind that when you are using it—there's no "get out" if it fails; it's got to work all the time.

The apparatus works like this. Your medium or performer has a miniature receiver which is usually about the size of an English Penny. This is carried on the person and allows the holder to hear anything that is broadcast by the assistant who speaks into the microphone plugged into the transmitter.

The two are not connected and complete freedom of movement is obtainable. The range on good models is often as far as a quarter of a mile when worked properly. It is possible to relay over a considerable distance—amounting to many miles, but such a set up takes a lot of trouble. There are three types of "receivers". The first works by direct volume—and you hear like as though listening to a miniature wireless set, the second known as the "bone conduction receiver" allows you to hear (and only you) by a process of vibrations carried on the bone (Usually the collar bone or the bone behind the ear). The last has no sound attached to it. It is called a "Pulse Unit" and the "receiver" attached to the leg or arm indicates by pulse signals what is being sent. The latter type needs a code and cannot be applied for direct voice transmission, therefore is not so good. With all types, it is impossible for the audience to see or hear anything at anytime—unless you want them to!

The majority of these sub-miniature radios are "one way" sending units. That is to say, the assistant can speak to the performer—but the performer cannot speak back to the assistant. However, two way models can be made. Nevertheless, a fantastic amount can be achieved with the one way unit, and more often than not the assistant is in the wings or very nearby the stage and can hear what is said. Another way out of the "one way" problem is for the performer to write his answers on a blackboard which can then be seen at considerable distance. Really it is not much of a disadvantage—at least, not as much as one would suppose.

The use of radio equipment presents a lot of problems and requires a lot of skill. The apparatus may well be perfect—but it doesn't end there. You have to be well trained and have thoroughly reliable assistance. You have to work out a really good application of the equipment, a thing which might appear very easy—but which is in fact remarkably hard. The great difficulty is deciding what to do. There is so much that you can do that you tend to lose your head a bit and find yourself bringing in absolute miracles which are *too good*. So good—that any intelligent member of the audience will say to himself—that man is using a radio or he's psychic! It's not a laugh—but a very true problem as anyone who has dealt with the subject will tell you.

To conclude, if you are thinking of this type of work for a two person act (or a one man routine) then I advise you to consider the following important points:—

(*a*) Find out if the equipment is a Battery or Mains model and if it is the latter be sure you get the right voltage for your locality. It won't work on the wrong voltage. If it is a battery model, be sure you can get replacements and have spares with you at all times.

(*b*) Remember you cannot work it alone (except for very few effects) and that you must have reliable assistants. Always teach the assistant how to work the controls so that they can cope with any emergency (*i.e.* turning up the volume, switching on and checking the microphone plugs).

(*c*) Don't think that a transistorised radio will make you a mentalist. Nothing but the ability to perform and the talent of showmanship will do that. It will give you wonderful effects that you can do—but you still have to present them.

(*d*)  Before entering this field, if you are a newcomer to the subject of radio-mentalism, get some practical advice from somebody who knows —you can waste a lot of money if you try and find out the hard way.

(*e*)  No matter what model you decide to try—or what is claimed of it, always have a check just before you are ready to use to see that there is no interference from outside sources. Certain types are badly jammed by Electric Shavers, Electric Lifts in nearby buildings, other Radio equipment and the like. If you should be using one for a programme at a Broadcasting Studio—be sure to see that their equipment does not "receive" from your transmitter.

To summarise this particular type of work, we can safely say there is nothing to compete with Electronic apparatus for two person mentalism. Moreover, that with present day equipment it is a practical proposition. The use of the old telephone system involving masses of wire, terminal contacts in the floor and suchlike are obsolete—and outside of the home, there is practically nowhere that such apparatus could be used today. The only danger from the mentalist's point of view is that with the progress of science, the knowledge that sub-miniature radios exist—may become widely known to the public. Even today, similar appliances are being brought into use in hospitals for calling doctors, large stores for detective work and diplomatic embassies. The future radio mentalists must therefore aim at convincing his audience that he is not using one of those things they have heard about!

## (3) Electrical Two-Person Communicator Unit: CODE

The next step down the ladder from advanced electronic equipment—is very simple but highly effective electrical apparatus. There are two or three different gadgets that allow two people to communicate for the purpose of mental magic.

The first we shall describe is probably one of the best. It is the invention of J. G. Thompson Jr., and the original form was published in Annemann's "Practical Mental Effects" under the heading of "Moonlight Madness". This appliance was very simple; a small pocket torch battery connected by a lead to a small bulb. The bulb was affixed inside the lining of the jacket at the back—and it was possible to see the light of the bulb through the coat material. By pressing a control, the performer, with his back turned to the medium, was able to signal by light flashes—anything pre-arranged in a code.

The advantages were many; no cumbersome visible signals were used, nothing was said, complete freedom of movement was obtainable and there was little danger of being caught out as the performer naturally faced the audience whilst signalling to the medium. The principle was very clever— simple and thoroughly practical, so we decided to work more on the apparatus with the resulting effect:—

### Improved Light Communicator by Corinda

The efficiency of the Thompson electrical unit was without doubt one hundred per cent good. One snag existed, since it utilised one light bulb—a time factor limited its use for any elaborate routine. For example, to signal the number fourteen—it took fourteen individual flashes which was asking too much. Likewise, a fairly complicated code had to be devised to cover everything that could be signalled in single flashes.

Working on the idea for quite a time, I finally devised a unit which although retained the basic principle, gave, in addition—many more possibilities and cut out the time loss and need for complicated codes. The unit I describe now is really *four* of the electric light outfits built into one system. It is very simple and inexpensive to make, an excellent appliance for two person mentalism and enables you to perform some outstanding effects.

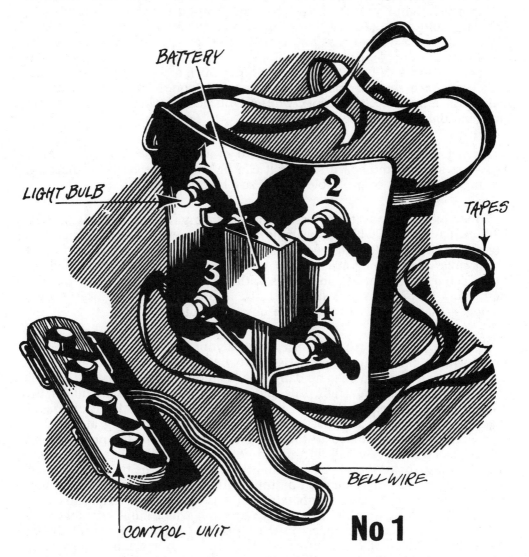

BATTERY

LIGHT BULB

TAPES

BELL WIRE

CONTROL UNIT

**No 1**

Diagram 1 shows the constructional details. A cardboard frame is used as the base because it is pliable and will bend under the coat to take the shape of the body. Fairly thick card is used and a square is cut to size 10 × 10 inches. From Woolworth's you get four small adapters and four 2½ volt torch batteries. Fix on adapter to each corner of the board so that they are evenly spaced with nine inches between each one. To the centre of the board fix a strap which will hold a 4½ volt flat torch battery. You also require a supply of thin bell wire and four push buttons similar to those used on most front doors.

The four push buttons are mounted in a row on a small strip of wood (3 ply) to make what we call the control unit (*see* diagram). To the strip of wood one fixes four safety pins which hold the unit in position on the coat when in use.  The complete control unit is about four inches long, the buttons being quite near together.

It is now necessary to wire the circuit so that when the first push button (I) is depressed, light (I) on the board goes on.  Similarly, when two is pressed, the light bulb at II goes on, III with III and IV and IV.  But—the circuit should also be wired so that any combination of I, II, III and IV can be flashed.  For example, pressing II and IV brings those two lights on together —or I, II, III and IV bring *all* on at one time.  Such a circuit is so very simple that I will save space by not giving it here.  Anyone who understands the basic principle of electrical work will tell you how to wire the bulbs to the push buttons and include the battery.

Having wired the apparatus one or two other fixtures are needed.  Four tapes are fixed to the board so that it can be tied to the back.  If elastic is let into the tape, a comfortable and steady hold is obtained.

To use the apparatus it is necessary to have the right coat.  A thick material will restrain the light which appears normally as a mere pin point at a certain position.  To allow for this, you can either wear a thin coat or cut out a small circle of the lining at the point where the bulbs will be positioned.  A tailor could make a neat job of this without any damaging effect to your best suit.  However, try it first—because more materials allow the light through—than do not.  The odds are in your favour!

To fix the apparatus ready for use, remove your jacket and strap the board on to your back.  Button the coat so that the material is then drawn fairly tight over the bulbs—there is no danger of them burning your coat.  Lead the main wire down to your right side and pin the control unit just under the coat at the point behind the right jacket pocket, where the hand can reach it easily if the arm is dropped to a natural position, hanging at the side. The Control Unit is pinned to the lining of the coat with the push buttons facing your body.  You will find that if you slip your right hand just under the edge of the coat, slightly curl the fingers and feel for the buttons, you will be able to put one finger on each button. With the hand in this position you can press any one or any combination of buttons without any danger of pressing the wrong one.  You just have to think which finger or fingers to use.  The pressure of the finger on the button is taken up by the palm of the hand on the outside of the jacket.  If there is any spare or excess cable from the board to the Control Unit, tuck it out of sight.  Also, if you find that the battery mounted in the centre of the board causes an unusual bump at the back of your coat, that can be removed and held in the hip pocket in place of having it on the board.  I prefer to have it all in one place.

Let us now consider the Light Communicator when in use.  The general set up would be to have the medium (your assistant) seated and perhaps wearing a fake (direct vision) blindfold.  She can see your back—therefore you will work near to the front (footlights) or well over to one side.  Clever use can be made of a blackboard.  Members of the audience are invited to write sums on the board which the performer, standing to the side of the board, can signal to the medium.  Diagram 2 shows the Unit in action.

254

**No 2**

### How to Code with the Light Communicator

Remember—practically all the coding that you do is SILENT. Not a word is said. To simplify the coding—all that need be known is the *type* of subject to be transmitted. For example, is it a word, a number, a card or what? If the medium expects a word—she goes on to the alphabet code and if she expects a card—then she starts looking for card code signals.

(*a*) **Numbers.** We have four lights and can actually work no fewer than TWENTY different combinations of lights. However, to use them all is not really needed for numbers so we use six combinations.

Each of the bulbs in Diagram I is numbered as you will see. When we flash Number I, we signal counts in units of ONE. Therefore if it is pressed three times it signals three. Now the next bulb is Number II so each time this flashes we count in units of two—*i.e.* 2-4-6-8, etc. The next is Number III so we count in three's and the last is four so we count in multiples of four. Now we introduce two combinations to count for five and ten. If we light the diagonals I and IV (to be remembered easily because the total is FIVE) we count in FIVES and lastly, the opposite diagonals Numbers II and IV signal TEN when both light together— or rather, units of ten like, 10, 20, 30, 40, etc. . . .

255

The result of this is that whereas with *one* light it would be necessary to press a maximum of fourteen times to signal "14" (less perhaps if a morse code was used) with the present facilities we can transmit the number "14" in no less than TWO presses. We flash once the diagonal "ten" code, and once the "four" corner bulb. We have signalled "14". Let us take a more complicated example; we want to signal "58":— Press "ten" five times, "five" once, and "three" once. A total of seven flashes and you have signalled 58. Not bad!

To transmit really high numbers we introduce a "key signal" which is "1-2-3-4" run quickly around the board at the very start. This means that the following numbers are to be MULTIPLIED and the signal ends on another "1-2-3-4". By such a means, we can signal something like "1,562" with comparative ease. The code would run:—(Key) 1-2-3-4: "ten" then "five" (equals fifteen) again "ten" (makes $10 \times 15$ now 150) and again "ten" ($150 \times 10$ now 1,500) end multiplication key with 1-2-3-4 and signal "62" by six flashes of "ten" and one "two". You have therefore transmitted the number 1,562 in eleven flashes which should take about ten seconds to send and receive.

As an alternative to sending a complete long number, you can of course signal it number by number—offering a distinct pause between each group. The medium then writes the answer on a slate or calls it out number by number. By this means a number consisting of any amount of numerals can be transmitted.

You must have a secret code between the two of you—to deal with emergencies. An often occurrence is the need for a "repeat signal". Either you make a mistake and want to correct it, or the medium missed the signal so coughs to ask for a repeat. In this case, at anytime during the signalling you can offer the "correction repeat key signal" which is four flashes of all four lights at once. This cannot be confused with the number code as meaning "16" as such a number would be signalled by "ten, five and one"—a shorter route.

(*b*) **Playing Cards.** This is a piece of cake! You have four bulbs so each one is designated a SUIT which is signalled before the value is sent on the same code as you use for numbers (Jack as 11, Queen as 12 and King as 13). The Medium knows that a *card* is to be signalled and so takes the first flash as the suit. Any card in the pack can be signalled with a maximum of three flashes (*i.e.* King of Spades:—one flash for suit, one "ten" and one "three" flash for the number 13). Any three bulbs lighted at the start signal the Joker.

(*c*) **The Alphabet.** Rather than learn long lists of objects that can be identified by a number—it is probably better to be able to spell out *any* word so that anything can be said. The easiest way to do this is for both performer and medium to learn the position of every letter in the alphabet —not much of a task. Then using the number code—you signal letter by letter. For example, to transmit the word "Beak" you send as follows: (B) one flash of "two" pause; (E) one flash of "five" pause; (A) one flash of "one" pause; and (K) One flash of "ten" with one flash of "one". All lights on for long pause—say three seconds—indicates end of word. Any letter of the alphabet can be signalled in three flashes as a maximum —excepting "Z" which takes four. Hence the speed can be pretty quick.

### (4) Summary of the Light Communicator

Considering the small expense involved in making this apparatus, it is really worthwhile. It requires quite an amount of handling and practice, but it works over a wide range with its capabilities and I consider it one of the best known methods for two person code acts. Worked on the lines suggested in the previous text, it becomes practical for stage or cabaret work and although the original model was invented for a more or less "mediumistic stunt"—the improved apparatus has the scope for use in a full act. In view of the fact that it is silent against the alternative verbal code—I would say it was better and probably involves a lot less hard work.

### (5) Miscellaneous Code Systems for Full Routines

We have dealt with three major systems of communication for full two-person acts, and before we deal with minor systems adaptable to single effects, we have space enough to outline a few more principles that given sufficient study, could be enlarged enough to be of use for a complete routine.

It will be understood of course, that any of the major systems will be of use either fully or in part for single effects—which we study in the next section of this book.

Bearing in mind the basic requirements of a full-routine code, the overall need for versatility and comprehensiveness, we can entertain the following ideas:—

### (a) Radio-Controlled Pulse Unit

During recent years toy manufacturers have developed ingenious small devices for the purpose of remote control over model ships, engines and aeroplanes. Today it is possible to buy such a remote control unit for a matter of a few pounds. It has a working range of about 1,000 yards under good conditions, it is nearly always worked from batteries and with very little modification it can be adapted to make a perfect two person communicator for mentalism.

With the control unit it is possible to guide a model boat and stop and start the motor or engine. The stop and start mechanism is all that we require. When the unit is switched on it operates a small lever at the receiving end, we can fix a lightweight hammer to this lever and by strapping the "receiver" to the leg—a code can be rapped out by constant off and on working of the control. The code will be silent and will work by feel alone. However, with a good amount of practice it will be possible to reach a fairly quick transmission speed. With two such units—two people could work wonders since it would be possible for both to send and both receive; the only possible disadvantage is that the wife can answer you back!

### (b) Action Signals

Given a lot of study it is possible to work out a silent code (non-speaking) by developing a series of visible signs and signals. The code will exclude any obvious and unusual movements and will incorporate such finer moves as the well-timed flick of an eyelash. Although it might seem pretentious to try and work out a full code for stage by action signals, in actual fact it is quite an easy matter.

There are one thousand and one *natural* movements that can be adapted to the code. Any false pose or movement of any kind should be eliminated;

257

the best way to do this sort of coding is to keep on the move all the time—but send the code signal at a prearranged moment so that the movement becomes part of a movement in itself. With this added subtlety, you move naturally before and after the signal and the code becomes literally impossible to detect. Moreover, when working on this type of code—bear in mind that every movement can be utilised. The feet—which way they point, the head, hands and body. The objects you hold and where you put them—the number of steps you take when you walk. Use the simple, natural movements of the body—you have more than enough opportunity.

### (c) Sound Reading

We have already dealt with the principles of Sound Reading in Step Two and it will be agreed that with lots of hard work at the start—an act which will defy beating can be designed. The application of Sound Reading will be somewhat easier than the practical examples given in Step Two. The reason is that *you* do all the writing and can make it easy for the medium to hear.

A blindfolded Medium sitting six feet away from a blackboard can tell ANY number, ANY word and ANY of the standard E.S.P. Signs that are written on the boards. All this is achieved by nothing less than the noise made by the chalk as it writes on the board. Let there be no doubt that this can be done, I quite often get a spectator to write a word on a slate and tell him what it is by listening to the sound. If you have any doubts—please refer to pages 38-39 of Step Two and try for yourself the test given there—it is almost impossible to fail. You will now appreciate that with the enormous advantage of having your own partner do the writing (*i.e.* slowly and deliberately)—the makings of a full act is at hand. I don't think it has ever been done—goodness knows why not—as it almost cuts out the initial hard work of code-learning. Just think, all that is done is to seat the Medium six feet away from the board—with her back to it. A spectator whispers any number in the performer's ear, he writes it on the board for all to see, the medium duplicates it on her slate. Not a word is said—the medium can be blindfolded it makes no difference. Only those people who try this will believe me—it is too easy to be true. To put people right off the scent, the spectator himself can be left to draw some of the simple E.S.P. designs which are so easy to detect by Sound Reading via chalk on the Blackboard.

Aside from direct sound reading of letters and numbers—you can transmit sound to the medium in many other ways for this type of act. One subtle example will be enough to show you what I mean.

The spectator is invited to write any number on the board—one single number so that all (but the medium) can see. This having been done, you rub it out. The medium duplicates on her slate that very number. The method is again natural and based on sound. When you rub out the number, the coarse cloth you use makes a distinct swishing noise on the board. The medium counts the number of strokes you use to rub out the number! Rub your hand on the table top to hear what I mean.

### (6) Conclusion of Major Code Systems

Enough has been said about major codes! If you can't find a method of working an act out of the systems already given—you wouldn't get anywhere on another fifty ideas. Whatever your choice may be, remember this, the secret to success is natural behaviour, talking, walking and moving as you would if you were not doing a communication act. The wise performer

258

will not stick at any ONE system, he will learn one major code and then two or three minor ones that can be introduced to divert from the main theme. The most successful two person teams have been people who could switch quickly from one Channel to another—keeping at least one ahead of the audience all the time. If you intend to work a two person communication routine—it is your job to be able to communicate with each other under almost ANY condition—utilising verbal codes, action signals and sound—with one or two of the minor codes systems given next, you will beat the best brains. May you never say a word out of place!

# PART TWO: MINOR SYSTEMS

This part of Step Eight deals with a few of the methods that can be used to signal from one person to another. There are very many methods that have been devised for a single effect or two or three tricks—and we need only cover a few which will be illustrative of the common principle.

It will be noted that we are dealing to a considerable extent with methods of *communication*. The reason is simply that nearly all two person mental acts are performances which require a secret means of communication between two people. The alternative type of two person act is simply one with a performer who does the tricks and an assistant who helps—but not to the extent of becoming a partner.

Our next concern is general methods for communication; some of these will be used in the tricks and routines given later, but it has to be understood that this list is by no means comprehensive—it is merely a series of examples which will be enough to guide you towards a general understanding.

### (7) The Pre-Arranged List of Objects or Numbers

This method of communication is not really a code—although one or two signals may have to be incorporated during the routine. It is a simple system which can be just as fooling as some of the more advanced ones. Both Performer and Medium learn a list of objects—about thirty to forty— and both learn them in the same order as they appear on the list. The objects chosen for the list will be items that are commonplace in any audience, such things as coins, combs, standard equipment from a ladies handbag, cigarettes and matches, etc. The performer must select objects from the audience that correspond to those on his list. The medium never really knows what he is holding—she only knows the order by the list and calls that out. We deal more comprehensively with this system under the tricks section of this book— where the method is seen in use.

Aside from Objects—the same idea can be applied to a long list of numbers and those of you who have read Step Three (ref.: page 78, section 3) will know that it is applied there for a routine. Mnemonics are utilised to remember the numbers in a fixed order.

### (8) Playing Cards in Pre-Arranged Order

Again in Step Three (ref.: page 73) we have explained the basic principles of the Stacked Deck. Many two person effects will be possible by virtue of having a pack of cards in pre-arranged order. The signal is easy and deceptive. The medium is allowed to glimpse one card and knowing the arrangement, can tell that the chosen one is one ahead in the stack. This may be applied to any number of cards.

## (9) Time Codes

This particular class of code is not adaptable to full two person performances but it has many uses for single effects or tests. It is particularly deceiving and is therefore a good code for challenge test conditions.

It is best described by an effect:—

Performer sits at one end of a table and medium at the other. A number is written on a piece of paper which is handed to the performer, he transmits that number to his medium who writes it down.

When the performer receives the paper he looks at it and sees the number. When ready to begin the signal, he blinks once. As he blinks, he counts "one" to himself—and the medium, seeing the signal, does the same. Now both parties count silently and with a regular beat until the performer blinks again. His second signal is given on the count representing the chosen number. It is obvious that *both* parties must count at the same rate—so we introduce a simple method to regulate the count. Mentally you are counting "one, two, three", etc. but between each number you count—you say to yourself "Concentrated" which has the effect of regulating the count on both sides; in effect, you are both talking to your self all the time—and there are no "silent" gaps which would cause misplacement.

So the count from the start goes (sending "4"):—

(Blink) "ONE - concentrated - TWO - concentrated - THREE - concentrated - FOUR (Blink).

The only requirement for this code system is good balance of timing between two people and key signals for starting and stopping. Various forms of this principle have adapted such things as the heartbeat, breathing, the noise of a ticking clock and the like—for regulating the count.

To adapt the system for more advanced work than sending single numbers, it is only a matter of working out the key signals to indicate which subject you are coding. For example, with numbers you could devise a signal which meant start at 10, 20 or 100—to cut out any conspicuous time lapse during the sending. Moreover, with playing cards—you would signal the suit first by sending the number either 1, 2, 3 or 4 (each representing a suit) and the value afterwards.

The Key Signals can be many and varied. Any form of noise or action can be introduced and the less conspicuous the key signal, the better the code.

## (10) Positional Codes

This is a very old system—but still good. To explain it simply, we will suppose that a card is chosen whilst the medium is out of the room; it is placed face down on the table and she returns and names it. Don't take that plot literally, it is not strong enough as an effect on its own—but is used just to illustrate the principle.

When the card is put on the table it is laid in a certain Position. You mentally divide the table top into squares and whichever square you use indicates the value of the card. The suit is signalled by the rest of the pack placed to one side. The diagram shows a table top and the squares are shown by the dotted lines—as you see them mentally. The card is placed in the fifth square so it would be a five and we note that the pack is in the SPADE cell.

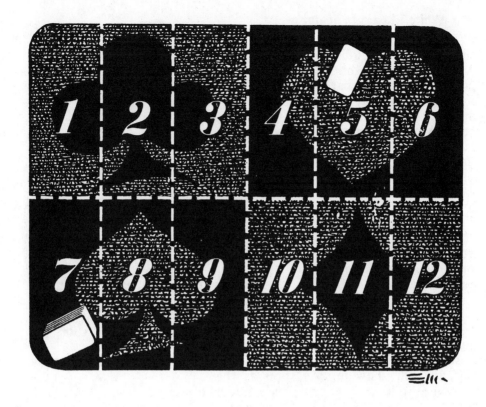

The principle can be developed to a high degree. Bringing in pencils of different colour or length, paper, visiting cards, cigarettes and matches, etc., it is possible to signal quite an amount of information. We will give an effect to illustrate the advanced form of this principle later in this book.

### (11) Graph or Chart Codes

There are a diversity of code systems based on what is called a "Code Chart". One example will suffice to illustrate the fundamentals of the principle. Under the section dealing with tricks in Step Ten, we find an effect called "Card Code" by Punx, the German Mentalist. This is a card-transmission two person stunt or routine and the method of transmission, although partly a verbal code, is also considerably improved by the use of a Key Chart. Reference to this particular trick will show you exactly how it works. Other charts for coding cards, numbers and letters have been devised as for example Al Baker's "Over the Phone" trick to be found on page 26 of Al Baker's "Mental Magic".

261

## (12) White Elastic Indicator

This is another rather old principle but it can be quite effective. A small piece of white elastic is pinned under the back of the collar (coat) or, alternatively, under the back of the jacket hem. A piece of fine thread is tied to the elastic which is then lead either through the legs and attached to the vest button at the front, or into one of the trouser pockets—or any other convenient position as may suit you.

thread under suit

When the thread is pulled slightly, the white elastic comes into view with about half an inch showing. As soon as the tension is released, it pops back under the collar with the result that by developing a code of longs and shorts (*i.e.* Dots and dashes) you can transmit to the medium with your back turned. Again it is silent and so deserves consideration.

It is quite surprising to find that at a considerable distance—this small tail of elastic is clearly visible. Since the merest touch is required to pull it into view, no conspciuous movement will be necessary and it will operate faster than you will want to use it. Another old, simple—but reliable method.

## (13) Conclusion of Part Two

Sufficient has been said to illustrate the basic simplicity of most systems of communication. In general we have tried to stick to methods which are known to be practical and although the selection is by no means comprehensive, it is more than enough to start you on the right road.

If you are genuinely interested in methods of communication between two people, you won't stick to any one code. As you progress, you will find that certain methods suit you more than others do and you will begin to enlarge upon the best suited method until you develop your own system. It is well worth remembering that if you do go to the trouble to develop your own system—it is time well spent because you alone know the answer!

Finally we end on another method which has not been awarded a heading of its own. The Stooge Signal System is one of the most powerful weapons for the two person routine. Everybody naturally centres their attention on the performer and medium which means that a third person, apparently a member of the audience, is in a remarkably strong position to give the signals. I don't think it's a matter of ethics, I wouldn't think twice about

262

using a stooge for any mental effect that I considered was worth it, I consider the extra person an added assistant who takes part in the act. Decent ethics are generally impractical in the field of Mentalism; you must be a first rate liar, cheat at least opportunity and stoop to any level which brings about a first class trick that entertains all and harms no one. Idealism is one thing, but the higher you go—the further you have to fall!

# PART THREE: ROUTINES

**(1) "The Lady is a Mindreader"'** By Corinda.

**The Effect.** Performer introduces his assistant who, he claims, has the ability to read thoughts. As an example of her powers she will conduct a test. The lady holds a card and pencil, one person in the audience is asked to stand for a moment and to concentrate on the date of any coin taken from their pocket. This person now sits, but keeps the coin in his hand. Another spectator stands and thinks merely of their date of birth. On a second card, the medium writes her impressions once more. Taking a third card, the Medium writes the thoughts of a third spectator who has been asked to stand and think "of any three numbers that enter his head".

The performer now takes the first card from the medium, explains that although any coin was selected—the medium has written a date. "Would the spectator who thought of the date please stand and tell all what were his thoughts?" As soon as he names the date, the performer reads aloud the date written by the medium and immediately hands the card into the audience for examination. It is correct—the Medium is right!

Next he takes the second card, asks the person in the audience to confirm his date of birth, or more important, the one he thought of, and again the Performer reads what was written by the Medium before handing the card into the audience. Once more the Medium has read a mind! Lastly, the Performer rightly explains that for the Medium to have divined a date on a coin and a person's birthdate—was quite an achievement—although not entirely beyond natural forces because by some strange means the medium may have known the coin and could, by a large stretch of imagination, have discovered the gentleman's birthdate. However, the last test will prove beyond all doubt the Medium's Powers—as now we deal with a set of three numbers, selected at random as they were, there could be no way of knowing beforehand what they were going to be. The performer takes the last card asking if the gentleman who thought of the numbers will stand. He asks if the gentleman will tell everybody his choice; immediately he does this, the Performer hands the card to a person in the front and says "And will you call out loud the number received by the Medium" . . . . it is the same.

**Method.** Medium writes nothing; Performer writes the answers with a Swami Gimmick as they are called by the audience. Two dozen methods of doing this are given in Step One—further instruction would be repetitive.

**(2) "Smoke Gets in Your Eyes"** By Corinda.

A few pages back we were talking about Positional Codes; this is one and it is used to good effect for a two person stunt suitable for drawing room.

**The Effect.** Medium leaves the room and during her absence, a card is chosen by one spectator who puts it in one of his pockets. This having been done, the medium is called in and proceeds to divine the name of the chosen card. First she finds the person with the card, next she names which pocket it is in and finally she names the card!

**The Method.**    We have three factors to deal with.  Which person chooses the card, which pocket he puts it in and what card it is.  The first factor, is best done by pre-arrangement; you both agree (secretly) who will be used for the test and when you come to offer the card, you go to the selected spectator.  The next factor is equally as easy.  When the medium returns she moves from person to person apparently trying to locate the bearer of the card.  Whilst this goes on, you blow your nose and when you put away your handkerchief, return it to the similar pocket as was chosen by the spectator when he put a card in his pocket.  Lastly, the card.  On the table you have an ashtray and you are smoking a cigarette when the card is chosen.  Each corner of the table represents a SUIT and you move the ashtray to the corner required to designate the chosen suit.  The ashtray is now regarded as a clockdial.  You put your cigarette in the tray pointing to a certain time.  If it is a King, keep the cigarette in the hand.  So that you both know where to start from, rotate the suits anticlockwise, H.S.D.C. starting from the corner of the table nearest to the door, and have position 12 o'clock on the ashtray-clockdial the point also nearest the door, moving around the ashtray anticlockwise.    The diagram shows a table top with ashtray and cigarette signalling "3 of Spades".

264

**(3) "All in Order"** by Corinda.

This is the application of the pre-arranged list of objects as described on page 259. To illustrate the principle we shall concern ourselves in this instance, with an effect for drawing room. Two people, namely Performer and Assistant or Medium are ready to demonstrate a power of mental communication.

The Medium sits on a chair in the corner of the room, she is blindfolded and faces the wall. The company is told to take objects from their pockets and hold them in their hands.

The performer moves rapidly around the room, en route he touches many articles of furniture, he picks up ornaments and odd things that come to hand. Every now and then he takes an object from one of the onlookers and that too is "transmitted". Each time he chooses an object—he calls out loud "What's This?" using the same words and tone every time. The Medium replies, naming the object and he then answers "That's Right" or "That's Wrong". Again there is no deviation from the wording or tone used.

**The Method.** We have already discussed the elementary principle involved; all that is left to work on is a list of objects that will be met in practically every drawing room and a few commonplace articles almost certain to be found in the pocket. However, aside from the list—there is the matter of presentation. We have to make the whole thing seem authentic and if you intend to use this type of routine, you would be well advised to pay attention to details—such things as making a deliberate mistake on one call, and coming back to it later in the pre-arranged code when it is named correctly after some "mental strain" on the part of the Medium. Also, aim at speedy presentation and make the descriptive answers humorous when the opportunity presents itself. A few examples are given alongside the list—what the Medium answers is given in brackets:—

*Suggested Pre-arranged List for Drawing Room:*

1. Clock.
2. Ashtray.
3. "Dustbin Lid", That's Wrong! ("Sorry—a Penny, I knew it was round").
4. Gentleman's Pocket Hankie.
5. Table Leg.
6. 1ST KEY OBJECT.
7. Cushion.
8. Wallet. How much in it? ("Not enough!").
9. Clock (We've had that once!)
10. Curtain.
11. Key.
12. Powder Compact.
13. Envelope.
14. Nailfile.
15. 2ND KEY OBJECT.
16. More Money. (There's a lot about tonight).
17. A Rabbit. That's Wrong (Sorry a human hair).
18. Tenth stitch down the right-hand seam of a gentleman's jacket coat!
19. Button.
20. Dust.
21. Bootlace.
22. Lampshade.
23. Pen.
24. Ladies Handbag. What colour? ("The Lady is white!").
25. 3RD KEY OBJECT.
26. Book.
28. Page 32 in the book!
29. Gentleman's Tie.
30. Performer holds up an imaginary object. ("Two inches of nothing")
31. Ring.
32. Buckle.
33. Wrist Watch. (What time does it say—I can't hear it speaking.)
34. Glass.
35. Disgusting! (Dirty hankie, book, etc.)

36. Cigarette Lighter. What type? (Bryant and Mays!)
37. Performer holds up someone's left arm. Which hand is this? (That's Left!) That's Right (No —That's Left!) Left's Right!!
38. Bracelet.
39. Picture.
40. 4TH KEY OBJECT.

Before the performance is started, both parties examine any four objects and learn them in order for the "Key Objects". When you come to these, you give added detail, *i.e.* "Ronson Lighter engraved with D.G. 1949—needs a new wick".

**(4) Reference to Effects for Two Person Telepathy in other Steps**

STEP ONE:    "Two Person Telepathy". Trick No. 10, page 19.
                "A Mediumistic Effect". Trick No. 11, page 20.
STEP TWO:    "Sound Reading". Page 38.
STEP THREE:    Use of the Mnemonic Number Code. Trick No's. 2, 3 & 4.
                "Take My Word". Page 79.
STEP FIVE:    Psychical Research Versus Mentalism. Page 146.
                Blindfold Noughts and Crosses. Page 155.
                The Blackboard Test. Page 157.
STEP NINE:    Mediumistic Stunts.
STEP ELEVEN:    Question & Answer Effects.
STEP TWELVE:    Publicity Stunts.

**(5) "Misdirectional Womentalism"** by Eric Mason. (*With apologies to the reader*).

**Introduction.** In a moment I will leave Eric Mason the honour of wording his own effect—or routine as it would be better titled. Before doing so, I think it only fair to say that I have seen Eric perform the routine on several occasions and it has been alarmingly successful. I have never made up my mind whether this success is the outcome of a good mental effect or the high sex appeal of the presentation!

**The Effect and Working.** Three people freely choose a Number, any City and a Card. They are all found to have been Predicted in advance and are discovered under novel and impossible conditions.

**Requirements.** A Beautiful girl with legs. The girl is attractively dressed and wears nylon stockings and she is "prepared" by having a white card approximately 3×4 in. concealed in the top of her stocking. Another card of the same size, but painted the same colour as the stocking is placed within the foot of the young lady's stocking—white side outwards so that it can be seen when the foot is lifted. A third card, same size and white is left on the table with a short pencil standing nearby. Lastly, a Brainwave Deck is tucked gently down the front of her dress and two handkerchiefs gimmicked to materialise a brassiere (!).

You will see that everything is simple in preparation with only the girl to carry around and it all looks indecently impromptu! Nobody will care whether your predictions are correct or not.

**Presentation.** Three people are asked to co-operate. One to say a number that comes into his head, Two names any City of the World, and Three to standby and simply concentrate on any Playing Card that comes into the mind. Make a few introductory remarks appropriate for the occasion and

266

then introduce your assistant. She stands in front of the table, turns round and bends slightly and you lift her skirt and clearly remove the card from the top of her stocking. Ask for the "thought of number" and as soon as you hear it—write it on the card with your thumbwriter (preferably a "Boon" as I get sixpence on each one you buy). Hand the card out for verification.

The first subtlety comes when the girl bends over the table. With her back to the audience, she quickly picks up the pencil and writes the name of the City on the card and then palms the card. No one will question the misdirection!

The girl turns back to face the audience. You ask her to remove her shoe and she does so—holding her foot to display the card in her stocking. She is asked to remove her stocking and take out the card, to do this she has to balance on one foot—so you "Support" her. Under cover of this action, you hold her hand and she gives you the palmed card. She removes her stocking and hands it to you bunched up. All you have to do is to turn the coloured side of the card outwards leaving it in the stocking—and show the palmed white card bearing the name of the chosen city—as though it had come from her stocking.

For the last part of the "routine" you pick up the two prepared hand-kerchieves and tie together saying that you will now attempt to appear the "thought of" card between these two hankies. You tuck them down the front of her dress. Have the card named for the first time and then pull out the ends of the hankies to disclose the brassiere! Apologise to your partner, dive down again and come out with the Brainwave Deck and finish in the orthodox manner.

The writer considered the present routine valuable because it accomplishes mentalism—when all the action is invisible and not suspected. Misdirection is used in the first part of the routine to produce the written word (whatever the subject matter). That word appearing on the card will be a mystery of the finest kind. The flow of movement up to the end is quick and amusing— the last part may be varied to taste and although some may find the dressing (or undressing!) a little indecorous—but then it can be changed to suit your taste. The principle is enjoyable in both rehearsal and performance in spite of the aesthetic twang.

### (6) Wrist Watch Code. By Corinda.

This is another subtle way in which a card is signalled to the medium. The lady (your assistant) turns her back or leaves the room whilst a card is chosen. She returns when all is ready and examines the hand of the spectator who chose the card. Apparently, by way of palmistry, she is able to divine the card.

**The Method.** I will make it very brief because it is almost self-explanatory, is that you use your wristwatch as a means to signal the medium. When the card is chosen you must know which one it is. You then patter a moment giving yourself time to set the hands of your watch to indicate a card thus:— Hour hand shows the suit dividing the clockdial into four, the hour hand can point to any of four sections each representing a suit. From 12 to 3 say Hearts, 3 to 6 say Clubs, 6 to 9 say Diamonds, and 9 to 12 say Spades. The value is indicated by the minute hand pointing to the number equal to the value of the card. Eleven o'clock is taken to represent a Jack, twelve o'clock a Queen and a King is easily dealt with by an added signal—fingers of the hand open.

Having set the watch, it should be fixed on the wrist face on the inner side of the wrist. The medium enters and you turn to the spectator and say — kindly show your palm like this (illustrate how) and let my assistant look at it. As you demonstrate you hold your hand out in front of the medium—who has nothing more to do than to look at the face of your wristwatch and note the time which tells her the card. You will have two and a half minutes delay time before the hands move out of position, which is more than enough for this purpose.

This principle may be utilised for signalling any two numbers to the medium. It will be found of use for book tests and similar experiments. Obviously one has to take care that the audience do not see you paying particular attention to your watch when you set it—but this is a simple matter if you behave casually.

## (7) The Third Man by Corinda.

I consider this to be an outstanding effect. It packs a real punch, literally flabbergasts an audience and is just right for large audiences.

**The Effect.** Medium is seated on the stage and turns her back to the audience. The performer has two Telephone Directories—both the same. He gives one to the medium and hands one to a member of the audience. The performer then gives the instructions. First, he explains that the medium will try and duplicate the action of the spectator. He tells the spectator to open the book at any page he likes—but first to examine the book to see that it is quite normal and contains some two thousand pages. The spectator finally settles on a page—the medium likewise chooses a page—and writes her page number in white chalk on a slate. Performer takes the slate—asks the spectator to call out what page he chose and then shows that the medium has written the same number. He does the same effect again with that spectator and again the medium is right. The book is now passed along the row a bit—another spectator chooses a page—again the medium is right. Finally the book is handed to a third spectator, he is told not to open it yet. This time the medium writes a number before the book is opened—then the spectator chooses a page—calls it out and has people on either side of him verify it—and the climax comes when the performer turns the slate around and shows that the medium has gone as far as she can—and predicted quite accurately the number that has just been selected!

**The Method.** Seated in the front row of the audience you have an assistant. He can hardly be called a stooge because of the amount of work he does! By any of the various code systems given, this "third man" is able to signal numbers to you. When you first hand the book into the audience—you give it to the spectator seated on his right. Naturally he looks over their shoulder and sees the chosen page. He signals the number to you—and you signal it to the medium (see "Technique" for methods). When you have finished with the first man in the audience, tell him to pass the book along the row, without much delay, your assistant grabs the book from the chap next to him and passes it to the man or woman on his left. Again he is seated next to the spectator. Finally, you ask that "someone else should take the book" whereupon the plant again acts lively and takes the book and keeps it himself.

All that remains is to make the best out of the advantageous position. You have pre-arranged a page for the finale and the plant chooses that page after the medium has written the agreed number on the slate. By this time the plant is above suspicion as several spectators have already taken part—and "Madam" has been quite successful. I don't think the method matters one iota—the effect is more than worth the price of a third man.

### (8) Musical Mindreading

**The Effect.**  On the stage is a piano—preferably a Grand for the sake of appearance. Seated at the piano is the "Musical Mindreader"—your partner, who is able to play reasonably well a pretty wide selection of musical excerpts. You, as the performer, go down into the audience with a large slate. You approach various people and ask them to whisper the name of any composer —preferably a well known one. No sooner do they tell you their choice— than the pianist starts to play something composed by that musician. Whilst this goes on, you quickly write the chosen name on the slate in bold letters —and after a few bars have been played, the pianist stops and you hold up the slate. The bulk of the audience will have recognised the tune played and will know the composer, now they see what was given and find that the pianist has by some strange means—found it possible to find the composer. This is repeated for a selection of some ten composers and each time the pianist is right.

**The Method.**  There are a diversity of methods by which this wellknown effect can be achieved. Punx of Germany worked the routine for many years by developing a system of visual signals to his versatile pianist. Each signal indicated a composer and Punx found that practically every composer had some pecularity that could be built into a visible signal, as, for example, the scratching of one ear—which would draw attention to the ear, signifying deafness—the key to Beethoven. Personal pecularities of the composers coupled with mnemotechnic situations (*i.e.* rubbing the chin meaning Barber of Seville for Rossini) made it possible for Punx and his co-worker to "accept" any composer named by the audience. On top of that, his pianist was a clever man who was able to play a popular selection from any composer chosen. Although the average musician will be able to deal with practically any composer—the system which I give now offers scope to the amateur pianist—since the choice is limited.

We have two main considerations for this type of routine. First we must be able to deal with a fairly comprehensive range of composers—including some of the lesser known people as the audience will doubtless try and stump you with an out-of-the-way genius of music. Secondly, since the whole thing depends on the fact that the audience recognise the tune and associate it with that composer, we should aim at playing the most popular and well-known piece from any works of the composer. To discover such relevant information I refer you to any good musician, record libraries, catalogues and sales statistics which to some extent, will indicate popularity trends. Choose one hundred composers dealing with those which are best known first. Choose ONE piece of music for each of the composers—the one piece that is most likely to be recognised. The pianist and you both arrange a list of the composers and form them in alphabetical order before numbering the list from one to a hundred. You write the composer list in pencil on your large slate, the pianist writes them on a music sheet and adds to his list a brief note alongside the composer which tells him the title of the piece he must play. You don't have to know the titles.

You will see now that it boils down to a code system—where by signalling any of the numbers from one to a hundred—the pianist knows what to play. The code system has to be an action signal, the effect would be ruined if you spoke directly to the pianist—in actual fact, you pay little attention to your hard working assistant. (You have enough troubles of your own!). We have already discussed the basic principle of action codes so it will not be a difficult task for you to work out a visual code system. You have the slate, a duster, the chalk, the spectator and yourself as materials for action codes; more than enough. Just one thing though, bearing in mind that the pianist has to see your signals from quite some distance, the signs should be bold and clearly definable. Just one thing remains to be said; your slate has the list of names on it but such a list is visible only at very close quarters. You can chalk over a pencil mark on a slate and later rub off the chalk. If the chalk is a soft grade—the pencil mark will not be affected. Alternatively, you can have the list on the other side of the slate—or better by far, though a little more involved, is that you (and the pianist) learn the full list off by heart, utilising perhaps a mnemonic system to help you in your work. (See Step Three).

This routine is a time-tested winner. It always appeals to an audience and it is a very fine presentation of mentalism. The musical mentalism principle has been used on stage, in the drawing room and occasionally for cabaret. It can be an act in itself—the scope is there for two hard working mentalists. As with all these effects of two-person telepathy, I give only the bare outline of working and describe the plot. All of them require study and working out with your personal presentation; don't take them literally and stop dead at the effect exactly as described, what I have given is but the starting point, the plot and basic method.

## (9) Conclusion on Two Person Telepathy

To summarise the entire subject of Two Person Telepathy, using the utmost brevity, we can say first and foremost that it is one of the finest fields of mental magic, that it is probably the most complicated and difficult to learn (outside of Mental Systems & Mnemonics) and that it takes at least twice as much rehearsal to make it successful. In a line, it's good enough to be worth all the trouble you go to—and all the time you invest.

270

# MEDIUMISTIC STUNTS

## BY

## CORINDA

### STEP NINE
IN CORINDA'S SERIES:—
## "THIRTEEN STEPS TO MENTALISM"

# STEP NINE in CORINDA'S SERIES

## "THIRTEEN STEPS TO MENTALISM"

## "MEDIUMISTIC STUNTS"

## CONTENTS

### PART ONE: TECHNIQUE

### PART TWO: PHYSICAL PHENOMENA

### PART THREE: MENTAL PHENOMENA

# MEDIUMISTIC STUNTS

With Drawings by
Eric Mason

# PART ONE

## INTRODUCTION

Those who concern themselves with the study of Mentalism will find that as they progress through the many and varied channels of magic of the mind, they encounter other branches of " The Occult " which closely relate themselves to the parent Art of Mental Magic. Mentalism in itself is a pure Art, a science of psychology, applied magic and physical experiment. However, the very nature of Mentalism is such that it lends itself to association with similar or Allied Arts. We find such things as Muscle Reading, Hypnotism, Mnemotechnics and Mediumship all find their place in association with the pure art.

Mediumship is one of the Allied Arts, one which links itself very strongly with magic of the mind, and understandably so. Mediumship and Mentalism differ in kind when the first takes on a physical nature and becomes demonstrative of actual manifestation; until then, existing as mediumship of the kind called mental phenomena, there is hardly any difference to be found.

Practically any good mental effect could be adapted to use as a demonstration of mediumistic ability; a few alterations in the general patter and usual type of presentation would make most mental effects basic material for the seance room. On the other hand, not all mediumistic effects could be adapted to mentalism simply because they are too involved, specialised or literally too far fetched for the average audience. The incredibility of the mentalists' audience is quite something, but compared with what one can get away with in the seance room—it's nothing. My experience is that there is absolutely no limit to what you can do in a seance room and I say that after a good many years at the game! (Lest that remark be misinterpreted, I had better qualify it by adding that " my game " was not as a Fraudulent Medium—a type which I consider to be the lowest form of animal.)

Mediumship or so called paranormal development is a study far too complex and vast to come within the bounds of one Step. Moreover, we are not really concerned with the subject as a whole; at this point we aim to deal with a selected number of tricks and routines that can be associated with Mentalism and a few in reverse, that can be adapted to mediumship. I have already written one book which deals specifically with the subject of Mediumship for Magicians and if you require comprehensive details of patter and presentation for Mediumistic effects, you would do best to refer to the publication.

The selection of effects given in this step have been divided into two classes; first we deal with what are called " physical phenomena " and next with " mental phenomena." We differentiate between the two by calling any effect that involves *visible action* " physical phenomena " (i.e. Levitation, Telekinesis, Materialisation, etc.) whereas any effect which is of a purely mental nature, involving action not seen by the audience, is termed and classed " mental phenomena " (i.e. Telepathy, Coincidences, Psychometry, etc.).

Before we give effects, a short section on presentation is given. This is merely a rough guide to the type of patter and style of presentation that is best adopted for these effects. In all probability, you will not seek to make a specialised performance of these effects so there is little demand for endless details; should it be that you are keen to study the field of mediumship with a view to full scale entertainment in this class (i.e. ghost shows, etc.)

275

then for your benefit I have added a list of books which I consider would be useful to further your studies of applied mediumship.

**Mediumistic Patter**

If you are going to present mediumistic effects, you may as well do it as near to the real thing as you can. The most important part of presenting these effects is the patter you use and the dramatic delivery of speech. To refer to your partner as an " assistant " would be grossly out of place. Performing an effect of this kind the "assistant" is always "the Medium". This serves as an example for substitution of phrase; you will find that most magical and mental terms have their counterpart in mediumistic jargon. The following is a compact description of the type of phrases that are commonly used by mediums:—

When you speak of Mindreading or Thoughtreading, substitute the phrase "Telepathy, Paranormal cognition, E.S.P. or Extra sensory Perception". For the magical phrase, Second Sight use the terminology "Clairvoyance" and for supernormal hearing the term "Clairaudience"; should you deal with supernormal feeling, the term is "Clairsentience".

Any equipment or apparatus should be referred to as a "Psychic Appliance" unless it is obviously something quite normal such as a Slate, when it is called a Slate. Reference to the audience or place of performance is made with phrases such as "Meeting, Gathering, Sitting or Seance" and direct reference to the audience is made by "Sitters, Friends, or The Gathering" (Avoid "Ladies and Gentlemen"). Speaking of The Dead, never use the term "Ghost". Always adopt the reference "Spirits" and for several, "Spirit Friends". The Medium usually has one special Spirit Friend called her "Guide" and when the Guide acts through the Medium, she is said to be "Controlled"—or the Guide is her "Control". Spirit Friends have a home, they are said to come from the "Spirit World" which may otherwise be referred to as "Beyond the Veil" or "From the other side". We, the Living, are said to be on "The Earthplane".

Never use the term "Trick" or "Effect". Always refer to the actions of the performance as "Psychical Experiments, Mediumship Tests, Phenomena", etc., using the specific phrase "Mental Phenomena" or "Physical Phenomena" according to the stunt.

When you use any Appliance which has been given a definite name, use that name. You may use such apparatus as "The Ouija Board, a A Planchette, Auragoggles, Spirit Trumpet, Gazing Crystal, Spirit Cabinet, Spirit Painting", etc.

Most of these appliances are devised to demonstrate various phenomena. Call the phenomena by its proper name, using such phrases as "Materialisation, Levitation, Apportation, Telekinesis, Dematerialisation", etc. In brief, to qualify these names, Materialisation means to appear as a spirit or part of one, although sometimes it may also be used to describe the appearance of something inanimate. Telekinesis is used to describe the movement of objects at a distance—usually visible movement. Dematerialisation is the magical equivalent of "Vanish" and may be taken as the opposite of Materialisation. Apportation explains the appearance of something apparently brought into the room by supernatural means. When something is apported it is generally moved from one place to another by invisible means, not to be confused with Telekenises, where the movement of an object is visible.  Levitation of course is well known to the magical fraternity. It means floating or suspending an object or person in mid air.

Any of the action phrases may be referred to as "Manifestations".  Special terms are used to describe specific manifestations like "Transfiguration" which is a visible change of appearance, usually confined to the face and is said to be caused by Spirits building their features over the medium's face. The material used for the Spirit Moulding process is called Ectoplasm or Psychoplasm and this will be found responsible for many manifestations which involve materialisation.

The partner or assistant is called "The Medium" who is said to have acquired her abilities by "Developing Mediumship".  She is said to be "Psychic" and works under "Spirit Control".  Frequently the Medium when under control is said to be "In Trance" and if the voice of the Medium is said to be the voice of her Guide or Control, then it is claimed that the Guide is talking "Through the Medium", probably delivering a "Trance Lecture" or "Spirit Message".

Finally, to gain the co-operation of the audience you request that they adopt a "Sympathetic Attitude" which will help you to establish "Harmony, Psychic Condition and Friendly Vibrations".

## Establishing "Atmosphere" in The Seance Room

Part and parcel of the Presentation of mediumistic effects, is the atmosphere that you have to create to give that authentic feeling to the programme. I would say that without any doubt, the most important aspect of presenting spooky magic, is the atmosphere that you create.  Effects hardly matter— it is surprising what little you have to do in the way of trickery—as long as the atmosphere is tense and expectant.  There is a subtle thrill to be gained from a serious and mysterious setting;  the audience become entertained with anticipation alone and given the right setting for a seance, any effect you do perform becomes quite exaggerated in its importance and achievement.  You cannot pay too much attention to creating the right "seance-room atmosphere".  A few suggestions that go a long way to helping you build up this necessary feeling are:—To get a mysterious setting, try to be unorthodox.  Avoid like the plague, anything that suggests or appears "Theatrical".  You will never really scare an audience if they feel they are watching a play, you must bring them into the seance room and make them feel they are taking part in the strange proceedings.

Your audience are human beings and you can stimulate or deaden their senses to help you create the right atmosphere.

Start off by creating a strange and exotic smell—use Joss Sticks or Oriental Incense which gives a weird, mysterious odour strange to the atmosphere. Keep the feeling on a serious plane by playing quiet background music most of the time.  No music is more likely to sober the atmosphere, than Church Organ Music.  The long playing Bach Organ Fugue (Columbia 33CX.1074, Vol. One, Albert Schweitzer) is one of the best recordings that I have found for this purpose.  Concentrate on unusual lighting schemes.  Make particular use of Red lamps for any part of the seance that involves physical manifestations.  Remember all the time, the darker the room, the better it is for you.

If you want to concentrate on serious demonstrations of mediumship, avoid any typical ghost-show activities, such things as playing Chopin's

Funeral March as background music and sticking in a Black Light Ballet with Dancing Disjointing Skeletons would make your seance what is best described as "Corny".

## The Stage Medium

Up to now we have concerned ourselves with the type of Mediumship that is as near to the "real medium" as you can get. However, it is accepted that many people will have no interest in such presentation. Quite a few Mentalists like to stick in a couple of spooky effects just to booster the act and that is as far as their interest goes.

The Stage Medium is the type that does a Second Sight Act, invariably question and answer routines, or may be one person who flings in a Spirit Cabinet routine for good value in his "Mental Programme". I think it's a bit dangerous to mix *physical* mediumship with a strictly all-mental act, but you must judge for yourself how far you can go before you make the act too incredible to believe.

There is a definite answer to any danger caused by using physical mediumship in a Mental Act, and that is to present it as a demonstration of "How Mediums Trick the Public". This is a time tested routine that always appeals to the public and they are on your side from the start. You perform a series of spooky effects which entertain and baffle the audience, but there is no necessity for telling them how you did it; on the other hand, they don't have to believe it as you have already said it is a demonstration of trickery. I would say that this is about the most favourable form of presentation for the Stage Medium. Such an addition to your programme is definitely good, even magicians doing straight magic will find that a few spooky stunts improve the show and by some strange psychology, a magician who does this sort of thing is always popular with the audience and often they credit him with far more ability than he really has!

There are many effects in this book which can be used for the purpose of Stage Mediumship (Exposé Demonstrations). Some of the best are The Spirit Cabinet Routine, Rope ties and Escapes, The Waistcoat Escape, Table Lifting, Spirit Writing and most of the Telekinetic Effects. The audience like to *see something*, so the best effects for this purpose are those which involve visible action.

## Reference to Mediumistic Effect in Other Steps

# BIBLIOGRAPHY — REFERENCE BOOKS ON MEDIUMSHIP

There are thousands of books on this subject and most of them will tie you up in knots! Very few explain how to do the actual trickery, most concern themselves with case reports and masses of "evidence for the supernatural". For the serious student of mediumship, I offer a selection of books that I consider are most practical. Some are listed because they offer historic facts, some a close study of the language used by mediums and other for their value as technical references on effects and schemes used by our "gifted brethren".

(1) *Searchlight on Psychical Research*, by Joseph Rinn.

Undoubtedly a valuable work for practical information. Rinn associated himself with Harry Houdini in various cavorts to expose fraudulent mediums. I recommend this book to anyone interested in the subject—it is both entertaining and educational.

(2) *Modern Spiritualism*, by Frank Podmore.

Two giant volumes that although very dry and factual, give what is probably the most comprehensive study of all round Spiritualism that has ever been written. All the famous mediums are described and not many of the tricks of the trade have been missed. Particularly good for information on table turning, spirit moulding, materialisation and the usual physical phenomena.

(3) *The Drama of Life After Death*, by George Lawton.

One of the best books for an unbiassed historic account of Spiritualism and other forms of Mediumship not associated with the Religion. Excellent for those who wish to understand the many weird and wonderful names invented by the mediumistic.

(4) *Behind the Scenes With Mediums*, Abbot.

Invaluable as a reference for technique. Particularly good for rope ties, slate routines, spirit cabinet effects and general physical phenomena.

(5) *Mediumship for Magicians*, By Corinda.

This book is by no means comprehensive but it is aimed at starting people (with a basic knowledge of magical principles) on the road to holding a complete ghost show. It's a good place to start if you are just entering the field—I will say no more lest I be accused of advertising!

(6) *The Dead do not Talk*, By Julian Proskauer.

Rather a bitter attack on mediums and their activities, but enlightening and most informative to the serious student.

(7) *Spirits in the House*, By Chislett.

Mr. Chislett writes a full account of his "home ghost show"—a performance which he gave regularly to visitors to his home. His book is particularly useful for information concerning Spirit Paintings.

(8) *The Fraudulent Mediums Act*, 1951. (H.M. Stationary Office).

Not a book—but the official publication which everybody dealing with this work should read and understand. As a matter of interest, there is also *The Hypnotism Act*, 1950, which would be worth reading whilst dealing with the other Act. There is no danger of you breaking the Law by performing mediumistic effect for *entertainment* purposes; but you do as well to know the Law as many times you will be asked a question that deals with the subject and it is the job of the mentalist to know about everything that deals with his Art.

This list should be more than enough to give you a thorough grounding on mediumship. If you read all these books and learned the tricks therein, you would know enough to out-fox the Fox sisters who "founded" Spiritualism in 1884!

## PART TWO: PHYSICAL PHENOMENA

### (1) "Spirit Writing"

Many years ago there was a famous Fraudulent Medium, a man who specialised in producing written Spirit Messages on slates. He worked from a platform, first giving an answer to questions service and then climaxing the proceedings by getting the spirits to write an answer or message for one of the gathering. This man was at the top of his trade and new most of the tricks of the trade and a few more. One day a magician attended one of his meetings and openly challenged him to get a spirit message for him! That magician was a man well known and his name is still a big name in magic.

The medium accepted the challenge, which was not an unusual thing in those days and agreed to produce a spirit message on any slate that the magician cared to offer. The next night the magician turned up with the slate; this the Medium inspected and cleaned, gave back for examination to the magician who was then told to sit on it. In due course the magician was told to stand and was asked by the medium if he would be satisfied if a spirit message had now been written. The magician was forced to agree that under these conditions, such an event would be remarkable. He was then told to turn the slate over and see if anything was written there—and chalked across the slate was his mother's maiden name!

The secret of this amazing test was a closely guarded one for many years. Strangely enough, it does not seem to have been picked up by magicians and used magically. It is a method of producing a Spirit Message on any slate— even one that is offered although you are not likely to be asked to do it!

**Method.** Those who know anything about Chiropody will know that you can get small sticks of Silver Nitrate. These sticks are exactly the same diameter as a common slate pencil and although silver nitrate is a white chemical, it decolourises on exposure to air and turns grey to black—exactly the same colour as a slate pencil. A gimmick is made by breaking one stick of silver nitrate in half and likewise, one slate pencil. Half of each are then stuck together to form one pencil about five inches long. Looking at it, everything seems normal. The only other requirement is a sponge that has been moistened with a saturated solution of sodium chloride (Salt water). The silver nitrate sticks are poison and should not be handled unnecessarily as the chemical has a caustic nature. Suppose you wish to "materialise" the name "Washington". The slate is taken and the medium proceeds to check that the "writing surface" is smooth and adaptable to the experiment. To do this, she merely scribbles all over the surface. The mass of scribbling is done with the slate pencil end of the gimmick—then, with a little mis-direction she turns the gimmick and boldly prints the name "Washington" across the centre of the slate. The name cannot be seen as it is confused with a mass of scribbled lines! Next, having satisfied herself that the slate is suit-able, she takes the sponge and wipes it clean. In doing so, the slate pencil markings are removed but the silver nitrate markings stay there although they cannot be seen whilst the slate is wet and black. Immediately the silver nitrate is brought into contact with the salt water—a precipitate of white silver chloride is formed which closely resembles white chalk. To force the drying of the slate, which is given to the spectator in damp condition, the subject is told to sit on it or, funny but practical, to "stick it up their jumper". If the latter is done the heat of the body soon dries the slate!

Chemical magic is usually a touch-and-go affair, but this particular test is one that is well worth doing as the conditions seem impossible and the effect is almost supernatural.

### (2) Spooky Stunts for a Blackout

Nearly all Ghost shows or demonstration seances climax the proceedings with a total blackout. Here, at the end of a lot of "conditioning" the audience will be inclined to accept all sorts of simple things as weird and frightening. The total darkness allows you to do all sorts of silly things which because you suggest are created by supernatural means, give everybody the creeps! On paper and viewed in the cold light of day, these things look downright silly, but you see them from a different point of view when your nerves are not too good!

### (3) Astral Signs

Cut out some squares of cardboard and paint matt black on both sides. Then paint on one side only with a good quality luminous paint—any sign that you please. Crosses, squares and circles will do. Hang these cards by a thread from a reaching rod, lazy-tong extension rod or pole and whirl them around. The effect created is the rapid appearance and disappearance of white signs in mid air.

### (4) The Spirit Hand

The same principal as above is used but you paint a hand with the fingers open on one side of the card and with the fingers closed on the other. If the card is whirled rapidly the hand appears in mid air with the fingers appearing to grasp at the audience!

### (5) Cardboard Skeletons

Cardboard skeletons are very easy to make and in the dark look as good as anything you could dig up in a cemetery. Paint them in luminous paint on black card and dangle them from threads suspended across the room. By jerking the thread you can make them dance and for a really horrible effect, try tearing one up in view of the audience—it looks as though the skeleton falls to pieces.

### (6) Fire Balls

If you throw a handful of luminous ping-pong (table tennis) balls into the audience—invariably they pick them up and throw them on again. Soon the room becomes full of travelling lights and weird bouncing noises!

### (7) " It "

This is something that has been used very successfully for creating a spooky effect without any apparent means of doing so. You have a luminous coat button in your mouth. You are seated on a chair and when the lights go out you open and close your mouth—the effect is surprising. If you are tied in the chair you can still do it and the effect is more perplexing. As a variation of this—you can have the sole of your shoe painted luminous and wave your foot in the air—although if this is used, it is not so easy to pre-expose the luminous surface without sitting at an odd angle!

### (8) Ectoplasm

Another materialisation that can be performed whilst you are tied in a chair is made possible by treating all but one corner of your pocket hankie with luminous paint. The hankie is then tucked in your top pocket (jacket outside) with the non-luminous corner sticking out. You are tied with your hands behind your back and the lights go out. Reach forward and catch the tip of the hankie in your teeth. Slowly draw it out producing a greenish glowing material which looks very ghostly. When it is all out of the pocket, wave it in the teeth and then tilt your head right back letting the hankie fall over your shoulder and down the back where the hands can grasp it and tuck it into the hip pocket. Alternatively, drop it in your lap and reach under your legs (stand slightly) to pull the hankie through to the back and out of the way. Few people will ever notice the absence of your pocket handkerchief when the lights go on!

### (9) Apports

With a fourpenny pea shooter and some peas you can have a lot of fun and cause quite a bit of disturbance. It is better to shoot the peas at a wall or at the ceiling so that they make a tapping noise, rather than to risk hitting someone in the eye by aiming shots at the audience.

### (10) Spirit Lights

Many weird effects can be achieved by brushing wire wool across the terminals of a pocket torch battery. Small sparks of light are emitted which can appear quite mysterious.

### (11) The Icy Hand

There are two ways of doing this and both are sensationally creepy. Have a wet sponge which you touch gently to the hands and faces of the sitters—it's a most unpleasant feeling in the seance room! The next method is even more horrible. Have a rubber bag in your pocket with blocks of ice from the 'frig in it. Leave your hand in the bag holding the ice until it gets really cold and wet—then go up to someone and take their hand! I can assure you they think they are shaking hands with the dead—and they don't hold on for long!

### (12) The Message in Mid Air

Another sensational stunt which looks like nothing on earth is to let the audience see the spirits write a message in mid air. To do this is quite simple. A fairly large blackboard and a stick of luminous wax is all that is required. You mix luminous paint with beeswax to form a stick of chalk. When you write with it—the writing appears slowly as you do it letter by letter—and the board cannot be seen so the writing suspends itself in mid air! To climax this you can turn the board around very quickly and the writing "dematerialises".

### (13) The Spirit Candles by Corinda

I have given many demonstration seances and of the numerous effects that I use, this is one that never ceases to create a stir. Usually I have the medium seated at a table working a ouija board with a committee member. The ouija board spells out a message from the other side which tells all that "they" are willing to try and produce some physical phenomena. Three candles light the table and the board spells out "Watch the candles". One by one they go out. Each time one goes out it gets darker and more creepy!

The method is painfully easy. Get three 1 by 6 in. white candles. With a sharp pair of scissors, groove out right down one side of the candle until you reach the wick. Remove the wick and with a hot knitting needle enlarge the hole through the centre of the candle. Now insert a lighter wick leaving the small wire drag-through on the wick. Allow about a quarter of an inch to stick up at the top, just like a normal candle wick and then carefully drop a blob of wax on to the top of the wick which will lock it in place until the candle is lighted.

Put a very fine strip of wood in the slot made by the scissors and then cover the wood completely with wax from another candle. It can now be viewed from all sides and nothing is to be seen. Prepare three candles thus and having done so, next obtain a *heavy* board and drill three small holes about four inches apart along the board. Get some fine thread or nylon and pass it through these holes fixing one end to the wire part of the lighter wick in the candle. Stand the candles thus threaded right over the holes in the board and wax them in position so that they will not move.

The board is placed on the table and the three "pulls" lead off to an assistant. (Usually a co-operative member of the committee!) Now when the candles are lighted the wax at the top melts but remains in sufficient quantity to prevent the wick falling down the tube. If however, the thread is pulled, the molten wax is not enough to hold the wick back and is therefore pulled down into the candle and out goes the flame. The apparatus is crude but reliable and the effect, which matters more than the apparatus, is really terrific for the seance room.

## (14) The Waistcoat Escape

This is a trick that I have used for many years and found a good standby for doing a stunt with little preparation. It is ideal for parties but can also be used in a more serious vein.

You borrow a gentleman's waistcoat (or use your own), remove your jacket and put the waistcoat on and then replace your jacket. You explain to the audience that you will demonstrate an old medium's trick of escaping from a restriction; that you will remove the waistcoat whilst leaving the jacket on *and* whilst a member of the audience holds one of your hands *all the time*. It cannot be done—so don't try and work it out!

When you put the waistcoat on, button it up properly and holding your hands in the air turn round slowly to let everybody see that it is being worn in the authentic manner. Next don your jacket and button that down the front. The action must of course be screened from the audience, so you borrow a sheet or blanket (a table cloth will do in emergencies) and have two people hold it up forming a screen. Before you step behind the screen, have one of the assistants take hold of your left hand and tell him to grasp it firmly and not to let go at any time. Step behind the screen which should be held so that your head and feet are left in view, allow the hand also to be seen held by the spectator. As soon as you are out of sight you go through the following contortions:—

(*a*) With the free hand unbutton the jacket and slip it off and down the left arm.

(*b*) Likewise, unbutton the waistcoat and slip it on to the left arm.

(*c*) Reach over to the left and pull the jacket through the left arm hole of the waistcoat making sure that it does not twist in doing so.

(*d*) Slip the right arm back into the jacket and button it again at the front.

(*e*) Bring the waistcoat on again—but this time it is OVER the jacket and not under. Quickly button it up along the front and the work is done.

Still standing behind the screen you explain to the audience that for many years the famous medium baffled the world with this escape—but tonight you have done just the same *and* gone further still—not only have you taken it off but you have put it back on again! (The audience suppose they will see no change!) Quickly now push the sheet aside and step into view saying—

285

"And to make it more of a problem, I have put it on over the coat just for a change!" People really believe you took it off and then put it on again—when in fact it never comes off at all. The drawing shows the basic moves made by the performer as viewed from behind the screen or door.

To summarise this stunt, it is really a paradox. When you know how it is done there is nothing in it—but I can assure you that if you had seen it and did not know the method, you would not find it easy to solve the problem. For best effects it is essential that you move quickly. I find that with a good waistcoat (one that has fairly large armholes) I can do the complete routine in just under fifty seconds. If you take too long, the routine drags so aim at a breakneck pace. Also, from time to time I have been unable to improvise a screen and when this happens you simply step outside the door and push your arm into the room allowing all to see the spectator holding your hand. The door is left ajar because it can be very painful when somebody closes it with your arm in that position!

### (15) The Stage Spirit Cabinet

### Routine

The Stage Cabinet Routine differs from the Seance Cabinet Routine. The first has to be quick and presented with an air of comedy; the second is deadly serious and dramatic—also usually a slow affair.

Normally the Stage Cabinet Routine consists of a demonstration of how mediums make the spirits manipulate musical instruments. A large cabinet, something like a beach tent is erected in the centre of the stage. The medium sits on a chair in the cabinet and is tied to prevent him using his hands. A small table bearing an assortment of musical instruments is placed within the cabinet and an assistant stands ready at the front.

At a given signal, the assistant quickly draws a curtain across the front of the cabinet and the very instant the front closes—the instruments begin to play! The audience hear several of them playing at once—and then the assistant quickly pulls back the curtain only to show all the instruments still on the table and the medium still securely tied in his chair! Again the curtain is drawn and again the music (of a kind) is heard; this time however, the spirits get a bit frustrated and the instruments begin to come hurtling over the top of the cabinet crashing to the floor. The curtain is again pulled back and the table is empty —all the instruments have been apported out of the cabinet but the medium is still firmly tied. In addition to playing with musical instruments other phenomena may be included. A spirit message is made to appear on a large blackboard, the medium changes places with another person, in Annemann's "Practical Mental Effects" there is a change of coloured shirts that is quite good and so on.

If you choose which musical instruments you use—by careful selection you will find that it is possible to sound many of them at the same time. The medium, although apparently secured can escape very quickly and get back into the tie. He has freedom of his hands, feet and mouth. First you have a piano accordian (any old second hand one will do, costing very little) you sound this by slipping one foot into the strap at one end and pulling up and down with one of the hands. The fingers operate the keys in doing so. With the other hand pick up any mouth instrument—a flute is quite good— and stick that in your mouth gripping it with the teeth. With the free hand again grab a large handbell and shake it like hell to create a real din! With the unused foot—tap on a drum giving a base rhythm to your unearthly concerto. Never mind about playing tunes or anything recognisable. To sound the instruments is enough and if anyone wants to know what was played, tell them it was Symphony No. 17 just written by Beethoven in the Spirit World. Have one extra instrument lying on the table that you use only for signals to your assistant. For example a hooter. Drop the others on the table and pick up the hooter and sound two "honks". Immediately your assistant counts five and then whips back the curtain. In the count of five you drop the hooter and slip back into the tie.

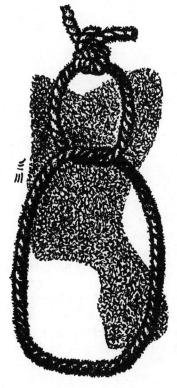

The most effective tie that I know is one taught me by The Great Levante who made a leading feature of the Spirit Cabinet Routine in his Stage Show. The performer sits on a chair and brings his feet together. About six feet of white rope is used for the tie. First it is passed under the performers knees and then crossed once on top. The performer puts his hands together as though praying, and places them over the cross above his knees. The Rope is then tied over his wrists with several knots. It is a simple matter to gain slack when the tie is made, all one has to do is to part the knees a little. Later when you want to free the hands, just brings the knees together and the rope goes loose; when you put them back in the loop, again force the knees apart which makes the tie appear tight and still secure. Diagram A and B show the position adopted for the tie.

### (16) "Telekinecards" By Punx

**Effect**

The performer prepares for an experiment in Telekinesis by giving an introductory talk on the subject. He connects Telekinesis with the power of the mind to move an object at a distance; he hands out five cards for examination and then has them mixed again. Five people each take one of the cards and do not reveal what card they have taken. The cards are E.S.P. Sign cards each bearing a different symbol.

Now the performer takes a fairly large wooden board which is a glorified card stand. He sits down and holds the board at the top; along a ridge at the front stand five duplicate E.S.P. cards facing the audience.

He now asks any person with a card to look at it and then to gaze at the duplicate of their design and to think that they have the power to move that card. Suppose they hold a square—they concentrate on the square on the performers board. As they watch, slowly and dramatically the E.S.P. Square card begins to move and it rises from the stands at the front, moves right up the board and then returns to its place on the ridge. The performer asks which card "was thought of" and the spectator names the square!

This is repeated with all five cards with correct results every time. On the last card—it rises to the top of the board whereupon the performer takes it and holds it up asking if that was the chosen one. This having been done, the spectators may come forward and examine the board if they so wish—it is in no way faked.

## The Method

"Telekinecards" is a trick which utilises a very old Spirit Cabinet principle that is known as "The Third Hand". If you look at the drawing given you see the board just as the spectators see it. Apparently the performer holds it with both hands one at each end along the top. In actual fact the left hand is a dummy, just a set of bent fingers that can be quickly clipped on to the edge of the board. The right hand is real—but it is held in exactly the same manner as the dummy. This means the performer, screened behind the board which rests on his lap, is in a position to move his other hand to whatever purpose he likes! The cards are lined with razor blades and the performer has a powerful magnet. The board is three-ply wood which does not obstruct the magnet from moving the cards where you wish. It is as simple as that—the only points to watch carefully are; make a good imitation of the hand—gloves could be used, but they are not anywhere near as good as a first class hand. Use a powerful magnet (about 12 lbs. lift) and stick a good amount of razor blades in each card. (Step Two deals with making magnetic Cards).

You could ask the audience to call out any card which you then force to move. But the effect is doubled if it appears that you yourself do not know what one has been selected. The easiest way to do this is to mark the set of cards that the audience take. Make bold and clearly definable markings on the back of their cards—they are not going to inspect them for trickery so make nothing of it.

The board is rested on your lap to take the weight. It should be size 1 ft. 6 in. by 2 ft. of smooth three-ply wood or smooth hardboard. Along the base run a strip of wood to form a ledge. To show the cards clearly, paint the board black. The second drawing shows the operation of the board from the back view as seen by the performer.

## (17) The Palladino Table Lift

There are several methods of Table Lifting which is an effect highly suitable for Stage Mediumship or Seance room. It can be presented as quite a mystery and the only trouble with the effect is that quite often the performers are tempted to go too far and a solid mystery becomes a "lark".

The Palladino method is for one person. Palladino was a famous medium who did a lot of table lifting; she had a special lightweight table that could be manipulated in the semi-dark by lifting it with her foot. Otherwise, there is the pin fake method which is very effective for single person operation—but you must have a light table. (A balsa wood one would be perfect).

In the top of the table you drive a pin with a fairly large head which is left protruding about one eighth of an inch. It is too small to be seen. On the middle finger of the right hand you have a ring which is slotted on the underside to fit the pin head. (See Diagram). It is simply a matter of engaging the ring on the pinhead as you place both hands on the table and then lifting. If you have two of these rings and two pin-heads—you can start with both hands on the table top, whilst floating in mid air, remove one hand and leave the table apparently adhering to the other. Replace that hand (engaging the other head as you do so) and free the one just used to support the table. Because of the amount of leverage you can get with the fake ring—you can, if you wish, pull out the pins at the end which makes the table free for inspection. It is not imperative that they are allowed to examine the table.

### (18) Table Lifting with Arm Hooks

This method requires an assistant, you cannot work it alone. Both you and your assistant are equipped with a set of gadgets called "Arm Hooks". These are strong steel hooks that are strapped to the wrist forearm. If both you and your assistant have two of these, one on each arm, you will be able to lift an amazing weight between you.

The best way to present this is to have four people, each sit at one side of the table—but you be sure that the assistant sits opposite you. As they all place their hands on the table with fingers stretched out, etc., you engage the hooks on the edge of the table and from then on its a matter of presentation. You will find that the sleeves cover the Arm hooks and make them very hard to spot unless the audience see directly under the table. (See diagram.)

### (19) Table Lifting with Waist Hooks

This is another two person method (or more) and by this means a really heavy table can be floated or, with very strong waist hooks, you can float a table whilst a small person sits on it! It has the advantage that both hands are free at all times although they must be used to steady the table whilst floating.

You have a strong leather belt about 2 in. wide. At the point around your waist in front of the stomach, you have a small steel hook. This engages on to the edge of the table as you stand and lean forward. Your assistant (opposite) does the same.  If you lean back and push on the table top with both hands, you have a very strong lifting position—so much so, that if any spectators are joining in around the table—they will not be able to push it back to the floor.  The table cannot be lifted very high as is obvious—but it can be raised well clear of the floor and moved around the stage with good effect.

### (20) "The Haunted Ball"

This is strictly a drawing room or seance room stunt—and cannot be done on the stage.  In effect, you have a card table (although almost any table will do) and it may be examined before the experiment and after.  It is in no way prepared.  You have also a table tennis ball which can be examined before and after—it too, is unprepared.  A spectator places the ball on the table—which is stood in the middle of a well lit room.  No one goes near the table and people can stand all round.  The Medium, demonstrating Telekinesis, proclaims that he will move the ball at any time suggested by the audience.  He waits until he is told to try and then stares profoundly at the ball.  Slowly it moves and gaining speed rolls to the edge of the table and falls to the floor.  Immediately everybody can examine everything and they are not likely to find the answer!  The Medium stands some ten feet away from the table whilst the effect is demonstrated.

### The Method

This is another of those ridiculous methods that achieve such good results.  It costs very little to rig up and it is quite reliable.  The room must have a carpet and you need a platelifter with a long extension of fine rubber hosing.  Run the plate lifter under the carpet leaving the bulb somewhere in the middle of the floor.  Note the spot where it is by looking for some marking in the design of the carpet.  The other end run well away from the centre of the room and leave that too (with the second bulb) in a place that you can identify.

Borrow a table, the lighter the better and have it examined.  Move it to the middle of the room and in placing it there—be quite sure that one of the legs stands over the bulb under the carpet below.  Now take up your position near the other end of the lifter and have the ball placed near the middle of the table.  To make it move, you only have to tread gently on the bulb below your foot and the table is lifted slightly causing enough tilt to make the ball roll off.  The tilt, which is about one inch is too small to be observed by the most observant watcher.  Yet it is quite sufficient to cause the ball to move.  If you like, you can lift your foot before the ball drops off the table, which will stop it at the edge.  Also, if you care to repeat the experiment, move the table so that a different leg stands on the lifter—and then the ball will roll in a different direction on the second showing!  If you try this as I have, you will find that an ordinary platelifter will lift quite a heavy table—it is more than surprising to find a small rubber bulb will lift a medium oak table—but it does.

Finally, if you do work with an assistant—make full advantage of the situation by having her work it whilst you stand wherever the audience decide—even out of the room if they insist!  One thing that must be watched all the time if the audience surround the table, is that no one of them stands on the feed pipe.  This would block the air supply and spoil the effect.  I have used this principle for challenge effects—where people defy you to demonstrate telekinesis—it has always won the battle for me!

## (21) "Spirit Guide"

One of the best methods of appearing and disappearing what seems to be a ghostly figure, is to paint a *crude* six feet tall spooky picture on a large black curtain or roller blind. The "picture" is a life size cowled figure painted in good quality luminous paint; alternatively an animal or a shapeless blob can be used.

To operate, it is simply a matter of slowly unfolding or unrolling the picture and then twisting it about in the dark to cause weird movements of the cloth. The effect is very good, the constant change of the shape causes people to imagine that they see all sorts of things materialise. Again, this is one of the simple things that look silly in daylight—but incredibly different in the dark and mysterious atmosphere of the seance room.

## (22) "The Dead Hand Writes"

This is another visible effect which has all the qualifications of good spooky magic. It is the glorified presentation of a Living and Dead Test—but how it's glorified!

In effect, a sitter is invited to write five names on a card—and to make any one of them the name of a Dead Person. He does not say which of the names is the Dead name nor does he reveal its position on the list. The card is taken and placed on a board. A box is brought in, it is opened and with great care a Hand is unpacked from cotton wool in which it is wrapped. The hand is laid on the board and a pencil placed between the fingers; a square of black cloth is laid gently over the hand and all is set.

It is suggested that in order for any "Communication" to be received in the form of writing, it is necessary for our Spirit Friends to Control the mediums hand or be allowed to manipulate a hand. The hand used for your experiment was "lent by a Museum" (don't say whether it is a dummy or an amputated real one—leaving a nasty inference!). For the test, the Spirits will form an ectoplasmic arm to join the hand (which may or may not become visible) and having done so, will write or make a mark on the card. So that it may be known that the communications is from Beyond, they will identify the dead name with their mark of the cross, a thing which would be quite impossible for another person to do!

The committee joins hands and wait in solemn silence. They watch. In due course there is an obvious slight movement of the cloth, this intensifies and becomes a definite upheaval that looks very much like a hand writing and moving under the cloth. Then it stops and the cloth is still. The Medium goes to the hand and lifts the cloth, takes the card and looks at it and sees a mark has been made. (Indicated to the audience by surprise on the face). Excitedly the medium calls to the sitter "We have a result—truly a manifestation—but they may be wrong—which name was the dead one?" The sitter replies as the Medium hands him the card with a flourish that conceals the neat little black cross just made with a Swami Gimmick!

All that remains is the working of the hand. In brief, get a heavy, old rubber or wooden hand (window display model will do) and about twenty feet of thread. Run the thread across the board a la Rapping Hand, Floating Ball and similar effects and lead it off to some place where you have a stooge, assistant or committeeman ready to gently tug at the right moment. Alternatively, for one-man working; run the thread from the *cloth* up to the ceiling and through a small hook. Lead the end back and anchor it to a chair

293

standing nearby. Thus when you back away from the board you may casually rest your hand on the chair and in doing so engage the thread. Screening the movement with your body by a slight turn, you tug away merrily until you think the illusion has been created. Another method is a platelifter —but I dare not venture into that one or I stand to be accused of having platelifters on the brain! Thread is good—thread works and that's all that matters. Never think twice about the method as long as it works; remember at all times you are demonstrating *effects*—not *how they are done*.

### (23) "Corinda's Ghost Walk"

There is an old maxim for ghostworkers that is as true today as it was in the beginning; "The more Ghosts in a Ghost Show—the better it will be". This is absolutely the last word in man made Ghosts. The apparatus seen in daylight is a laughable heap of nonsense, but paraded in the gloom of the seance room—it is the ultimate in spookery.

In effect, the performer (usually the Medium) reaches the point where it is necessary to climax the proceedings—and naturally the aim is to make this the very best you can offer. The onlookers have seen mild manifestations, ghostly effects have come and gone but nothing *typical* of the classic ghost has been seen. Now we come to such an effect. Our Medium prepares the path by delivering an address in which she tells that for the final experiment, she will call upon the Spirit World to send a fully materialised form. She explains that all must be patient, everybody must join hands and under no circumstances should anybody touch anything that materialises. (By the way, there are several reasons why people should hold hands and one of them is so that they will not be tempted to grab at your ghost and thus expose the ruse! Other reasons are best left to the imagination of the Reader!)

The gathering sit in near total darkness waiting for the materialisation of a Spirit Friend. Quiet organ music is to be heard in the background and the Medium is to be seen breathing heavily in trance condition. (To affect Trance Condition, flop into a chair and act as though you have just drunk a bottle of Gin!). Slowly but surely the door creaks open and then in glides a full size Ghost. This ghost can be anything from five to ten feet tall, it flows into diverse shapes as it moves, sometimes touching the floor, sometimes floating in mid-air. It glows with a greenish light (which is said to be ectoplasm) and it does not flop around within two feet of the door—No! It comes right *into* the audience, flows within inches of them—they see it and some see through it. More! It touches them with icy cold fingers and whispers or groans odd sayings into the ear of any disbeliever! Then it oozes back to the centre of the floor and there, in full view of the audience, slowly begins to dematerialise until it shrinks in size from feet to inches and finally vanishes completely. The lights go on—the Medium recovers from her ordeal with the Spirits (not Gin!) and nothing is to be seen which explains such unorthodox goings-on!

Before disclosing the modus operandi I will relate briefly a memorable story concerning my apparition. It happened some years ago whilst my time was spent in cavorts to expose Fraudulent Mediums. Very few were to be found that ever did anything worth exposing—but one man (a Medium) did occasionally, and for the right price, "materialise" a Spirit Friend. On one of these occasions I had the good fortune to "get in" with another friend. We waited throughout the usual rigmarole until "Mr. X" declared that "they" would come through—and at this he departed into a large screened Cabinet.

294

In due course a rather small misty shape emerged from the cabinet and uttered unintelligible sentences which sounded remarkably like the Medium talking with a peg on his nose! In time the little one disappeared and another slightly larger came forth. However, more or less as this appeared—so did something else! Nowhere near the Medium but well within the seance room when it was seen—a six foot monster groaning and slithering towards the cabinet was soon spotted by the Medium who rapidly came out of his trance and dashed from the cabinet quite horrified that there in his seance room was a ghost that he didn't materialise!! Nothing can be more embarrassing to a ghost worker—than to have a ghost turn up that isn't "one of yours"—and our spook, which we took along, nearly gave the Medium heart failure. That was how the ghost walk came into being.

To make such a monster as I have described, one requires about six yards of fine white net or nylon material (54-in. wide). This material one forms into a crude shroud—cutting a billowing head cowl and allowing the rest to drape loosely. No arms are required. The shroud is then daubed with a good quality liquid luminous paint and for best effects, this is done in a haphazard manner for strangely enough, the rougher the painting the better the ghost.

The next requirement is an assistant who wears all BLACK clothing. Over his shoes he wears a pair of black socks which allow footsteps to be deadened. The appliance is exposed to a bright light (electric will do) and then donned by the assistant. When ready he has but to enter the room and go as near as he likes to the sitters. It is strange that the luminous net over black cloth creates an illusion of transparency, which in effect makes the ghost look entirely vapour. To make the monster more fiercesome, the assistant wears a skull mask that has been similarly treated with luminous paint and a pair of white gloves that have been treated adds the finishing touch.

If you so desire, the Ghost can be materialised actually in the seance room. All you have to do is to pre-expose the shroud and accessories and stuff them into a black bag. In full view of the audience (with the lights out that is) you pull out the material bit by bit, which allows the Ghost to slowly form. From then on it can be donned by an assistant in the room (perhaps from the audience) or may be paraded around without being worn at all. Finally, the black bag is used to dematerialise the ghost. It is simply stuffed into the bag—but for best effects, slowly bunch it up first to create the illusion of diminishing in size before entirely dematerialising. Sometimes I have had the black bag tied to a black rope—and after the ghost has been "bagged" an assistant pulls the bag away into another room or into some convenient hiding place. At the worst, to use a current colloquialism, you can "stick it up your jumper"—there is little bulk to it all when well bunched up.

As a final word on the Ghost walk I feel I should add that, on occasion I have used the apparition to entertain friends at home—just for the fun of it. This I no longer do as experience has taught me that it is too frightening and I think it should be confined to the seance room where people expect and hope to be scared. Under no circumstances should it be demonstrated to any children—it would be liable to cause considerable harm.

## (24) Spirit Moulding

In the History of Spiritualism we find that some "investigators" have managed to get the Spirits to mould their hands and faces in wax. The method is a bit messy but undoubtedly sets an air of mystery as to how such a thing could be done.

On the seance room table the medium places a bowl of luke warm molten paraffin wax. (Low melting point wax is obtainable from suppliers to Histologists). Alongside she places a bowl of cold water. The lights are put out and the sitters wait. After a while the lights are put on and now to account for slight noises which happened in the dark, we find a perfect hand moulded in wax—floating in the water bowl. It could not have been made by the medium or anybody by just putting their hand in the wax and then into the water—as it would be impossible to withdraw the hand from the cast without breaking the mould.

The method I can reveal in a few lines as once you know the secret it is obvious. You have a thin rubber glove which you inflate by blowing up. This you dip in the wax and then into the cold water which sets the wax quickly. Release the air from the glove and remove it through the wrist hole and there is your "spirit hand". Specialists in this sort of trickery have gone to the trouble of making a fine mould of their own hand, from which is made a rubber glove with their fingerprints on the outside. When this glove is used for the Spirit Moulding process—it forms a cast with fingerprints on the *inside*—which "proves" a hand must have been used to form the cast!

The moulding of faces is less dramatic as it offers no problem as to how it is done. If you want to do this the best thing is to use ordinary face masks but keep them slightly oiled to prevent the wax sticking. As a matter of interest, in the Museum of The Society for Psychical Research there are Spirit Hands (moulded) to be seen on show today. I do not know how the Society explain their origination.

## PART THREE: MENTAL PHENOMENA

### (25) "Phoney Business' By Corinda

**Effect**

The experiment takes part as one of a series of demonstrations of para-normal perception. This time a telephone is used to prove that it is possible to control thought over a considerable distance.

The performer conducts several tests. If the demonstration is outside of a seance room—playing cards are used; if not, Tarot cards are used. The performer explains that he knows a Medium who lives, shall we say, in Brighton. (He chooses some place away from the scene of action). He tells that arrangements have been made with the medium to conduct a series of E.S.P. by telephone. He explains further that arrangements have been made so that the medium can signal the audience by ringing the telephone from her end of the line.

First about four cards are selected from a pack and then replaced and mixed with the remainder by the audience. Next a number is written by a spectator and the information is kept to himself for a while. Lastly a word is chalked on a board.

The performer now asks a member of the audience to dial a number which is the home number of the Medium. He tells the spectator to ask if she is ready and if she will ring the phone three times as soon as the receiver is replaced. The spectator does as told, telephones the Medium who tells him she is ready. Next he replaces the receiver and immediately the Medium rings the phone three times. The performer picks it up again and tells her that everything is working correctly and that they are ready for the first test.

He explains to the Medium that four cards have been chosen from a full pack of fifty two. A spectator will hold them one at a time over the telephone and will she try and identify the selected cards by ringing once when the spectator happens to be holding one over the telephone?

The spectator quickly passes the cards one at a time over the telephone which stands with the receiver replaced. Four times the telephone rings and on each occasion—the spectator is found to hold one of the selected cards! At the finish the performer lifts the receiver and congratulates the Medium on a perfect score! For the next test he writes the complete alphabet on the board. He tells the Medium that a spectator will run along the row of letters and asks her to ring "stop" on each letter required to name the word that has been selected by the audience. He replaces the receiver and instructs a spectator to begin. The telephone spells out the word.

The final experiment concerns the number chosen by a spectator. The bell on the telephone rings out a series of numbers and these are chalked on the board. When the last number has been signalled, the performer asks if the spectator will stand and for the first time announce what number he decided upon. They agree!

**Method**

Before you can perform this effect it will be necessary for you to make yourself what is called a "Body Ringer", which is a similar appliance as is used for electrical Spirit Bell Routines. The Body Ringer is simply an electric bell, a battery and a flat push-button wired to function properly. The Bell is strapped to the leg (thigh) and the battery is carried in the back trousers pocket. The push-button is affixed with elastic bands to one knee and is adjusted so that when both knees are pressed together, the bell is sounded. The tone of the bell should resemble the tone of any normal telephone bell although absolute likeness is not imperative since the real telephone bell is at no time sounded and the audience cannot compare the two noises.

Other necessary equipment for this routine is a Telephone, Playing Cards or Tarot Cards, Chalk and Large Slate or Blackboard and some means of getting a carbon impression of the number written by the spectator. This may be obtained by way of a Clip Board, Impression Wallet or the Clip Book which is described in detail in Step Seven.

If you can arrange it so that you have a friend standing by ready for a telephone call from the seance room, you can use a real telephone and have the spectator dial the number and ask for the Medium. If this cannot be contrived, it matters not as you dial any number and act the part of talking to a Medium. Once the arrangements have been made at the start of the routine, the Medium actually rings off and you do all the ringing with the appliance on your person. When on occasion throughout the routine you lift the receiver to congratulate the Medium on her success, you act the part again because in reality, the telephone line is dead.

By now the procedure should be clear. The cards selected by the audience can be marked so that you can identify them as they pass over the telephone. The word is easier still, as you have only to watch carefully and ring your bell when the required letter is reached; the number is known to you because of the carbon impression which altogether means you have very little work to do outside of acting! The last thing to add is that it may be as well to telephone the seance room number from an outside telephone and leave the receiver off so that the line remains engaged and cannot be called accidentally from an outside source—if such a thing happened it could be quite embarrassing!

## (26) "Yes-No" Slate Gag

There are two ways of presenting this swindle—and it depends on what sort of audience you have—as to how you work the trick. The first method is for laymen. The performer enters holding a slate and chalk in the hand. He points to someone and asks "Can you read minds?" Whatever the reply, he proposes an experiment. He writes vigorously on the slate and holds it so that no one sees what is written as yet. He now asks the spectator to be quite honest, and to say outright if they can tell him what he has written on the slate. Invariably the reply is "No" whereupon our wit turns the slate to reveal the word "NO" chalked boldly across the slate. A mind has been read! It's a corny gag that gets a good laugh—and the number of gags that get laughs in Mentalism, are few and far between. Just one thing has to be watched when writing "No". You go over the same lines several times because it can become obvious from your arm movement what word you are writing on the slate.

The second variation is a sucker effect for magicians who know the first version! Performer enters with slate as before and goes through the same procedure, asking a spectator to try and read his mind. However, after writing "No" on the slate it is "accidentally" flashed to the audience who get a glimpse of the word and naturally presume they know what's coming! Again you ask the spectator to be quite truthful—and say outright if he knows what you have written on the slate. This time he answers "yes" because in truth, he has seen the writing. Slowly, and with amazement on your face, you turn the slate and there in bold letters in "Yes" . . . !

The method, which I should think is obvious, is simply a flap slate. Under the flap on the slate itself you have previously written "Yes". The flap is put into position and the slate is shown clean with a casual wave before you write "No" on the flap. It is dumped on a table for a brief second whilst you do something like putting the chalk away in the box—and then picked up again leaving the flap behind. As a final word, take great care with both methods—that when getting the spectator to answer "yes" or "No"—you phrase your question so that he cannot reply in any other manner. This is not too difficult.

## (27) "Cryptopsychism"

Another simple mediumistic mental effect is this stunt where the medium leaves the room and stays outside, the performer has the committee write a list of objects and some of these are chosen. The list is taken out to the medium who proceeds to tick off the chosen items. The test can be repeated over and over again and it may be done impromptu.

It is very, very simple but also very deceptive. The performer in the room explains that certain objects have harmonious relationship with others. He asks the spectator to write down a list of about a dozen objects. He then glances at the list and names two or three items that he thinks are linked by this so called Harmonious Relationship. He instructs the spectator to take the list to the medium who will name any objects that she feels have this binding factor—and she names the same because all she does is to look at the second letter of the first word, and to tick off every word in the list that has that letter in it. You have named the objects by virtue of the same principle.

It will be seen that the code will probably vary each time the test is done and although it would be a simple matter to devise continuations that would withstand rigid inspection, it is hardly necessary as it is only a simple parlour stunt that you can use to fool a few friends. Do not be inclined to scorn the simplicity of the code, Fogel and I have used it with very good effect and it's one of those effects that if you do have a spectator solve the code—it makes him very happy because he supposes he is more intelligent than the others! A little psychology goes a long way!

### (28) "The Ouija Board"

Of all the forms for novel revelation of a chosen word, dead name, spirit message or what-have-you, this is one of the best and most suitable for seance room Mentalism. Although I have used a Ouija Board for many purposes, I did not think of it for this. I credit the idea to Al Koran and the angle, although only a twist on presentation, is really good.

Most of you will know what a Ouija Board is—but for those of you that don't I will describe it briefly.

The Ouija Board is usually a plate of glass square or circular in shape and around the rim are stuck small pieces of card or paper which bear the letters of the alphabet; additional to 26 letter cards, there is usually a "Yes" card and a "No" card. In operation, a small tumbler is placed on the glass and the medium (sometimes with a sitter or two) places her fingertips on the bottom of the glass. (It goes upside down on the Ouija Board). It is now purported that the Spirits, acting through the Medium, move the glass around the board going from letter to letter thus spelling out a message.

Those of you with lesser morals than myself, will readily see the wonderful opportunity to push the glass where you want it to go—and to Summerland* with the Spirits! So with the knowledge that we can easily make the Spirits spell out a word—it remains a matter of getting the word. In Step Six on Billets I gave you the easiest method in the World—the Centre Tear, and this would be a good place to use it. (See page 166). Alternative methods would be forcing, carbon impressions, pencil reading and billet switching; all these are to be found on the lower rungs! (Steps 1–8).

*NOTE.—Purely as a matter of interest, "Summerland" was the name given by an emminent Fraudulent Medium to the "home" of Spirits— the world from which they come. One should picture the location as a sort of Astral Vineyard.

### (29) Spirit Writing on a Slate

There are very many methods of producing a spirit message on a slate, and during the course of time I think I have explored the best of them. This one I have used very often and it is quite good.

**Effect**

Four people sit round a table, you have a slate cleaned by the sitter opposite you and then you both hold it under the table for a brief moment, having given the Spirits sufficient time to materialise a message the sitter pulls up the slate and there is chalked a few kinds words from Granny!

The modus operandi is cheeky—that's why I liked it. You have two slates and one of them is prepared with the message written in chalk. This slate lies in your lap as you sit opposite the victim. To your right is an assistant—although nobody knows it. All you have to do is to show the clean slate and take it in the left hand—as you go under the table you simply pick up the other slate in the right hand, push that forward into the subject's hand, but, at the same time, cross your arms and pass the clean slate to the assistant on your right who takes it into his lap and then sticks it up his jumper. This can be done without any conspicuous movement. Usually at this point I would give the assistant a chance to dispose of the slate by turning to him and saying "would you please get a duster—we may need it". He would get up and go for a duster, leave the other slate and return leaving the whole phoney set-up as clean as a whistle!

If you have one of those tables with cross bars just under the top—you can rest the message slate on the bars in place having it in the lap. It is all very simple and bewildering—which is what good spook stuff should be.

### (30) "Strike a Light" By Punx

Usually any effect which involves putting all the lights out—is a waste of time, but in this case—working in the seance room—we have every opportunity for doing so and the trick is very good.

### Effect

About a dozen people sit around the seance table. The performer works alone; he throws a box of matches on to the table and then turns his back to give instructions to the gathering. He asks any one of them to open the box and select any match from the thirty or forty therein. This done he tells that person to give the match to any other person who is then to mark their initials on the stem—at the end away from the head. The match is then replaced in the box and is thoroughly mixed with the others.

Now the performer turns round for the first time. He takes the box and calls for the lights to be turned off. As soon as they go off—within a matter of seconds the audience see him strike a match and with it burning in his hand he goes round the circle looking into the faces of the sitters. In front of one man he stops—and calls "Lights". As they go on—he blows out the match and hands it to this man saying—"this is the match chosen from the other fifty and you were the man to mark it with your initials!" He is right.

The match is examined by all—it is indeed the original match chosen by a spectator and it has the initials on the stem. All others in the box are also open to inspection and there is no clue to the mystery.

The method is quite simple. You have two boxes of matches. The first box which you throw on the table at the start contains matches which have all been dipped by their ends into luminous paint. When the lights are on this is not visible! So a luminous match is chosen and when this has been done you remark casually "can I have the box back please". Having regained the box—it is an easy matter to switch it for a box of untreated matches whilst your back is turned to the audience. The initials are marked on the chosen match and you throw the box behind you on to the table so that they can mix the luminous match with the untreated ones. This done you have nothing more to do other than to have the lights put out. As soon as this is done you open the box and there will be one match glaring at you. Hold it by the tip so that others do not see the glow and strike it. As you do so you will find it an easy matter to read the initials on the stem and knowing who those initials belong to—go round the faces until you recognise that person.

DE MILLE

**NOTES**

# CARD TRICKS

## BY

Corinda

## STEP TEN

IN CORINDA'S SERIES :—

## "THIRTEEN STEPS TO MENTALISM"

STEP TEN in CORINDA'S SERIES

"THIRTEEN STEPS TO MENTALISM"

## CARD TRICKS

## CONTENTS

# INTRODUCTION TO MENTALISM WITH CARDS

It has been argued by my friends and colleagues that there is no place for card tricks in the Thirteen Steps to Mentalism, on the grounds that playing cards are suggestive of trickery in as much that they are so commonly associated with conjuring. With this argument on my hands I have been forced to form an opinion once and for all on this troublesome question, and I have decided to make a stand and stick by my guns. The answer is the existence of Step Ten.

I firmly believe that it does not matter what you use for a mental effect as long as you use it correctly. In the first place it is no excuse to condemn playing cards in the mental field because they are solely suggestive of trickery. It may be as well to recollect that playing cards were used for divination, prophecy, and for occult purposes as much as they were used for games, and indeed today cards are widely used for fortune telling.

On the other hand there is no doubt at all that playing cards can be devastatingly dangerous to the mentalist. They could be his undoing. as they could also be his making, and it all depends on what you do and how you do it. We must therefore pay a certain amount of attention to the best way in which playing cards may be used for mentalism. We need not concern ourselves too much with cards other than playing cards because, for example, a set of E.S.P. cards or Zenna cards are such that although in shape they resemble playing cards, their very designs help to keep them in a class of their own. Something that is not suggestive of the apparatus of the ordinary conjuror. So let us concern ourselves solely with playing cards for the moment. The following few simple rules are points which are worth noting and remembering and if followed will go a long way towards making your conjuring tricks into mental effects.

(1) Probably the most important point of all is this first one and that is to handle the cards in an unskilful manner. Never make a neat pressure fan, never shuffle the cards with digital dexterity using some fancy flourish. Even go so far as to avoid the weave shuffle. Use, and be satisfied with a common, somewhat clumsy overhand mixing of the cards. In other words aim to register psychologically with your audience that to you a pack of cards is a foreign thing. Set out and succeed in creating the impression that you are by no means able to manipulate playing cards even if you wanted to. In order to achieve this do not be too proud to look really clumsy at times. For example drop a card or two when shuffling. Make an occasional deliberate mistake when naming a card as though the suit was not a familiar thing. Hold the pack in a firm deliberate grasp and not with the delicate air that is to be expected of a manipulator who may be obliged to display the cards poised at the finger-tips.

(2) Take care of your language when referring to playing cards and what to do with them. Avoid anything that is typical of the magician and try to speak in terms that would be used by anyone just familiar with a pack of cards for the purpose of playing games. For example it is probably better to say " mix the cards " rather than " shuffle them." It is undoubtedly better to call a pack of cards a " pack," rather than use the term " deck " which has all the suggestive characteristics of the professional card man. Never use wording such as: " When I riffle through the deck I would like you to call stop at any time." Phrases such as that can be enough to destroy

the illusion and to cause the audience to think in their minds, here is a man at home with a pack of cards, just like a conjuror, he knows what he is doing.

(3) Never at any time use any of the well-known, clever ways of revealing a chosen card if it involves a flourish or a surprise appearance, for in doing so you make it obvious that magic is there. If a card is mentally selected from a pack that lies on the table, and a spectator is invited to cut the pack and finds that he has reached his card by pure coincidence, you have a mental effect on your hands. But if the same card was made to rise from the pack, although you have a good trick you do not have a mental effect and nobody on earth would ever believe that you did it by mentalism. So make up your mind whether you want your card effect to be mentalism or a conjuring trick, and whatever you decide stick by it, don't mix the two because that would be quite fatal. In other words don't suppose that you can do two card tricks as a conjuror—flourishing cards, fanning them beautifully, shuffling them skilfully, and then, five minutes later suddenly change your personality to become a mentalist and " manhandle " the cards and alter your patter. *You must be consistent all the time.* You are either clumsy and unfamiliar with a pack of cards, or you are a manipulator. If you are the latter you cannot succeed in mentalism with playing cards. That is if you are an *obvious* manipulator.

(4) A considerable number of mental effects require that a card is selected and then replaced in the pack. It is a very important thing that you learn to have the chosen card remembered by the audience and when a card is chosen, (whenever it is possible within the scope of your particular effect) have the spectator show the card to other people. Sometimes this is not practical because the trick demands that only one person sees the card. But in a case of this nature consider if the card may be marked or signed, so that there may be no question as to its identity. I have recollections of once being an assistant to another mentalist on the stage and my capacity was that of a member of the audience who had gone up to help him. The mentalist asked me to take a card, look at it, and put it back in the pack, all of which I did. But unfortunately I did not pay particular or very close attention to the card and I really forgot it. It was not a deliberate thing; it was just the sort of unfortunate occurrence that can happen to anyone and although I am to be blamed for my poor memory, the mentalist is also to be blamed for not drawing my attention to the card and insisting that I remember it for sure. So that is another little rule which is important.

With these few things to bear in mind and consider, I think there can be no doubt that by using ordinary common sense and here and there a touch of psychological misdirection, playing cards are as much use to the mentalist as they are to the magician. This step contains a selection of mental effects of all types. Some are for stage, some are for close-up. They all involve cards of one type or another—sometimes playing cards, sometimes geometrical designs cards. Whatever they may be, keep in mind all the time the few simple rules mentioned above and always do your best to make card magic mentalism and not mentalism card magic.

### PHOTO-MEMORY *By Hans Trixer*

This is a trick which is a lesson in simplicity itself, and one which suits Mentalism because it is presented as a feat of memory. The effect may be repeated two or three times and it is quick and direct.

308

The Mentalist borrows a pack of cards and has them mixed. He takes them back and then ribbon spreads them face upwards on the table or floor. In doing so, an effort is made to display every index. He explains that with a certain amount of training it is possible to memorise the position of every card in the pack—and that when in form, it should take no more than half a minute to do so! Beginning from one end of the spread he moves his finger along the row appearing, to all intents and purposes, to memorise the cards as he goes. Having studied the position of each card in the spread, he picks them up and asks anybody to name a card. As soon as a card is named, he ponders for a fraction of a minute and then declares its exact position in the pack. Suppose it to be the Four of Hearts—he might say " Twenty four " and then counts to the twenty-fourth card and removes it to show it to be the Four of Hearts. The effect may now be repeated with a few more cards—and if need be, the pack can be shuffled again and re-memorised as many times as you wish.

**The Method.** After the cards have been shuffled and spread face up, all you have to do is to note the first card in the spread. (Top card of the pack when assembled). Whatever *number* is called—name the *top card*. Next count very slowly and deliberately to the chosen number. Suppose it is ten; you hold the pack face down and slowly count nine cards from hand to hand—keeping them in order as you go. When you get to ten you remove that card and drop it on top of the pack. As you do this, turn to the spectator and say " I said ten—and you said ' Three of hearts ' " and, as you name the card, double lift from the top and display the Three of hearts which was the top card! Principally, that is all there is to it—but the trick deserves the introduction of a finesse or two, so change the method of introducing the top card as much as your personal ability will allow. For example, other changes could be accomplished by the Top Change, Mexican Turnover, Curry Turnover or Guyatt Exchange (See page 317).

Should you be one of those unlucky people that find all card sleights a problem—then moisten the back of the top card with saliva before you start the count and then you can push off two as one without even doing a Double Lift.

If you propose to do the trick three or four times running it is a simple matter to find out what card is next to the top. Do it once and when you reach the chosen position, remove that card and look at it—then misname it for the one you gave them and proceed as normal. The one that you have just seen will be the next card to name for the call and so it progresses.

### " CORINDA'S INCREDIBLE SLATE TEST "

The principle of this effect I have already used in two other items both of which have received quite a bit of attention. Basically I draw the mechanics from my " Khan Slate Test " which is a marketed E.S.P. effect and therefore cannot be described here.

In this trick, which can be for stage or drawing room—we have a spectator select ten Alphabet Cards (Lexicon Cards will do) and then arrange them into any order he likes without seeing the faces for the moment. When the cards are shown it is seen that the spectator has managed to choose ten cards that make up a word, and that they have arranged them in the right order to spell " INCREDIBLE "—but to top it all, you show a slate which predicts the chosen word—and chalked in bold letters is the word " Incredible."

If you study the plot you will observe that it is composed of three impossibilities! First it is phenomenal that out of some fifty cards, the ten that can be used to spell " Incredible " are selected. Next it is remarkable that the spectator should manage to arrange them in order without seeing their faces, and at the close your Prediction. The effect is therefore reinforced from all points of view, and you will be pleased to learn that the working is absurdly simple although you will have to go to the trouble of making a simple fake slate.

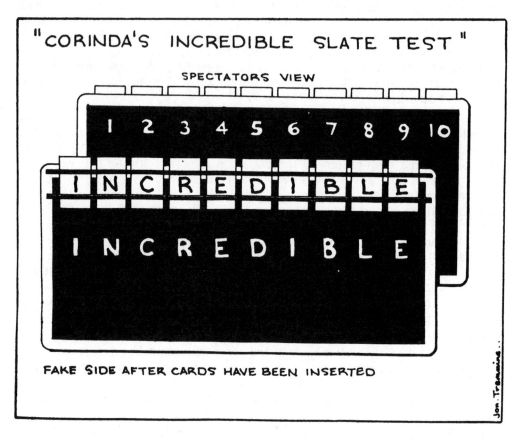

To make the Slate take a board of 5-plywood and cover it with black " Contact Adhesive Plastic " which resembles the colour of a genuine slate. For the sake of appearance, a border of grained " passe partout " may be run round the edge to act as substitute for the frame. This " artificial " slate appears very much like the real thing at very close quarters and it is by no means essential that it should be perfect.

On one side of the slate affix two lengths of white elastic (about ¼ in. wide elastic will do) and have these placed so that they run right down one long edge of the slate with a distance of two inches between them. (See diagram). The elastic is easily fixed with staples or small nails.

All that remains now is to fix a set of ten fake cards on to the elastic bands so that they are held firmly in position. Take ten alphabet cards that spell the word " Incredible " and arrange them in order. Now cut about one inch off the end of each card so that the centre portion which bears the letter, is of a width just a little less than the distance between the two elastic bands.

These centre portions of the alphabet cards are now stuck with glue to the underside of the elastic bands and then small pins are placed between each card to form a guide to the real cards which are inserted behind the fakes during performance.

This brief description along with the drawings should make it possible for you to follow the technical details so now we can get down to the working.

The slate lies face down on your table.    You must have some *Soft* white chalk (which writes best on the plastic material) and the Alphabet pack (which is best composed of 52 cards)—two of every letter in the alphabet.   With these things you are set to perform.

First pick up the cards and hand them to a spectator asking him to look through the pack to satisfy himself that there is a good selection of letters. Next he is asked to mix the cards himself to give them a thorough mixing. In the meantime, you pick up the slate, and without displaying the fake side take the chalk and write the numbers 1 to 10 in a row along the top edge on the back of the slate.  (See " spectators' view " drawing).   Put the chalk down, turn to the spectator and ask if he is quite sure that the cards are mixed.   Then tell him to reverse the pack and remove any ten cards without looking at them.  (If you have the facilities, it is a good thing at this point to spread the pack in jumbled order face down on a tray and have the spectator pick up any ten cards).

When ten cards have finally been chosen the others are placed aside or preferably left with the spectator for a while!  Once more the spectator is told to mix his cards and when the ten have been shuffled they are taken and laid in a row on the table or floor.   If they are left with the spectator, he is liable to cheat half way through the routine and look at a card thus exposing the ruse.   You have every excuse for taking the cards from him as the trick depends on the fact that he has no idea what cards he chooses or where they go;  this you may emphasise!   The only important thing is to make it clear throughout that no " phoney " moves are made.   It doesn't matter at all what cards he chooses so let him " chop and change " his mind and keep the selected ten in view all the time—lest it be suspected that you have changed them.

The effect is nearly done, the big build up to the finale comes now.  You explain briefly that on one side of the slate you have written a prediction in chalk, and that you have two elastic bands ready to hold the cards.  You do not show the slate (fake side) to prove it!  You point out that the numbers one to ten have been chalked on the other side of the slate, which now faces the audience.  You pick up the first card in the row (or any other you choose) and hold it back towards the spectator asking him where the card should go. He has merely to call out the number.  Whatever he said slide that card into position so that it goes behind the fake and leave some projecting over the edge of the slate so that the card does not entirely disappear from view.   This is repeated with all the cards.   It should now be apparent that no matter what cards were chosen or what order they were placed in the fakes force the appearance of the word " Incredible."

For the finale, the slate is turned to show the cards arranged in this order and below them, chalked on the slate, your prediction is to be seen—the word " Incredible " corresponding letter by letter to the cards above.

311

I think it fair to say that this effect as a mental trick is one that is outstanding in quality and simplicity. Because of the mechanics it is one of those rare items that could be performed almost without practice; however, no matter how sure-fire the apparatus, there is always scope for a blunder somewhere and it is therefore as well to rehearse the routine at least a few times before you put it in your next T.V. show!

### THE MILLION DOLLAR TEST *By J. G. Reed*

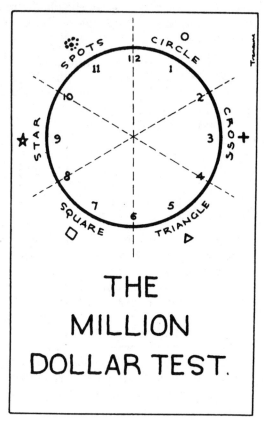

**Effect.** The "medium" helping the magician adjourns temporarily to an adjoining room. The magician displays six E.S.P. cards and a spectator points to one of them. The spectators are asked to concentrate on the chosen design, the magician snaps his fingers and the medium shouts out, (from the next room) the chosen card. The effect is repeated over and over again, and each time the medium is 100 per cent. correct.

**Method.** The method of working is perhaps one of the simplest and yet the most subtle ever devised. The medium and the magician are each equipped with a watch which has a large second hand. Before the show both watches are wound up and the second hands are synchronised. The watch face is mentally divided up into six portions, each portion representing one of the E.S.P. cards:—

| | |
|---|---|
| 12–2 o'clock—circle. | 6–8 o'clock—square. |
| 2–4 o'clock—cross. | 8–10 o'clock—star. |
| 4–6 o'clock—triangle. | 10–12 o'clock—spots. |

Consequently when the second hand is in the portion representing the chosen card the magician snaps his fingers and codes the design to the medium who reads it off her watch. During the actual performance, the medium can look at her watch quite openly because of her isolated position. but the magician must have his behind something, so that he can steal discreetly the information.

**Note.** The routine above is described for use in a private house, but the method can however be easily adapted for stage use without much thought.

### THE BIRTHDAY CARD TRICK *By Jack Avis*

Arrange the following cards on top of the pack (X denotes any card). Top card; X, X, X, X, X, X, X,; Queen of Clubs; Jack of Clubs; Ten of

Clubs; Nine of Clubs; Eight of Clubs; Seven of Clubs; Six of Clubs; Five of Clubs; Four of Clubs; Three of Clubs; Two of Clubs; Joker.

See that the Four Aces are in the lower section of the pack.

**Presentation.**

Explain to your spectators that, as a change from the normal run of " take a card " effects, you will attempt something a little different. In fact you are going to have a card selected making use of the physical and the mental faculties. First for the physical selection. Here you remove the four aces from four suits, and by physical means you are going to have one of the suits selected. Turn the four aces face downwards, and in the action of mixing them control the ace of clubs to the top position. Hand the four aces in a face-down packet to a spectator and ask him to place the top card on the bottom of the packet, the next card he is to place face-down on the table, next card to the bottom, then a card to the table etc., until he is left with just one card. This last card he is to place, still face down, to one side of the table. This card represents the physical choice of the suits.

Your assistant now thinks of a value between one and twelve, but he is told not to reveal his chosen number until asked. You now say you will attempt to penetrate the mental and physical barrier and so discover the chosen card. Ask your assistant for the month and date of his birth. From his reply appear to make a mental calculation and announce that his guide number is twenty. You explain to your assistant that as you deal the cards onto the table, for every card dealt he is to add one to his secretly-chosen number until he reaches his guide number of twenty, at the count of twenty he is to call " Stop."

Commence dealing cards from the top of the pack, and on command from your assistant stop the deal. Before revealing the last card dealt, proceed to build up the climax as follows. First have the assistant turn face up the odd ace card that was his physical selection. This of course proves to be the club suit. Next he is to reveal for the first time his secretly-chosen number. Let us assume that this is SIX. Combining his physical and mental choices gives us a value of a playing card, in this case the six of clubs. Turn up the last card dealt and reveal it to be . . . the SIX OF CLUBS.

## E.S.P. TEST *By J. G. Reed*

**Effect.** Half a dozen or more spectators are each given an envelope. A display stand holding a number of design cards is shown. The spectators are asked, whilst the magician's back is turned, to select one of the design cards and each seal it in his envelope. The envelopes are then mixed up. Tearing one of the envelopes open the mentalist removes the card and openly displays it. Eventually he manages to " guess " who originally selected this card and hands it back to them! This is repeated with all the envelopes.

**Working.** This trick requires a small amount of showmanship and given this it will be a big hit. The method is very simple because the envelopes are marked. The mentalist knows who gets the various envelopes and consequently when he tears them open he looks at the marking and returns the contents to the original owner. The method you use for marking is a matter of personal preference but pencil dots take a bit of beating. Although the method is simple if you put plenty of showmanship into the trick then to the audience it will appear to be an astounding effect.

## THE TRIO *By Sidney Lawrence*

### Two Minds—a Single Thought

**Effect.** Two spectators are asked to assist the mentalist, they each cut themselves a packet of cards from a freely-shuffled deck. Whilst this is done the performer turns his back and remains so whilst each spectator counts the number of cards in their separate packets. Our performer does not know how many cards are chosen. This completed, the performer takes both groups of cards and places them together in one packet. He now proceeds to pass the cards one at a time from hand to hand showing the first spectator the face of each card as he does so. He instructs the spectator to watch out for the card which appears at his number (i.e. the number according to the amount of cards that were in his packet at the start.) The spectator has simply to look for this card, and is asked to say nothing when he spots which one it is.

The same process is repeated with the second spectator—who is asked to note which card falls at the number accrued by the total cards in his packet at the start. However, when he sees the card, he is to remove it and place it face-down on the table without saying what it is.

The performer now asks the first spectator to name his mentally-noted card and the second spectator states that his was the same card. The result is proved when the card on the table is shown to be the one named by both spectators.

**Method.** As the performer takes the two packets from the spectators, he places them together in his left hand with the face of the packet to the audience. He then transfers the cards slowly from left hand to right, showing them to the first spectator. The cards are placed one behind the other in the right hand *except* for the last card which is placed *in front* of the packet. The effect is now self-working.

### Before Your Very Eyes

This is a trick with 52 cards. First of all you take the cards in your hand and ask the person to select as many cards as he likes, you don't have to know the number of them. But let us say for example that they have taken a number of cards and are going to count them. Let us say for example 12 cards. Now he has selected any number of cards. You ask him to think of any number he likes and say he thinks of three he looks at the third card down from the top of the pack that he has counted out before. You take the cards away from him and cut the cards. When you cut the cards from the bottom to the top remember how many cards you are cutting. This time, for example, four cards from the bottom of the pack to the top. Now at this stage neither the performer nor the spectator know the position of the card. To make sure you do not know where his card is request him to take the cards behind his back and think of the number he thought of. If it was three he is to take three cards off the top and place them onto the bottom of the pack. He does this, brings the cards forward and then you ask him to hold them before his eyes. He is then looking at them and while he is looking at the cards you ask him to concentrate on it. While he is concentrating on it you go over, and without looking at the cards select his card. The way you make your selection is because you have your key number which in this particular case was four, that's the four cards you cut from the bottom of the pack to the top and all you have to do is to take the fourth card out.

That will be his card.

## Gamma Location

The pack of cards is given to someone to shuffle. Being satisfied that they are thoroughly mixed they select a number of cards. Let us say they select five cards. You ask them to put the selected cards in their pocket and ask them to give the same number of cards (without telling you how many) to the person on the left. Thus he also has five cards. The rest of the cards he has in his hand you ask him to shuffle.

After doing so he looks at the top card—in this case the Ten of Spades. You must make sure at this point and you ask him to agree that you could not know his card. As long as he is satisfied it is all right but if he is not satisfied then he can change it. After he has looked at the card you then ask him to select any pack he likes (his pack or his friend's pack). These cards are then taken and placed on top of the pack. You now explain that you cannot possibly know the location or the identity of that card. Having done that you then shuffle off the cards, and this is where the " hokus-pokus " comes in. You moisten your thumb and count off the top of the pack any number you like, e.g. fourteen. You shuffle the fourteen cards. In other words you reverse the cards as you count them. One; two; three . . . thirteen; fourteen, and you place them back on top of the pack. You now take the cards from the other gentleman's pocket and place those on top. You do not know how many cards the gentleman had in his pocket but your key number is fourteen. You now take the cards, place them on the table, make a false shuffle and a false cut. Your card is still now the fourteenth from the top.

Now there are many ways this card can be revealed. You can for example ask a person to name any town he likes, e.g. Birmingham. Now he counts Birmingham, dealing the cards as he spells. While he does so you silently count the cards—ten. So you have four more cards till your fourteenth card. You now ask the gentleman if he knows any person in Birmingham, e.g. Philip—Phil for short. You then ask him to spell Phil onto the table which brings us now to our card (the fourteenth card). He turns it over and there is the Ten of Spades.

# BEYOND THE VEIL *By Patrick Page*

**Effect.** The performer allows a spectator to select one of two packs of cards. The spectator is then invited to cut his pack anywhere and name the card of his choice. This done, the performer takes the other pack and spells out the name of the card. At the end of the count the card reached is shown and is found to be perfectly correct! The effect can be repeated as often as the performer likes, yet he is always able to find the correct card at the correct spot. The effect can be presented as a mystery. The performer explains that as soon as the spectator selects a card " unseen forces " from Beyond the Veil will arrange the cards so that his card will always be at the right spot.

**Method.** Two packs of cards are used both of which are arranged in a special order. The first pack used by the spectator is made up of fifty-two regular cards half of which are short cards, and the remainder normal. The cards are all different but should be arranged with one long then one short from top to bottom. It does not matter what order the " pairs " are in, and the pack can be shuffled like a Svengali deck if necessary.

The performer's pack consists of fifty-two cards all different but with a set-up. These cards of course must not be mixed. The exact order of the pack from top to bottom (back upwards) is:—

10D; 5H; 8C; 10C; AH; 6S; AC; AS; 4D; 2H; 3H; 2D; 3D; 6H; 5D; 6D; 7D; 10H; 9D; QH; KH; QD; JH; AD; KD; 9H; 4C; 8S; QS; 4S; 2S; KS; KC; JS; JC; 9S; 9C; 7S; 7C; 5S; 5C; 3S; 3C; 2C; 8H; 6C; QC; 7H; JD; 4H; 8D; 10S.

**Presentation.** Throw two packs of cards on the table and ask the person to select one. Force the correct pack. Invite him to open his pack and to cut (by the narrow ends) and show the face card. (If you prefer, you may hold the pack yourself whilst he cuts—to be sure of forcing the cut at the narrow ends; or you may instruct him to count to any number he names, having him turn up either the last card of the count, or the one following, whichever causes him to land on an even number. Check that you start with a short card on top to use this method. Having had a card selected proceed as follows:—

(1) If the selected card is a Heart or Diamond you count from the top turning the cards OVER on to the table as you do so.

(2) If the selected card is a Spade or Club you count from the bottom turning the cards over onto the table as you do so. (Both methods keep the pack in order for future use).

(3) Whatever the card is, always COUNT its value first, allowing eleven for a Jack, twelve for a Queen and thirteen for a King. Follow this with two more cards spelling out " of "—and then finally spell out the correct suit.

(4) Having shown the last card of the count or spell to be correct replace it in its *original* position and carefully replace the remainder from the table so that your pack is set for a repetition.

**Example.** Card named: " Two of Hearts." Start from top turning over and dealing in a pile on the table count " one, two " (two cards) follow with " of " (two more cards) and finally H, E, A, R, T, S (five more cards) and there it is!

## CARD EXCHANGE *By Terry Guyatt*

**Introduction.** This card exchange is not in itself an effect, it is fundamentally the means to perform many effects. It will be agreed that a considerable number of mental effects become possible if the mentalist is in a position to exchange one card for another without the audience knowing that he has done so. Moreover the more effective the exchange or the more deceptive, the wider the range of tricks that become possible. This particular one—the Guyatt Card Exchange is one that I have seen used on several occasions by Terry Guyatt himself and I consider it to be a remarkable switch. Earlier on in this book we mentioned one effect by Hans Trixer where the use of this exchange would be invaluable, and there are countless other card mental effects which relying on a good exchange or switch would be made possible by knowledge and understanding of this principle.

I leave you now to read through the detailed description which has been kindly provided by my good friend Terry Guyatt.

You must be seated at a table in a relaxed position and leaning backwards slightly, the body about a foot from the table-edge upon which both fists, loosely clenched, are placed.

The card to be exchanged, say the King of Diamonds, lies face-down on the table with one long side nearest yourself. It should be about ten inches from the table-edge. Another card, say the Ace of Spades, lies (unknown to the spectators) face-down in your lap.

Bring your body slightly forward and raise your right hand about three inches in a casual gesture as you make a remark about the card on the table. Now forget all about your right hand as you look at the King of Diamonds on the table and reach for it with your left hand, letting your right hand drop unobtrusively into your lap. Pick up the King by the nearest left-hand corner with the left first and second fingers on the back and the thumb underneath, drawing it towards the edge of the table and turning the face of the card to yourself. During this movement the left first finger moves from the back of the card to join the thumb on the face. The card is now clipped between the left first and second fingers. The thumb takes no part in the grip, but remains touching the tip of the first finger.

Meanwhile the right hand has secured the Ace of Spades in your lap, taking it by the right hand corner nearest the body—the index corner—with the thumb underneath and the first finger on top and raising it to a vertical position with the face of the card towards yourself. One long side should be parallel to the floor. The card is moved up until it's just out of sight of the spectators, below the table edge and at right angles to the table-top. There should be no suspicious movement or stiffening of the right arm or shoulder.

You should fix all your attention upon the King of Diamonds during the pick-up and forget all about your right hand in your lap. Both hands should move at the same time, the Ace of Spades out of view and the King of Diamonds in view immediately above it and in the same plane. This position is held for a second only.

Now comes the actual exchange. Make a remark, raising the left hand slightly for emphasis; then take your eyes from the King of Diamonds and look the spectator straight in the eye, leaning back, relaxing your body and dropping the left arm below the edge of the table at the same time. The

King of Diamonds passes between the table and the Ace of Spades, and immediately it is out of sight it is released by the first and second fingers and allowed to drop into the lap. The thumb and first finger collect the Ace of Spades, clipping it by the non-index corner in the same way in which the King was held. As soon as the exchange is made bring the body forward again, making another remark and bring up both hands into view—the left hand containing the Ace of Spades and the right hand empty. All this time you must look at the spectator—not at your hands.

The card should be out of sight for a split second only; and, if the misdirection is applied correctly, that split-second is when the spectator looks at your face. By the time he has looked back at the card the exchange has been made, and, except for the card, the hands are empty and in view. You appear to gesture and speak, pick up the face-down card and look at it and gesture and speak again. The whole action should be performed casually and without haste, and should take about three seconds from beginning to end.

### BLIND COINCIDENCE *By Michael Mence*

**Effect.** A spectator is asked to shuffle the pack and then cut it into two parts handing one to the performer and retaining the other for himself. Both the performer and the spectator take the packets behind their backs, take a card at random, and bring face-down card and packet into view (one in each hand). At this point the performer and the spectator exchange their unknown and face-down cards, take them behind their backs, reverse them and place them in the packets which are face-down behind their backs. The two squared-up packets are then brought to view again, both fanned through simultaneously face-down, and the two reversed cards are both found to be kings—" Blind Coincidence."

**Method.** Before the performance place two kings (it is more effective if they are both red or both black) behind your back clipped under your belt which is of course masked by the suit-coat. This means that the effect can be performed at any time during the act, provided that the incomplete pack does not have to be used previously. If you intend to repeat the effect then of course you must have two pairs clipped under your belt. The first time the performer's hands go behind his back, he takes out one of the kings from his belt and brings it out face-down as his card. The performer and the spectator now exchange cards. Both sets of cards disappear from view again and the performer places the spectator's card back in the pack, steals the second king, reverses it and pushes it into the pack. All that now remains is the revelation. For the greatest effect the two packets should be brought to view face-up, the cards then fanned simultaneously until the appearance of the face-down cards. Only then should the fans be turned over to reveal the " Blind Coincidence."

### MENTAL CARD TRICK *By Terry Guyatt*

From an unprepared pack give four people six cards each face down. Do this without appearing to count the cards and without drawing attention to the number each receives. Each spectator fans his cards and thinks of any one he sees. Then he shuffles his packet so that his card is lost among the others.

Place the balance of the pack aside. Take back the cards from the spectators in the reverse order to that in which you gave them out; taking No. 4's first face down; putting No. 3's face down on top of these; then No. 2's; and lastly No. 1's on top of all. You should now hold 24 cards face down, the top six are No. 1's, and the next six are No. 2's and so on. Say that you will mix all the hands together, cut below the twelfth card and make a perfect shuffle, retaining top and bottom identity. Again cut below the twelfth card and make another perfect shuffle, still retaining top and bottom identity. Place these 24 cards back on top of the balance of the pack. Pick up the pack and cut below the 26th card, making a perfect shuffle, again retaining top and bottom identity.

Give the pack a false cut, and, holding it face down, fan off the top eight cards without appearing to count them. Show the faces of these eight fanned cards to the spectators and ask if anyone can see his card. If anyone says " Yes " you immediately know his card thus: the first card to the left of the fan belongs to spectator No. 1, the next card is an indifferent one, the next belongs to No. 2, the next is an indifferent card, and so on through the fan. The first, third, fifth and seventh cards were all in the original hands. Put these cards on the bottom of the pack and fan off the next eight. Deal with these in the same way and carry on throughout the pack. Each time you fan off eight remove them from the pack to show them. By going through in this way for six packets all the cards can be found alternatively. When four packets have been dealt with in this way there are only two alternatives for any unfound cards. Fan the entire pack, face towards yourself, and dealing with each spectator left in turn, ask a leading question—" Red ? " " Picture ?"

**Footnote.** To simplify the cutting to an exact number for twelve, sight bottom card of second person's hand. For the 26th card: when you explain in first place sight second from top as you display cards.

### " TWO OF A KIND " *By Terry Guyatt*

This trick is a mental card effect which we can classify as a coincidence. Two packs of cards are used, one red, one blue. What appears to happen is that the performer has one pack and the spectator another, both mix their cards and then go through the same manoeuvre. Both parties hold their cards in a fan face downwards, extract any one card, turn the fan face upwards and replace the card anywhere in the pack. Both packs have been in full view all the time, and now when a check is made to find which cards were chosen and reversed at random, and it is seen that by some strange coincidence the performer has reversed the identical card as the spectator and vice versa. Not only does it match in colour of course, but the suit and value are the same. Surely, a coincidence under these circumstances with two complete packs of cards, in full view without any apparent subterfuge, is one ideally suited to one who performs mental magic with playing cards.

**Method.** As stated two packs are used. One of these packs, e.g. the blue-backed pack, is stacked in Si Stebbins order (See Step 3).

Produce the two packs of cards and if you like give them a shuffle making sure however that if you shuffle the blue pack you use a false shuffle that will not disturb the set-up. See that the spectator gets the blue pack which of course has the set-up. Instruct him to be most careful in following the directions which you give to him, and yourself be most clear so that then there

319

will be no misunderstanding which would spoil the effect. As a nice touch if you prefer, at the opening stage here when you produce the two packs give him the red pack and ask him to shuffle it whilst you take the blue pack and give it a false shuffle and no matter how clumsy your false shuffle may be you have a certain amount of misdirection because he himself is concerned with mixing his cards. This having been done you can point out that you don't know the position of the cards in his pack since he has just mixed them, and that he does not know the position of the cards in your pack. Therefore you exchange packs and you are both unaware of the order in the packs. The next stage is to give the instructions and see that they are followed carefully. You give the directions to the spectator and also follow them yourself.

Hold the cards face-down as for dealing. Then both of you cut the cards and then complete the cut and then remove the top card holding it still face-downwards. The deck is now turned face-up and the card is pushed into the deck at any particular point that you like. That is to say that you have pushed the card into the pack and the spectator has done the same. However when he turns his deck face-up you will note the *bottom card* and will therefore be able to calculate quite quickly what is the top card, or, what really is the reversed card—that is why the deck is stacked.

Now you appear to demonstrate what to do. You run through your cards to show only one reversed, holding your pack face-up. In doing so you watch out for the duplicate of his reverse card in your pack. When you see it, hold a break under that card but continue to run through the pack in order to show that there is only one reversed card. Then square-up the pack and casually cut to the card held at the break, bringing the top half below the bottom half of the face-up pack. The effect is that the top card of your pack is now a duplicate to the reversed card in his pack. All that remains to be done now is to gain the necessary misdirection in order for you to perform the Top-change. Normally this might be a problem but it is easily overcome in this instance when you turn to the spectator and ask him to run through his pack the same way as you have done, until he arrives at his reversed card and then to remove it and lay it face-down on the table.

Whilst he does this you simply do the same with yours removing the reversed card but quietly and furtively do the Top-change making the card which you place on the table an identical one to that which he has apparently chosen by the fairest possible means. The cards are " Two of a Kind."

### " BIRDS OF A FEATHER" By *Corinda*

On Page 180 of Step 6 the promise was made to give you an effect with the simple apparatus described on Page 178 under the heading Billet Pull. This particular mental card trick utilizes the apparatus described there to good effect. This is what happens.

The performer has somewhere in the region of fifty to sixty small pieces of cardboard spread out on the table or on a tray. These small pieces of card are in fact quarters of ordinary playing cards and they are made by taking a score of cards from an old pack and simply cutting them in half and half again. The pieces are all face-down on the tray and are all well mixed, and as far as possible they are approximately the same size so that there is no conspicuous difference between any one piece and another. However the cutting of the cards does not call for absolute precision.

The effect is one that I suppose should be called a coincidence—in actual fact a quadruple coincidence. As far as the audience is concerned what happens is that from the quite substantial number of small pieces of card four are selected quite freely by members of the audience and when they are examined it is somewhat amazing that by sheer coincidence four different people have each selected a corner from one card and when the four corners are assembled together they match perfectly making it once more a complete card. The mathematical chances of such an occurrence need hardly be explained. The method is not particularly difficult. It is a little cheeky. It is a question of timing, of presentation, and of course, the hard work, such as it is, is done for you by our old friend the Billet Pull. I am pretty sure you won't be surprised to know that the four pieces of card that the spectators choose are not the same pieces of card that they later on examine and find that they will fit together to make up one complete card and the reason for this is because you switch them.

It is a very simple matter. Have the pieces spread out on the table face-down, mixed well. This done point out that there must be somewhere in the region of one hundred or so odd pieces of card there. For the moment don't say that they are all different. There is good reason for this. Say that you would like to have any four pieces chosen at random and therefore ask any four people (if you are sitting at a table) to just reach forward and touch any particular piece that takes their fancy. When they have done this ask them to draw the pieces out from the main pile keeping their fingers on them, and then, making it casual and as though it is not particularly important, remove a paper clip from your pocket and take the four pieces one by one, clip them together, saying, " Now we have them all together, there will be no mistaking them or getting them accidentally mixed up in these." Then, still holding them invite the four people to turn all the other pieces on the table over and to satisfy themselves that indeed they had quite a wide range of odds and ends to choose from. Then, when they go to do this, their attention for one brief second is diverted from the paper clip in your hand to the cards on the table and, in this instant you perform the billet switch described quite clearly to you on Page 179 (any of the versions) and interrupt the proceedings with the words " Perhaps you would be good enough to hold the selected pieces of card whilst our friends here examine the remainder." Hand the real four corners of the card which you have pre-viously clipped and matched in readiness, to a spectator seated at the side.

In actual fact the drawing of the handling of the Billet Pull in Fig. 21 on P. 180 of Step 6 illustrates the method of switching corners of playing cards. It shows a rather important point and that is that when the four pieces are gathered together, from the spectators, they are clipped in a face-down position and like-wise when the switch is performed the real corners appear in a face-down position. It is a little finesse which makes a lot of difference. That is one version of Birds of a Feather but if you so choose there are diversions from the main theme. Quite a number of versions which may appeal to you as alternatives. The following are a couple of variations.

The cards, that is to say the corners of the cards, are spread out face-down on the table as before, four are chosen, switched and then matched together and found to be four matching corners. Then when the bulk of the re-mainder of the cards are examined, it is found that by an odd coincidence all the other cards were blank face, and by sheer luck the four pieces (that were selected quite freely from the 100 or so odds and ends) happened to be the only pieces with faces. That of course is another variation. *One thing that is worth noting in any of the variations*, is that it is good policy to use the distinctive card for the finale. That is to say a court card if cut into quarters and then matched together again gives plenty of opportunity to the spectator to see how accurately it does match, because there is plenty of printing and colour used. In particular the Ace of Spades from a pack is very good, because when you cut this card into four you will notice that all four corners are different and cannot be matched together in any other way except in the original way no matter how you change around the corners. On the other hand with a well printed court card or pip card and with accurate cutting it is indeed possible to vary the order of assembly at the end. If you have a look at the Ace of Spades in a pack of cards and think about it you will see what I mean.


Variation No. 2 is based along the lines where you start with a pack of cards and have one of them chosen and initialled in the four corners. This having been done it is torn into quarters and then the spectator is invited to take another dozen or so cards from the pack, and likewise tear them into quarters. Whilst he does this you have previously got ready in your pocket another card already torn into quarters, (it does not matter what it is) and with his attention diverted with the tearing of the ordinary cards you exchange his signed card for the four pieces you had in readiness. Those pieces with his initials on them are discreetly clipped together with a paper clip in readiness for the Billet Pull Switch a little later. So up till now it appears that the spectator has taken a card, signed the four corners, and torn it in four and has now obtained a neat pile of about fifty small cards by tearing up a few more cards from the pack. You now point out that if you take the four corners of his card, holding them face-downwards so that he cannot see what they are, and were to mix them in with the others, (which you do as you talk) it would be most improbable that at a random choice he could pick any one corner of his card. You invite him now to choose any four. He chooses any four and piece by piece you take them from him and put them into your paper clip (as on P. 179). You ask him to turn the cards on the table over and see if he can find any cards with his initials on the corner which gives you the time and the necessary misdirection for the Billet Pull Switch to bring back once more the four pieces that have his initials on them and that will match again the card which he originally chose quite freely from an unprepared deck.


The reading of this particular variation gives the impression that there are two switches used, but in actual fact it would be unkind to describe the first change as a switch, in as much as that there is so much time on your hands and so much misdirection there is no need for anything but a bold and slow exchange of the pieces. As I said at the beginning it is mainly presentation that makes this trick, and not very much work. But for all that one cannot decry the effect. I leave you with this theme " Birds of a Feather," but in doing so, I am sure that you will realise that even now with three variations, the principle has not been fully exploited and that there are still other opportunities for progress with the basic theme.

# "TELEPROGNOS" *By Corvelo*

By combining some well-known principles in magic you sometimes get an excellent effect. With this introduction you will have already got the idea that you will not learn something really new in principle, but I still urge you to try out the following effect just once and you will be rewarded by the good reception it will receive.

**Effect.** The mentalist asks two spectators to assist him and while the spectators are coming up onto the stage he shuffles a pack of cards. After that he asks spectator No. 1 to take a card and to remember it well. This card he has to place into a small envelope which is then sealed. Both he and the other spectator each take three more cards, but they do not have to remember the identity of these cards but simply place them into separate envelopes. The envelopes are now mixed by the second spectator and he is asked to hold up the envelopes one at a time while the mentalist stands a little way away from him. Suddenly the mentalist calls "Stop" and tells the spectator that he now holds the envelope which contains the Three of Clubs; the card the first spectator had thought of. The first spectator acknowledges this and when the envelope is opened it is really found to contain the Three of Clubs.

This is the first part of the experiment and the mentalist tells the audience that as the experiment has been so successful he will try to do something more difficult. He attempts to make a prediction. He takes a slate, writes on it, and places the slate in full view on a stand but with the blank side facing the audience. He now takes the remaining six envelopes and tells the spectators that he will count the envelopes one by one and that the second spectator may now say "Stop" at any time he wishes. When the spectator calls "Stop," the envelope that the performer holds in his hand at that moment is handed to the first spectator. He is asked to remove the card from the envelope and to announce clearly its identity, e.g. the Nine of Diamonds. The mentalist turns the slate over and on it is written: I predict that "Stop" will be said at the envelope which contains the . . . e.g. Nine of Diamonds.

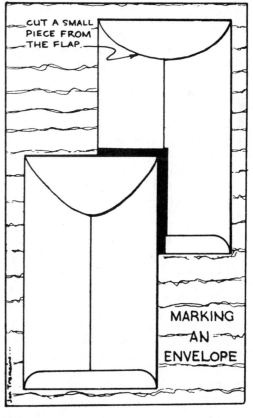

CUT A SMALL PIECE FROM THE FLAP.

MARKING AN ENVELOPE

**Method.** The pack of cards that is used is arranged in the Si-Stebbins set-up or any other system which you prefer. You also need six duplicate cards, e.g. Nine of Diamonds. These six cards are put in pay envelopes.

Seven more similar envelopes are also required. One of these envelopes is marked by cutting a small piece from the flap so you are able to recognise this particular envelope (See diagram).

A slate and a piece of chalk complete the apparatus and instead of a slate you may use a piece of paper and a ball-point to make your prediction. The six envelopes which contain the duplicate cards are placed in your left coat pocket, which is divided by a piece of cardboard. Now you are ready for the performance. Ask two spectators to come up onto the stage and while they are coming up carelessly cut the cards a few times. Make a " rough " fan (because you are a mentalist and not a magician) and ask the first spectator to take a card. When he has done so you cut the cards at the break you have held at the place from which his card was taken. By noting the bottom card you will know from the set up what card has been taken.

From the group of seven envelopes hand him the marked one and ask him to seal his card in it. Give the other spectator the pack of cards and ask him to take three cards (which he does not have to remember) and put them into envelopes too. The first spectator may take three more cards and these are handled in the same way. The reason for this procedure is that it has an important bearing on the second part of the effect. If they have looked at the cards each will think that the predicted card was with the three cards the other person took. Also by handing over the pack of cards they will afterwards think that the first card was taken in the same way.

After the cards are sealed in the envelopes you ask the second spectator to count the envelopes by transferring them slowly from one hand to the other while you are concentrating. At the same time you are looking for the marked envelope and when you spot that one you call " Stop." You tell the spectator that the envelope which he now holds contains the card the first spectator had in his mind and that the name of the card is . . . . . . . You now ask the second spectator to open the envelope while you take hold of the six remaining envelopes. While he is doing so you have taken the envelopes in your left hand and are standing right profile. In this position the left hand has all the time to enter the left coat pocket, deposit the six envelopes behind the cardboard partition and take out the other six. When the spectator has verified that the envelope really contains the card you tell the audience that because this experiment was successful you will try something more difficult with the remaining six envelopes. You make a prediction which you write on the slate.

You tell them that as you count the envelopes from your left into your right hand the spectator may call " Stop " any time he wishes to do so. Of course it does not matter when he calls " Stop " because all the envelopes contain the same card. When the word is given you hand over the envelope and ask one of the spectators to open up the envelope and announce loudly the name of the card that is in it. When that is done you turn over your slate and your prediction proves 100 per cent. correct.

Instead of using playing cards you may use geometrical design cards with a special order. The twenty-five designs given in the drawing page 325 are those which Corvelo has recommended. If you study them closely you will see that each particular design has some special characteristic by which it may be associated with its apparent number. For example we see that No. 1 is a circle and we may therefore introduce the mnemonic one. No. 2 composed of a cross—two lines; No. 3 a triangle. The first in this series you will note are similar to those which we have suggested already in Step 2. No. 5 itself introduces one of the Roman numerals—a V. No. 6 has six lines—a cross with two and a square with four. No. 7 is revealed mirror-wise. No. 8 consists of two circles. No. 9 IX, and so on throughout the series till you come to things like No. 20, where you discover the figure two has similar appearance to the letter Z. So you find as for example with 22, a double Z, and 25 where there is a little sketch or a design composed of a V (Roman numeral 5) and a Z. This is thus a compound of two of the systems. However there it is, a set of numbers which can quite easily be associated with a table of drawings, which in turn may be arranged into some order for the purpose of this particular routine, and doubtless the purpose of many other mental effects where it is necessary to use geometric designs and at the same time work with them in some specific order.

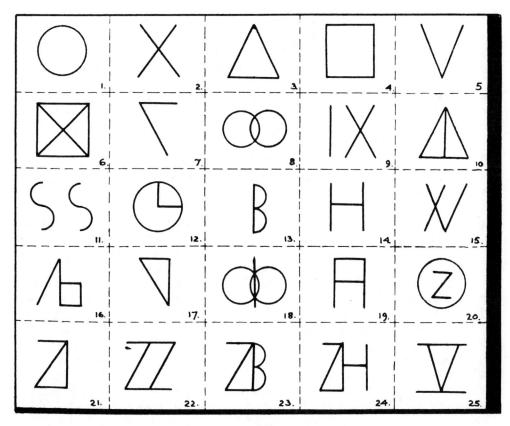

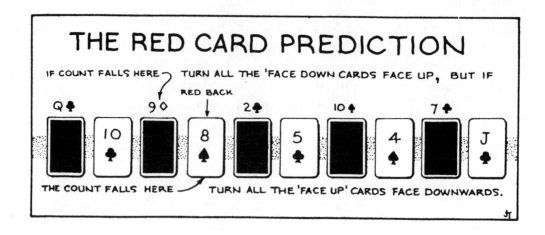

## " THE RED CARD PREDICTION "

**Effect.** The performer has ten playing cards which he places in a row on the table, some face-up, some face-down. He takes a slip of paper, writes a prediction which states: " I predict you will choose the red card." He gives the prediction to the spectator but does not say what it is as yet. He then invites the spectator to give him any number he likes from 1-10 inclusive and the spectator has a free choice. This having been done the performer counts to the chosen card and, having arrived there, it is found that by some strange coincidence it is indeed the only red card out of the ten on the table.

**Method.** It would be nice to give credit in the right place for this particular effect especially as the method is worthy of some praise. Unfortunately there appears to be a considerable amount of uncertainty as to who really has rightful claim to the origination. A similar set-up to this was once described in Abracadabra, the effect being titled " Poor Man's Supersonic," and those who have suggested improvements and variations include Arnold Liebertz and Dr. Jaks. However here is a method which works and whosoever may be responsible for the origination let us hand him our respect for a good trick.

The following cards are required and are placed in the order given in a row on the table. First the Queen of Clubs which is placed face-down. No. 2 is the Ten of Clubs which goes face-up. Next the Nine of Diamonds face-down. The Eight of Spades face-up. But this is very important. The fourth card is the only one that has a red back—all the others are blue-backed cards. That is why this face-down, face-up order is used as you will see later on. No. 5 the Two of Clubs which is face-down. The Five of Clubs face-up. The Ten of Spades face-down. The Four of Spades face-up. The Seven of Clubs face-down. The Jack of Clubs face-up. You will observe that all the cards excepting one (i.e. Nine of Diamonds), are black-faced and that all the cards excepting another are blue-backed. You will also observe that the two cards (the one with the red face and the one with the red back) are positioned third and fourth respectively. Now it so happens that no matter what number is given to you by the spectator it is possible to reach either the third or fourth card by a perfectly free count. However it is necessary to vary the method of counting according to the number given. And so first and foremost write your prediction which simply says: " You will choose the red card." Then invite the spectator to give you any number he likes between 1-10 inclusive, and adopt the following procedure of reaching a red card according to the following table:

| | |
|---|---|
| 1—Spell o—n—e. | 6—Spell s—i—x. |
| 2—Spell t—w—o. | 7—Count from the right-hand end |
| 3—Count 1, 2, 3. | 1, 2, 3, 4, 5, 6, 7. |
| 4—Count 1, 2, 3, 4, or spell. | 8—Do the same as for seven. |
| 5—Spell f—i—v—e. | 9—Spell n—i—n—e. |
| | 10—Spell t—e—n. |

You will see that by virtue of this system it is possible to arrive at a red card regardless of the number given. However there is one little touch necessary. Should it so be that the card you arrive at is the third card (the Nine of Diamonds), you simply turn over all the cards that are face-down so that the spectator can see quite clearly that there is only one red card there. You do not touch the fourth card. On the other hand if they should arrive at the fourth card you simply turn that card over and show the red back, and turn the others over to show all the backs are blue. In doing so you discreetly hide the face of the only red pip card the Nine of Diamonds. In other words you have enough " get-outs " to be on the winning end no matter what the spectator may decide. A nice clean mental card trick is thus performed.

### " ACROSS THE VOID" By Paul Marcus (New Zealand)

**Effect.** After speaking of his medium's ability to receive thoughts from a distance, the mentalist writes her name and telephone number on a business card which he places beside a telephone. One card is now mentally selected by a spectator. The identity of this card is not recorded in any way and it is known only to the spectator until the completion of the effect. A card is selected by a second spectator who shows it to the audience if he so wishes. Any spectator rings the medium who names both cards.

**Preparation.** To present this effect you will need three packs of cards with identical backs.

Pack No. 1 consists of 44 cards in the following sequence: 10S (Top card); 2D; 9H; Joker; JC; 5D; JD; 6C; 8H; 4S; KH; 7S; 3H; KC; 8D; 10S; QD; 2D; 9H; QS; 5D; 6C; Joker; 8H; KD; 4S; JH; 7S; QH; 3H; 8D; KS; 9D; AS; JS; 2C; 5C; QC; 10H; 3S; 4D; 9S; 6H; AH; (Face card). You will notice that the following eleven cards have been duplicated: 3H; 8H; 9H; 2D; 5D; 8D; 4S; 7S; 10S; 6C; Joker. By using cards that have been handled frequently, and consequently have thickened a little, it will not be noticed that the pack is short of the usual 52. This pack, in a card case, is anywhere at hand.

Pack No. 2 is a one-way forcing pack consisting of any low heart, other than the three. As I use the Five of Hearts in this description I shall assume it is the card to be forced. This pack, also in a card case, is in your right coat pocket.

Pack No. 3 is an ordinary pack of cards which you have loose in your left coat pocket.

**Presentation.** After setting the *mise en scène*, write the name and telephone number of your medium on any convenient writing surface which you then put near the telephone. Remove Pack No. 1 from its case, hold it face-down and give it several false cuts. Turn it face-up and fan it casually (remember you are demonstrating a mental effect, not card fanning) allowing the faces to be seen freely. Keep the cards slightly in motion and the duplicates of some will not be noticed. Close the fan and square the cards, still holding them face-up in the left hand. Ask a spectator to take the pack into his own hands, cut it, and run through the cards, " like this." Here you demonstrate how he is to do it by running the cards singly into the right hand without reversing the order, i.e. each card goes beneath the one before it. Do this so that the audience too, can see the faces of the cards.

Stop when you reach the Nine of Diamonds. Do not ask him to fan through the cards or he may notice that some are duplicated. Tell him to cut the pack, run through a dozen or so cards, and think of any one. " Please do not select the Joker or a court card; they are very difficult to transmit mentally." Direct him to step away by himself and turn his back while he follows your instructions. When he tells you he has thought of a card, toss the card case to him and ask him to put the pack in it. Take the card case from him and drop it into your right coat pocket. Decide almost immediately, as an afterthought to have a second card selected and remove pack No. 2.

Give the pack a quick casual cut or two before spreading the cards face-down on the table. Turn your back while one card is selected and returned to the pack. Ask a spectator to telephone the medium and ask for the names of the cards as you pick up the tabled pack. While attention is away from you, put the pack in your hand in your left coat pocket leaving it there you bring out pack No. 3. Place this pack facedown on the table. Because of the instructions given for the mental selection of the first card the choice is limited to one of the following ten cards: 3H; 8H; 9H; 2D; 5D; 8D; 4S; 7S; 10S; 6C. The medium does not know which of these cards was selected, but " pumps " the spectator on the telephone who repeats each statement aloud and has it confirmed or denied. Each " statement " is actually a question, and she does not proceed until that statement has been confirmed or denied. At the most she can make two mistakes, but a plausible explanation for any errors will be given shortly. Ask the first spectator to answer only " Yes " or " No " to the spectator at the telephone.

The medium learns first the colour, then the suit, finally the value of the mentally-selected card by means of the statements below. As no two suits contain the same two cards, a different procedure is adopted for each. This " pumping " may seem obvious, but due to the nature of the effect, it does not arouse suspicion. Each " statement " should be made hesitatingly, but not too slowly.

**Statement 1.** The card is red. (*a*) If correct: It is a Heart. If the card is red, but not a Heart, obviously it is a Diamond. (*b*) If the card is not red: It is a Spade. If this statement is incorrect, the mentally selected card is the Six of Clubs.

The procedure for each suit is as follows:

| | | |
|---|---|---|
| *Hearts* | (*a*) | It is an odd card. (If incorrect: It is the Eight of Hearts). |
| | (*b*) | If correct: It is a low card—below six in value. (If incorrect it is Nine of Hearts). |
| | (*c*) | If correct: It is the Three of Hearts. |
| *Diamonds*. | (*a*) | It is an even card. (If incorrect: It is the Five of Diamonds). |

(b) If correct: It is a low card—below six in value. (If incorrect: It is the Eight of Diamonds.

(c) If correct: It is the Two of Diamonds.

*Spades.*    (a) It is an even card. (If incorrect: It is the Seven of Spades).

(b) If correct: It is a low card—below six in value. (If incorrect: It is the Ten of Spades).

(c) If correct: It is the Four of Spades.

Should the medium make a " statement " which the first spectator denies, she can blame the second spectator for concentrating too strongly on his card. Thus, if the mentally-selected card is black, she says she picked up (mentally of course) the colour of the second card which she immediately states is a Heart. Have this confirmed at once. If the first card is a Diamond, she uses the same " out." If she wrongly " states " the first card is a low one, again the blame is put on the second spectator. Having the second card selected gives you the perfect " out " if one of the medium's statements is corrected.

The second spectator's card is named in a similar manner: first colour, then suit, finally value. As the medium knows the identity of this card, she need not wait for one statement to be confirmed before making the next. You may prefer to use three sets of " force " cards instead of two with fewer indifferent cards at the face of the pack.

In 1957 Charles Wicks of Australia showed me an effect using a pack consisting of six cards repeated. I extended the number to ten, added the elimination of court cards, and finally the selection of a second card. At the time I was using it as a one person effect. The idea of making it a two person telephone thought transference effect was an afterthought.

## BACK TO BACK

**Effect.** The mentalist explains that it is possible to develop the sense of feeling to a very fine degree. To illustrate this the mentalist bends over, his feet about two and a half feet apart, and his hands on his knees. He asks any spectator to shuffle a pack of cards, select one at random, show it to the rest of the audience, and place it face-up on the performer's back, resting on the part of the spine between the shoulder blades. (The mentalist explains that the spine is one of the most sensitive nerve centres of the body). After a few seconds contemplation he names correctly both the suit and value of the chosen card.

**Method.** When this effect is performed a friend of the mentalist is standing four or five feet directly behind him. As soon as the card is selected, the friend notes its identity and codes the selection to the mentalist in the following way. Because of the mentalist's position he is able to see the feet of his friend who is standing directly behind him. The friend only needs to move his feet inside the shoes very slightly to code the value and suit of the card.

For example a single movement inside the left shoe represents Hearts and two movements Diamonds. One inside the right shoe Spades, two Clubs. The value can then be given in the same manner with either foot. To prevent a mis-reading with the value, it is better to use the foot which has not been used to code the suit. For example if the *left* foot was used to code a Heart, then the *right* foot should be used for the value.

Although the method is extremely simple it is an astounding effect on the audience and is an ideal effect for drawing room or party entertainment.

# Dr. Thornton's "COINCIMENTAL" *by permission of Ed Mellon*

**Effect.** The performer shows and shuffles two packs of Alphabet cards. From one pack he chooses four cards and arranges them backs out in full view of the audience. A spectator is allowed to choose cards from the other pack and from them form any four letter word he desires. As soon as the spectator's letters are arranged, the performer turns his around . . .

Coincidence number one: They have both chosen the same letters!

Coincidence number two: They have both formed the same word!

Yes, any of several words could have been formed; the spectator can even change his mind if he likes. There are no confederates, no switches and no sleight of hand. It is as direct as that.

**Requirements.** Two packs of Alphabet cards. One is an ordinary pack of 26 letters cards; one for each letter of the alphabet. The other pack contains only 25 cards and consists of five " E " cards, five " S " cards, five " P " cards, five " T " cards, and five " F " cards. They are arranged in this order: T, E, P, S, F, repeated five times.

Also required are two simple card stands.

Notice that when the spectator has chosen these five cards and is requested to form a word with four of them, he will lay aside the " F " as it is impossible to make a word using the " F " with this combination of letters. This leaves the letters T, E, P, S. As you can see it is possible to form several words from these letters. The most frequently formed is STEP. The next most frequently formed word is PETS. The third possibility, though not often formed is PEST.

**Performance.** The performer shows the two packs of Alphabet cards. Laying aside the stacked deck for the moment, he mixes the pack in his hands by cutting—*not* riffle shuffling (not so important here, but when repeated with the other pack will keep the cards in their arranged order). Then he looks through the pack selecting the letters P, E, T, S. These letters are arranged on the card stand, backs out, in this order: PETS.

The remainder of the pack is laid aside and the " stacked " deck is picked up and " mixed " by straight cuts. A spectator is requested to remove several cards from anywhere in the pack. (Of course held out to him face-down). Here you need only be sure that he removes the cards together; not one here, one there. You then ask, " How many letters do you have?" and if he has taken five, O.K.; but if he has taken less than five, hand him the other from the same place in the pack. For instance if he has withdrawn three say, " Here, take a couple more," pushing two more out with the thumb, being sure that they were next to the ones first removed. He now has TEPSF.

Now you state that you want him to use any four of the letters chosen to form a word and ask, " Can you form a word from the letters you have?" Obviously he will answer yes, so you add: " Form any word you like." He places them in his stand with the faces towards the audience and as he arranges them you remark about the possibility of a number of words which can be formed by the letters he chose.

If he made the word STEP, you simply pick up the stand in which your cards rest and turn the whole thing around. If he made the word PETS, you begin at the left (facing the backs of your cards) turning around one card at a time replacing each on the stand. If he has made the word PEST, you begin at the left and turn the " P " and the " E " around separately and remark " Well, it seems that we have chosen the same letters." Then you pick up the last two cards at the same time and swing them around at the same time (which reverses them for your climax), " And it seems that we have thought of the same word!!!"

LUCILLIE AND EDDIE ROBERTS

# NOTES

# QUESTION AND ANSWER (READINGS)

## BY

Corinda

## STEP ELEVEN

IN CORINDA'S SERIES :—

## "THIRTEEN STEPS TO MENTALISM"

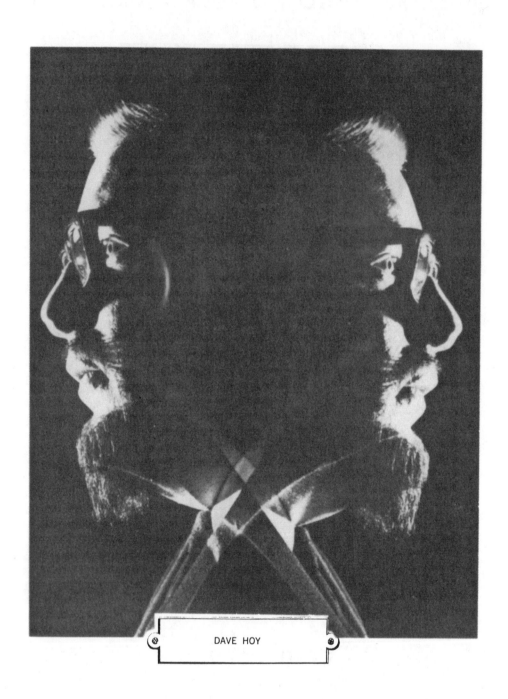

DAVE HOY

STEP ELEVEN in CORINDA'S SERIES

" THIRTEEN STEPS TO MENTALISM "

QUESTION AND ANSWER (READINGS)

## CONTENTS

# INTRODUCTION

Millions of pounds and dollars have been made by people who have acquired the knack of telling others what they want to know. Mindreaders and Mediums have spent a lot of time and study on the psychology of answering questions that are put to them by members of the public, who, supposing that the mindreader is gifted with some divine insight, presume he has the ability to foretell the future and see the past and present.

It is possible to tell the future and see the past and present! What is more, anybody who cares to do so—can do so; the qualifications required are few although their application may be harder than one might at first suppose. In order that you may consider time in a person's life, thereby providing the means to answer a question, you require experience of life, which we shall call worldliness, you must be skilled in observation of detail and you need a good memory along with the mentalist's best friend—the ability to talk.

Armed with these few qualifications, you are a powerful person. You can deal with people and what is equally as important, people want to deal with you! Shall we consider *why* there has ever been a demand for people who can answer questions? If we understand why the questions are asked, we understand what sort of reply must be given—and that is a most important thing to bear in mind at all times.

Starting at the beginning; when we are troubled with our health, we go to a doctor because we know he can answer our questions. Likewise, in a problem of law, we go to a solicitor. With all our material problems we find someone somewhere who is qualified to render advice—but when we step outside the material and find we are troubled with the intangible—whom then do we consult? Who is best qualified to deal with indecision, uncertainty, doubt, fear and hope and any of the emotional twists of our human make-up? A clever man knows that half his trouble is solved when he finds out what the problem is—so who do you go to when you are troubled and cannot pin-point anything or anybody with the blame? Some people go to mediums, some go to mindreaders and some go mad! Others find their answers elsewhere but we are concerned with those who go to mindreaders.

Most people who seriously ask our mindreader to render his professional advice, do so because they hope (and occasionally believe) that his unusual abilities give him something the others have not got. In the first place they presume he has something more than others because in general, the approach to the interview is something quite extraordinary; in fact, considered in cold daylight, it is more than extraordinary—it is absurd. The character with a problem wants to come up to our mindreader and sit in front of him with perhaps three words of greeting. From then on (in theory) our gifted seer reveals past, present and future, states facts right, left and centre and ends up with the perfect answer to all problems! It is not so—that's what they want and that's what they think they get—but by half a million miles it is not so. Very shortly, we shall see what diabolical deceit is used to make something so hard—seem so simple; it is the art of giving answers to questions.

To boil it down to a few words, when someone asks you a question there are TWO replies you can give. There is that which *they* want to happen, and there is that which *they* do not want to happen. If you tell them the first, they will believe in you and like you. If you tell them the second they will doubt you and dislike you. It's as simple as that, or is it?

339

The trouble starts when you find out *what* they want and yet to advise it would be doing what you know to be ethically or legally wrong. People don't always want to do the *right* thing, very often they want the opposite and if you encourage them, do you not become a party to their guilt? So how do you get out of that fix? Again it is simple when you understand.

Your first objective is to find out what they want—that is to say, when dealing with a serious question. Having done that, you call on your experience of life and work out within reason, whether or not you are in a position to give any advice at all. If no harm can be done (and we shall say more on this later)—then go ahead and say what commonsense tells you to say keeping your advice as near as possible to their secret wishes. If harm can be done, fall back on the old friend to Mediums—deliver a warning carefully worded but above all shroud the answer in ambiguity. Admit nothing, suggest nothing and insinuate nothing. Give out a long winded spiel that seems to answer everything and answers nothing. Play safe and remember that it is better to give no advice than wrong advice.

Exception to this can be taken when it becomes widely apparent that strong, sensible advice will do some good. For example, if you are confronted with a question that looks as though medical treatment would be the answer, don't be afraid to suggest a visit to the doctor. Never presume you can advise on all matters and leave technical problems to those qualified to handle them.

Many of the questions that people ask are concerned with medical problems and so we can take this type of question as illustrative of the right approach to giving an answer. Let us reason with commonsense. When a question has anything to do with health we can safely assume the person is worried on medical grounds. If nothing is wrong we could advise "you have no need to worry" BUT without the qualification of a doctor and a medical examination—how do we know that there is nothing wrong? We don't—so we offer good advice; we suggest a visit to the doctor. This assures that a satisfactory condition is reached because at the visit, if the person is told there is nothing wrong—then there is nothing left for them to worry about and on the other hand, if something is wrong, the fact that it has been discovered and can now be treated can hardly be considered in any way as harmful as a result of your advice!

Some readers might begin to think that I am rambling a bit too far from the main theme of this step—but I am not. If you propose to poke your nose (as I do) into other people's business, set yourself up as one who can advise on any problem or answer any question, you have got to be mighty careful. You are dealing with people's lives—not a dead pack of playing cards and you must accept responsibility for your own judgment. You must aim to be kind and firm, above all understanding; you need a broad mind and a controllable sense of humour and if you want to—you can do a lot of good, which is contrary to the average opinion that this sort of thing is a lot of bunkem and does no good.

For a long time I have frowned on mit-readers, pseudo-psychologists and the Tarot divinators. It took me quite a while to wake up to the fact that they do more good than harm and I have by now enough personal experience of people made happy by them. Hundreds will disagree with me on this—but the joy is that I'm writing the book and what I say goes in print!

This business of answering questions can be a fascinating aspect of Mentalism.

At the start it all seems very boring and unimportant and it takes time before you realise how very personal it is—and slowly you begin to see that this is an advanced field of mental magic, a field where experience counts for more than anything else. Nothing can teach you more than experience in this business and if you stick at it, by virtue of your experience, you will develop an uncanny knack of telling what they want, why they want it and facts about the person you are dealing with at the time. It's wonderful training for the mentalist because in the main it forces him to fall back on personal ability, shrewdness, perception, logic and mental analysis of situations and people. In the beginning, you may well take to apparatus as a means to gain information, you may call upon Clip Boards, Billets, Systems and so forth to booster your personal ability; but in the end you will not.

The true Question and Answer man does not use gimmicks because he does not have to use them. I have worked with professional readers and I have seen how they can fathom a situation and analyse a person—and these professionals don't know the first thing about mentalism and what is more, they don't want to! They fall back on experience and if you aim to specialise in this work, that too should be your objective because there is no higher standard and no better system.

Those experienced in answering questions know that if you were to invite ten thousand people to ask a personal question, the bulk of the questions received could be classed very quickly into a very limited number of groups or types of questions. You would not get ten thousand different questions as you might suppose if you were inexperienced. In fact you would probably be quite amazed at the large number that seemed to be much the same. If you decided to remove all questions that dealt with Money, Health and Sex in shape or form(!)—you would have very few left from your ten thousand. You don't have to be a psychiatrist to reason that these three things are predominate interests in the average life.

In view of this, which is an established fact and not a crackpot theory, we can anticipate what the question will be to some extent. Since the classification of questions is a statistical theorem, we cannot guarantee what the question will be. but what we can do is to save a lot of time and trouble by dealing with the most probable question first and so on down the scale until we arrive at the actual problem on hand. Sometimes people tell you what they want to know, sometimes they don't and then you must find out. Without recourse to trickery with apparatus (i.e. Clip Boards) you determine the question or problem by a process of verbal conjuring called "pumping". This again is a skilled art. It means you have to make them tell you what they want to know—and yet they must not know that they have told you. All very ridiculous when you think of it—but part of the game nevertheless! We shall deal with "pumping" a little later—but now we know what it is and why we do it, let us see how it fits in with our statistical questions.

Does it not stand to reason that if you have a pretty good idea of what they want, you not only know where to go with the opening gambit, but also you know how to deal with your discoveries and you save a lot of time and avoid nasty blunders of conversation that may otherwise occur. Without a clue, you may well start off on any blind alley. Why not ask them if their problem has anything to do with chrome-plating sardine tins? Answer is simply that more people have trouble with sex than sardine tins—so sex gets priority! Along these lines we can learn from those who have answered thousands of questions and pay attention to their views which tell you what subjects are most likely and in graduated scale form, which ones are most unlikely.

We shall give a table of probabilities which is based on an analysis of many questions to show what statistics say you should expect.

For the moment we need not consider the exception to the fact which invariably exists where statistics are concerned, because no matter what we say or what we prepare for, there will always be the catch-question, the ambiguous question and the lunatic's problem. We shall prepare for them by having in stock a couple of good replies that will fit any doubtful question and our budding mentalists should not be discouraged by the thought that someone may ask him "What is the I.Q. of my French Poodle?". Those who deal with Questions and Answers stick their necks out a mile or two when inviting ANY question—and you cannot limit the choice without impairing your status, but for all the risk it's great fun playing the mental-detective and finding out what they don't want to tell you and then telling them the same things in such a manner that it all sounds and seems frightfully clever.

It is frightfully clever at that! "Cold reading" means you start off without the slightest knowledge about the person and end up telling them a long list of personal data. Is that not clever? Maybe you will disagree, but one thing you can't argue about is that it's commercial. As stated earlier, quite a number of people have made quite a number of fortunes by acquiring the ability to do it. One or two moralists will stand up and call the whole affair a dirty business—and ten to one they don't know the first thing about it. Of course it can be a dirty business—and so can Mentalism and Magic if you choose to make it so. I know a group that use conjuring tricks solely for the purpose of performing pseudo-occult manifestations at meetings of so-called Black Magic. That's dirty magic—but you don't have to do it. When it comes to Questions and Answers you can be clean all the way—and should be. If you set out to amuse people and help them with some sound advice when you can—it does no harm whatsoever and I wouldn't care a damn what the critics say or think. I know from experience that half the visitors to a friend of mine, went there not because they wanted advice or solutions to problems—but simply because they just wanted someone with whom they could discuss their headaches. Having talked things over, they were quite relieved and nothing more than that did a lot more good than harm. So don't be too sensitive about dealing with Questions and Answers on the grounds that it has been—and will remain, open to attack from those who "think" but don't "know". Set yourself a decent standard in the work and stick to it. That is to say, resolve to keep your mouth shut about other people's business. If they are going to talk over personal problems with you—maybe you will learn a lot about them. Let that be a professional confidence and don't compare notes with other readers or advertise what has been confided in you. Don't get mixed up with any of the groups or Religions that allow scope for a question and answer man. Steer very clear of anything that can be labelled "Supernatural" and consider yourself to be more in the class Mentalist-Psychologist rather than Mentalist-Medium. Don't try and fool people who are guided by Spirits—either liquid or astral; some of the money earned from Question and Answer performers has been made from the mediumship level—but it's not such a high level so keep away from it.

Anything which deals with very personal matters is naturally a delicate subject and that is why Question and Answer workers have to be so careful. There are still many pitfalls that the unthinking performer will slip into. It may be an act from the stage with a Question and Answer routine thrown in. For general entertainment, the act may be guided along comedy lines—with witty, clever and taunting replies. However, you never really know if someone sitting out front is desperate for sound advice—or maybe someone is hurt by your joke. Therefore it is generally a wise policy to play safe when dealing with questions, and to assume that they are serious unless it is obvious that a prank or catch is intended. When it does happen that you get a catch-question or one that is quite obviously intended for fun, then you are at liberty to reciprocate in like manner, and your aim should be to out-wit the witty. We shall explore the usual catch-questions and give a few examples of how to deal with them. This will come later in the book.

The other type of question that we may receive is serious but dangerous. It is not just a light-hearted catch-question, but a "bait" question which has been cooked up to expose you as a fraud. If you are caught on this one—you are in trouble and you have got to be very sharp to talk your way out of it. Therefore the best bet is to play safe again and don't take chances. If you smell a bait question—try to avoid dealing with it altogether and when that is impossible, give any answer that commits nothing, approves of nothing and if the question warrants it, go so far as to insinuate that you doubt the sincerity of the question. Every now and then we get a real beauty, known as the "red-hot bait Question" and usually they are framed in aggressive language so you can, if you feel confident, reciprocate with a powerful answer. We give a few hints on how to deal with hecklers and sticky situations a little later.

So now let us get down to the business of studying now to deal with Questions. So that we can tackle this rather expansive field in some sort of syllabus, let us divide it into two main parts. Part one we shall call "Dealing with Questions that are known" and Part Two, "Dealing with Questions unknown". It is important that you read *both* Parts as there is a considerable overlap of technique and the two cannot be completely isolated from each other.

## PART ONE

### Dealing with Questions that are Known.

To clarify exactly what we mean by "Questions that are known" let us regard any Question or Problem that is written, conveyed directly or spoken outright as a Known Question. No pumping is required—the person has either written their question (which means you will read it somehow) or told you outright, or someone else has told you and so without more ado you know.

Starting off with knowledge of the problem on hand makes it all much easier for you although you must not forget that if they *tell* you their question, it is less impressive than when they do not tell you. Consequently, it is a good thing to find out what they want to know—right at the beginning, and if you can, keep it a secret that you have discovered what they want to know.

To do this, we can resort to several standard techniques of Mentalism which, having been dealt with already in other Steps—do not require further explanation here. However, for your convenience, the following reference to such technique is given here:—

## HOW TO GET INFORMATION

(A) Reference to Technique in Other Steps.

Pencil Reading (Step Two)        Billet Switching (Step Six)
The Centre Tear (Step Six)       Three Little Questions (Step Six)
The Clip Book (Step Seven)       Pellet Switching (Step Six)

(B) Other methods (not mentioned in later studies).

**(1) Alcohol or Chemicals.** A story is told of a well-known professional reader who worked nightclubs. He had people write questions and seal them in envelopes, these were then collected in a bunch and thrown into a pile on the table. Throughout his act, the performer swigged liberal quantities of whisky and in fact appeared very nearly drunk. But for the fact that he gave brilliant answers and nobody knew how he found out what to say, he may well have been booted out. His method was simply to keep his glass well topped with whisky and to "rest" an envelope on the mouth of the glass from time to time. With the proof spirit contained in whisky the envelope was rendered transparent enough for him to read the message inside—and so it was done. It may not be the best of methods, but I don't know a better excuse for drinking whisky! !

However, coming back to sobriety, chemicals that render an envelope transparent can be used but it is my experience that these methods are messy and not worth the trouble. If you must do it this way, I suggest you look into chemicals other than Alcohols (which in any case has to be pure-white and not the cheap "Meth" variety) and explore the advantages of Carbon tetrachloride. This achieves the same effect and has less smell. You can get wonderful transparency with ether or any of the highly volatile solvents, but generally they give off fumes which make the room smell akin to an operating theatre. Not to be desired!

The only real qualification for using chemical methods is that you need to read the message inside an envelope and then RETURN the envelope unopened to the writer. Hence you have other things to consider. If they are going to get it back—there must be no stains on the envelope and another thing which can be very troublesome today, no "running" of ball-pen ink used to write the question—a thing which is easily caused by the solvent action of many chemicals.

With these complications and with the option to use alternative, but equally as effective methods, I recommend that you do not involve yourself with chemical techniques unless you enjoy performing troubles.

**(2) Light.** Again we are dealing with reading a question sealed in an envelope and with the intention of returning it to the writer. Light is simply another method of making most envelopes transparent. Gimmicks have been made for this purpose so that an envelope can be "X-rayed" with light BUT once again we encounter snags.

First, if we are to use light then it has to be done secretly and that is not an easy matter. Nelson Enterprises market a gimmick which is suitable when you are using a stack of envelopes and there is a model of a Light-screening unit built into a book which hides the apparatus successfully. However, although you may choose the right cards and right envelopes for this technique, you will always get someone who fails in your instructions, and *folds* their card before sealing it in the envelope—and what then? Once more, there are easier methods if you want to use them.

**(3) The Window Envelope.** It is generally the case, that anything *simple* is *good*, and the Window Envelope is both. You have a stack of a dozen envelopes and the top one has been treated with a razor blade. A large section has been cut from the back. The questions are written on postcards and envelopes are given out to all people excepting one. You ask him to turn his card face downwards before taking it yourself and sliding it into the window envelope—as if showing the others what to do. There is no need for more than one window envelope as with the facility of knowing one question—you are in a position to work the Washington-Irving-Bishop Test, which as you all know is the One Ahead System! If you like to work with smaller sized envelopes, you use pay-packets in conjunction with visiting cards and apply the same principle.

**(4) The Clip Board.** Now we come to the group of apparatus that is designed primarily for the purpose of getting information—and very useful too in the right circumstances. In the general run of things, a Clip Board, particularly in England, is not a widely used or accepted appliance. However, where you are intent on having lots of people write lots of questions, it is not wrong to suppose that some sort of rest would be provided. A Clip Board is simply a square wooden board which has several sheets of paper held in position ready for writing—by means of a bulldog clip at the top. It is so constructed that a carbon impression is made and can be removed or seen after the top sheet used by the spectator has been removed and retained by him. Some Clip-Boards are very simple and some are cunningly designed with trick mechanisms that open panels, etc., and they range from a few inches to two feet in size, Likewise, their price on the commercial market varies according to method, size and model. The simple "Draw-out" type now available as a standard Dealers' product is good enough for all general purpose work. [For CLIP BOOK See (A) Reference page 344.]

There are other appliances which work along the lines of a Clip Board. That is to say, function on the impression or copy technique. Such apparatus includes a leather wallet (which I use quite frequently) which by virtue of its smooth yet soft surface, allows a clear embossed impression to be made when anything is written with a ball pen on a sheet of paper rested on the wallet. Having experimented along these lines, I find a black leather wallet to be the best colour for this purpose and since no faking is required, it is a very useful and natural appliance to use. The embossed impression incidentally, can be removed by pressure with the thumbs rubbing over the surface—so it can be used time and time again.

Another appliance was designed by the English Mentalist Eric Mason and is now a marketed item called "Dubbul". This is a wallet-type pocket writing case made in leather, and it gains the information by means of a direct carbon impression. It is very easy to read the impression with this wallet and so it is a very good idea. The original model of this item which was manufactured in plastic was a very poor example of the apparatus but since then it has been improved to a standard which makes it highly practical. Dubbul is obtainable from most dealers for the sum of about two pounds.

Finally, we have a number of clear-plastic or perspex boards which take an impression by use of special paper. Waxed paper (white candle wax) can be used, so can white powder and so can Silico paper. The only object behind the clear clip board seems to be the desire to prove that it is not faked. I object to that on the grounds that if you handle ANY clip board properly, it should not occur to your audience that it could be faked.

**(5) The Record Card.** This is a trick of the trade, usually confined to use where a reader is dealing with one person at a time—but suitable for more than one when required. ANY information is an asset when dealing with Questions and Answers, so when the visitor calls, he is asked to fill out a "record card" which is handed to him. This is a simple innocent looking filing card which has been printed with the terms as shown in the drawing. It is inferred that the purpose of the card is simply for "the record" of the visit. However, you see for yourself how much information you acquire immediately the card is completed!

|  XX  |  ZZ  |
| --- | --- |
| Name<br><br>Address.<br><br>Date of Birth<br><br>Question. | Name ........................<br><br>Address ........................<br><br>Date of Birth........................<br><br>Telephone No. ........................ |

As you will see, two varieties of Record cards are given. One of them asks you outright what is the question you want to ask! The other, less conspicuous, gets you off to a good start with lots of personal data about the sitter. A large number of professional readers have adopted these techniques to save time and to be sure of getting somewhere with the client. One might suppose the whole thing becomes blatant when these cards are used, but I can assure you that handled rightly there is no danger or even a suspicion as to their actual purpose. "XX" shows the layout of a question card and "ZZ" a less presumptuous hybrid.

It has been known for many years that one professional reader gave her clients a foolscap questionnaire that, by the time completed by the sitter, gave the reader enough personal data to sit back and write a biography on the client! If you possess the impudence, you can get away with murder. (Without prejudice!)

**(6) The Stooge.** Here we go again! Everytime I say "stooge" I get fifty letters telling me it's all wrong. Let me come back to something I said in Step Four. Stooges are there to be used if you want to use them, and need not be used if you don't want to use them. You do what you want—and let other people do the same!

I was reminded of this swindle whilst talking about Question and Answer effects with Fogel. It's very old—but very good. Working a hall or from stage the mindreader hands out envelopes and cards for questions. All are sealed by the audience before they are collected by the performer. On his way

346

round he gathers up the envelopes and takes one from his stooge seated in the audience. As soon as he gets it from the stooge, he looks back at him and asks "Did you sign your name?"—the fellow says "No" so the performer hands him back the envelope to open, sign and reseal in another envelope. What actually happens is that the performer gives the stooge a *different* envelope from his own—one that has just been collected. The stooge opens it, reads the question, copies it quickly on the outside of the envelope and seals it. The performer collects it and is now set for a perfect One Ahead Routine with Sealed Envelopes.

**(7) Switching of Envelopes.** We shall see that for work with large audiences, it is a practical proposition to collect a lot of sealed envelopes into some sort of basket or bowl, and then to switch the lot, lock, stock and barrel. All that remains to be done then is to open the real ones, read them, copy out the main context and convey it to the Reader. Methods of conveying questions to the Reader, will be considered in the next section of this book. Before that however, let us speak briefly on Switching the bulk stock in the first place.

Quite a number of professional theatre-workers have found it quite an easy matter to have questions written in the foyer by incoming patrons. The envelopes or folded slips being dropped into a Ballot Box, Bowl or Basket by the writers. An attendant is used to collect the full box and take it to the stage where it is dumped in full view of the audience. En route from the foyer to the stage, there are a dozen opportunities to switch the complete box for a duplicate box which has been ready loaded with dummy envelopes or slips. The fact that the method is blatant should lead you to suppose that it is liable to suspicion. The acid test is that it has been used time and time again— with a modicum of success.

Alternatively, we may resort to trick apparatus, switch boxes, fake-load-chambers, and the kind. My personal feeling is that they are liable to fail and what is more, they are by no means essential. Clip boards used in the foyer enable you to bring the real questions on to the stage and work with the information gained from the carbon copy questions when this procedure is adopted. It is a good method.

**(8) Planting of Envelopes and Slips.** Another rather subtle dodge is to have many envelopes collected but to ADD a few of your own to the supply. It is such an easy matter to do this that we need hardly bother with it here. As a matter of interest, Question and Answer acts have been devised where the performer answers about twenty questions and has no time for more. The twenty which consume his time are all planted by him and not one of them is genuine. By acting the part "talking to 'someone' in the audience" the rest of the house is convinced the whole affair is proper! Rather an ingenious swindle and one which takes a creditable amount of nerve to do! In any case, nearly all Question and Answer acts for large audiences, should consider the addition of one or two (at least) "spicey" questions which are going to guarantee a stir in the audience. Every question does not have to be ac-knowledged. You can always come up with the old spiel "The next question is one that I think is far too personal, and since it involves stolen money, I will not embarrass the writer by identification now...." with such an introduction, which sounds plausible, everybody is dead keen to know who is the crook and they are interested before you start the answer! What is more important is that you can say what you like—because the whole thing is fictitious and there is no danger of being prosecuted for slander.

## HOW TO CONVEY INFORMATION

On many occasions a Question and Answer routine is based on the old principles of stealing envelopes and opening them, getting carbon-copies or sneaking information by way of personal interviews. Generally, when this is so, it is a matter of *getting* the information from an off-stage backroom to the Reader who is on stage working, or ready to work. We shall not bother to detailise the methods—but content ourselves with listing some of the many; most of which suggest for themselves the method that is used.

We should know this, however. Our questions must be analysed, abridged to the minimum of context without losing any vital facts (i.e. names, dates) and written clearly though in very small letters. Bearing in mind that the Reader must hide this secret information from the audience and yet he must be able to see it clearly enough to read, we must be practical in our method. Sometimes the Reader himself will write out his questions, copied from the originals and listed for a handy reference for himself whilst performing. We have methods of doing this—since it would be far too confusing to try and remember some thirty or forty different questions in detail.

Fogel has advised me considerably on this matter and does so with good authority as one who has performed Question and Answer routines during his professional career. He suggested that a sample "code" be developed to reduce the context of the question to a minimum of writing. For example, he would write . . . "D!!MOORE/Mr/Tr/1907" which would result as the coding of the question "I have travelled as a soldier during the war and I am now fifty-two-years-old, do you think I will go back to where I was stationed?", signed D. MOORE. We see the basic points are Name, M. MOORE; Sex, Male—indicated by Mr.; Subject, Travel—we use Tr.; age, 52—we write his birth year. Space permitting, we could include "Soldier" and "War"—but already we have enough to go on. No complicated code is needed, simply abridge the question to a bare minimum of writing so that you can understand what was originally written—and quite often you will remember the complete question, word for word, when you see your code guide.

We see now that by coding the questions to reduce their length and along with the ability to *print* small but distinctive notes, we can write very many questions in a very small space. About twenty questions could be coded on to the back of a Postage Stamp (English 1d. in size), although this economy is hardly called for!

Just one last tip before we deal with actual means of conveyance. Do the writing whenever it is possible with a good *black* ink—which shows up well unless the method calls for writing with chalk, pencil or methylphenolatetri-iodide.

## GENERAL MEANS OF CONVEYING INFORMATION SECRETLY

**(1) Hand Rollers, Faro-Boxes, Slip-Boxes.** These are gimmicked apparatus which are operated by hand movement bringing questions into view and taking away those which have been dealt with. Nelson's "Encyclopedia of Mentalism" is a book that adequately describes the apparatus.

**(2) Pencilled Slate.** Many questions can be written on a slate with ordinary pencil and are hardly visible from a short distance. Similarly, a blackboard can serve the same purpose.

348

**(3) The Thumbnail.** Quite a few questions can be abridged and written on your thumbnails. Your hands are then free of cumbersome apparatus. Ink can be used.

**(4) Cigarette Holder.** Fogel gave me this and the next method. Questions are written along the stem of a cigarette holder which of course, in the hands, is easily seen.

**(5) Roller on Microphone.** Another Fogel dodge was to have a simple hand roller which clipped on to the stage microphone and was made to look like part of that apparatus! Very cunning and practical.

**(6) Watchface.** A small piece of paper stuck over your wristwatch face gives you another handy source of supply. Remember, you can get twenty questions on a postage stamp?

**(7) Cuff.** A method which can be used if you do not mind the laundry bill! Notes are made on your shirt cuff—just where the Victorian toff played noughts and crosses when teacher wasn't looking!

**(8) On a Small Card.** Questions are coded and then neatly printed on a visiting card which is not hard to conceal in the folds of a handkerchief or black velvet drape used to shroud your crystal.

**(9) Large Card or Blackboard.** Questions written in large handwriting and displayed on a large card concealed in the footlights—or chalked on a blackboard which you can see in the wings. It has been done successfully.

**(10) Written on Glass.** Questions can be written on a drinking glass in ink, or on the water jug that is brought on stage to you. Every time you take a sip you glimpse another question.

Once we appreciate that many questions can be reduced to a very small space we understand that there is not much of a problem when it comes to conveying the coded questions to the reader, or, recording them for his benefit. We have suggested but a few—obviously there are many more.

## SELECTION OF SUITABLE QUESTIONS TO USE

This concerns Question and Answer routines that deal with an intake of a wide selection of questions. If you have a small audience and about a dozen questions are provided, you have no choice other than to accept what is given. On the other hand, with a large audience—you should aim at getting anything up to a hundred questions 'in' so that you can browse through them and sort out the most suitable for your act. Which ones are most suitable?

Any question which offers an intriguing situation is good. Any question that blurts forth a lot of facts is good. Any question which infers sex (Will my baby be a boy or a girl?) in any shape or form is good—if you can deal with it and not involve yourself! Any questions off the beaten track— ("Am I overfeeding my alligators?") is good.

Questions which are no good are catch-questions ("Can you tell me my mother's maiden name?"). Questions that are disinteresting to everybody and lack enough material to give you any scope ("Am I healthy?"). Questions that lead you to fall into a legal trap ("What is the name of the man who goes with my wife?") and finally those (which you will get) which say "I dare not ask you now, but can I see you later please . . ." As a general guide you can refer to the Table of Probabilities which to some extent indicates what the majority interest will be—an assumption founded on the fact that most people ask questions concerned with the top topics. (See page 355).

Having sorted your questions and coded those you intend to use, it remains now a matter of performance—giving the answers. Since this part of the book deals with Questions Known—our speed of delivery (i.e. answering) will be quicker than Questions Unknown—as we have no pumping to do and we have facts on hand.

## ANSWERING QUESTIONS KNOWN

Primarily, there are two species of answers to questions. There is the answer that entertains and interests everybody, and there is the personal reply that usually remains of interest to one person only. If you are performing a Question and Answer routine as part of a mental act—then your first concern is entertainment so your answers will be framed accordingly. On the other hand, if you were giving a Private Reading—there is no need to be entertaining—since your audience is composed of one and that one is far more concerned with personal attention than amusement.

With this difference in mind, we can foresee that almost any question will do for the personal reading but for "open" readings (i.e. from stage or platform) we must become a showman. We have already considered the best *type* of question and now let us consider the best type of answer.

The personal reading is easiest to describe so we shall deal with that first. Your prime concern is to make the subject happy. No matter what they tell you or what you deduce, sort out something from the interview that can leave you in a position to advise a pleasant change very soon. There is no need to be commital. Ambiguity is the very essence of personal reading—and so is the art of introducing happiness. Try to discover what interests the subject most, and if it is money—advise a gain shortly to be met with; if romance, advise new friends, new faces and contacts from old associates are on the way, etc., etc. Speak in broad terms, never specialise or pin-point your suggestions too much. Allow the subject to create a meaning to your words—as they will if you do it rightly. Reflect for a moment that since the days when Shakespeare wrote in Hamlet "To Be or Not To Be . . ." tens of thousands of people have sought their own meaning to that most ambiguous phrase. It suits ideally any of the vast number of problems that do occur in every life—and people, forgetting all about the original intention of the line from Hamlet —seek their own meaning.

Flattery can be a sin, a deadly weapon and a medicine depending upon how it is used and when. The Mentalist should study the uses of flattery and particularly so when it comes to readings. An obstinate client can be inflated to an endless degree of self-importance, and then become quite a chatterbox when the tongue has been loosened with a few flattering remarks! A self-conscious timid client can be relaxed when you tell him that his talents are more than he supposes, that he is too tolerant and considerate. With an understanding of the use of flattery, you will find that this alone can be the means for you to bring success to your private reading. Very, very few people are immune to the effect of flattery and whenever you discover a talent or skill in the client, build it up as though it is something worth having and something to be proud of—again using your personal judgment in the matter. For example, having discovered that your client was a first class burglar— it would not be advisable to flatter and thereby endorse his talent!

To reduce the requirements of an answer given to a personal question, to the very minimum, let us say this. First find out what *they* want and as far as possible, twist your answer round so that you say they will get it. Keep the interview "alive" with suggestions and inferences of good things that may happen. Stick in a couple of sure-fire predictions for good value and act the part throughout. For example, during the reading you vary your attitude. Sometimes you are serious—the matter is grave, and sometimes light-hearted, the future is bright! One thing is vital knowledge to the Reader and should never be forgotten; that is, nearly all clients ask a question which has already been considered by them and they have invariably formed their own opinions as to what to do. More often than not—if you advise against the decision they have already formed in their mind, you are conflicting with their wishes and they don't like that. As long as you can, make it a rule to find out what they have decided they should do—and you advise the same. The only time to break this rule—is when you know without any doubt that it will cause lots of trouble, if it is illegal or extremely dangerous. If you keep in mind the slogan "Tell them what they want to know"—you will be successful.

## ANSWERING QUESTIONS FROM PLATFORM

There is a distinct difference between the Private Reader and the Stage Reader. We have seen what sort of answer is given by the first and now we must consider the second. Bearing in mind what we have said that "Entertainment is the prime object"—our answers must appeal to the mass and that is why you carefully choose the *right* questions in the first place.

There are numerous styles of presentation for the Stage Reader. Some performers prefer to start off by calling out the initials of the person who wrote the questions, having them hold up their hand for identification and then replying to them. Others answer the question first and have the spectator identify his question afterwards. Some do not have any identification or acknowledgment from the audience and some mix a bit of each and everything. The very last is the best.

It means that sometimes you start off asking "Who is 'M.G.B.' please?"—and sometimes "This is a question about buying a church—our friend is somewhere here tonight and we shall see who he is later . . ." However, since we have established a pattern that varies—i.e. sometimes we identify at the start, sometimes not, we leave ourselves with a delightful loophole. Every now and then we answer a question that is nothing bar a figment of our imagination! With a large audience, a bold performer will often take a fictitious question and start off by asking "who is 'B.B.'—the lady who wants to know if she should go to a marriage bureau?" He then glances around and finally "sees" a hand raised at the back . . . "thank you" he replies to a lady somewhere in the audience—but in fact non-existent! Timed and acted correctly, there is little danger of anybody knowing that you did not receive a reply. It takes nerve, but it adds authenticity to the presentation.

So we have the pattern to work to; now and then we use real questions, sometimes we use fakes. It is practically essential to have some fakes lined up to give spice to the routine and as an emergency reserve. Learn to memorise which type of question goes over best—and get a solid reply ready worded in your mind. This is your fake and reserve question. Think nothing of the fact that you are cheating by using fake questions—because only a hypocrite declines the use of fake questions and then goes on to answer the real ones with the pretence that he knows what he's talking about.

351

The answer you give to any question should be directed to the audience as a whole. Occasionally you speak loudly and specifically to the person concerned. You frame your reply so that it *appeals* to *everybody*. Grab at any chance for a witty or comical reply (without hurting anyone's feelings.) Learn to infer that you know much more than you say. *Keep* the spectator saying "YES" as much as you can—even on reply to statements of fact. For example, a written question:—

"Will my daughter become engaged to the Doctor...? Mrs. Freeman".

You can score at least five 'yesses' out of this alone, without a few lucky hits on the road. During the spiel, you feed in the *facts* and each time put it as though you had made a discovery and wanted confirmation. For example. at various points along the road we can "enquire" . . . "We have a lady here who is concerned with her daughter and a professional man—will the writer please hold up her hand?" Thank you. Madame—I believe you are a married woman (YES) and therefore you understand and appreciate what I will say. First, let me ask you, or better still, tell you—that I feel your problem does concern marriage, although it has not yet taken place? (YES) I would say that there is in fact an engagement with a view to marriage in the air? (YES). Now let me deal with a gentleman who has a very great bearing on this matter, who also has a very noble profession—the man we have in mind is a doctor isn't he? (YES) and there is a great deal of personal feeling in the family for this gentleman? (YES) . . ."

From this example we see that everybody is drawn into the question. We do not make cryptic replies that mean something to the writer alone. We let the audience hear by a continuous stream of yes, yes, yes—that you are right! They all think you are doing fine—how could you know all that about a stranger? And the lady is also none the wiser as to how you know—although as one in hundreds she may suspect you have read her question. Now you see how it appears to the audience as a whole, and when you think of it, you have not yet started—you have only used a few scraps of information. You can always scrape a few more 'yesses' by such statements as "might I say that you have indeed been concerned with money of late?" Just think about it. How many people can honestly say "No?" There are dozens of lines like that which you can sort out for yourself as they are easy to formulate. Whip them in quick and get on to something else before people stop to think how blessed silly it is!

The sure fire prediction is the emergency exit of every reader. When he can't get along with any spectator—the facts are few and acknowledgements less, you fall back on time honoured policy and talk about the *future* which cannot be denied there and then.

Within reason, you can go to town with the future. You can always call upon the "Letter soon to be received with surprisingly pleasant news" and "A journey to meet a strange man—something to do with your father's side of the family". You can take a small chance now and then and be specific. An old one that hits nearly every time—is "I see you have a scar on your knee," this, said to males, nearly always causes astonishment because few stop to think that most every male does have a scar on his knee. Try it—I'm not talking tripe (this time!).

Always keep a handy stock of sure-fire predictions in your mind. We all know that when you are right—they remember what you said and when you are wrong they forget . You are not going to have the audience sit there for five years to find out if what you say is really going to happen—so don't hold back. Blossom forth with visions of money, promotion, travel and friendship. Paint the future bright and keep them happy.

Make use of fake questions—don't just sling them in to fill space. If you are playing safe (and you are with a fake) make it hot. Let me give you an example of a fake question and how you would create interest with the audience as a whole.

"This next question is something which I don't like to handle. It is very risky for me to offer any advice at all, but I can see that the writer needs help and so I will offer a few strong opinions. This is a very personal question so I will not ask 'G.D.S.' to raise his hand. You have asked me to help you with your weakness. I'm going to be very strict on this and say I don't approve of any forms of unnatural behaviour. You are not even trying to help yourself. You should go to a psychiatrist for professional treatment and I think there is no doubt that you will become involved with the law if you don't stop these activities. Now you know what I mean, make an effort—you are in great danger the longer you leave it".

To analyse that question and reply we see that it has all the essential material for general interest. If I wrote that paragraph on a slip of paper and asked fifty people to read it and say what they thought was the trouble—I would get many different opinions. That's good—it's the old "To Be or Not To Be"— we make them form their own opinions and jump to conclusions. You come pretty near the mark in the Question and Reply—but you are not commital. Nothing really terrible is said but lots of inference is given! It has the suggestion of seriousness—(a psychiatrist is needed), of scandal (the police and the law), of sex (although you don't say it—our word is behaviour)—it has everything and yet when you read it as it is—there is NOTHING in it. Everything is *inference* for the proof is that every detail of the question and reply would fit to perfection either a timid kleptomaniac who stole green combs from Woolworth Stores, didn't know why and couldn't stop doing it. He would be in danger of arrest for stealing and need psychiatric treatment—BUT also, we might visualise a sex-maniac. It all depends on the thinker, how they think, what they think. Politeness forbids me to enquire what you were thinking when you read it!

Perhaps I should make clear that it is an accepted licence that you use inference to dramatise a Question and Answer, and yet you are bound by the laws of common decency to keep it clean. Some houses would love to have a dirty session and it would not be difficult for you to provide it, but you have a status to maintain if nothing more, and your position as professional Mentalists should keep you above the level of smutty, sordid and shameful behaviour on your part.

As with scandal, money and travel you have three popular and workable topics, so with all the minor interests like family, health, marriage, etc. Aside from these which you can use, there are other strong topics which, although strong, you cannot use. Without giving any explanations why and wherefore, please take my word for it that one rule you must set yourself and stick to—is keep off Religion and keep off Legal Matters. Another runner-up is keep off Politics. It is a fact that by Law you could become involved in a case simply by what you say. It is one thing to entertain and it is another to do ten years for opening your mouth at the wrong moment!

Aside from these pitfalls we have the other type of trap which is less deadly than a Legal error: we get the catch question and sometimes the heckler in the audience who wants to make you look two inches high. The answer is simple. Keep calm and remember all the time your first obligation is to be polite and that you are there to entertain everybody and not argue with one nark. If you can, be more clever than he is. Nine times out of ten they will try something that has been tried so many times before—that we know the answer by experience. We get the usual catch which is thought to be a brilliant trap by the inventor:—

"What will be the name of my wife when I marry?" Any experienced performer will not hesitate to give the stock reply—"A gentleman wants to know the name of his wife when he marries—who asked that please? Ah, you sir—may I call you by your name—who are you? Mr. Henry Coates, thank you. Well, Mr. Coates, it may come as a surprise to you—but there seems to be little doubt that when you marry, your wife's name will be Mrs. Coates—thank you!" He swallows the bait and tells you his name and you get a laugh and you are out of trouble.

When you get a technical catch question as sometimes you do, just pass it off quick with a joke. You might get "What are Streptococci?" and you can deal with it simply . . . "I am asked what are streptococci? Well ladies and gentlemen, I do not claim to be a qualified bacteriologist—a subject which I believe deals with streptococci—but if the writer is that keen to know, he should turn to Volume Eleven, page 1,325 of the Encyclopedia Britannica and there on the right-hand page, left column, seven rows down—is given a most comprehensive explanation! It is reasonably safe to assume that no member of the audience will have with them the thirty odd giant volumes of Encyclopedia Britannica. Don't be afraid to get a good laugh when dealing with these routines. Let me give you a few more examples of quick replies to catch questions. Replies given with a view to getting rid of the question quickly or getting a laugh:—

Q. How can I win lots of money on the pools?
A. *Very simple. Get eight draws correct on the Treble Chance for six weeks running.*

Q. Are you really a mindreader?
A. *No! Actually I'm a millionaire—but I do this to pay my taxes!*

Q. M.H. asks, "Can you lend me five shillings?"
*My reply is simple. Only just!*

Q. G.Y. Asks, "I've got lots of little troubles—can you help me?
A. *Have you tried insecticides?*

Q. (Can be faked for laugh). "Am I good looking?—H.B."
A. *In reply to H.B. who asks if he is good looking—can I say he's the prettiest bricklayer I've seen in a fortnight.*

Q. Can I stop smoking?
A. *Give me your cigarettes and I'll try for you!*

Q. Which of my teeth are filled with gold?
A. *If you give them to me for a moment I'll soon tell you!*

Q. I'm troubled at home, what's good for mice?
A. *Cheese is about the best thing I can think of!*

# SUMMARY

Let us summarise the important points to be remembered for dealing with questions known. First for Private Reading and then for Platform (stage) Reading:—

## PRIVATE READINGS

(1) Avoid dealing with Legal matters.
(2) Avoid, if you can, Religion and Politics.
(3) Make the reading happy.
(4) Weaken the subject with flattery.
(5) Discover their interests and tell them what they want to know.
(6) Be ambiguous: say nothing commital unless it is a sure-fire prediction.
(7) Never say word for word the exact text of the question showing you have read it.

## PLATFORM READINGS

(1) Strictly avoid any Legal Matters and don't chance Politics and Religion.
(2) Use plants (stooges) in audience and use fake questions to enliven the show.
(3) Pick questions which offer appeal to everybody and not one person.
(4) Use inference to create a situation that may not truly exist.
(5) Vary the way in which questions are acknowledged from the audience.
(6) Get the spectator to say "Yes" as often as possible.
(7) Use wit and cleverness to deal with trouble. Not temper and argument.

## TABLE OF PROBABILITIES
### (Subject of Question)

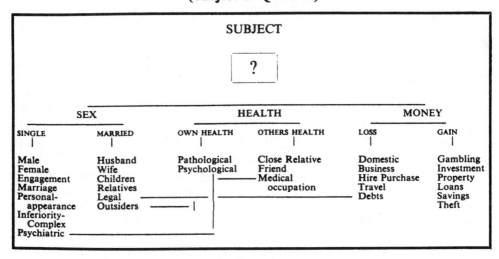

# EXPLANATION

The Table of Probabilities is designed to show what subject is most likely to be encountered and in what order subjects most frequently occur. For example, we note that there are three major probabilities: Sex, Health and

Money. Then we perceive that subdivisions of these topics can occur, and that in the sub-divisions there is a distinct order according to position in the list. We find for example that there is more likelihood of a question dealing with a physical complaint of health, than of a mental complaint. We find more people ask questions on Gambling than do people ask questions on Savings. Similarly, we accept that to some extent there is a link between major subjects and their subdivisions. Our table illustrates for example that a question on Mental illness could fall under several headings. It could be personal illness, it could be concerned with sex and it could simply be that the question writer was employed in a Mental hospital. Other obvious associations between subjects have not been given.

We have already explained that by knowing what subject is most probable our time is saved and we refrain from wild and unsystematic guesses. We always tackle the most probable first and then work down the list. Very often this will mean results straight away as trial and error during performance will prove to be the case.


## PART TWO

### Dealing with Questions Unknown

We have clarified the meaning of Questions that are Known, so now let us say what we mean by the opposite. We are concerned now with one of the highest forms of Mental Magic; it is the art of Cold Reading, a process of mental analysis with a subject that leads you to discover their problems without having any direct information conveyed to you. Nothing is written, nothing is asked outright as a question, nothing is told to you by a third person. You do not know the subject at the start, you have no idea what they are, who they are and what they want to know. You find out and deal with the information obtained to give them what we call a 'Reading'. That's it!

On the face of it, the accomplishment to do anything like that we discuss, seems to be no mean achievement. Indeed, it is no mean achievement—and yet it is not so hard as some people would have you think it to be.

Admitted that it takes years of doing it before you can hope to be any good, but all the same, with a system behind you at the start, your work is not so hopeless. We can devise a practical system and we do have one for you. It is a method that has been evolved by a study of what others do. I have been fortunate in having the facilities to make a close study of good cold readers and to see their work. Also, with a keen interest in the subject myself, I have tried many of the ways I suggest and can therefore endorse the practicality.

Let us encourage ourselves at the start by estimating the odds against success. We shall assume that we have a Private Reading on our hands, one person sits with us in privacy and want "professional treatment". They don't want to be bothered with writing down their question—they have no wish to introduce themselves. You have not seen them before. It doesn't look so good, does it? But we think to ourselves, this one is about the three thousandth client. I already know what they want—they have a problem—otherwise they wouldn't be here now! What is more, I know what problems are most probable and what are most unlikely. I have other advantages, they do not suspect that I am going to adopt a subtle cross-questioning system so they will not be on guard as they might be if they happened to be a criminal

356

being interviewed by the Police. I also know that if I flatter them, they will talk about themselves and tell me what I can tell them! Then I shall remember what they say and when I tell them the same thing a little later, they will have forgotten that they told me because they are not prepared to remember words of conversation as I am .... there is *much* in our favour!

In that little paragraph we just about told you what to do. We can enlarge a bit more! Let us outline our main objectives and then formulate a plan of attack:—

## MAIN OBJECTIVES WHEN COLD READING

(1) Develop a high degree of observation. Look for personal details.

(2) Learn to use your voice so that you can ask a question in such a way that you seem to be stating a fact.

(3) Learn to put two and two together. A black tie suggests death.

(4) Be a good listener—as well as a good talker. Give them chance to *tell you*.

(5) Never forget a fact, Remember names, places, dates especially.

(6) Always be prepared with a twist of conversation to change the topic when you are wrong. Never leave yourself without a 'get-out'.

(7) Give them time to forget what they have said, before you tell them the same.

Now to enlarge upon these essential qualities. let us give a list of a few things that suit our first objective. Observation. From this we can tell no end, and yet we do not accept anything we see until it has been checked. We are careful for example when we see a wedding ring on the correct finger—and we check that our subject is married. It is a strong guide—not a fact. It is a start for conversation and that is a priceless gift to the cold reader.

There are hundreds of things to look for and things which help you along. Let me give you a few examples to show you what I mean:—

(a) Fingernails bitten; suggestive of nervous trouble, especially in adults.

(b) Makers tab on inside of overcoat that you hang on the door as they come in. Think what this alone may well convey. The information is unlimited—have a look!

(c) Jewellery—real or artificial. Real jewellery suggests financial standing.

(d) Quality of clothing—particularly condition of heels on shoes, speak for themselves.

(e) Condition of hands; Clean, dirty, groomed, workers' hands.

(f) Articles carried by the subject; a carrier bag marked 'Hamley's of Regent Street, London'.

(g) The subject's voice; vocabulary, cultured attitude or otherwise.

(h) Badges worn in the coat; membership to some organisation.

(i) Engraved property; a cigarette case, ring, watch, lighter, initialled handbag.

(j) Age; (very few people of ninety are concerned with marriage!)

(k) Condition of health; thin, fat, limping, anything which implies medical disability.

(l) Their manner of approach to you...i.e. "confidential" or "curious?"

You see by this small list that before you is a living index of information— all you have to do is be observant, look, work it out yourself, check and use it.

357

Next we have said learn to use your voice to advantage. Many, many times you will want to know something about the subject—and if you know how, you can literally ask her—simply by the way you do it. You want to know perhaps if the subject is married. You do not say "Are you married"—you are supposed to be able to tell that! You cook up something like this. "There's a certain illness 'in the family' that has been causing you some concern—have you been worried, do you understand what I mean?" Our victim has only to mention "Husband, son, daughter" and we have solved that one. Because you are a cold reader, you don't have to show it. Be subtle and as a magician uses misdirection with apparatus, you use misdirection with words. You don't have to advertise out loud that you are a glorified fortune teller—your signature tune is well aloft from those who say that they are, thus destroying the belief in what they can do! You may get my meaning from the words of La Traviata:—

(The Chorus):   "We are gypsies—come from afar.
                 We can read everyone's future in his hand,
                 We can consult the stars, no fate is hid from us,
                 And we can predict what fate holds in store for others!

If you want to be a gypsy, say so and expect a gypsy's payment—"Cross my hand with silver". Thus it is unwise to say that you are anything but "A consultant" and that you can do anything—don't blow your own trumpet at the beginning of a session. Let results speak for themselves.

What do we mean by No. 3 "Put two and two together?" It means, to use the vernacular, "Use your Loaf". Think. When you see a lady with a wooden leg, you do not suppose that she is troubled with problems concerning mountaineering. Gold teeth don't grow in rice fields. Where there's a bruise, there's a blow. Those who relax are those who don't worry. All of this adds up to one thing. By what you are told and by what you can see, with half an ounce of worldliness, you can put two and two together and get a pretty good idea of what it's all about. I repeat; Use your Loaf!

Number four and five of our Main Objectives for Cold Reading, tell us to be a good listener and remember what facts you are told.

It stands to reason that if you do all the talking the subject is not given the chance to tell you anything. It should all seem natural. A conversation between two people, sometimes you talk and sometimes you listen. It may well seem superfluous to make such a point as this, but the downfall of many a learner is the uncontrolled desire to make it a one man lecture. Keep it in mind, it's important, you learn more as you listen more.

Furthermore, it's a fat lot of good being a good listener, picking up names and dates from the conversation and then forgetting them. The information you gain will be the information you use—so get it right. Make a particular point of remembering what you think is a strong point for later use. Some professionals go so far as to "doodle" whilst talking—and the "doodle" hides a host of brief notes gleaned from the talking.

Our Sixth Objective is to be prepared at all times to handle the conversation, to twist it along the road we choose and to side track unwanted topics. The most important point that has to be made here, is that you must have the ability to "cover up". That is to say, you are pumping for information, you say something which quite obviously is miles from the truth and seeing your mistake, you cover up very quickly with glib patter. Learn to "pass it

358

off", get to know the value of the simple phrase "Well if it hasn't happened yet—it will do so very shortly . . ." for such a phrase turns your blunder into a prediction and leaves you still master of the situation. To be quick and to be ready for this misdirection of attention (which it is)—the only answer is learn before you start; train yourself in such a way that you can sidetrack any doubtful point. Amass a stock of parrot phrases which you stand by for occasions of this kind. Don't wait until you blunder and then think what to do. Never admit defeat and bear in mind that you can avoid a lot of trouble in the first place by wording the statement right before it is denied. The more ambiguous your statement is, the more loopholes are left for you to escape in case of error.

Cold Reading goes on like this all the time. You are as a detective of the mind and it becomes a continuous stream of pumping, finding, checking, stating and rejecting. Needless to say you are not going to be wrong all the time and when you do get a right—don't waste it. Enlarge upon your discovery, exaggerate now to make it seem quite clear that *you said it was so*—and not that you tried to find out! With very little experience you will be able to tell whether you are right or wrong. There are many ways that a subject may reveal his thoughts. Watch for reactions. Look out for any sign that says "No" and any that say "Yes". Watch the hands, watch the eyes and it will not be so hard. Half of the time they tell you Yes or No anyway, so you then have nothing to worry about.

Finally, a skilled performer knows what is meant by "time" in Cold Reading. He gets to know how long it takes for the subject to tell you something and then forget it. He also knows the crucial moment when it is best to use what information he has got. Time is hard to explain, it is something almost intangible and it will vary in so many ways with so many different people; and yet is it so important. We can see the gravity of time in Cold Reading when we visualise what might happen if we gave no consideration to it. Our subject tells us they have just bought a house. Two minutes later we tell them they are concerned with buying property . . . almost immediately they turn back and say "Well you know that—I told you just now I had bought a house". You see, the time factor is all wrong. You must give them time to forget what they have told you—or cleverly force the pace so that so much is said, it is too much to be remembered in detail. Information is useless to you unless you can use it as though it was NEWS to them! Even if it is only news that you know about—it's news.

## CONCLUSION

This is a small book compared with the giant volumes that could be written about the Art of Questions and Answers in Mentalism. However, I have tried to include all the major points and although very brief, you have here the essence and very foundation of the Art.

No writer or teacher can ever give you as much as actual experience from practice. I would assert that half the qualification you require for success— is worldliness and that comes from meeting people and going places. A Reader cannot be a Dreamer, he is a man who knows the facts of life and he has to be prepared to drop any Victorian niceties, and admit (at least to himself) that sometimes, some people do nasty things. Life can be very vulgar in reality and the Reader will meet with every vulgarity that has been conceived. You will have to be prepared for all types and every situation and must therefore study all types and different situations. This does not mean you have to become a crook by studying criminals. If we can walk with Kings and keep the common touch—it is just as important. You cannot learn about life unless you study it. You have got to know about life to be a Reader.

We have seen that there are two approaches to Reading. We can get information or get a question and by trickery find out what it is. We can be more presumptuous and start cold. The latter, being the hardest, should be the last to try if you are a learner. Perhaps a good plan is to start with gimmicks that get you information and then to drop their use bit by bit until you finally work with nothing but skill.

A wise Reader will always know a couple of ways of getting information by trickery so that at anytime when things get really tough, he can fall back on the Centre Tear (Step Six) or any other classic method.

To end this Step let me say that I firmly believe that of all the Arts and Crafts of Mentalism, there is nothing more advanced, more difficult and yet more satisfying than one who is a first-class Reader. It is the ultimate in Mentalism and if you can reach this standard—you will never get any higher —nor will you have to. It is a paradox that entertainers seek to create a fantasy and yet the fantasy of this art is reality.

RONNIE GANN

# NOTES

# PUBLICITY STUNTS

## BY

## CORINDA

## STEP TWELVE

IN CORINDA'S SERIES :—
## "THIRTEEN STEPS TO MENTALISM"

# NOTES

STEP TWELVE in CORINDA'S SERIES

" THIRTEEN STEPS TO MENTALISM "

" PUBLICITY STUNTS "

## CONTENTS

### PART ONE

### PART TWO

# PART ONE

## INTRODUCTION

This Step does not deal so much with tricks and technique as do the predecessors, it confines itself to Publicity, a subject which is of equal importance to the trickery side of Mentalism, and one that cannot be ignored by any who propose to make a living by professional or semi-professional entertainment.

The world of entertainment is Showbusiness—and as the latter half of that word indicates—it is indeed, a business. Like any other business, what you have for sale, has to be advertised, displayed, marketed, whether it be the sale of broom handles or a mental act. So it is that in the Twelfth Step we come right down to the mercenary side of Mentalism and consider a few ways that can be used to sell your act.

Publicity is a very important thing to the showman, and it is by no means an understatement to say that the average semi-professional man does not pay enough attention to the subject. He is inclined to go so far towards designing an act and then seems reasonably happy to sit back and wait for bookers to come along and purchase his talent. The real professional knows better. He cannot afford to sit back and wait, he gets out and goes to the right places and right people and sells his act so that next week, like last week, he may continue to eat. Moreover, contrary to common belief, eating is at times a luxury even unto the professional! The only man who knows for sure where his next meal is coming from, is the magician who has a rabbit in the act. So let's blast the wind out of "magical stardom and money galore". The chances of being a star at anything in showbusiness—are pretty rough; the chances of being a star as a magician or mindreader are ten times worse. It's no good hanging on the history of magic and kidding yourself that your chances are good. They are not. Your chances of professional success are, to put it mildly, lousy. I might add to that by saying that without some knowledge about Publicity—you have no chance at all.

I do not sit back and grind forth these bold statements without reasonable support to what I say. First, let it be clearly understood that I have no axe to grind. To put it mildly, I do very well earning my living out of magic and mentalism and I don't care how many stars there are or there will be. I hope there will remain a good demand for magical entertainers and I aim, in the writing of this Step, to help some people along the road to success. But I confess I am one of those odd people who like to see things as they really are, and I have no time for dreamers who wish to imagine that today magic is the easiest thing on earth. I have no time for bad performers who should either improve or get out of magic and leave it to somebody who can do better. I have no time for magicians and mentalists who try and kid me that magic is getting more and more popular every day. It is not. In fact, the way it's going magic could die completely—and if this happened, nine people out of ten would blame "Television", Lack of Theatres—Cabaret Conditions, etc., and the odd one would admit that nothing harmed magic more than bad magicians.

Publicity concerns the professional class of entertainer and so we have to consider the truth because it's no good trying to sell something if people don't want to buy it. It has been my good fortune to know quite intimately a large number of professional magicians and mentalists. Of all those I know, very few would tell you that their job was an easy one—all of them have to be on their toes all the time and it's a constant battle to keep going. Only dreamers sit back and think top line magicians drive around in a chauffeur-driven cadillac, sit in front of roaring log fires at their country mansions and guzzle champagne by the gallon. The average "pro" sits at home staying up late at night working on everyday problems. He has to scheme out new tricks, try and improve on something he has already done for ten years, think up new and topical patter, consider new Publicity angles that will bring him in more work and keep up a constant demand for his talent. With his cup of tea he works on two major problems; getting an act that can be done under present day conditions and then finding a way to sell the act to bring him work. In previous Steps we have given material that can be the foundation of many an act, in this Step we go into the selling side.

This is not a Step for the timid and it is not intended for the strict amateur who does his magic for personal amusement (and has every right to do so). Amateurs who do not presume to ask for payment for their performance, have an unquestionable right to be good or appalling. It is their hobby and their delight and who are we to interfere with the enjoyment of others? But up the ladder a bit we find the chap who grades himself between amateur and professional—the "semi-pro" (*i.e.* Alistair Crockleforth—who runs a fish and chip shop, and can do Troublewit, The Asrha Illusion and Seven Keys to Baldpate—with or without chips—as a sideline!). The "semi-pro" is a man on dangerous ground. He is the man who can do so much good and so much harm to magic. A full professional has got to be good—and be good all the time or he is out of work. The semi-professional is on a safer footing. He usually has another source of income and magic is simply that which supplements his pocket money. As this is so, there is no imperative need for quality; should he perform badly and get paid little, he still has his regular income and it doesn't matter so much. Yet out of this comes much trouble.

We find that people who pay to be entertained by a magician expect to be well entertained. Why shouldn't they—they are paying for it? Then we find that some who don't have to be good, step into the breach and do their half-rehearsed, unprofessional tricks and ruin the market for good. Such a thing affects the field of magic as a whole, it reflects badly on professional men, it causes disinterest in magic and it causes bitterness within the fraternity. Yet none of this need be if only those who accepted payment—gave value for money. There are very many semi-professional magicians and very few of them will admit they are poor performers. Quite a lot of them are very good and some of them should pay the audience for the ordeal of twenty minutes of boredom.

Not in the habit of doing many things without reason. I will now explain why I write all this before getting down to Publicity Stunts. What I have said has been put in the introduction because you now know that if you do not have a good act to perform—you have no right to try and sell it in the first place. Don't try and put a shoddy product on the market—this book will tell you how to sell what you've got, but get *something worth selling before you start*.

## THE LAW OF SUPPLY AND DEMAND

There are two fundamental ways of selling anything. Either you are able to supply that which is in demand, or you create a demand for that which you can supply. If you understand this you are a good business man.

Let us regard Mentalism as a Product for Sale. If we are right at the very start we think to ourselves "now what do they want?" and finding the answer, we go ahead and create an act that fits present day requirements.

On the other hand, maybe we have an act already so our problem is different. We think this time "How can I create a demand for this act?".

The two are not the same and so it's no good thinking about Publicity Stunts until you decide which is which. If you are concerned with the second contingency, that is having an act and selling it, you may be in for a few headaches. It is quite possible that you have worked for a long time to perfect a series of tricks and to routine them into an act. Then, when everything is ready to go, you suddenly find that nobody "wants that kind of thing". You have spent five years working on something that isn't in demand.

On the other hand, you might think you are a shrewd fellow who looks around and spots everything that's going well and you decide to do the same. So you spend five years perfecting a new act and when it's ready you find that what was in demand is now decidedly out of fashion. It's not as easy as it seems.

So we have two headaches. Let us deal with number one first—selling the act that already exists!

**Creating a Demand**

We presume that in the first place you have an act. What is more, we presume that it is a very good act, it has been tried and tested as best you can, everything has been fully rehearsed, you know how to do all the tricks with your eyes closed (we speak figuratively!) and all in all, you have faith in the quality of your act. If you don't have any faith—you won't convince anybody else that it's good and even if you do—it won't be long before they find out that it's not what you claim.

Before you decide upon a Publicity Campaign—which has to come, you must first decide *where* you want to perform. You will direct the mass of your publicity in one field (*i.e.* cabaret, theatre, dinners, etc.), so consider very carefully the best type of places for your work—a thing which is governed very much by the type of act you have created. Obviously, big illusion acts cannot be done in small rooms where you get dinners held. Close up magic and mentalism looks silly on a large stage. So fit the place of performance to the act—and even modify the act when necessary to fit the place of performance. Ideally, you should have an act that you can do almost anywhere. It will go on T.V., it is angleproof for the cabaret floor, it is large enough for the stage and it can be squeezed into a fairly large room for dinners. Any "pro" will tell you how easy it is to get an act like that ! !

Fortunately, the Mentalist has the advantage over the Magician when it comes to creating a "versatile" act. The Mentalist does not have to work with big props and a personality can fit into any room or fill any stage—and I don't mean with tonnage!

When you think of it, you realise that a Mindreader is primarily supposed to read minds and if so, any apparatus—no matter what it may be, is something which does not fit the picture of the true Mindreader; our conception of the authentic telepathist is the man who simply stands there and tells you what you are thinking. Bearing this in mind ourselves, we may rightly suppose that a commercial act which purports telepathy, can be one which uses very little equipment. An important point to remember, because the less equipment you have—the more places there are for you to perform.

So we analyse our act and then decide where we can best perform it. As an example, we can assume that we decide Dinners, Small Audiences at intimate gatherings and perhaps small halls, are the places where we can best perform. (Remember, this is only an example—it need not necessarily be so).

Our next concern is to decide outright how much we want to get for our performance and that financial conclusion will direct our attention to some particular class or level of society. Quite a few of my friends make a steady living playing what we call "Working Men's Clubs"—but these places do not pay what fees can be expected from Cabaret at society restaurant places. How much you expect to be paid is something which decides what you do, what quality you exercise and what standard you have to maintain. It is wrong to suppose that a sophisticated Cabaret Act is just the thing for an 'Old Army Reunion Dinner', etc. Both classes are open markets for a good performer but it's no good trying to kid yourself that a strongly worded and rather naughty show for Army Camps is highly suited for the Savoy Hotel. Also it is wrong to suppose that all the money is to be made from the best places. You might get paid more for work in high class places, but there is more work to be had as you come down the scale of social entertainment. Many "old hands" I know earn as much in a year with regular bookings at Clubs and Dinners as do quite a few top line professionals who now and then get a Cabaret booking. The best place for anybody to work—is the place where they feel best suited.

All this might seem irrelevant to the Question of Publicity as a subject, but it is by no means so. Only a fool will go madly ahead and spend a small fortune on an artistic and expensive brochure that sent to club organisers gets him a booking that would have come just the same from a duplicated letter. And on the other hand, a cheap duplicated letter sent to a Cabaret booking agent does not bear out a sophisticated act that it suggests. "Lady X" who wants a distinguished performer at her house party next Friday—likes to see a four-page, art paper, professionally drawn, coloured and designed Brochure. Mr. Roberts, a busy club secretary and organiser of social evenings can't be bothered—he wants to know quickly what you do, how long and how much.

Decide what you want to do, where you want to do it and then, and only then, get down to creating a demand by perpetrating a Publicity Campaign.

We are taking for example a performer who decides to work for small gatherings and we shall take it that he aspires to a medium level and intends to work in a class above the barrack room and below cabaret. There is a big market in between.

Let us consider for example a few of the many places which may call upon his services. We have social parties, wedding anniversaries, twenty-first birthdays and the kind; there are Church activities and there are a diverse number of Clubs of the semi-sophisticated class. We have annual affairs of industrial companies that often call for an entertainer at their Dinner and Dance. There are Masonic Dinners—entertaining at private licensed rooms for groups which hire these premises for meetings, there are receptions of various kinds and Charity Banquets. There are many "private engagements" to be had—which are held at private houses of the well-to-do (and often pay very well) and there are quite a few exhibitions to cater for your services. Last, but by no means least, now and then work is to be found with a Concert party or Variety group.

From this we see at once that, although we have indeed cut down our field in which we intend to perform, we have even so, allowed plenty of scope for our work.

Now we decide to create a demand in this field and we consider how to do so. Our policy should be to achieve two things. First to become known and to get in—and then to maintain the bookings so that year by year you go back. Do not aim at a short sighted policy which suggests you go once, do it and forget it. In our present field of work (the example) there is much demand for "repeat orders" so work with an eye to the future.

To qualify the last sentence, let us take it that if you push your prices up to the top—you may well get in once, but you may well be "overlooked" next time. It is almost a sin to undercharge and it is foolhardy to overcharge. Be reasonable.

Maintaining the bookings with the same agent is the consequence of good work at reasonable prices, which speaks for itself, so we can deal with the first part of our policy and see what publicity can do for us to "get known".

## Personal Publicity

There are many different types of publicity and we shall deal with a few of them and later we shall give examples as are used and that can be used. One type we term Personal Publicity and that is what is often called in show-business "a gimmick". A personal publicity gimmick can be literally any-thing; it's very vague and yet there are many good examples to be found. It can be something you say or how you say it—and become noted for those words or that expression. It can be a laugh (our English Magician Tommy Cooper soon wins an audience with his gimmicked laugh) or it can be a mannerism or personal feature. You would be surprised to learn what a perfectly bald head did for Yul Brynner the actor! You need not necessarily shave your head bare as he did—but it was an angle which as a gimmick was "it". If you can create a personal gimmick and live with it (!) it hall-marks you for life and that means publicity. If you are not born with some-thing different to use, make one; one of the greatest men of showbusiness is Charles Chaplin—he wasn't born with two feet stuck sideways and a bent cane in his hand—he made the gimmick and the gimmick helped to make him. Anything is better than nothing; even being nasty like Richard Himber makes you famous! Although he's the most horrible man I know—I still have a healthy respect for him and he's one man that knows and uses publicity. Take a look at the world of showbusiness; nearly everybody who is anybody has got a gimmick, and not without reason. The acid test of a good gimmick is one that if used by an impersonator, people would recognise *you* without being told who was being impersonated.

## Personal Advertising

Under this heading we cater for such things as Business or visiting cards, brochures, handouts, headed writing paper and novelties which advertise you and your business. Later in this Step we give some examples of advertising used by a well-known American magician which show the practical side of the subject. Let us here, satisfy ourselves with a brief consideration of the subject on hand:—

## Visiting Cards (or Business Cards)

Things which are so cheap and useful that there is no excuse for being without them. However, little as you may pay for them—you should go to the trouble of having them done right. Choose a good quality card—and have the printer use what style of type you think looks neat. Most important of all, get the wording right on the card. The basic essentials are your name, address and telephone number and profession. Sometimes, it is enough to have your name and profession only but in any case, avoid the common mistake of over-wording on a visiting card. Keep the professional status to a minimum and avoid overflowing lists of achievements like:—

| | |
|---|---|
| Mr. T. Corinda<br>Mindreader | Available for dates . . . . . .<br>Mr. T. Corinda, M.I.M.C., I.B.M.<br>Magic, Mentalism, Hypnotism &<br>Puppets<br>(For Children & Adults)<br>Address : 65 Mortimer Street,<br>Tel. Lan 2491          London, W.1. |
| EXAMPLE " A " | EXAMPLE " B " |

We have two examples. In "A" we have achieved what a visiting card is supposed to achieve—it tells them WHO you are. In "B" we see what is nearly an autobiography and yet we see the type of thing so often. It is not good—it is a sign of culture to know what to say and what not to say—even on a visiting card.

In example "A" we could use the name "Mentalist" in place of "Mind-reader". It does not make a lot of difference—except that everybody knows what you mean by Mindreader and not everybody knows the meaning of Mentalist. Also, we could add the name of our agents (if any) or our address, if we wanted it known.

In example "B" we find a host of sins. To start with, there has always been something wrong with the phrase "Available for dates . . ." It suggests unemployment! It is wrong to put anything like Hypnotism and the words "for Children" within a mile of each other. It is wrong to appear a "Jack of all trades" because having read it the only conclusion is "well what the hell is he?" Lastly, you may have magical qualifications like Member of the Inner Magic Circle, but to put them on your card as M.I.M.C. means everything to Magicians who know and won't book you—and means nothing at all to outsiders. The Magic Circle is a famous club and sometimes it carries weight when getting bookings—so if you want to use any titles, and having the right to do so, say what they are and don't abbreviate. Better by far to leave such qualifications to the brochure which is read by people who want to know about you.

## The Brochure

Paying attention to our earlier discussion we must remember that different types of advertising must be used for different fields. We maintain our example and continue to imagine that our field is small audiences. Our first consideration is how much do we want to spend on a brochure and is it worth it? Well, the last part is easy to deal with—of course it's worth it. If you work it out in businesslike fashion, you find that you need as little as one per cent. result or booking from your circulation to pay the material cost, which leaves you with all that publicity if nothing more. At our Magic Studio we have often sent out ten thousand circulars and when we get one hundred replies it is very good business. The same applies to almost any form of mass advertising—you need so little back to pay the cost. Although we do not suppose that you will be sending out thousands of brochures, it is quite possible that you will dispose of very many over a period of time. Remember, as a professional entertainer you are in business, and in any form of business, advertising is usually an investment and not an expenditure.

The amount of money you want to spend on your Brochure will obviously be the factor that determines quantity and quality. The initial expense can be quite considerable as you have to cost art work, original printing blocks and the kind. Once this is overcome—they cost very little.

My advice to you is to have a brochure and moreover, have a good one. I would suggest that for economy, you have your brochure designed so that from one page, it folds into four. For example, take a quarto sheet and fold it twice and you get a leaflet with four small faces and one large when opened out. This is quite adequate for the unpretentious! It means also that from the printing side, it is an easy "run". Your printer will set up to run twice only (for one colour) and one must bear in mind that the more runs involved the more the cost. It is a matter of taste as to what style you want but for those who cannot decide, I would suggest the following as a reasonable guide.

Size quarto which *you* fold into four as they are needed. A good quality white art paper (just the same as this Step) and at least two colours. The more colours you use, the more the expense, but no less than two colours; better three or four. (Your printer will tell you that with careful selection of four basic colours, many other colours can be created at no extra cost; my advice, consult a good colour printer or commercial artist.) Quantity: first run 1,000.

Design and layout. I would recommend that you regard each small side as one page and utilise these as follows. Front—a first-class drawing and a few words which present your name. Sometimes you can use a phrase which invites people to look further . . . "Can you read minds?" and the next page tells them you can! Sometimes an action photo is used on the front cover —but make it good if you use it. I prefer, as I say, a simple introduction.

We unfold the page to inside left and start there with information about yourself. Who you are, what you do, where you have done it. Make sure that it is in good English and don't be ashamed to give yourself a bit of a build-up—remember this leaflet has got to sell you! Our next page, inner right is best devoted to what others say, a time honoured advertising technique, and we cover this with photo copies of press reports, cut outs from complimentary letters and perhaps a final plug which tells them how they go about booking you for their function. We are left now with two "pages". The very back and the full size. I feel that the best place for a full-size photograph (professional pose) is the small back page. A close-up head shot is good for this. Admitted a photograph could go on the inner large page— but there is one thing against this and that is, because of the four-fold page arrangement, there would be two big creases bang in the middle of your photo' which is not to be desired.

We are left with the full quarto middle page and can use this in several ways. I have seen some excellent cartoons which drawn by the right men, go a long way to describe the "product" (you) in a nice way. I have seen the continental fashion which runs along the lines of contemporary art (line drawings) which psychologically suggest "Magic". There is something in historic plates—and there is much to be said for a "mixed" or "scrambled" layout of action pictures. The latter, if they are available, are very good because they show what you have done. You pick shots which give views of large audiences, you on a Television screen, a few close-up showing the expression of amazement on faces of members of the audience. and for good effect, you can stick in name headings from daily or well-known newspapers and below in smaller type, use favourable comments given by critics. As you will appreciate, it depends a great deal on what material you have available.

Once we have planned the design, layout, size and shape we assemble all the material we have and make a note of any ideas that might be good. We then set out to find the right man to do the job. Ten to one you are not an artist and you can't beat the right man for the right job. You don't go to the dentist to get your boots repaired so spend a few pounds or dollars and have a professional artist draw up the brochure for you. Unless you happen to be first-class yourself—do not try and do it yourself (as some do) because you cannot afford to have an amateurish brochure.

There are people who do nothing but design brochures for a living and these are the best people although usually they are the most expensive. I know one English magician who recently paid £140 for nothing more than art work on a brochure. But what he has is a work of art.

Any good commercial artist knows about colours, design, etc., and almost certainly, can handle the job. Tell him just what you want and then listen to what he may suggest as improvements. Have him produce several drafts or rough sketches that give you an approximate idea of the finished product. Finally, settle for what you think is so good it cannot be improved, and have the "master" drawn and designed. Your artist, knowing about block making and printing will produce the originals in such a size that they can be reduced to the desired size of quarto. The drawing will probably be five or six times as big as the finished product and they will be photographically reduced by the block makers. A helpful artist will tell you where to have blocks made and recommend a good colour printer. He will also handle the whole project if you pay the right money—remember, it's his job so he knows what he's doing.

One final word concerning the "quarto leaflet brochure". You will appreciate that once the art work is done on a grand scale, reduction may be made to any reasonable size and so you may like to think about two sizes of brochures made from the original drawings. This means twice as many blocks—but a tiny pocket brochure can be a handy thing to carry around.

We have described very briefly one type of Brochure. Needless to say, there are others much more expensive and some cheaper. If you have sufficient ambition, publicity material and money, there is nothing to stop you producing something "Out of this world". You can get something that looks almost too good to handle. A six-page booklet; velvet or cloth covers, sophisticated embossed lettering, scroll work in gold and black, tinted papers, cellophane protective inserts, and every copy personally signed by you with ink specially prepared by Soulies of Bond Street (Three guineas a bottle) but . . . . we have already said that there is no need to advertise above the level of your intended market. It may be as well to remember that no matter how good your brochure. you still have to go along and prove you're good on the day!

## Photographs

There is not much to say about this because a lot can be taken for granted. You will need quite a few copies of good photographs of yourself. This means, without any arguments, a good photographer. Your pal with his Brownie camera might take good snapshots but they are not in the least any good for you. Go to a professional photographer (or have him come to you) and get it done properly. Normally, the more copies you have printed from the negatives, the cheaper it gets, so look ahead and have as many done at once as you can afford. Two sizes are advisable, theatre display size, usually about 10 in. x 7 in. and postcard size, about $3\frac{1}{2}$ in. x 6 in. Lastly, in case you are unacquainted with the fact, there are people who can doctor your photos, working on originals, to make them look much better than the first print. Unless six chins is your gimmick—have an artist blot out five!

## Headed Paper

The last subject we deal with under Personal Advertising is the business of having at your disposal, Headed writing paper and maybe envelopes. Personally, I do not like name-advertising on envelopes and think it better to use a plain one. However, it is pretty important that you have a good headed paper. In saying what I am about to say, I do not wish to be personal to anyone in particular, but during the course of each year I should say I receive some thousands of letters from Magicians and Mentalists and to be quite truthful—the usual standard of headings used on their business papers— is utterly appalling. To start with, I loathe corny names; stage titles adopted by people who having no imagination think "The Great Faggo" fits in well with a cigarette act. An accurate check of my records at the office shows we have no less than seventeen people calling themselves "Mr. E." (all of them claim they were the first!) which cannot be a good thing for the other sixteen "Mr. E's". It cannot be a good thing to have a name that can be confused with another person.

Your headed paper should look like the rest of your advertising material— tasteful and neat. An artist-drawn block is very good and inexpensive and once again, don't overload your private paper with personal data. (See Visiting Cards). It is literal etiquette to put your address on the right of the page, so don't stick it on the left. It is an accepted licence in business to run your address with your name as a heading or across the top of the page.

## The Publicity Campaign

If by now you can remember our introductory remarks, you will recollect that we are dealing with publicity for an act that already exists. It may be superfluous to point out that it is not an easy matter to design (for instance) a Brochure—when you have done nothing and whatismore, you don't know what you are going to do! Remember, a brochure is part Promise and part History, it's a promise of what you will do and history of what you have done! Therefore, you cannot conduct a Publicity Campaign until you have an act.

The basic structure of your campaign is founded on a very simple formula. Get something to sell, let them know you have it for sale, sell it, keep on selling it. Four stages which we can break down as follows:—

(a)  Get something to sell. In other words, once again, have a good act ready to do and ready to describe in your publicity matter.

(b)  Let them know you have it for sale—means you are ready to go, and the easiest way to arrive is with a bang. That means a fairly big Publicity Stunt, and the more your ambition, the greater must be the stunt. For this, in Mentalism, we call upon Headline Predictions, Football Pool or Racing Predictions, Blindfold Drives, Challenges (with no risks attached) and things of that kind. They are the stunts that launch you like a battleship—and sometimes you end up in deep water!

(c)  Having done the big stunt, it's a fat lot of good sitting back and waiting, so you exploit any publicity you gain and bring it to the attention of those who will be impressed and give you work for it.

(d)  Having got a booking on the strength of your Publicity Stunt, you now play it out—and keep getting bookings since your object is to stay in work as much as possible. Therefore maintain your publicity and keep yourself to the front. No matter how famous you are, throughout your career it is necessary to booster your name with another publicity stunt. So keep at it and when the fame of the last stunt dies down, start working on another to rekindle the fire.

## PART TWO
## PUBLICITY STUNTS

Having surveyed the reason and purpose behind Publicity, we are now in a position to get down to details. We know what we want and why we want it. The following Publicity Stunts are a mixture of those that serve for a major attraction ("B" in the Publicity Campaign) and some that provide the means to maintain Publicity as is needed. ("C" in the Publicity Campaign)

Our first concern is "Plots". We are not going to bother too much with method now as in past Steps we have given plenty of studies that reveal the necessary technique of Mentalism, and the actual trickery. There are quite a few tricks on past pages that can be twisted from a Mental Effect to a Publicity Stunt, so all we lack is ideas and plots—the raw material of publicity. The only point which has to be made is that although you may well be using a standard and very simple mental trick for your publicity stunt, you must grossly exaggerate the effect; we aim for magnificent and spectacular presentation as though our effect was being performed for the Nation instead of for one small audience.

If you want to "reach" the Nation, cause a big stir, get known and become talked about—if you think it out, there are very few medias to convey your fame. It comes down to methods of mass-communication and there are three outstanding methods, Sound Radio, Television and Newspapers. The common pattern of a Publicity Campaign runs along these lines. You collaborate with a well-known Newspaper and do a Stunt which gives them a "Story". They report on you and your activity and if it's interesting enough, you stand a good chance of appearing on T.V. or getting on the air in any of the short interview programmes that deal with topical events and personalities of the week. That is the ultimate, the ideal pattern for a major publicity stunt because it exploits what you have done to a maximum degree. If it works out really well, you may get "follow-ups" by way of Press agencies— circulating your story in many smaller papers, magazines and with a bit of good fortune, you may even get a newsreel film run on you.

Such a glorious success as we describe in our last paragraph may seem too much to be hoped for by the average man. That is because the average man does not "think big" and does not give the essential material "a story". Big thinking brings big results and Newspaper Editors like a story about the outstanding and the unusual. So in your presentation of a publicity trick, do it "big" and let there be material for a story that's outstanding news.

## PUBLICITY PLOTS AND IDEAS

### Radio Prediction

About two months ago I was working on a series of B.B.C. Radio Programmes with my good friend David Berglas. Halfway through the series of thirteen programmes we decided that a Publicity Stunt would do everybody a bit of good! The occasion will serve as a good example of how a plot is thought out and then exploited.

Our first concern was to "think big". My job was to get ideas and David's job was to do them; normally I reckon that given time I can work out a stunt which is big enough for any occasion, but Mr. Berglas is a "stunt eater". I'd think up something that would scare the living daylights out of the ordinary performer—and David would look it over as though it was a new novelty for kiddies. He talks in terms of "Vanishing Nelson's Column" and "Stopping all the traffic in Piccadilly for three minutes". (It took me three days to talk him out of the last fantastic scheme which would have landed us all "inside" for a short holiday!) So the situation demanded something big and David Berglas was the right chap to handle it. Those who know him as I do, will appreciate that there are not many like him—and when it comes to Publicity Stunts, David is an expert.

The plot for our Radio Prediction was basically very simple. A prediction would be done. Now came the problem of dressing it up to giant size so that it would interest several million listeners who weekly followed the radio programme. Not to be satisfied with several million listeners, David decided that the general public and press should be trawled in—the more the merrier!

We decided that the Prediction would be sealed in a fairly large box and this had to be displayed very prominently for quite a while. The usual run of things like "leaving it in a bank vault" and "the Editor keeps it in his safe" were out. Not big enough. Two million listeners would suspect your uncle was the Editor and the other millions wouldn't care. After rejecting twenty ideas, it was agreed that the best place to display the box was to suspend it in mid-air—and make it somewhere so that everybody and anybody could see it —yet nobody could get at it.

After three weeks of arguments, debates, bribes, swearing and threatening, David had been to every official outside the House of Lords and finally gained permission to suspend the box on a wire cable hanging right over the middle of London's prominent thoroughfare—Regent Street—within a few feet of Piccadilly Circus which we call the "heart of London". It stayed there causing curiosity, traffic jams and alarm from old ladies who thought it had come from

377

Mars, for no less than one week. During that time—thousands upon thousands of people must have looked up and wondered what the hell it was. Press people naturally followed the interest and a brief mention on the air brought many more to see nothing less than a big box marked with a query swinging thirty feet over the main road.

By the time the week was up—and the Stunt taken place, there was a keen interest by half the Nation to know what was going to happen. The B.B.C. were delighted that the listening public increased their tuning in to the programme. All was well, David came on as Resident Mindreader on the series; members of the audience provided information to make up an imaginary passport. They supply the name, address, age and nationality, etc. .... when this had been done in the Studio, a team of officials, supported by a B.B.C. outside broadcasting unit—hauled in the box through the windows of a Famous Hotel and opened it up. There inside, where it had been for a week is a genuine passport issued especially to David Berglas a week ago— and it predicted with amazing accuracy the facts just supplied in the Studio! Amid the gasps of amazement there were one or two quieter sighs of relief as a couple said to themselves "it worked!"

Now for the judgment, was it worth it? The answer came that night. David had been booked to appear six times at weekly intervals on the radio series. That night the Producer wanted to know if he could possibly continue and stay in until the series ended—another seven weeks. David did thirteen programmes.

This particular occasion served as a first class example that big results demand big thinking. I make no attempt to bother you here and now with how it was done. That was unimportant—the trick itself was child's play, and who cares how a good trick is done—as long as it is done well?

## Personal Column Advert Stunt

Leslie May of Edinburgh reminded me that a very good publicity stunt is one where you insert an advertisement in some prominent daily paper. The original idea comes from an early Jinx and to my experience, Joe Elman our contributor of "Sightless Vision" in Step Five, is one person who has made good use of this for many years.

Practically any trick will do—a simple card prediction, a word for a book test, a name etc., you merely word out a small advert which goes —

AT THE SAVOY tonight, Mr. Eric Mason will select the Ace of Clubs.

.... LESLIE MAY (Paranormalist).

You insert the place of performance of course, and use the name of the Chairman or President as the one who will select the card. Ending with your own name. You see that you have a copy of the paper with you when you arrive at the place of performance and say nothing about your advert until, by some means, you have forced the Chairman to choose the Ace of Clubs. Then comes printed evidence of your prediction being correct. Not to mention the curiosity that can be aroused by other people who spot your advert in the Personal Column. (Leslie May suggests two adverts in one paper; the Personal Column and Entertainments Section would result in a good tie-up). The easiest way to force the Ace of Clubs is to keep it under glass in bright sunlight—a la tomato plants ! !

At this point I will ask to be forgiven for sidetracking Publicity Stunts to come in with a true story, told briefly, which concerned David Berglas and a printed prediction set in The Radio Times.

David at a Studio in London worked a stunt with a lady in Manchester (another Studio—linked up). She had been told to choose a newspaper, choose a page, tear it up into eight pieces and choose one piece. Tear that bit up and finally came the order from David "and now you have one piece left, please choose any side". For half a minute there was a deathly silence and then David heard laughter and some unscripted remarks from the compere at the other end, who on this occasion was Cyril Fletcher. Naturally, David got a bit worried at this unexpected turn of events, and as best he could on a live broadcast, he asked Cyril Fletcher "What's going on . . . ." Back came the reply, "Well, our guest has done what you told her to—she is chewing the paper ! ! " The lady obviously mistook "Choose" for "Chew" and there she was chewing the vital slip that was intended as the prediction to tie up with the Radio Times advertisement! If she had swallowed, it would have taken an operation to prove the prediction correct, as it was, a sad and rather well-eaten slip of paper was deciphered, and with lots of giggles it turned out all right in the end. There's no accounting for taste!

### Registered Letter Prediction

Another Stunt which goes well when you know in plenty of time, the place of performance; send a registered letter containing a prediction to the organiser (or, to anyone who will be there on the night). In actual fact, the envelope is empty—only to be loaded with a prediction from a billet knife or billet pencil (see Step Four) when you come to use it during the act.

You don't want the organiser to open the prediction before time, so what you do is send him the prediction sealed in an envelope which is enclosed within another envelope (the registered one) along with a note telling him to bring the enclosed envelope to your performance and to safeguard it intact until that time. They will co-operate if you do it tactfully.

If you are the proud owner of a Prediction Chest, this may also be sent via registered mail and worked accordingly.

### Fogel's Bullet Catching

From time to time performers have utilized the dramatic stage trick "Catching a Bullet in the Teeth" for the purpose of a Publicity Stunt. Legend has it that Ted Annemann once did a stunt, catching a bullet, and nobody knows how. Reading the description of this in Dexter's book is most interesting and quite impossible! Who cares? Annemann knew the difference between performing effects and demonstrating principles!

The Bullet Catch is a good Publicity Stunt because it fringes on play with death. However, it is not a toy that is something to be done by a fool. There are many safe methods; there are just as many unsafe ones. Some people insist that *any* publicity is good—but they go wrong when you hit the headlines with "Mindreader blows his brains out when stunt goes wrong". So you're in the news ! ! ?

I will not commit myself to methods for Bullet Catching, all I say is that here we have good material for Publicity Stunt on a grand scale—and if you are very careful—there is no more danger than there is from dropping a Svengali pack on your foot and breaking your toe.

Two years ago I had the great pleasure to watch the greatest Publicity Stunt I have ever seen. Maurice Fogel does the trick. Fogel does everything the book says: takes a trick and makes it big.

On stage a team of six crackshot guardsmen. A colonel in charge of the "Firing Squad". Regulation army rifles—sandbags and anti-ricochette boards around. A plate holding eighteen live bullets—and each guardsman loads any bullet he likes. Twice they fire a salvo of six rounds at a plate which disintegrates under the impact of six bullets. The din is terrific, the atmosphere tense. Fogel now stands in shirt sleeves ready to face the onslaught of catching six bullets at once. The Colonel gives the order . . . "Load, Take aim, FIRE!" Another deafening bang and Fogel totters forward and crashes flat on his face. Everyone is on their feet with one thought "it's gone wrong" . . . thirty seconds later, after what seems to be ten hours of utter silence—Fogel stands to his feet—turns and smiles and six bullets array themselves in his teeth! They drop on to a plate, eager committee men rush forward and grab them—identify markings, they match —they are *the* bullets.

I doubt that I will ever see a more frightening, dramatic and gripping performance than on this occasion. Primarily, Fogel did it for a Publicity Stunt. That night and next day nearly every paper in the country carried the story and many held front page pictures. Three newsreel films went out and brought the story on film to the public for six months afterwards.

Many plots for Publicity Stunts can be conceived by performance of some daring and unusual act. Once it was the fashion to go over Niagara Falls in a barrel, and as many who hit the headlines—hit the obituary column! We know about people like Houdini who utilised underwater escapes for dramatic Publicity Stunts. However, our prime object is to publicise ourselves as Mentalists—so the stunt must be one that savours of mental skill in addition to manual daring. Since there are many stunts which do not involve any risk of physical injury, it is not worth bothering or chancing anything that may land you in hospital.

**Example of Personal Publicity: Raymond Hafler**

A few pages back in this Step I criticised some of the letter headings and visiting cards that Mentalists use. Now we go to the opposite end and examine publicity of the personal kind—that we feel is in good taste.

Raymond Hafler of California, U.S.A., is a good friend and fellow Mentalist and his status in Mentalism we would call semi-professional. That means he does not do it for a living (although he is more than capable if it were necessary). Most of his time nowadays is taken up with professional work at the Municipal Courts of Long Beach. This means that he doesn't have to have good personal publicity—but Ray, a Mentalist of many years experience knows the value of a job well done, and I asked him to allow me to reprint here samples of visiting cards and leaflet handouts. The card, you see, is direct, simple and sophisticated. The leaflet has been carefully worded and is given out as a small, single fold card. Our reproduction of this handout shows you both sides. The front is a straightforward drawing and bears his name. The inside tells you all about it and the back tells you he can be booked by telephone. Since Ray Hafler has been good enough to permit us to reproduce samples of his personal publicity, I will ask you to respect his property and not to copy these reproductions; they are merely illustrative.

## "MAGIC OF THE MIND"

Raymond W. Hafler, world traveler and lecturer of the science of Extra Sensory Perception is most qualified as a propounder of the startling discoveries and findings of this comparitively new science.

His travels have led him to those corners of the earth, Asia and the Orient, known for their intensive search to lift the veil of the secrets of a science hitherto placed in the category of mysticism. Steeped in the wisdom and the fruits of knowledge accumulated by those ancient civilizations, Mr. Hafler has truly gained a unique insight and familiarity within his chosen field that has resulted in a most successful and productive quest of the unknown.

It has been stated by Mr. Hafler, "Nothing in this world can be supernatural, but on the contrary can and must be subjected to the analytical mind of logician and scientist." Consequently, his lectures and demonstrations are presented from a purely unbiased standpoint and solely for the purpose of entertaining his audience.

His demonstrations include illustrations of the various characteristics and functions of that sixth sense, Extra Sensory Perception, e.g., the discernent of a person's thoughts; intuition; control of other minds; and the prophecy of occurrence.

He uses individuals in his audience who are unknown to him for his telepathic demonstrations. He makes them the actual recipients of telepathy and mental pictures which he climactically reveals. Interest and thrills await those viewing this most unusual lecture.

Aside from becoming an example of good personal publicity, Ray Hafler serves to prove another point. When he gives out his leaflet it reads good; it sounds very much as though they will get someone who knows what he's talking about—and has worldly experience. Anybody who can write English can turn out the spiel—but as we said at the very beginning, you have to back it up with action and proof. Ray Hafler shouldn't be a bit worried that his leaflet oversells him to the bookers. If we look at his personal history in brief, we find he had 24 years in the U.S. Navy and ended up a Lieutenant Commander. During his service he performed endless varieties of Magic and Mentalism in many countries of the world. Ray tells me that whilst on the USS. Breckenridge alone, he played to cabin and troop passengers well over a hundred shows—which adds up to two things. He has the experience and ability to back up the claims in his leaflet, and he must be capable of a good entertaining act, to be wanted for over one hundred performances. We see that he has "something to sell" and now we have seen his personal publicity and know one method by which he sells it.

There's nothing special about Ray Hafler to say why he should be used as an example in the Steps; only that he is a rare example of a non-professional who takes the trouble to do it properly. Some who read this will think to themselves "it doesn't strike me as being very much"—and nine out of ten who think so, will be Mentalists who have nothing like it to offer themselves!

## Visiting Card Gimmick

I have played with this idea for quite a while and it seems to be a good way to stop people throwing your card in their wastepaper bin as soon as they get home.

On one side of your card you have the normal name and address as on any card. On the back you have specially printed a mass of numbers in rows and columns. From one to a hundred mixed in any order will do—using the cards all the time, you soon get to know where the numbers are roughly speaking. Now to use the visiting card gimmick. It's very simple; one side of your card says you are a mindreader and you let them see it, invariably they look at the back also and in doing so—they are curious about the numbers. You tell them they are there for a simple mindreading test you do. Take back the card and ask them to think of any number from one to a hundred. Say you will circle the one they are thinking of . . . pretend to mark one with a pencil; ask what they chose and then do the rest with a swami gimmick. This is not much to carry, a few cards and a swami gimmick (see Step One for technique) and they are sure to keep the card as a souvenir and probably it will be shown to many of their friends when they relate the experience!

## The Haunted House

Once again we find Fogel tied up with something big and unusual. As a Publicity Stunt—something that is sure to make good reading in the Newspapers, you (as a Mentalist) knowing a thing or two about poltergiests, go to a house that is alleged to be haunted and "lay the ghost".

Usually this is a fixed and phoney set up. A friend lends their house for the occasion—claims they are being disturbed by strange noises, etc., over a short time they build up the plot, local spiritualist association have a go and get no results, psychical research team fail to stop the disturbance, etc. Finally they ask you if you can do something to help. You go in (with local press, police, the vicar and whosoever else you can ensnare!) and hold a seance.

382

The last time Fogel went through this palava, he was actually invited to try and exorcise a ghost. Surrounded by officials he held a seance and some mighty queer happenings took place. By some strange co-incidence, a spook sent the message that it was restless, but now promised to leave and would never cause trouble again! Not only did it make good reading in the press write ups, but the house owners were no longer disturbed and were indeed truly grateful to Fogel.

## The Challenge Seance

There's a lot of work in this stunt—but a lot happens and I have done it several times with good results. As a Mentalist—you challenge a Medium to produce any supernatural phenomena that you yourself cannot outdo or duplicate by methods which, you claim, are natural.

To give it all a certain amount of attraction, a big money wager is offered, press, local dignitaries and officials are invited and away you go! Step Nine gives you all the information you want on what to do—all else that matters is the Medium. I am sure you will be too intelligent to be disappointed, when I tell you the best way to get a Medium for this sort of stunt, is to train one yourself! You haven't got a chance in a million of finding a physical medium who will accept a genuine challenge from you, and even if you did find one— you stand to lose your bet if the medium suddenly pulls three yards of ectoplasm from your left ear—and you don't know how!

No doubt we could find a small-time mental-medium who would be pretentious enough to demonstrate clairvoyance or psychometry as a challenge, but it's not big enough for our purpose and in any case, it is almost impossible to dispute clairvoyance which offers no material evidence of trickery. In fact, less than two years ago a well-known professional medium stood on the stage at the Magic Circle in London and for two hours demonstrated clairvoyance; but for a few hecklers who were soon outwitted in cross-fire conversation, the medium had it all his own way! Watching this demonstration, I could not fail to acknowledge the medium as a brilliant speaker and thought what a perfect Mentalist this man would make.

However, back to training our own medium, that is the safest way and that's what I normally do. You need a man or woman who can act and you teach them a few tricks of the trade to put them in business against you!

With the right person to act as medium on your side, you can't go far wrong and it will still seem legitimate. In case you should doubt that, I have tried it out before highly critical audiences and still got away with it (*i.e.* Magic Circle, Society for Psychical Research, Newspaper Reporters, etc.).

There is good publicity material to be gained from stunts between Mentalists and Mediums. The market has not yet been exhausted and there remains plenty of scope today. In the past it has always been a reasonably safe bet for publicity. I have many press records of stunts in the past and some of the names, to mention a few, include Harry Houdini, Carl Hertz and his challenge to Madame Dis Debar which held a full page in the London Times to say the least, Julien Proskauwer, Harry Kellar, and of course, Maskelyne and Devant. Needless, to say, there are many more.

## Headline Predictions

Probably the most used Publicity Stunt of them all, is the prediction of the Headlines in some prominent newspaper. The reason for its popularity is that it nearly always get a story in print and this is mostly the outcome of providing press material that is personal to the newspaper itself.

On the market, magic dealers have about ten good ways of performing the feat. To mention a few, Prediction Chest, Billet Knife or Pencil, Fogel's headline Prediction which is sealed in a bottle and so on. Most of them achieve the effect by simple means.

There is barely any need for me to discuss technical details; all that is lacking, generally speaking, is good presentation. My advice to those who aim to do this type of stunt, is first get a foolproof method (like any of those mentioned) and then forget the mechanics and concentrate on building up the stunt. For example, let us suppose that we have arranged to forecast the headlines in our local paper. To create as much interest as possible, we seal the prediction in a box and then arrange to have this box prominently displayed in the window of some big store and surround it with showcards which tell the public "this box contains an Amazing Prediction made by Oscar Oswald—mindreader" and "£1,000 offered if he is wrong!" etc., etc. It doesn't take long to work out a few eye-catching slogans and it costs very little to have a few showcards done. The box displayed there for a week is seen by many before it is opened—all added material to your story, all added publicity which you don't get if the box is left in the Editor's safe for a week.

Other presentation plots on headline predictions include an idea from Punx. He has the prediction chest opened after a week or two—and out comes a roll of "ticker tape" with brief headlines for ten leading newspapers throughout the country. I have yet to hear of a better disguise for a rolled piece of paper in a box! ! Then we have the headline predictions performed from stage in the theatre. The box has been suspended from the dome of the theatre from the start of the show. Finally, I had no trouble switching a small length of recording tape which made it possible for me to perform a novel headline prediction—by tape recorder.

**Glorified Muscle Reading**

I rebuke myself for not using this as an example earlier when speaking on little tricks that are blown up to an enormous size to become Publicity Stunts! This little trick is a book test—and the method we claim is muscle reading—or whatever you prefer to call it.

You start off in the Editor's office. You wait there and keep a small committee amused with a few mindreading tricks—whilst they send someone to any public library in the town. That person is told to go where he likes, choose any book in the library and select any page or word—make an accurate note of all the details such as name of book and page number, etc., and then return to you. He is instructed most carefully to return the book to the exact position as where he found it.

When he gets back you have him seal the record paper in an envelope and hand this to the Editor or Sub-Editor (whoever is free!). Now you start out with a group of three of four people. For your own benefit, the group is best composed of one reporter to write up the details, one cameraman to take a few shots, the Editor to see that everything is above board and the man who picked the place and book for the test.

You call a cab and off you go to the library. You find the right floor and then tour your group around sections and divisions through thousands of books. You get warm at the right shelf, you find the book, you open it at the right page and with a sigh of exhaustion—underline with your pen the chosen word! You ask the Editor to open the envelope and check your findings—and if it's favourable publicity you want after that palava—the contents of the envelope had better be right!

I suppose there must be a good ten ways of doing this stunt—but for those who can't think out a method, I suggest you work alone. Send the scout out to choose his word, etc., telling him to *remember* exactly the facts. When he gets back—find some excuse to get him to write the facts down—"I want the Editor to have a copy in his possession all the time—before we leave" . . . a sheet of carbon paper stuck inside a newspaper will then get you a copy. Another method, with help this time—is simply to have the scout followed by a friend. By this you will be able to find the book and maybe the page—and proper muscle reading will find you the word. (See Step Two). The best way for your friend to signal you is to have him waiting outside for you to come on to the street with your party. He then calls a cab and you do the same. You guide your cab driver in the same direction as the friend drives. The chances are you will know the library as soon as the cab starts as there are not that many to choose from if you consider how long it took the scout to go and come back! At the library you again "pick up" your friend and he goes to the shelf and selects a book from there—but not the chosen one. Browsing through the book he keeps it open at a page number which tells you how many books along the row is the chosen book. Then he turns his pages to give you the number of your page, etc., as long as you keep an eye on your assistant, there is no need to stand beside him. He can leave the book open on a table and then walk away—you spot the page number as you pass by.

## Publicity Pencils

It is not commonly known that for very little outlay, you can have your name and a few words inscribed on ordinary lead pencils. It is economical to have about one thousand done at once and the cost of this number is somewhere in the region of fourpence each.

I have some which bear my name and also the inscription—"The Pencil Made for Mindreading". As you may guess, give one of these to anybody and the first thing they want to know is "why is it made for mindreading?" . . . . which immediately provides the excuse to get them to write something down ready for one to do the Centre Tear (see Step Six). When they have written a word, their name or telephone number, I go through the usual procedure and destroy the billet. Now I take back the pencil and on another piece of paper, slowly reproduce what they wrote! This ability I attribute to the pencil—explaining in brief the principles of automatic writing and give a good example by describing a planchette. By the time it's done—not only do they keep my pencil as a souvenir, but also, they remember every time they use it and frequently tell the story to other people. Every time you give away a fourpenny pencil, you get a pound of publicity!

In a small way, the Publicity Pencil serves to illustrate that anything which arouses curiosity—is good for publicity. The more interest it creates, the better the gimmick. To arouse the inquisitive instinct is one of the few ways to get people to *ask you* to show them your ability—a better thing than you trying to force them to pay attention!

## Blindfold Drives and Walks

Not to be forgotten whilst on the topic of Publicity plots—we have Blindfold Drives and Walks. We have already discussed the point that anything which breeds danger attracts attention and is good for publicity, and this is in that class. So much so in fact, that today in many big cities of the world—Blindfold driving of cars or bicycles is forbidden and the necessary permission from the Police is unobtainable. This is rather unfortunate because it stands to reason that when you drive blindfolded, the more the traffic on the road and the larger the city, the more impressive the stunt becomes. To see the local Vicar peddle around the village green on a penny farthing is less dramatic than watching our budding mentalist shoot up busy Oxford Street in a steamroller. So the first thing you do before you even bother to think about blindfold drives, is to find out if they will allow it where you want to do it. If they will, Step Five tells you everything you need to know about blindfolds to make it possible.

Blindfold walks on their own—don't mean a thing. You need a plot and to give you some ideas—a good stunt at Hampton Court; find the middle of the maze whilst blindfolded—a thing which most people cannot do under normal conditions! Or try and bring in the danger element—if you care to, walk a plank which crosses two buildings pretty high in the air. At the zoo, lead a committee to the cage of any animal they care to nominate, in a museum, lead the group to any object they name. It would be unworthy of me to pass the subject of Blindfold walks without mention of Pierre Dufont. This gentleman led six officers of the British Army for two miles across a field whilst blindfolded. The only extraordinary thing about the episode was that it was an enemy minefield in France during the war. When asked why he did it and if he was scared his reply was very simple. He said that if he had remained behind, the chances were he would have been caught and shot—which was a good excuse for going forward. He later confessed that before the war he had been a showman, and he decided on the occasion to die a showman if fate would have it—so he wore a blindfold! There seems to be little doubt, according to the report in "The Soldier" that if Dufont had followed the usual paths across the fields (which he would have done without the blindfold) they would all have been blown to bits.

## CONCLUSION

Sufficient plots have been given to illustrate what makes a good publicity stunt and all that remains now is to summarise all that we have studied, so that we get the bare essential of that which is needed for good publicity. Here they are:—

   (1) First have a good product to sell; have a good act.
   (2) Organise Personal Publicity; keep it in good taste.
   (3) Attract attention, create mass interest and arouse curiosity.
   (4) Think big.
   (5) Whilst you remain in showbusiness you need publicity. Keep it up.
   (6) Don't take unnecessary chances—they are not worth it.
   (7) A Personal gimmick is worth a ton of printed matter.
   (8) Learn to commercialise your publicity and not to waste it.
   (9) Be dramatic and grossly exaggerate any trick you do.
  (10) Be as good as your publicity says you are!

# PATTER AND PRESENTATION

## BY

## CORINDA

## STEP THIRTEEN

IN CORINDA'S SERIES :—
## "THIRTEEN STEPS TO MENTALISM"

STEP THIRTEEN in CORINDA'S SERIES

"THIRTEEN STEPS TO MENTALISM"

PATTER AND PRESENTATION

## CONTENTS

Printed in England by H. Clarke & Co. (London) Ltd.

Published by

# INTRODUCTION

It is a bold and somewhat presumptuous step to take, when anybody sets out to write even a small booklet on Patter and Presentation. A subject of this kind demands a lifetime of experience and a keen understanding and appreciation of magic as a whole. As writer of this book, I have neither of these qualifications and I would make it quite clear in the beginning that I try to do nothing more than express my personal views on Mentalism. When necessary, I have taken the advice of those more qualified than myself and I am grateful for the considerable assistance of my many friends.

Since this " Step " expresses that which I presume to be a reasonable approach to presenting mental magic, it is naturally confined to Mentalism which I like. It may not include mental magic which is favoured by others and it may even be incomplete when consideration is given to the whole field of Mentalism—a vast subject. However, it will be wide enough and comprehensive enough to give those who want to know—a knowledge of one way to perform Mentalism. The way which I have chosen is the one which favours simplicity, straightforwardness and impact. Naturally, I have done my readers the courtesy of trying out these principles, before writing about them, so I have the satisfaction of knowing they work and I am confident that anybody else can do the same if they want to.

Now to get down to work and discuss in detail the little things that make a weak trick appear as a miracle or, alternatively, the miracle seem a flop. In this short sentence alone, we have the very essence of mentalism; it is not the trick that matters one fifth as much as the way you do it. I would go so far as to say that in the hands of a good performer, any trick, no matter how bad as an effect, could be made into something. Indeed, it is possible to perform several things which are not even tricks—and still bewilder an audience by dint of first class showmanship. Nothing is more satisfying than to fool an audience, when you haven't done anything!

If we can appreciate this, we must realise of what value good presentation is to mental magic. It is in fact quite indispensible since you cannot perform good magic without it—and that means regardless of how brilliant your tricks (as tricks) may be. It is a common failing to suppose that a first class trick or effect, needs less attention concerning presentation than a weaker one. One is almost misdirected into believing that a startling effect *must* be good when performed. But it is not so. There are two distinct things to be done before you achieve the ideal performance; first you get the best possible effect and then you get the best possible form of presentation. To get the effect and stop there is to stop half way to perfection.

In my profession I meet magicians and mentalists all day and this gives me a fair opportunity to see how most of them work. I mean no offence when I say that in my opinion, the average person is not in the least interested in proper presentation, and good patter is likewise badly neglected. There appears to be an insatiable urge to find new tricks (which is entertaining and interesting) and there is hardly any inclination to make these new tricks worth performing properly—(which is not so interesting although far more profit-able). Really there is no need whatsoever for new tricks as there are more than enough already, and as an inventor and dealer I am as guilty as anyone for propagating new monstrosities! My honest advice for what it is worth, is to spend less time searching for new effects and more time working on those you already have. It is an achievement in one life to be able to do six tricks perfectly and if you get this far, then you are entitled to play games and fiddle with novel diversions. The odd thing about magicians is that when this sort of thing is said, everybody agrees and at the same time everybody thinks it applies to somebody else. It could be you!

## THE ESSENTIALS OF GOOD PERFORMANCE

No one thing makes a trick right or wrong—many things go together. To name a few of the more important subjects, we have:—

(*a*) Personal appearance.
(*b*) Manner and speech.
(*c*) Patter.
(*d*) Good effects.
(*e*) Handling.
(*f*) Timing.
(*g*) Misdirection.
(*h*) Co-ordination.

Let us deal briefly with each one in turn but at the same time, let us remember that they are not isolated in performance—they must all come together making, in effect, the complete picture.

### (A) PERSONAL APPEARANCE

When you look good, you feel good. When you feel good, you work well. Personal appearance is important and can easily be overlooked. When you are a performer, people have to look at two things, you and your magic. Both should be pleasing to the eye.

You do not have to be rich in order to dress in good taste and there is no excuse for dirty hands and fingernails which can be an alarming distraction from the magic your hands do.

There is no such thing as a typical costume for the Mentalist. This is a good thing because it means you don't have to dress up into some make-believe role each time you wish to perform. Contrary to some schools of thought, I do not believe that the stage mentalist has to be garbed in flowing Eastern robes and crowned with a turban. The only time I would endorse such extravagance would be in the case of an Eastern Mentalist who rightly dressed in native style. That would be natural and what is natural is most important which brings us to the next point.

Personal appearance has a lot to do with the way the audience regard you. Consider what you *want* them to think of you. If you wish to present your mentalism as supernatural phenomena, then you are almost obliged to appear supernatural. One has to picture the common mental image of a character part as seen in the public eye. Question people and ask what they think a Medium looks like—and few suppose that such a personality is an ordinary looking person. Introduce the supernatural and you automatically introduce alongside the Occult. Now we anticipate our mentalist a la Svengali; a freakish man with the evil eye, pointed beard and what have you. As a further example, there have been half a dozen or so films made which involved a Medium. In nearly every instance, the Medium always turned out to be an eccentric grey haired old lady, garbed in flowing dress and heavily bedecked with chains of beads, bangles and odd trinkets. Never once was the medium an ordinary looking person, which in fact is what they all are, as it did not matter what they really were like, it was what people expected them to be that counted. Remember one secret of showbusiness is to exaggerate the ordinary so that it becomes a change from the commonplace and therefore is interesting to watch.

Bearing this point in mind, and others which we will discuss, we come to the question, " is it worth pretending to be supernatural?" I have little hesitation in giving my answer as No! At least, not for the mindreader. It is an artificial role which is hard to play, hard to maintain (since you have to keep it up) and to cap it all, it is quite unnecessary.

So now back to personal appearance; what should you look like? Well you should look clean, suitably dressed to meet the company which you entertain (*i.e.* Pink jeans are not worn at a Duchesses Dinner Party) and for your own benefit, dress comfortably. If you are not sure at anytime as to what to wear, play safe and wear a quiet suit and tie. All this might seem minor detail, but it is by no means so as you may, if you care to, learn the hard way. For instance, one professional mindreader from England turned up to play a Casino in France two years ago, he was not allowed through the doors because of a House rule that all gentlemen wore ties. He missed the engagement because on a hot day he arrived in an open neck shirt. Then there is another aspect to consider. When you are not well dressed and you arrive in company that is, naturally you feel different and can easily become embarrassed. How can you possibly work at ease when you are self-conscious about your appearance? If you are one of these people who like to claim you don't care a damn what you look like then you might like to know that the people who pay for an artist to entertain their guests, frequently expect somebody who looks like a gentleman and not a tramp. They care.

Before we leave this topic, let us say just one thing. Although you are committed to dress respectably, you are not barred from a touch of personal taste as long as it is reasonably good taste. You don't have to turn out like a tailors dummy—for instance, I have often worked from a stage wearing a maroon corduroy jacket (rather like a smoking jacket) and with clean shoes, shirt and tie I think I felt almost civilised.

## (B) MANNER AND SPEECH

When you meet a strange person you form a quick impression of them by the way they dress, speak and behave. Quite often your audience meet you for the first time and they will form an opinion about you. They can arrive at three conclusions. They like you, they do not like you and lastly, they can't even be bothered to think about you.

We have discussed the importance of correct dress and see now, once more, that it helps to form a good impression at the start. However, immaculate as you may appear, sooner or later you have to say something and once more you can make or break yourself.

What you say and the manner in which you say it will have a decided effect on the audience, especially at the beginning. There are certain golden rules to follow. Speak clearly so that people hear what you have to say, talk loud enough without shouting for everybody to hear, and speak as best you can in the best possible English. (For an English speaking audience, since even the best Oxford English may not be appreciated when addressing a batch of Zulu tribesmen).

When it comes to the manner of speech, the first thing at all times is politeness. Nothing creates a better and more lasting impression than good manners. Very few people study etiquette and it is a definite point in your favour if you can do the right thing at the right time. To know that one addresses a Bishop as " Your Grace " and not " Mac " or " Mate " is what one might take as a sign of culture! If you don't know what to do, almost any Public Library will have a book telling you about it.

Aside from politeness with manner of speech, there is attitude. You can win an audience—or lose them in seconds—simply by taking on the right or wrong attitude. The right approach is to appear confident, friendly and professional. The wrong one incorporates nervousness, big-headedness or conceitedness, amateurism and vagueness. Try to appear as though you *like* being there and like doing the job. Never appear bored and disinterested. Oddly enough, you will find that as you feel so this, in some peculiar manner, goes out into the audience. You have to make yourself feel good and feel confident and then they feel the same and soon accept you. When you are nervous—often you make the audience nervous, especially in close up work and this is almost useless for the role of a commanding mindreader.

To sum it up, a good dodge is to become introspective by assuming that you have an entire audience of professional cold readers (See Step Ten) and imagine how they will see you. If you were a cold reader you would look for dress, manner and speech—so look at yourself.

## (C) PATTER

It is practically impossible to perform a mental act or routine without saying something. Magicians are a little more fortunate than mentalists in this respect, if they like, they can evolve an act, a so called " Silent Act " and nothing is said. Hardly any mental tricks explain themselves to an audience by vision alone and because of this, we are forced to meet the demand for good patter during performance.

Patter is the name we give to a story we tell and the casual asides of conversation that come during performance. Not to be confused with speech which is, as we have seen, another thing. One concerns voice production and correct use of a language and the other (patter) deals with what you say and why you say it in order to make the effect presentable.

One of the outstanding weakspots in the amateur mental programme is usually patter. More often than not, budding mentalists buy good mental effects from their dealers, and then go ahead and perform the mechanics of the trick as given in the instructions supplied and forget to add the very necessary talk to the effect. A dealer cannot hope to supply every client with correct patter for every trick he sells. He can suggest plots and themes for patter that go well with the trick, but it's your job to find the right words to be used at the right time.

There are people whose profession it is to write words for others to say. Scriptwriters as we call them are of little use to a mentalist. The best scriptwriter for your mental act is yourself, and this is something that you should actually do; devise a script and learn it.

The important thing is to understand the purpose and value of good patter. When you understand, you will realise that others cannot write words for you and that imitation of another person's patter is likewise useless. We go back to manner as discussed earlier and try to visualise what the audience think of our work and ourselves. I believe that it is very important to be yourself and let it seem that what you do is natural to you. This you cannot achieve with artificial patter. Your words have to be the sort of thing you say naturally and a scriptwriter doing the job for you would have to be a psychiatrist at the same time, in order to create words that were natural to you. Later, when we discuss Misdirection, we shall see the added importance of behaving in a natural manner.

Now let us discuss the true purpose of patter. It is not just a case of having something to say to break up the silence, there is much more to it than that. Good patter is the means to an end—perfect presentation. It can be used to draw attention to your tricks (or apparatus) and when this happens, attention goes away from yourself. I know of several excellent tricks which would fail absolutely without the use of one or two right words delivered in the right manner at the right time. To think that one little word can often be the making of a great trick!

Let us examine examples of patter being applied during performance as a means of trickery. You will remember in Step Six on Billets we discussed in detail the Centre Tear Routine. We went through several stages and arrived at the most difficult part of the trick, we had to steal one piece of paper from several others held in view. This was achieved by using correct patter at the very right moment. A few natural words (" Have you got a match please?") took the attention from your hands to your face, and the trick was done. Another example, the crucial point in the Al Baker billet switch is reached, a few simple words, but right words (" Did you write it in English?") are spoken, and the trick is done. The Punx-Mier variation of the centre tear is a classic example of applied patter and serves as another example (See Step Six).

Now we begin to appreciate that it's not just " Words, words, words . . ." There is reason and cause behind all this. So how do we begin to get the right patter for the mental act?

Start by writing your own script; fit the effects into the pattern we call a routine, and then write down everything you think you should say from beginning to end. In the beginning, overload your script, write too much because you can always cut down by editing, which comes later. Allow for a straightforward introduction to each trick and for what you have to say during the performance of the effect. Finish by scripting your comments that go at the end of your trick. Completeness is essential. At this stage the script is in its crude state. It is simply a record of everything you might say. Now comes the editing. First find out if the present script is reasonably long enough for the running time of your tricks. The easiest way to do this is to run through a few mock performances. The use of a tape recorder in these trial and error stages can be a considerable help.

Having got enough on paper to last you during performance, now work to improve what you have already said. Start with the words that matter most and see if you can find a stronger word for any point where patter is part of the trick itself. Find the right word for that point, the word which suits the actions you make, the trick you do and the manner you do it in. Then go back over the rest of your material and see what can be done to improve it. Look for words that are ambiguous or unsuitable and change them to something which makes the trick clear, simple to understand in effect and entertaining to watch and listen to.

For each and every trick there is a good pattern to follow when devising the patter you need. Start off by finding the best way to explain to the audience what you are going to do (as far as your trick permits). If you cannot explain what you are going to do, and we know it is not always possible or desirable, then tell the audience what you are doing at the time. Moreover, when you do this, tell them in such a manner that you do not insult their intelligence or bore them with statements of the obvious.

(Avoid the bad habit acquired by many of naming each and everything they touch. " I am removing the cards from the case and cutting them . . . " that is an example of rather stupid patter. People can see you do this and if you can think of nothing better to say, then utilise the brief pause by making a quick aside that amuses people and entertains them.)

Having found the best way to introduce the trick you must find something to say whilst it goes on. As far as possible, stick to patter which deals with what you are doing. Remember you can distract attention with words and you do not want to perform the trick twice because people were more interested in your words than your actions! This part of the trick the middle part is the point for natural talk, the point where you exert your personality by saying the right things in a casual relaxed manner. Nothing will help you more to relax than knowing what you are going to say. You don't have to tell the audience you are working from a script. When you see a professional artist at work you see his relaxed talkative manner. He appears natural and what he says seems impromptu, but very probably he has said the same things hundreds of times before and by now those words are natural to him.

The last thing in the pattern is how to end the trick. We have to find suitable patter and our first concern is to find words which clearly indicate that it is the end. The word " Thank you " said in the right voice and accompanied by a suitable applause position on stage—signals the audience you have finished and they can applaud or throw tomatoes as the case may be. We shall discuss stage work later, but for those who are not sure about applaud positions, as an example, stand facing the audience and stretch out both arms facing the hands palms to roof. You adopt this position and loudly state " Thank you " and you have the right word with the right action to finish a trick or an act.

If it is the end of a trick and another is to follow, a definite finish to the trick is made and then a nice touch is to make a quick joke or comment before striding into the introduction of the next trick. It is worth noting that when you make a joke, people laugh and relax and this is the ideal time to get ready for the next trick or get rid of the evidence from the last one. There is powerful misdirection to be gained from a simple joke.

Now we have to deal with another completely different aspect of patter for mentalism. We are obliged to consider what type of things to say; how to introduce Mentalism to the public and what claims to make by word of mouth.

Well it is all a matter of opinion as to what you should or should not do. Some think you can claim to be the world's most phenomenal brain and others like to suggest that what they do is perfectly normal and could be done by anyone.

My personal opinion leans towards the last suggestion as opposed to the first. However, not to the extent that I openly admit that anyone could do the things I do. (Referring to performance of mentalism as seen by the public). I have experimented with numerous approaches to this problem and these days I find myself more and more in favour of a psychological trick of presentation which I find to be the perfect answer.

Whenever it is possible—and this is nearly always so when working mental magic at close quarters with an audience, I make a short introduction which tells them that I would like to show them a few interesting things that can be achieved if you like to train the human mind to do them. I openly state that it is my belief that everybody could do these things and that it is simply a question of study and practice. I flatter the incredibility of the human brain and not myself (which would be a wrong manner to adopt). I go on to explain that people could quite easily think there was something psychic about the things that can be done, and add that it is by no means so; certainly it takes training, a lot of hard work and a fair understanding of psychology—but all the same, it is something which anybody can train their mind to do!

As you realise, it is practically telling them the truth—but you need not fear the modesty of your claims will in any way effect their appreciation of your ability.

Having adopted this approach, I phrase the patter in straightforward language. I do not go off the deep end with long winded pseudo-scientific phraseology that supposedly sounds good. I prefer to use down to earth understandable language. I call a trick an " experiment " or a " simple test " and now and then I allow a technical term like " E.S.P." to slip in, just for effect. Whenever I use a technical term, I always add quickly an aside which explains it as it is quite wrong to suppose that the average man understands one half of the fancy names you can use. Most of the fancy names have been devised by psychologists and mentalists and I am sure they are not in common agreement themselves as to the meaning which is intended. I know of three books which use the term " Pre-inferential Cognosis " and none of them use the term as it was originally intended. The only time I would think of using any term such as the last mentioned one, would be as a joke to the audience. Having done something I would pass it off with the comment, " and I expect you would like to know how it was done? I don't mind telling you, it is nothing really, simply a case of pre-inferential cognosis —but don't tell everybody . . . " Used in this vein you pass away a technical phrase as a joke and that's about the best you can do.

Generally speaking it is easier, safer and altogether more convincing to use language that people understand, and to act as yourself rather than attempt to create an artificial personality. Nothing appears more ridiculous than a performer who starts off with a Chinese accent and ends up talking like a Cockney. Moreover, by using your own personality and speaking as you would normally, you find yourself at ease so much that although working to a script you are still able to ad lib remarks and witticisms into the proceedings —giving it all the more personal touch and making it all so much more natural.

Ideally, whilst performing, your talk should seem free, unrehearsed and natural. That is why one should avoid the over use of technical terms. Remember it is not a lecture, not a case of reciting poems and not a monotone announcement. When you introduce a trick don't make it sound like the usual voice heard on a railway station—the one that drones on telling you

397

the 10.50 train will stop at Fagsend and Doggit. Try and sound interesting, to some extent, what you say about the trick you intend to perform, will decide how much attention they will pay to the opening stages of your effect. If you arouse curiosity and interest at the start—the battle is half won.

I have no intention of giving you examples of patter for Mentalism. I think it would be downright stupid to do so. I have already explained that what suits one person rarely suits another and any examples I gave would naturally be those I use and may be quite unsuitable for you. Better by far that you do as I suggest; write your own script, keep in mind the purpose and uses of patter, experiment yourself to find that which suits you and then you have patter for the tricks you do.

Finally, the specific use of patter for misdirection is discussed a little later—that of course you can and should copy—as it fits anyone.

## (D)  GOOD EFFECTS

The prime purpose of this discussion is to analyse the makings of good (or bad) presentation. Therefore we must give some consideration to the actual effects that are performed. It is easy to say and nice to think that a brilliant performer could take any old trick and make it into a veritable miracle during performance. I am inclined to disagree with this hypothesis and in any case, if you know what you are doing, you do not have to use weak effects. Your aim is not to prove how good you are by showing your ability to take a weak trick and make it presentable. Better by far that you start off right at the beginning with strong, good mental magic; there are plenty of good tricks to choose from and the best way to assess their value is to put each trick to a simple test. We draw up a short list of questions and see how many of them permit us to answer yes to any one trick. The more yesses we get, the better the trick. The questions are those which are most important:—

(1)  Can it be done without much preparation or expense?
(2)  Is it absolutely reliable and sure to work every time?
(3)  Can it be performed without using assistance of any kind?
(4)  Will the *audience* understand what has happened?
(5)  Will it be accepted as a mental effect and not magic trick?
(6)  Can it be done without excessive apparatus?
(7)  Can it be performed anywhere; stage or close up?
(8)  Does it suit your style and can you find good patter for it?
(9)  Is the effect strong enough to fool everybody?
(10)  Are you capable of working the trick?

Now we have our table of questions and we can find any trick we like and put it to the test. Few tricks will come out of the test with ten points out of ten—but there may be excusable instances. For example, you may find a trick which takes a great deal of preparation and gives you the answer " No " to No. 1 question. However, if the effect is so good that it warrants a lot of initial work—then you may wisely choose to adopt it for your act.

The ten test questions I have devised can be altered as you wish. You may decide that there is another important feature which you think every trick should have, and if so add it to the list. It is a simple way to run through a great many tricks in a short space of time and sort out those which have a potential value to your act. You know at the end of a test run that you have tricks which are worth working onb ecause they stand up to some pretty tough questions. Do bear in mind that every trick will not stand up to ten out of ten—but on the other hand, keep in mind that the higher the score, the more suitable the trick. Also keep in mind that you can alter tricks so that you improve them and with that in mind, if you are sure a change can be made you naturally answer yes to what might otherwise have been no. I find this a simple and time-saving system. I lay no claims as to the originality of this system as I am confident that anything so painfully obvious must have been thought of by everybody who, like myself, has blundered through reams of diabolical mental magic—hoping to find one trick!

What else goes to make a trick good or bad? Well, to a large extent it is a matter of taste and we must allow for a considerable amount of personal bias. I know what I like and what I do not like, which is a good thing. However, what is better than that, I know why I don't or do like an effect and maybe if I describe briefly what I feel is a good trick, you will have something to guide you.

First I feel that it is absolutely imperative that the trick is one that can be explained to an audience. By that I mean, performed in such a way that they will understand what has happened. It might well seem a very odd thing to say—but one sees so many tricks of mentalism these days and quite a few of them are so involved or over subtle that at the end nobody is quite sure what has been achieved. That, to put it mildly, is a fat lot of good! The only advancement on this type of effect is the one that cannot be understood by the audience and the performer himself is not so sure what has happened. Yes—they exist.

One thing you have got to bear in mind all the time and that is *you know* what happens because you have read the instructions or invented the trick. That's all very well but the audience see it for the first time and they have to grasp the effect first time or it is useless. So first of all, be sure the audience understand what you do.

This leads us automatically into my second demand for a good trick. That is simplicity. I like straightforwardness. Invariably, a trick which you find simple to understand is a trick which is simple to perform. This does not mean the trick has to be weak. Anybody who knows anything about magic will acknowledge that some of the most beautiful masterpieces of trickery are so simple that they outclass the mass of tricks. If you bother to think about it, you will find that you personally get far more satisfaction by fooling somebody by a very simple dodge—than you do by a complicated and drawn out routine. So the trick should be simple to understand; you did this, you did that and the result was so and so, and it should be simple to perform. The less worries you have whilst performing, the better will be your act. The easier your tricks are the less worries you have. Never be ashamed of simplicity, it may not impress the boys at your local magic club but if you don't tell them how, a simple trick is just as likely to fool them as it is sure to deceive a lay audience.

The third standard which I expect of a good trick is that it is worth doing. I qualify that by saying there are many effects which although of the class mental magic—they are just not strong enough or unusual enough to be worth performing. You have to achieve something good. To have a card taken from a pack, remembered and returned, and then found by a couple of quick looks through the deck—that is the sort of thing which amuses those

399

who take this subject as a hobby—but it is not good enough for public presentation. If you like to dress it up and make it into something that's a different thing, but you belittle yourself by performing rather silly small tricks. If you know one good trick and nothing more, do the one and then stop. If you go on and add a few half-hearted catches you reveal yourself. If you do nothing more they are never sure how much you could do if you wanted to! It stands to reason that you now want to know how you can tell when you have done a good trick? Very simple. At the finish of the effect look at the audience; if they have gone white in the face, froth at the mouth with excitement, shake at the knees or get down on the floor and salaam you —it is quite a fair trick. If they snore or ask you what time your bus leaves— take a hint. I used too think one way to judge a trick was to wait and see if they said " Do it again." I made the mistake of thinking that if they said this, they liked it so much they wanted another dose. Now I know better. Often people say " Do it again " because you were so damn clumsy the first time that they caught half the trick and they now want to see the other half so that they know how it works. It is a great thing to make mistakes because that is the best way to learn!

Finally, a few minor standards for the making of good mental effects. The trick should be reasonably short, as a guide you might say that the more people you have watching a trick, the quicker it should be done. If you are working to an intimate audience of six or so seated around a table you are in a position to introduce one or two lengthy routines. The six people are close enough to enjoy the company of the performer, to see everything that happens and to hear everything that is said. On the other hand, on stage with an audience of one thousand it is by no means the same. This time you cannot be with every member of the audience and there is much more chance of them missing something you do and not hearing something you say. Therefore you have to struggle to catch and keep attention from start to finish. Nothing is more likely to cause a drop in attention than something which goes on and on and on.

If you have a first class effect which you feel must go into the stage act and yet it takes quite a time to perform, you must try and divide the performance of this effect into stages and make each stage a short, separate entertainment for the audience. A joke is enough to break the monotony—a funny gesture at the right time, can be the saving feature in a trick which will have a stunning finish if anybody waits long enough to see what happens. Consider at all times what you are supposed to be and what you are supposed to be able to do. You are a mindreader and you " should " be able to say to somebody, " Think of a name!" and three seconds later you blurt out " Dr. Livingstone " and the victim nods his head in reply. Any deviation from this theme is a stride away from what you would do if you could do the real thing. So when you have a member of the audience clean and examine twenty four school slates, keep in mind that you are the only person in the world who can understand what slates have to do with what you are supposed to be.

This brings us to another important point and it is something which connects the running time of a trick with the value of a trick. Primarily you have to entertain your audience and it is easy, very easy to get carried away with a trick that you like and forget that it may not be so interesting to an audience. You have an appreciation and liking for mentalism, try to avoid

400

the pitfall of entertaining yourself without at the same time, entertaining the audience. This sort of mistake is made more often by an enthusiastic amateur mentalist, than by the professional man who tries continuously to see everything from the audience viewpoint.

Everything must have a beginning and an end. A good trick must have a good and decisive finish. It is part and parcel of showmanship to be able to tell the audience " Now you can clap " and the stronger your finish, especially with the last trick in the act, the better off you will be. It is a very common mistake among inexperienced performers to take a few tricks and build them into an act. Then they hear the word " Continuity " and think this means that one trick must run smoothly and faultlessly into the next, making the whole a continuous routine. This is all wrong; utterly wrong.

If you have an act you might say you have a routine with six tricks. You have got to remember that it is six tricks and not one routine that you are showing. You should get at least six rounds of applause, one for each trick and each round of applause represents a break. If you make your six tricks run so smoothly one into the other, you do not finish one before you start the next; you do not give the audience a chance to applaud or to have a break. You need both, which we call applause-breaks during every performance. They serve more than one purpose. A break relieves the tension. You start a trick and build up the tension using showmanship and effect to scare or amaze an audience, then you break off quickly and let their emotions fall back to normal and give them a chance to let off steam by applauding your work. Then you start again rather like a see-saw, causing elation and then relaxation. Added to this pattern of psychological mistreatment, each trick should be followed by a stronger one if possible, so that each time you elate the audience a little more than last time. Now you achieve the purpose of routining and that is to go forward in steps until you reach an outstanding peak. Then you end.

I gained a lot of experience and understanding about breaks when I used to perform ghost shows. The necessity is not so apparent when doing ordinary mental magic (although it is still there) but when you go into the business of frightening people you find out that obvious breaks are imperative. You are performing a ghost show and you see and feel the tension building up: if you don't stop it gets unbearable, the audience become so tense that you feel as though an explosion is due to occur. You have to create breaks which act as safety valves and let the audience unwind a bit every now and then, it does them good, it does you good and to come back to the beginning, perfect routining does not achieve this when the continuity is overdone. Some while ago I watched a very good mental act at the London Society of Magicians. At the end, my friend turned to me and said he thought the act was good but it didn't seem as though the audience liked it much as they only clapped once. To me, the answer was very clear. Excepting when the man walked off the stage, the audience hadn't been given a chance to clap; there were no breaks.

So to come back to our original discussion, a good trick is one that enables you to make a strong obvious finish. Although you adopt an applause position (*i.e.* as suggested on page 396) to show the audience you have finished, the trick itself should also seem completed. Some tricks depend on a flash back principle; the performer does something and then slowly stops and smiles. The onlookers seeing him smile begin to think and suddenly realise that what he did half a minute ago was very clever, now they smile and show their appreciation. For some working conditions, close up for example, this technique can be quite good. But for stage work it is bad. You cannot afford the time to let people think back over all your movements before they realise you have done a trick. It has to be more obvious than that—avoid the flash back type of trick for large audiences.

Now what about the most important trick in the act, the last one you do. It is the most important because it is the one that leaves, or should leave, the final impression you create. To find a really good ending trick is not at all easy. To start with, unlike all the other tricks in the routine or act, this one has to be a trick which at the end leaves you and you only, on the stage. Quite clearly, for close up mentalism it is not the same and does not matter if you are left alone or not. But it is extremely important when working from the stage. It is quite wrong to conclude a performance and attempt to take a final call when you are standing on the stage surrounded by half a dozen people who have come up from the audience to help you during the act. If the last trick requires assistants, as it probably will do, it will have to be constructed so that you can politely dismiss your helpers back to the audience before you finally end the trick. Therefore, talking of good tricks, one that allows you the opportunity to do this is one worth having and you know where to use it. As a detail, I think that the last trick is also best if you can finish empty handed. It is not imperative—but at the very end you should think of every way to focus attention on yourself and try to eliminate anything that may become even a slight distraction. If you are forced to finish with some thing in your hands, do so and when the final applause has ended walk off with the object. Don't cross over to a table and put it down. Make the end, and end and be done with it.

Now what about all the little things that go into making a trick good or bad. We can argue about the type of prop you use, how it should be decorated if decorated at all; we have to consider visibility, angles of working, variety of effect (*i.e.* no one act with six consecutive prediction effects) and so on.

These things are all details, they are the little things which are quite frequently passed over and forgotten. To do anything properly, you have to pay attention to detail. You don't have to give yourself headaches worrying too much—but keep the little things in mind. For example, suppose you have a good effect that uses a prop which looks fancy and magical. The answer is very simple, if the effect warrants the use of the apparatus, go to a bit of trouble and redecorate the apparatus to make it appear less conspicuous and more suitable for mental magic than conjuring proper. As a rule, it is better to use things that seem commonplace with preference to anything that looks as though it has been designed for the purpose of tricking an audience. Nearly any piece of conjuring apparatus can be skilfully explained away so that it becomes usable for Mentalism. You may remember how I gave you an opening mental effect in Step Four—and the apparatus used was the common design of Card in Balloon.

Bear in mind that aside from the appearance of the apparatus you use to achieve a trick, what can be just as deceptive is the way you use it. But all the same, it is my opinion that the best mental tricks are those which do not require very much apparatus, and if they do, the apparatus is such that it will not attract attention.

If you are not using apparatus you rarely have to worry about angles. If you are, then here again pay attention to detail and see that the trick you want to use is one that can be performed without revealing to part of the audience some secret flap or gimmick that may exist. If you have a prop which is subject to angle trouble, bear in mind that if you keep well back on the stage, you give the people at the side less chance of seeing round the corner.

To end this discussion which concerns good or bad tricks, let us take examples of the best possible tricks, what are they? Again I have to remind you that what I say is simply my opinion and does not have to be taken as Law. But I think that there is no question at all that the very best mental tricks are those you can do anywhere, at any time and with practically no preparation. In previous Steps I have given a fair selection of tricks that fall under this category. The Centre Tear Routine given in detail in Step Six is worth its weight in gold. Sometimes people tell me it is limited to close up work; they are wrong. If you present it in a big way, you can do it from the stage if you like. A good test for your ability and for your tricks, or those you know and can do, is to be able to go anywhere and suddenly you are called on to perform a short show. You should be able there and then to do a pretty respectable routine with a few pieces of borrowed paper, a pencil, maybe a pack of cards or whatever else you find comes to hand. That is Mental magic at its best and tricks that you can do on these occasions are, I think the very best.

## (E)  HANDLING

We have talked about the type of trick to do and now we concern ourselves with the handling of these tricks. What is the right way to handle mental effects? The answer is, the way that suits you best.

Many tricks which utilise apparatus are supplied with instructions which tell you how the thing works. Sometimes the instructions go further and tell you what to do when and what to say as you do it. Cut this part of the instructions away and chuck it in the wastepaper basket; it is a waste of time if you want to learn serious mental magic. We have already said that patter for one person is rarely suitable for another, and the same applies to handling. In the first place, do you want to do and say the same thing as everybody else does? Do you realise that a dealer may sell 500 of a good mental trick—all with the same instructions? If every one of the 500 customers did and said the same thing—audiences would get so used to that effect it would be quite absurd. As a human being you are gifted with the ability to think and originality in patter and presentation is simply a question of thinking for yourself. Only lazy people are satisfied to do just what instructions tell them to do.

The first thing you have to do is to find out how to do the trick. No matter what bright ideas you have of your own, you must be able to do the trick. When you have mastered the mechanics then you start to work on effect to make it suitable for your type of work. You have to get the right handling and this means smooth, clean and natural work. When you pick up a fake slate from the table, you have to know just where your fingers go to get hold of the slate. When you hold a small visiting card in the hand to do a mental prediction with a Swami gimmick, you have to know just how to hold the card. I gave you paragraphs of explanation in Step One which told you just how to hold a card and why. To many readers I have no doubt those words were wasted and considered to be padding. It is now more apparent to my readers that you were given important details.

When you know how the trick works, you are left to find out how to work it in the manner that suits you best. How do you do this?

What suits you is that which suits your character, your personality and your style. If you can't fathom this out, look at yourself. Watch what you do in every day life so that you find out how you behave when you are behaving naturally. Do anything just as you would do it normally, but watch the way your hands hold a pencil, pick up a book, light a cigarette. Watch and observe, you are teaching yourself how you behave! When you know yourself and you know what you do, try to mould the tricks around this natural manner of yours; you are out to achieve something very clever, you will achieve something very clever if you do it. By being yourself you have created the most powerful misdirection in the world. You have made it possible for yourself to relax and do your work in the easiest possible manner and to enjoy what you do.

## (F) TIMING

What is timing? It is doing the right thing at the right moment. Not to be confused with " running time " which we cover later on. It is the factor that co-ordinates movement with speech during performance. Many tricks depend on split second timing when it comes to doing something vital to the making of those tricks. Good timing is invisible, bad timing stands out a mile.

Remember again in the example of the Centre Tear—we arrived at a point where you said a few words and then did something (removed the centre to the pocket). Split second timing of words with action enabled you to make a vital move. If the timing had been wrong, the words said before the hands were set to make the move, before the spectator had been misdirected or before you were standing in the right position, the whole thing failed. In a short while we are going to debate what is called Co-ordination; when we do, you will find that one outstanding factor is timing. Unless things are linked together in the right manner at the right time, the picture is out of focus.

How does one acquire a sense of good timing and learn to make use of it? First disregard the timing of showmanship which we shall discuss later, and let us deal now with basic timing; the co-ordination of action with words. Remember a few pages back we were dealing with patter, what to say as you performed your tricks. Now we have to be sure that the words not only suit the action—but go with the action in time. That is to say, it would be ridiculous if your patter, spoken from script, went on " Take a card, look at it and simply think to yourself the name of that card " . . . as you say this, you have handed a pack in the case to a spectator. You continue rapidly, " and the card you are thinking of is the three of clubs." The spectator may well reply, " I haven't looked at one yet." Your timing in this case is vastly wrong. Obviously, you have to watch them and give them time to take a card, look at it, etc., before you commit yourself. It is therefore necessary to pace the patter to suit the actions of performance. If you need more time, you use more patter; if you want to cut down the time, you use less patter or choose words that hurry the spectator.

Because it is essential that actions go with speech hand in hand, it is important when writing a script of patter for tricks that you perform the effects as you devise the patter. If not, what may well happen is that you find yourself trying to do two things at once. It is as though you had your patter recorded on tape and simply mimed the tricks. You would be forced to work

404

to the speed of the tape, sometimes slowing down your actions and sometimes speeding up in order to keep in time with the recording. Naturally, you do not have tape recordings but all the same, working from a script you tie yourself down to a pretty rigid pattern.

So that this difficulty may be overcome, we allow ourselves a licence of speech which is called in the business, " Spiel." This is off-the-cuff padding or *ad lib* patter. Fundamentally, it is something which you add to your script or general speech for fixed tricks, and not something which you use haywire or uncontrolled—unless you are an absolute expert at talking. It is a common mistake for people to think that they can start at the beginning and go on to the end using unrehearsed speech all the way. Undoubtedly it can be done, but those who can do it well are few and far between. Better by far that you have a solid script which covers the bulk of what you have to say, and fill in with spiel as your time, tricks and personality permit.

To return to the subject on hand; Timing. There are other aspects that we have to know about. Let us deal with Running Time.

Running time is the total length of your performance. Up to a few years ago, running time was not so important as it is today. Music Halls and Theatres expected an act to run for " about " ten minutes and as much as one minute under or over the mark was a margin that the producer could afford to allow. In some fields today—a one minute overlap would be quite disastrous; I refer to Television of course. If you want to work on Television, you have got to know quite a bit about running time. You must understand in the first place that on a T.V. programme you are one small unit of time which makes up a full hour (maybe more or less). The best way to think about it is to bear in mind the cost of one second on peak hour commercial television. Time doesn't seem very important until you think that ten seconds over running may cost somebody fifty pounds or more. That's what it can amount to.

You may get booked for a television show and you are expected to work two or three tricks and appear for three and a half minutes. If you finish before the scheduled time, you may unbalance the entire programme and your short act may seem to have a poor, rather drawn out finish. If you exceed the given time, a worse fate can happen. It may be necessary for the producer to fade out on your spot in order to get the next act in on time and from the viewers point of view, they see half a trick. Therefore the answer is to be on time. This is by no means an easy matter, as it is so difficult to allow for unforseen events that may consume valuable seconds during performance. Naturally you will do your best by selecting the right tricks, that is to say, those which you know can be performed within a certain rigid margin of time. You will select a type of patter that gives sufficient breaks from script to allow you to rush or slow the proceedings by inserting spiel. But you cannot allow for the behaviour of an assistant from the audience who comes to take part in a mental effect. Almost invariably a Mentalist has to work with somebody—if you are going to read minds, you have to have somebody's mind to read, and the weak spot in your time problem is the spectator who assists. The most sensible advice that I can give towards solving this problem is to choose tricks for a short T.V. programme that enable you to do most of the handling and let the spectator do as little as possible. You know what you are doing and how long it takes to do; the spectator does not know what to do until you tell him and is not worried about how long it takes to shuffle a pack of cards for example. The best you can do is to estimate by trial and error how long it takes the spectator to do certain things and when you do so, play safe and allow them more time in your schedule rather than less. Remember all the time that it is easier for you to draw out an act for half a minute than it is to cut it short.

During a television programme you will probably see a man making weird signs at you. A lot of studios have a timekeeper who sticks fingers up and down in the air telling you to speed up or slow down. The T.V. producer of the show will explain to you what the signs mean and what he wants you to do when you see them. Don't mistake the timekeeper for a cameraman who is learning to be a bookies' tic-tac man! Work to time using the studio clock, the timekeeper and your rehearsed schedule for the act. Do not look at your watch as though worried about the time; if you must look at your watch at any time (unless it's part of a trick) do so with a spot of misdirection. This applies to any type of performance.

Anybody who manages to get on a T.V. programme to do a few tricks in a given time, and has not rehearsed those tricks, is an idiot. It has been done, and if you are lucky you may get away with it, but for comfort of mind and efficiency of work, know what you are doing to the tenth degree. The only exception to this rule is when you happen to be a guest artist and unexpectedly you are called on to show something. When this happens, the time you take is their problem not yours and ten to one the organisers have allowed time for you to do a trick. To make it easy for them, make it snappy. However, as those who know anything about work on T.V. will tell you, there is hardly a thing done or said at any time which has not been discussed or arranged beforehand. Mistakes of any kind are not encouraged and rightly so.

We have discussed two forms of Time as it concerns presentation. Now we deal with another meaning and that is what we call the Timing of Showmanship. It is by far the hardest factor to explain as this is very subtle.

Briefly, there is a point or a phase in every trick you do—when you reach the perfect time to surprise people. There is another point when you reach the ideal peak to finish your act. Another exact moment when a few words delivered dead on time will bring the house down or change an entire act. One of the most noticeable applications of good timing in show business, is the job of the comedian. Watch a good comedian working and see how he waits for one joke to hit and register before he delivers the next. Listen to some specific jokes which depend on the speed of delivery alone. Many jokes wouldn't be funny at all if there was no distinct pause between certain words in a sentence.

A good trick is one that goes on until the time is reached that the audience feel something is due to happen. Then it happens—but not what they expected—and so results in a pleasant surprise. A good act is one that builds up trick upon trick getting better and better and then you seem to reach a peak—and that is the right time to end. Nothing is worse than an act that exceeds its peak time. From that point onwards the act begins to die and starts to bore.

How is it possible to tell the right time, or better still, the ideal time to do something which will incur audience reaction?

One way to tell is to think of the wrong times and see what that leaves you. For instance, you can do something too quick. The build up was insufficient or the effect so rapid that the audience were not given a chance to understand the accomplishment. When we say " something " we mean the part of the trick that actually reveals the achievement; we do not mean the preparation or actual working. On the other hand, you can do something too slow. The initial preparation is too involved or so long that the audience begin to lack interest; as a result, when you reach the ideal point you unwittingly go on and from then onwards you expose yourself to the danger of boring your audience. A good showman is able to build up the atmosphere (theoretically working to the climax of his trick) and no good showman goes beyond the peak. If he does this, the audience are liable to feel frustrated and pay less attention to a second attempt to stimulate their interest.

Now we know that we can go too slow or too fast, and we are left to decide at which point between the two comes the ideal time. An excellent way to discover this is to use the audience as your guide. Make them your clock! If you are running too slow or going on too long, you will see plenty of movement and hear people whispering to each other. They are obviously restless and that is because you have not absorbed their complete attention and held it. If you are on a stage and cannot hear whispering or even see the audience because of bright footlights, you will still " feel " the reaction you are getting. In fact, it is to what extent a showman can judge the feel of an audience— that makes him a glorious success or a blithering flop. To end this discussion, let me add a suggestion that acts as a fair guide. When you perform tricks, do things which you like and which please the audience also; make them as quick as you can without spoiling the effect by over haste and try to avoid the common pitfall of going on too long. Occasionally one sees a trick performed and after waiting perhaps nine minutes to reach the end, you are never sure whether they clap because they liked the trick or because it has reached the end at last. Whenever I see this sort of thing, when it gets to five minutes I pray the thing will work because it scares me that in the event of failure the performer might have another go from the beginning again.

## (G) MISDIRECTION

I cannot stress too strongly that Misdirection is one of the most important things for you to study. It will make your work perfect and it will make your work easy.

How good or powerful can misdirection be? It can be so good that if you were seated alone in a room with one man, and through the door came an elephant which had been especially prepared with black and white stripes, on its back a Scotsman playing very loudly Highland Lassie on a set of bagpipes (out of tune)—and the elephant complete with escort thumped through the room, in theory your spectator wouldn't know it had happened.

And why not? Because you misdirected his attention!

For those of you that do not have an elephant to test this remarkable feat, I will discuss the general theory of Misdirection.

Generally speaking, there are two ways of distracting attention. First, by what you say and second, by what you do. Misdirection by speech and Misdirection by action. Sometimes the two go together. Occasionally one finds a prop that has been designed or decorated in some particular fashion, with a view to distracting attention (or even attracting attention) and this is more often a case of disguise than Misdirection proper as we know it to be.

Aside from the two obvious ways to apply Misdirection (*i.e.* Speech and action) there are other methods which from time to time are usable. We can adopt the use of sound, touch and smell all to good effect. I recollect that one of my psychological tricks which I entitled " The Powers of Darkness " was a routine involving Misdirection by touch and sound as the main stimuli and speech as a minor help to the effect.

Forgive me for mentioning one of my own tricks that is on the market, but I say this purely for your benefit; if you want a study in Misdirection—" The Powers of Darkness " is a lesson worth having.

Casting aside everything that Magicians do, what sort of Misdirection is strong for Mentalists?—that is our concern. The answer is this: anything that appears to be done *naturally* either by you or to a spectator is powerful misdirection. A mistake is the most powerful of all. Allow me to give you a trick which I have devised to illustrate the application of a mistake used as misdirection. Study this and try it. You will find that without the mistake—the trick is lousy and fools few people. With the mistake I guarantee it is a good Mental effect.

What happens? Nothing much. You have five cards face up on the table, they are these cards:—10S, JH, QD, KH, AD, in your hand you have five more cards and these match in value and colour those on the table. That is to say, you have 10C, JD, QH, KD and AH and this, you explain to a spectator. You ask anyone to merely think of one of the cards that they see on the table. You read their mind, remove one card from your fan and lay it face down on the table as though for all the world you have no doubts that your selection will match their choice. You remain holding the others. Next you point out the free choice and ask them to name the one they thought of. Whatever they say, you look surprised and disappointed, grab at your card on the table, look at it again and then show that you understand why you went wrong. " Sorry, I've got them in the wrong order," you say and replace the card from the table in your fan and commence to rearrange them, back outwards. Having done this to your satisfaction, you explain that this time you will go a step upwards and ask the spectator to try and match the cards. You hand him the five cards face down so that he cannot tell what they are, and instruct him to deal those cards in any order he likes, one on each of the cards on the table. This he does. When they are turned over, every card matches perfectly, every time it matches and you do nothing whatsoever. You did the work earlier on—using misdirection and acting.

Now you want to know two things. From where do you get the cards and how to do the trick. Last thing first. The trick is achieved by using five double face cards and five double back. You didn't have any cards to look at but the mistake you made convinces them you had! They get the five double backed cards and it doesn't matter where they deal them as when you turn them over (in pairs using the old Two card move) they see the other side of their own cards. That's all there is to it.

Lastly, you will be delighted to know that although the standard double face pack is a haphazard assortment of cards; the five you require will be found in any double face pack and that leaves you with nothing to do in the way of preparation.

In order that you may appreciate the importance and value of a trick of this kind, which functions on the principle of misdirection coupled with good acting, you would be best advised to try the effect both ways. Try to perform the trick on one audience without the preliminary error. Judge the reaction and then later try again on another audience and this time include the opening mistake; I guarantee you will find the effect ten times stronger.

In this discussion I have already said that one very strong form of misdirection is the mistake. In Step Five mention was also made to show how blindfold routines could be made to appear all the more authentic by the introduction of an occasional mistake.

It may well be thought that it is not a good thing to make a mistake at any time. On the face of it, it is not the right thing—but it all depends very much on how many mistakes you make, and in what direction you make them. In addition to this, there is a certain psychology between the audience and the performer which creates a feeling of sympathy when an error occurs. The audience tend to relax completely and their attention comes sharply off the trick and on to you; a very convenient condition at times!

For those of you that think a mistake of any kind is a bad thing, we can point out that quite often we allow the spectator to make a harmless mistake —or force the spectator to make one. An example of this principle is to be found in the Punx-Mier variation of The Centre Tear (Ref. Step 6). Personally, I do not think it matters if you make a few mistakes as long as it is not overdone.

The next form of Misdirection which is of use to the Mentalist is that which I like to term " Demonstrative Misdirection." It can be applied for work with billets, books or cards and the principle, although very simple is extremely good.

In effect, suppose you want to switch a pack of cards. One deck is in your hands and one deck in your pocket. You could go into a ballet dance of movement which might enable you to exchange packs, or alternatively you could do it by demonstrative misdirection. You want the spectator to have the deck in his pocket and so you simply say " I want you to keep this pack of cards in safe custody, not to open them, not to look at them for the moment— and to be sure that nobody else touches them. Take them please." (You reach forward handing him the pack in your hands and then as he is about to grasp it, take it back and say . . .) " No, better still, put them in your pocket like this and put your hand over the outside so that nobody can even get at the pack . . ." (Calmly put the deck in your pocket and leave it there; remove the hand and show him how to hold his hand over the outside (" Demonstrative ")—and having finished your explanation, casually reach back into your pocket and remove the second deck handing it to him for safe keeping. The pack is switched.

The above procedure could be used just as well to exchange a small dictionary, box or billet. It requires two things to be good. The key is natural behaviour and because of this, go slow and suit the action to the word. The best way to act the part when doing this sort of thing, is to try and believe yourself; pretend with as much conviction as you can, that what you are doing is simply showing him what is to be done. Forget you are switching a pack of cards, the only time you have to remember this is when it comes to knowing which pack is which. You can stand one on end in the pocket or contrive any sort of simple division to tell you by feel which is which. Such a thing is obvious so we need not discuss it.

We have spoken about natural behaviour as an important feature of applied misdirection. Let us see how far you can go. A classic example of the next form of misdirection, that which I call " Repetitive misdirection " is a trick which I believe should be credited to David Berglas. When I have described exactly what happens, you may doubt that it can be done. All I ask is that you try it and see for yourself.

It is safe to assume that the more times an audience see the same thing the less attention they pay each time they see it done. This is a weakness that we can use to advantage. For example, David Berglas will do several card tricks in succession and most of them start by having someone take a card, look at it and return it to the deck. After a while a minor miracle pops up. Spectator takes a card and replaces it anywhere in the deck and immediately shuffles the pack to his heart's content. The performer does not touch the pack again and yet he successfully names the selected card.

The method is repetitive misdirection. For the first few tricks the spectator is told to take a card and they are fanned face down to allow him to select one. For the last trick, they are fanned face up! The whole thing is quite absurd because you see which card they take but you must add a few touches to conceal the fact. The cards are fanned face up and you ask the spectator to select any one he likes. As soon as he takes the one he wants, you casually turn your head away and quickly turn the pack over saying " Look at it to be sure you remember that card and then replace it anywhere in the pack (hand it to him face down) but be quite sure that I cannot tell where you put it—I'll look away while you do it." The audience are so concerned with hiding from you the place where the card will go—that they never think that you looked as he chose a card. To progress upon the effect even more, you could work this in conjunction with a pocket index to achieve a very strong effect. Having seen the card of his choice, give him the pack and whilst he is busy mixing them you locate a duplicate in design and value from a pocket index. (Step Four for details of Pocket Index.) Have this card palmed so that when you now take back the pack, it can be loaded on top.

This done, you ask any other spectator to call out a number. " Our friend here has chosen any card and mixed it with the rest, our other friend has given us any number. Wouldn't it be a strange thing if this gentleman's card was to be found at the gentleman's number?" You count to the selected number and use any of the simple sleights to make the top card appear at the chosen number. (See Step Ten on card tricks.)

It is not necessary to perform the continuation with a pocket index. It is quite enough, or strong enough to name the card selected.

To summarise the general principles we have discussed we can extract the essentials of misdirection for mentalists.

Our aim is to use misdirection as a means to achieve tricks. This can be done by drawing attention to something or taking attention away from something. For example, in Step One we discussed the many uses of the Swami gimmick. We used a pencil to suggest that the prediction was written *before* it was. An added touch of misdirection would be to use a white pencil —a conspicuous pencil so that psychologically it registers with the audience. On the other hand, a few Steps ago we discussed a card trick where you located one card in seven by touch. Six were marked and the chosen one was not. Attention was drawn away from the actual means of achieving the trick by using a simple rather obvious method.

The use of the word obvious in the last sentence brings to mind another anomaly of misdirection. That which is obvious is not always apparent. People do not think of the obvious explanation; generally speaking they try and credit you with far more skill than you have. Another weakness. The more simple, natural and outright your misdirection—the powerful it becomes. To sum it up; never try and be clever when you can be simple because nothing fools more than sheer simplicity.

## (H)  CO-ORDINATION

We have gone to some lengths to describe all the minor features that go into making mentalism presentable. Now we discuss, very briefly, the importance of co-ordination, or doing things in tune.

Imagine your assets of performing ability as various instruments of an orchestra. You know about patter and timing, misdirection and movement and all the other things that matter and consider each to be an instrument. What sort of overture emerges from this collection if there is no governing body? A true orchestra is ruled by a conductor, a man that co-ordinates the strings with the brass. You are the same; you are your own conductor. You have to do things to tune. The real secret of performance is the moulding of all things into one harmonious picture. Any one item on its own is not enough. Knowing the right things to say without knowing the right things to do is as bad as a half-finished symphony. Like music, everything has a time and place and more than that, it has a time and place in parallel with other things. All things mould together making one magnificent show and if not, that which lags behind or races ahead is that which goes out of tune. Conduct your performance as a man with an orchestra to care for and the result will be entertaining—and that is all that matters unless you seek to be a mentalist because it pleases your vanity.

# AN INTERVIEW WITH CLAUDE CHANDLER

## INTRODUCTION

Claude Chandler, now Vice-President of the London Magic Circle has spent a lifetime on the stage. As actor, magician, producer and writer he is well qualified to give advice; we attended a lecture given by Claude on the subject of Acting on the Stage and the Importance of Production and Presentation. In our humble opinion, this lecture was brilliant and we were so impressed with the practicability of it all, that we arranged for him to come to our Studio and tape record an interview on the subject of Stage acting and Production for the benefit of our readers. Like the Interview with Fogel in Step Seven, it is considered that a great deal of advice can be given and taken by these cross-question interviews. It may be pointed out that Claude Chandler is not a Mentalist. But those of you who have worked on any type of stage will readily agree that no matter who you are or what you are, Production and Acting counts one hundred per cent. If you learn to be an Actor you can play any role and a Mentalist is simply one role; therefore let us leave you to learn from the experience of a man who can act.

## THE ACTOR *By Claude Chandler*

*Corinda:* We start off Claude by asking you a little bit about your personal career in show business, how long you have been at it and what sort of places you have played in your time.

*Claude:* Well, I'm not a Mentalist of course although any actor could play the role of Mentalist; as you know, I am a professional magician and ventriloquist. I wouldn't like to say how far back I go!

412

*Corinda:* Well how many years have you been at it?

*Claude:* Ever since I was a boy at school—and that's quite a while. I've done a great deal of private entertaining of course, and worked in the days when you went to the lovely country houses of England and most of the Theatres and music halls in the country.

*Corinda:* Interrupting you there Claude, I suppose it is worth mention that you have played Royal Command Performances?

*Claude:* I don't think that's the most interesting—I have worked for members of the Royal Family but I think the most interesting thing from magicians and mentalists points of view is the fact that when I was a young man, and the great and famous David Devant finally realised that through illness he would never perform again, he actually chose me to carry on with his work. I didn't know him, he saw me performing and asked me to come and see him and the outcome was I presented nearly all his most famous illusions in a show that ran for nearly an hour and a quarter. The Artists dream and the Golliwog ball, all the wonderful things that were his, which I performed for a number of seasons at Maskelynes and I suppose that is the most interesting thing in my career from a conjuring point of view. Needless to say, Devant himself was an Actor and I've always been extremely interested in Acting which brings us to the subject of this interview.

*Corinda:* Would you say you learnt a lot from Devant as an actor?

*Claude:* I don't think I learnt anything directly from him as an actor except of course that he was a very accomplished actor and he always mixed with actors and understood the value of acting, in magical presentation.

*Corinda:* May I ask you did you learn your acting from an acting school or did you learn it by experience, by constantly being at it?

*Claude:* I learnt it from experience, I never went to a school of acting, but I made a study of it; I've always studied acting and considered it, thought about it and read about it. Everything I could do, I did to find out about acting and the art of the actor. Then I learnt to apply it to magic as I think many people ought to do.

*Corinda:* How would you advise somebody who was interested in making a study of acting—what would you recommend to them. Should they go to a school?

*Claude:* Well, they can go to a school of acting of course, it's an excellent thing and if they can do it, although it is rather difficult and takes a long time, it is a wonderful thing for them. It would not be money or time wasted if they wanted to go in for magic or mentalism seriously. A course of acting would be a vast step forward. Otherwise, they must just find out what they can about it and study it from whatever point of view they are able.

*Corinda:* Off hand, can you think of any good book that you could advise to help on this subject.

*Claude:* No I don't think there is any special book for me to recommend. There are books undoubtedly published and many are to be found in every library.

*Corinda:* I believe I'm right in saying that in your career you have indeed done several Royal Command performances.

*Claude:* Yes, I have on a number of occasions because, as I say, I used to work to people referred to as landed gentry and on many occasions, Royalty were there. This includes our present Queen and her family.

*Corinda:* And lastly, talking about you, I suppose you have played theatres and music halls?

*Claude:* I suppose I've played almost every theatre in the British Isles.

*Corinda:* And today, I believe I'm right in saying you do quite a bit of producing and you are also the Vice-President of The Magic Circle.

*Claude:* Quite true.

*Corinda:* Well now, Claude, what I want to do is to ask you some questions that I think will help readers of this book to understand more the acting side of show business. Most of my questions are drawn from a lecture you gave recently on stage craft and acting, and having made some notes at the time I would ask you now to give us more detail. In general, we are concerned with points of interest to Mentalists as you realise this book specialises on that subject.

*Claude:* I'd like to break in there and say I don't think it matters what you are doing—if you are giving a stage performance, whether you are a comedian or a Mentalist, a magician or any form of stage performer, you are employing the art of the actor and the better actor you are the better performance you are going to give to further your medium.

*Corinda:* This prompts me to ask you whether the same principles apply for stage as for close up?

*Claude:* Yes. Let us talk from the stage point of view, it's easier to talk that way. But the same principle applies wherever there is entertainment. If you have mastered the technique for stage you can apply those principles anywhere—even a drawing room.

*Corinda:* I remember the first thing you spoke about was deep breathing. At the start I thought it was unimportant—but half way through your lecture you had me convinced I was wrong.

*Claude:* Yes. Although it seems a strange thing to say if you do learn the simple process of deep breathing, it can be a great help; I will try and describe it briefly to you. You take air in through the nostrils and fill the lungs and then expel the air out of the mouth. The way to do it is to empty the lungs, one thinks for deep breathing that you have to fill the lungs, but the important thing is to empty them first of all—because you can't fill them up with fresh air if you've left some stale air in there. Fill up by taking it slowly through the nostrils and breathe it out slowly through the mouth. But as you take in, tighten up all your muscles, grip your hands, and flex your arm and shoulder muscles—and as you let the air come out, relax everything.

Now I didn't describe in the lecture until later on the use of deep breathing —but I think it best if we do that now in this case.

*Corinda:* Yes, please do or readers may well think you are talking a lot of nonsense.

*Claude:* Well, if you have mastered deep breathing, that is to say, you must practise it a bit, you cannot do it suddenly—it has to be acquired, you will find that one of its great values is when you are standing in the wings waiting to go on. There is nothing for you to do, everything is ready and all you do is to stand there and feel more and more nervous. Now deep breathing apart from the good it does you, will steady your nerves, gives the blood oxygen and *gives you something to do*, something to mildly occupy your mind just at that time when you are at the height of your nervousness waiting to go on. You will find it is a most valuable thing at that particular time.

*Corinda:* If I can pop another question here. Later you will be speaking about voice control, I believe I'm right in saying that you said there is an important connection between deep breathing and voice production?

*Claude:* Yes. That is another use which we shall discuss presently.

*Corinda:* Right. Let us leave that for further discussion later on and start now at the beginning of a performance. Can we ask you for tips for making an entry on to the stage. What is the right approach?

*Claude:* Yes, before I deal with that, I should say that an actor looks upon everything he does as playing a character. And it can be very helpful to mentalists if you think of yourself as playing a part. It's a bit like the ordinary individual at a part; dress him up and he behaves in a manner according to his dress or character. You will find that if you have formulated in your own mind that you are playing a part—you are the Mentalist or whatever you want to be, you step into that character and its almost like putting on a disguise. You will be less nervous if you do that.

*Corinda:* Well Claude, in your opinion what character is a Mentalist. I mean, how can you tell so that you can portray that?

*Claude:* No. Simply form in your own mind a character, whatever you feel you would like to be on the stage. Your stage character may be just that little bit different to you. You may feel that when you want to walk across a room you like to slouch across; but in your own mind, you feel that the sort of man you would like to be on the stage is not a man who slouches so you cultivate for that character a more upright walk or a better walk. Maybe a more commanding appearance or manner, something a little more dynamic than you have in the ordinary way. It is a character, something a little different to yourself.

*Corinda:* Would you say it was wrong for mentalists to create a belief in himself to the extent that during his act he actually believes he can do that sort of thing?

*Claude:* I would say that it was essential for the mentalist to do it. As long as you bear in mind it's not playing a part in a play where you can make all sorts of exaggerated statements, here you must be careful that you do not overdo it and land yourself in trouble. Mentally—if you are playing a part you should believe you have these powers—that's the actor.

*Corinda:* Can we return to our earlier question about walking on.

*Claude:* One important thing to bear in mind is to stand well back. Don't stand close to the wings so that your first step brings you right on to the stage. Get well back off stage so that when it's your time to appear, you take at least three or four, or even more steps before anybody sees you. Then you are well walking, travelling at a good speed by the time the audience see you. Don't appear as though you have jumped out of the wings.

Another important thing there. As you walk on, *look* at your audience. Directly you get on to the stage, look at them. The power of the human eye is amazing and if you don't look at them you look a fool. We might say that's a golden rule.

*Corinda:* So to sum it up, stand well back to arrive on stage at a good walking speed and as you come on turn your head to face the audience. Then where do you go?

415

*Claude:* You arrive centre stage normally.

*Corinda:* You mentioned the danger of standing too far forward on the stage because the footlights can make you look funny.

*Claude:* True. Take a reasonable distance, depending on the stage and your set up of props and what you have got. I would say as far as you can say, if you keep a few feet from the footlights without falling over your props you will be all right. It is very bad to stand on top of the footlights and you should always try and avoid it.

*Corinda:* When we were speaking just now about looking at an audience, I meant to ask you more about that. In your lecture you described how to do this.

*Claude:* Many beginners and often really experienced people fail to know how to look at an audience. Some people will tell you to look over their heads, to look here, to look there . . . the actual secret is that you look in the *direction* of the audience, but you do not focus, you do not allow your eyes to focus on any particular thing or any particular person. Then you will give the impression that you are speaking and looking at everybody. Your eyes casually move around up into the gallery or circle and down again. Never look directly at any one person—an actor doesn't look at the audience because he is playing a part. If you are in a scene or a play, you don't look at the audience, they are the " Fourth Wall." On the other hand, as an entertainer walking on to address an audience, then you are going to speak to the audience and so you do look at them.

*Corinda:* What happens in the case of some theatres where the lighting conditions make it almost impossible to see the audience?

*Claude:* You look in the right direction just the same and the audience will not know you cannot see them. It makes no difference.

*Corinda:* Can we get on to a very important subject—that of Voice Production, correct speech and talking so that everyone can hear you.

*Claude:* Well of course, it's a big subject. One can take elocution and have your voice trained and that sort of thing, but broadly speaking first of all is the correct production of the voice, what is known as a " Forward Production" and that means the voice must be pitched just behind the front top teeth. Pitch the voice forward and not down in the throat. A good way to assist you, if you don't think you have a forward voice is to use what is called the nasal voice—that is talking through the nose; if you do that, and then leave the nose open, you will find the voice is in that forward position.

*Corinda:* People usually believe that if you get on a stage and talk to the back row of an audience, everybody must hear you, would you say this is correct?

*Claude:* Yes. Definitely. If you feel that you are talking to someone who is sitting in the back row it will work. But be careful not to shout. Again it comes back to deep breathing. You have a good lung capacity and you can hold a lot of air, and you can conserve air. The more air you get behind your words, the more force you can give them without shouting.

*Corinda:* There was a tricky point in your lecture where you were forced to show that you could perform deep breathing on stage without visibly blowing yourself out in view of the audience.

*Claude:* No. You do the deep breathing in the wings before you get on stage but it can still be done gently whilst actually on stage.

*Corinda:* And you had something to say about speaking good English and not clipping off the ends of words.

*Claude:* Yes you get that in Elocution. One of the things they teach you is to sound your consonants clearly. Also, not to clip off the endings of words —finish a word. You would be surprised, if some of our entertainers could make tape recordings and listen carefully to what they are saying, they would be very surprised to hear how many of the endings of their words they clip off. In a big hall or theatre it means that those words just don't get over. Pronounce your words clearly and finish them.

*Corinda:* Do you vary the volume of your voice according to the size of the place in which you are performing?

*Claude:* Yes. Obviously you must do so. To go to an extreme, you may be performing in open air. Due to inexperience you may find yourself inclined to shout; if you would only realise that you can be heard in the open air as long as you speak clearly and distinctly. In a hall or theatre there is always a certain amount of vibration which brings the sound back to you so you can hear yourself speaking. In the open air your voice seems to disappear and you worry, thinking you are not being heard. Always try to avoid shouting.

*Corinda:* Now to change the topic again, I remember you said the hardest thing for an actor to do is to stand still on the stage. What can you add to that?

*Claude:* True. Many an actor finds it extremely difficult to stand still on the stage. The secret is to plant your weight firmly on both feet, don't have your weight on one foot. Let your arms hang by your side and *relax*. If you put your arms by your sides and your muscles are stiff, it will betray any nervousness and you won't look at ease. You must relax completely.

*Corinda:* Why do you consider it important that an actor or mentalist does stand still?

*Claude:* I think that it's important to stand still because when you do move it has dramatic effect. If you are constantly moving about it serves no purpose, it becomes monotonous and you lose people's attention. If you stand still as you should do when you are talking to an audience, then, when you do move, it is definitely dramatic.

*Corinda:* In your lecture you mention quite a bit about bad habits concerning movement on stage. Can we speak about them?

*Claude:* That was the various things you can do through nervousness. The sort of things that people do, not knowing they are doing them as a result of nerves. A common habit is nodding the head in emphasis and another is shifting the weight from one foot to another. People don't realise it but eventually they form almost a rocking movement which is most irritating and means the performer lacks repose. Another bad habit is to gradually wander forward a little bit and then wander back. Again you see you have unnecessary movement.

*Corinda:* I have another note on your comment that an actor never does anything on stage unless he knows that he does it. What did that mean?

*Claude:* It is a very hard thing for the inexperienced performer to grasp. A trained actor is in complete command of himself. Every intonation of his voice and every muscle of his body, every look in the eye and all he does is known to himself. He does not do anything on the stage without knowing

417

he does it and the danger with so many of our performers—many that I have seen in magical societies, is that they have so many bad habits and they do things not knowing they are doing them. You can do whatever you like on the stage—it may not be successful, which is a matter of trial and error, if you want to do your Mentalism standing on your head, you can—if you wish, but you should know that you're doing it! You can do it on one foot if you like—the awful thing is the man that does it on one foot and doesn't know he's standing on one foot.

*Corinda:* A complication occurs to me listening to you Claude. You say that it's important that an actor knows about everything he does, his speech and movement, does that mean a person must watch himself whilst performing. How can a performer overcome the difficulty of watching himself and not paying enough attention to the audience?

*Claude:* Well, it's a curious thing and I suppose it only comes by long training or long experience. There is an essential difference between the inexperienced performer and the experienced performer, be he actor or any other form of entertainer. The experienced performer constantly thinks of the audience, he sees everything via the eyes of the audience. The inexperienced performer is constantly thinking what he's doing. " I'm walking on a stage, I'm picking up this, I'm standing here, etc. . . ." he can't help it, even he would change with experience to the professional attitude . . . " the audience see me walking on a stage, they see me picking this up, it's having this effect on them . . . " all the time, the effect on the audience as they see it.

One must stand outside oneself and learn to look at oneself and see what is going on.

*Corinda:* Speaking about stage movement, you gave some useful advice on the right way to walk on stage.

*Claude:* An actor is taught to walk the stage for an example, a mentalist stands in the middle of the stage. He has to turn up stage towards a table, pick up something and return to the centre of the stage. Now if you turn round and approach that table and bring your feet together—you cannot get back to the centre without a lot of shuffling of your feet. If you arrive at the table with what we call the upstage foot (that's the foot furthest away from the audience) with your weight on it, and the downstage foot is more or less allowed to hang behind, in that position, you find you can turn and come back with almost no movement of your feet. It is difficult to describe but if you try, you will find that if you bring your feet together you can't turn round and start off back again without an awful lot of shuffling. That's the kind of thing one learns in walking the stage.

*Corinda:* Dealing more with movement, what would you say is dramatic movement?

*Claude:* I think almost anything that he hasn't done constantly, is dramatic movement for the mentalist. It brings me back to my point, if a man is constantly walking back and forth there's nothing startling in any movement he may do. But if he's been standing still for quite a time and he suddenly moves and turns upstage, that sudden movement can be arresting. Any gesture or movement that is done fairly quickly and held can be dramatic. Another example. If you point your finger to someone in the audience, or straight out into the audience, and stand there pointing it's bound to be dramatic as long as it has some bearing.

*Corinda:* Let us leave this now and change to another topic. What would you say are some common faults with patter?

*Claude:* The outstanding fault is not learning patter. Patter should be learnt and I think the mentalists are probably the greatest offenders. A mentalist has to do so much explaining and the whole of his script should be edited with the greatest of care so that he has an economy of words, otherwise it gets lost and fogged with verbosity. I would say a vital thing is to write out your patter first and learn it after some editing has been done. Get it clear and concise. I've seen many a good mental performer fail because the audience don't quite know where they are with this awful jumble of words.

*Corinda:* I feel I should point out in defence of Mentalists, that we have to use what is called spiel—very often an almost impromptu fill-in of patter.

*Claude:* There we have the peculiarity of this subject—so you allow patches in your script which are there for the purpose of ad libbing or spiel. The other points should be linked up by definite patter.

*Corinda:* I gather that you think the average mentalist uses too much patter?

*Claude:* Not too much. It seems overburdening because he hasn't got it cut down—he could say all he has to say with less words. A mental act is bound to be very wordy so let's get it as clear and concise as we possibly can. The only way is to write it out and then edit it.

*Corinda:* Can you offer any tips on how to learn patter?

*Claude:* An old dodge is to read it over before you go to sleep—any actor will tell you that. Merely read it—no need to keep saying it over to yourself. Remember patter has so many uses and it is therefore important. It can be used as misdirection, it is not what you do, but what you make the audience think you do and patter can help you to achieve that.

*Corinda:* Now what about props—you mentioned the importance of planning where you are going to put your stuff on stage.

*Claude:* It is vitally important. Every prop on stage should have its place. Where it comes from and where it goes to. Moreover, if you have one trick with props that is to be followed by another, it's important to know what you are going to do with the props in between. If you need time to get rid of the props from your last trick, start talking about the next one whilst you are putting the props away. It is what we call continuity—things must go on smoothly. You must hold the audience's attention all the time.

*Corinda:* Well Claude we have covered a pretty wide selection of subjects, but we have yet to deal with the very end of your act. What advice can you offer to our readers concerning curtain calls and exit?

*Claude:* One very important thing is to check at every theatre to find out which way the tabs close. If you want to make a quick and smooth movement to the front to take your curtain, you must head in the right direction through the tabs. Look up at any time in your act if you have any doubts, and don't leave it too late.

*Corinda:* In conclusion in your lecture you mentioned some rather important points about having assistants in the act—and the difference between an assistant and partner when it comes to curtain calls.

*Claude:* Yes, well I did mention that because so many magicians and mentalists do have their wives and friends as assistants, and the point is this with full time experienced professional men who have assistants, male or female on the stage, the assistants do not take a call. The performer who has been assisted by his wife is in a difficult position because she will want to take a call, but strictly speaking, as an assistant, she should not do so.

If the performer feels she has to be there to take a call, the best way is to give her a little more to do in the act and then she becomes more important and she equals a partner and becomes entitled to take a call.

*Corinda:* Well Claude, I'm sure there are many other things you could tell us but we have to stop somewhere and we are thankful for all your advice in this interview.

---

## ERRATA AND ADDITIONS TO THE FULL "THIRTEEN STEPS TO MENTALISM"

However careful one tries to be, there is always the mistake. Many readers have kindly informed me of errors published in this series and for the benefit of purists the following alterations and additions should be made to existing copies:—

STEP ONE: Pp. 16. Madame DISS DEBAR should read, Madame DIS DEBAR.

STEP THREE: Pp. 66, para 2 should read: "Alternatively start with the number above the Key (*i.e.* 38) and when you reach a Key Square subtract two. (Diagram C.)

Also on this page Diagram "B" and Diagram "C" should have a black star added in top left hand squares. (Square number 52 in "C" and the equivalent in "B".)

STEP SEVEN: Pp. 229, para. 8. For Houdini read Houdin.

STEP TEN: Pp. 309. Photo-memory by Hans Trixer. Either method may be used. The number called and performer names card or the card called and then performer states at which number it will appear. Line 23 should read "You said Ten and I said Three of Hearts."

Pp. 316. Beyond the Veil. Readers were not informed that in the pack, the cards which should be *short cards* were:—

8C, QC, AC, 10D, 2S, 4C, AD, QS, 10S, AH, 8D, 8H, 4D, AS, JH, 8S, 10C, 4S, JD, KD, 6S, 4H, 5H, 9H, 6C, 7H (total 26 cards). The other 26 cards not mentioned consist of the remainder of the pack. This deck, arranged in long- and short-pairs, with cards in any order, will allow you to spell out from the stacked deck when instructions, as given in the effect, are followed.

A final note on The Thirteen Steps to Mentalism. Those of you who have seen or read this complete series will appreciate that I owe a great deal to many fellow Mentalists for their advice, help and general support. To all those who have so generously given us tricks and routines, I express my sincere thanks. To those who have given us tricks without knowing it, I say thanks again, and leave in modest consolation the words of Hans Trixer who, speaking of those who steal or borrow tricks—writes . . .

When you steal one trick, they call it plagiarism.

When you steal many—they call it research.

## THE END

*Page*        *Page*